The Diaries of
JUDITH
MALINA
1947·1957

The Diaries of
JUDITH
MALINA
1947·1957

GROVE PRESS, INC./NEW YORK

First Hardcover Edition 1984
First Printing 1984
ISBN: 0-394-53132-9
Library of Congress Catalog Card Number: 83-048293

First Evergreen Edition 1984
First Printing 1984
ISBN: 0-394-62450-5
Library of Congress Catalog Card Number: 83-048293

Manufactured in the United States of America

GROVE PRESS, INC., 196 West Houston Street,
New York, N.Y. 10014

For Julian

ACKNOWLEDGMENTS

In the preparation of these diaries for publication I was fortunate to have the aid and encouragement of a number of friends who generously gave of their time, talent, and energy to help me through the complex decisions which the work entailed.

My deepest and now forever unexpressible gratitude is owed to the late James Spicer who first suggested to me that these diaries should be a book, and who first edited them, and spent many years working on them, typing them and promoting them.

With Julian Beck I shaped the first draft in Brazil in 1971, doing most of the work when we were in jail together in Belo Horizonte.

With Julian and Hanon Reznikov I edited the final version in Rome in 1982. I thank them for going over the typescript with me again and again during long tours and years of love.

I thank Hanon for giving me the courage to overcome so many obstacles—personal, artistic and literary—as well as for his perceptive eye and his well-tuned ear.

Pierre Biner has my warmest and affectionate gratitude for his valuable notes and research, and for going through the holograph with me to check out every word against the typescript. To Paul Goodman I owe the heart of my matter. That I thank him posthumously is my great grief.

Thanks to my friend Karen Malpede for her loving encouragement and for her care and critique of the diaries and (for) the faith shown in writing about them over many years of our friendship.

My thanks to Berenice Hoffman and Hal Sharlatt, and Austryn Wainhouse and Mark Amitin. Thanks to Robert Projansky for his help in rescuing the manuscript from oblivion. Thanks to Rubin Gorewitz for guidance through troubled waters.

Thanks to each and every one of the members of the Living Theatre who have lived these diaries with me. Thanks to all those whose names appear in the diaries, in the hope that they will bear with me and interpret mildly any injustice that I might have done them.

Special gratitude to Barney Rosset of Grove Press for his encouragement and enthusiasm, and to Lisa Rosset for her patience and sensitivity to my needs.

Thanks to Garrick Beck for reading through the manuscript and making helpful notes on the events of his infancy and for supplying valuable research assistance.

Thanks to Isha Beck for her sufferance of the many hours of her mother's attention that she relinquished to these pages.

The Diaries of
JUDITH
MALINA
1947·1957

1947

June 4, 1947

"*Schon einundzwanzig, und noch nichts für die Unsterblichkeit getan.*" Twenty-one already, and I still haven't done a thing worth immortality.
Secretly, I had expected a sudden and decisive change.

I wake early. My mother has set out the traditional birthday table with dainties and gifts.
I dress in new clothes. I feel a sense of freedom at quitting my job at the bookshop where I haven't been happy.

Julian comes and brings presents: Cocteau, *Götterdämmerung*, César Franck.

Then I go to Harald's, where a tall red candle burns on a cake, and blue crêpe paper covers his baggage. He gives me these three notebooks, asking me to keep a record of my thoughts and actions. I promise to send them to him when completed, but I will avoid writing as he would have me write. A journal kept for someone else is a letter and not *ein Tagebuch*.

Our love is saddened by the awareness of our coming separation.

In the evening, to the Cherry Lane, where I'm rehearsing *Ethan Frome* for the On Stage Company.
I'm still struggling with the character of Zenobia Frome, but there's some comfort in playing in a theater where I've worked before, along with Lola Ross, my classmate at the Workshop.[1] While waiting for Julian to return from his Sierra adventure last summer, it was to Lola that I confided the earliest plans for the Living Theatre, the most important work of my life, for which I am now preparing.

June 9, 1947

In two days Harald returns to Europe. I try to spend as much time with him as possible. This morning I study my lines with him and then accompany him to various consulates.
Now he's across the street at the Dramatic Workshop, where we first met and studied and rehearsed. I'm waiting for him in the Ritz Coffee Shop because I may not enter the Workshop until I write Piscator a letter of apology.
I've put it off from day to day. It's difficult because I'm in the wrong and don't have an adequate excuse. It was a strained and late dress rehearsal of Sartre's *Flies*. Harald and I had quarreled and I was crying and wasn't in costume. Piscator scolded me and I answered him rudely. Now I must write him before it is too late.

June 10, 1947

Harald and I talked about Vienna at the Algonquin over cocktails. I had a Pink Lady, a tart's drink. Then we went to the Village to see *No Exit*.

We came home and drank champagne. When we made love I could only think, "This is the last time," and I cried because it's of his own will that he leaves and this must be against all the principles of love.

June 13, 1947

Harald stood at the ship's rail, and I on the pier, and we talked till the whistle blew and the ship pulled away. Under the shriek of the whistle I sobbed as I ran to the end of the pier. Through my tears and the blinding sunlight I watched the great ship turn and grow smaller. I waved a small handkerchief. At the other side of the pier I saw a girl waving a white hat with a black ribbon.

On the walk back up the dark pier I stopped crying.

I got on the crosstown bus and the girl in the white hat sat down beside me. She said, "Is he coming back?"

"He isn't sure," I answered.

June 14, 1947

He is three days at sea and has become a phantom.

It is six in the morning. In a few days it will be better. And in a year.

June 15, 1947

I write Piscator:

I cannot vindicate myself with alibis.

My only appeal can be to your understanding of my feelings toward you, your work, the Workshop and my own ideals in the theater. I have learned to believe what you believe in, to strive in my way for what you strive for. You are my teacher, the one in whom I have the most faith, in whom I trust, from whom I learned and still hope to learn.

This is my only excuse: All that I ever hope to be I owe to you, and therefore hope with all my heart that this apology will be acceptable.

June 16, 1947

On Stage has decided to produce *Juno and the Paycock* with the original Dramatic Workshop cast, to give us more time to rehearse *Ethan Frome*.[2]

Yesterday I bought Hallie Flanagan's *Arena*. How exciting these first chapters in which she describes how she created the Federal Theatre to speak to the people, to the workers; a theater using all the forms, new and traditional, verse and prose, in all the languages that are spoken in the U.S.A., in every city and village, and on wagons for the country people and for the poor . . . I look at the scope of this book and I think pridefully: "It can be done. She did it. So can I."

Continuing our search for a theater. Julian and I look at the former Labor Stage, now occupied by the Experimental Theatre of Equity and the Belmonte, now showing Spanish motion pictures. No hope.

June 17, 1947

The pain that I've kept down to the vanishing point manifests itself as melancholy. If only the Living Theatre were a reality.

To still my restlessness I order my theater collection into files.

In the mail I receive my diploma from the Dramatic Workshop, but for "Acting" instead of "Directing"!

Now I'll have to go and protest, and tell the whole story: how I entered the Dramatic Workshop fervent to be an actress and, after a few days of watching Piscator's work, knew I wanted to do the more encompassing work that is called directing.

Piscator looked at me coldly: He does not have a high regard for the staying power of women in the masculine professions. He expressed his opinion that I would "get married and forget about the theater," that for this reason I had better study to be an actress. I pleaded with him, swallowing my humiliation at his low opinion of my qualifications because of my sex, and he, somewhat reluctantly, allowed me to take the directing course. Thus I was able to study not only acting, but stage design, theater management, lighting, and above all, take invaluable directing classes with Piscator.

Now they've sent me an acting diploma, and Piscator isn't even in New York for me to protest to.

All through my school years I tried to prove my worth to him and I haven't yet.

I'll go and ask for that directing diploma even if no one ever sees it.

June 21, 1947

For *Juno and the Paycock* I'm working on the role of Maisie Madigan again. Recreating a role, I remember each line reading and have to work hard to avoid imitating myself.

Last night Julian came to discuss the Living Theatre. Once again we went over all the empty theaters and halls. I don't see much hope of an empty motion picture house big enough to mount Cocteau's *Infernal Machine*, though I am as anxious as Julian to open with Cocteau instead of the simpler one-act plays by Stein, Kreymborg, and Goodman.

We made a list of artists whose work we admire. We composed a very formal letter asking them to guide us by their experience, and call themselves sponsors of our enterprise.

June 23, 1947

I see much of Julian. He comes to *Juno* rehearsals. Saturday night we went to see *No Exit*. And then to Coney Island.

Here in a waxworks, tortured bodies and murderers moulder beneath a thick layer of dust. We walk by the water, carrying our shoes and stockings. Wading from Coney to Brighton Beach, we improvise songs and throw stranded fish back into the sea.

Three letters today! And I read them now in the dim backstage light between acts. Harald has been to Paris, gotten my letters, possibly spoken to Cocteau. He has been to Zürich, spoken to Kalser, written me on a train from Le Havre to Paris, while I, unexcited by opening night, play Maisie Madigan.

The only glimmer of joy is Julian's opening night telegram:

Out of the darkness a slim hand so lovely carries a rich bunch of red roses for thee me TLT.

June 27, 1947

A letter from Paris. Harald loves Paris. I become insanely jealous at the thought of his being happy away from me.

He has tried to see Cocteau, but Cocteau is making a film and is hard to reach. Harald, however, is drinking champagne at an outdoor café with a young *régisseur* of the *Comédie Française* who says he will speak to J.C. for us about translation rights.

Ethan Frome rehearsals. Mike Gazzo complains that *Ethan* cannot possibly go on in ten days, blaming my lack of concentration. Calmly, I bow out. I'm sorry, but my lover just left me and I have no heart left.

The next day there's another letter from Paris. What he writes about the beautiful city no longer makes me unhappy. It makes me want to be there.

He has contacted Cocteau concerning the Living Theatre. Cocteau is upset about a bad translation of one of his plays, and while drunk gave away the American rights to another. He doesn't remember how *The Infernal Machine* stands. But Harald thinks he will let us do it.

June 28, 1947

Bob Ramsey announces that he is going to play Ethan. Of course in that case I want to play Zenobia and prove that I can have the role ready in eight days.

June 30, 1947

I was tired after a nine-hour rehearsal, but Julian had promised to help me with my lines and we went to his studio and immediately immersed ourselves in our theater collections: that mass of photographs and clippings and programs that Julian and I have been hoarding all our lives. Now we decide to merge our collections, and begin to sort and file till at 12:30 I realize that I haven't studied my lines. I'm furious at myself. Julian says I have a block against learning the role.

July 7, 1947

Tonight *Ethan Frome* opens. Last night we had our first run-through. Have not yet seen a costume. No dress rehearsal!

A walk with Julian after rehearsal. The air cool and fine. We talk about the Living Theatre. How well it will be organized and how smoothly its dress rehearsals will take place.

At breaks in rehearsals I go to 10th Street and stand across the street from Harald's house and watch for him in the window. I will run across the street. He will open the door. . . .

I need to think of quiet things to keep me calm for tonight. I will do what I can with Zenobia and not fret over my unrealized potential.

With Piscator I developed every interpretation and inflection under his harsh but careful direction. Without such guidance I find it hard to feel the slippery inner edge of the character.

July 7, 1947

Opening night. A fight with Mother about Harald just before the show. She sees Harald as a deceiver who exploited my innocence. She considers me a fallen woman.

I run out into the street desperate and humiliated, but Mother follows, talks reasonably and gets me into a taxi just in time to rush into makeup and get on stage. I perform through misery.

Julian sent fourteen roses.

July 8, 1947

When I arrived at the theater the whole play had been redesigned and rebuilt to take place on a unit set. Action to flow directly from bedroom to kitchen to bedroom. I make a few fifteen-second costume changes upstage-right in a black cubbyhole curtained off by a blanket. Scenes end with black-outs as at Piscator's Rooftop Theater. The play went far better.

July 9, 1947

First rehearsal of the Auden/Isherwood play, *The Dog beneath the Skin*. Alexis Solomos is directing this difficult play for On Stage. I play Mildred Luce, driven mad by the loss of her sons in the war.

Dog beneath the Skin has seventeen sets and a cast of sixty-five. Auden promises to write a new ending for us and the *New York Times* has already written about this "first American production."

July 14, 1947

Rehearsals of *The Dog beneath the Skin*.

For years I rejected Stanislavsky's sense-memory theory. In Raikin Ben-Ari's class I used the last scene of *Iphigenia in Aulis* to demonstrate that I could play the famous tearful plea with my mind empty of all but the most prosaic thoughts. I said: "A painter does not weep when he paints a weeping figure." Yet I exploited my own emotional turmoil when I played Cassandra. And in the role of Mildred Luce, what alternatives can I find to the sense memories of grief?

I'm reading *Back to Methuselah*. Julian ambitiously thinks it could be a Living Theatre production.

July 17, 1947

Finished *Back to Methuselah*, Shaw's cycle of plays.

In his preface he writes a critical appraisal of Darwinism, a refutation of atheism, a detailed defense of Lamarckian evolutionary theory, a Fabian analysis of Marxism, materialism, vitalism *et al*. When I take issue with him, he invariably downs my arguments in the very next paragraph. He is the perfect Sophist.

As to the play, I am uncomfortable in utopias. From St. Augustine to Thomas More, from Huxley to Shaw, the utopias are ugly because they are not human and our only criterion for beauty is a human one.

July 20, 1947

Last night *Ethan Frome* closed. Tomorrow *The Dog beneath the Skin* opens.

I arrived at the last performance of *Ethan* hoarse from rehearsing the cries of Mildred Luce. Zenobia's last long tirade, the pickle-dish speech, was not spoken but literally torn from my throat.

We rehearsed *Dog beneath the Skin*, from ten A.M. to midnight. It took eight hours to run through. Technically everything is confused but the quality is astounding.

Alexis works keenly, unsmilingly, impersonally; a knife, with short, thorough strokes. Piscator slashes through to the meaning of the play in one clean sabre cut. I'm afraid I will work like a saw, arduously and laboriously. What makes the best cut?

July 21, 1947

At the theater to do crew work. I paint two Rembrandt self-portraits in fifteen minutes each. The vandal showman "Destructive Desmond," shreds one at every performance and I will have to paint a masterpiece daily.

I am intoxicated with the theater, I love the paint smell, the rushing about, that feeling when looking around a room that you know everyone is working for the same end and that you are part of it. Like communal singing. The spell of tonight's opening enhances everything.

My first scene is over. Mildred's hysteria more hard-hitting than in rehearsals. Now I must wait until the last scene, in which I stagger on to kill the hero.

The emotion comes by itself. I am not sure whether I "feel" it or not. Piscator compares the actor with too much technical training to the centipede who walks along smoothly on his 100 feet until someone asks him which foot he moves first; at which he becomes so confused that he cannot take another step.

Yes, it is an intoxicant. And suddenly, as I'm saying my goodnights after the show, I realize that I am at last an actress who takes her daily work for granted.

July 30, 1947

Julian fulfilled a four-year-old promise to me, taking me to visit Marsh Pond, with which he has been in love ever since he first came upon it as a boy scout.

In the Berkshires, near Winsted, set quite high, and full of lilies and lily pads, its unique feature is an aura, a steady, quiet aura.

Julian planned the future: the house where he would paint . . .the library. . . . He spoke often of "we."

August 3, 1947

The Dog beneath the Skin has become a success. S.R.O. nightly. Friday night Christopher Isherwood came, introducing himself as "half a playwright." He stood on stage and spoke to the cast, his manner self-effacing, like a man asking for street directions. He thanked us all for "letting him come" as he had never before seen a production of it. He admired Gene Saks' Vicar no end. Said he agreed with Auden that the sermon should have been cut because no audience would sit through so long a monologue at the end of a long play—until he heard Gene do it.

Gene in turn praised the poetry and Isherwood said it derived from Melville's sermon to the whale.

Is it mysticism that makes for so much modesty? Auden's haughty distractedness is a severe contrast. Isherwood no doubt was the restraining influence on the unbridled whimsy of Auden.

August 7, 1947

I work all day every day on the Living Theatre.

Our plans are to open with *The Infernal Machine* and then to add three one-act plays: Alfred Kreymborg, Gertrude Stein, and Paul Goodman. After that, Cummings' *HIM* and possibly *Troilus and Cressida*.

Every evening after my opening scene Julian meets me backstage and we make plans and write letters.

Monday night we got involved in a love scene. I don't know how to think about it. I am embarrassed because he is the close friend with whom I speak lightly about such things, yet there are some things I cannot discuss deeply even with myself. I censor thoughts. But can I in deepest earnestness say that I would not marry him?

August 14, 1947

At last a letter from Harald. He is an assistant director at the Salzburg *Festspiele*. So our lives turn into different lives and the inevitable separation of the heart follows. I can visualize that aristocratic glance at home at last— and dead to me.

Julian: We have come closer to love than we admit to ourselves. At heart we both want it and dread it. There is so much to do. The world will find a way to turn, I hope.

August 19, 1947

The Dog beneath the Skin closed Saturday night with a cheerful and sentimental cast party.

The season is over, the first season that I have played through and I feel unattached after having belonged to a theater.

At the party, Paul Johnson, who saw *The Dog* nine times, says to Julian and me that he has the equipment to make 16 mm movies and is looking for a group of actors, a director, and a script.

I said immediately that all these things were available.

Now Julian and I are working on a scenario at a frantic pace.

Reading *La Belle et la bête, the Diary of a Film* by Jean Cocteau.

Several films at the Museum of Modern Art: *Die Dreigroschenoper* with its allegorical finale, as the beggars disperse slowly into the shadows.

It is the interpolator again, the Greek chorus in modern guise. The chorus is dear to the audience because it bridges the gap—being part of both the audience and the secret mystery of the play.

Valeska Gert[3] plays Mrs. Peacham in *Dreigroschenoper*, with great control of the *grotesk* style for which she became famous.

By 1943, when I worked for her as waitress/singer/hatcheck girl, she had become the grotesque character she played, as Jarry came to resemble Ubu. I wish I hadn't destroyed the diary I kept while working in the Beggar Bar.

Other Museum films: *Mädchen in Uniform, Emil und die Detektive*, and *Fährman Maria*.

Some images touch us where the deep fear lies: In H. G. Wells' *Things to Come*, the world lies in ruins and a plague strikes the people. It is called "the wandering sickness." The words float across the screen, as a thin woman's figure moves slowly across a plaza away from the others. We see her hypnotic motion, her distant look and hear a euphonious whisper: "The Wandering Sickness. . . ."

It haunts me.

There are other such images: the aged face in *Lost Horizon*; the burning of the cholera victims in a furnace in a film about a ship; the screams of a woman being dragged to the firing squad in *Michael Strogoff*.

"Wandering . . ." I shudder.

Is it the Wandering Jew? The wandering mind?

August 27, 1947

Last night at Paul Johnson's garret, we saw his film *Chimera*, in which the actors, none of whom had had any acting experience, planned each scene just before they played it for the camera.

I visit Erica Perl at *Vogue* magazine. She rushes out to greet me in a black New Look dress with a wide ballerina skirt. A young man takes pictures of a smiling sun painted on her forehead. They seem like children, half playing, half serious. Erica thinks the glamour frivolous and is leaving *Vogue* to become art editor of *Opera News*.

We eat in a small Italian restaurant, discussing her love and mine.

August 31, 1947

At the Museum *Olympia*, Leni Riefenstahl's record of the 1936 Olympic games in Berlin, with Hitler smiling under the swastika flag.

I'm amazed at the beauty of the great-armed, long-torsoed athletes, throwing the javelin or poising the pole to leap. Divers plunge across the screen, silhouetted bodies flying like swallows, human birds, faster and faster across the sky.

At night a drive with Julian to La Guardia Airport.

The planes roll down the runway, slow and cumbersome, shining in the blackness. Then their silver bodies speed along the ground like creatures charging prey. The wheels rise and like a wisp the thing floats up, changes, becomes a distant silhouette.

I hope soon to fly in one of those superb birds.

September 1, 1947

All afternoon Julian and I work on a sponsor letter to Joan Junyer. Julian writes letters the way he writes poems; every word must be perfect. At this rate our correspondence will take the better part of our lives.

September 8, 1947

Early this morning, Alfred Kreymborg phoned in response to our sponsor letter. Happy to hear that we planned to do his one-act *When the Willow Nods*, he hastened to tell me about a three-act play in the making, and a play about Tristram and Iseult "based on a medieval legend that they took the love potion because they had been playing chess all the way from Cornwall and didn't know what the hell they were doing."

We made an appointment for two tomorrow.

After weeks of fruitless job hunting I thought I had found a job as a receptionist in a doctor's office but tonight they told me no and left me quite depressed.

Julian and I went to see about renting the Fifth Avenue Playhouse. The manager seemed amenable but is asking $2,000 a week, and a certified check in advance for two months rent—$16,000. Is there that much money on earth?

Stopped in at the Cherry Lane where Bob Ramsey gave me my season's paycheck for $44.76.

September 9, 1947

Julian and Kreymborg liked each other immediately.

We talked about our adventures in looking for a theater but soon the old poet began talking about his friends, his work, his plays, and from then on the stage was his. He read to us for several hours the first two acts of his play in progress about the Trojan War. A weighty, unplayable play, written in what he calls "poeticized prose." We lied in our teeth, our praise falling on whatever praiseworthy aspect of playwrighting we could think of. We held hands till

Kreymborg politely asked us not to. Thereafter we sat mutely until he looked up for a comment and we nodded "wonderful."

He was at his best after dinner when we sat in Washington Square and he indulged in stories of the old bunch: of "Tom" (T. S. Eliot); of Ezra Pound; of "Red" (Wyndham Lewis); of H. D.; of Gene (Eugene O'Neill); of the Provincetown Playhouse; of the early struggle to hoist the flag of free verse; of Edna (Millay); of Gordon Craig with his great cape and other idiosyncrasies; of *Broom* magazine, which swept clean.

Of course he won our hearts.

September 14, 1947

Julian and I go to the Museum film showings as often as possible to study techniques: cuts, panning, editing, frames.

We found Paul Johnson at a garden table in discussion with Julian Sawyer, disciple and disseminator of Gertrude Stein.

Sawyer was defending the Hollywood product, which he sees as a vast cultural seduction, and expresses his complex theories with the passion of the seduced. PJ had to concede.

Yesterday another call from Alfred Kreymborg. He had just finished *The Wooden Horse* and would I come over to listen to it right away.

Julian and I had worked arduously over our first letter to Kreymborg and chose him as the first sponsor to consult out of respect for his poetry and his plays.

He conducted himself as the "grand old man of letters" and confirmed my preconception. His professional behavior placed me in the role of the listening neophyte and there I made myself comfortable. Now, suddenly, our relationship changes.

Kreymborg imagines that he is in love with me. He hallucinates a romance with a young girl in a poem he reads to me: "My Swan, Your Spring Song."

Kreymborg is a superb lyric poet, a romantic of sorts, and a gentle old man, but I am dismayed and don't know how to cope with his approach to me as a lover.

As to the play, he has finished it as badly as it was begun. His Greek farmers and soldiers all read and write. For his Greek Venus and Jove I suggested Aphrodite and Zeus; at first K agreed but then decided instead to add a preface "To the Scholar Out Front," explaining that the American public is more familiar with Venus than with Aphrodite.

He gave me a copy of *The Little World*.

September 25, 1947

The Passion of Joan of Arc[4]
I couldn't stop crying.

After the film we drove downtown to Alfred Kreymborg's.

I sobbed uncontrollably while Julian and Kreymborg talked. Then Julian and I drove north, out of the city. I grew calmer.

We talked.

We talked about our love and our peculiar relationship, and we spoke of marriage.

Julian hesitated, but I urged him to decide then and there.

Sitting in the darkness at a wooded roadside stop in upstate New York, we decided to get married.

October 20, 1947

This morning we put a deposit of $500 on the Malin Theater. Without a lawyer, Julian and I struggle with the wording of the receipt.

Strindberg's *Briefe Ans Intime Theatre*. His theater had 150 seats. The same old story: the complexities of rentals and government regulations caused the bitter genius more anxieties than the artistic aspect of his productions.

A letter from Cocteau, almost illegible, about the Wildman translation. There is a sort of hieroglyph that makes one sentence read either "Follow the text carefully" or "Don't follow the text carefully." I hadn't intended to stick closely to the Wildman translation though I would like to know whether Cocteau is with me or against me.

Cocteau suggests that we translate *Les Chevaliers de la Table Ronde*. I find this strange, since he knows so little about us, and wonder whether we can consider it an authorization. Paul Goodman would be a logical translator.

Read through *Ubu* in my fashion. Dictionary is no help when Jarry coins his own language. Ubu is a tremendous character.

The paper is signed. The bank exchanged slip for slip, duly stamped and dated. The Malin Theater is under option to us for a $500 deposit. Now I know that I will soon be doing what I really want to do.

October 21, 1947

Judith Anderson in Robinson Jeffers' adaptation of *Medea*.

She is a beast, half goddess, half hunted wolf.

At the Dramatic Workshop, Arla Guild played a savage Medea in a production directed by Al Mulock, and Margaret Wyler was superb in the production for which I was assistant director; but I never knew Medea till Anderson ripped away the mask of humanity revealing the ferocity underneath, boundless, terrible and wondrous.

Among the first nighters is Tennessee Williams, who sits beside us. He takes the play lightly and laughs at the Nurse's tragic message.

He and Julian were close friends in Provincetown three years ago, when Tennessee was writing *The Glass Menagerie*. Now Tennessee is famous and he is cold, and when Julian talks to him about the Living Theatre he seems unmoved.

October 25, 1947

Yale at night. All shadows Julian and I walk the stone paths among the excellent fake gothic structures. Through a leaded window I see a young man close a book; two latecomers, roommates, echo in an archway; a laugh. Distantly, someone tries a few notes on a piano. Stillness again. A cricket and a tree and the scholar's dream of the conquest of knowledge. Hamlet. Wittenburg. Faust. Heidelberg.

The Yale-Harvard football game. Cold, fair weather.

Yale won. Celebration. Dark night.

We stood under the pseudo-Egyptian portals of the Grove Street Cemetery. Above us, engraved in the granite: "The dead shall be raised."

And we quarreled about love and we parted.

We parted because I tried to force Julian to declare his love for me. And he doesn't want to marry.

I am broken-hearted and repentant, but Julian does not want to marry.

We abandon our plans.

We talk of abandoning our plans for the Living Theatre.

October 29, 1947

E. E. Cummings answers our letter with a friendly postcard (unpunctuated) making an appointment for tomorrow.

Robert Edmond Jones calls this morning. Caught off guard, bewildered at the idea of talking to this legendary man, I swallow hard and make an appointment for the fifth.

October 30, 1947

Kreymborg gives me a copy of a play, *The Other*, by Miguel de Unamuno. A metaphysical, unidimensional play.

We manage to postpone signing the lease till Thursday, when we hope to be incorporated as The Living Theatre, Inc.

A few evenings back we had a session with Paul Johnson at which he suggested filming Alexander Pope's long poem *Essay on Man*.

November 1, 1947

Yesterday we visited E. E. Cummings in his little house in Patchin Place. Normal trepidations at meeting the great poet who has influenced Julian so much. Rain. We entered like two dripping cats.

A tall woman opened the door and immediately dispatched Julian to the corner bakery "to get the cake for Mrs. Cummings" and disappeared into the kitchen leaving me alone in a room that was informal, almost unkempt, with figurative paintings on the walls, an ebony elephant. . . .

Cummings came in wearing work clothes and talking the way his poems read—lively, exaggerated, concise. He had a repertory of stories and comments on every subject.

Upon Julian's return we had Dubonnet and cake. We talked about language and the misuse and disrepute into which adjectives like "lovely" had fallen, about tall buildings and about the dead art of burlesque. We talked about the strangely reactionary tendency in modern poetry. He said he had heard T. S. Eliot say, at a lecture at the 92nd Street Y, that it was all right to read Milton again.

"But of course," said Cummings, "we had never stopped reading Milton."

We talked about *HIM*. And about the Living Theatre. Cummings seemed pleased with our ideas, though I thought we talked far too little about our work plans.

He gave us permission to go ahead with *HIM*.

The talk was two hours old when suddenly Cummings leapt to his feet, shook our hands, and said: "It is time for the poet to go to work."

Julian is troubled by his abrupt departure. I thought it fitting.

A few days ago Julian and I visited Paul and Sally Goodman. Paul sees swiftly through everything; he is as honest as hay. I expected a whitewashed orderly life from the author of *Communitas*. But his home is an easy, carefree setting for their baby to grow in.

He talks philosophically, deeply, wisely. He says he will be a sponsor of the Living Theatre.

We showed him Cocteau's letter about the translation of *Les Chevaliers de la Table Ronde*. He says it's his favorite Cocteau play, that he admires Cocteau even as much as I do, and will make the translation for us.

November 6, 1947

Yesterday: Robert Edmond Jones.

His setting: A high, huge, square room. A tall mantel, with a clay Hindu figure at just such an angle. A mirror, antiqued so that one sees nothing in it, framed in ormulu. An uncarpeted floor; an immense square gray screen with a black, plain border; little light.

The distinguished artist receiving aspiring artists in his atelier; a glass of sherry to toast Mr. Jones' wide range of ideas.

He criticized acting in all its forms and styles and seemed to disagree with the whole world. He seemed pleased with all that we wished to do.

We discussed the Jeffers-Anderson *Medea*.

The men think it immoral to justify Medea's infanticide by rescuing her in the end. They miss the point. They think the play condemns Medea. But it is Jason who is guilty. Medea the avenging instrument set in motion by his betrayal. She cannot do otherwise.

Jones gives us much strange advice: He suggests Duse's great success, D'Annunzio's *Città Morta*, for our repertory. He says: "Anyone who has a good voice, or trains his voice, can read *Hamlet* and *Prometheus*. To read well is to act well."

We make another appointment to show him plans and drawings.

November 19, 1947

On Friday, Julian and I race to finish the last of the costume plates and the models to show Jones.

The set for the Kreymborg play, a series of gauze-covered wire forms positioned at different levels, is a collaborative effort by Julian and me which we sign Garrick Damona.

We put together the portfolio and the two still-wet models and run all the way from Julian's studio to Jones'.

Jones admires everything. He looks at Ramsey's drawing for *The Infernal Machine* and says, "Appia," pulling from under his fingers a book of Appia's drawings, showing us a setting of platforms and ramps for which Bob's might have been a first draft.

"It proves this sort of thing is in the air."

And of the Appia design—it was for *Orfeo and Euridice,*—he says pensively, "This is the most beautiful set in the world."

He praises each of the costumes, especially the Sphinx as Nemesis and Oedipus' coronation robe.

As for Julian's drawing: "I wish I'd done that," says Robert Edmond Jones.

Jones admires the economy of our models for the one-act plays. He likes the tinfoil, the glass, the wire, the string.

"If only you had a smaller budget!" he complains.

He begrudges us *The Infernal Machine* cyclorama and plastic plinths.

"Do it for nothing. Do it with ingenuity."

But I point out that we must pay rent.

"Do it here. Do it right here in my studio. Do it with these cushions as a setting. Use this room."

He gestures toward the high ceiling and the tall square walls.

We should have accepted instantly.

Jones sums up. He had expected us to go further. He wanted us to build sets out of sound, out of dreams, out of who knows what. He wanted something "totally new."

Robert Edmond Jones may be one of the finest designers alive, but for all his zeal for the new he never was revolutionary, not even when everyone else was. And now when everyone else has settled into a complacent artistic groove, when they speak of "Ah, yes, the wild twenties when we were experimenting," he is among those who designs perfectly charming, conventional sets and costumes like those for *Lute Song.* Yet he expects us to come to him and say that we have the secret of the next step, "the answer," and he is disappointed that we only ask the question.

He offers to help us. Good enough. He says such improbable things. One comes away from his room strangely unsatisfied as from an unfinished dream.

December 13, 1947

I haven't written for a long time and I conclude this notebook to be taken up again at the beginning of the year.

I cannot heal my breach with Julian, and we suspend plans for the Living Theatre. The record of these weeks must remain incomplete.

I look forward to a better year to clarify the confusions and to calm the distress.

1948

January 1, 1948

A quiet day. A big snow. Followed by sleet and ice. An air of emergency. Julian and I see *Mourning Becomes Electra*, a cold, hard film.

January 2, 1948

I'm trying hard to find a place to do some small plays. Not the Living Theatre by any means, but a kind of foothold. In Greenwich Village I inquire about using the basement of 230 Wooster Street as a theater.

The room consists of a pit surrounded on four sides by a wooden stage on which a play could be performed for an audience of approximately forty people. The form puts the spectators in the center like the Elizabethan "Wooden O." I must go ahead with some work, now that the Living Theatre is only an uncertain hope for the future.

January 3, 1948

Howard Friedman is directing *The Spook Sonata* at the Dramatic Work-shop and invites me to play the Young Lady and the Mummy. Rehearsals are exasperating. I never liked improvisation. I favor a well-planned action and considered movement. It is my much-abused intellectual approach.

Piscator: "Malina takes one eye in her hand and holds it at arm's length to see what she is doing."

It's true. I've been trying to work more freely, in looser forms, since my own direction of *Spook Sonata* last year.

Howard swears by improvisation. In order to portray the malady of the Young Lady, he makes me improvise an irate shopper cheated by a butcher. I'm trying to follow his direction even when my judgment balks.

January 5, 1948

In order to escape my strained situation with Julian, I apply for a job as a psychiataric aide in a mental hospital in Hartford, Connecticut.

Drang nach einem Zauberberg, nach einem Kinderheim. Hans Castorp of the lazy soul. Surely my old patterns will reestablish themselves.

A rehearsal for *Spook Sonata*.

January 6, 1948

In Cocteau's film *L'Eternel retour* the protagonists are not aware that they are acting out the Tristram and Iseult legend. Nietzsche's concept of "returning eternally," without the pomp of Wagner or the authority of the old poem.

Cocteau permeated with magic. It was his subject in *Beauty and the Beast* as it was in *Orphée* and *Blood of a Poet*. In *The Infernal Machine* Oedipus is impressed into the service of the dark arts, and in *The Eternal Return* the power of the myth is magical. Cocteau uses magic without mysticism or metaphysics.

The magic is potent only because we believe it.

January 12, 1948

A letter of acceptance from the Institute of Living in Hartford.
I will leave right after playing *Spook Sonata*.

January 13, 1948

At lunch with Helen Jacobs, I refuse to say that the Living Theatre is dead. I refuse to believe it. I blame the postponement on our inability to procure a theater. Meanwhile I wait.

January 14, 1948

Lunch with Alfred Kreymborg. He is in the thick of the Henry Wallace election campaign and can talk of nothing else. He serves up his whole political history—from the time he ghost-wrote Woodrow Wilson's campaign speeches—as a side dish to my salad at Kresge's.

"Wouldn't we be responsible for the possible election of a Republican president, if we support Wallace?" I ask.

"Wallace," he says, "answers that by calling a Democratic vote a vote for the lesser of the two evils." But in that case the Republican victory is the greater of two evils, and a third party vote seems to favor that possibility.

Kreymborg has written a dramatic poem called "No More War," which *Esquire* magazine has published. He'd like to see it performed. He will recommend my directing it at the Dramatic Workshop to Piscator, but of course Piscator will never let me do it.

January 17, 1948

Last night Howard tried a *Strange Interlude* rehearsal of the last act of *Spook Sonata*. We spoke our thoughts aloud between the lines. Soon Louis Criss and I were carried away by the reality that emerged from expression of the internal dialogue. The hysteria rose. The harp didn't play.

January 19, 1948

Yesterday we rehearsed *Spook* all day without the stage. . . .
As the Young Lady I'm wearing the Cassandra costume Mother sewed, with a silver sash and pearls. It's rather ragged, having been made for *Agamem-*

non,[5] out of dyed old window curtains and time has not been kind to it. For the Mummy I make myself a costume of burlap.

January 20, 1948

The Spook Sonata performance.

The Mummy: In the parrot scene I screech at Hummel across a great distance. Alexis Solomos seems very far away as I mock him through the mesh covering my face.

I couldn't make contact and, like the character, I played for effect.

The Young Lady: Only when we reach the frénzy and the agony of the death scene do I feel comfortable.

I secretly prefer my stylized production with its white-clad ghost surveying the whole play from atop a black ladder. The past itself looking down on us. And dominating us.

After the play, Piscator told us "how it was when I played the Student."

With evident pleasure he recalled that production in Königsberg in 1920, in which the chairs of the house were like spiders, infesting the old house as representative of the decadent society. The young student representing the future defying the past.

I couldn't stay to hear Piscator's whole talk as it was my last chance to be with Julian before leaving for Hartford.

January 21, 1948

My early faith in Piscator was based on what I knew of his past achievements at the Volksbühne in Berlin. Then for years I watched his cruel, wonderful directing, laboriously untangling his expressive theories from his insufficient practice. I wanted a great play from him and played in his audacious *Aristocrats*, a constructivist masterpiece in the Russian style, and I played the leader of the chorus of Flies in his *Les Mouches*, always uncomfortable in its classic frame. But tonight in Robert Penn Warren's *All the King's Men*, I finally see Piscator working in the presentational style with an epic play.

The story traces the political career of Huey Long. As in Toller's *Masse Mensch*, the best political play that I know, good and evil are clearly recognizable.

Piscator creates a stage space that one can play on, under or around. A spiral staircase rises from the center of a ramp, a small platform atop it, permitting the graphic enactment of the upward striving for power. The small stage seems to expand; a revolving platform allows cinematic effects of action in motion. Actors walking on a turntable that revolves against them, or single spot-lit faces function as theatrical equivalents of the moving camera and the close-up. Piscator is not an actor's director. But he is present in the style of all the actors.

January 25, 1948   *Hartford, Connecticut*

Hartford. I am a psychiatric aide at the Institute of Living.

Connecticut snow-covered and monotonous under a white winter sun. A short bus trip from the station takes me to the spacious grounds. It is plainly a hospital for the wealthy. Nowhere do I see bars or walls or even a gate.

After registering and receiving a smock and keys I'm shown to comfortable quarters, which I share with another girl, in a Tudor-style building on a campus of Georgian and Gothic reminiscent of Yale.

Dinner in a noisy, chattering cafeteria.

Then to Pickwick, a social club for off-duty aides. The atmosphere is high-strung; the experienced aides try to frighten us newcomers with tales of bizarre episodes with the patients, violent assaults, escapes, close shaves.

I won't believe anything except what I see or learn in class. My first class is tomorrow at eight. Good reason to stop writing as it's past one o'clock.

January 27, 1948   *Hartford*

On my third day here I feel acclimated, although I haven't yet seen a patient.

I've learned a new vocabulary: a patient is called a "guest"; there are "sick" guests and "well" guests, many such euphemisms.

The Institute is centered around the nineteenth-century Hartford Retreat, which, when it was built in 1822, was still called an insane asylum.

Everywhere there are facilities for recreation: the "Golf House," a social room and soda fountain for well guests, the "Huntington Club," with a bowling alley and squash court, indoor and outdoor swimming pools, etc.

My days are spent in classes. A splendid supernurse, Miss Eaton, is giving us a week in psychiatric background.

The Institute's therapy is explained as "Re-education, Re-adjustment, and Re-habilitation," with the expedients of insulin, electric shock and hydrotherapy in curing gross symptoms. When the symptoms disappear the patient is considered cured. The ability to socialize and to understand reality in its accepted perspective is considered a "cure." It seems like crediting a clever cosmetician with curing smallpox. Psychoanalysis is not one of the therapeutic procedures at the Institute.

January 28, 1948   *Hartford*

Some classes in basic biology, some in nursing procedures. And we learn how to approach a guest and how to deal with escapes.

Now I know exactly what to say when someone points to an ordinary table and says, "How do you like this 1947 Studebaker?"

We are taught to treat irrationality by confronting it with reality and by treating every situation as a normal one.

January 30, 1948   *Hartford*

My first contact with the guests. Our week of classes is over and that's all the training we will get before assuming responsibility.

There is a system of residences to prevent sick guests and well guests from meeting. The worst cases are in the ominous South and North halls.

I'm assigned to a hall known as Todd I. There I found a group of women knitting, and playing cards; as I came in one of them was changing a Schoenberg record for Schubert *lieder*. One young woman taught me to play Russian Bank and beat me at it several times. A girl came in waving a *Saturday Review of Literature*, opened to the personals page and said, "Look, girls, here's someone for us all to write to: 'Young neurotic man seeks neurotic young lady to compare therapies.'"

Everyone laughed.

At the end of the training period I signed what is known as the "Florence Nightingale Pledge," vowing not to reveal any information given me by the patients except to doctor, and promising not to reveal the identity of guests to an outsider.

Last night to a jazz concert: Stan Kenton and his band.

In the afternoon to the Wadsworth Atheneum: Serge Lifar's collection of ballet designs by Picasso, Bakst, Modigliani, Berman, de Chirico.

Browsed in the bookstores of Hartford. I discovered two scrapbooks of actors' pictures collected in 1901, from Bernhardt to Lillian Russell. I spent more money than I could afford.

January 31, 1948   *Hartford*

I walk with Phil Purdy, a fellow aide, along one of the quiet streets. The *Hartford Courant* posts its headlines in public places on broadsides. In the window of a barbershop:

GANDHI ASSASSINATED

I stop in the middle of the street. I stand there so still that Phil says, "What's the matter with you?"

"Gandhi's dead."

He raises one eyebrow and says, "So?"

We walk on in silence. I'm heartbroken not only because Gandhi's dead, but because I see how little it means to people.

Tomorrow will be my first day on duty.

February 1, 1948   *Hartford*

I'm assigned to "special" Miss Gerber[6], a quiet, elderly, extremely depressed woman. To "special" a guest is to see to their comfort, report on their behavior, keep them occupied and under observation as they are often suicidal. I tried to draw her out. She didn't protest when I set checkers in front of her and she played a good game.

In the afternoon we went for a car ride. The Institute maintains a corps of thirty Lincoln limousines, driven by uniformed women, which tour the countryside with one guest and an aide. The route took us past Winsted near Marsh Pond, of which I once dreamt, and perhaps still dream, of making my home with Julian. I shut out uneasy thoughts with sleepiness.

February 2, 1948   *Hartford*

I'm reading *The Canterbury Tales*. The sweet sounding Middle English tongue is pronounced like German and reads like music.

The flavor of another culture is pleasing in this place where an embryonic science has fascinated everyone into ignorance of cultural tradition. In the prologue, Chaucer introduces his Doctor of Physik and the "quaint devices" of his cures. Here the "quaint devices" of hydrotherapy and electric shock are accepted quite as blindly. The pity is that these admittedly undeveloped devices are so cruel, matrozol and insulin particularly, and so frequently unsuccessful.

February 5, 1948   *Hartford*

I was assigned to South I, which new aides generally don't get to see for a long time.

Some of the guests lie naked on the bare linoleum floor or wander about gesturing, or grimacing or holding conversations with hallucinations.

We are told it's impossible to keep them dressed because they tear off their clothes or defecate in them. Shoes, we have learned, are a potential means of suicide or assault. They scratch their faces and tear their hair, and they can't be kept in constant restraint.

As I came in a gray-haired, desolate creature approached me and begged me to let her out the door, pleading that she wanted to go home.

A young woman with tears streaming down her face asked me the date. When I told her that it was the fifth of February, she screamed at me not to lie.

Along a large open ward is a row of seclusion rooms, each with a high window and a bed and nothing else. Each has a door with a square of thick glass at eye-level for observation. I was assigned to be one of an escort of three who bring dinner to a patient who is rumored to have killed several aides and nurses.

The door opens. She is young. Her face is torn, evidently with self-inflicted scars, her expression barbaric. She grabs the food. We retreat.

An elderly woman sat on the floor mumbling scatological words. They say she will be given a lobotomy, a prefrontal brain operation so drastic that the whole behavior pattern changes.

The patient became violent, screaming sexual words in a throaty monotone with occasional shrill notes like some deep-voiced actress. The aides who came to calm her giggled. Her face had a permanent look of contempt.

She was put into a "cold pack," a device for calming hysteria. She is laid naked on a table on which wet sheets are spread out, hanging down like a tablecloth. Two aides hold her at the feet and shoulders. Four other aides, facing each other across the table, quickly wrap the wet sheets, folding them from alternate sides, over the naked, screaming, squirming body. The cold, wet sheets are smoothed around the body, covering it like mummy bindings from feet to neck.

Blankets are wrapped over several layers of these sheets, enclosing the patient completely. Now she can neither kick nor move her arms but as she can still roll off the bed, a restraining canvas is tied over it. For a while she will struggle vainly; but eventually the body will warm the cold sheets. The effect of this changing temperature serves to readjust the circulation so that the patient falls into an exhausted sleep. Till then, she lies there, wrapped and jabbering, no longer a human being, but the Mummy of *The Spook Sonata*, gibbering her painful life in parrot cries and baby talk.

I was assigned to a ride with a patient who was, or says he was, a Yale student. I had been warned that he prevaricates constantly.

As soon as the car started he began to talk about his experiences hunting dinosaurs in Africa. Not fossils, but live ones. He describes the dangers of dinosaur racing and their feeding habits.

Then he came to object/subject of his derangement: the dinosaur, he confided, will only feed on "dead niggers." I expressed my disgust with his ugly fantasies. And then he laughed and asked me how much of his nonsense I had believed. I said none of it.

His mood changed. Self-deprecating, self-berating: he was brought up in poverty, eking a miserable living out of his father's delicatessen store. They saved for a lifetime to send him to Yale. But then he says he couldn't get into Yale, because his blood was "tainted with colored blood." He became emotional, saying he was unfit to talk to me, denigrating himself.

At length he laughed disarmingly, and I was bewildered like—the servants in Pirandello's *Henry IV* when the madman pretends madness but leaves room for doubt as to whether he playacts or is what he seems to be.

For the past two days I have been specialing a heartbreaking patient, a lovely girl of about eighteen. When I was assigned to Bobbie I was warned that she was "assaultive, incoherent and violent," that she ate soap, had to be spoon fed, was aggressively lesbian, and would give me a bloody nose at the first opportunity.

She was living in Carolina, the most luxurious of the cottages. I found her sleeping fitfully. Her resemblance to the newly-married Princess Elizabeth of England struck me.

She had just spent two days in hydrotherapy: tubs of warm water in which an agitated patient is placed for six to forty-eight hours.

When she woke she began to murmur disconnected words. She paced, gesturing and speaking more and more loudly: "No it isn't couldn't Egypt not in the Egypt money oh he isn't but smash it rip it tear it I haven't and what then? Oh thank God what then? What then? Money Egypt never I didn't what then money isn't isn't isn't. Thank God. Money money money money foot foot Egypt."

I ran after her, talked to her, held her hands, and when she quieted she looked at me very solemnly and said, "Thank you."

But then she ran into another room, snatched some crackers, Kleenex and magazines, and slammed the doors. Because of this she was moved that afternoon to Russel Cottage, which is considered the exclusive annex to the South wards.

I had heard that Bobbie was still in contact two weeks ago, but last night I learned that the doctor had pronounced her "incurable." It troubled me, that phrase, and my night was full of dreams of madness.

Today when I was assigned to Bobbie again, I realized as soon as I saw her that I had to control my feelings of affection. We've been warned that aides suffer when they become involved emotionally with the progress or retrogression of a guest.

Today she was more coherent. She took both my hands and asked me very sincerely, "Please don't call me Little Runky." I promised.

In the afternoon Bobbie sat watching a badminton game in South Gym. The crowded room and the noise soon brought on the hyperactivity so dangerous for her. She jumped up and wrested a racquet from a player and struck her with it, hard across the arms. The guest screamed. Bobbie ran around brandishing the racquet, trying to hit people. It was difficult to catch her as she was wearing a slippery mink coat. I tackled her running down the bowling alley. We grappled in one of the lanes while the guests gleefully continued bowling, aiming the balls at us. When I succeeded in getting the racquet from her and quieting her, she said in utter innocence, "But she was hitting the bird."

Something is drastically wrong with what is being done for Bobbie. She gets insulin and electric shock treatments, but the human element is missing. Her doctor came in, said "Hello" and walked out. She is given a new aide every few days, some of whom admit they dislike her. Her illness is rooted in family relationships but the Institute doesn't accept psychoanalysis.

February 10, 1948   *New York City*

Back in New York for my days off.

We work four days in twelve-hour shifts. And then, to rest from the tensions we have three days off. I'll spend them in New York.

Visit Adolph Giehoff, who is making some commercial surrealism for Macy's window displays. Even though Dali has already dragged surrealism into the store window, André Breton and Paul Eluard little thought of Macy's when they named that strange semiconscious writing *"surréalisme"* in honor of Guillaume Apollinaire's *"drame surréal."*

In New York everyone is curious about the Institute and its inhabitants. I find myself talking about little else.

February 11, 1948   *New York to Hartford*

At lunch with Helen Jacobs she suggests the small stage at the 89th Street Synagogue as a possible theater. There also lurks in my mind a large decaying theater, the Japanese Gardens, atop the Riviera movie house.

An all night bus ride back to the peace of the madhouse.

February 12, 1948   *Hartford*

Electric shock therapy. We are not allowed to observe the shock treatment until we are experienced aides. But I watch patients coming out of shock when the treatment is over. We learned that a current is passed through the brain at the temples. The patient feels acute fear. In the patient's mouth a rubber gag prevents her from harming herself during the spasms.

I watched two patients (I almost wrote "victims") coming out of shock. They were still spitting, their eyes tearing and red, around their mouths a deathly pallor. Gradually they grew calm; the gags were removed, and they regained consciousness.

I helped one of them back to the hall where she rested and claimed on awakening to remember nothing of the treatment. Some of the guests confirm the position of those who justify the cruelty of the treatment by the ensuing amnesia.

One woman reported: "You go out, not gradually, but suddenly, and you remember nothing between the time the gag is secure in your mouth till you are back in the hall. Then you feel nauseous all afternoon, or you have a headache or something."

Is suffering less actual when it is not remembered?

The patient is not unconscious as under anesthesia; she feels intensely and emotionally. Miss Eaton explains it as an overwhelming fear of dying. The ten seconds of "deep shock" is unthinkable to us who have not experienced it. Though in a sense no one has, since no one recalls. They say the results indicate a percentage of successes. But what is crueller than to inflict the deepest bearable fear on a human being? We are back at the masked dancer frightening away the devils. The specter of psychosis exorcised in a trial by worse-than-fire. Ah, but she does not remember, they say. And the trauma in the unconscious?

They say it does not harm. Because they don't remember. Neither do the dead.

Something tells me that experience is actual, apart from and beyond the memory of it.

Today Bobbie was able to hold a coherent conversation with me. She told me about her large family, about her father, a tycoon whom she calls by his initials.

She told me her fears. First she mentioned only a fear of cancer, of which she says her mother died, but then she spoke at length about "the terrible pain" which she tried to avoid and which she dreaded beforehand. "I didn't mean it," she said, "but there had to be the pain and now I have to be in an insane asylum and the pain is getting worse."

Her modesty about the location of her "pains" made me suspect their genital origin, and later she admitted that she feared she was pregnant and dreaded having or having had—an abortion.

She believes that living with her unaffectionate family, along with fears about sex, are the cause of her sickness. But according to the Institute, "we do not know the cause of schizophrenia."

I become more and more convinced that the science of psychiatry is banging the patients' heads against a wall of innumerable therapies which harm and warp and ultimately kill.

February 14, 1948   *Hartford*

For Valentine's for Julian I make a montage of a heart cut from a magazine, a slow snail, a swift butterfly, a detail from Matisse, with citations, "Now is the winter of our discontent," and "When winter comes can spring be far behind?"

February 17, 1948   *Hartford*

For the past four days I have been working in a Group Room.

The sickest of the group room cases is a white-haired, dignified old lady, Mrs. Lee, whom I specialed. Completely shattered by the death of her husband nine months ago, she trembles and will not eat. Tonight "they" will come and take her away "to a dungeon." "They" will cut off her hair. "They" will brand her. Her food, she claims, is poisoned. If I drink half the cup of "doped" eggnog, it does not convince her of its harmlessness.

She wrestled with me down the stairs to the X-ray room and I would never have succeeded in getting her there if a strong nurse had not happened by. Once there the poor woman pleaded with me to let her out before they tortured her. Her resistance makes me cruel in my own eyes.

I spend this evening at a Tony Pastor concert trying to forget for a while the misery of these unfortunate women.

February 18, 1948   *New York City*

I live half in Hartford and half in New York. The bus journey is long and there is no light to read by, so I watch the still cities that seem uninhabited, except for the live neon.

Eva Le Gallienne is playing *Ghosts* at the Cort Theater. Exactly two years ago I was in this theater with Julian, seeing Anouilh's *Antigone* with Katharine Cornell. When Antigone stood up against Creon's cold, pragmatic justice the whole world seemed ripe with possibilities. I think of that night, and Mrs. Alving seems drab as I sit alone in the second balcony.

February 23, 1948   *Hartford*

Since I have been away from home I haven't eaten meat, even on my weekends in New York. If there seems to be less variety in the meatless diet, it is compensated by a sense of lessened suffering.

I still eat fish, but I say "still" because I intend to put an end to that soon. However, there are too many arguments about vegetarianism at the table.

Tonight an attractive young man argues with me at dinner. I explain that I feel it's an evasion of reality to be able to eat a lamb only because it was someone else and not I who had to cut its throat.

He asks irrelevantly: "Do you believe animals have souls?"

February 24, 1948   *Hartford*

A long-awaited letter from Julian, arrives. A letter as enigmatic as he himself.

Forgive the impersonality of this letter. Behind it all is enormous feeling. For I have more feeling, for you, dearest dearest Judith, than for anyone I have ever known I think. . . .

I will not answer yet because I do not want to write in the first flood of emotion.

February 29, 1948   *Hartford*

From Elizabeth Chapel I hear the faint sound of "A Mighty Fortress Is

Our God." The evergreens are loaded down with thick snow. I think of Julian. I'm unable to enjoy what I can't share.

Friday night in New York at the Ballet Russe's *Giselle*, Julian said that when we admire opera or theater, we don't necessarily want to be singers or actors. But at the ballet we long to be one of the dancers because the ballet creates a world in which miracles occur, where what is most tragic is most beautiful, where death is sad but never disgusting.

March 1, 1948   *Hartford*

The daily events of the hall called Brigham II become routine. Mrs. Lee struck me so hard in the solar plexus this morning that I fainted. But I'll have forgotten it after lunch.

Reading: *Beowulf*, the counterpart of our comic strips—the superhuman hero and the supernatural monster.

Gide's *Journals*. He has a monumental mind, but he is cruel. And these early journals are merciless self-dissections. He suffers in order to learn the mechanics of suffering.

Though Gide hints at it, he says he can't explain why he writes a journal. He records his experience to savor or to learn from it, but I write in order to become increasingly involved in it.

When Gide describes Africa it is as no man ever saw it. It is Africa in Gide, not Gide in Africa.

This, too, I admire in him.

March 2, 1948   *Hartford*

Motionless while awaiting a letter from Julian. I'm glad that nothing happens.

Gide writes: "I was like a sailor who drops his oars and lets himself drift; at last he takes time to look at the shore; while he was rowing he saw nothing."

Every day I record the fluctuating emotional behavior of my patients on the hospital charts. Every day they change. Every day I am the same.

March 3, 1948   *Hartford*

Suddenly everyone is depressed. Mrs. Lee will not even dress herself.

A tall professor's wife, Mrs. Fagin, is brought to the group room. Her husband drove her to the Institute for an electroencephalogram in connection with her epileptic seizures. She signed a paper thinking it was for the EEG, and suddenly her husband was gone. Someone emptied her pocketbook, ushered her into a hall and told her that she would have to stay. I hear the same story from everyone who has "committed herself": that they never realized that they were to be locked up. The discovery of the keys is horrifying and we who keep the keys are the living embodiment of that horror.

I warn her that the only way to go home is to show no agitation, no matter how deeply felt. She agrees to act the role.

The atmosphere is thick with unrest. Fortunately I have three days' respite.

March 4, 1948   *New York*

On the bus to New York I read Gide. He is less cruel with age. I feel shamed by his learning. How can I justify never having read Stendhal or Montaigne at the age of twenty-one?

But where is the time to read? And to work? And to live?

March 7, 1948   *Hartford*

On the bus to Hartford I read in Gide's journal his experiences in waking and sleeping on a train through France: glimpsed landscapes and a drowsy awareness of geography.

And of his devoted reading of Stendhal's journal over a period of two years, as a great delicacy which he allows himself only in small daily portions. He expresses the wish that one day his journals might influence some young man as he was being influenced.

It's like that box of cereal on which there is a picture of a woman holding a box of cereal on which there is a picture of woman holding a box of cereal, until the picture becomes too small to see. Am I the one too small?

Now I want to read Stendhal.

March 8, 1948   *Hartford*

Mrs. Lee grows thinner and bit by bit the vestiges of refinement give way to a fixed expression of terror. She carries her head thrown back and to the side and looks at me with a kitten's amazement.

There is no joy in this work. Next week I will be on "night duty." To sit silent all night in the half darkness and listen to sleep.

It's nine o'clock. I wish I could stay home and read and write, but I feel the need for others. Gide's fortunate love of solitude: "I am delightfully sufficient unto myself." Happy he. I must go out.

March 9, 1948   *Hartford*

At noon I am told that Mrs. Lee is to be moved to South II. This morning she entered the dining room terrified that she was to be taken to "the very bowels of the earth." Now, when I have to tell her that she is to be moved, my palms are wet with anxiety. She looks at me quietly. "I knew it," she says. "I told you this was coming."

"You know we only try to do what is best for you," I tell her. But my words sicken my stomach and sound painfully stupid.

She sits passively watching me pack her belongings into a large laundry hamper, but puts up a vigorous fight when we go.

The damp warmth of South II nauseates me as I lead Mrs. Lee past the forty-bed ward to the crowded sun room. She repeats over and over again: "Miss Malina, Miss Malina, let me stay with you!"

When she is through the door I have to shut it forcibly, careful to keep from slamming her fingers that still reach for me.

She looks at me dumbly through the inch-thick glass. My feet seem to stick to the clean linoleum as I make my way back.

I compose an elegiac poem for an unborn child, inspired by the exotic names of the flowers and the shrubs on the campus.

The boy Garrick, the most ambitious dream of Julian and Judith.

March 10, 1948   *Hartford*

The Department of Educational Therapy gives me a record album of Blitz-stein's *Airborne* Symphony for a music appreciation class that I am required to conduct.

The war theme agitates the guests, who burst into tears, forcing me to stop the machine. They hurl accusations:

"Don't you realize that most of us are in here because of the war? Because of what the war has done to us?"

"Don't you realize we don't want to hear war music?"

They don't like me anymore.

At lunch, gruesome news of a knifing in North I, the most-disturbed-men's hall.

A dream: about Bobbie and me—and Julian: A nurse comes to understand her patient's gibberish as the real truth behind the myth which the nurse has built around a remembered incident and an elusive man. The gap between wisdom and well-being closes. The dream ends in an ode to joy: "Tochter aus Elysium."

After work I try to write. Clean desk and room. Regulate temperature. Turn away the face of the clock. I use only the tiny reading light so that the whole room is in darkness except the paper.

I take the pen and push thinking of Piscator's admonishment, "Every man can learn the alphabet and how to write words. But he can then utilize this knowledge to write business letters or to compose Goethe's *Faust*." I turn out a banal dream story about a nurse unhappily in love.

I turn the clock around: 9:30. The frustration is complete. I go out in a strangely good humor.

March 14, 1948   *New York*

Yesterday Julian called Mother to ask for the script of Paul Goodman's *Hagar*. He didn't know I was in New York. We were happily surprised to hear each other's voice.

In his studio we pore over the playbill collection. He gives me a drawing from 1944, bright orange censored and confined by a vague but assertive black circle. More than his other work, it is an angry drawing.

Antony and Cleopatra: Julian arrived after the curtain was up and stood with me at the back of the theater.

Gide says he weeps in the theater and that the name Agamemnon spoken on the stage is enough to make the tears come. My copious tears antagonized Julian at Olivier's Oedipus. He didn't weep.

March 16, 1948   *New York to Hartford*

Through Harlem and now over the small black water that marks the end of Manhattan. I look with interest at this darkness which I shall come to know well; tomorrow I will be on night duty.

Night is the time to remember Pancho. I visited him impulsively today in his miserable little hotel. At the door, the pale revolting odor of stale alcohol reminds me of the room on 64th Street which Val and Julian rented for Pancho in the days when he was revered for his decay and idealized for his usefulness to society.

Now the ruin eats away the memory of the memory of the drunken poet I adored at Valeska Gert's. His hands are horribly burned. I don't let him touch me.

March 17, 1948   *Hartford*

It grows dark. I am about to go to work. Julian's long letter is about poetry, plays, painting:

> . . . Passing thru Yale was a little dead, I suppose it was a result of my attitudes towards school. Perhaps it was my natural, or unnatural, rebellion against authority. Perhaps it is the fact that school is a sort of marking-time place that puts limits on the possible areas for creative expansion which in me seems to be a need that is akin to the sexual need. . . .
>
> I am writing some poems—partially because I want to write poems and partially as exercises before starting the play. . . .
>
> There are three plays in my head and I am working on the notes for the three of them. . . .
>
> Then there are the paintings—I am still doing drawing after drawing—they are a means of quickly getting out of my system the innumerable visual experiences that I had in the six months that I did no painting while working on the theater. . . .
>
> I shall parcel post to you a drawing. In my mind's index it's called The Ribbon Pond. Since it's a pastel you'll have to put it under glass.

March 18, 1948   *Hartford*

The night shift was a long, futile struggle against sleep, watching the sleepers. I walk up and down the dark corridors not daring to sit, for I no sooner sit but I sleep. At the midnight break I fry two eggs. Everything seems absurd as in a dream.

I'm going to make a request for disturbed duty in the South wards, where it's impossible to fall asleep because there's always action.

March 21, 1948   *Hartford*

Writing in South I:
Disappearance of sense of time and place and, exquisite fear, alerting every energy. Nothing in my mind or body dares to give less than full awareness.

A screaming girl, uncontrollable features, cross-eyed, devoid of memory, to be put in cold pack. When we undress her, her perfect body is both small and generous; small breasts, pale bright skin. Twelve hands push the naked body across the wet sheet. All of us oblivious to the person, solely involved with physical restraint. Wrapped like a mummy, only the contorted face screams.

March 22, 1948   *Between Hartford and New York*

The long, pink worms squirming on the walks when I left work this morning were beautiful. But the motionless, squashed ones made me walk carefully.

Last night I was in charge of Brigham II. Rushing requests for food and medications on every side. I was alone and responsible for charting every guest, weighing them, and hearing out their complaints.

All night long the work kept ahead of me, like a horse on a carousel.

Morning. The carousel streaking into a nightmare. No sleep the day before either.

But in this bus the open window blows summer into my face as I write and I feel completely fresh.

At Westport the bus stops at a noisy restaurant where George Bartenieff is playing a pinball machine, looking very tall and adult.

He was twelve when he played Pinocchio and I played the cat in Mme. Piscator's Children's Workshop. He is still with Mme. Piscator, playing Bottom in *Midsummer Night's Dream*. I envy him his air of familiarity when he talks about the theater as though saying "*du*" to her.

March 23, 1948   *New York*

Coming home yesterday too active from sleeplessness to go to bed, I went to the studio for which Julian had sent me a key.

He is at work on a drawing. When I arrive he stops work and we compare the theater programs which we have accumulated during the week: Bernhardt, Edwin Booth, Modjeska.

At Shaw's comedy *You Never Can Tell*. I talk to old acquaintances. Everyone is "doing something." They all say, "What are you doing now?" Or, "How is your theater group coming?" And I struggle to say something.

I like talking to people at intermissions. Because the conversation is of a specified length, because there are no awkward partings, because the conversation never comes to one of those baffling standstills as there is always the play to discuss, and lastly there's a mutual compliment in the fact that we are all at the same play.

March 24, 1948   *New York*

Amiel's journals. He plunges directly into the subject of deity and devotion. He even dislikes eating and walking which he calls "coarsened thoughts."

It's Purim; in synagogue the *graggers* accompany the melodrama of Ahasuerus, the vulnerable king and Esther, bartering her beauty, and Mordecai, wresting reaping honors from Haman, and his harsh wife, Zeresh. I see them as subjects for a comedy, till I think of Racine's tragedy.

March 25, 1948   *Hartford*

Not having slept on the bus, I was afraid that I would fall asleep on duty.

In desperation I broke open a benzedrine inhaler, tore off a piece of the drug-soaked paper inside, and dropped it into a Coca-Cola. It worked well. Too well almost. I regret that my spirits are not always as fine as they are this morning. Finished Gide's *Journals*, but only the first time through. Wrote a short story. No title yet. All night I concoct plans for the theater.

March 26, 1948   *Hartford*

Restlessness. There's a filthy damp in South I that I can't wash off.

I go home to sleep, but I can't sleep. To work without sleep.

I learn that Mrs. Lee was moved back to a less-disturbed ward yesterday, and today the aide who was specialing her found her dead, hanging by her belt in her closet.

March 27, 1948   *Hartford*

The routine aspects of living become the most difficult. Only when the life of necessity is under control can any deeper life develop.

Facing another night's work with three hours' sleep.

March 28, 1948   *Hartford*

I wake this evening from an unremembered dream with the vivid sense of my father's presence. Too rarely do I permit myself to think about my father, and yet there the roots of my character lie buried. . . .

The pain of his death when I was thirteen; my mother's unquenchable grief hidden in her silence; the strength that his history inspires.

If only she had let me talk of him, all these years, but her sorrow is too much for her—or for me—and his name is never spoken in our house, so that he has become both myth and taboo.

His struggle set the pattern for my life:

When there was yet no power behind the National Socialists he felt the hatred rising and—when I was two—he took us to New York from the Germany that didn't want us anymore. Thus I was spared when most of our family was murdered.

Here he founded a small congregation, living in discreet poverty, veiled by a refinement that forbade even a moment of coarseness.

He was the acknowledged spiritual leader of our community, my mother his *"Frau Doktor Rabbiner"* and a certain standard was expected of me as their daughter.

I failed it often. But it set a standard for my life.

He conducted services for his German speaking congregation in borrowed chapels and in rented halls. He edited a small newspaper, *Der Zeitgeist*, and later *Das Jüdische Familienblatt*, which published his appeals for the rescue of the Jews of Germany and Poland, among more theoretical pieces by Gutkind and Buber.

All the while he was trying to move heaven and earth to save the Jews from the death camps. He gathered with the famous, conferred with the rich and the great, formed committees with congressmen, with Einstein, campaigning to convince Roosevelt to raise or suspend the immigration quotas. . . . Devoted himself totally—and died at forty-two—at the height of his vigor.

His cause was not a pacifist one—He wanted the United States to intervene. How we would have argued about isolationism . . .—when I was fourteen.

But he was struck down by leukemia, suddenly and painfully. I wonder if he would have become an American patriot. I think not, for he taught me, "They can always take my country away from me. But they can never take my Torah away from me." He was asking me not to put my faith in princes or in nations, but to put my trust in the truth.

The brevity of his life and the suddenness of its end have set before me the specter of death, making me aware of how little time there is.

Then I think of his great spirit and his great struggles. His struggle for a synagogue to worship in; his relentless battle with political people; his ability to keep burning with the original brightness of his belief; then I remember his love.

March 29, 1948   *Hartford*

I move into my own room. The first room of which I am the sole occupant.

My privacy is complete. Working at night, I never speak to anyone. It is very pleasant.

Julian writes:

" . . . The world news of the last week has been so distressing that the other morning I awoke and the combination of wasted time and the state of the world projected me into a profound depression, which placed me for a good ten hours on the verge of tears. . . .

. . . You know I like to flatter myself into believing that I am doing something for myself and for others by painting or writing things that will either bring beauty or shed light. But it seems such a minor contribution, seems to affect so little, so few. Oh you know you know you know what it is that I am trying so painfully to say. . . .

Our last meeting? The forced laughter you mean? Ah, Judith, you and I are terrified of the false sound, the uneasy moment, the seconds of untrue conversation. And we try to cover over the uneasiness with all kinds of artificialities. We are not natural when we are with each other. We guard every word. If we would only remember that we cannot hide things from each other. We do, we do, we do know each other too well. We know each other so well that the little poses, the little hidings glare all the more. . . .

I have been reading plays at a rapid rate. It is quite impossible for me to begin writing a play when I have not read more than half of Shakespeare. My most astounding confession to date. There! What intimacy! You are the only person to whom I could tell that. Who knows what comes next?"

South I. Specialing Tessie Bauer. I see her through the glass square of the seclusion room clutching a piece of blanket in a catatonic stupor. Suddenly she looks up. Hideous.

Have I really finished this notebook of 200 pages in three months? What have I done? Played in *Spook Sonata* and taken a job in a hospital in Hartford. Hoped and waited. Waited. Waited. Waited.

> Now the white lady and the murmured law
> Dissolve into an image in the mind
> And the blind slumberer who dreamt he saw
> Awakens and is blind.

April 1, 1948   *Hartford*

I learn that Bobbie is to be given a lobotomy. Murder!

April 2, 1948   *Hartford*

I hand in my resignation at the Institute of Living.

April 3, 1948   *Hartford*

No sleep. I roam through South I active with benzedrine.
My last night of work.

April 4, 1948   *New York*

I arrive in this city trembling with excitement. My little room in Hartford is empty. A few vivid memories of my last night at work; especially of the slap delivered by Mrs. Liggett. The movement of her hand. A sharp light ringing as of metal.

Of Mrs. Gosling, a tragedian. With arms outstretched proclaiming, "Look at us, look at us, caught in the web of our achievements. . . ." I dream of South I.

April 5, 1948

I find a job in the cosmetics department of McCreery's Department Store. A vulgar profusion of odors. Places where I've worked with strong odors: the kitchens of several restaurants; the unique stench of Valeska's Beggar Bar; the smell of damp heat in Consolidated Laundries; South I.

I am supposed to sell a hair-coloring crayon to cover streaks of gray, but I didn't sell a single crayon all day. Women of all sorts walk by the counter and I'm supposed to address them, "Madam, do you want to cover your gray hair?" But I can't bring myself to say it.

At lunch I walk among thousands milling around the garment district. A union election is about to take place and the workers have stuck cards in their hatbands reading Vote Bessie Weissmann or Vote Dore Schwartz. They are handing out leaflets. Meanwhile a sound truck is campaigning for Henry Wallace; and the two elections compete for the interest of the clothing worker.

Another truck is loudly petitioning for the withdrawal of United States troops from China, and some people are marching with placards reading "Our guns are killing our boys." Someone in a high building pours torn paper from the window to express his sympathies. The confetti excites the crowd to even more vehement expression. I push my way back to my job on Fifth Avenue.

April 6, 1948

Julian wants to start work on the Living Theatre again. I am overjoyed!

Immediately we resume planning. We count up those who were lost in the melee: Donald Oenslager, Aline Bernstein, Norman Bel Geddes—three designers with whom we had made appointments we didn't keep because of our separation. Can we approach them again?

Mr. Malin, however, is still holding our $500 deposit and is still saying that the theater will be complete in ten days.

April 8, 1948

On a walk with Julian through a softened, misty night we talk about the future of the Living Theatre. Then by the East River we embrace and fears and barriers are broken down.

April 9, 1948

On my last day at McCreery's I spend the hours thinking about Ibsen's *Lady from the Sea*. I shall play Ellida and Julian will direct, dreams of Duse and Gordon Craig.

We see *Macbeth* with Redgrave and Robson and talk for hours afterward at Sardi's.

Though I had promised myself that I wouldn't, I speak of our bitter fight.

But the anger is gone, and as I speak I realize that our misadventures only bring us closer. It's a kind of turning point and I want to say that I love him, but he is Julian, and I am afraid.

April 11, 1948

Yesterday was Army Day and Mother and my cousin Josie went to watch the uniformed men march with their guns up Fifth Avenue. They don't understand my horror at this. They say to me, "But this is our only safeguard against war!"

Spent most of yesterday and today with Julian. We laugh a great deal and only the haunt of the state of the world sours our spirits.

August 14, 1945:
It is the night of peace; Julian and I crowd with what seems all the rest of the joyous world into Times Square. Cheering and kissing, crowned with streamers and embraced by intimate strangers. From now on, we

believe all humankind will work for life not for death, and the whole world will turn toward peace and closer bonds of love.

The front page of the *Times* today reports Russia's vetoes in the United Nations; stirring up fear and hatred; headlines Palestine torn in battle; revolution in Colombia; crisis in Czechoslovakia; riots in Italy. Distrust and violence everywhere. Where is the peace we celebrated?

Julian fears the draft and I say that I would never let him go to war, and we look at the world around us and we shudder.

It begins to dawn on me why the wise Paul Goodman chooses to count himself among the strange anarchists.

Yet one cannot step aside to let the worst take over. And yet, and yet . . .

April 19, 1948

After a long trudge of job hunting, I get a job at the Johnson O'Connor Aptitude Testing Foundation.

Before I start, I must take the whole battery of tests. I'm a failure at the mathematics and I find the Seashore Pitch Tests painful to my ears.

April 21, 1948

When I complete the aptitude tests, they give me a booklet called *The Too-Many Aptitude Woman.* I'm pleased, and even take a little pride in the fact that what I can't do I do very badly, as though this implied that my accomplishments are proportionate.

The Ballet Theatre: *Billy the Kid* with Copeland music; *Apollo,* a *nouveau classique; On Stage.*

Why was I bored? I am out of patience with watching. I want to go beyond the roles of the dancer actor writer into some greater immediacy. Yes, it's impatience, not boredom.

April 22, 1948

I begrudge this evening the time it takes to make these notes.

My great crime: indolence. Under it every virtue is obliterated. My crimes against myself in the order of their gravity: 1) Indolence = Satisfaction with the superficial. 2) Disorder = Impatience. 3) Underestimation of my abilities = Inferiority complex.

The remedies for these crimes: work.

April 23, 1948

Asleep through most of the Seder. In this way I express my antagonism and miss the meal. I can't expect Cousin Recha, Aunt Jenny and Ismar to understand why I won't eat meat.

Last night I had a dream about this Seder and my unwillingness to eat meat. I dreamed that I rose to ask the מַה נִּשְׁתַּנָּה, the four questions, and lifting up my wineglass, I said instead of the traditional words:

He prayeth best, who loveth best
All things both great and small;
For the dear God who loveth us,
He made and loveth all.

Then with dramatic emphasis I drained the heavy goblet. The dream delights me.

The Seder is an ordeal. Ismar, my cousin Recha's new husband, conducts the ritual without poetry. My father used to make me feel all the suffering of the years in the desert and the rejoicing at our release from bondage.

"With a love I seemed to lose with my lost saints."

My father's voice, my father's prayer.

April 25, 1948

Spring gloried on the walk to meet Julian, the whole city covered with yellow-green forsythia buds. I forgot everything, floating along in that air.

At Julian's studio. How can I describe what I do not understand? Julian both wants me and does not want me. When he finally breaks through the barricades of feeling, he stops because he fears a definite step.

He assumes that I want him without qualification. I acquiesce. This is no time to argue. Julian's own struggle is enough for him. So I let him lead me anywhere.

But the truth is I do not want Julian unqualifiedly but with love . . . that's what I want from Julian and anything less is inadmissible.

April 26, 1948

In the lawyer's office the details of incorporation are finally attended to. I am named secretary and vice-president while Julian bears the title of president. We acquire an intricately embossed book of stock shares and a corporate seal that stamps out The Living Theatre Incorporated 1947 New York.

And still there is no theater.

April 27, 1948

Of Hans Richter's surrealist film *Dreams That Money Can Buy*, one might say with Strindberg, "It is very beautiful, but is full of imperfections."

The first dream, called "Desire," is Max Ernst's mid-Victorian concoction with Ernst himself and art dealer Julien Levy in surreal-romantic roles. "The Girl with the Prefabricated Heart," by Fernand Léger with lyrics by John Latouche. Man Ray's "Ruth Roses and Revolvers." Marcel Duchamp's "Nude Descending a Staircase." Alexander Calder's "Ballet," with Paul Bowles' music. Calder's "Circus." And Richter's "Narcissus."

How can we look to these older artists with anything approaching reverence? They were the tradition breakers, but in this film they have left us nothing. The young artist works without any heritage, betrayed by the early "moderns."

May 1, 1948

Going to work I find police blockades all around Fifth Avenue for the two May Day parades. One, the traditional workers' gathering, the other a "Loyalty Day" display antagonistic to the first.

Yesterday Julian took me to a City College production of Marlowe's *Edward II* in which Julie Bovasso, a girl of sixteen, shone as an amazingly mature and gracious Isabella.

After the play we went to the home of a college friend of Julian's, Pierre Garai and his very French mother. Pierre is intimidatingly intelligent.

The young men discuss obscure French poets over port, while in the kitchen, Mme. Garai, making tea, wrests from me intimate confessions about Julian.

"Ah, I can see you are madly in love with Julian and he with you, but wait. You have time. First comes the theater."

"Ah," she says, throwing her arms sideways in a gesture replete with knowledge and despair, "you need not wait to have your *stationery* to write Cocteau. Ah,"—gesture again—"my dear, you do not know Cocteau! Ah, darling, Cocteau would love you!"

This evening, the premiere of Balanchine's *Orpheus*, one of the most beautiful performances I've seen in any theater. Stravinsky's music, Noguchi's settings and costumes.

Three sculptures by Noguchi are the only objects on the stage. In the center a dancer turned away from the audience, his head bowed. Women carry gifts to Orpheus: with the bow and the lyre on their clasped arms, they lead him to the underworld.

And when they lead him down they do not dance; they walk, a slow, dramatic walk as a white translucent curtain wafts down like a wave in slow motion. Behind it Noguchi's forms ascend, the earth rising as the dancers sink into the underworld.

If only I could recapture one iota of the tragedy of that walk for Oedipus and Antigone when they go to glory in *The Infernal Machine*.

A startling moment for applause: Noguchi, Balanchine, and Stravinsky taking a curtain call together. Julian shouts "bravo."

After being bored by theater and ballet for a long time, despite the moments when I doubt the value of all false face and mimicry, I'm glad to feel the wonder again.

1943:
I'm walking with a former dancer of the Joos Ballet Company, now old and sick and down-and-out. I had just bought him a cup of coffee and suddenly he pulls me across the street shouting, "Isamu, Isamu darling. I want you to meet the most fantastic actress in the world. Isamu, this is Judith."

Noguchi extends his hand. I murmur, "How do you do?"

Finally my friend says, "Isamu, darling, give me a dime."

The sculptor complies.

May 3, 1948

I go to work for the Johnson O'Connor Institute, housed in a dilapidated mansion. Among the crystal chandeliers and the brocade falling in tatters, I sort papers for the filing cabinets.

Three music tests are being given in the room where I am writing: Pitch Determination, Tonal Memory and Rhythm. Several examiners have suffered nosebleeds from these recordings.

I sit in the rear and mark yesterday's tests: Design Memory, Finger Dexterity and Vocabulary.

May 5, 1948

I see Julian often. *Fluctuat nec mergitur.*

May 10, 1948

The first sultry day of summer has made me pliable and quiet like the air. Nothing presses me, not even Julian's affection. No impatience.

May 11, 1948

The first performance of the Poet's Theater at the 92nd Street YMHA, organized by Maria Ley Piscator.

Paul Goodman's two Noh plays, *Dusk* and *Stoplight*, open the program.

Excessive choreography belittles the bare and thoughtful plays, which Paul intends as the modern equivalent of the Medieval Noh.

At intermission the talkative and ebullient John Myers, who organized the evening, describes the second part of the program as a *pièce de résistance*, a work of great importance.

It is Genet's *Les Bonnes.*

Its theme is servitude: the love of the maids for the mistress, a *Weltbild* in a lady's boudoir, full of possibilities, ready for all sorts of theatrical things. But the direction was seduced by the chic instead of repelled by it; the acting frivolous.

After the performance, friends of Paul invite us to discuss the plays.

The choruses in Paul's Noh Plays lead Julian to ask at what point and by whom the chorus was first used during the action rather than as interlude.

Paul says, "Probably Shelley."

"*Prometheus Unbound?*"

Paul says, "The chorus is classically the voice of the poet; it's a new invention to use the chorus in the action. The Greeks never used it that way. The Greek chorus was always of a lower class than the protagonists and represented the townspeople, the slaves, the women."

May 13, 1948

Thunder shook the high French doors and lightning illumined Mr. O'Connor as he spoke during our staff meeting. He is a man who constantly smiles. Someone from the staff explained that this is due to his being "extremely objective."

During working hours I read *Rosmersholm* and reread *The Lady from the Sea*.

The Habimah Theatre presents *David's Crown* by Calderon on Broadway. Julian says the language sounds as he imagines Greek to sound. I like the extravagance of Hannah Rovina and the sounds the actors make—the groans, the shrieks, the extenuated wails.

May 14, 1948

The declaration of the Jewish state of Israel. I have strong and divided feelings about this important news. A dream 2,000 years old, the fulfillment of the Diasporan hope.

I've said too often "If I forget thee, O Jerusalem" to feel unaffected. But it is not Zionism that moves me. Zionism is not the establishment of the true Zion. The true Zion reconciles Jew, Arab and Christian. The true Zion can never be nationalistic. Nationalism always courts bloodshed and competition and the horror of war.

Holy War? How can one hate the Arabs for defending the land they have lived in while we Jews were dispersed over the whole earth?

May the viciousness of the battle never rouse me to hate.

Now armies from Egypt and Iraq are attacking by sea, air and land. The United Nations broadcasts diplomatic courtesies that take up hours of the time for decision. They are discussing a "mediator of Palestine" and argue over wordings and amendments superimposed for some interest.

Last night I saw the national theater of this new nation act out the strife of brothers over the crown of David. In the final scene David rejects the crown because it is the cause of bloodshed.

I lose my job at Johnson O'Connor for no stated reason. It may be that I am not objective enough.

May 15, 1948

Mother is having a birthday party from which I have momentarily escaped.

Bobby Jastrow's parents are here proudly announcing that their son, having just received his doctorate in nuclear physics, is going to go to the Princeton Institute for Advanced Studies, where he has been invited on a fellowship.[7]

Robert, who explained (with anatomical charts) the mysterious ways of sex to me at his Bar Mitzvah party, the first time I wore high heels, is now one of the architects of the future.

We were discussing Wallace and the split vote with the Jastrows, and I am trembling with all sorts of emotions. The atom, its fearsome weapons, in the frail hands of men. I flee to the bathroom, the only private place in the apartment. Here I ponder: What within my tiny scope can I do? I am small, yet I am strong. It is not beyond my power to make choices. But it's so difficult . . . so insurmountably difficult. I must stop.

Reading, in French, Cocteau's *Le Foyer des artistes* and, simultaneously, a review of French grammar. When Cocteau's language eludes me I turn in defeat to the list of irregular verbs.

May 16, 1948

A family visit to Bernard Suhl whom I haven't seen since I was a child. His mother has just arrived from the new state of Israel. A superb old woman, she tells stories of the guiding spirits and other folkloric tales with serene belief.

Last night *Medea* closed. Seeing the play for the third time I become aware of the perfection of the plot.

Afterward, Julian says extraordinary things to me. He imagines in some fatalistic way that he loves me. But love, to him, is the forbidden and undesirable breaking of the certain seal of self. . . .

May 17, 1948

Alfred Kreymborg asks me to come hear some new poetry.

Kreymborg reads me political tirades in blank verse. One against Churchill. He is embroiled in the political battle and talks mostly about Wallace and Washington and the radical position.

After lunch in the co-op cafeteria we walk in Washington Square. Kreymborg talks all the way. He does not like me to talk. He doesn't like anyone else to talk because he has very much to say.

May 19, 1948

Paul Ransome from the Dramatic Workshop asks me to read my role in *The Flies* for a recording.

Consequently, this morning is spent at the New School. I pass the time in conversation with Dr. Franz Engel, just returned from Europe. He is pessimistic about America's political future. The Russians, he assures me, are not as villainous as the American press makes them out to be. And America is just as jealous of her power in Europe as the Russians, if not more so. He points out that the Americans used all the means at their disposal, as did the Russians, to sway the Italian elections.

Europe, he feels, is entering a renaissance while the United States is heading for a decline.

Mike Gazzo says that Irving Stiber's Interplayers have started rehearsals for *The Infernal Machine.* Alexis Solomos is directing.

I talk with Alexis. He says apologetically that he imagined that we had dropped the idea of doing *The Infernal Machine.* I tell him that this is not so. But I tell him that we should not think of ourselves as rivals. He pretends that he will consult me on production problems.

May 20, 1948

We write to William Carlos Williams asking for a meeting and the rights to one of his plays.

Walk by the river. The row of lights reflected in the Hudson when a slight fog dulls the Jersey shore.

The news from Palestine, the new State of Israel: The Jews are fighting a losing battle for Jerusalem. Many are trapped in the old city which is now almost entirely in Arab hands. Britain continues giving aid to the Arabs.

May 21, 1948

At the Metropolitan Museum of Art military police are guarding an exhibit of paintings taken from Germany during the war for safekeeping.

Array of treasures: Botticelli's study for his Venus, his tender Saint Sebastian, Vermeer's *Lady with a Pearl Necklace*, Rembrandt's *Man with a Golden Helmet*, and his *Moses* smashing the tablets.

To the modern painters on 57th Street: a fierce and brilliant Picasso show at Knoedler's. I feel only abstract appreciation for these masterpieces. I try. Julian thrills to them. I am far behind. Le Corbusier's show. Robert Motherwell's show. Eugene Berman's show. Now I have looked at too many paintings.

We go on, however, to the Pierre Bonnard show at the Museum of Modern Art.

The sun is suddenly exquisite on the way to the Museum. Church bells. Brightness. Almost too much.

It was the right preparation for Bonnard's sunlit room and his wholesomely set table.

May 23, 1948

In the Sunday Times the publication of the second volume of Gide's journals is announced. I've never looked forward to a book with greater anticipation. In the same paper a note about the translation of Stendhal's journals, which served Gide as a model.

Habimah's *Oedipus Rex*. All the choruses sung in a Semitic melody. Some stylized movements for the blind and very ancient Tiresias. A setting of columns and levels. Julian murmurs "Appia."

May 26, 1948

I get a job at the Book and Card Shop. I sell "Belated congratulations on my sister's anniversary" and "Congratulations on entering the service of the Lord" cards.

I called Fabienne Loy; her mother answered the phone. I told her that I was an admirer of her work.

"What work do you mean? You don't mean to say you have read something I've written? I didn't imagine anyone knew I existed anymore."

She was excited at my assurance that there are many people who still read and admire Mina Loy's poetry.

"You know, I have no idea where they find it. Recently someone wanted to get a little volume together and I couldn't find the old poems and have only a few new ones. Do you know where any of them were printed?"

I had just read some in *Others* at Kreymborg's house last week. And there were some that Julian knew of. She grew quite excited.

"I'm certain this is an omen. It would change my whole life if I could find those old poems."

I told her I would make a list of her published work.

May 27, 1948

Lost my job.

I fluctuate. I listen avidly to advice. I am swayed by everything I look at. All things seem potential examples for me. When I see Julian I observe the pitfall and promptly jump into it. There I indulge my vices.

May 29, 1948

An exuberant letter from William Carlos Williams. He is more than anxious to see his plays in production. The good news and encouragement fill us with energy. He writes:

My dear Judith Malina and Julian Beck:

You've got me shaking in my shoes! Nothing in and perhaps out of this world could possibly give me more satisfaction than a performance on an actual stage of a suitable play by me. And that's putting it mildly.

BUT are my plays "suitable" for any sort of performance? The doubts rise like a fog creeping over the sun. Is my first play, the one that appeared in the issue of New Directions, witty enough to carry the dialogue? I had hoped that it was so and perhaps the ability of the actors may be able to add just that edge that would make the lines successful—but I am scared! scared to think that what should sound light might sound heavy—to the unwilling. In other words, it's a battle I see before me, a battle to sell myself to you and a possible audience. With help I might do it. I deeply appreciate your wish to give me the opportunity to put up a fight.

I'd be delighted to have a conference with you over the plays at some early date—give me some idea where I may find you possibly on a Friday afternoon. And here's to the future full of rose edged clouds.

Sincerely,
W. C. Williams

May 30, 1948

Kreymborg recommends my work to an actor, Lou Polan, who is active in the Third Party Campaign. He's amiable, and eager to talk about Henry Wallace and his party.

He asks me what my plans are. At the mention of a new theater company he attacks me, "Would you want to direct a theater under a fascist government? Because that's where we're heading unless . . ."

He is pessimistic, as any reader of newspapers should be. He is enthusiastic. I agree with him about peace, freedom and the possibilities of radical politics. And when he asks whether I wish to become a member of the PAC, the Political Action Committee, I know I will have a tough time defending my negative response.

I cannot, for the present, see myself allied to any group. At this point my thinking demands freedom to develop its own channels. First I want to know what I believe, then look for those who believe as I do and help them in their cause, because it is my cause.

Lou Polan asks whether this means that I will never be one of those who form the important dissenting minority in any group. It means I won't support a party which supports policies of which I disapprove.

Lou Polan calls this lack of faith. He promises, however, a performance for any play that I prepare for the campaign as long as it has a message that furthers the cause.

We decide on Kreymborg's cantata, *No More War*. I agree to get music and actors.

June 1, 1948

Yesterday: Julian's 23rd birthday. He says he feels old.

I am as one possessed today. Anxieties and hopes set off by thoughts on my reluctant place in the political structure, my immense dissatisfaction with all existing orders.

To construct a political philosophy, I must

1) Develop a theory of social behavior (abstract);

2) Develop a historical understanding of what contributes to human happiness (concrete);

3) Be able to suggest procedures for integrating the ideal social situation with the real, individual, human factor (active).

And, in addition to that, a wide knowledge of practical things: economics, food, housing, everything, everything. . . . before I am equipped to take political action.

During my thoughts the mail brings *Resistance*, the anarchist newspaper, which I have been receiving ever since a young poet named Honig, attempting to convince me of the anarchist position, put my address on the subscription list of the magazine that was then called *Why?* I am surprised to find it full of pertinent material.

> 1942 or 43:
> A meeting of a Village poetry circle; Loker Raley and the Raven (later called Paris Flammonde) gather some poets in the little cellar of 230 Wooster Street. I think, "What a good place for a small theatre!", and we each read aloud our own works. Honig, nineteen, in a black shirt, black trousers, announces aggressively, "I only write one poem each year." He reads his two-line poem for the year, as if to mock our wasteful epics. We sit embraced on the divan the rest of the evening.
> He whispers to me, not of love or of poetry.
> But of social responsibility and of anarchism as its proper function.

Till now I had hardly paid attention to the magazine, even though Paul Goodman writes for it. Because I distrust militant politics. And though Kropotkin writes splendidly on the future society, I don't know how to share his faith. I have tremendous respect for the anarchist ideal. Yet all the anarchists I know except Paul seem to live such disordered lives.

The anarchists' insistent refusal to participate in authoritarian politics seems irresponsible. There is no ideal situation. Certainly compromise belittles the human being. But in the face of total evil—Dachau, Belsen, Auschwitz—there seems no choice but struggle even though struggle is admittedly evil and a compromise. And yet, evil exists in the world and our refusal to participate in it doesn't seem an adequate response to it.

Paul has an article in *Resistance* on vegetarianism, in which he examines the problem of free choice and the intellectual insight that free choice demands. He looks into the causes of behavior, the frailty of people, and loves them because he understands the genesis of their failings. His honesty makes me look with horror at my own self-deception and the treachery that my right hand commits against my left. He is wise like an elder.

Kreymborg calls. To him, as to Lou Polan, I pretend that I have already assembled actors. At the Dramatic Workshop I find the theater closed for the summer. Now my choice is limited.

The employment problem. I sit for hours waiting for a ten-minute interview, the result of which is always "We will let you know." Meanwhile I fall into debt.

The newspapers and radio report disasters, floods, wars. The United Nations asks for a Palestine truce. Arabs and Jews agree under conditions that will make peace impossible.

June 2, 1948

Can't find a job. It's hot and humid.

Now I am up against it about the actors I lied about.

At the office of Brandt and Brandt, Janet Cohen tells us that Irving Stiber has the rights to *HIM*. She says that when Cummings first saw an announcement about the production he wrote her curtly, "Who are the Interplayers and where the hell did they get hold of *HIM*?" But since then he has talked to Irving and approved their doing the play.

June 3, 1948

Mother's sickness is serious. She suffers, but she doesn't want to talk about it. Thus it becomes a taboo, always in the forefront of our awareness and always suppressed. She dreads the prospect of even a few days in the hospital, is pale and sleepless.

The doctor's report is not optimistic. I hesitate to write here what I can't speak about freely.

Can't find actors for the Wallace play. I've called everyone I know.

June 4, 1948

Another birthday. Sadly I think of Harald's room, of the lighted candles, the dates and chocolates and apricot brandy.

This year I can't celebrate. Mother's illness upsets me too much.

June 7, 1948

William Carlos Williams sends, *A Dream of Love*, with a third enthusiastic letter. The play, to be published by New Directions, is in galley form and Williams had a few copies pinned together and sent us one. It may be a wise choice to open with. The opening of the Living Theatre seems remote, though we speak glibly of September.

Mother must go to the hospital tomorrow. The doctor saw her today and said the faster the thing is taken care of the better.

Julian tells me that he is going on a four-day bicycle trip. These four days of all the days I know him! The first time I need him! But he does not realize this. When, after I tried hard to hide it, he sees me cry, he asks, "Why?"

When I tell him he says nothing. He is in his insular world of which he is the unique inhabitant.

The human loneliness. The eggshell enclosing the individual. We can't reach beyond it to touch one another. Does love ever come close to spanning that breach?

Julian's Achilles' heel is his inability to break this all-enclosing shell. Achilles' heart. It is vulnerable.

June 8, 1948

Mother is examined at Mt. Sinai Hospital. The clinic is crowded with the sick poor, sitting on wooden benches while waiting to embark on the desk-to-desk journey involved in hospital admittance.

The Babel of the languages, the complaints, the emotions rise and fall like a tragic chorus. I am peculiar and over-dressed among them. It seems ridiculous to sit here reading Thomas Mann's essay on Faust. Endless lines, files, interviews, questions, benches, papers.

Efficient doctors examine and reexamine Mother. What they really find I do not know. They look grave.

This evening Julian is full of penitence. He understands now. But he does not say: I cannot go away when I must be here with you. He doesn't say it. I remain calm.

We read *The Lady from the Sea* under a lamp beside the Hudson. And the dark river is not as dark as I.

Slowly my eyes become accustomed to the dark, the dark with which Julian has veiled himself, and I begin to see.

It makes no difference to love.

June 9, 1948

Julian has really gone. His promised call does not come.

A grueling day at the hospital. One cannot but be frightened. Fear sits tyrannically on my stomach, allowing no food, no rest, no relaxation to unthrone him from the domain he has usurped.

June 10, 1948

Lou Polan has made several changes in *No More War* on the suggestion of the Political Action Committee. This has served me as an excuse for not having actors. I'll see Kreymborg this afternoon.

Julian calls from Burlington.

Mother will remain at home until she receives word from the hospital.

To Kreymborg's house. He is irate at the changes in his script.

"Polan is naive," he says. "Unenlightened."

He reads to me, for the second time, the Churchill poem that I do not like.

After I leave Kreymborg, I wander a while in the Village.

I pass the Provincetown Playhouse where they are rehearsing *The Infernal Machine*. Loren Denny, who is painting something black, explains the set to me. Louis Criss raves about the last act. Alexis is growing an artistic beard till dress rehearsal; he is too busy to shave. Irving Stiber pretends to be surprised that we had ever planned to produce *The Infernal Machine*. I congratulate everyone.

I encounter Bob Ramsey on MacDougal Street. He is in an exuberant mood and I am terribly grateful for his remark, "Yes, I'm going over to wish the dirty bastards good luck too."

We curse them awhile.

Bob offers to help me cast the Wallace play.

The June 10th sun is hot in the Village. It might, for all the difference it makes to time and place, be last year.

June 14, 1948

Dr. Rothschild gives me insulin injections to gain weight.

We meet Pierre Garai at Theodore Stamos' housewarming party. A wide loft apartment filled with driftwood, shells, insects, a doll under a glass bell. All the young artists. Julian talks a long time with Mark Rothko's beautiful wife. We leave early.

Terrible days of waiting for Mother to go to the hospital.

June 15, 1948

Alfred Kreymborg calls and says that I must see him whether it is convenient for me or not . . . and now!

Kreymborg behaves so ardently that I have to reject him brusquely. He almost cries. I'm regretful but adamant, and very much in need of a playwright to organize the clumsy scene.

Finally he promises, "I will never try to make love to you again, but our artistic collaboration shall continue."

He says, "Piscator told me: 'Malina has some rough edges that life will have to wear off.'"

June 16, 1948

Waiting at home with Mother for the letter admitting her to the hospital. Waiting. Mother runs away from herself in movies, walks, anything, but there is not far that she can go. Time seems endless. She is very brave about it.

Yesterday we received a friendly letter from Jean Cocteau—"*Chers amis (vous permettez?)*"—in which he expressed pleasure at being translated by

Paul Goodman and at our producing *The Infernal Machine*. He is apparently unaware of the Interplayers' production.

Full of trepidations, we go to see the Interplayers' version. They approach it as a technical problem with no love, no triumph.

June 23, 1948

Julian and I read *Iphigenia in Tauris*. I feel the urge to act again.

Mother and I go to Butler Davenport's Free Theater, where she often took me as a child.

Davenport has grown old. He was to have played Molière's *Affected Young Ladies*, but his cast was decimated by summer stock and he carried the evening alone with monologues: Chekhov's "Swan Song" and "An Interview with Mark Twain."

I'd seen "Swan Song" often and was always impressed, by this potpourri of *School for Scandal, Merchant of Venice* and *Hamlet*. I never noticed how drab the stage was because I believed in that darkness then, nor did I notice Davenport's failings as Shylock, Hamlet or Cardinal Richelieu because I believed in him.

Now the old actor was apologetic because he had to alter the ending of his plays to get offstage to pull the curtain; there was no one else to pull it.

At the act break, he made his long speech to the audience about social betterment and birth control. It has a quaint, oratorical quality.

A solitary actor in his fortress.

He passed the basket for support.

June 24, 1948

Mother goes to the hospital. Julian accompanies us. He is a restraint to the emotion. There is a long wait. Afterward we go to the studio and spend some time on the theater collection. Then back to visit Mother. She is unhappy in the ward.

Predominant: Instability. Deceptive Assurances. Moments of Certainty. Everything completely dependent on State of Mind. No other standard.

June 25, 1948

Early call from Mother. She is upset about the ward. Julian and I go to the hospital and disturb the doctors with her request. Nothing, however, can be done. She refuses to permit the operation.

Julian is with me all the time. He is very good to me.

June 26, 1948

We stay with Mother in the hospital until time for the operation. She is calm now and looks wan and more beautiful than ever. The change is remarkable.

I spend this day, like all these days, with Julian.

In the evening I try to work on my unfinished libretto *Cassandra of Ilium* but I no longer understand what Cassandra's death resolves.

July 1, 1948

The days go by and the sense of escaping time is like a sea in which I am drowning. I clutch at the water, which, like time, takes no notice of me.

We meet with Marcel Aubry, Cocteau's agent in America. He claims that no one except he or Cocteau can authorize performance rights to the plays. Why then, has Oxford University Press offered them to us?

"I have a lot of trouble with Cocteau," says Aubry. "He gives away rights and authorizes translations by a scribble on a bit of paper to someone with whom he happens to have dinner."

We do not mention that we possess just such an authorization for the translation of *Les Chevaliers de la table ronde*.

On Wednesday I went to a meeting of "Operation Culture," a section of the PAC. A cluttered room on Park Avenue replete with toppled files, stacks of leaflets piled on the floor and other cultural equipment for a presidential campaign. There were some young people to whom I showed the script of *No More War* and I asked them about actors. Thereupon they told me that we must bring culture to the people, that America is in the midst of a cultural revolution, etc., etc.

July 4, 1948

Hospital visit. A scorching day.

Mother is not doing well. She dreamt about mice while feverish and the superstition that a dream of mice foretells death persists in spite of her better judgment.

Julian and I argue about mountain climbing. I protest that adventure does not justify the risk of life, which has a more important purpose than conquering stones for the thrill of conquest and the conceit of overcoming hazards.

Julian says, "It is the response to challenge, man's conquest of the powers of nature. It allows a man to fulfill his duties because he has done this thing."

I understand him better than he knows. To him the world is a challenge, and death as yet not real.

July 5, 1948

With Mother back home a little order may enter my life. Good. Good for order.

I read: Huxley's *Antic Hay*, Henry James' stories, Cocteau's poems, Stein's *Four in America*, Sartre's *La Nausée*, Carolyn Spurgeon's scholarly book on Shakespeare's imagery.

I always begin by liking Stein but get irritated after fifty or sixty pages. She is splendid, but it takes a stoic's patience to withstand her impudence.

In *La Nausée*, written in the form of a journal, Sartre notes the diarist's compulsion to expand on the fact, to exaggerate, to include external factors that embellish the subject.

Have begun to translate Tieck's *Gestiefelte Kater (Puss in Boots)*. First making a rough, sight translation in longhand, which I'll revise without reference to the German. Then, I'll check back to the original.

Last night at an Operation Culture meeting, Jules Shirer talked for hours about incipient and overt fascism, and of bringing culture to the people of America; beside him is a prop box with a sacklike costume emblazoned "Food Prices" hanging over its edge. The whole "skit" about prices flashes before me. I despair.

July 12, 1948

Occasionally Mother is in pain, but mostly she suffers from weakness. It's calm in the house. Cousin Josie pores over his chemistry formulas and tomes.

Hot, quiet days at home. Work on *Puss in Boots*. Read Henry James' "Story of a Year." Early work.

Saturday Helen, Pierre, Julian and I at Jones Beach.

He is pure, this Pierre. And he is aflame. He is not one of the blue-eyed people, but makes his agony visible in his almond-shaped eyes. Helen is dressed according to *Vogue*'s latest requirements for the seashore, her red hair crinkling into cherubic curls.

Heroine Helen walking on the beach with Pierre Garai. I, in Julian's arms, longing with him for some unknown excellence.

July 15, 1948

Last night one of those hot sticky meetings at the Wallace headquarters on Park Avenue. They are sending out "caravans"— cars carrying six people with skits and songs. They discuss ideology of a very basic nature.

There are few things these days that do not irritate me. I say to Julian, "When I grow up I want to be an old crank."

July 16, 1948

The entire day in reading. Finally, Swinburne. Julian and Pierre, in a delirium, declaim parts of "A Forsaken Garden" in chorus:
"Like a god self-slain on his own strange altar,/Death lies dead."

July 19, 1948

At the Wallace headquarters the political atmosphere is not satisfying. I want some consistent ideology, but I find no standard in the world.

Because I can't condemn I can't believe. Whichever way I turn I am confronted by irreconcilable contradictions. At sea among the concepts.

The anarchist and the utopian socialist.

The communist ideal and the cold war.

The blockade of Berlin.

What do we know? Except *No More War*.

And the war? Who will tolerate it?

Who will denounce it? I will.

O God, can it be that peace is impossible?

We have made monsters: great nations and their pride; great sciences and the power for destruction; ambitious men who have the power to act, but not the power to reason.

I am searching for personal ethics, but every solution is a trap.

July 23, 1948

A frightening political situation. The arrest of leading Communists in a sudden sweep, including all the highest ranking party members and the *Daily Worker* staff. What can this mean but that the government is inculcating in the American people a warlike spirit to justify the draft? The more imminent a war appears, the more tractable people become.

We have no access to the facts, but interpret from signs and symbols what does not see the light.

Julian lives in fear of the draft.

If there is no choice in America, except a prison sentence or service in the dealings of death, there's no reason to stay in this country.

The studio is hot and a depressing rain falls outside.

Yesterday at the Museum I saw *Birth of a Nation*, the work of a great ego, a work of arrogance and artistry.

And this morning comes the announcement of Griffith's death. I imagine him to have had some of Piscator's qualities, both being masters of the Epic.

July 25, 1948

Yesterday, sunbathing on the roof of Julian's studio. I read to him a malicious passage out of Gide's journal: a discussion of Léon Blum and Jews. Gide's cruelty is superb. He uses it against himself so that becoming intimate with it he can use it against others with expert dexterity.

With mixed feelings I see the Interplayers' version of *HIM*.

July 26, 1948

The day as clear as any *Märchen* would have it. We drove to the Garais' in the Becks' Futuramic Oldsmobile.

Pierre in white trousers and checked shirt. Madame Garai in a white dress and sneakers.

"Where are you going?" she greets us gesticulating. "To Deauville? To the Lido? You are so dressed for going splash." She vibrates.

On the slow drive through Sunday traffic we listen to the convention of the Third Party on the radio. Pierre opposes it. His politics are sad with disillusion. Or is it old with disillusion?

He says he was an idealist when he was a child. At ten he became a vegetarian. Later he put his heart and soul into his hopes for the Spanish Republic, till his disillusionment with the Communists in that struggle shattered all his beliefs.

His hatred for Stalinism is deeper than his hatred of war and he would willingly go to war against the Soviet Union. Though he calls himself a Socialist, despair makes him assume a pose of elitist arrogance.

"I want to live to write six novels; after that, to hell with the world. I am interested in my life and the lives of a few friends. As for the rest, I hate them one and all."

Our mock flirtation, like all pretenses, touched the fringes of reality, as all pretenses sooner or later need to.

On the return trip through infuriating traffic, we sang loudly and lustily. Pierre sang with his head on his mother's lap.

July 27, 1948

I copy the following from Gide's journal of June 1914:

> Dramatic art must no more seek to create the illusion of reality than does painting; it should work through its own special means and aim towards effects that belong to it alone.
>
> Just as a painting is a space to set in motion, a play is a space of time to animate.

In looking for those "special means" and those "effects that belong to it alone" many means and effects have been devised: the bioconstructivism of Meyerhold, the expressionism of Kaiser, the Dadaist antilogic, the superrealism of David Belasco, or Reinhardt's sentimental grandeur. All efforts to theatricalize the theater.

But today all these structures have been debased into superficial devices.

Broadway buries itself under a sugary realism and the experimental theater devotes itself to various forms of fantasy; Hollywood inserts surrealistic dream sequences into banal love stories.

Only the dance continues to explore, and it is there that our best advances are made.

In the Living Theatre, we have avoided the word "experimental." But Gide's concise paragraph reestablishes it in my mind. To experiment in the theater is "to aim towards effects that belong to it alone."

July 30, 1948

After an exhausting workday I lie here in the heavy heat almost undressed on my bed. I've found a job. Selling French fashion magazines to Seventh Avenue dress designers. The office is in the elegant *Librairie Française* at Rockefeller Center, where an amorous gentleman is my boss.

Julian drove us to Princeton last night to see Gertrude Stein's *Yes Is for a Very Young Man.*

August 1, 1948

In the heat of the beach, Pierre turns on me with sudden open unpleasantness. He says, "It's ridiculous for you to be in love with me."

I say nothing. This burning that I marked in him will kill him if he cannot kill it.

He expresses interest in this journal, lying on the sand. He insists that I admit my love for him in this notebook. If he read it that is exactly what he would read into it and still he would be mistaken.

The sea is rough. Julian and I wander out to an unpopulated stretch of beach. Sandpipers scurry up to the water's edge and then retreat with uncanny alacrity. Giant gulls, sensing our approach, glide into the air with soundless excellence.

"What did you talk about with Pierre?" Julian asks.

Josie and Mother want to visit Roosevelt's home. Julian comes early to drive us there.

Hyde Park is the home of a man too aware of his greatness. The study contains a reproduction of the Winged Victory of Samothrace. Nearby, the wheelchair and the black cape.

We walk with the sightseers from room to room, Julian and I, wrapped up in conversation about Pierre. "Is it that he envies my productivity?" asks Julian.

Why are we so strongly affected by him?

In the formal flower garden, the perfectly proportioned block of marble marks Roosevelt's grave.

August 4, 1948

I lost my job. Can't sell magazines.

This day devoted entirely to finishing the first draft of the Tieck translation.

Yesterday an evening with Larry, who is in the National Guard after serving overseas in the war. He talks like one in a fever. "After seeing people die the way I did, I wouldn't want to see a mouse killed. . . . To see a man die by your own hand . . . I relive it so often that I've killed that man a thousand times." And his face had a fearful look.

Yet he trains recruits. He says it is his duty as an officer.

August 11, 1948

Every morning I look for work in the columns of the *New York Times* and every afternoon return home exhausted.

Pindar's *Odes*. Pindar inflamed by the Olympic contest, while the current Olympics incite national pride.

Gide, too, amazes me with his patriotic narrowness. And yet he accuses the French Jews of overdoing their patriotism. But then, he accuses the Jews of every vice.

I complete the first scene of a new play, *Damocles*, full of workable anachronisms. I am writing by the Hudson. Above me the planes move on the air while small insects creep across my notebook.

Julian has spoken to Pierre on the telephone. Pierre puts off seeing him.

So the old myths go, but there are always new ones to take their place.

August 14, 1948

Nobody remarks that this is V-J Day, the anniversary of the war's end. Julian says, "Because it is not yet over."

August 16, 1948

Mother, Josie and I take a trip to Midland Beach. I read with Josie from Sartre's *La Nausée* to make some headway in the French language.

For a few melancholy moments I wandered away and stood contemplating the watery carcass of a long-drowned animal, a dog, or possibly a sheep, thrown up on the beach by the tide. And anyone is congruent with any other.

The evening is splendidly spent with Julian. We had determined to work on the Living Theatre, but in the end found something even more profound to do.

August 22, 1948

Yesterday, a day filled with a rambling radiance. A day of gardens and paintings, poems, theater, and friends and talk and love.

In the morning to the Metropolitan only to pay our respects to the Etruscan Warrior and the early Christian mosaics.

We note, newly engraved in marble on the list of museum benefactors, Gertrude Stein's name.

Then to the garden of the Modern museum, and while we await Pierre, we drink a bottle of Mountain Sylvaner. How fine he looked walking toward us through the sculptures.

Julian and Pierre engaged in literary talk. And, of course, they joked. Will there ever be another soul with whom we can joke that way? I think not.

We wandered among the sculptures. The wine roused us and the summer light in the garden.

In the afternoon Julian and I talked seriously about the draft, conscientious objection, evasion, his future. He can't go into the army. The problem is only the means.

After this serious talk we have a frivolous dinner of vichyssoise and watermelon because Julian has been reading F. Scott Fitzgerald. Then to a frivolous Broadway musical called *Inside U.S.A.* because we want to see everything.

And we end the happy day in a splurge of love-making.

August 23, 1948

At Bernard Suhl's, I agree to work on a revision of his translation of Constantin Brunner. My father shared with Dr. Suhl a deep respect for Brunner, but in the few pages I read I find him too satiric a philosopher, though he expresses himself passionately.

I spend most of the day on *Damocles*. The play progresses.

August 26, 1948   *Lake Hopatcong, New Jersey*

I am here with Mother in a crowded but charming country house. I have with me *Paradise Lost* and "Lotte in Weimar" and Dewey's *How We Think* and of course, *Damocles*.

This country weekend deprives me of Julian and an anarchist meeting to protest the draft.

Monday I go to work as a salesclerk at Barnes and Noble Bookstore.

As a child I thought that if one always does the right thing one is certain to be universally appreciated. At adolescence I realized that we can't always do the right thing because we don't know what the right thing is. This explained the evil in the world, but it gave me the horrors. My childhood peace was destroyed once I discovered that I couldn't always tell the difference between right and wrong.

From the time of this discovery we are no longer happy. We are adult. All our energies are directed toward the search for certainty. The great dramas are on this theme: the Faust, the Hamlet, the Oedipus search.

We look with envious suspicion at those philosophers and happy few whose actions seem consistent with their ideas.

August 30, 1948   *Lake Hopatcong*

Milton's description of the fall from grace is almost too strong for these turbulent days. I turn gladly to Thomas Mann's ponderous and precise "Lotte in Weimar."

September 5, 1948   *New York City*

My work at Barnes and Noble leaves time for a good deal of reading.

Surrounded by thousands of books and wanting to absorb them all, I go about tasting now a French grammar, now a book of English verse, a book on psychosomatic medicine, a book on the odds in gambling . . .

Standing behind the counter I read Kafka's "Metamorphosis" in snatches with constant interruptions by customers.

September 7, 1948

A little biography of Beatrice Webb. Admirable, solid woman but not enough nonsense about her.

Pierre Garai's review of Camus' *La Peste* is published in the *New Leader*. He gropes a little, but I suspect that Camus gropes too.

September 9, 1948

A letter from Jay Landesman at *Neurotica* saying they are holding my poem "A Woman Met a Walker" for consideration. They have turned it into a prose poem titled "Voyage" and cut the last stanza, an alteration with which I have no sympathy, but honestly, the idea of publication is so gratifying that I accept these changes.

Julian and I have a long conversation about having a baby. We speak of marriage. There seems little else left open for me and in the end I admit it. What I am afraid to lose is my struggle to assert my "person" as an individual distinct from Julian or any other.

I will find a way. Even in this.

September 12, 1948

Julian is going on a five-day trip to Vermont with Pierre. How can he do this under present conditions. I am aghast that he can leave me now.[8]

Finished "Lotte in Weimar."
An appalling revelation in Mann's essay on Goethe.
According to Mann, when Goethe was a member of the government in Weimar in his late years, he sat in judgment on a case trying a young girl for killing her baby. There was a plea from the court for mercy, but Goethe *signed the death sentence* because "he placed justice above mercy."
Mann defends Goethe's stupid cruelty in the name of order. Mann writes: " . . . It bears witness to a stern self-disciplining of his own kindliness and pity and their suppression in favor of established order.
"For order the mature Goethe held in such honor that he openly declared it to be better to commit injustice than tolerate disorder."
Farewell to the moral teaching of Goethe or Mann. Goodbye to literature!
. . .

September 13, 1948

We dispatch two letters.
One to William Carlos Williams in answer to his wonderful letter suggesting that we produce *Trial Horse No. 1: Many Loves*, which is the Williams play we really should do, rather than the more conventional *Dream of Love*.
The other letter is to Marcel Aubry asking about rights for Alfred Jarry's *Ubu Roi*.

September 14, 1948

I note that it is five years today that I met Julian.

September 15, 1948

Waste the evening at a hideous war film glorifying people's ability to "take it." If people weren't so willing to take it, it wouldn't be that way.
What primitive times we live in. For those born 100 years from now the problems will be more subtle.

September 19, 1948

Julian returns from Vermont. He brings news.
We walk down Fifth Avenue discussing a new beginning. All the stores have special displays for the Golden Jubilee of New York City. The windows are in gilded, gold dresses, gold jewelry, golden lights. The Public Library, lit in gold, looks misty and decadent.

September 21, 1948

Damocles is finished. The last scene somewhat too melodramatic. So far only Mother has heard it and of course she likes it.

Two films: Gide's *La symphonie pastorale* and a short film on Matisse.

Matisse, in a garden full of soft, thin trees appears in a great cape, hatted and shawled, and moves slowly down an old stone stairway. Halfway down he pauses in the sunlight, opens his book, sketches a leaf.

Susan and Erica Perl return from Europe. In Salzburg they met Harald and he sends me his regards.

Oh, heavens, is it possible? His regards?

September 24, 1948

Paul Goodman and Sally were crying as Julian and I came in. Paul: "We were having a gloomy argument."

He shows us the first act of *Faustina*, his new play, a parable about the wife of Marcus Aurelius. Many of Aurelius' speeches are from the *Meditations*.

This is a play that the Living Theatre must do.

The talk turns to the draft. Paul thinks Julian should have registered "under protest."

"I am not basically a pacifist," says Paul. "I am only opposed to these mass-organized wars that involve no personal issue."

He's right that vengeance and rage are unavoidable passions, but they are only that: passions. War can't be justified by the passions involved.

What of the defensive war?

What of invaded Holland?

Clear and divine Reason, help us to see clearly!

September 28, 1948

We go to a hearing at City Hall on a zoning regulation to establish whether or not we can use the Malin Theater.

Malin has been deceiving us. There has been no prospect of a theater since May. The tenants of the residential district on 22nd Street object to the noise that a theater would make.

A circle of old men who look as if they are about to indict Joan of Arc read the petitions in droning monotones. Except for the noisy woman who represents the 22nd Street tenants and exclaims over and over again, "But, your honor, we have to sleep!" till the chairman stops her.

"There used to be a church there," she says, "and we would hear the sermons like they was right in our own room."

"That didn't do you any harm, did it?"

"Oh, no, your honor, we liked that. But this wouldn't be like that."

Everyone laughed except Helen, Julian and me.

Leaving City Hall in defeat we follow a lead to a decrepit opera house, large and available! There would be considerable expense for alterations: an air vent and five metal doors.

So here we are again in a state of expectancy.

Mr. Malin, on the telephone, says, "Call me next week, I have another theater that I think you'll like even better. . . ."

October 4, 1948

William Carlos Williams in his bright yellow Rutherford house is cheerful and unassuming. He welcomes us like a country doctor and begins to talk a delightful blue streak that can hardly be interrupted.

His wife, Flossie, sits in an oversize chair like a figure painted by Grant Wood. She says very little but is quietly friendly, solid as the floor.

Dr. Williams seems far more the doctor who writes poetry than the poet who is also a doctor. But he understands his importance and his tremendous influence on the world of letters.

It is difficult to speak of the theater at length for he interrupts our slow, carefully planned expositions with gay little tales of the Provincetown in the old days when he played in Kreymborg's *Lima Beans* with Mina Loy and William Zorach, or of the Rutherford little theater where one of his one-acters held the audience spellbound because the audience knew the woman who played the lead and was "eager to see if she would really go to bed with this young man."

His son came in, the one who is beginning to practice as a doctor now, and drank beer from a bottle. His other son is a businessman who commutes daily to Brooklyn and was out bowling. Williams serves us water from an underground stream, "purer than Rutherford tap water."

A William Carlos Williams story:

"When I was a young intern at French Hospital in New York in 1908, they were building the Pennsylvania Station. It was a tremendous task since it all was dug out of solid rock. There were many accidents and they were brought directly to the hospital.

"One day a husky 200-pound laborer who had fallen from a ledge onto the rock pile below was brought in badly injured.

"He was taken over by the nurses to be undressed for a thorough examination. Suddenly the nurses came from behind the screen all flustered, 'Oh, doctor, come look at this!'

"We went in to see him and there he lay, this husky, rough man, and beneath his laborer's clothes he wore pink, lacey lingerie with bows here and there"—with both hands W.C.W. pointed to his chest and knees—"and silk stockings and all.

"Later, an extraordinary, distinguished gentleman came to the hospital and ordered the best care and no expense spared for the laborer. This elderly gentleman had small white curls neatly arranged close to his head, carried himself with grace and elegance, and was altogether the most extraordinary fairy I had ever seen. We learned that he was the brother of a high government official. It is after this man that, forty years later, I modeled the character of the Producer in *Trial Horse No. 1.*"

As we left, Williams said that his whole life was leading up to the moment when his plays are produced, that that was the great day for which he lived, and that he hoped we might bring it about.

October 8, 1948

Last night the Beck family came to discuss the engagement of their son. It was relatively pleasant.

We want to marry in the first week of November and they want us to marry in June, but at that time we will have a one-month old child.

Mr. Beck talks a good deal about money.

I'm quiet and try not to antagonize anyone.

October 11, 1948

I try to be sociable. But when Julian's father defends every reactionary cause I can't stand it. I find myself so enraged that I hastily say I have a headache and tearfully leave the house.

Out on the street Julian confronts me. Why am I not tactful?

I can't. I can't. I cry out against the whole way of life.

Julian asks me what I really want. And I tell him the other side of the fantasy, the dream I have of being in the real world doing something useful.

"I want to go to Detroit . . . and I want to talk to the men who work on the assembly line . . . and I want to find out. . . ."

But I don't know what I want to find out. Something about why the factory worker lives in a real world and I do not.

Not long ago, I worked in a factory too, and I thought I would be trapped there, in a world not my own, forever. And now I'm on West End Avenue. But I don't belong here either. I don't belong to the bourgeoisie.

Can Julian understand this? Not now. He looks at me blankly when I say, "I want to go to Detroit. . . ."

October 14, 1948

Julian doesn't know about the horror, neither its workings, nor its causes, nor its manifestations. He is unaware of the minuteness of the individual in the universe. In his own concentrated self—which he imagines to be eternal—he conceives the universe. All things revolve around his consciousness, even the distant stars.

October 16, 1948

The imbecile pettiness of the forms through which I must pass in order to exist within the social group. How narrow all the passages are!

Mother, after three nights of sitting wide-awake and brooding, goes about with a grim face and speaks with Tolstoyan solemnity about "shame" and "moving away from the neighborhood" and "the Jewish way of life."

At the Becks' last night she was staunch and charming. Julian's brother, Franklin, and his wife, Shirley, and her mother complete the company. I am frantic with the small talk. At dinner I am dismayed by the maid with the tray and the formalities. These things panic me.

I read only now and then. Maxey's *Political Philosophies*. Ezra Pound's *A B C of Economics*.

Pound proposes a four-hour work day and "certificates of work accomplished" (money) to be distributed to workers. And just when one has agreed that plenty, leisure and social equity are excellent ends, he takes advantage of one's assenting humor and praises the dictator as a superior intellect, specifying Mussolini as a man to be so praised.

It's not enough to be disgruntled at Pound's irrationality.

I'd like to understand the principles that make money, banking and interest necessary. I'd like to have an inkling of what can be done to undo the economic mess.

"Life is short and the art long, the occasion instant, decision difficult, experiment perilous." Seneca.

October 18, 1948

Ruth Gordon opens in her own play, *The Leading Lady*.

In the audience Marlene Dietrich, like a dream of herself, in black lace, diamonds and rubies around her throat, white mink wrap reaching the floor. She wears a constantly lively expression, and heavy, heavy makeup, her eyes focused carefully so as not to betray her awareness of being stared at.

Celebrities crowd onto the stage after the performance and Gordon kisses them heartily. From the darkened auditorium, Robert Sherwood carries on a conversation with Raymond Massey, who is on the stage among the crowd around Gordon.

The audience gave a good performance.

October 21, 1948

Our license and blood tests are attended to, but there remains the shopping. The endless banalities of the marketplace.

Everything seems full of evil and deception.

Julian says that lying is justified when the truth would cause unhappiness, that we shouldn't bring out the evil in a person by telling him truths that would bring out his "evil forty percent." I argue that we can't be deceitful in order to bring out someone's "sixty percent good" because . . . ends and means.

October 22, 1948

Following a hectic taxi ride to City Hall minutes before closing time, Julian and I were legally married in a short ceremony.

We arrived in the nick of time and learned that it would be necessary to find witnesses. Julian ran into the corridor and brought back a handsome couple who had just applied for their license, Charles F. Heller and his bride, who agreed to be witnesses for us.

Signing the marriage register, Julian broke the pen, spreading a great blot that obliterates the names recorded today. The chapel had been papered in a rose pattern by a patriotic ladies' association to make more homey the quick marriages of soldiers on leave during the war. The chancel is flanked by two American flags.

I broke up with laughter during the whole thing, because I react to pompous situations that way.

We had no wedding ring. And so when the justice of the peace surprised us with a red cushion for the ring, Julian detached the keys from his keyring and placed it on the little pillow. The justice of the peace picked it up and said disapprovingly,

"It should be an unbroken band."

So we put my engagement ring, which was Julian's mother's, on the cushion.

I wear the broken band of the keyring now, along with the family diamond.

October 27, 1948

Legally married. But I'm not to live with Julian till after the religious ceremony: Mother doesn't count the legal marriage as valid. I feel sick most of the day and so terribly tired, washed away, whitened, bleached. Misty, changeable, placid. Pregnant.

October 29, 1948

Julian and I argue about all the bourgeois wedding preparations on which our parents insist. We shout at each other because we feel trapped. In anger I take the subway downtown and walk around Washington Square. A warm fall night. I walk leisurely, desiring only to be one with the beauty around me, to fade into the scene.

This calm spirit guides me to the door of 230 Wooster Street. I have a long talk with Bryce Porter, the photographer whose studio it is, about education and anarchy, labor unions, primitive societies, rationality, and the use of his room as a theater. There seems no obstacle to our going ahead.

At home Julian and I exchange loving apologies. He says, "Such behavior is everything we are fighting against."

November 2, 1948

In Julian's bedroom. In Julian's house. 11:30 A.M. Julian still fast asleep. I have been awake and reading for about three hours. His room is painted a dark, icy blue. There is no warmth in this house.

Saturday evening, Mr. and Mrs. Beck drove us to Danbury to be married in Jerome's synagogue.[9] Only Mother and Josie were with us. We were stopped by a Halloween-Election Day parade through the center of Danbury, the streets full of children in disguises.

The empty synagogue had been decorated for a big wedding to take place the next day, and so we were married among flowers and elaborate decorations. Jerome, who carries on the rabbinical vocation of our family, conducts a simple ceremony which reminds me of the ceremonies my father performed in our living room.

Jerome spoke of our love as "an affirmation of faith in a world that by its nature could easily destroy all faith in man and man's works."

We stayed in Danbury overnight in the Hotel Green, notable for its pillared portico and an atmosphere straining for refinement. A double bed and a Gideon Bible.

Sunday. A beautiful autumn day. We took a bus to New Haven.

In the green room of the Yale theater, students of acting sit with their cardboard containers of hot coffee, joking while waiting for their cues. I love the insipid wit. I feel with them the excitement of this dress rehearsal. Seeing this theater, I yearn to work in the theater again.[10]

We walked around New Haven until exhausted then boarded the train home.

This morning in spite of many trepidations we will vote in this ridiculous election.

November 4, 1948

We sat up half the night watching the returns on television.

Truman maintained an early plurality. Everyone was certain that at any moment the tide would turn. Every prediction pointed to a Dewey landslide. Dr. Gallup looked weary. Walter Winchell made jokes. Henry Wallace trailed far behind expectations.

To sleep with the radio talking all night. Waking in the morning to find Truman still in the lead and talk of the decision going to the Senate and House. Shortly before noon Dewey conceded.

Helen visits. We make plans for the Wooster Stage:

Two performances a month requiring two rehearsals on stage.

A seating capacity of thirty. Seats to be sold by a membership subscription, as we don't have permission to operate a theater and can't expect the fire department to grant a license for that funny little cellar.

A practically nonexistent budget consisting of rent, chairs, occasional royalties, mailing and properties. Costumes will be devised.

Initial investment about $200. My $100, $50 from Julian and $50 from Helen.

Possible programs: Pound's translation of the Noh plays, Eliot's *Sweeney*, Yeats' *Four Plays for Dancers*, an evening of medieval Mystery, Miracle and Morality plays, Wilde's *Florentine Tragedy*, Hardy's *Queen of Cornwall*, Cocteau's *La Voix humaine*, some of Thornton Wilder's one-acts, Ibsen's *Lady from the Sea*, Paul Goodman, Kreymborg, Cummings. We visit Marcel Aubry, the agent, who says Alfred Jarry has no heirs (he calls them "hairs") but royalties would have to be paid to the *Société des Auteurs*.

November 7, 1948

Now it's three A.M. and at six I will get up to manufacture my first homemade breakfast for Julian.

Late, time, rush, now, later, wait, do, hurry, hour, clock, worry, run.

November 8, 1948

Reading. Ezra Pound's book on the Noh, and looking through many Mysteries, Miracles, Moralities.

Meanwhile, I'm halfway through Paul Goodman's *Art and Social Nature*. The free man (libertarian), says Paul, chooses his place to "draw the line"; that is, at a certain point a man must say, "I will be coerced so far but no further."

Once the line is drawn, he says, it matters little where, since the fact that it is drawn at all means taking a stand and defining a position.

November 9, 1948

I find myself going to pieces in this house. Without the theater, without work, this West End Avenue environment sends me into spasms of weeping and complaining.

Julian suggests psychoanalysis. I like the idea.

November 10, 1948

Dinner at Paul Goodman's. I enjoy Paul and company and their peculiar other-worldly beauty. The little boy, Matthew Ready, is still awake and dirty and pagan.

At Paul's class at N.Y.U. a guest speaker, art critic Jerome Melquist, lectures while Paul smokes a philosophical pipe.

Melquist talks about form and representation. "I don't usually care for the surrealists, but I like Magritte's painting of a pipe, underneath which he has written: 'This is not a pipe.'"

Paul (waving his pipe): "An artist is great when he teaches us something."

Back at the Goodmans', Paul reads us the end of *Faustina*. The best new play that I know.

Matthew Ready is asleep, the huge dog, Tinker Bell, is quiet, and the atmosphere calm.

We tell Paul about Wooster Street. He muses, then says "chamber drama." Appropriate and useful. The idea expands.

David Sachs, a guest of Paul and Sally, teaches philosophy at Rutgers, and now constitutes one of the Wooster Stage's sixty members.

November 16, 1948

This morning a letter signed "Uncle Alfred" comes from Kreymborg wishing us joy in our marriage.

Spent most of the day in inquiries about the rights to this and that play. When I inquire about Pound at Macmillan, his publishers, they know only that "he's in jail."

November 18, 1948

Am I married? Is this my home? Is the child I am expecting a real living person-to-be? Are these strange, cool people now "related" to me? Is this my life that I am living? Is it for this that I prayed and hoped through all my childhood? For this emptiness? What of the dream? What of the woman that I was to be?

Enough of these haunts, it's morning and I should try to use the day.

November 19, 1948

Psychoanalysis: Julian has been going to see Dr. Frances Arkin for four years, ever since the draft board intimidated him into it.

Now he asks Dr. Arkin to recommend an analyst for me. She suggests Ralph Jacoby.

Now I have two Park Avenue doctors: an obstetrician and a psychoanalyst.

Dr. Jacoby succeeds in obliterating his personal characteristics, as the analyst is meant to do. But this rouses the curiosity of the patient who feels challenged to "discover" the analyst and wrest his secret self from him.

Doesn't the patient resent the one-sided opening of her nature with so little reciprocity from the guide who never becomes a companion?

He has a shabby waiting room: a frazzled carpet, a large oriental chest, a round table spread with *Vogue*, *Bazaar* and *Life*.

His inner office has the prescribed gray wallpaper with an annoying pattern.

We talked only of business and why I came to him. He is willing to take me on immediately.

The kind of gray day that makes me suspect that I may really be a character in a novel.

November 29, 1948

I lie down, half numb, half asleep. They say this is part of pregnancy. Maybe it's indolence.

We begin work on the Wooster Stage. We've decided to begin in the middle of December with three medieval plays.

Alfred Kreymborg gives us a long list of names for our mailing list. We've sent out 400 printed announcements of dates and repertory. Kreymborg is childishly enthusiastic and completely optimistic about audience response.

Meanwhile my analysis goes on every other day. I'm irritated by Dr. Jacoby's quietness. I lie back and I can't see him. Nor does he speak.

I simply talk about my life. At first everything sounds condensed and incomplete. I postpone intimate reflections until I feel more confidence in him. At any rate, it is pleasant to lie back and talk about oneself.

December 1, 1948

We find actors and then they take Christmas jobs at Macy's, or at the post office, and leave us in the lurch. We read through the plays at Helen's house.

December 2, 1948

Julian has become increasingly ambitious since yesterday's arrival of the first subscriptions in the mail. In spite of their scarcity, the quality is beyond expectations: Babette Deutsch and Robert Edmond Jones are the first two subscribers.

Some progress after two rehearsals with two new actors. Costumes are to be made out of scraps. Julian, designing, has elaborate ideas but does not begin work. He does everything with a nervous haste that upsets me.

Learn to be the calmer of two people.

December 6, 1948

Rehearsals progress. Tomorrow we see new people from an announcement in Actor's Cues.

Assortments of curtains, old clothes, bits of ribbon and furniture covers result more in masquerading than costume work.

Our days are devoted to work on the Wooster Stage. I go to sleep late, rise late; Julian and I find no time to make love.

My analysis progresses well. Dr. Jacoby continues quiet though more human. It's a difficult relationship and for all one's recognition of Freudian transference, it comes unexpectedly.

December 8, 1948

Impasse concerning Wooster Stage—neither enough actors nor subscribers.

Helen and Julian are of the opinion that it should be given up. I want to try a while longer. Either my stubbornness is making everyone work for a lost cause, or the cause is lost because I don't have the guts to insist. The decisive factor: If I call it off now, the year ahead is bleak.

The fabled Maria Jeritza sings a gala performance of *Tosca* in the Mosque Theater in Newark, her first appearance after many years of retirement. She carried far too many flowers, but her voice was rich and rounded.

In a white and scarlet gown with a heavily beaded train scraping behind her, she danced as she sang Tosca's betrayal.

Her arms tremble tragically. Her blond hair scatters over her head. She looks twenty.

Her *"Vissi d'arte"* is legendary. She sings it lying flat on the ground, her face buried in the floor, her body wrapped in the train of her gown.

Tremendous ovation and flowers in such profusion that it was impossible to get them gracefully off the stage.

December 15, 1948

Everything ruined. The whole plan ended.

I went to the *Daily News.* They won't accept our ad. I pleaded with them for an hour.

"The police," they said, "the police!

"The police see that, they say it's a lure for a brothel or a white slave ring. You can't put in an ad for actors to come to a place like that."

No actors. No ads. Fear of the police.

I cry at Dr. Jacoby's.

The money is returned to the subscribers. The costumes packed away. Helen and Julian attend to these things. I have no heart for them.

Now? Now at least a year, perhaps more, till I can work again. Now wait.

"But the faith and love and the hope are all in the waiting. . . . So the darkness shall be the light. . . ."

Tonight—winter's first snow. We remain at home.

"Teach us to sit still."

December 18, 1948

Plans for a trip to Mexico including three days in New Orleans and two days at Acapulco.

In my sessions with Dr. Jacoby we never seem to touch the thing that's important.

An Equity Library production of *The Eagle Has Two Heads.* When Tallulah Bankhead played the Queen she was exuberant in the face of the anarchist's threat and love, but Joanna Roos plays a political encounter with a cast conscious of their roles in the struggle with Azrael and Anarchy.

December 31, 1948

My impatience is not dispelled by theater-going, operas, reading or company. It is quieted only by a feeling of progress in work, which is now impossible, except for writing.

Not even writing. Just wintry day-to-day existence with Julian, for he is making nights late, risings late, days pleasant.

The film *The Eagle Has Two Heads*, directed by Cocteau himself, eulogizes rather than exposes the characters.

Cocteau spoke at the theater but we came too late and missed him. He returns to France immediately. Fears that I may never see "Cocteau plain."

New Year's now. No resolutions. My resolutions were made long ago. They gradually take on form, color, solidity. Their outlines begin to appear. But not overnight.

1949

January 1, 1949

It is frightening to enter the new year, the year in which my child will be born.

On New Year's Eve we went to see the film of John Steinbeck's *The Pearl*. The perfect pearl brings tragedy upon tragedy. In it the father sees a happy future for his child, but it causes the child's death, and he throws it back into the sea.

How is this to be interpreted?

At one minute to twelve a clock flashes onto the screen and ticks away in seconds. Then the word NOW appears and everyone in the theater shouts "Hurrah."

January 8, 1949

Reading: Ruth Benedict's *Patterns of Culture*, Julian Huxley's *Man and the Modern World*.

My impatience longs for facts. Art is a slow, luxuriant way of learning.

Julian says that my impatience with literature and the arts is only temporary. But I need some understanding of the physical order of the universe.

I allow myself, however, the lyrical splendor of Claudel's *Satin Slipper*. Billowy, high-flown, bursting with the exploding image.

I am impatient, irritable, changeable. . . .

What Dr. Jacoby claims is progress seems to me haphazard talk of no importance.

January 23, 1949

Disorientation. My awareness lingers between remembrance and aspiration.

Plans play too large a part in my life. They have engulfed everything else.

Plans for the baby, for an apartment, for the Living Theatre, for changing ourselves—the subject of the ongoing discussion between Julian and myself—plans for the trip to Mexico. We leave tomorrow.

If I've written little about the approaching child it's because I don't yet comprehend it.

I don't feel real in this half-rich home in which I live as a transient. I can't believe in this marriage in which I play a child bride and Julian a little boy. It's not real. My dreams are more real. Their landscapes more scaled to my size.

January 25, 1949   *En route to New Orleans*

From the train window, an impoverished land; stretches of red scraggled weeds and weatherbeaten, gray shacks.

Last night a stop at Danville, Virginia, and the memory of its verminous jail, where my trip ended the first time I tried to get to New Orleans.

The detachment of being unmoving in a seemingly moving world. The landscape changes. I remain.

This morning there's a change. Tangled firs, fallen trees and palm leaves on the water.

We take brief walks in the cities at which the train stops: Atlanta, peopled with hard-looking men; Mobile, a dismal city with wide streets. Montgomery has the vilest outskirts. Shacks crowded with impoverished Negroes, shabby, saddening.

But coming out of the stations we always see the poorest neighborhoods.

We began to talk about what could be done, not only for this misery, but for the large segments of the world's population that live in such poverty. What use are theories dealing with "advanced man" and the hope of a humanistic libertarianism here?

It is night. We near New Orleans. I am reading Whyte's *Next Development in Man.* Julian is reading Santayana's *Last Puritan.* We have just finished disputing the relative value of reading and experience.

New Orleans

We walk around the French Quarter, in air moist and dense with camellias and heady sea odors from the Gulf of Mexico.

We eat at the Court of the Two Sisters in a courtyard dominated by an enormous weeping willow, and in the candlelight everything shines.

The heavy air tires us. We will fall asleep quickly.

January 27, 1949   *New Orleans*

The people of New Orleans are good-natured, tell rambling historical stories.

Dinner at Antoine's, *Hamlet,* the film with Laurence Olivier.

Then to a nightclub in the French Quarter where "Tirza Takes a Wine Bath." A shower in a dark red liquid, which she rubs all over herself. A master of ceremonies explains that this "erotic dance to Bacchus" commemorates the self-sacrifice of a Babylonian maiden who drowned herself in a fountain which thereupon turned red as wine.

January 28, 1949   *New Orleans*

Our last day here, a boat ride in the rain, on the yellow-brown Mississippi. Gulls. We stand the furthest end of the ship where we savor the wideness of the murky river.

To a production of *Macbeth* so bad that the play itself seemed bad.

Tomorrow we leave this city, but not without an argument. Julian doesn't look deep enough beneath the courtesy of the people of New Orleans. He puts aside the issue of their racial discrimination. He is too eager to see the good.

January 30, 1949   *Mexico City*

There are the very rich and the very poor. There is the grandeur of the *Palacio de las Bellas Artes* and the squalor in front of the cathedral.

Barefoot beggars stand at the entrance of our hotel, the sumptuous Del Prado with its murals by Rivera. No line divides the city into sections of rich and poor. They intermingle, emphasizing the grotesque in both.

Rivera is to painting what Piscator is to the theater: a crusader, a mass-inciter, creator of "crowd scenes" who makes every work a banner.

We walk to the Zocalo, the square that has been the center of Mexico since the Aztecs built their pyramidal temple where the cathedral now stands.

There is a throng of poor peasants in front of the cathedral selling lottery tickets, tortillas and religious pictures. There are the aged and the crippled, begging, shoeless. Girls of fourteen and fifteen carrying their babies in their shawls. A man with no arms is weaving baskets with his toes.

Pushing past them, we enter a cavernous space surrounded by chapels and shrines of beaten gold on which the dust hangs heavy. The statues have dirty faces and the paintings are invisible under the grime.

The poor drop a few *centavos* into the church boxes and carry away little colored pictures of saints. They kneel in the dusty dark while a priest chants in Latin over organ music.

The bright sunlight outside the cathedral is a relief, but the beggars descend on us.

What right have we to cultivate ourselves?

Julian says that we seek enlightenment in order to best serve others, but the crying need here is too immediate to reconcile with our indirect commitment as artists. I don't know of anything that I can do, but I will not forget that the truth told must be the truth for everyone and that my work must be valid for all the people and not only for the patrons of my theater.

At the Bellas Artes they are playing Strindberg's *Danse Macabre*.

February 2, 1949   *Taxco*

From Mexico City to Taxco. We take a car with a guide, Señor Gomez, who looks as though his private thoughts were not his expressed thoughts. When he addresses a waiter his tone changes from the polite charm he uses toward the tourists to a passionate arrogance. It is also evident that he dislikes tourists.

Driving through hilly country; the earth is yellow and dry.

All along the way we pass Indian houses of round stones, of straw, fenced with tall cactus. The men walk along the roads in white trousers and straw hats or drive burros so laden that only a mass of moving straw is visible. Women too, carry huge loads tied onto their heads with a strap, the body bowed into a crouch under the weight.

In Taxco, primitive conditions are maintained by the government for the benefit of the tourist. The cobbled streets winding up the hill on which the town is built are intact. The mines attract tourists seeking silver ornaments. The jewelry is of one series of patterns; the prices are uniform and not exceptionally low. Neither the miners nor the craftsmen reap the bulk of the profits.

On the slanting streets, fat hogs and thin dogs push their snouts through piles of refuse.

We walk away from the street of the silver shops up a steep slope to the village. The Indians plod uphill, their babies wrapped in their shawls. Their bare feet are hard and gray on the rough stones.

I walk cautiously among the cobbles in my high heels. Julian is looking in a shop window. A boy approaches me to beg.

I look into his face and see his sightless eyes. They are two sores that bleed a pus, like tears along his cheeks.

I want to give him, not a few *centavos*, but all my care, my devotion, to cure his eyes—to stay in Mexico and cure them all—the entire plan of my life lies open in his sore eyes—and I realize what I have to do—because of what I am able to do—and because of what I am not able to do, I screamed—

so that I frightened the child, and I ran, with my eyes closed, because he could not see—

and I knew that the boy thought that I screamed in revulsion though that was not true—

I screamed because I was leaving him, but in that scream I also promised myself to him, to do the work that I have to do for him, because in his pain and blindness he made it clear.

I run to Julian. He sees only that I am hysterical.

We quarrel at night, and reconcile; it's our way of screaming.

February 3, 1949   Mexico City

We left Taxco early.

At Cuernavaca, an ancient, crooked town, we visit Cortez' palace and the market. The palace is full of historical paintings, including the famous picture of Juarez flirting with an Indian maiden in a garden.

Here also are murals by Rivera.

Since we have been traveling Julian and I have been completely vegetarian.

It's not hard to eat well without meat. And I feel, in my body as in my mind, the relief of not partaking in the slaughter.

The hardest part is to maintain the social graces, to refuse food that is offered in friendship, to set oneself apart from one's carnivorous fellows. To avoid insulting friends with a holier-than-thou attitude, to explain to waitresses who regard one as a difficult crank, not to make the painful subject the one and only table talk, to send back food with "just a bit of pork" floating in it, not to be a martinet, to make it a positive thing even while it is a negation of the custom.

February 4, 1949   Mexico City

We walk through the Merced Market of Mexico City.

In streets lined with stalls we encounter odors that recall the old Essex Street Market on the Lower East Side.

But as we walked deeper into the market the streets narrowed, the sunlight shut out, and the fumes of the frying food thickened the air.

We see female children holding to their breasts their own tiny infants wrapped in rags, and the old, bent and half-blind leaning over their wares or arduously making their way through the crowded lanes.

Boney dogs with diseased eyes sniff about searching for scraps, the stench and confusion increased by their presence underfoot.

Between conscience and disgust.

Between guilt and abhorrence.

We try to get out. But every direction leads us deeper into the market. Trapped in the crowded passage, we can't just push past the sick and the old and the blind.

And there among the blind our eyes began to open. And we saw who these people are in the world, and what the world was like.

We wander further into the district where the poor live, often ten in a room. Each plastered one-room house with its holy shrine; many with caged birds in the doorways.

There seem to be no middle-aged people. Those who survive are old already.

We come to a square, blank like a dreamer's landscape, chalky and deadly, devoid of all beauty.

In the plaza, a church, an acrid room. Candles light the corners. A glass and gilt casket holds a sick and bleeding Christ wrapped in dusty sheets. A moribund god. A woman wrapped in black kneels before it.

Smell of dirt and incense.

In that darkness we saw a little more clearly.

The sun sets and we begin our walk to the hotel, talking about what we have seen.

We discuss "direct action" and what it means. We come closer and closer to more basic questions.

In our hotel, the luxury becomes repellent.

February 5, 1949   *Mexico City*

The great mountains Popocatepétl and Iztaccihuatl. Snow-capped, aloof monarchs without love for the world below. My eye too human not to see them as cruel.

At Cholula we visit a pre-Aztec pyramid that is being excavated. The passageway is a long coffin-shaped tunnel that rouses a claustrophobic panic in me. My palms are wet, and the sweat collects on my forehead. The sensation is physical and the fear unreasonable. At the very breaking point of my self-control the guide turns us back.

In Puebla we visit the hidden convent of Saint Monica, where a group of penitential sisters lived after the banning of convents by the revolution. They arranged a section of an apartment house to include a chapel, a burial ground, a room for relics—the withered heart of an archbishop preserved in alcohol, and a petrified tongue.

At night, back in Mexico City, we go to the theater to see Cantinflas in a lavish musical comedy called *Bonjour Mexico*. At Cantinflas' entrance the audience stamped and shouted as though with political fervor, the wildest ovation I've ever heard. Julian says Cantinflas is the heart of every member of the Mexican audience, the clumsy wise man lost in the sophisticated world.

The play is gaudy—five showgirls play five white grand pianos suspended in midair—but the audience waits only for the reappearance of their hero. At 1:30 A.M., no finale in sight, we left during an Apache dance.

February 6, 1949   *Mexico City*

In the morning in the romantic floating gardens of Xolchimilco we board a flower-decked boat, the Juanita, which moves along a lake on which the

Indians once cultivated flowers on barges. The barges settled into the lake bottom and are now islands on which the slenderest of trees grow.

It is a little artificial, but we like it perhaps because the sun is just right.

Is it real? Am I in Mexico with Julian? Are the years of longing and desire for Julian so perfectly resolved?

I can't imagine the future. The present is enough.

Even before we came to Mexico, Julian and I had had bitter words about the bullfight.

He had seen it at sixteen and was overwhelmed by its color and pageantry. He holds bullfighting in high esteem as an art and as a sport. I will be glad to get it over with.

Señor Gomez tells us that tourists used to leave after the first bull but now they stay to see the killing of all six.

The bull enters the ring: this distorted-looking black-hunched monster is not nature's creature; bred and inbred over generations for all the qualities demanded by the *corrida*, this is the work of eugenics.

The bullfighters in gold and pink and red and silver, slim and graceful against their misshapen opponents.

The first bull rushed out with insane fury. He struck his horns twice against the wooden walls of the inner ring and then with a crazed leap jumped over the *barrera* and got wedged between the bullring and spectators. Two sweepers were behind the barrier; one got out easily, the other was trapped beneath the bull's trampling feet. No matter what happens in the *corrida*, the fight goes on as long as the bull lives and will do battle. The maiming or death of a man is ignored; a second replaces the fallen one.

The bull would not budge and the crowd on the sunny side, where the less restrained audience sat, began to make sounds of impatience.

I could see the bull from my seat: his look of fury and confusion.

Twisting at his tail did not help. He looked as though he were protecting himself from what was to come and a wrenching pity rose in me.

Suddenly the bull sprang out. He was tamer now. The *picadores* did their dirty work.

The bull began to bleed, streaming light red blood down his silky hide. The *banderilleros* stuck him with barbed pink and green ribbons. The matador, using his cape both for protection and provocation, exposed himself to the bull's horns. The crowd demonstrated its approval.

The staggering creature panted and scraped in the sand. The matador, at excruciating length, drove home the final blow. The beast staggered backward, its front legs buckled, and it dropped.

The carcass is dragged out of the ring by horses. The matador is applauded. The bullfight rouses an atavistic blood lust, calls up the life and death struggle in its original fierceness, and the crowd is moved.

The second bull wounded a bullfighter. Not badly, but at the moment when the man is tossed into the air and thrown to the ground it's not possible to see whether or not he has been killed.

I remember only Julian's intensity, his paleness. He screamed. But after his moment of anguish, he stayed and watched with greater and not less equilibrium.

My senses dulled. The bulls no longer seemed ugly. The matadors no longer beautiful.

The fifth bull was, according to the accolades of the people, well killed. Once tired and hurt and struggling, the beast was "given his chance at the bullfighter." Velasquez, with much pretty capework, came nearer and nearer as the shouts of the crowd urged him on to greater danger.

Straw hats showered down on the ring. After the killing, the crowd waved white handkerchiefs to signal the judge that the matador deserved reward. Velasquez thereupon received an ear and the tail, and paraded several times around the ring holding his dripping trophies aloft.

The bull was also deemed to have put up a good fight, for which it received the honor of being hauled around the ring.

We left before the sixth bull.

In the taxi we hear over the radio of the goring of the last bullfighter. The announcer says again and again, "*Sangre, sangre!*"

Julian shudders. We are grateful to have missed it. Here he can accurately use one of his favorite words, "monstrous," for the bull is bred to be a monster and the men fighting and breeding him become the monster's monster, the worse for being wiser.

The fight is dependent on the short attention span of the bull, who reacts to the immediate stimulus. The cape is more immediate than the man. The method is interesting but unreliable.

The fight is not brute force against the mind of man. It is the feeble brain of the beast against man's heartlessness.

I am depressed this evening, and the world seems monstrous. When my spirits are low I cling to Julian. I love him. The goodness of his nature tips the balance against the world of wrongs of which I am so unwillingly a part.

February 7, 1949   *Mexico City*

In the ruins of pre-Aztec Mexico we climb the Pyramid of the Sun. Carried away, Julian and I wish to be archaeologists, but that will pass in a few hours.

We visit the shrine of the Virgin of Guadaloupe, patroness of Mexico. The peasants press their hands against the glass enclosing her icon and then rub their ailing bodies in hope of miracle cures.

February 14, 1949   *New York*

Our last week in Mexico was spent in Acapulco, in a cottage surrounded by coconut palms and a profusion of red flowers, atop a yellow crag rising out of the Pacific.

Heat, and the sound of raging surf in the cove below us. Sometimes we hardly spoke. All ambitions dissolved. No reading or writing. Only the sun, the distinctly tropical sun.

How good it is to be back.

I woke on the plane to an unparalleled sunrise, then slept and woke again in a thunderstorm, flashes of lightning illuminating the bright aluminum wing.

Customs in San Antonio, and the health station. Everyone woken at two A.M. and shepherded into a room with a machine vending hot coffee.

Re-adjustment to the city.

February 18, 1949

What is the task? The first task is to identify the task.

What have I done since Mexico? A prisoner of family life.

From Mexico we wrote Dorothy Pound, explaining the demise of the Wooster Stage due to suspicions that we were running, not a theater, but a front for a bordello. Pound sends a penciled note scrawled on a postcard: "How *else* cd a seeryus tee-ater support itself in N.Y.?" Ez P.

February 20, 1949

Julian and I probe, read and discuss, absorbed in those issues that Mexico raised for us.

From meager knowledge we derive a limited ideology. Opinions form too quickly.

We must be as ready to discard every philosophy that is outworn as to accept new ideas.

From the Beck's living room the sounds of women playing mah-jongg and men at cards. Julian is reading Lenin in "our room," to which we have retired after the meal. Julian's parents insist that the door be left open as a concession to sociability.

Yesterday we lunched with Kreymborg, who related his successes in the literary world: elections to honorary societies, his work on the Pulitzer Committee . . . (he tells us in solemn secrecy that Vierek is the forthcoming prizewinner).

The old rebel inflamed with himself; the venerable radical.

Julian and I indulge ourselves in fantasies, planning a superb trip through five continents to last ten years, following two years' preparatory study!

February 22, 1949

Last night *Pelléas et Mélisande*. Julian says it's a masterpiece. He values the exquisite too highly. Its very distance from life, which gives it its beauty, detracts from its worth.

Every evening to the theater: Tonight: Richard Whorf's *Richard III*.

March 1, 1949

Here am I and what am I? I wait. There is nothing to do but to wait and to wait is to make time the tyrant. Time cancels everything.

These are the years that matter. This is my young life and how do I pass it, my young life, my only youth? With waiting.

Dr. Jacoby says that I rebel. I do. My rebellion is all that I have. I rebel against my impotence, against time. Must I grow old to achieve anything?

Time is occupied.

I go to the theater: Wagner's *Siegfried, Tristan and Isolde, Madwoman of Chaillot* by Giraudoux.

Sense of losing ground. I am so heavy with the pregnancy.

Julian's patient nature. And now at last, Julian's love.

March 4, 1949

Reading in a book on evolution: "The longer the intrauterine period and the longer the infancy of the organism is prolonged, the higher that organism is in the evolutionary scale."

The Living Theatre's gestation period: almost three years already!

Too much theater-going. *Red Gloves* by Sartre. A dry political play.

March 6, 1949

Oh, to have a still and ordered mind. To be changeable and stormy, calm and temperate, and retain, like the seasons, my continuity.

Oh, to move smoothly through the world like the seasons.

March 7, 1949

We seek vainly for living quarters. Yesterday there was a tenement fire down the block from Julian's studio. Two children burned to death. We don't want to have the baby in Julian's parents' house and had been planning to move into the studio but now we dread the prospect.

Reading: Whyte's *Next Development in Man*. Childe's *What Happened in History*. Hume's *Morals*.

No fiction or poetry. A sort of ascetic period.

March 10, 1949

I see far too many plays and operas. I create nothing. I only absorb.

Salome at the Metropolitan. Welitsch, in the reddest of red wigs, tears at her hair. She throws herself on the ground. She dances and she sings.

Dr. Jacoby nags endlessly about my rebelliousness. I vigorously defend it. Progress is made out of rebellion, and out of dissatisfaction made active comes the future of the world.

I suffer from countless pens such as this that take my thought from what I am writing with their splotches.

Again tonight to the theater: *They Knew What They Wanted*.

March 14, 1949

I'm afraid that the baby will mean isolation for me. Work in the theater will be impossible and other work is only a substitute. I can't wait for years. Driven by the inner necessity.

Dr. Zakin examines me and finds the baby in good condition.

We begin fixing Julian's studio into living space. No heat, three flights to climb, and a terrible fire hazard.

March 18, 1949

I can't write poetry. The poetic image is stifled by Mexico. Nothing glows because I can't give the enthusiasm that I once possessed to anything.

That's why my reading is on such a factual plane. But there are things I do not want to lose: "holy, glowing heart."

Julian and I talk at length of how we miss the ecstatic moment.

March 21, 1949

At the Braque show, Theresa Bernstein, in a charming, aggressive manner describes the excellence of her husband, Maurice Meyerowitz, as a painter, a baritone and a wage earner. She recites one of her poems, which treats of success:

> And when you get there,
> You just don't care.

March 25, 1949

To New Haven to see Yale's production of *Faust*. In the audience: Piscator, Chouteau Dyer and Dr. Colin.

A near perfect stage: a high arch of stairs rising in a spiral crescendo, scrim and cyclorama imbued with mystery. The witches' kitchen, steaming cauldron under skeletal bats' wings against a green sky. To this scenic display add Goethe and what does it come to? Nothing.

It came to nothing because the play was not played for the meaning, but for the effects. We speak to Chouteau during the intermission.

"No story, that's all, no story. . . . That's a very good phrase, 'No story.' It says a great deal."

Piscator says nothing.

On the train back to New York Piscator is glum and surly. He needs a big theater. He, who planned the Total Theater with Gropius sees the facilities of the Yale Theater misused. He should do *Faust*.

I remember it as a March of Drama reading my first week at the Dramatic Workshop, where the muses and scholars met under the aegis of Piscator, the master.

Virginia Baker's Gretchen seemed the highest art and Eugene Van Grona's Mephisto inspired me to a school-girl infatuation. As for Robert Carricart's Faust:

February 1946:
The day after the reading, in theater research class, Piscator complains of Bob's shallow Faust. "You do not play the great scholar, Carricart," he says. "You do not play the man who has studied medicine and theology and who knows everything already. You do not play the beard."

"Oho!" Carricart jumps up from his seat, "he had a beard! I didn't know he had a beard. I would have played it differently if I had known he had a beard! I thought he was a young man."

Piscator closes his eyes in pain.

Dr. Colin insisted he saw the poodle which the Yale production had left imaginary.

"But I saw it stage left," he insists.

"Good fantasy," says Piscator.

"An excellent subject," says Chouteau.

As we approach New York, Piscator praises my cantata for *The Aristocrats*. My work remembered!

March 29, 1949

We hear that distant relatives of the Becks are moving out of their apartment across the street at 789 West End, and that if we care to gamble we could have it.

They have no lease nor the right to sublet. We could move in only to be evicted, but we could fight to stay.

We go to look at it. A seven-room apartment, practical for Julian's painting and the baby.

We jump.

At midnight we began carrying over cartons of our belongings. This morning they move out. We move in.

April 1, 1949

Last night we visit the painters Meyerowitz and Bernstein. In their high-ceilinged studio we listen to Winston Churchill's warlike speech on the radio. They admire his delivery (he quotes Pope). But he says appalling things about the "thirteen men in the Kremlin," and their "church of communist adepts whose missionaries are in every country as a fifth column."

April 3, 1949

Read the first part of *Iphigenia auf Tauris* in German with Julian before going to see Bergner's performance. Mother tolerates our bad German in silence.

April 5, 1949

In the morning, Dr. Zakin hastened my labor by a week, a process of which I have never heard, and which scares me.

In the afternoon the irritating monotony of Dr. Jacoby.

In the evening, we travel to Brooklyn for the Red Cross course for expectant parents. A pleasant nurse explains the female genitals.

April 12, 1949

Today is spring here. Julian is going to work for his father. He feels vanquished.

City College is on strike against the racial discrimination practiced by the administration. Headlines of "riots" and cries of "communist." The facts are confused. We get very little information and the newspapers print nonsense.

Helen comes for a last visit before her trip to Europe. We go to the Hudson to watch an eclipse of the moon.

I would like to write a play with Akhnaton as the central character, a play about a rebellious free spirit, an obsessed West Wind figure.

April 13, 1949

The Akhnaton idea has taken strong hold of me. Dr. Paul Zucker's classes at the New School first gave me a glimpse of his revolution and his art. Whyte says Akhnaton's influence affected only the short span of his reign and vanished at his death. Because he was too far ahead of his time.

Rostovtzeff outlines his career. Today I read Hall, who considers Akhnaton a madman, possibly even "a cretin influenced by females," a fanatic who brought war and dissension.

His achievements are remarkable:

He refused to fight even defensive wars for Egypt because he believed that all men are brothers.

He produced realism in the representational arts because he knew that nothing is as beautiful as reality.

He is called the inventor of monotheism because he knew that God is One.

All this amidst preparations for Passover. Dispute with Julian concerning the rationale of ritual.

But tonight's Seder was friendly and informal. Through the Haggadah a talk with Josie about the Egyptians and Akhnaton.

April 20, 1949

For the last few days the baby is heavy to carry. I tire, tend to be irritable, trying hard. Some good writing: two poems.

Reading Weigall's *Akhnaton* in the Egyptian rooms at the Metropolitan Museum of Art.

April 26, 1949

Many films: *Mary of Scotland; The Fugitive; Blood of a Poet; Day of Wrath; Zéro de conduite.*

We are reading Rhine on telepathic communication. We experiment with the simpler image transference tests. We have had some scant success. Curious about the mechanism of the mind. Physical aspects of thought.

Curious? Anxious.

April 27, 1949

Reading Pound's *Cantos*. It's a long time since I have read any poetry at all.

May 2, 1949

A small group of writers at Paul Goodman's house tonight. Paul says little, is tolerant, probably on the basis that there is some truth in most things.

Johnny Myers is here with a quiet girl, Zenia, who was once John Cage's wife. David Sachs sets up intellectual enigmas. Edouard Roditi gives him definitive answers in an authoritative tone and is in fact a little frightening. Hayden Carruth, an editor of *Poetry* Magazine, completes the group. And of course there was Sally and the beer-drinking baby, Matthew Ready.

A great deal of talk about homosexuality, about psychotic states and about the personal relationships of certain writers.

They dismiss Pound as a madman, divide Europe into Catholic and communist, agree that Catholicism is bad for writers but psychoanalysis is good, decide that there is no "perfect lyric" and all this amidst more gossip than a sewing circle ever dreamed of.

"Our dried voices when we whisper together are quiet and meaningless as . . . rats' feet over broken glass."

May 3, 1949

All day feeling ill. I can't even write.

Last night I wanted to write about Mexico. Julian came home to find me bent helplessly over the typewriter. I describe my frustration. He writes differently: He can write anytime. "I write a poem when I have time."

"But can you think in terms of poetry at any time?"

"I think the same way whether I speak or write poetry." Yet he doesn't even *speak* in the same manner when he is poetically or emotionally moved.

He tries to pin it down.

"Look for the image." But my images are the result of, not the instigation of, feeling.

May 6, 1949

We see Herma Briffault about the rights to her translation of the Picasso play. She talks quickly, with a nervous energy that exhausts the listener.

She is agreeable to our doing it but insists that we option it. We're not in a position to option anything.

She is shrewd, though, and knows what she does.

May 9, 1949

Julian's painting *Sierra Nevada I* in a group show at the Laurel Gallery. It stands out in its departure from the lines (of least resistance?) that the other young painters are following. Abstraction seems a contribution to the development of a style, not an art form in itself. Abstract art will be followed by a more representational style which will have learned a great lesson from these forms.

Julian speaks of "opening eyes to help people to see and to experience."

Julian's mother and mine come to look. Both "do not understand modern art." Both are polite about it.

Still in my ears, the jangled pitch of the Chinese opera. Under Manhattan Bridge is a large hall filled with oriental faces. The trains passing directly overhead can be heard and felt. The stage is a mass of gilt, sequins and jet. The orchestra sits on stage dressed in street clothes. The actors are elaborately costumed.

Bright red makeup around the eyes, and black lines that accent the direction of the glance. The forehead is left white, as is the bridge of the nose; the black line of the eyebrows marks a sharp division between white and red.

The women sing in a piercing voice; the men are coarsely shrill.

A Chinese man beside us explains what is happening, translating while scanning a synopsis in Chinese.

We see first a tragicomedy about a man who kills his adulterous wife. The second play is a battle piece of sword dances. And finally an Aristophanic piece in which a serving man is attacked by thieves while relieving his bowels in the garden.

We eat ice cream, purchased from a vendor who walks up the aisle hawking his goods in loud competition with the singers.

A remarkable performance. The elements of stylization are so different from our conventions that they challenge our conception of theatrical production.

May 13, 1949

Dr. Zakin says the child is ready to be born and has only to pick its time.

This was the predicted day for the baby. I am incredulous. And what will it be like, this creation, this new human?

May 17, 1949

I have a son. What joy could ever surpass the first sight of his delicate face and small shut eyes. He is a very tiny baby. How beautiful! Oh, sweet, small mouth, and little dark, round face. Oh, how beautiful!

As soon as we arrived at the hospital Dr. Zakin gave me an amnesiac and told me that I would have a baby about sunrise.

The next thing I remember was the nurse asking, "Well, have you had your baby?"

"Oh, no, not yet," I replied, my hand reaching toward my belly.

"Yes, you have. A little boy." And my hand came to rest on my flattened abdomen. Happy and tired, I went to sleep.

Just now, the doctors came. They spoke sternly about the baby's smallness. They frightened me with their caution. The little one is in an incubator.

When they leave I panic. I'm not allowed to see him. The nurse says she can't help me. In desperation I get up to look for the baby. I don't find it hard to walk at all, but the nurse sees me in the corridor and is horrified!

Terrible fear. I want the baby near me. I dread the worst things: The doctors were so solemn. The head nurse takes me back to my room.

I have a long talk with my roommate. She is really a whole segment of womanhood: intelligent, but depressed by her helplessness. She wants "to do something with her life."

Her husband works for the F.B.I.

I'm wakeful, worrying about my beautiful baby boy.

Longing to see him. Longing for Julian's visit tomorrow. Longing for my baby to be safe, a strong boy. To exult in him with inevitable love.

May 19, 1949

In the hospital: helplessness and isolation.

It is monstrous that mothers can't see their own children. I want to call out, "He's mine, I made him, give him to me. I made him. I can still feel the pain of making him and the joy. Let me see him. Let me hold him. Let me feed him."

But he is in an incubator. Small, fragile one: My fear for him redoubles my love.

Unfriendly night.

Each human being is irrevocably and eternally alone. No companionship exists, no reaching. My baby caged in his warm tent must feel so isolated, so helpless there.

If only there were prayer; it would be so helpful to be able to pray, to say:

"O God, help the helpless, the incubated, and the isolated in this solitary world."

May 19, 1949

We have named him Garrick
Because it has a noble and theatrical sound
And because we thought of it romantically
Long ago, and it was our dream
To have a child named Garrick.

Mother makes a terrible scene on learning the baby's name.

She thinks it ugly—not in the Jewish tradition. I plead that his middle name, Maxwell, carries on his grandfather's name, Max.

I think it has a good sound; Garrick Maxwell Beck.

But mother storms and weeps and says she will never look at the child because of his name. He will win her over, Garrick Maxwell Beck.

I spend the time drawing, trying to learn the body, copying studies of da Vinci and Michelangelo, and the smooth Bouchers, though I don't attempt the free lines of Delacroix.

It's a good time to draw figures because I feel my own body so intensely. My own changed proportions and the violent experience of childbirth increase my sensitivity to skin and muscle.

The doctors tell me that Garrick will have to remain incubated in the hospital after I leave. I try to be stoic about this. I am a mother, yet I have no child. A hard way to learn patience.

Julian brings me Gide's *Travels in the Congo* and Woolf's *To the Lighthouse*.

May 20, 1949

Garrick has a fever, and though the doctor reassures me he is better than ever, it may be necesary to move him to another hospital. "It's only the heat," says the pediatrician, yet they are giving him penicillin and streptomycin to be "a thousand percent sure."

My roommate left with her baby this morning, and already the bed is occupied by another mother, and from another housing project.

She is from Stuyvesant Town, "where," she complains, "you feel out of place without a baby carriage." Human individuality seems to crumble in these Brave New World projects.

"Where does your husband work?" I ask her.

"For the government."

Evening. Garrick's temperature is normal. He breathes well, has eaten well. They will not have to move him. These fears were a trial that has strengthened my desire to be with him. I can soon go home.

May 21, 1949

I am awake at night and go up to the solarium to read Gide's *Travels in the Congo*. His amateur naturalism wavers between sentimentality and a callous capacity for hunting.

Gide, Goethe, Strindberg: amateur naturalists. What others belong to this list? (No writer makes me adopt so quickly his tone as does Gide.)

I read his description of the cawing of the exotic birds of the Congo as I hear the crying of the tiny people in the nursery, including, perhaps, the cry of my little son.

May 22, 1949

I am at home but Garrick's room, tenderly painted in white and blue, is still empty and I yearn.

Before leaving the hospital I saw him again. His black eyes open so wide. Grow strong, Garrick, and come home, Garrick.

Julian's warmth and kindness are boundless.

May 23, 1949

The third volume of Pound's *Cantos*. I read them in the editions in which they were first published in order to benefit by Julian's annotations. Also Pound's history of China.

I am not disappointed.

May 24, 1949

I hear that our boy is doing well, gaining weight. But we may not see him yet!

For all the times that I will be impatient with him, for all the times I will begrudge him my time . . . let me remember this time.

I finish the *Pisan Cantos*. Pound, imprisoned, learns pity (like Wilde), becomes affectionate and human.

May 27, 1949

Whyte speaks of a new "heuristic principle" capable of changing the nature of man from a dissociated personality to a unified personality. Even as Galileo and Kepler discovered a new principle of measurement.

Reading *Inside Europe*. Sick, corrupt, decadent, evil. No hope there, according to Gunther, the old world is dead.

May 29, 1949

We visit the hospital. Through a glass we see Garrick held up by a nurse. His tiny face like a philosopher's. He somberly shakes his head. He looks like my father, pensive and wise.

He is coming home tomorrow morning!

May 30, 1949

Garrick has come home.

Will all my days pass as quietly as this? Will I write? Will I have time to go out? Will I be able to accustom myself to long hours at home?

Perhaps I can use this time to order my life.

May 31, 1949

For Julian's birthday and mine, his parents give us an 8 mm movie camera, a projector, screen, lights. To photograph the baby.

Headache. Sleep. Too quiet.

June 4, 1949

On my twenty-third birthday: Until the theater materializes I want to devote as much of my time as I can to writing. I have enough plans: *Nora's Dream*, a long one-act on Ibsen's play; Akhnaton; completion of Cassandra; Mexico, a long poem; many shorter poems to be revised; even the beginning of a film scenario. That would be a full year's work.

June 5, 1949

A long walk last night around Midtown. We wonder at the aberrations of our fellow man. What is it that we find so ugly and crass? I want to know more the negative, so dark and hard to define.

June 6, 1949

Garrick cries often and lustily as he gets stronger and bigger. Each new movement is meaningful.

At the Cherry Lane: Stein's *Yes Is for a Very Young Man* done by still another company that grew out of On Stage.

I feel a maternal almost grandmotherly pride toward these groups. Toward On Stage which grew out of Ramsey's impatience with our theater, toward Interplayers and New York Repertory Company. And now Off Broadway, Inc., with Bea Arthur, Mike Gazzo and Gene Saks from the Dramatic Workshop.

June 7, 1949

I strive for self-discipline with the same intensity with which I reject outwardly imposed discipline. An inner discipline will serve each individual according to her needs and *her demands upon herself*.

But how to dispel the idea that discipline is synonymous with deprivation?

June 9, 1949

Our first attempt at entertaining. Peter Miller and Rhoda, and Professor Leffert.

The professor attacks Joyce. Soon he is reading aloud from *Finnegan* to prove that it is incomprehensible, while Julian reads from Tennyson to prove it is equally so.

June 18, 1949

Garrick cries as much as eight hours at a stretch, sometimes all night. Julian can quiet him when everyone else fails. Patiently he paces holding him and singing to him, over and over till dawn, "Maxwellton's Braes are bonnie where early fa's the dew. . . ."

June 19, 1949

The Prester John Company, an anarchist group, is performing Paul Goodman's *Faustina* in a loft on Eighth Street occupied by Robert Motherwell and Barney Newman's art school. No stage, no raked floor, no facilities. Only folding chairs and a stifling heat. A packed house. The audience is young; in these people there's a wide-eyedness, a wakefulness, a lack of ennui.

Jackson Mac Low, who writes for *Resistance*, played Marcus Aurelius in a soft-voiced, stoic tone. He also directed.

It deals with the empress of Rome; her husband, Aurelius; and a handsome gladiator, an unwitting sadist, who discovers that he tortures the beasts he kills. The empress is torn by deeper, undecipherable compulsions.

A resolution is found at the advice of a soothsayeress played as a grotesque by "Doc" Moe Moscowitz, one of the anarchists who invaded a Christmas party at my house two years ago carrying a toothbrush in his coat pocket to indicate homelessness.

The gladiator is sacrificed and his blood runs, still warm, over the body of Faustina.

Aurelius: Why does he call out? Is this the spontaneous outcry in such a case?

Frontius: What would you cry out in such a case?
Aurelius (quietly): I am in such a case, and I am crying out.

June 24, 1949

I've broken off my analysis with Dr. Jacoby. He tells me my neurosis relates to my feelings about my mother, and he is right.

June 25, 1949

Garrick in his carriage goes out to see the world for the first time. He sleeps peacefully through the adventure.

Walking in the adult world with my child I feel a child myself, playing house with a doll and carriage.

July 18, 1949

Panic at the sight of Kafka's Gregor in the kitchen. I force myself to clean it. The baby has been sleeping for some hours.

In a book opened at random I find the phrase: "Whatever is is holy."

July 20, 1949

I read this line in Agee's *Let Us Now Praise Famous Men*: "Everything capable of being believed is an image of the truth."

Is that true? What do I believe with any certainty? In innate goodness? Is evil then, a spontaneous manifestation, or is it innate goodness somehow gone wrong? How can existence be defined as good or evil?

In some way everyone is trying to do right, and in so far as that is true: "Everything capable of being believed is an image of the truth."

July 24, 1949

Two splendid days in the country. Mother comes along and the baby chores are divided. Garrick is pleased by the driving and the country air, but cries with displeasure in the sun. No Akhnaton he.

July 30, 1949   *Woodmont, Connecticut*

Julian's childhood summers were spent in Woodmont.

He shows me an old hotel, remembering picture hats and garden parties; a crusty shore along the sound, jagged striated rocks with evocative formations.

"This," says Julian, "we called the 'Great Throne,' this the 'Canoe.'"

I see him as he must have been, clambering on the rocks, inventing his own games.

Reading, while feeding or rocking Garrick: Rabelais; Sheean's *Personal History*; Campbell's *Hero with a Thousand Faces*; finding universal symbols within the diversity of varied mythologies.

I am making a notebook of drawings of flowers found on our trip.

I take Garrick to the library to renew my library card. Holding the baby I fill out a form with the librarian's help. When she comes to "occupation" she smiles at Garrick and says, "I can see you have no occupation" and writes down "house."

I try to make the best of what I feel and even smile.

August 14, 1949

Troubled talks with Julian about the state of the world, impending disaster, the bombs, the war. Why do we sit calmly and make our pretty paintings while someone is tugging at us frantically screaming "Fire!"

August 18, 1949

To Centre Street to apply for a permit to learn to drive.

In front of the United States Courthouse demonstrators supporting the twelve communists on trial march with placards. The pickets are mostly youngsters with the proud, energetic faces of radicals, a little tired but affecting tirelessness.

Placards read: "Judge Medina, don't be a fool, real Americans don't stool," and "Free the communists, arrest the lynchers" (carried by a young Negro).

An older man calls out a chant which everyone takes up: "Somethin' really must be stinkin' / When they jail you just for thinkin'" and "Let's take democracy out of the deep freezer." (Several important Washington wives, including Mrs. Truman, are said to have received "gifts" of deep freezers.)

Inside the courthouse I join a line of people who have come to see the trial of the United States vs. the leaders of the communist movement in America. Most of the people on line are communists and have the snappy, well-informed air of the left. But though they are cheerful and enthusiastic they are bitter in their hatred for such institutions as "the press."

The handsome young man beside me has been on the picket line. "It's good for the soul," he says. He's unemployed, wants to make documentary films, talks about Maya Deren, and was on Okinawa during the war.

An Italian man passes around a copy of *Stars and Stripes* in which his son, now stationed in Okinawa, is mentioned. Soon the young man beside me is drawing rough maps to show the old man where things are on the occupied island.

The copy of *Stars and Stripes* is examined for its tendencies. Surprise is expressed at the inclusion of certain news that was "suppressed here."

On the line, as inside the courtroom, there is the feeling of an historical event, that more than the fate of twelve is at stake. More, even, than the fate of the American Communist Party.

The courtroom bristles with hostility, tension and seriousness. The jury files in looking bored and stupid.

Judge Medina enters and sits down to rock back and forth. Not once does he stop rocking.

Alan Mack, the managing editor of the *Daily Worker*, is cross-examined. At every question by the prosecution the defense interjects, "I object to the question."

And each time, Medina rocks back and forth and mutters, "Objection overruled."

This has been going on now for four months.

Communism is not the issue. The freedom to disagree with the government is on trial. When these men speak of revolution, are they thinking of a revolution of arms and barricades, or of a social revolution? Is the word "revolution" simply a name by which to catch them?

Who is not misled? Who sees it clearly? Who is not tangled in the web of authority? That web has become a shroud called "the law," in which the human mind lies buried.

August 24, 1949

In *The Hero with a Thousand Faces* Campbell says that all action is illusion. But to give up activity is a denial of function. As long as we are alive, we can suppress it only partially and the effort of such suppression is itself a life activity.

Campbell's tract on myth sinks me into *Weltschmerz*.

August 31, 1949

In the trivial externals a pattern becomes visible that is in itself *not* trivial. I want more. Whatever I have, I want more.

Learning is slow. Dreaming is learning. Attending to the trivia is learning. The frustration of having no time is learning.

Julian and I speak of writing a book called, "The Free Society." The problems of lawlessness. Could laws function as a practical guide for those who choose to use them if no one were forced to submit to decisions by authority?

How can people solve the daily problems of social life without delegating authority?

If only I could think these things through. If there were time. "If that the world were always young, and truth on every Shepherd's tongue . . ."

I write some poetry and send it to publications which reject it. I read. I attend to Garrick, the sweet.

Tonight, movies of Garrick's early months. I wish we could use this camera to make a serious film.

September 6, 1949

The City, a documentary about smog-covered steel/coal-town slums by Pare Lorentz. Wooden shacks in hilly rows are juxtaposed with Lewis Mumford's ideal community. I'm reading Mumford on utopia.

In the film, utopia is a sprawling industrial town which has put a stop to dirt and poverty, but also to life itself. Who would choose to live in this sterile, limited community?

What would I put in its place?

September 12, 1949

Lawrence Maxwell gives a cocktail party at his bookshop for Gershon Legman, the author of *Love and Death, a Study of Sadism and Sexuality*. Legman, a gruff and forbidding man, is one of the editors of *Neurotica*. With an author's pride I see them sell my poem, along with his "Case against the Comics," which appears in the same issue. . . .

September 21, 1949

In a sudden spurt of straw-clutching I make the rounds of theatrical offices while Mother watches Garrick. I have an inordinate love for the crowds and for the racetrack atmosphere of Broadway, so distasteful to Julian. After a time I'll despise it again, but right now it's a refuge.

September 28, 1949

Life has always seemed to me inevitably tragic and I am surprised to find that it is not.

I am only happy among people. Mother says it's my fear of missing something, and she may be right.

I write this with Garrick beside me on the bed. He interrupts me with his wordless call. He is watching my writing hand and trying to reach for it. I give him my left hand to play with.

Julian and I spend time discussing time. The time to live and the time to make love.

October 1, 1949

After reading Vincent Sheean's description of Rayna Prohme's exemplary life in *Personal History*, I begin Gertrude Stein's *What Are Masterpieces?* I am put off by her aggressive style. I discuss this with Julian for hours. I compare the sincerity of the nonliterary Sheean, the journalist, with the imposing edifice of Stein's work.

I say, "Of what value is keen observation which is, to use an obsolete term, 'soulless'?"

Julian's repeated symbol is the mask which becomes the wearer and is truer to the wearer's nature than his unmasked self.

What is this struggle for honesty?

Julian says he is honest with himself. But I'm sure that I deceive no one as constantly, as carelessly, as myself. (Didn't I almost let my pen slip now to write "carefully"?)

Confusion. There is only confusion without an absolute like God or good. Or the magnification of some other value such as revolution, society, art, fame, science, war, medicine, construction or accumulation as a motivating force.

October 4, 1949

Through Yom Kippur with godly books: Julian reads to me from the Bible. I finish *Paradise Lost*.

An easy fast, and an uninspired service in a nearby hotel with neither the shallow virtues of pomp nor the deeper virtue of piety.

October 9, 1949

To theatrical offices. Today I get to Jules Ziegler. This large Jewish man with cigar stares up at me and wheezes, "Yeah?"

I talk very quickly to counter his rudeness. After which, he: "Well whadda ya do? Ya sing? Ya dance?"

In spite of this sort of thing I never enter an office without the quickening hope: "This time it's for me." The idea that "chance" can't constantly go against me.

While buying tickets for the Goethe bicentennial productions at Hunter College, I stop in at the new Elementary School. The great fire of 1936 left nothing of my old school except my memory. In the playhouse a class of small children in costume is rehearsing an Indian dance to the piano tinkle of what Anna Curtis Chandler, the famed story-teller, supposed to be an Indian theme. Proustian flash that I had danced this dance to this very tune.

October 17, 1949

He has grown, my infant, into Garrick, the assertive person who "wills" and "wants." Every morning I bring him to Mother's house and make my dutiful rounds.

"Piscator?" says a television director, when I mention my background, "He's completely impractical. I can't afford to be artistic."

I'll try to compose an audition piece.

Julian paints.

To the Motherwell exhibit at Samuel Kootz'. Collages that seem brilliant flashes, the result of spontaneous inspiration, but Julian says that Motherwell labors arduously over them. Motherwell says, "Beneath each painting are six lies."

October 20, 1949

E. E. Cummings reads from his poems at the 92nd Street Y.

No tricks of speech or gesture. He reads softly with a lyrical simplicity that belies the bombastic appearance of his printed page. He gives the impression of modest behavior masking an outrageous ego.

Claude Fredericks and Milton Saul accompany us home afterward along with Harold Norse, a poet Julian knows from Provincetown, and Walter McElroy, who translated Tristan Corbiére for Claude's Banyan Press.

Claude and Milton are tender people. They live in Vermont where they grow vegetables and publish finely wrought hand-printed books. Claude's gentle manner gives him a mystical air. They seem to be genuinely involved in the seasons.

Harold Norse is an anarchist. "Is it possible to be a saint?" he asks. And then, speaking for himself, he replies, "Yes, it is very possible. It is very easy to be a saint."

When I was a little girl, I thought it would be easy to be good and couldn't understand why everybody wasn't.

Our poet friends speak about the word anarchism. They judge it faulty because of its association with chaos, disorder, violence and destructiveness.

Can "anarchism" apply to a cooperative, moneyless, self-determining society? It is, of course, a word that makes enemies because it implies the breakdown of the existing system.

But this breakdown is part of a process in which the resulting reconstruction must be noncoercive, otherwise the breaking-down leads only from power structure to power structure. The real change brought about by the anarchist principle is a whole other way of organizing our lives.

Harold says, "Life has become too complex."

I say, "We must adjust to becoming healthy individuals inside a corrupt society, not outside that society. Within it, but not involved in its corruption."

It gave us hope to hear someone assert, "Love is the eventual solution." And, "Only by personal example is the world made better."

It's no dream. It's a realizable hope.

October 26, 1949

This morning reading de Jouvenel's *On Power*, I am moved to tears by his description of war. At such moments I am seized with the desire to do some useful work with my voice, my body, my hands. Some work to make peace. I dream of ways to say it, to show it, to act it out.

And so, not having solved my own life, I wish to go out and solve everyone's.

October 31, 1949

Housewarming for Mendy and Mary Jo, in their Village apartment. Very elegant people. Everyone touting their own accomplishments.

Mary Jo, pregnant, in a Dior dress cut away to the very points of her breasts. Many fashionable ladies: Stella Adler in black and rhinestones, Herma Briffault exuberant. To Bob Ramsey she says, "And who has the Cherry Lane this year?"

"I do."

"Ah, then you must have luncheon with me tomorrow."

"Tomorrow I shall be busy all day signing things."

"Ah, then we must have champagne."

"Well, then call me."

"You see, champagne, it always works."

Vincent Sheean says the relation between the world and the individual is the only theme. I want to partake creatively in the immediate struggle for survival.

November 3, 1949

Instead of working this morning while the baby sleeps, I read: first a story by Mary McCarthy on psychoanalysis, then some poems in *Tiger's Eye*. No time to write now. Quickly I take a pastel and fill a sketch pad with drawings of nude women with languorous, sad, elongated faces.

Now late. Rush. Hurry. Baby wakes. Still undressed. 12:30. No ink.

November 4, 1949

Julian moves out of his studio on 59th Street. We decide to give our whole theater collection to the New York Public Library.

Relief. It had become an albatross.

November 16, 1949

Helen, returning to America, tells me what they are saying in Europe.

"There will be a war," they say. "In 1952," they say. "New York will be the first place to be bombed in a surprise attack by Russia," they say. "And it is inevitable," they say. "In Europe they are hungry, sad, unsmiling, bombed out, bullied. The world is tight and terrible and there will be," they say, "a war."

Helen shares the pessimism of the Europeans. "Destruction is inevitable. The present is all we have. No plans, no hereafter." Her attitude toward suffering is to turn away.

I: "Yes, I, too, turn away. I want to make all of life my immediate concern. The survival instinct forbids me."

November 21, 1949

Dick Gerson visits. He was working with the United States army's propaganda department in Europe. The army censors all news coming from overseas. There's an emphasis on anti-Russian literature. He cites *Russia through the Ages, a History of Tyranny*.

Dick has become a World Federalist. He and Julian knew Cord Meyer, the president of the World Federalists, when he was an editor of the Yale Literary Magazine. Julian recalls Meyer's lengthy critiques of the poems he submitted. Meyer has written a book called *Peace or Anarchy* which suggests an international federation modeled on the constitution of the United States!

While there is something noble in the World Federalists' struggle to create the world that they envision, I don't know how to point out that for all their advocacy of peace-making, world government backed by armed force would by its very nature be an absolute tyranny.

Garry Davis' case shows a reckless kind of courage. Though he was never an anarchist, and is no longer even a World Federalist, the destruction of his passport and the renunciation of his citizenship is an anarchist act. What is admirable is his individualism and his courage in performing a sensational action in a time of timid whispering.

Do I overestimate the dramatic act? No. The dramatic act is the mouth-piece of the thinker.

November 24, 1949

I make the rounds. But the awe has gone out of the professional theater for me. Quite simply, quite suddenly vanished.

A long conversation with Dick Jessup, who studied at the Workshop and is now a sailor. He is searching for something he calls Christ, though he says it is not a religious search. He wonders if he is a "Red." In a year on ship he read 700 books ("any books, good and bad"). His wife and four-year-old daughter live on Long Island while he ships out on banana boats. He is too aware of his attractiveness.

Thanksgiving dinner at my mother's with Josie and some European friends. Talk of politics with these young men who deny their leftist leanings. Mother's extreme sensitivity about politics, her hatred of Germany, her fear of the Russians, her blind trust in the United States, inhibit free discussion.

We speak of film as an influence on political thought and note the lack of pacifist films such as those that appeared after the first world war: *All Quiet on the Western Front, Grand Illusion, Nurse Edith Cavell.*

December 1, 1949

In Proust: the superb leisure of the characters as of the plot. And the writing is careful beyond human understanding. But on what all this care is expended I am not certain.

I'm interrupted by the baby and now resort to rocking him in the bassinet while I write. I have learned to rock him with my foot. So I steal time from the fates.

He is so big, my boy, and incredibly endearing, because he is all possibilities and all future.

Again at work on the Living Theatre. Each time with fresh hope. Now the costliest project of all and entirely unfeasible.

We plan, since no theater seems to exist, to build one. And in order to do this inexpensively, to build it in a quonset hut, one of those metal sheds that the army developed.

A representative of the Great Lakes Steel Corporation gives us the figures: about $5,000 for the shell. He tells us some of the legal requisites for places of public assembly: swinging doors, reinforced steel. But the price of property in New York City is fantastic. The whole thing is fantastic.

Paul Goodman will speak about it with his brother, Percy, who has built a quonset synagogue on Long Island.

At least I am married to an optimist.

December 6, 1949

Torquato Tasso with Herbert Berghof presented in German by the Players from Abroad at the Barbizon Plaza.

Tasso, as Goethe drew him, is the free, uncompromising spirit that Goethe could never be but regarded with longing.

Paul tells Julian that Percy says quonsets are not permitted in New York City. The quonset company told us otherwise. I will inquire at the Building Laws Department, or whatever it is called.

At the Municipal Building everyone is helpful and attentive.

The quonset problem is a new one, not provided for under the housing laws but taken care of by special ruling. I wend my way through drawersful of files of the Great Lakes Steel Corp., but I can't find a thing about public buildings. The borough superintendent, I'm told, will have to make an interpretation.

At the borough superintendent's office I speak to the chief engineer, a thin, sober man named Faiella, and a stocky, white-haired man who stands beside him. White-haired man explains to Faiella what an experimental theater is and that one of them discovered Eugene O'Neill, so they can't be entirely bad.

Faiella knows nothing about this, he says the law would have to be amended.

December 7, 1949

McElroy and Collins visit again. Walter is the most civilized of poets and the most refined of intellects.

Americans don't refer to themselves as intellectuals, as Europeans do, because of the American notion that intellect is undemocratic since it is not equally available to the whole population.

December 8, 1949

Paul Goodman discusses anarchist and pacifist morality. Paul's quiet, assured talk. My rashness, my overdrawn examples.

I feel freer all the time. Even people who would once have awed me now must bear my impertinence.

My irritation sometimes takes the form of a romantic spirituality and at such times I find Julian cold and unpoetic and foreign.

December 14, 1949

The New York Dance Company: José Limón, Doris Humphrey, Charles Weidman, Valerie Bettis. Fine work.

Recollections of the wild days of our youth. I think I still love that free, insane, outrageous and beautiful Julian, the mad, unfettered, homosexual poet who has disappeared so completely that he himself does not recall him, not even as well as I do. And when he does, it is without any love for his lost liberty. Julian forgets that his old brashness was only the cuttingness of glass being shattered to let in the air.

But now? We find ourselves in a kind of life in which contentment is supposed to replace the ecstasies of misery, but . . .

December 15, 1949

Chouteau Dyer directs the reading of Dick Gerson's *The Thirteenth God* at the Dramatic Workshop. Robert Carricart read Alexander. I was moved, though not to tears, by his passionate looks. I read Statira, Alexander's Persian wife.

It was gratifying to use again the range of my voice, the gestures of the eye or the clenched or open palm, to live that life, even so tentatively and so temporarily—the life before an audience. Oh, yes, I do want to act.

December 16, 1949

The Burning Bush at the Rooftop Theater. Even Piscator's genius could not do much with this play about the trial of Hungarian Jews accused of ritual murder.

Piscator is wrong when he says he can "direct the telephone book." He cannot make an epic drama out of a courtroom melodrama simply because of its social theme.

The opening night audience was sumptuously beminked, and intellectual—even on Houston Street.

December 19, 1949

The preposterousness of the quonset idea is beginning to have its effects.

At Gordon and Freed's, architects, Mr. Gordon says that we can't get permission to build the quonset unless we first put in a bid on a plot of land. But we can't buy land until we have money, and we can't get money until we can prove that it's legal.

December 22, 1949

I walk around the Village looking for land.

We consider for production three adventurous plays: Padraic Colum's *Balloon*; Michael Fraenkel and Walter Lowenfels' *USA with Music*; Picasso's *Desire Trapped by the Tail*.

December 26, 1949

We met Claude and Milton at Gotham Book Mart, where we had a long discussion with the mad Frances Steloff about feet and shoes. She's eager to tell the Queen Mother of England about a space shoe moulded to the foot by a craftsman named Alan Murray. She is convinced that the Queen Mother would promptly fly to America to have a pair made. E. E. Cummings browsed in the shop while we talked.

At a Christmas Eve party at Walter McElroy's we meet Dollie Chareau, widow of the architect and a patroness of the arts, with a friend, Leon Kochnitzky. Mme. Chareau is a spirited and jovial woman of distinct tastes and bearing. She teaches French and offers to give us lessons. "*J'ai honte, j'ai honte,*" I kept saying.

Julian talks to Gene Derwood about her plays. She is studiedly eccentric.

"I can't give anyone my plays unless they first promise to produce them. God is the judge of my work. I have my demons."

When Julian refuses to play such games, she says that she was testing his integrity. She goes off to read Claude's palm by the light of a candle.

I chat in the kitchen with her husband, Oscar Williams. I tell him that my husband is a painter.

"Does he paint you?"

"No, he paints abstractions."

"But all legitimate abstractions are based on reality."

"That's true. He does derive everything from subject matter, but he has never chosen me as a subject."

"Do you write poems for him?"

"Yes, many."

"And he doesn't paint you?"

"No."

"Then why don't you divorce him?"

"I love him."

"Even though he doesn't paint you?"

"Yes. It is possible to love someone who does not paint you."

Look of complete defeat behind thick-lensed glasses. End of poet's conversation.

Paul Goodman is with Sally and some good-looking youngsters with whom he carries on.

December 27, 1949

I visit Mary Jo Weisgal. She's in her seventh month, and we talk about babies and sex.

Mendy is on tour with *Streetcar Named Desire* and she is content to have her baby alone, an independence that I admire but could never attain. She makes me ashamed of how I cling to Julian, I who can't bear to be alone for even an hour.

December 28, 1949

Read Gertrude Stein's *Doctor Faustus Lights the Lights.* Her words are symbols, a quality that is becoming to the theme. I want to do this marvelous play. Carl Van Vechten, who has the thumbs up or thumbs down on Stein plays, will probably not give permission.

Also read Brecht's *Good Woman of Szechwan*. A good play, but it's difficult to do parable propaganda theater.

As the year ends we work on plans for the theater.

We need a legal adviser for the theater who can work in our spirit. We need to recruit artists for a fund-raising portfolio of production designs. We need to prepare directing books. We need to look for land. Julian is set on building. I doubt we can raise the money.

January 1, 1950

The night was not ruined by celebration. As the birthday is a private measurement, so the New Year is a universal aging.

At the distant whistles, I go into the bedroom to grasp the passing moment alone, but Julian follows. We talk sentimentally over champagne. Now it is daytime and different.

Claude brings us his play *The Idiot King*, in which a just and good king suffers while a saintly nun survives sorrow by transcending it.

We want the Nun's joy, but we want the real world with it. Because the real world contains it. I feel great sympathy with Claude as he speaks of the world beyond mysticism, which is part of the soul's experience, and its best part, at that.

We talk until five A.M. and Claude sleeps over in the cold studio. At breakfast he tells us he is going to Van Vechten's New Year's Day party, and will ask him about permission for *Doctor Faustus Lights the Lights*.

January 3, 1950

At the opening of Mark Rothko's show at Betty Parsons Gallery we ask him to do some designs for the Living Theatre.

Rothko is very drunk and it isn't easy to speak to him, for he wavers from one subject to another. His new paintings are large, flat areas of juxtaposed color.

Robert Motherwell is there and tells Julian that he would like to work with us.

"Theater design has not used the knowledge that painting has given us," he says.

January 7, 1950

In the real estate office with Julian fantastic sums are spoken of casually: $25,000, $40,000. No matter. One is as easily pronounced as the other. The idea of a theater built to suit us is beyond belief. To raise that much money is beyond belief.

Rothko says no. He has abandoned the theater. Working with Madame Piscator on Paul Goodman's plays for the Poet's Theater he realized that designing for the theater means conforming to other people's specifications.

Special awareness of fine weather and of church architecture since reading Proust. Also Gide with his minutiae: a leaf, a wind, a transient sensation carried to mystical limits.

January 13, 1950

My son is sitting beside me munching zwieback.
When I'm tired things glow with that soft greenness that makes mysteries.
I like tiredness, though it feels unhealthy.

January 14, 1950

Robert Motherwell says he would like to design *Tamburlaine*.
His ideas come freely and quickly and are as much intellectual as visual.
He appears very handsome because his blue eyes light directly into yours with
a sharp aim. He immediately grasps the idea of the Living Theatre. He feels
the urgency.
He speaks of plasticity and fluidity: "A set should be designed on the stage,
as a picture is painted, with the changes made directly in the medium." Motherwell wants to create his paintings in the setting in which they are to be seen.
He has painted his own studio and plans to paint an exhibit in the gallery
where it is to be shown. Of course it would be ideal to work directly on the
stage, but certain limitations would be imposed by the needs of the play. Unless the set were the play's subject.
The Van Gogh show at the Metropolitan: the light! They are painted with
light.

January 22, 1950

Last night we attended the opening of T. S. Eliot's *The Cocktail Party*.
It's a drawing room play, in which things occur that touch the soul—the
soul which the theater has neglected—it seems a confession of sentimentality
even to admit its existence.
The awareness of the uniqueness of the individual is the revelation that
leads to the disillusionment out of which change is born.
I am moved, but belief is transient. The spirit of the occasion is lost. The
glamour of the opening night besmirches the dream.
The Duke and Duchess of Windsor cause a stir in the theater and a crowd
gathers outside.
The first nighters push on to Sardi's. Vincent Sardi favors us with a pre-
ferred table.
The play is lost like a Sunday sermon.
"Oh, Lord, what is man that thou regardest him?"

January 23, 1950

Barney Newman's show at Betty Parsons. Strange canvases. Surfaces of flat
color with a stripe down the center. He says, "It's a concentrated statement
that I'm obsessed with."
Julian addresses a mustering of assembled artists: Jacqueline Lamba, Breton's wife; David Hare; Bill and Ethel Baziotes; Hans Hofmann; Bob Motherwell; Jimmy Ernst.

January 29, 1950

A cocktail party for Anaïs Nin at Lawrence Maxwell's. Very crowded, hot room.

Kreymborg talks endlessly about himself. Paul Goodman is talking about the Living Theatre and Kreymborg.

There's a new magazine, *Flair*, that features a badly written article describing the "New Bohemia." It seems decadent to be part of it. Yet these are our people and I don't see any escape: This is the world we must work within. The peak we seek to scale is no higher than a thimble. Oh, vanity of vanities!

Save me from the clever conversationalist. Save me from the chic. Save me from the despair of caring so terribly.

January 30, 1950

Last night Julian read to me from the *Times* about the hydrogen bomb, H-bomb, Hell bomb, and all night I dream of war.

I tried to reconcile myself to sleep by reading Proust. I read the passage in *Cities of the Plain* about the bee which fails to pollinate the flower, a parable of the perversion of which the wars are a part.

But the deluge has not yet come and it's our work to hold it back and not to be discouraged. If we are small we'll play the boy who put his finger in the dyke till the ocean crashes down over us.

I am almost ready to begin.

Last night at Martha Graham. She is a noble artist, but I am impatient with the spectator's role and with the aesthetic of her World Pictures. I am moving in another direction. All things extraneous to it become diversions.

February 4, 1950

Julian and I go to the top of the Empire State Building to talk about a Peace Plan. The recent reports on the hydrogen bomb convince us that we should put our energy and imagination to stopping this planetary forest fire.

How to rally our strength. Julian suggests a peace pledge to rouse everyone's conscience.

February 5, 1950

Tuesday night we saw Julie Bovasso and Shepperd Kerman in *Salome* and spoke to them about working with the Living Theatre.

Wednesday, Seymour Rutkin, a young architect who studied with Mies Van Der Rohe, came here with grandiose ideas about building a glass shell theater on the far shore of the East River.

Thursday night, Gil Orlovitz, a poet sent to us by Claude, came and left his play, *Stevie Guy*.

Friday at Harold Norse's: Helen Thigpen and David Allen and the composer Howard Swanson. These musicians have the nervous artlessness of actors and the personal animosities of writers.

This has been an important week. And for all our cultural comings and goings, I could become completely committed to the peace work.

February 8, 1950

Julian asks Paul Goodman to come here and talk about how to stop the wars.

How to stop the wars?

"Remove burdens," says Paul.

That is the way of the saint.

I protest that in the forest fire there's no time for splendid projects.

Paul says people need violence, but he really means passionate expression.

The tenets of love annul petty concerns and express ardent rebellion against confining circumstances. Paul doesn't make the distinction between ardor and violence.

Yesterday at the opening of Bill Baziotes' show. The social device. The lying eye.

February 10, 1950

There is No End, a shattering play about war, at Piscator's workshop. I can't bear it when the sacrifice of the innocent for the sake of a greater cause is shown that clearly.

In a sweat of anguish, I feel like one going insane who acts with calm gravity so that no one will suspect her. Can this pain be good because I can make use of it?

In the face of the moral dilemma Julian experiences with me what seems to be the most incommunicable of perceptions.

We say one must be mad not to take political action, although we've found no answer that in one way or another does not stink with sin.

Stop being a pragmatist. Revert. Go back to purity.

Once you are aware, there is no way out of awareness back into ignorance.

Now I understand the story of Eve and the temptation: that awareness of good and evil is indeed expulsion from the paradise of our ignorance.

A visit to Pancho. The light through the Mondrian shutters throws me backward through time.

I switch on a lamp. Pancho is asleep among debris on a never-made bed. A mountain air on the radio: "You can't love the brother of the wild red goose."

Pancho woke and asked me to read aloud some melancholy stories he has written. There was great suffering there, dim and unreal as that man beyond sanity whom once, long ago, I imagined that I loved.

We spoke of insanity and sainthood and I could cry forever if I dared to think fully about any one thing.

I am going to write in a smaller notebook that I can carry about more easily.

February 11, 1950

The Portable Journal.

On a Saturday afternoon shopping trip we meet a stranger, Jack Dolph, in the Vanderbilt Bar under the Purple Tree. He speaks in a theological tone, is a writer of mysteries, a member of the Committee for a Free Europe, an ardent idealist and a partisan of the theory that sometimes it is necessary to kill. I refused to accept his argument.

"Get out your soapbox, kids, and get a tent, because that's what you have to do the way you talk," and we said that we knew that. "Then what the hell are you doing drinking martinis in the Vanderbilt with me?" And we did not know.

So we three sat under the Purple Tree like Buddha under his bamboo and contemplated the same problem.

There were no answers.

February 13, 1950

A special delivery letter from Chouteau Dyer asking me to read Cassandra in the March of Drama's *Agamemnon* tomorrow night.

But tomorrow night is Irving Beck's birthday and they have bought tickets for *A Member of the Wedding*. The reading means a lot to me, and I'm furious that I'm prevented from going out of indebtedness to Julian's family.

The realization that I am not free is much more important than the reading. Julian says, "Don't make a symbol of a situation which the situation does not warrant."

Then the mood exhausts itself. I will get out of this.

February 14, 1950

A Member of the Wedding. It should have been a good play about loneliness. But the new poetic realism (a pseudoneurotic style as expressionism was a pseudopsychotic style) depicts only a psychological state idealized by distance and, ultimately, falsifies the reality.

February 16, 1950

Claude and Walter McElroy talk with us about the H-bomb.
Claude asks, "Where will you go to preach and organize?"
"Where there is despair."
"How can we stop the terror in our hearts?"
How can we not feel terror? Never before has it been a question of total destruction. Of everything. Would the vegetation survive?
It is unthinkable. That means I will not think of it.
When I am with Claude I am aware of my artificiality and am ashamed.
Claude says he values his journal above his other possessions. We preserve the past.

February 17, 1950

Gide's *Les Nourritures terrestres* is a dangerous book breeding dissatisfaction; a beautiful book breeding insights.

He gambols with Arab boys under an Algerian sun. My kitchen is piled with dishes and my typewriter is still. Yet I will write:
  1. Akhnaton

2. Band of Angels, a dramatic poem.
3. A book on a free society to be written together with Julian.
4. Nora's Dream. The night of Nora's departure.
5. A novel with God as the protagonist.
6. A final act for Cassandra and a revision of the whole opera.

But time won't let me. Even to retype *Damocles* is taking weeks. Meanwhile I burn. And burn.

February 19, 1950

Old faces at the Dramatic Workshop Alumni Meeting.

Piscator talks. Some flame that is not forgotten revives. Among all the small voices, his clear, strong voice is alive with an inner excitement. And that silver head, a very medallion of a head!

He speaks of his disappointment that the Dramatic Workshop has not produced a vanguard army of political theaters across America. He speaks derisively of certain alumni who have ignored his political inspiration. Tennessee Williams is cited. Piscator says, "I wish to make of every actor a thinker and of every playwright a fighter."

And his regard and intentions seem to select me, to accuse me, to want to force me into willing action.

There's a performance of *There is No End* for the alumni, but I can't bear to see it again, and so during the performance we take a short trip across the Hudson: "This is not a river," Julian says on the ferry, "it is an estuary."

Over the roofs of Weehawken the fists of the New York skyscrapers rise up like a threat.

We walk west toward the marshes. The street swoops steeply past a large graveyard beyond which lies a tangle of flat houses cowering against the flat ground. The sticky air carries the sickening odor of the burning marshes.

Between some of the houses, the lifeless, beflowered cemetery can be seen, and between others the flowerless swamp.

Just beyond the gray street the swamp begins, like the fabled edge of the world, that thrusts the unwary mariner into boundless space.

This landscape like the sun-drenched poverty of Mexico becomes part of our burden and call to action.

Suddenly back in the city at 42nd Street after a bus ride through the coffinish tunnel; Eighth Avenue is a welcome sign of life.

We return to the alumni meeting where the performance has just ended. We too, feel that we have been witnesses during this time. Robert Hilliard, the student who first suggested to me that I could make my own theater, insists that the playwright needed a Marxist on stage to resolve the dilemma with a real dialectic.

When we question Piscator about the next step, he speaks of the need for mass action.

"Individual action is not enough in our time."

He, too, speaks of Marx. "We must do our work," he says, "as a personal contribution, and join the party whose politics most nearly express our own as a social contribution."

But Marx didn't do that at all. He formulated anew as we must formulate anew. The individual action can inspire mass action when nothing else can. If only we do not resign ourselves to war. In fact, we must not resign ourselves to anything.

February 22, 1950

Yet I am tormented by a kind of spiritual wasting.

When I suffer in this insidious, silent way, I seek turbulence and violence. Then my daydreams are overwrought and I find in everyone a source of secret pleasure. I dissemble. I romanticize.

It's hailing. I can hear the tapping, so different from the tapping of the rain. And that will alter everything.

The panic is overcome. Calm this evening.

The Baziotes are here. Ethel and Bill.

Bill is easy to talk to, naive, but thinks himself a great fellow and all in a most pleasant way. Ethel is like a country girl in citified clothes: forthright and without pretension.

Discussion of the state of modern painting.

Helen hears us repeat our proposal for a moneyless anarchist society again and again to our guests. But how amazingly often we draw a positive response.

February 23, 1950

Today I am calm and practical, I said on waking.

At noon two copies of Paul's book *The Dead of Spring* arrived. I only looked into it. The fantasy frightens me.

Now I am upset again. Tense. Excited. If I were uncontrolled I would be hysterical.

Is this brought on by looking into a book?

Of course not.

Going outdoors might help, but I am alone with the baby and there's snow outside.

The sweaty foreboding of calamity, as if something were about to happen. I am aware that this is not so. But it makes me write so fast, as fast as I can, and still the terrible frustration at not being able to write more quickly. . . .

February 25, 1950

Julian reads to me from *Life* magazine about the H-bomb. Figures about anticipated deaths in the millions.

Anouilh said, "In a tragedy everyone's destiny is known. . . . The whole sky has fallen on you and all you can do is shout . . . not because it will do any good, but because saying these things teaches."

Julian comes to me after I have been crying, after I have thrown the *Life* magazine out of the window and seen it break apart and shatter in the cold river wind. He comes to me and says: What are we to do? And I must answer, nothing, for I know nothing. What is there, then?

But now, when I looked at the Anouilh quote, I see another line of Antigone's spoken as she is about to commit the rebellious act of burying her brother under the very nose of the forbidding authority. Willing to die rather than not make the gesture, in spite of the futility of her action, she says, "I know all that. I know it. But that much, at least, I can do. And what a person can do, a person should do."

February 26, 1950

Last night to hear Dylan Thomas at the Poetry Center. His is a tragic style. He reads in a daring, rich, oratorical, theatrical voice. His sea, stone, bird image is always the image of the spirit.

March 1, 1950

Garrick crying all night until five A.M. and I lose patience. Julian wakes and shouts at me. Julian's screams fill me with loneliness. I go into the kitchen and listen to the five to six A.M. radio music and weary talk till the farm programs bring cheerier voices about crops and weather.

How alone one is when the lover becomes distant and unknowable, when the gulf deepens between the self and the other.

Ljuba Welitsch's histrionics in *Tosca* are not as violent as Jeritza's. She sings the *"Vissi d'arte"* as a prayer and speaks the recitative in German.

After the opera, a testimonial for Edward Johnson's retirement as manager of the Metropolitan; the great singers of his tenure on the stage in their favorite costumes: Bori, de Luca, Martinelli, Svanholm, Marjorie Lawrence, Novotna, Welitsch, Tagliavini, List, Baccaloni, Schoeffler, Tibbett, Munsel, Peerce, Albanese, singing like the aunts and uncles at a family party, "Hail, hail, the gang's all here."

The Strange Case of the Oklahoma Leopard.

Three days ago a ferocious leopard freshly imported from India escaped from the Oklahoma City Zoo by jumping over a 20-foot wall.

Since leopards are among the few animals that kill for pleasure (among them the species of which I am a member), the city stayed indoors. Squads of armored cars and bloodhounds sought the beast, which, like Dillinger, became fascinating.

Why am I interested in this? The hunt is enthralling because we are torn between our desire to find the quarry and our desire for the quarry to escape.

Yesterday the leopard was returned to his pit by being fed drugged meat. Shortly afterward he died, and this morning's newspaper headlines the death of the leopard.

Was my sympathy always unwittingly against the people? I feel guilty about my sympathy for the beast. Until I hear the radio say: "Oklahoma City is in mourning for her leopard." It's to be stuffed and put on a pedestal.

March 3, 1950

A long, long Chinese opera by the Sun Sing Opera Company in the theater under the Manhattan Bridge. The odyssey of a girl made invulnerable by a magic hoop. Ultimately she is killed, only to be reborn singing for twenty minutes while emerging from a lotus blossom.

There is something to be learned here, among these brilliant costumes and exotic forms—something that we need—

To take us beyond our theatrical conventions.

March 5, 1950

Julian returns from work with a torn leg tendon, having flown down a flight of stone stairs. The pain mounts and he is confined to bed.

At night, he lies surrounded by guests who came not knowing of his injury: Gil Orlovitz, Harold Norse and Dick Stryker sit like visitors to the aged Voltaire, or the ailing Goethe.

March 6, 1950

Days with Julian home, but busy as hell with two mothers directing everything like the Lord's traffic cops.

I see myself on a television program called "Candid Camera" looking uglier than seven Satans. Glad to have seen this ominous film, as I learn from it: 1) never to move my face while listening except in response to the speaker; 2) to avoid grimaces when speaking; 3) to look at the person I address; 4) to look up; 5) to think first even if it creates a silence, then speak.

March 11, 1950

The New York City Ballet Company's *Age of Anxiety*, based on Auden's poem about the unavailability of each of us to the others. *Firebird. Illuminations*, based on Rimbaud.

March 15, 1950

Last night with Mother to the opening of *The Consul*, a Menotti opera. This sentimental music play is done so well that all its flaws seem virtues. Toscanini in a box applauds slowly at his own tempo with no regard for the rapid, noisy applause of the rest of the audience.

The producers are Efrem Zimbalist, Jr., and Chandler Cowles.

1947:
We are rehearsing *Androcles and the Lion* at the Dramatic Workshop.
Chandler is playing the Handsome Captain.
I'm working on props and costumes.
I'm fixing his sword or his belt or something.
He's writing a letter, sitting up on the windowsill in his white tunic.
"What are you writing?"
He shows me a letter from Henry Miller, part of a long correspondence dealing with existentialism and financial problems.

I meet him at the theater door, where he is greeting friends in the traditional manner of the producer.

How innocently political theater can involve one in commitments which imply a willingness to defend them (albeit not violently) and thereby can eventually get one into trouble. Not that Chandler is taking risks as the producer of a political opera, but the theme of *The Consul*, with its presage of persecution, arouses these qualms.

Taxi causing bad handwriting as we drive up the West Side Highway and pass the great ships on the Hudson. Early twilight. Just enough light to write. To my right, the lighted skyscrapers against a still-daylit sky. I'll stop writing to enjoy the river to the west, the city to the east.

March 17, 1950

Among the bookshops on Fourth Avenue. The proprietor of the Raven Bookshop tells me he's a pacifist who takes no particular political line.

"When *I* tried to evade conscription they said, 'You are not a pacifist, you're just a Jew.'"

I work out a very adequate plan for a 299-seat theater with my own architectural drawings. Nothing extravagant, but it could serve our minimal purpose. Quite proud of my renderings.

March 21, 1950

First day of spring with snow falling but not sticking.

Mother comes here bruised and shaken after an accident on the bus. The door closed on her foot as she was boarding and the bus began to move, dragging her along.

Garrick's high temperature, which I thought the result of teething, proves to be a virus.

He also has an infected ear and throat and a disturbed stomach. He howls at his penicillin injection. Poor bird.

He is still restless at two A.M., but Mother and Julian insist on my going to bed. Mother will sleep in Garrick's room and now Julian is rocking the crib.

March 27, 1950

Daudet speaks of his son's sudden exposure to all the philosophers in school and of the depression that this brings about. He suggests that children be left to learn disillusionment from life as they encounter it.

The peculiar sadness of all things seen in a particular light. Fog. Low sound of fog horns on the Hudson bringing the river in through the windows so that my whole body feels damp.

We drive through Central Park. The mists shut out the skyline and the Park becomes an expanse of orderly woods, a sort of French countryside. The burning beauty of the lake.

Sometimes the beauty makes the melancholy all the more unbearable.

March 29, 1950

My wedding/engagement rings are stolen from my bureau drawer. I notice it but don't tell Julian's mother for fear of a melodramatic outburst.

My grandmother's ring is gone, too, a peculiar twisted gold band that I liked to draw as a child. And a filigree ring with a small diamond that I received for my sixteenth birthday.

When Julian tells his mother about the theft she doesn't see why we don't call the police.

At her insistence, we ask the police if we can get help in retrieving the jewelry without pressing charges.

At the police station: A detective, Mr. Collins, a fellow made for the villain's role, discourses at length on the methods of burglars. As for retrieving our things: "The police consider it a crime not to bring a known criminal to trial.

"If everyone felt as you do," he said, "there would be no property." That's true.

We do not leave our names.

April 1, 1950

Downtown to a *Resistance* meeting while Julian paints.

Today's topic: "Is an Optimistic View of Human Nature Laughable?"

The people who publish *Resistance* meet in a loft rented by a group of Spanish anarchists. A few elderly men sit smoking and reading in the small hall. Under a big plaster bust of a martyred comrade, an old radio shouts in Spanish. There are posters, and a kettle on a stove and rope-bound cartons of books marked *Bombas y Marxismo* and other such titles.

The first to arrive is David Wieck, who writes the lead articles in *Resistance*. He is badly/madly dressed and wears the firm, clear-eyed expression of the career anarchist.

A friendly young man introduces me around. He is Charles Wellman.

"I'm not a pure anarchist," I tell him. "I don't even approve of the word 'anarchist,' because it smacks of violence and has an historical background of violence." I had to leave before the discussion began, because Passover starts tonight and I must bring Garrick to Mother's for the Seder. But I will come back.

In the taxi home the driver explains the relationship between prizefighting and sex.

Seder.

April 5, 1950

Yin/yang days of despair and exuberance. Passover. Sending out poetry. Shopping. Garrick has four teeth, claps hands, uses toilet. Some poetry written. Proust. Some old pamphlets. I buy Garrick *At the Back of the North Wind*, which he won't be able to read for years.

April 6, 1950

In the great dazzle of the sunset a small, black airplane fills me with gratitude that not even the sky shuts us out; we are rivals to the sun.

The poems I'm writing are religious poems derived from my father's style. I suppose I wanted to be the saint he was, or the saint he wanted to be, though I always knew I must remain outside the religious vocation. Yet I'm tied to its imagery, to the language of religion, and to religious forms.

Reading: Proust's letters, Malatesta and other anarchist pamphlets, purchased at the *Resistance* meeting.

April 9, 1950

Back to the anarchists on 13th Street. David Wieck wrote me a note after last week's meeting addressing me as "stranger" and apologizing for the late start and hoping that I would come again.

When we arrived, Paul Wattick was saying that the planet is headed for an all-powerful world government and the work of the anarcho-socialist is consequently becoming impossible. He believes that the disorder brought about by an inevitable future war may make this work possible again.

No one agrees with his dark views.

Even I speak—the first time at a political meeting.

I say, "We stand outside of wars. Our personal example is a useful political action in spite of Wattick's contention that it is a limited expression. Gandhi's action, and Christ's too, began as limited expressions."

But Wattick doesn't agree. His point is that it's necessary to organize the workers, since spontaneous workers' action is impossible within the present structure (including the unions).

Jackson Mac Low, with his disciple's beard and thin hands like my father's, pleads for the validity of individual action.

Wattick holds out against us coldly and belittles Gandhi's achievements: "Hitler freed India, not Gandhi."

What can we say to him about violence?

These anarchists are anarchists for personal reasons. What other reasons are there?

There's nothing wrong with rebelling against the state's authority as a form of rebellion against the father in the Oedipus analogy. If the state has become a tyrannical father, let's freely rebel against it and admit the psychological part of it without hesitation.

Afterward to Harold Norse's. Dick Stryker, Glynn, and Walter are there.

Dick was a conscientious objector for which he suffered three years in prison, his eighteenth to his twenty-first.

Harold also had invited the Goodmans, but they refused on the grounds that they were enjoying connubial bliss.

"Guess who I'm madly in love with? Sally, of all people. My God, it's wonderful!" quotes Harold of Paul.

Everyone is pleased as though some family black sheep had settled down, to the satisfaction of aunts and uncles.

April 15, 1950

At the Frick Gallery only to look at the three Vermeers. The perfect painter.

At the anarchists', a discussion: "Should Every Act Be Good in Itself?"

Julian takes an active part.

"Good," says Julian, "is the extension of life."

Some of these people do not approve of the terms good and evil.

They speak of the inevitability of the healthy person making the right choice at the right moment.

They speak of an unwillingness to be subjected to rules, even those of sociability.

Afterward we talk with Jackson Mac Low and Charlie Wellman. Jackson says he wants to talk to us more about the inevitability of the right choices.

April 17, 1950

A film called, *The Man on the Eiffel Tower.*

The City of Paris. Homesickness for a place yet unvisited. Who has not carried a little map of Paris in a notebook, reciting, and even memorizing the names of the boulevards? Unvisited, she is the phantom of unimaginable and illimitable pleasures.

April 18, 1950

There was a child who asked her mother when the first war took place. The mother answered, "When Cain killed Abel."

"But," said the child, "that wasn't a war, that was only between two people."

"Yes," answered the mother, "but at that time there were only four people in the world, and that was half the world's population." Remembering this, I am impressed with the shrewdness of my mother's observation.

Every year I experience things less personally. As a child I identified with my surroundings and my belongings. But now I feel almost a spectator.

April 19, 1950

The Scapegoat at the Dramatic Workshop. Piscator's staging of *The Trial* skillfully underlines the parallels between Kafka's paranoid vision and Senator McCarthy's investigations.

April 24, 1950

To another anarchist meeting. The poet Howard Griffin was to speak on poetry and pacifism, but chooses to speak about personal responsibility. His heart is in the right place.

The concept of nonviolence is not clear to these people. They regard pacifism only as a form of resistance to the state and its wars; they seem to have no fundamental objection to killing.

Garrick is with us and is angelic at first but soon disapproves of being quiet in public and forces us to leave.

How is it possible to love one's enemies when it is so hard to love one's friends?

April 29, 1950

Premonitions of disaster. Not yet disaster: unrest.

New York begins to resemble post-World War I Berlin.

An elevator strike affects most of the city. The picketers are all over the street.

High school students strike for higher wages for their teachers.

Rioting at City Hall.

Meanwhile the McCarthy hearings continue to be the most pronounced symptom of the government's fears.

Today, testimony by Earl Browder, leader of the United States Communist Party and Louis Budenz, a former editor of the *Daily Worker*, now testifying against his former comrades.

A witness disappears and makes headlines. Then no further news about the incident. Hushed up, swallowed into silence. Like Joseph K we feel accused, tried, found guilty.

Everything, even the peculiar experimentation with rainmaking now going on (tampering with the cycle of the life-giving powers), conspires to make the time seem out of joint.

I've been writing poems all on the theme of sorrow and destruction.

May 1, 1950

On the street today, the Loyalty Day Parade, to spite the May Day Parade. A Russian contingent passes us just as we cross the street. Large signs: "Cossacks United: Fight Communism"; and "Ukrainian Peasants' League of New York." A large woman in a white and lavender uniform passes by toting a flag. Embroidered on her hat: "President of Westchester."

May 3, 1950

We become friends with a couple named Telfus who own a small stationery shop near here. Both are physically handicapped. They have recently had a baby, Amy.

Reading of the defeat of liberal congressman Claude Pepper by a Dixiecrat this morning, Mr. Telfus couldn't eat his breakfast. He tries to be cynical, but they worry about the world and feel personally responsible for it.

May 4, 1950

The river is broad at this point; the blue-gray mist, heavy and warm.

My God, that bridge! That wonder of man's hand in God's world.

I am interrupted by a small boy who asks what I am writing. I tell him I am writing how beautiful I think the bridge.

He looks up at it, thinks a while, and says, "It's not so hot."

He is carrying a cigar box in which he is collecting mica.

May 7, 1950

Maria Collm is singing in a little restaurant, gorgeous in silver brocade. She sings with no voice, but exudes her personal drama. Her perversions, her odyssey, her lovers, her contracts are tales melodramatically told. And tales of Valeska Gert's Beggar Bar on Morton Street, when she was the singer and I was the hatcheck girl. We reminisce.

At the Dramatic Workshop for a reading of *How Does Your Garden Grow?*, a social spook story that shows how "power corrupts and absolute power corrupts absolutely." I read the role of a woman driven insane by money.

May 10, 1950

Three new poems all on the same theme. "Odious Climates," my most cohesive poem; "Pilate Washing His Hands" and "Premonition of Passing Bells." The latter two are narrative and loose, but I am satisfied nonetheless. I mean them all to be hopeful, but no one will interpret them that way.

May 13, 1950

Reading: Sheean on Gandhi, *Lead, Kindly Light*. Sheean sees Gandhi's political actions primarily as religious practices.

Also: Gertrude Stein's *Things As They Are*. Printed with the sad note that "this is the last book to be printed by the Banyan Press." Claude is going to Europe without Milton; the press is being disbanded. There was something about those two in Vermont printing books and writing and farming, with an understanding between them that seemed exemplary.

The book is a theorem about three American college women involved in a romantic triangle. Stein's title: *Q.E.D.—Quod est demonstrandum*.

At the waterfront to buy bamboo window blinds, we walk around that section of New York where old warehouses stand near the river along a strip that has not yet been demolished for the tall business establishments.

We see the remains of Castle Garden, our old aquarium, a relic without the splendor of a ruin, now only a part of the demolition.

May 14, 1950

A ride to Staten Island to visit Oma's grave.

We intended to have a picnic and Josie was eager to visit Edison's Laboratory at West Orange, but we got lost and returned depressed.

The depression is of two sorts. The first makes me irritable with Garrick's crying. The second makes me mourn for the world and its spent light.

May 17, 1950

Garrick's first birthday. Much celebrated with guests, gifts, champagne.

May 20, 1950

This morning's mail brings the *American Courier* with my "Mountain Poem," retitled "Names."

En route to see the Vienna Collection at the Metropolitan Museum, we pass the Armed Forces Day parade. With a sort of childish defiance we cross Fifth Avenue against the parade, half-hoping to be stopped so that we may resist. We are not stopped.

The Vienna Collection is decadent and opulent. There are four Judiths with Holofernes' heads, one Salomé with Jokanaan's, two raped Lucretias, and the King of Rome's cradle decorated with Napoleon's gold flies.

But, among these—Vermeer's flawless *Artist's Studio*.

We should have gone straight to pick up Julian's painting at the Laurel Gallery, but reckless as usual, we hurried to an exhibit at the Museum of Modern Art. From there Julian called the gallery to ask if they will be open for another ten minutes. . . . Yes, Mr. Ritter will wait for us. When we arrive he tells us that in those ten minutes he sold the painting.

Julian is very excited about his first sale. Priced at $100 and sold for $75, minus commission = $60. *Sierra Nevada I* lost forever. Or maybe not.

Garrick takes his first steps at an afternoon *Kaffee und Kuchen* at Mother's. He was not aware of walking, and everyone watched hushed.

May 25, 1950

Party at Larry Maxwell's.

Anaïs Nin is in orange. Julian speaks to her for a long time. She is shy, he reports, more shy than I. He talks to her about my journal. Her diaries, though still unpublished, are already famous. Lengthy, and probably terribly literary. I sometimes wish mine were lyrical and artful, but I have already embarked on something different.

We know Stuart and Susan Perkoff from the *Resistance* meetings, where we argued with them publicly, but privately we agree on a great deal. They are young and bohemian and revolutionary in their very bearing. He has just lost his job at the Gotham Book Mart, where Frances Steloff told him that the forces of the universe were displeased with his work.

They say they are very poor. We take them to dinner.

Stuart has been in prison for refusing to register for the draft, but he questions the value of the jail sentence. "After all," he says, "the object of one's refusal to register is to be free."

Paul Goodman calls this choice "registering for jail." Jackson Mac Low registered "under protest," which is what Julian has done.

We spoke of our planned book about the free society, and the revolution based on the cessation of the use of money. At first Susan and Stuart argued that a moneyless revolution was "not militant," but they conceded that it was consistent with the anarchist idea of a general strike and encouraged us to write the book.

Stuart tells us that there is internal strife in the *Resistance* group over the religious question. Pieces are published in the magazine by unanimous consent of the editors, and a single line in a poem—"Christ said it thus on the Mount"—is causing a deadlock.

May 28, 1950

We walk around our neighborhood up to 110th Street on Riverside Drive and back down Amsterdam Avenue, observing the fantasies of Victorian architects: nymphs and graces jutting boldly out of squat, graceless buildings. Cherubic granite caryatids wreathed in laurel, nude muses dangling over the street in semiclassical postures. Out of the windows lean the forms and faces of Puerto Rican tenants.

At a neighborhood church, we stop to hear a Lutheran sermon in Spanish. The minister speaks proudly of his American forbears and tries to persuade us, gently, to join his congregation.

I lay Proust aside for Sheean and *Prison Etiquette*, mostly because I don't want to finish *Remembrance*; loath to leave that pale, nostalgic world.

May 31, 1950

Hurt my eyes looking too long through a telescope at the full moon. Can't read or write.

This is Julian's birthday. I didn't want him to go to work, but he insisted.

June 4, 1950

Twenty-four. Nothing is accomplished.

Julian's gift: a beautiful guitar.

A walk along the river with Mother, Josie and Julian. The park bright with a crowd that might have been painted by Seurat.

That was the good part of the day.

June 6, 1950

A sleepless night during which I alternate between Djuna Barnes and Sheean's Gandhi. Nightmares follow.

I have to make a clearing before new structures can be erected. If I could rid my time and my environment of all excess, I could work at the moment when the desire to work is strong! Woe to us who make the bitter excuse of being able to work only on inspiration.

June 7, 1950

Prayer for remission of sins not yet committed. If I am tempted without temptation, how shall I not fall when tempted? Punishment is so primal that if it is withheld the transgressor will mete out the punishment to herself in order to restore harmony.

Anagram: transgression/O stranger's sin.

Unbelief is a glass bell inside which faith is trapped. There is no clue in physics or philosophy as to the boundary, which is translucent, ineffable, fragile.

I wait to contend with winds, while the breeze of my painted fan is all that stirs around me. The fault is not the atmosphere's.

I am not unhappy. I am restless in my hand-embroidered Elysium.

June 16, 1950

Last night at the Master Institute, the After Dinner Opera Company did

Chekhov's *The Boor, Savitri,* based on a story from the Mahabarata, and Meyer Kupferman's setting of Stein's *In a Garden.*

I tell Julian that I want to write an opera libretto. He suggests Héloïse and Abelard.

June 17, 1950

City Island and Fire Island. I see no birds.

When I see the ocean at twilight I always become sullen and unsocial. Like Ibsen's Ellida, I imagine that I am a sea creature out of her natural habitat. My seaside birthplace.

My fear of drowning?

Fire Island is reached by a launch which cuts across the nine-mile bay. The sand is littered—shells, sea-worn boards, boxes, skeletons of sea things. There is a feeling of the inhuman, or better still, the prehuman and the su-perhuman.

Garrick takes these trips well. He points to what he desires and refuses substitutes. He eats mostly rye bread.

June 21, 1950

Robin Prising, a young friend of Claude's, comes expressing interest in the Living Theatre. He is handsome, well mannered, romantic and idealistic.

We listen to a radio program about atomic energy called "Year of Deci-sion." It concludes with two statements: one by Truman about the importance of armaments, and one by Einstein, lauding Gandhi for showing us a way to do battle using nonviolent means.

Einstein, like many brilliant people today, supports world government. In a newsreel a few days ago, we saw a group of World Federalists in Paris prac-ticing passive relaxation as the police carried them off, for protesting against atomic weapons.

June 22, 1950

All my rejection slips have compliments scrawled on them. Of my short story, "How They Live and Die in Mexico," *Accent* magazine writes: "This is very interesting and potent, but why don't you try to work it into a short story?"

Like Gandhi, I would like a day of silence every week.

June 24, 1950   *Philadelphia*

The Art Museum, in Greco-Babylonian style, can be seen from the center of the city, crowning its height. It houses Picasso's *Three Musicians,* and two masterpieces hung facing each other: Cézanne's *Bathers* and Matisse's *La Danse.*

Behind the museum is a small aquarium. The fish, which of all higher creatures are least like us (even the insects breathe our air and move on our earth), look at us nonetheless with human expressions.

Then the Rodin Museum and the Museum of the University of Pennsylvania, where I pause a long time in front of the flawless crystal ball made for the empress of China.

At the Philadelphia Library, while Julian browses, I recollect an earlier visit to this place:

November 1944:

Mariya and I have run away from home intent on hitchhiking to New Orleans. We take refuge from the cold in an all-night movie house in Philadelphia, watching a film about a caterpillar. In the morning we go to the public library hoping to doze awhile in a corner of the reading room. We hide behind the largest books we can find, trying to nap unobserved, but can't sleep and continue on our wintry road, getting as far as Danville, Virginia, where we are arrested.

I read some bits of *Finnegans Wake*, which chances to be lying on the table where I sit down.

June 25, 1950   *Philadelphia*

A delegation of Texan women with large badges and large bosoms swarms out of three large buses into Independence Hall. They photograph each other in front of the Liberty Bell . . ."with your hand on the crack."

We are lured inside Christ Church by a vestryman who then clicks us in on a counter.

The sermon concerns a war in Korea, which the minister compares to the Italian war in Ethiopia. Just what he is referring to I do not understand, for I have heard nothing about the present political structure of Korea or what disrupts it. But I am disturbed.

In the Philadelphia Cathedral, we buy a tract called *Thou Shalt Not Kill*. It explains how Christian morality allows for plenty of exceptions. But exceptions to "Thou shalt not kill" are the whole world's morality. The really non-violent, the Quakers, the pacifists, the Gandhians, are always a minority. We have to recognize the fact that people approve of inflicting death, to try to understand their justifications so that we can discuss it without hatred.

Philadelphia's a messy city, a lady who's forgotten a glove in the Victorian era and is racing to retrieve it in a 1930 Chevrolet.

June 27, 1950   *New York*

Korea. People are hoping that the explosion will happen far away in Asia and thus relieve them of participating in it. The world is round. I am bound to Korea, to China, to Russia, to wherever it is. What are we to think? We who cannot think what they tell us to think?

June 29, 1950

The news reports are terrifying; all the news, war news. The battle in Korea fluctuates in favor of one side and then the other. The American people are resigned to American soldiers fighting there. Yes, there is a war far away. Yes, we know that there is no longer a "far away." Yes, we are dying in it. Yes. Yes.

But I say that it is I myself; I, and not a stranger; I, and not a foreigner who dies and lives out the killing.

It's time to mourn. No one expects things to get better, but they'd rather not hear, like people playing bingo in a bomb shelter. And they don't want to hear because they don't know what to do with the fact if they face it.

Perhaps I should mourn for the American flyer critically injured and flown to Tokyo. Perhaps . . . I mourn for all the dead dying by each other's weapons.

In the awareness of my own mortality, I feel through their death, my death.

In the last war—and yet not "the last"—I was too young. Now I can scarcely bear to read newspapers, though I listen to the radio. The torment less pictorial.

But I recall one night when I was about eleven and home alone:

1938:
Hitler is going through Europe taking small nations one by one. I am in bed in New York City thinking about it. Suddenly I'm overcome by claustrophobic horror. The very walls seem nearer and menacing. Burning fear stifles me and I say aloud, "It's too hot." Then the feeling passes, but that moment is the war for me.

June 30, 1950

An evening with Gil Orlovitz, Helen, Robin Prising, and Bob Kerrigan.

First there was a murmur about Korea and the bomb. Robin sensed the look of war on the faces of people coming out of theaters. Gil smiled and said, "It is only an incident."

"Do you think there will be a war?" he asked me.

"There is a war."

Gil says that America's participation is only a question of geography.

Is a war in Korea, in China, in Formosa, our war, a war, the war?

No one is an isolationist this time. We've learned that we can't say it's not our battle. And yet we have to say that in order not to be inside it. How? By being mourners and not murderers?

Nothing is easy for responsible people.

At two A.M. Bob and Julian were discussing a free society.

July 1, 1950

A seance. Unlikely as I consider the existence of disembodied beings, much more do I doubt their susceptibility to manifestation by ritual rigamarole. Why would an unearthly spirit in its orbit of infinity make mundane predictions in the primitive setup of the seance and convey ideas by means of the tapping table?

The seance took place at Harold Norse's. Harold invoked the spirit in a rather arrogant, commanding manner. We sat there for a while with our fingers touching on the table top.

The table moved. The first moment I was startled, but neither before nor after that did I believe anything supernatural occurred. We asked tentative questions about Garrick's future and the Living Theatre. The answers were vague.

Dick left and went to sleep. As he did, the table moved with only my hands and Harold's on it.

I became suspicious of myself; I felt that I was moving the table. Harold was asking about the success of his work, and I couldn't help feeling responsible for not disappointing him. It seemed that if I exerted the slightest pressure on the table, it produced the desired taps. I don't believe I resisted the desire to produce the result, but I can't be certain as to how much I controlled it.

Then Julian joined us. The table "seemed to want to communicate with Julian." By taps it finally gave voice to Leon, the respected patriarchal figure among Julian's dead uncles. The table tapped out a message for Julian using the laborious system of one tap for "A" to 26 taps for "Z." The presumed message read: "Turn to look to peace, Julian. Russia plans war. Who postpones size of royal gold votes Russia. You touch m . . ."

Then dawn came and the tapping stopped.

I believe that Julian controlled the tapping, but I'm sure that he did so unconsciously.

I leave a margin not for the spirits of the dead, but for the unconscious mind trying to speak.

At dawn, New York is at its most spectacular. We stopped to see Adolph Giehoff's display paintings in the windows of Bergdorf Goodman's: landscapes with unicorns and satyrs. They were like the city: an atmosphere of dream into which real objects thrust pale shadows.

July 3, 1950

Julian is painting for the first time in months. The smell of linseed oil and turpentine enters the bedroom like incense. His South American painting that had been white, and then yellow and black, is now tinged with lavender by a process called *frottage*.

July 9, 1950   *Montauk Point*

Montauk Point. The seaweed thrown high, reeks in the sun. The dead gulls, dead fish, and dead crabs are less ugly than the carcasses in butcher shops.

A live red-winged blackbird, a catbird, a sandpiper; a hare, especially endearing. We look at each other; he waits a long time for me to move as he looks up from the underbrush.

July 11, 1950

Mother leaves for Europe. To visit her long-lost brothers, Leon and Bernard, and the old cities.

The *Batory* is a Polish ship that sails under the Russian flag. It recently served as an escape route for Hanns Eisler, the composer who was persecuted here as a Communist. Before the trial he went aboard the *Batory* as a visitor, disappeared as a stowaway, and is now in Eastern Europe. This scandal caused the cancellation of visitor permits to the *Batory*, so we can't go aboard.

The baby fell asleep in Julian's arms. Mother, on board, waved, smiling happily, and then the ship moved out, turned in the river, the tugs pulling it around. Everyone ran to the end of the pier to wave.

Seance. Night with storms. This time we conjure here in our library with Harold, Dick Stryker and John Nerber. The spirit stamps out its name as Anne of Brittany. Anne is a mighty hefty spirit. I feared for the floor.

The subject matter was the same as it is in our conversations: To where should we flee?

Harold spoke of Nigeria, which Howard Swanson had recommended. Guatemala, Southern California, South Africa were considered. The radio reports plans to move the industrial centers out of New York. When they move the factories it will be time to go.

Anne said: "War. Flee New York."

We asked: "Now?"

"No."

"When?"

"Fall." [We gave ourselves leeway.]

"Where to?" No reply.

"Will New York be bombed?"

"Yes."

"Is it safe in the western hemisphere?"

"No."

"Is Europe safe?"

"No."

"Asia?"

"No."

"Africa?"

"No."

"Australia?"

"No."

"Where shall we flee?"

"Nowhere."

Harold asked: "To God?"

No reply.

Harold: "Is there a God?"

No reply.

Dick (under his breath): "Get *him!*"

Then Anne was asked if she had a message for us.

Anne: "Don't worry."

Harold, the medium, is very angry at Dick and me for laughing. I claim I am allowed to laugh because of my disbelief.

Harold, in a gossipy way, asks the spirit "not to mind Dick."

Anne gives us each an individual message. To Harold: "Work." To Dick: "Don't be afraid." To John: "Publish." To me: "Patience."

At my message I lift my fingers off the table slightly because I would rather not be responsible for it. Let them compose it. But, strangely enough, they spelled it "pateince"—my frequent misspelling of the word.

There was no message for Julian.

Dick calls the spirit a bitch. The tapping stops.

Another spirit then takes over, a very violent one who refuses to tell its name and ferociously taps out "hate!" We end the seance. Dick is much blamed.

What interests me is the way a tacit agreement is made between participants in the group so that no conflict occurs. The control is not necessarily the medium's. In our two seances Julian and John Nerber controlled the table.

During the thunder I worry about Mother in a possible storm at sea. She is always seasick.

July 20, 1950

We've begun work again on the Living Theatre. Like a woman with several miscarriages who has no courage to admit to another pregnancy, I hesitate even to mention it.

July 30, 1950

The war progresses.

I gaze stupefied at the man who speaks of going again to the front lines, unable to believe that people who have suffered one war can tolerate another. Young men enlist and their wives and mothers don't throw themselves in front of the troop trains.

The newspapers vie with each other to report the atrocities and the *Times*, its solemn air of truth making its reports seem semiofficial, is the grimmest of all.

A peace petition from Sweden called the Stockholm Petition is being circulated. Julian and I sign. Today the radio talks of it as "vicious communist peace propaganda" and warns: "Hundreds of Americans have been horrified to learn of the real nature of the cause to which they have given their names."

We decide to paste up labels bearing four messages: 1) Answer War Gandhi's Way. 2) Don't Let Politics Lead You To War. 3) War Is Hell. Resist It. 4) All Politicians Make War. Don't Vote.

We buy sheets of gummed labels and type our messages with six carbons. These are to be posted on lampposts, houses, mailboxes, subways, wherever we can put them. Even if it's futile, it will make us feel that we are not submitting too quietly.

When we discuss the war, Julian's mother says, "I feel that I am the most infinitesimal small fry being swept along by the tide."

Among our friends the talk is about getting away from the Bomb. I'm not yet thoroughly convinced that war will bring death to this city so quickly.

We talk about the draft with Robin, who asks advice on how to stay out of the army.

August 1, 1950

Rumors say that the United States is deliberately stressing its losses in Korea in order to prepare people for the draft, increased armaments, and the sacrifices of wartime.

Last night at the movies a newsreel: young men on troop trains, their faces shallow, yet innocent and alive. The blankness: a form of fear and of disguising fear.

Sudden cut to young bodies on stretchers, neatly row on row on the ground.

I scream. A long horrible shriek.

Julian moans: "My God. My God."

All the faces turn toward us. The film keeps rolling on.

I accuse the people in the movie house, "You are crazy to let this happen."

And then Julian cries, "You are crazy to let them make you kill and destroy and not protest."

We get up and run out through the lobby; an usher, a candy girl, and a distressed manager make way for us.

We ride downtown on a bus wondering what effect we've had on the people in the movie house.

We put up labels in the bus: "Don't Let Politics Lead You To War" and "Answer War Gandhi's Way."

We walk along 42nd Street at Times Square. There are a great many mounted police. We learn that earlier 5,000 peace demonstrators clashed with police in Union Square during what the newspapers called a "communist rally." Nowadays all peace actions are regarded as communist by the press. The news moves across the light strip on the Times Building. Relentlessly.

August 4, 1950

At times like this the desire for action makes my pulse quicken and my breath come short as though I had run a distance.

Then I decide to write my journal and can't find my pen. I try a straight pen but the inkwell is dry; the ink bottle is in a cabinet which is stuck. I finally find my fountain pen but I can't fill it. No ink. Search. Then ink. Just as I fill it the doorbell rings and the telephone rings and Garrick wakes up. Now it's four P.M. and Robin is at the door.

In the park with Garrick under a shade tree I listen to tales of Robin's loves.

Robin stays for supper and then sleeps over. We talk of finding a place in the West to set up a free community and do our own work and perhaps farm and live out the crisis there.

August 5, 1950

The theme of evacuation develops all day.

We climb up High Tor with Robin and with Garrick in arms. Romance in the wind and the great vista of that "far seeing" place.

I'm half asleep. Will write about High Tor tomorrow. Robin and Julian are in the library having a seance. I've become skeptical enough to prefer sleep. Robin is trying to reach Isadora Duncan.

August 6, 1950

Yesterday's ascent of High Tor. The wind came up and the path was steep. I was in black taffeta with high heels and jet necklace, not quite a hiking outfit. Robin leaped over the rocks, in sandals, his shirt open, and made a great staff from a fallen branch and put vine leaves in his hair and a yellow flower.

The sun came out as we reached the top, looking down on the river and the town of Haverstraw.

Suddenly, black clouds appeared and we raced the storm down the Tor. We kept Garrick content by feeding him sweet ripe berries picked on the way.

We reached the town just as the rain came.

We went to Robin's river-view room, cluttered with photographs of his idols—Isadora, Duse, Le Gallienne, and Gielgud, alongside books by Gibran, the Vedanta and the Bhagavad Gita. He approaches the mystical as an educational activity like the dance or elocution.

August 7, 1950

At the theater last night we saw an unconvincing production of *The Lady from the Sea*.

I'd play it on a set made of driftwood with the sea mist as the only prop.

I am at a point where all art seems too indirect, and only action has any bearing on my needs.

August 12, 1950

There's a mass depression such as I have never witnessed. Everyone says, "I can't stand reading the newspapers." "I dare not listen to the radio."

Thursday night party: Bill and Ethel Baziotes talk with Robert Price, the shy poet who lives with Stamos and says Pollyanna is his patron saint. (I've cribbed the phrase from him innumerable times.)

Bill Baziotes says every painter paints from his awareness of the social situation in which he lives, and calls his abstractions social paintings. Politics is, after all, more than government.

Bob Kerrigan held out against strict nonviolence, with God and Aquinas on his side, while Bob Price, who fought in the last war, sat silent.

Other events of this week: *The Storm Within*, an English film version of Cocteau's *Les Parents terribles*, *Rasputin* with Harry Baur, and *La Bête humaine*.

September 1943:

It's raining. There's a rehearsal at my house for a U.S.O. soldier show. I'm playing Little Nell in *He Ain't Done Right by Nell*.

The phone rings. It's Julian. He and Gaugau are going to *La Bête humaine*. It starts in 20 minutes. Will I come? I'm committed to the rehearsal but I don't dare say no, for I've only seen Julian once before. And what if he never calls again? I hardly know him and I love him already. I go upstairs and call off the rehearsal.

Everyone is furious with me, but I am ecstatic.

We didn't see the film that night.

August 15, 1950

In our search for some kind of action, we begin a letter-writing campaign and plan a system for distributing the labels, and beyond that we can only "trouble deaf heaven with our bootless cries."

On the radio, a breakfast program troubles the air. Dorothy [Kilgallen] and Dick [Kollmar], one of the popular husband and wife teams who usually chat about innocuous matters, have asked their listeners to write them, not whether we should use the atom bomb, but *when* we should use it against the Russian people.

Robin is here and we are all writing letters. My letter is too heroic and emotional. The typewriters clang away at messages of peace.

I am content tonight because I saw the yellow light of approaching evening, which can be seen only with a quiet eye. Remembered times of peace seem always to have been yellow evenings.

Julian has decided to give up his job. How happy I will be to live with his constant presence, whether we stay in this dangerous city or move to some far-flung corner of the earth.

Friday, the Becks will take Garrick overnight and we hope to deluge the city with 6,000 labels: "Answer War Gandhi's Way" and "War Is Hell. Resist It."

August 18, 1950

Day: Silent, endless rain. Breath of Strindberg. Swathed in gray netting.

Night: Some No Doz tablets, the little caffeine pill that prolongs wakefulness harmlessly, it says on the label.

But it puts a suspicious beat into the pulse.

Midnight: We meet Robin at Columbus Circle and divide our labels. Julian is in his white suit and I am wearing a long black lace dress and white cape. We walk along the streets seen by too many. Too conspicuous. It's too early, so we go to a soda place and sit for a while. More No Doz. Then to our work.

On every street, the police car passed us several times. Passersby began to look like plainclothesmen. In the gutters and on the sidewalks there are dozens of revolting waterbugs, some scurrying, others crushed, dead, dying.

Three A.M. We start at 59th Street from Eighth to Madison Avenue. Then we go east to west and west to east along 57th Street. The whole world seems awake.

We move through the streets like criminals. At Fifth Avenue a police car pulls over. We have rehearsed all possibilities. Our object is not to be arrested, therefore not to provoke.

We answer quietly, respectfully, innocently. While the older policeman phones the precinct, his partner talks to us,

"Do you really think you'll stop the war by putting those up?"

How we wished we could have said yes.

"If we can awaken one conscience . . ." said Julian.

The policeman argued as he must.

He motioned to a cabdriver standing on the corner next to his taxi.

"Hey, Mac, you see those labels?" He pointed to the bank on the corner on whose pompous marble columns our little labels shone white.

"Go read what it says on them and tell us what you think."

He complied. Returned. "I think what you think."

"What do you think?"

"The same as you."

"Well, tell us, we're interested."

"Yes," we three echo, "we're interested."

"I don't think those were put there by an American. And in the first place they shouldn't be there."

"Thanks, Mac."

The senior officer returned, told us to go away, and "if you're seen around here again. . . ."

We went our way wondering whether or not we should take the car (in which some 5,000 labels were secreted) or return for it in the morning. We decided to risk it. Drove around for a while. Some time after five A.M. we went to sleep.

It is all that we can think of to do. And in Antigone's words: "What one can do, that one must do."

August 20, 1950

Joe Turner, with whom Julian climbed the Sierras, gives a party consisting of young couples, one or both of whom teach philosophy. Hysterical joking about the war and the army; a suggestion for a Krafft-Ebing Division, with a masochist brigade and a sadist brigade.

This morning, Dorothy and Dick read Robin's letter on the radio. Robin is asleep in the studio and comes out to listen wrapped in a bedsheet. He sits on the kitchen table. I feel great pride at one of us being heard. His passionate cry for peace rings clear, though Kollmar didn't read it well.

They belittle both his appeal to reason and Gandhi. They express contempt for passive resistance as impossible "except in a country like India where the average person does not expect to live beyond the age of thirty."

"How long can a man close his eyes to the fact that someone is going to punch him in the jaw?" asks Dick Kollmar.

"What does he suggest? That we sit still and wait for them to do anything that they want to us?" asks Dorothy Kilgallen.

Dorothy summarized well when she said, "I agree that everything he says is true, but it just won't go with us."

August 21, 1950

Julian's letter is read on the radio. His phrases resound nobly though Kollmar prosefies the writing and can't handle his complex sentence structure. Dorothy scoffs at the phrase "an ugly weapon."

"I wish we didn't have to use an ugly weapon. I wish we had a perfectly lovely weapon."

"I'd like to be able to sit here and just think beautiful thoughts, but that won't stop the Russians from coming here and taking over."

August 24, 1950

On the same lawn in the park where I took Garrick on his earliest excursions I write now while he sleeps.

Reading Gandhi's *Letters to a Disciple*, which I had hoped would make me a little more content with my daily life. He writes of diet and spinning, his walks, his weight; his own life compact and unshatterable, in the midst of world-shattering events.

Reading the fantastic L. Ron Hubbard with his panacea, dianetics. And Proust.

August 27, 1950

Saturday we intended to spend the night putting up labels in some quiet area.

But then Harold Norse called, wanting to bring Michael Fraenkel here, and I was to meet one of those people with a gift for stirring and altering lives.

I knew very little about him except that he was the coauthor, with Henry Miller, of *Hamlet: A Correspondence*, the editor of the magazine called *Death*, and author of some poetry on the subject of death.

He looks a sage and makes certain rabbinical gestures which are etched in my memory as characteristic of the wise man.

He is an anarchist, and is appalled by our idealism.

Robin speaks of beauty and I speak of political and social potential.

Michael Fraenkel accuses us of inaction.

We disclose our labels, talk about our letters, our plans for speeches, pamphlets, and propaganda. Fraenkel approves.

His strategy is based on "getting out of 'the system,'" on weakening it by not partaking in it, by not working for it, by not paying taxes.

He is obsessed by this villain which he calls "the system." He emphasizes its power in silencing the artist.

He owns a plot of ground in Indiana on which he grows vegetables and on which he, like Thoreau before him, built with his own hands a house of the earth. But now, feeling that his recent writing endangers him in this country, he plans to work in France. He suggests that we settle on his farm after his departure.

We drive our guests home and continue downtown to paste labels.

We feel that Fraenkel has had a decisive influence on us.

In "planting the seeds," as Julian calls our labeling expeditions, we are developing pacifist tactics, though one might think that we were secreting bombs instead of slips of paper the way we go about it as a criminal business.

Night covers nothing. On the contrary, it casts suspicious shadows on innocent acts; it's too melodramatic.

The work was easier after dawn came. The city magical in its primal hours.

Harold calls in the evening. He has turned down a teaching post at City College to go to Europe, but would remain in America if we all go to Indiana. It seems too perfect: a group of friends living and working together.

August 28, 1950

I dream. I plan. I schedule. I consider. I contemplate. I wonder. I evolve. But what do I do?

August 30, 1950

5:30 A.M. All the beds in the house are occupied: Julian and I in the bedroom; Michael Fraenkel in the studio; Robin on the front couch; Harold Norse and Dick Stryker in the back room; Garrick in his crib.

The night grew long in talking about our fleeing to Indiana if Fraenkel goes to Europe. But Harold still wavers between the farm and the desire for Italy. Robin is interested in Rome and a *castello*. Cuernavaca appeals to me. Dick may not be able to get a passport because of his record as a conscientious objector, but he could go to Mexico since no passport is required.

A seance is suggested, but they tap without me. The message: "World war. You touch money without love."

No more rappings came after that. The interesting thing is that it concluded Uncle Leon's message of two months ago: "You touch m . . ."

Michael doesn't believe in the seance. He talks of practical matters. He describes how to build rammed-earth houses. He and Daphne built their own for less than thirty dollars; for five-dollars' worth of seeds they had enough vegetables for the whole year.

He envisions the formation of large anarchist communities, their organization, their economic and human possibilities. We imagine our small group of eight farming, sharing the work, creating art and political action.

August 31, 1950

With Garrick in the park, reading Gandhi's letters, I am shamed by their calm.

Robin has gone to see Duse's *Cynara* for the fourth successive day at the Museum. Yesterday he came home in tears because the audience laughed at her.

Our Thursday evening brings together George Berger, who desires a baroque palace, and Peter Farb, the features editor of *Argosy*, the Complete Man's Magazine, who is a southern agrarian, and Paul d'Avila, a conscientious objector who will take noncombatant service, in a vehement discussion of war and anarchism.

September 2, 1950

Yesterday at work, an order for batteries to be shipped to Korea gave Julian his cue to leave Beck Distributing Corp. Working for the war is out of the question.

A prolonged, tense discussion with Julian's parents. No understanding of our desire for another way of life. As to the war contracts, our disapproval is discredited as sheer insanity: "Anything you did, except nothing, would be an aid to the war effort."

Julian agrees to remain only until he can be replaced.

We go out to put up labels, but the streets seem haunted and we think we are being followed. We eat at Chumley's, where we join a group of gorgeous young people playing with a bouncing, melting, snapping substance called Silly Putty. When we leave, a laughing young woman calls after us: "Soon everyone will be busy with this. No time for war. No atom bombs. Silly Putty will end wars."

September 4, 1950

Michael Fraenkel has told Harold Norse that his plans to go to Europe are still too indefinite for him to promise us that we can live on his Indiana property. Great disappointment.

Saturday. Garrick points at the paintings in the museum and says "Dada" when he approves (the painting is as good as dada's?). He likes *Les Demoiselles d'Avignon*. He particularly dislikes Pascin, expressing his disdain with a violent "ne ne ne ne."

Sunday. We were to have gone to Bearsville to see Holly Cantine and Dachine Rainer, the anarchists who edited *Prison Etiquette* and print *Retort*. They had been suggested to us by the *Resistance* people for printing our labels and broadsides.

But en route the car skids into a taxi causing enough damage to make us drive back home.

The skyway leads over a murk of factory wastes, smokestacks breaking the flat sorrow of the marshes.

In this dank atmosphere we talk about our trap.

Then all the world's a prison.

The image of the closing trap realizes itself like Oedipus' prophecy. Yet in my earliest dreams I felt it more deeply. I feel nothing as deeply as when I was a child.

September 5, 1950

When Julian tells his parents that we intend to leave New York for fear of the bomb, they are more hurt than when we said we were going to live "poorly" in New York without Julian's working at Beck's.

Now Julian's father offers to pay our rent so that we can do the work we want to do. The offer is tempting—it would give Julian time to work on his paintings—but he puts up a certain amount of resistance.

To accept money is the same bitter bit no matter what money it is. If I were moral I would refuse to touch money, to take it into my hands, no matter what the provocation, and live possessionless and devoted to work.

This is by no means the state in which I find myself. The self fights for survival.

Hier stehe ich, ich kann nicht anders. Gott helfe mir.

If we are expected to take pride in the achievements of our species, should we not also be expected to take responsibility for the failures?

Does the murder victim, then, share the responsibility for his own death, insofar as he, along with the rest of us, has been unable to prevent the misdeed?

September 7, 1950

A harrowing day at the pier to greet Mother on her return from Europe.

The crowd is angry because the docking of the *Batory* is delayed by the F.B.I. Rumor has it that they are afraid that this Polish ship may be carrying the components of an atom bomb, to be assembled and exploded in the United States, instead of being flown over and dropped by plane!

But their search turns up only a bedraggled stowaway, who has reached his destination only to be tossed back. Mother saw him taken away in handcuffs.

Visiting her family has relieved Mother of her sense of isolation. I haven't seen her so full of life in years. Happy, glowing, excited.

September 10, 1950

Rounds: The indignities are so many, the reward so meager, the odds against you.

Haunted all night by dreams that the war has started.

September 13, 1950

Rosh Hashanah. The centuries are at work in me and my father's teaching asserts its strength.

We go to a Conservative German congregation and I am not touched by the service. But the fact of the date is enough.

Julian and I talk about the distance from reality which he calls nonparticipation. This depersonalization which daily grows more severe for me is for Julian a state in which he has always been.

He can't remember feeling differently, while I remember when things and people and experiences were real and immediate.

It seems to have turned when I was about ten years old. Julian imagines that for him too there was a turning, but that it occurred at the age of three or four.

Are our social concerns a defense against our feelinglessness? I prefer to think our commitment is a rejection of our coldness.

Harold, Dick, and Robin come for a farewell for Michael Fraenkel, who sails for Europe tomorrow.

September 18, 1950

There was no summer; this year only a few hot days, a light without light's usual power to penetrate. And suddenly it's fall.

The war takes a turn. The United States moves north of the front. They speak of the war ending soon. The only possible good news.

Even I grow inured to the fact that men are murdering each other daily, to the maps and statistics, the feature magazines with their bloody pictures, the newsreels. . . .

September 19, 1950

The world is tightening up—like a trap—and those who want out will be the hardest bitten.

Do the whole thing without hatred. Edith Cavell's way: " . . . no hatred or bitterness toward anyone."

Neither the politician nor the policeman is the enemy.

It's harder to do the day-to-day than to perform the heroic. Or if not harder, it is at least less satisfying.

September 21, 1950

Yom Kippur. When I consider Gandhi's twenty-one days, how can I find this single day's fast difficult? But then he fasted with deep belief.

Tonight at the Kol Nidre service, a paragraph on the four kinds of death inflicted by the courts: burning, stoning, beheading, strangling.

I imagine death by stoning . . . the skull-splintering impact. . . .

But such deaths are antiquities. Why do I trouble about them? Aren't there injustices enough in our daily life, in the contemporary world?

But I need to atone also for the historical, to feel the pain afresh in order to make this fast meaningful.

I dedicate it first to those who commit the crimes as well as those who are falsely accused, then to those who pass the sentence of death, then to those who carry out the execution.

September 24, 1950

How passionless we have become.

How bright, how light we used to be. And if we were irresponsible, thoughtless, unproductive, at least we loved ourselves and lived for the moment and for the future and felt the whole universe to be ours.

Julian has been painting and has already completed several canvases since he left his job. . . .

I have been writing letters to producers, trying to break into the theater safe in which they keep their cheap goods tucked away so securely. I would like to ruse my way in and then blow the place to gold and yellow bits.

Last night to the ballet. The Sadler's Wells company holds no interest for me, still less the sardonic commentary of John Simon, who sat beside us.

The Metropolitan audience attacks Frederic March and Faye Emerson demanding autographs, demeaning the already faded glamour of the venerable opera house. But glamour is always vulnerable.

October 1, 1950

A recital by Ruth St. Denis, who at 73 astounds us with her magnificently supple body. Ted Shawn stands at the proscenium presenting the dances, which are religious, and plunge into the poetic phrases of which most artists are afraid; it is her willingness to overstate that makes for the excitement.

I wonder how much her dancing derives from Isadora's. Both Shawn and St. Denis speak often of Duncan. She has a fragility that I doubt was Duncan's, whom I imagine as massive and positive. She dances, like Duncan, to bad music.

October 3, 1950

Now we have settled into some kind of routine and what we call routine most people would call madness.

Julian paints constantly.

October 8, 1950

A long, hard party in farewell to Walter and Glynn. Smoke engulfing about 70 people sitting cross-legged on the front room floor. Bill Baziotes, Gordon Ricci, Jean Garrigue, Ed Mahoney, David Sachs, Oscar Williams, Gene Derwood, Sally and Paul Goodman. Paul with a flock of handsome young disciples: Jo-Jo LeSueur, Gianni Bates, and Bruce DeJohn; Paul plays Socrates as his young students develop his ideas in their dialogues.

Anaïs Nin and Ian Hugo. We talk about the bullfight, which I had expected Anaïs to defend because of her love for Mexico. But she leveled those mystical eyes at me and said, "But the bullfight is anguish. I have known it always. My grandfather waged a campaign against the bullfights in Spain at a time when attacking the national ritual was close to treason." Hugo says that to love the Mexicans you must first understand that they are a cruel people, bred of a cruel soil, a cruel sun, and a ruling class that keeps the people enslaved to cruel customs.

But I don't believe that it's worse in Mexico than anywhere else, only that the cruelty glitters in the bullring.

Cruel people too at the party. Insults and smashed glasses.

October 9, 1950

Television auditions: I've begun work on a speech from Djuna Barnes' *Nightwood*, the Doctor's maniacal monologue; guaranteed to scare the shit out of them.

October 10, 1950

Charlie Chaplin in *City Lights*: Do pathos and tragedy differ? Chaplin shows us pathos as a form of tragedy. Man is pathetic and this is his tragedy, and therefore it is difficult to laugh at the comic scenes.

At a pier in Brooklyn we see Walter and Glynn off to England on the *Marengo*, a small freighter carrying six passengers.

Kit Barker, Gene Derwood, and Oscar Williams are engaged in tense little conversations mirroring the envy of those who are not going for those who are.

And what does it come to? A handshake and a polite bustle that forms around the farewell and the farewellers.

Only now do I discover that the closeness that I felt with my parents is not to be expected of my friendships.

With Walter and Glynn I would have liked to have made a lifelong irreversible bond. In real relationships there can be no breaking off.

But everyone is so objective, so civilized, that all the power goes out of knowing each other.

October 17, 1950

Piscator hands me a German script, *Heimkehr*, by Ilse Langner, which he asks me to translate. He describes the plot in his abrupt, magical manner. He is as magnificent as ever, surrounded by his aura. I talk to some of the students, and find that they still deride their great teacher, find his flaws, his ego, his self-sufficiency intolerable. Among the alumni who use the school as a headquarters for making the rounds there's no longer any apparent love for the theater, only talk about jobs.

Lunch with Dick Jessup. His conversation is sinister and sexually provocative. He is the prototype of the seducers of fiction.

We walk down Broadway and meet Al Mulock, who says to me, in front of Jessup, "Do you remember the passionate love we made backstage at *Tonight We Improvise?*"

"I thought it was *Circle of Chalk.*"

"No, no," he said, "it was Pirandello."

Further down the street we meet Bob Carricart hectic with excitement. He tells us he's reading for *King Lear;* first he was misplaced among the spear carriers, "And me with two Broadway Shakespeares under my belt!" And in a fit of fervor declaims, "Of God and bastards!" loudly to the Broadway throngs.

The street brightens and for a moment the lights of Broadway and the jumbled version of Lear collide, recognize each other, and embrace.

A woman comes jiggling a can of coins for orphans.

"I'm a starving actor, ma'am." Bob shrugs his shoulders proudly and goes off.

News to chill the spine: A friend of Julian's, Bill Cannister, a law student at Harvard, after many tries at suicide, riding in a subway car with friends, puts his head out of the window and beheads himself.

October 18, 1950

Langner's *Heimkehr* is all that Piscator promised, a moral play dealing with postwar Germany. Translating it is complicated by the Berlin dialect.

October 23, 1950

It is scarcely possible to keep pace with myself. As Gide complained: While one is leading an eventful life, there's neither time nor patience for journal-keeping; when one has the leisure to make long entries, it's a certain sign that the time is uneventful.

The past three days spent at the typewriter with Mother's and Julian's help, translating *Heimkehr.*

I live in the world which my eye perceives, and I live in the world in which my mind modifies what my eye has perceived, and I live in a world that is beyond perception.

I do not act according to my deeper feelings, but according to exigencies of the external world. What is untouched underneath is immune.

October 24, 1950

Bursting with anger at the sound of the brass band playing for the opening of the new recruiting station in Times Square, I lose my temper with a policeman who orders me to move away from the curb. "Will you move?" he bellows.

Visions of handcuffs and Black Marias float in my brain as I hear my timid voice say, "No.

"Why don't you try to stop this display of war-mongering in the middle of our city, instead of shooing people off the streets?" I protest.

But he turns and walks away; there's a large crowd listening and he's avoiding trouble.

October 25, 1950

Reading Harold Norse's poems: the work of a wholesome nature. Like Julian, Harold thinks cumulatively and believes in the arithmetical result. Even more than Julian he believes what he sees and trusts what he feels.

Donald Pippin has become a conscientious objector, and been given a 4E classification. Over and over we hear people express their unwillingness to participate in the war. This time there will be a fantastic number of objectors. Our friends recount their draft board experiences and how they answered the first question: "Do you believe in a Supreme Being?"

On their way home, Harold, Robin, and Donald are stopped and questioned by the police. No reason given. We hear the police are making a "pre-election roundup."

October 28, 1950

Julian has painted a large, dark canvas of a palace with strong colors reaching out of the black with whole histories of forms, lit by strings of lights. He's finished one painting every week since he's been home, and all the time taking care of Garrick, while I've been out making the rounds.

Am I an actress? Am I an artist? On the rounds I only remember that I need to make connections, that I have to look well, try hard, know him, go early, write a letter, see a secretary, smile. But heart? Art? Nah!

Julian's eager to sell his paintings, regardless of size, for a uniform price of $100, and all drawings for $35. I'm in favor of this.

"The important things," says Hans Hofmann's wife to us at her husband's opening at the Kootz Gallery, "are, after all, the paintings. They are the only things that count and all this politics—what does it matter?" When she says politics, she means money.

Edith Sitwell reads her poetry at the YMHA on 92nd Street. This is a triumphal season for the Poetry Center, which promises us even the Buddha's tooth, T. S. Eliot.

Sitwell is regal in a gold and red brocade cape that falls to the floor in a richly folded clerical cut over her black satin dress. Her stern, hawklike face is ennobled by her imposing stature. She speaks sharply, but reads softly. Her poems are the essence of wordplay and avoid the heavier imagery of modern poetry.

Doctor Sitwell handles the question period with a witty, superior air. She objects to the poet who sits down to write about an idea: "This is to be left to amateurs."

To a question about her poetic affiliations, she replies that she feels closest to the Elizabethans. To a question on the quantity of her work: "I don't write very much, but I write very well."

When Dylan Thomas reads Sitwell he redeems her lightness with his profundity. She refers to his reading of her poems as "masterful."

In the crush moving out of the hall we meet Tennessee Williams who is now part of the inner circle.

So much of our effort is wasted in trying to penetrate the inner circle; what an idiotic drive inwards. Most of the participants, like myself, are antagonistic to the pattern, but what can we do?

October 29, 1950

Saturday afternoon *Resistance* meeting. A lecture on Gandhi turns into a discourse by Paul Goodman.

Paul asks: "And how do we know our deepest self?" And answers himself: "By our actions."

In the end we do the right thing if our action is consistent with our deepest self and springs from our deepest knowledge.

And, again, Paul, speaking of principle: "What is principle? Principle is that which is deeper than I know. At the crisis I must decide whether I shall trust what I know or whether I shall trust what is deeper than 'I know.'"

There follows a dialogue between Paul and Isaac Rosenfeld about Gandhi's psychosexual development.

I like this dirty hall, its footloose occupants, its old Spanish radicals, its wooden tables, its incendiary literature.

October 31, 1950

A color on Julian's newest painting has darkened because of the incompatibility of titanium white and purple. And he works in his peculiar temper to find the original shade.

At the Soutine exhibition at the Museum of Modern Art: Edith Sitwell in another fabulous cape, this one of yellow and gold, accompanied by Sacheverel of the mighty mane. She peers boldly at everything, including Lincoln Kirstein, horribly handsome tonight, and any number of other people who were not looking at the pictures.

November 3, 1950

Shaw's death, much too soon, even at 94. A symbol of longevity shouldn't die so young. We need his spirited rebellion. Julian had always sworn GBS would live to be 115 and I share his disappointment.

Through and over everything this gloom. And it's by no means confined to me.

Deaths and wars. The Korean War lengthens. The draft increases. Our friends prepare for prison terms. No talk of peace. The word "peace" is subversive and "red." It has been stripped of its dignity.

An attempt to assassinate the president in the name of Puerto Rican independence. At the price of three lives—one guard killed, one revolutionary killed, one revolutionary captured and doomed—the knowledge of this independence movement is brought to the American public.

November 6, 1950

At work on the *Heimkehr* translation with John Bohn. He works with an even, relentless drive that I trace to his West Point training.

A circular from the Workshop in this morning's mail announces *Heimkehr* for the 30th of November: Apparently Piscator wants to rush another play into production.

Chouteau Dyer stopped by last night preoccupied that the Workshop may have to give up the theater, if the next play does not make money. And the school without the theater is nothing, says Chouteau.

I am wounded in my love for the Workshop, in my love for Piscator, and for his very ambitious theater, failures and all. And I hate to hear its students deprecate it without any conception of what Piscator is really trying to do.

Dick Gerson wants Piscator to do his Alexander play and comes to me for advice.

A party in the Tolstoyan setting of the *Sociedad Internacional Anarquista.* The weather is terrible and the damp wooden room seems to creak. Beer and sandwiches.

Across the street two policemen skulk in the doorway of a clothing store observing our comings and goings.

Stuart Perkoff suggests that Julian and I speak on pacifist revolution at a *Resistance* meeting.

It will be the first political lecture for both of us.

We choose the title: "The Ends as Means: Techniques of a Peaceful Revolution." Julian insists on being carefully prepared. For such an informal group, I'd prefer to be more spontaneous.

Since few of the *Resistance* group are pacifists, we expect some challenging opposition.

November 8, 1950

Rounds: Moving aimlessly among the brass and marble underpasses of the bowels of the RCA Building, the soul narrows down, context vanishes. Jostled out of an elevator into a room filled with dozens of Negroes in red satin outfits rehearsing jazz routines. Then, lost in a four-directional corridor, I tap a lady in peasant costume on the shoulder to ask directions, and find myself face to face with Lillian Gish.

November 10, 1950

A call from an agency sends me to my first television reading, for "a sweet but not syrupy" beauty carved out of wood by a hermit who, like Pygmalion, has brought her to life. I don't read well. Can't bridge the gap.

November 18, 1950

4:30 A.M.: At work on our speech for the anarchists tomorrow. A fine time to do it. Confused by stray citations from Thoreau, de Jouvenel.

Julian will open with the connection between pacifism and revolution. Then I'll take up the technique of creating revolutionary change by eliminating the use of money. Then Julian will discuss some of the foreseeable results of a moneyless revolution. And I will end with a plea for nonviolence.

November 19, 1950

Our first political speech meets with a lack of faith among these anarchists who, of all people, should have most faith. They are deeply resentful of this world (as they should be), often so much so that their concern with destroying the existing order overshadows the work of building a better one. Their attitude is that since revolution is at present impossible and the general strike too difficult to organize, all we can do is break down faith in the existing state. Valuable work, but by itself too negative. And love does not always enter in.

"You're much too optimistic."

"You can't organize production if you haven't first instituted syndicalism."

"The parasites would live off the workers."

"You won't get enough people to agree to it."

Their main concern is the means of production and they scoff at the idea that overproduction should be halted.

They are still thinking in monetary and socialistic terms. Marx's "To each according to his need, from each according to his means" is cited to justify compulsory employment. They are rejecting revolution as "too difficult"; a revolution that means hardship instead of bloodshed is deemed inconceivable.

A few people agreed with us wholeheartedly. Charlie Wellman was the most enthusiastic. He is trying to live an exemplary life. He works as a janitor, earning twenty-five dollars a month, but having found that he needs only fifteen dollars a month to live, he's refused the rest of his pay. This way he feels that he's not using money, but only subsisting.

A chiropractor who calls everyone "comrade," quotes Kropotkin in a Russian accent. She wants to give the comrades a talk on health foods.

Among the opinions voiced there was very little true anarchism.

David Wieck and Irving Feldman, a former CCNY classmate of Julian's, left early. Stuart and Susan Perkoff came late and said nothing. Jackson Mac Low said he needed a regeneration of his faith in man.

An old Spanish anarchist who always sits there reading Bakunin tells us, with tearful eyes, in broken English, of the heroic deaths of the Spanish martyrs.

In contrast to our comradely SIA hall, the elegance of Piscator's home to which we go for a cocktail party, puts us ill at ease among a clutter of Victorian bric-a-brac, engravings, paintings, sculpture, and portraits of Madame.

Mme. Piscator greets everyone with an embrace, introduces people with fantastic ebullience: "This is Mr. and Mrs. Beck. She is Malina. She went to the Workshop and is now a writer and an actress and"—a pause and a sigh—"she is lovely."

Stella Adler, dressed in the vamp tradition, practices wiles on Julian. Alexander Ince pretends to be shocked by my low neckline and tries to adjust it more modestly. I insist that it is as it should be. With the innocent expression of *Mitteleuropa* he says, "I don't know such things. I'm just a beginner."

Piscator, while accustomed to such parties, is obviously not happy.

A person named Kahnert tells John Bohn that the English rights for *Heimkehr* are to be divided as follows: 50 percent to Ilse Langner and 50 percent to be divided three ways between Piscator, Bohn, and Malina.

Kahnert smilingly assures us that present day Germany has solved all its problems. "It was black for a while, but now we are politically very fine."

He is here at the invitation of the State Department, and tells us cheerfully, "I am living on your taxes."

November 21, 1950

Tracy Woodward suggests that he audit me dianetically.

Rounds in freezing weather.

November 22, 1950

Donald Pippin has been invited to a ranch in California where some musicians are doing advanced studies. At a small farewell at Harold and Dick's, we sit around a hearth, while Donald plays the piano.

Julian presents Harold and Dick with a painting called *The Birthday Party*. Superbly lit by the fire, its textures change constantly. It shakes slightly at the El train's passing, as does the Picasso drawing hanging opposite.

Isca sings a magnificent Habanera. Her beauty is entirely original.

I go uptown to Tracy's on 106th Street, where he has overdecorated two tenement rooms in an oriental flavor.

The dianetic trance may be all imagination. It's easy for me to imagine returning to a situation, even to one I haven't been in. Tracy asks me to name a date, then tells me to flash back to it. I describe a scene in my high school lunchroom, those present, and the conversation. Then another scene in which Charlie de Coro first kissed me. Then suddenly Tracy says, "Go back to conception."

Having submitted to the indignity of being ordered back to my own making, I make the best of it, set my stage in my mind's eye, and experience according to the book. I feel chills and aches, and squirm a bit, feeling altogether ridiculous. But Tracy believes that I actually returned along the time track to conception.

In Tracy's bathroom, little mice run about with amazing alacrity.

November 23, 1950

When I feel that I can do all that I want to do, I become elated and industrious. Then, in my ardor, I work faster and faster until the ardor exhausts itself in nervous energy. I've just experienced such an elation, but the cycle hasn't yet run its course. Now I grip my pen so hard that my fingers ache and can't write quickly enough. My anxiety mounts. Impatience takes over. I'll scream. Then I don't.

Instead of turning away from the theater, I have to approach it in a different way, a way frowned on by theater people, but the only way possible for me.

I've forgotten that I'm an artist. I've forgotten that I am a woman.

Daily on my rounds I become a "character ingenue" and I'm ashamed.

November 25, 1950

A great windstorm hits New York. The double-headed street lights have fallen from the lamp posts, their massive tops lying on the streets or embedded in the tops of automobiles. Garbage and broken glass fly through the air breaking windowpanes. I battle the wind up to Tracy's for a dianetic session. Through a series of painful incidents, he leads me to return to the most painful: my father's death.

I recall the moment when my mother told me that my father was dead, but I don't reexperience it, feeling it would be disrespectful to rehearse so meaningful a pain in this setting. I go on to Harold's departure over which I weep profusely. Later I imagine that I am four months old, being examined by a doctor in a Copenhagen hospital. During this examination, I am accidentally struck across the eyes by a stethoscope.

Three A.M. Robin calls: "Julian, 448 West 55 Street. Come quickly. I'm hurt." He has been robbed and beaten. He was left on the streets clutching pictures of his mother as a Gibson girl and of Isadora Duncan.

Now that they're on their way home after patching and bandaging at Roosevelt Hospital, I'll make some tea.

November 30, 1950

I watch a magnificent stretch of gray and gold cloud pull its soft weight across the Hudson in a haze of winter sunlight. I want to preserve it, but it will dissolve into the composite memory of a thousand clouds and try as I will I will fail to keep it apart—save only—ah, subtle craft—by writing this.

The fear of a world war. Defeat threatens the U.S. in Korea. Rumors that the government is "considering" the use of the atom bomb on Peking: The great East-West catastrophe for which civilization has been preparing for a thousand years.

December 1, 1950

When I am elated is it due to dianetics? I don't believe in dianetics, but I do credit Coué and suggestion.

Last night Charles Wellman and the Perkoffs.

Charles is one of the pure souls in the world. His goodness shames us. But he does not change us. The tragedy of a modern saint. Or of any saint.

O pure spirits, enlighten me. Save me from possessions and misdirected passion. Take me outward through inwardness, and inward through outwardness. Remove the need to be admired; replace it with admiration and a love of solitude. Address only yourself in prayer, Malina.

December 2, 1950

Decades pass in minutes. Growth and decay flash by; I can't write what I think. Events can be recorded, the memory of a feeling is another feeling entirely foreign to the original.

Julian's paintings constantly excel themselves. His last, completed today, is a strong poetic gray mass with stones embedded in the paint.

Here comes Puss to be read to.

At my unfortunate suggestion, Harold Norse, Dick Stryker, and Richard Miller decide to see Tracy about a dianetic auditing.

In that madman's castle Tracy terrorizes them, scrutinizes them with a merciless unpleasantness, a brash authoritarian tone, and harasses them into becoming patients. They are furious with him.

But he audits well. Whatever it is that he can do he does with an almost magical facility.

He has intimidated Dick into early morning sessions. He will go to Tracy at 6:30 A.M. before work, a feat Tracy accomplished by accusing him of "being unwilling to make sacrifices." The dictatorship of the psychotherapist promises to be the most corrupt of all.

December 4, 1950

Harold calls at night, quite excited at having recalled conception.

Too crowded to get seats for the T. S. Eliot reading at the YMHA. We listen in an adjoining lounge, where a speaker system carries the elegant, dramatic voice with its crystalline enunciation.

The nobility of the work breaks the mirror of our image over our heads. He reads from "The Wasteland," "Sweeney Erect," and all of "Dry Salvages." He reads of what we are and what we can be and how we can use it.

I'm not interested in what I can't use. What I can best use inspires me most.

December 5, 1950

Harold is buying a car to take us out of the city should we need to flee suddenly.

I don't want to leave New York. I don't want to consider the destruction of New York as a possibility. Nor do I want to sit for impatient years in the country cursing the sweet woods, languishing for the cruel pavements.

What of "the war"?

The deaths are numbers and the men who die are hardly missed except by their mothers.

December 6, 1950

Julian has paintings flowing from his fingers; his best work comes from him quickly.

Today, an audition that went well. When I strayed from the lines, I managed to improvise on Djuna Barnes' monologue.

Tonight I tried my hand for the first time at an oil painting, using Julian's leftover palette.

The wasted hours sit on all the chairs, smile at me from corners of mirrors, chivalrously open doors for me.

December 8, 1950

I stagger into bed at four A.M. with a plate of hot soup. Just time to write this while Julian and Robin talk in the kitchen. Julian says, "The days are getting weirder and weirder." Today, for example:

At the Workshop I give a grand, explosive reading of Lady Macbeth, which, however, they will not let me play.

"Malina is too little, too Malina, to be Lady Macbeth. . . . Malina is fit to do translating and dramaturgy. Otherwise . . . Oh, no, not Malina."

With the stage lights in my eyes, I tranced into a realization of being where I belong.

More rounds. Then I meet Helen and we wander around the ten-cent store looking for a Chanukah present for Julian. Then to Mother's for supper. Then home to find Robin dancing to Beethoven in a bizarre outfit as Julian's father listens thoughtfully to the music.

Tracy enters this skelter to overhaul the back room as an office for his dianetic practice. Then he begins to order everyone about the household.

December 9, 1950

I'll curl up in a corner and meditate. In the mirror I'm astounded, again and again, at how closely I resemble myself. To be more and more like myself.

Now the philodendron beside me smells so strongly that I am inclined to move away. I never realized it had an odor.

Tracy antagonizes everyone, especially provoking Julian with his commands.

"We'll have to move this desk out. It's horrid. How about putting it in your studio?"

He wants to paint the ceiling dark blue and to change the numbers on the back door.

Meanwhile, Alex Burdett comes to deliver a manuscript by Gleb Botkin called *The Seduction to Goodness*. Alex has been converted by Botkin, an Aphrodisian priest living in New Jersey.

December 14, 1950

A talk with Julian wherein we bare much to each other and yet do not touch upon the spot of loneliness.

In the evening, we go to Chumley's and play chess. How natural that I lose every game.

December 15, 1950

At the Workshop this morning Piscator will not even listen to my reading of Lady Macbeth.

December 17, 1950

An anarchist evening at home. The Perkoffs, David Wieck, Gil Orlovitz and Joe Turner.

The conversation is limited by a lack of hopefulness. No light in that darkness.

Stuart pretends to be callous. David expresses only despair, though pure intentions sprout from him unwanted like weeds. Still they won't be dissuaded from the dismal road. Instructive opposition is rare.

To a party at Isca and Joop's, where I meet Willem de Kooning. He has a placid Dutch manner unlike his paintings, which I have always found too violent. But now that I see his face, I see the freedom rather than the anger in his paintings.

Isca's singing teacher wears handcrafted terry-cloth and latex shoes which would solve the vegetarian shoe problem except that they are not waterproof.

December 19, 1950

Julian Sawyer came last night and let Julian in on the great secret about Garbo—that she is a man named Gareth Hughes who left Hollywood the year that Garbo arrived. He shows us photographs to document his extravagant fantasy.

Also of the male sex: Jean Harlow, Anna Magnani, Mae West, Ingrid Bergman, Lynn Fontanne and Elsa Maxwell.

December 20, 1950

Julian Sawyer will do Eliot's *Cocktail Party* as a monologue in our front room. In its entirety. With props.

December 21, 1950

Dick Gerson has rented the Cherry Lane and is pressing us to produce, direct, and design *The Thirteenth God*. He doesn't allow a moment's rest between telephone calls.

December 22, 1950

I wait with Garrick in the hallway of one of the brothels on 99th Street while Julian stands in the snow negotiating with a young man about a 1935 car. For fifty dollars from my bank account, we get the half sheet of paper that makes this trap ours. Julian doesn't dare try it at night on a slushy hill, so it stands where we bought it and who knows if it shall ever move.

Yet this car is intended to get us to Connecticut tomorrow. Harold has bought a house and farm near Canterbury, some forty miles from Hartford, where we could live and build a studio cottage.

Though we go to Canterbury, we resemble not so much Chaucer's pilgrims as Boccaccio's refugees fleeing the plague.

December 23, 1950   Canterbury, Connecticut

Written by flashlight in a snowbound colonial house amid acres of woodland, lush and golden. Harold offers us a room and a studio and a child's room on the second floor with a north-light window facing the hills.

I too often forget the vital things, but the air of the woods is fraught with them.

A snowfall frightens us, for our small car will not move in the snow and the land outside is whitening quickly.

December 24, 1950   Road between New York and New Haven

Even in the car, bouncing along a wet road, it is easier to write than lying on that cold floor last night.

In the morning we walked across acres of fir and maple, nut trees and grape vines, wild roses, winter ferns pushing green through the fresh snow. On the path, we speculate on the tracks of creatures. Not a moment but I think of Thoreau.

Later, at the garage, we saw a magnificent gray and yellow deer leap up through the woods. The mechanic said, "All I need now's a good shotgun."

Harold is troubled by the hunting on the land; a round of shots popped through the air this morning. "No Hunting" signs are legal, but don't make good neighbors. Harold goes so far as to fear that they might burn down his house, but that doesn't seem like New England.

Our nearest neighbors are the Ames family, the former owners of the house, ruled by the patriarch, a man of 81, tall, gaunt, white-haired; he sends a gallon of milk up to the house along with some oil lamps.

Our car, named "The Pardoner," as one who "wends his way to Canterbury," is driving perfectly, only that the emergency brake must be hit on the top with a hammer before it will move.

I love this part of earth, the gentle Connecticut. And to live here, even away from New York, would not be much hardship.

December 27, 1950   New York

The dianetic and analytic techniques that Tracy uses create a dependence on the therapist. This week Dick is collapsed with a cold. Harold is unable to sleep at night or stay awake during the day. And I am rapidly losing patience with this therapy.

December 28, 1950

We agree to do The Thirteenth God. Many faults in the play. However, many advantages in working at the Cherry Lane as a preparation for the Living Theatre. It's a sort of practice run.

December 31, 1950

At year's end, try to recount:
I feel that my life took place in the forties.
Julian considers this a fruitful year because it has brought into being his best paintings.
I've written some good poetry and if I were a writer I'd feel encouraged; but theater work needs coworkers, and not the solitary desk.
This has been the year of Tracy, his hypnotism and mumbo-jumbo.

Now there's *The Thirteenth God* half in this year and half out. The rent on the theater is paid and the date is set.

Nothing passes. All things return. Life is reunited by its loose ends and makes circles around itself. There's no unfinished moment.

Eternity consists of this. Out of this flash of eternity we construct a new existence like a phoenix. If I could move one millimeter away from myself I would be God.

The year's events have passed by like landmarks, bits of topography seen from a speeding conveyance. A stop or two. No idea of destination.

The future is a dream to which I cling as I hope one day to cling to the present.

Rabbi Max Malina. March 28, 1948: "His struggle set the pattern for my life. In 1928 he took us to New York . . . where he founded a small congregation. . . . He edited a newspaper, *Der Zeitgeist,* in which he published appeals for the rescue of the Jews of Germany and Poland, among more theoretical pieces by Gutkind and Buber—And died at 42."

March 28, 1948: "My father taught me, 'They can always take away my country from me, but they can never take my Torah away from me. . . .' My mother was his *'Frau Doktor Rabbiner'* and a certain standard was expected of me as their daughter."

October 29, 1948: "Julian and I argue about all the bourgeois wedding preparations on which our parents insist."

May 17, 1949: "I will never forget the first sight of the little face . . . as beautiful as anything I have ever seen—O sweet small mouth and dark round eyes!"

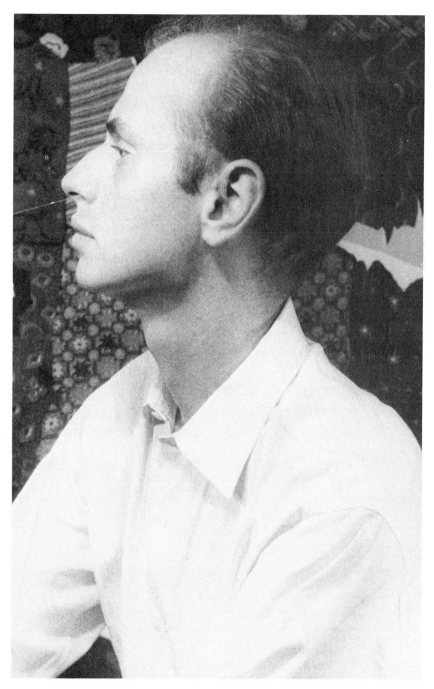

August 23, 1951: "Carl Van Vechten . . . photographs Julian against a patterned cloth . . ."

1951

January 1, 1951

Dressed in oriental style and veiled in tulle and silver, I feel more like a bride to the New Year than a celebrant and am inclined at this moment to accept the omen.

We had no desire to celebrate, but Robin, Harold, Dick Stryker, Richard Miller, Alex Burdett and Charles Wellman have come.

The boat whistles and sirens announce the turn of the year, while our gloomy talk centers around the destruction which such alarms might herald.

We recalled the celebrations of VE and VJ Days, the joy of victory, the joy of peace.

Harold asked for some oriental music to which he could dance. An ensemble was put together with Garrick's toy piano and xylophone, from which the two Richards, Stryker and Miller, extract pure Eastern sounds. Harold asked me to be his partner; I put on my Persian skirt, my Balinese earrings and a silver tulle veil. At Harold's insistence I added a caste mark to my forehead. He dressed in a Japanese kimono, Robin's Martha Graham pants, my Roman silk sash, a Chinese hat, Julian's Japanese sandals with a white satin blouse improvised out of an old coat lining.

Harold, who had once been a dancer with La Meri's company, showed me two basic movements. The furniture was moved to one side. The musicians started, and I was amazed at how well I was performing.

After us, Robin danced, leaping in a circle, and straining to free himself, like Isadora, from all impositions.

Harold danced a satirical Salome in German expressionist style to Welitsch's singing.

Robin read from Krishnamurti. When we talked of ethics, Charlie Wellman guided us with prodigious modesty. He was a conscientious objector in Chillicothe, the same prison where Dick Stryker served his time.

Harold praised Eric Gutkind as a moral thinker. What a panoply of memories that name unfolds: the beautiful philosopher who used to sit talking for hours with my father, of the spirit and the world, of the Kabbalah, of the Chassidim, and of the horrors of war. I listened from the other side of the room, where I sat with my mother and Lucy Gutkind at *Kaffee und Kuchen*.

The Gutkinds live only a few blocks away at the Master Institute. I resolve this New Year to get in touch with them.

Then dawn came. Instead of going to sleep we went to work on *The Thirteenth God*.

I finish *Remembrance of Things Past* after two years.

And it was evening and it was morning the first day of 1951.

January 2, 1951

I spend the day at the Dramatic Workshop looking for an Alexander and a

Hephestion for *The Thirteenth God*. Dick Jessup could play Alexander but probably is too proud to work without pay, not to mention too poor.

In the evening while cutting *The Thirteenth God* with Dick, a frightful argument about the war erupts. When we talk of personal responsibility and guilt, he challenges me to go to Korea and try to stop the war. The red of my own blood flashes in my eyes.

"Tell me how. How can I get there? Where's the ship? How can I get on it? You said I should go, now get me there! I'll hold you to it. . . ."

He tries to calm me.

It seems as if a lifetime of frustration had to burst out. I continue until I'm exhausted. It was four in the morning.

January 3, 1951

Jessup is eager to do the play. He would make an attractive Alexander and cruelty is a part of his beauty. He shows us a photograph of himself taken by his friend Karl Bissinger. Tiny planet, little webs.

At Tracy's we reach what is called "basic-basic," the postulated earliest engram, or painful experience. And from this, according to the book, great changes should spring. I await the changes.

January 4, 1951

Jessup, helpless with a headache and unbecomingly pale, reads Alexander. Julian is teaching Harold to drive.

Harold reads both my poetry and Julian's. He liked "How They Live and Die in Mexico"—the first praise I've had for my favorite story. He's now reading *Damocles*.

January 5, 1951

Shaken by a remarkable dream from which I haven't quite awakened as I write it down:

I am traveling along an American highway with a caravan of cars, bound on a kind of crusade. All the voyagers are young and eager to accomplish the mission.

The cars slow up. Ahead I see the superstructure of a gigantic bridge being towed upward by immense cranes, hoisting it to the top of a high cliff rising directly from the side of the road. The work starts a landslide. Rocks crash down. I am afraid. On the opposite side of the road is a body of water. Deep below me a ravine. All this on a superhuman scale. I cannot run away back down the road.

I find myself huddled against the guard rail between the road and the water. I'm afraid of drowning should the road and fence be broken by the plummeting stones.

Men are at work transforming the cliff into a vast dwelling. The work is dangerous and proceeds at great cost of life.

Just as terror threatens to overwhelm me, a young man comes toward me and puts his arm around my shoulder.

Workers are constantly being killed and falling down from the superstructure. Their bodies appear like divers against the light sky. Then a shuddering scream rises from the watchers followed by a hush, a sort of memorial by workers and spectators to the fallen men.

We are not the spectators, but an inner circle whose duty it is to witness this. The real spectators are a crowd of poor people who occupy a viaduct between the road and the river, out of danger's way.

At night we break up our watch and retire to our rooms, which are primitively furnished cabins on wheels. I occupy such a room with the young man who had had his arm around me.

As he embraces me, the "order" comes that men and women may no longer occupy the same room. I plot to change my room "officially" and then return through the camp to the young man, but before I can accomplish this, day breaks and we return to our positions.

The spectators on the viaduct are already there when we arrive. We discuss whether we should move farther from the danger but choose to come closer where we can hear the conversations of the workmen.

Where the cliff stood, a tremendous basement is being constructed. I dare not look down into its dizzying depth.

But I have the reassurance of the certain figure beside me, a reassurance that applies not only to myself, but to the project itself.

The work is accomplished. The project's wonders are demonstrated by a fast-talking department store salesman, who makes the great work puny by his description. Consumed by gadgets and pettiness, it shrinks beside the importance of the young man who enabled me to witness this terrible building.

January 8, 1951

Yesterday morning we went to the downtown law office of Dick Gerson's father to mimeograph scripts. On a Saturday, the canyon district, without its stench of gasoline, smells of the sea.

At night, Julian Sawyer awaits us, impatient to set the stage for his monologue performance of *The Cocktail Party*. Having been kept waiting for more than an hour, he greets me with a screech, "Cart that baby off to bed!"

Then he tears the front room apart, to turn it into a suitable stage setting.

I retire with Garrick into his room while Sawyer rants.

"Curse everything! Damn it! Damn everything!"

Harold and the two Richards stay in the kitchen so as not to disturb the actor preparing. Dick Gerson is in the library stapling *The Thirteenth God* together.

Sawyer's *Cocktail Party* amazes everyone. The monologue has a forcefulness that I would not have suspected. With change of voice and stance and gestures in the tradition of the oriental theater, he unfolds the play as one man's dream of the world as a cocktail party where the characters grope in their spiritual darkness, blinded by the chandeliers.

January 9, 1951

The front room still a stage. The library a shambles. Parties and plays and what else? Casting office, home and nursery. I'm running a circus.

I'm overwhelmed by ANTA's production of Lorca's *House of Bernarda Alba*, a document about sexuality. Can any other contemporary playwright write tragedy? Such tidal wave writing is rare. Paxinou was pure tragedy in its bareness and horror. Mme. Piscator, in the lobby, laments, holding her head in her befurred arms, "I hear such comments in the audience! Such stupidity! What is one to do? What can one do?"

Garrick has an ear and throat inflammation. He is limp with fever and passive when held in arms. It's hard to concentrate on the work. But how good it is to be working. Like a raging in the blood, all-demanding and physically delightful.

January 10, 1951

Jessup is burning to play Alexander. If he can put as much passion into the role as into his desire for it, he should do well. I commit my own opinion in his favor.

Calls from actors all day and it's obvious that from now on life will be more hectic.

Through the aisles of Brooks Costumes. Under the hand, the cloth that clothed Anthony and Jason and Helen of Troy crumbles to tatters and torn tassles. There's nothing here for Alexander. We will make our own costumes. Julian will design them.

Memories burst into the modernized interior of the St. James Hotel as I wait there for Dick Gerson:

Memories of my first meeting here with Julian when Gaugau introduced us to each other; and of Tommy Scott who disappeared from the earth's face so that neither his family nor the F.B.I. could find him; memories of Genius Incorporated run by a hungry, lean Leo, who is now the magnate of Shull Publications; and of that world of *demi-mondaine* actors who dwelt in that hotel in a kind of communal sin, hallowed by their tired spirits and their apathetic humor.

I was 17 and gave them my enthusiasm. They were brutal and vulgar and terrifying, but my innocence was implacable.

It was different at Valeska's Beggar Bar. There the decay was an historical style elaborated by the person who gave birth to it.

Where is that bohemia now? The rebels are in Paris, the pioneers in California, and the artists are afraid, timid and afraid.

January 13, 1951

This afternoon to the Metropolitan to work on costumes in the Museum library. In the oriental exhibits, the bodhisattvas radiate such patient calm that I go more slowly and do fewer things.

This book is a record of my impatience. I write quickly. I look forward to completions.

"Politics are awful," says Johnny Myers at Bill Simmons' party last night. "They're so impersonal. I'm a very personal person."

And of art, "I simply can't look at Picasso anymore. Victor Hugo, *hélas*. Picasso, *hélas*." He straightens his bow tie while he speaks.

January 15, 1951

The house is a casting office. Robin greets actors at the door, sweeps them into the library, and announces: "Miss Malina, the director."

During a good session at Tracy's, a call from Dick Stryker about our back room, the one Tracy had claimed for his office. Now Dick wants to move a piano in.

Tracy has convinced Dick Stryker and Harold that their cohabitation is aberrative for both of them.

Dick decided to move into Donald Pippin's room, which had been occupied by a mad lady doctor who has been removed to Bellevue, and thus the room was ostensibly Robin's, who in turn wished to give it to Dick.

The landlord, however, informed Robin this morning that the doctor, insane or not, is being sued for back rent and furthermore Robin is to have his things and Donald's things out of there by ten this morning.

Here comes Robin's stuff, Donald's stuff, and Dick's stuff, in addition to Dick and his piano.

Tracy says, "Tell him to get the hell out of there."

Suddenly I see them as strangers and our maniacal laughter as a symptom of our estrangement.

January 16, 1951

An opening of Grace Hartigan's work at Johnny Myers' new gallery, the Tibor de Nagy, a friendly, fashionably remodeled old apartment, sponsored by Dwight Ripley. A Gidean character this Dwight, a chapter to himself in someone's chronicle. Not mine. Not here.

Grace Hartigan uses the name George because of the prejudice against women painters. She says she took the George from Sand and Eliot. Her brush work is bold and her compositions complex. Her sensitivity is female, but she paints with a vigor that men claim as exclusively masculine.

Maya Deren enters like a wild woman, her broad, tense face circled with hysterical ringlets, an enormous earring and a band of pearls protecting her hair and face. She enchants us.

Another tempestuous fight with Gerson. He still has a four-and-a-half-hour script and refuses to cut a line.

January 18, 1951

Jessup read for Alexander to my satisfaction. Gerson and Julian agreed. Renee Masse, Gerson's lover, will play Olympias.

January 19, 1951

Are we like the young artists who gathered together to inspire each other in the first part of this century?

When I imagine that Julian's painting and my theater, and the music, the dance, the poetry of our friends will become a true movement, then this communal home takes on meaning.

January 23, 1951

Today a frightening number of young ladies came here to read for Thaïs and Antigone, the camp-followers of Alexander.

The hardest task is to refuse actors the roles they covet. Woody Parker read Alexander admirably but finally had to be told that Jessup was playing it.

Mother is depressed about the death of Selma Panofsky, my father's secretary, and my childhood companion; she is dead by her own hand.

January 24, 1951

Charles Wellman invites us to the Wednesday meeting of the Peacemakers, at Mount Morris House. Once called the Harlem Ashram, it has served as a haven for radicals, the oppressed, the resisters. Dick Stryker stayed there during his turbulent career as a conscientious objector. Unlike the SIA hall, here the spirit of revolt is permeated with a humility lacking among the aggressive anarchists. In this world of disgruntled souls, these are the best.

I feel uncomfortably well-dressed. Mine are the only high-heeled shoes and the only earrings.

The meeting is informal. Most of those present are residents of the communal house.

I had read in the *Times* about the arrest of three Mount Morris House Peacemakers at a protest against "The Ways of Love" at the Paris Theater. They are out on bail and are here to tell their story: Some Catholic groups were offended by the film which is about the torment of a possessed religious woman, Anna Magnani, who believes that her child was fathered by St. Joseph. Our three friends were a part of a counterpicket of Catholics supporting the film.

First to be arrested was handsome, young Jim George, who described his experience with humor and innocence.

The police asked if had registered for the draft. He said he was a nonregistrant and submitted to arrest. As did the other two pickets.

When they were taken away, they went limp, which Jim George explained as a way of avoiding the temptation of responding to violence with violence. He described being dragged first up the stone stairs and then down again, feet first, his head crashing against each step.

"I guess God took the strength out of my arms because he did not want me to pick up the picket sign to hit anybody."

In the artistic milieu in which I live, personal religion, prayer and petition for direct intervention, or trust in divine inspiration, are regarded as childish. But I feel no such disrespect.

After the meeting, time was set aside for meditation. The lights were dimmed and everyone fell silent. I looked around blankly. Several people were sitting still with closed eyes; one sat in lotus position. At first I was embarrassed, but in a minute or two I relaxed and my hands lay still. I stopped observing the others.

The hope of the world is in such handfuls of good people—a "cell," they call themselves—and the light of the world is in their silence. Such is the kinship between them that they call one another "brother." In the silence, I felt myself partake of their vision. Then the light was turned back on and a general talk began.

January 25, 1951

Casting a play is cruel work. Friends feel cheated and scorned. The worst part is saying no.

Dozens of young ladies file by to read for the camp follower, Antigone. I try to put them at their ease, but I am myself not easy. I too am playing a part.

The director may be dispensable. Piscator goes so far as to say that art itself is dispensable, that the aim is to abolish art, that is, to destroy the need for it.

I am disturbed by the authoritarian position, which, like all power, corrupts. I try to overcome it with a friendliness which I tremble to think unconvincing.

This passage was interrupted by Garrick, who tossed this whole volume into a bathtub full of water and my writing time has gone to an archaeological reconstruction of the year.

January 28, 1951

About the casting. Woody, with painful resignation, accepts the Hephestian role. He answers the phone with a sarcastic, "Has Jessup dropped dead yet?" And Jessup pales at the sight of him, though they are polite to one another.

This is the rivalry between Alexander and Hephestian. It will be in both their performances.

Val calls Julian, the Val Cogan of the old millennium, Julian's idolized and idolizer, teammate of his wild oats.

"Julian, has anyone ever loved me as you loved me? Julian, I may need you very much soon. Will you be there?" He will meet her at the Algonquin this evening.

February, 1944:
A room squint-eyed with smoke. Val, the lousy Medusa, shouting "Nay, nay" and kissing me as Julian burns every flammable object in the room. A whispered warning, "Keep knives away from Julian." A secreted note inadvertently found, "You are my Nile. Go on when I am dead." Mornings by the Hudson. Nights in Valeska's cellar.

To banish these thoughts, I go with Dick Gerson to the night club where Renee is singing, adored by the young men who sit for hours perched on their barstools. I enter what I try to escape. Memories of Valeska loom in the dim light.

When I return home, Julian says, "We saw each other, but there was nothing to say."

Harold Norse has read some of my poems to Harold Vinal, the editor of *Voices*, who has promised to publish five of them. Most of them had been sent to *Voices* and returned without comment only a month ago. Vinal didn't remember. I'm certain Harold's reading to the half-blind Vinal did them more than justice.

January 29, 1951

John Garfield plays Peer Gynt as if Peer were an unsuccessful Faust; a characterization full of Group Theater mannerisms, nursed by director Lee Strasberg's neo-Stanislavskiism.

February 3, 1951

At a cast meeting for *The Thirteenth God*, everyone sits stiffly around the front room. No one knows anyone else. Gerson talks to the actors about the play. At least one good feud begins.

February 4, 1951

Jessup resigns. Woody Parker to play Alexander.
Geraldine Page, a dazzling creature, gives a dazzling reading for Antigone, the camp follower.
Dick Stryker is working at the music.

February 5, 1951

Terror and shyness as I face a rehearsal in the role of director. Woody is cold to me sometimes, but to Julian he is unwaveringly warm.

Conventions are a form for communication. The abolition of any convention meets resistance because we are afraid it will make communication impossible. But the revolutionary who tries to abolish convention wants to take communication to a higher level. In order to do this he becomes his own means of communication.
Revolutions are in themselves the language of the gap between our present form of signaling and our next form of signaling.

February 6, 1951

The world recedes from me as from a moon-bound passenger. I used to feel it especially when I walked alone through the streets, but now it is worst in company. Numb behind a glance, I observe that even the observation is a mirage.
Last night a reading of *The Thirteenth God*.

February 7, 1951

The second reading was better. Both Woody and Steven work sensitively, quickly, adroitly—and I adore Woody.

February 8, 1951

Marooned on a corner of separate earth, working at what I wish.
Last night's rehearsal excited me. Julian all day drawing the sets, scene after scene, with a few props, and the slides that we had planned. The slides

are a developmental arc, a shuddering undercurrent. He draws a series of masks, to be projected on the entire surface of a silver backdrop. The masks portray Alexander, at first the handsome familiar portrait, then more and more creased and tormented, until the mask finally crumples and falls, when Alexander dies, revealing a face transcendent and calm.

Dick Stryker has a sketch for the prelude and the "World Wide Wedding Day" music.

February 9, 1951

What a pleasure to work, to direct these actors, particularly Woody, who is as self-possessed as Alexander himself.

This morning I am elated, almost suspiciously elated, vigorous, energetic. The sensation that nothing is real is gone.

Six A.M. The difficulties of the play. A whole new first act is written. Meaning a whole new staging.

No matter what a director does, the occupational hazard is power.

Dawn's light calls me to bed.

February 12, 1951

Richard Miller's birthday party. He has a mad mother, who moves through graceful poses and speaks in a high sweet voice. The room is running with roaches. The guests sit in a circle like children at a party at a loss for games.

Among them: Lou Harrison, whose piano works Dicken has been playing for me. He is a man with a sudden smile that vanishes just as one is about to smile back.

The pleasure of feeling the play grow as I mold it, the emergence of action from words, the dead script vibrating to my touch.

I work wildly, passionately. As the evening grows late, I stage the whole banquet scene jumping up and racing through several roles in pantomime.

Worked with Woody all afternoon on our love scene and it embarrasses me.

February 15, 1951

My wish is that the passions that possess me subside and my consolation is that they always do.

What subtle tortures the heart practices, and then the body, traitor to the mind, sides with the heart and allows itself to be inflamed, and then the myths begin. . . .

If I am not for myself, who will be for me? And if not now, when?

In my poetry, I revert to my biblical image. I call myself Miriam hidden among the bullrushes.

It will pass, I say to console myself. Yet my desire is to cling to it.

February 20, 1951

City life is too full of incident. I think of Gide's quiet journal and of how he coped with Paris.

Gide's serious illness strikes us all with foreboding. And Robin, adoring tragedy, "I shall telegraph Bill: 'Alas, Gide is dead!'"

Woody claims to have no human emotions. "I don't care about anything, I don't want friends, I don't want a home"—enumerating on his fingers—"I don't want a wife; all I want or have ever wanted is success as an actor."

February 21, 1951

The rehearsals are the whole day for me. And at night I dream of them. I dread the day they will end.

Yet the work almost goes to pieces with incessant homosexual jokes. Is it the taboo that creates this snickering innuendo? I joke too and say, "My next play will have an all-girl cast," and one of the actors says, "What do you think you have here?"

I appeal to Geraldine, "What does that make us?"

She shrugs regretfully, "That means no one makes us."

February 26, 1951

I pour out my heart to Julian in the Rhineland Cafe. All my fears and frustrations to the higgly beat of the German jazz. The play has become real and life unreal. The actors and the characters express contradictory and unreal propositions.

March 1, 1951

A silent snow reminds me that external excellence is unchangeable.

By what mystery was the world, now cold and white, warm and autumnal only a night ago?

I made a ritual for Aphrodite with scents (I was not mistaken—the charm exerted its power) and for Cassandra's patron, Apollo.

No, I don't even remotely believe in these things. But like a piece of music they change my pitch and tone.

At the bar across from the Dramatic Workshop, I induced a young man to buy a round of beer for the thirsty rabble. There was Helen Fortesque, who opened this evening as Piscator's Lady Macbeth, and Bob Carricart, who is in *Rose Tattoo*, and Walter Mullen, whom I used to kill every night in *Dog beneath the Skin*. Walter was with Helen but we slipped out and walked through Central Park. The buildings gleamed in the sky-filled lake and the night cleared and the stars were warm.

Just as pain exists, so does its compensation. Sometimes the winter wind can be warm and the turf tender without trespassing on the uncomfortable places in the heart.

And after, we sang together in the streets *"E Lucevan' le stelle."* Why not romantic? Why not?

March 3, 1951

I am elated by a good rehearsal and depressed by a bad one. The difference depends on my control over the cast, and on Woody's humor.

March 5, 1951

Our first run-through was rough. I have no third act at all. But my first act is almost an act.

Jan Kindler of *Dog beneath the Skin* cast has joined our company as Kleitos.

We work on the platforms tonight. Our living room a jungle of bamboo poles and levels. I work on costumes.

March 6, 1951

Mysteriously, as though beyond our making, it becomes a play. Out of the scattered scenes, sequences.

Woody has dyed his hair orange gold. His desperate eyes look quieter under pale eyebrows. But the arrogance of his heart is tight and cold. I've developed a strange, hostile passion for him and a fantasy about pain and death.

March 11, 1951

A dream about theater: Downstairs Cornell is playing in *Antony and Cleopatra*. On the top floor we are rehearsing a campy gay musical. The rehearsals are lewd and the actors revolting. I keep running downstairs to see the play in which Cornell is being applauded, but cannot stay there as I must return to the noisy, smoke-filled hall where a piano is running over the paces for some painted chorus boys.

During this I must cross a bridge, which loops and dips like a scenic railway. Helen and Henrietta try to help me across but each time I touch the bridge, I get a painful electric shock. When I fail to cross, I go back to the rehearsal.

This dream, on the night before we go into the theater.

March 12, 1951

The Cherry Lane. The smell of it. The musty, stale odor of it. The historicity of it. Dreams that flood back in cascades of scent. The dressing rooms still imprinted with our names: Bea Arthur, Gene Saks, Irving Stiber, Walter Mullen, and the scoreboard of Zeena and Mattie. The stairway on which I wrote my first journal. The shelf on which I framed Harald's picture, tacked Julian's telegrams.

A run-through of the whole play. If I could hold on to every gossamer moment: "*Verweile doch, du bist so schön.*"

March 19, 1951

At six in the morning the light board gave up in a flash of blue agony.

At seven A.M. a flood of water inundated the stage.

Tonight a preview for an invited audience. In the makeup mirror I am faced by a green-skinned Toulouse-Lautrec in a coffee dream.

Evening. Not tired now. The preview is on. The Plain of Issus scene just beginning. I am waiting for my entrance.

March 20, 1951

Opening night. Before my entrance.

I begin to warm beneath the skin; that hot flash of terror. My stomach leaps; breath is short. It will go well.

The end of the Plain of Issus. Then the shrine in Egypt.

I go downstairs.

2:30 A.M. Gone in an iridescent light. Like phosphorus glowing in the darkness of memory.

Everything went wrong: the cyclorama, the lights, the props. But what is that when we work by the light of constellations?

As I went on for my last scene I felt the ground reel. The lights blurred and I went through my lines automatically. But everyone praised me. The distracted director and the distracted princess combined.

Afterward we were exhilarated. I still am. With Julian, Robin, Dicken, Lou Harrison and Remy Charlip to a restaurant.

Lou charmed me from the first with his buoyant brilliance, his music— and those enchanting looks of terror and turbulence that fleet across his face.

He comes backstage breathless with praise and holds my hands very close. We kiss and plan a meeting.

I am suspicious of our drunkenness and of the role of Statira, in which he knows me. And does not know I'm not, and can never be, the cold white queen.

March 22, 1951

Last night Alfred Kreymborg's face loomed large from the third row among the empty seats. Having recognized him, it was hard not to play toward him.

Kreymborg likes the play, calls it a strong indictment of fascism, while other intellectual friends are angry at us for producing it.

Harold says we shouldn't discuss changing the world and then do a play which is not a work of art.

Lou calls. There is a laughing nervousness between us. He shares my fear of the telephone. We agree to see one another tomorrow, but in 15 minutes he calls back. Tonight then. If this is impatience, I would be very happy.

Now I am nervous before my entrance.

March 24, 1951

On Thursday night after I made my last entry, I gave a performance full of flaws. Woody, in the wings, held back his white robe in one trembling hand and pointed the other hand into my face.

"If you ever destroy a scene of mine again I'll slap your face right on stage."

There was still his death scene to play and I managed to get through it.

When I returned to the dressing room, Julian told me that Lou had been in the theater, but left without coming backstage. I broke down and ripped my costume with a prop sword. Julian found me crying in the dark at the bottom of the cellar stairs and I got dressed and he took me to Sardi's, the way my mother used to take me to Geiger's Cafe when I was sad.

The next day I called Lou. Again the promise, this time not taken with trust, that he will be at the theater after the performance.

Is it true?

Interrupted by the play . . .

March 25, 1951: Easter

Lou is . . . Lou is . . . What can I say Lou is?

Half saint? Half beast?

One walks through curtains approaching him; up against crystal walls (the image is his) when close to him. Look at him too closely: The crystal breaks.

Since he is afraid, I become the seducer. Then I fear his fear and I retreat to allow him to pursue.

He constantly battles my reality. His courage is heroic, but he doesn't recognize his own strength.

Lou tries to be honest, but he constructs an imaginary world to which he retreats. He understands its illusory quality, but then he encounters demons.

His room is taken up by a fine grand piano, bits of stained glass, a brass mobile and oil lamp, oil stove, a photograph of Remy, and the atmosphere of Lou as rich as the world. Powerful, strong, strange.

The moon filtered through a blue velvet curtain accompanying the purity of the Easter morning.

Lou lives in symbols; he sees me as Woman and not as Judith, but with an innocence that would be cruel to betray.

At breakfast, he is suddenly taciturn, distant. In spite of our lovemaking, perhaps because of it, he is afraid. He talks of going to North Carolina that same afternoon, of going to Paris in the summer, of going to California. He leaves me at eleven, angry and depressed.

But the Easter Sunday light on Washington Square is the light of hope and awakening.

March 27, 1951

I am not strong enough for such a relationship. I am not impervious to pain, even if self-inflicted.

I must put him out of my mind in order to function.

At peace again. This rise and fall, as though the pull of the moon's gravity took me mysteriously as the tide.

Before the play, I try to call Lou. His phone has been disconnected.

The play went abominably.

March 28, 1951

Love, like all things, requires practice. It all takes place in my mind. I suffer. This suffering is the pang of luxury.

Orson Welles' *Macbeth* film. The strength and weakness of a giant who wields power without heroism.

March 29, 1951

Dicken and I begin work on a one-act opera on Héloïse and Abelard. We plan a two-part work with a sharp discord in the middle to represent the rupture of love. The characters might be three: Abelard, Héloïse, and the Devison. The Devison to be the narrator, antagonist, uncle, devil, and finally the Divinity—all forces that separate the lovers.

Harold Norse is writing a libretto for Lou Harrison. They have chosen Cupid and Psyche for their story.

March 30, 1951

My television debut is a prosaic affair, rather startling in its absurdity. Excerpts from *The Thirteenth God* on an NBC breakfast program.

March 31, 1951

Research for our libretto. Lou has lent his copy of Waddell's *Abelard* to Dicken, though he does not know for what purpose.

Two more performances of *The Thirteenth God*. The closing of a play is a death and all the people involved are mourners.

Reading some Provençal troubadour poetry, the *Chanson de Roland*, and some studies of early French music.

April 1, 1951

Yesterday, midday awakening. Then to Jean Erdman's concert at the Weidman Studios.

We are ushered inside by a charming and handsome man such as inhabit the dance world.

Remy greets us—he's running lights for the concert—then Dicken, having sneaked out of work to play in the percussion group for Richard Miller.

I see Lou walking back and forth with distracted steps. He comes toward us: "I can sit here now for a while." Then panics: "I must go see Richard."

Richard Miller waves to us from the wings. Just before the program, Harold arrives and completes the circle. We sit together.

Richard has composed a saraband for gourd drum, bamboo pole, pebbles, camel bells, and glasses. The musicians are Remy, Richard, Dicken, and Lou.

Also an enchanting light piece by Lou.

After the performance, Lou introduces everyone to everyone and then scurries away as though he had committed an indiscretion.

Among the people to whom he thus introduces us are John Cage, Merce Cunningham and Erdman's husband, Joseph Campbell. I had imagined Campbell as a dry scholar, but he is the attractive young man who had ushered us into the theater. I tell him that I spent some weeks much disturbed by his work. Why? Because I had pigeonholed everything differently and he juggled it into another frame. I was speaking of *The Hero with a Thousand Faces*.

Harold mentions *The White Goddess* and Lou suddenly runs into a corner as though he had seen a friend to greet, albeit the corner is empty.

Everyone to a restaurant afterward. Lou sits beside me and the world goes well.

A line of Harold's poem, "God is a circle whose center is everywhere," is turned into "the goddess. . . ." Lou turns to me quietly, "I favor the goddess." I say I'm surprised to hear it. Then he flashes disturbingly at me. "You should have known it"—with an unaccustomed vehemence.

Tracy sits in my dressing room and mocks Botticelli's *Primavera*, which I've put on the mirror.

"What if Lou found out that you are not the Botticelli?"

"I'm not hiding anything."

"And when he discovers you're not 'the white goddess'?"

"Perhaps I am. Perhaps I'm not as imperfect as you think."

After the play we go to Lou's for a rhapsodic, free evening. Lou and Julian talk together and I am happy.

Lou transforms when he plays the piano, and lights up as though from within. He plays his Mass, the "Magnificat," and his "Pastorales."

At six in the morning we leave him and his mad, rich laughter.

This should have been a sad night because it was the closing of the play. But I'm not sad.

April 2, 1951

Garrick, back at home after spending the opening week with his grandparents, is flourishing, though his hair is cut and he looks unfamiliar. Julian's mother pens a note regarding the disorder of our house and "the poor infant you have brought into the world."

Clearing out the Cherry Lane. Garrick running through the dressing rooms.

In the afternoon we meet Lou at a gallery. I long for a friendly word.

The paintings are by John Heliker, who portrays Italian cities in forms that derive from the Cubists. He talks of Italian architecture under Julian's nervous questioning.

My eyes follow Lou around; he seems to be looking for someone.

April 4, 1951

The postplay depression has caught up with me. I work on Héloïse and Abelard. Dicken suggests that we model the third character, the Devison, saint and devil, after Lou, who has enchanted us all.

Lou doesn't keep his appointment tonight.

Restless. Painfully restless.

April 5, 1951

I meet Susan Perl on Fifth Avenue and she gives me news of Harald.

She and Erica stayed with Harald's mother in Maximilian's castle at Traunkirchen. Harald drove up in an elegant automobile elegantly dressed and then drove off to Vienna, Paris and North Africa, leaving his mother in tears.

How strange to hear of the past as if it still existed.

I dreamed last night that I was in an eerie, corrupt part of a city in which barbarians lived in paper shacks, filthy, depraved, and sinful. I went there often and was not afraid.

April 7, 1951

Some threads are being put into place. It is a time of mystical awakening. There are "signals" which I lightly attribute to the Fates, but which are really my own heightened awareness.

There is *Finnegans Wake* with its earth symbols encompassing all the myths. And there is my devotion to Lou Harrison's mythology, which has led me also to read *The White Goddess*, an object of worship among people who praise what they fear. And then there is Cocteau's film *Orphée*.

The Woman as Death, evokes the lineaments of the goddess. I too readily identify with Casarès' mannerisms, her style, her acting.

Cocteau's film poems taken together are an epic of "The Poet, Death and the Woman" of which *Blood of a Poet* is the synopsis. With *Orphée* we have almost made a circle back through Death's mirror. In *The Storm Within* (the Woman as Mother), we returned to the Poet's childhood, and in *Beauty and the Beast* (the Woman as Beauty), to his childhood's myth. The Woman as Power in *The Eagle Has Two Heads*, the Woman as the vessel of the Eternal Cycle in *The Eternal Return*, and finally the Woman as Death in *Orphée*, leave but the *Ewig Weibliche* to transcend them all through the Poet.[11]

April 9, 1951

Dicken shows me a postcard from Harold Norse to Lou.

"Dear Lou:

Terrible troubles. I feel like Psyche with the grains of sand. Surely Venus was referring to footnotes . . . so nobody will see much of me for another three weeks. And if I fall into a dead sleep at that time, you will know that I too have been at the source of hell. Is it all a preparation? *De Profundis.*

Harold."

To "The Goldbergs" for casting. Gertrude Berg stands me up against a tall man and says, "We're set. Come in tomorrow for rehearsal." No reading, no interview. Nothing.

Graves' *White Goddess* is a tedious compilation of historical facts, but then that becomes part of the incantation.

April 11, 1951

At rehearsal Gertrude Berg's personality shines on everyone. Like the mother of the world, she presides, orders, loves, rules everybody.

I'm to play "Day Is Done" on the bugle, which is more than I had bargained for. I am a professor's wife and play "Taps" as accompaniment to his lecture on camp life. The professor is Ferdi Hoffman, whom I immediately recognize as the imposing Christ of *Dear Judas.*

At midnight, Richard Miller calls Dicken about a party at Lou's.

Dick was at work on his music; Julian stretching a canvas for a new painting; and I was about to study "The Goldbergs" script. But, to the party . . .

April 12, 1951

At the party, Lou was rudely cold to everyone, especially me. Richard Miller and Dicken talked about problems in atonal composition and Lou fled from one room to another. Suddenly Lou came into the room in which Julian was trying to stir up conversation and said, "Everyone please go home. I'm tired."

Dick calls Lou a dangerous angel. Because he inspires love but does not give it.

April 13, 1951

I had imagined that "The Goldbergs" rehearsals, with twenty years' experience behind them, would go smoothly. But no, I hear the same "No, we can't do it that way . . . go back and try it the first way . . . try it the third way again . . . no, go back to the first way."

The director is a young man who has no authority over Gertrude Berg, who keeps him entirely in check.

My scene causes controversies. My role has become a teapot for a tempest, changed its significance, and consequently no longer suits the lines. It may be my fault. The character has become too strong and is in need of more action and speech. Of course I keep this opinion to myself. An additional rehearsal is called for this afternoon, just for Hoffman, Buloff, Mrs. Berg, Philip Loeb, and myself to straighten this out.

Philip Loeb took me to dinner last night.

He says: "I love sweet young girls like you."

I easily assume a rather girlish attitude. I like to be what people expect me to be.

He accompanies me to Carnegie Hall where the long-awaited *Wozzeck* is to be performed.

This is the most moving opera I ever heard; the most violent, the most tragic.

Two insane crescendos on a single note as Wozzeck comes to the full comprehension of the act of murder. The rising sound needed to resolve in a full explosion, and that explosion never came. Only the sound of a beer-hall tune on a piano, tinkling like a fever.

The pathos is so overwhelming that one comes from it maddened rather than somber. Dicken says, "As in a Greek tragedy, the catharsis is achieved and we find release through suffering."

April 14, 1951

The next rehearsal with only Gertrude Berg, Hoffman, Buloff, and myself is very tense.

Upon discovering that I can't play the bugle, Mrs. Berg decides she likes the way I sing, and I now sing "Day Is Done," while pretending to play the piano.

Then to the New School where a piece of Lou's was to be played. But Lou was dissatisfied with the rehearsal, and a Henry Cowell piece had to be played in its place.

Along the back row sit Dick, Richard Miller, Harold Norse, Tracy, and Lou, who glares at me furiously.

Harold is afraid that the opera, *Cupid and Psyche*, may be in jeopardy. Lou says, "If we ever do it . . . We may never do it." Dick is worried about his lessons. Richard Miller is at odds with everyone and maneuvers to trap Lou like a prize unicorn.

Robin takes me to a party which is enlivened by Julian Sawyer's scenes from *Ninotchka* and *Anna Christie*. Afterward we go to Sawyer's spotless room, lined with neatly framed photographs of Garbo, and his exhaustive Stein collection, immaculate and in mint condition.

Since *Wozzeck*, I have wanted to write a cantata for voices and instruments in which the orchestra plays the dramatic role. I use this night to do it.

I've written a poem setting music and man in opposition, in the form of a double fugue. The subject is Lou and the struggle between music and madness.

April 15, 1951

Julian comes in from a telephone call with Dicken.
"What is the most surprising thing Lou could do?"
"Nothing he would do would surprise me."
"He has just announced that he is getting married."
How do I manage to smile? When I need to cry, I cough.

Worthington Minor comes to "The Goldbergs" rehearsal making changes and suggestions. He stands extremely close to the actors and subjects them to his scrutinizing eye.

8:30 P.M. at Bonnie Bird's dance studio for two of Lou's works. I didn't want to go to another of these difficult scenes, but wanted to see the Cocteau ballet, *Marriage on the Eiffel Tower*.

April 16, 1951

Eiffel Tower: Cocteau's whimsical poetry with Remy's sparkling costumes and Lou at the piano playing his tender, lighthearted score.

Wozzek is still in my mind drowning out all other music.

I talk a long time with Mary, the music student whom Lou intends to marry. She expresses herself modestly. Lou doesn't speak to me.

Remy gives a party at his house after the performance. Lou and Julian argue about whether the arts are revolutionary or conservative. They argue in difficult languages. I stay out of it and talk to Remy.

Because of the few who are like Remy, the rest of us may be redeemed.

"If ten good men shall be found there, I shall not destroy Sodom," God promised Abraham.

TV: In a former movie house, a fantastic assortment of cables, catwalks, and paraphernalia. The cameras have eyes like mouths. The mike booms sweep out like the feelers of a cold and terrible metal insect.

The show begins. I feel like sneaking out the back and never appearing in civilization again. I watch the beginning on the monitor; then realize that I get too nervous that way. Millions of unseen eyes are watching, those million-fold Arguses. Trembling.

I seem to be always awaiting cues, journal in hand.

If only I didn't have to sing.

April 17, 1951

It went quickly. No time to be nervous. I sang "Day Is Done" without a flaw. It was only possible to act at what seemed a gallop, and the work is suddenly finished without fanfare.

The celebration that attends even the smallest theatrical production is lacking. Abruptly the good-nights have been said, and the street is dark and unfriendly, and one belongs nowhere.

April 20, 1951

Library work on *Héloïse and Abelard*.

I talk with Remy till dawn. About Lou. His devotion to Lou is extraordinary. He is disturbed lest he wound Lou by making love to me. We talk by the river and it is cold and the moon is cold like a Ryder moon swathed in mists.

We return home and the world becomes real like a murder weapon doing the unretractable. It is fearsome to exist, but also very beautiful.

The circle makes its final turn and closes in an embrace. We say very little of one another. We talk only about Lou.

Remy exalts the dawn through the drapery. As did Lou. A *leitmotif*. In the same words, the same surprise.

I am sitting in a restaurant on Park Avenue and 59th Street.

Paper blows through the streets, remnants of this morning's parade to welcome the homecoming General MacArthur. We listened to the thunderous demonstration on the radio. The scandal ensuing from his recall by Truman has made him a national hero and he may become president, this man who called the sight of mauled dead North Koreans "a sight for sore eyes."

Dicken, whose hatred of war sustained him through the prison years, listens with a strange look.

My paycheck from "The Goldbergs": $141.89 after taxes. A fantastic sum for so little work.

April 25, 1951

When confusion and difficulty become too great, a turning point is reached and we take on a protective calm, an armor that prevents us from going mad.

Every night my "weird" assaults me. A wretched impatience that my best efforts cannot conquer. This only happens at home; when I go out I feel free.

There is a cocktail party this afternoon for Chester Kallman and René Bouché at Gotham Book Mart. Chester, an old friend of Harold's, has just published a book of poems called *Elegy*. But most of the talk is about *The Rake's Progress*, the libretto Chester and Auden have written for Stravinsky.

The Gotham party was a politic affair. John Myers concocts a strong punch.

April 26, 1951

Billy Budd is a morality play: Melville's story of the sea, war, the ship as small world within the world, the captain as God.

I leave the theater in that tearless state on the threshold of tears.

Dicken asks why I can't read *Moby Dick*. Is it because I have a deep cruelty in me, or that I fear cruelty so deeply that I am unable to bear it witness?

Julian and I go down to the Village. I need the buzz of populated places, that other kind of loneliness.

We go to the San Remo Cafe which I've heard so much about but where I've never been. It's a good bar, gay and intellectual, rather close to my notion of a Paris café.

Here we listen to Chester Kallman talk about *The Rake's Progress* and Stravinsky. He is highly opinionated about opera. By four in the morning, the sadness, along with all other feeling, has left me.

A Thursday: Peter Farb, Helen, Dicken, Joe and Marilyn Turner, and Jackson Mac Low. Jackson, the unhappy anarchist whose good will is trodden bare by his cynicism, stays late and we talk of the world.

April 28, 1951

A German film about Carolina Neuber, actress and director who founded a theater which gave Lessing a stage to write for. Amid stories of love and intrigue, the same worries: the faithless actors, the search for stages.

"We'll play even if we have to perform outdoors on the free fields."

En route home, Mother quotes from Lessing's *Emilia Galotti*, which also figures in the plot of this film:

"*Wie geht die Kunst?*"

"*Die Kunst geht nach Brot.*"

"*Das muss sie nicht, das darf sie nicht, das soll sie nicht. In meinem kleinem Städtchen besonders nicht bis ich selbst keins mehr hab'.*"

("How is art doing?")

"Art is running after bread."

"It must not do that, it should not do that, it shall not do that—and especially not in my little town—till I myself have none.")

April 29, 1951

A party for Conrad Aiken at Oscar Williams and Gene Derwood's loft atop an office building on Water Street, one of the few streets left of old New York, where before long the skyscrapers of the financial district will take over.

No one lives down there. At night the watchmen go from door to door, and the little O'Neillian bars cater to seamen.

The Williamses are mad, but surely divinely mad. I had misjudged Gene: She displays a rare goodness and a daring individuality.

Conrad Aiken sits among us without speaking a single word, though his wife is friendly and chats.

All around the small room are Gene's terrifying, grotesque paintings. Also some creditable portraits of Dylan Thomas and the inevitable mobiles.

Gene talked wistfully of Walter McElroy. I believe she was even more attached to this flown poet than I. And Oscar gives us a photo of Dylan which he had recently taken.

I try to speak to the silent Aiken, but he will not be drawn out.

Dick saw Lou today and reports that he is "ready to begin complicated things again."

Dicken writes a pastorale in honor of Harold's completion of his thesis. Julian paints a splendid Orpheus. Lou implies to Dicken that he, Lou, should have been asked to pose for it.

April 30, 1951

At Dick's lessons, Lou says with that humor that is only a feint for speaking shocking truths, "I destroy all my pupils."

Reading: Herodotus, Plutarch, and the insidious *White Goddess*.

May 4, 1951

At a casting office, I meet an old friend, Glenn Bryant, who was the Husky Miller of *Carmen Jones* when Mariya and I were usherettes at the Broadway Theater. Glenn recalls our mischief backstage when he and Luther Saxon, who played José (Joe), used to joke around with us, and later, when Mariya and I ran off to New Orleans, Glenn, who was a police officer on leave from the department to sing in *Carmen Jones*, had an eight-state alarm put out to find us. Now, in the safety of time, I thank him for returning us to our homes.

May 5, 1951

Film: *Seven Days to Noon*. A scientist steals an atom bomb and threatens to destroy London unless the manufacture of the monstrous weapon is stopped. The film then proceeds to prove that 1) only a madman would want to stop the manufacture of atom bombs; 2) the government can do anything.

I was prepared to applaud the first pacifist speech, which, however, never came. When questioned directly about his motives the scientist said, "I do not wish to discuss this with you."

My applause when he finally said that he hoped other scientists would take courage from his example, was promptly followed by a barrage of hisses.

One image redeems the film: the scientist in a London museum, in the shadow of an extinct creature's skeleton. In his hand, the little satchel containing the instrument of extinction. Was this the hidden intention? Or am I dreaming a dream in which men know right from wrong?

May 6, 1951

Another quiet day reading the narratives of Herodotus. I love these daylight hours. But at night, how different! Last night I was so glum that I went to a gruesome technicolor epic of the South Seas, and then was relieved to be back in my own world. As Abelard writes his friends, "I shall relate my sad history so that you shall see your troubles are as nothing compared to what I have suffered."

So when the technicolor maiden walked into the volcano to save her people, my own troubles were as nothing.

May 7, 1951

The other day, when I dwelt at length on the subject of portrait painting, Julian asked whether I record this kind of thing in my journal. No, I waver between a record of events and a diary of feelings. In the first years, I had reservations; now I am shameless.

I want to act out the adventure. And with my body. In the light. With my voice and my head and my whole being.

But waiting for several hours in a theatrical office to be given a blunt no, and then to the next office for the same. Well, 'swounds, where's the art in that?

I describe "the rounds" to Dicken. He exclaims, "But that's sheer masochism. Why don't you stay home and become the American Miss Sitwell?"

There's a compliment. But I haven't the temperament.

May 8, 1951

Tracy has wanted to befriend Lou for a long time, and now Remy, Tracy, and Lou are having dinner together. This dinner infuriates me. Everyone who is male has a right of *entrée* that a woman does not have, a right to make offers, invite, suggest, call, visit, that a woman does not have.

Cocteau's romantic *Ruy Blas*: nothing of the poet's genius to redeem it.

This last paragraph written at Carl Fischer's, where Dick, who works as a clerk, has put me in a booth with Josquin des Près.

In the evening an interesting concert: a sinfonietta by Henry Cowell; a fantastic concerto for piano and strings by Alan Hovhannes played by Maro Ajemian; a pleasant string thing by Frank Wigglesworth; a piece by Ruggles; and Lou's "Alleluia."

In Cowell's Sinfonietta, Cowell, Wigglesworth, and William Masselos swing thunder sticks over their heads, creating a whirring buzz like the wings of giant insects. This over and under a cello solo.

Lou has written an Alicat Press pamphlet on Ruggles in purple praise. I heard nothing but a sweetness that was almost sentimental.

In Lou's "Alleluia" the key phrase sounds like:
"It will be morning."

At intermission, Lou spoke to me more civilly than usual.

The most attractive man there was Joseph Campbell.

May 9, 1951

Harold Norse lends an erudite air to the house, writing a review of Rexroth's *Beyond the Mountains* and researching the Greek plays.

This evening, John Nerber and his wife for a quiet Thursday with Helen, Dick, and Harold.

For a long time I've talked about doing plays in our front room for a small invited audience, perhaps with Noguchi's glass-top table as the well in Yeats' "Only Jealousy of Emer," 15 to 20 people per performance could sit on chairs and cushions.

Harold is keen about the idea and reads to us from Yeats' article in *Theater Arts* called, "Instead of a Theatre":

. . . My theatre must be played upon the floor, the players coming in by the same door as the audience. . . . My theatre must be the ancient theatre made by unrolling a carpet or marking out a place with a stick, or setting a screen against a wall.

Dicken, who wants to compose for such small performances, has many ideas. The purity of Dicken's values is instructive.

From impatience I am swept toward enthusiasm. At last we have other artists to work with us and we may finally materialize a small, inventive theater in a room.

May 10, 1951

Then bang!

Where is the lucidity, with which I understood myself yesterday?

Then bang!

Like a seashell's enigmatic perfection, dead, white, useless. Lou is terrifying and foolish, and I adore his lyric no less than his *Stummheit*.

Sitting through the concert wishing it were done with and wishing it would be there forever.

A duo for two tubas by Richard Goldman sets the fanciful tone of the evening.

Between Ardevol's trio for two oboes and cor anglais and Ellis Kohs' chamber concerto, Frank Wigglesworth and John Cage scurry about the stage moving pianos.

Along with the applause, there is a hissing in the balcony—those opposed to atonality asserting their taste.

Not until the preparation for Virgil Thomson's "Capitals, Capitals," does Lou Harrison appear as stagehand, looking elegant in a dark suit. He moves things clumsily with helpless gestures and looks of shocked dismay. Julian says he looks like Schubert.

In the Thomson-Stein combination, four singers feast with great humor and enjoyment on Stein's phrases. Virgil plays the piano part spiritedly.

At intermission there's Remy with a ghastly toothache and Tracy cool and unfriendly. Then suddenly there's Lou. With a big embarrassed grin, saying, "It's nice to see you again" and I know that I'm lost.

Then a very funny cantata by Paul Bowles for soprano, four men, and a harmonium.

"Thomsoniana" is a setting by Peggy Glanville-Hicks of three reviews of Virgil Thomson's music. Her satires of Stravinsky, Satie, and Schoenberg rouse the hissing section to hoots and howls.

In "March Suite" by William Russel, John Cage plays the piano with his elbows. It is scored for a different tempo for each instrument and a metronome is set atop the piano, but the ticker doesn't have a chance against John's vehemence and topples with the early blows.

Cage's impetuous face seizes upon the spirit of the music, qualified as always by his innate efficiency and order.

Then Lou's "Canticle Number 3 for Five Percussionists."

A great to-do on the stage setting gongs, brake drums, cowbells, ocarina, guitar, and pipe lengths in a complicated array on tables and chairs.

Lou conducts. His hands move like miraculous birds. There is precision in disorder and precision out of disorder. He is transformed, regulating sounds with decision and poise.

The ocarina opens the canticle with a dream cry. The brake drums follow, sweet, clear gongs. John Cage plays in this too. Instead of conflict, there is change; instead of contrast, realization. Nothing is left in doubt. It's the only piece at which the hissers don't hiss. And the bravos are many. Lou smiles when he turns for applause. . . . I'm no longer sad.

The program then takes a technological turn.

"*Fugue aus der Geographie*" by Ernst Toch is a recording of place names spoken nine times faster than speech and his "Soundtrack" experiments with the optical track of a sound film.

The last piece, by Cage, innocently named "Imaginary Landscape No. 4," is scored for 12 radios and 24 players. Silence is an important component. Cage conducts explicitly and very smartly. He is stiffer than Lou, and more of a showman.

Julian says the composition suggests driving swiftly across a night landscape catching bits of light. Among the radio players are Richard Miller (all polished, a tie, but no socks), Dick Stryker, Lou Harrison and Jean Erdman.

After the concert Lou acts as if he scarcely knows any of us, as he busily packs up the instruments while we stand watching.

Virgil Thomson comes up on stage fluttering his hands in the air. "Someone just asked me, 'Who is that wonderful composer, Lou Harrison? His music sounds so Japanese.'"

Julian suggests we help Lou pack and everyone exits with bundles. I take a brake drum, but Lou won't let me, insisting it's too heavy. When all the instruments are piled on the sidewalk, a hearse drives up.

John and Remy pile the silent music into the vehicle, which drives off trailing a funereal gloom.

"Don't forget to record this detail in your journal," says Harold Norse, who is always very much concerned with what I write here. I'm flattered.

We decide to go to the San Remo where one can sit in solitude among people, like Proust writing *Remembrance of Things Past* in his little glass booth in the lobby of the Ritz.

May 12, 1951

Harold's finished-thesis party: "I had overprepared the event."

But unlike Pound's guests, ours came.

At midnight Lou and Remy arrived, the spirits in the fairy tale.

Bob and Rose Anderson brought a painter, Norris Embry, who carries with him some German records.

Pink champagne. Dancing. Dietrich and Lenya.

The police and the mad psychoanalysts from downstairs complained.

Norris Embry danced alone, a tangle of strange contortions.

Lou to me, "He's very released, isn't he?"

Lou played a little piece that he wrote for Harold, and danced with Isca, by whom he is captivated. I danced with Joop.

The dawn is heavy; I can scarcely lie under it. The blue light in the window is too sharp. I turn on the electric light to write. And to stay the day a little longer.

May 13, 1951

Here at a lecture at the ANTA Playhouse, I trust that I look as though I am making notes on the lecture instead of writing in my journal. Stark Young, speaking of Duse and Bernhardt, tells hackneyed stories in cross-country lecture style. On the stage is the set for tonight's opening, *Getting Married* by G. B. Shaw. The old-fashioned set matches the speaker.

Young drones on about the successes of Duse at twenty. I turn to Julian with a look that echoes "twenty!" He says, "The life span is longer now."

But I don't work hard enough. Too much of my energy goes into futile romantic attachments and dreams.

In *Getting Married*, a vulgar, sensual woman in a trance of religious ecstasy delivers a great poetic tirade on love within a frivolous pastiche.

Harold, who baby-sat with Garrick, spent the evening writing a birthday poem to Lou, which trips me into an abyss fraught with dreams of vengeance. And all for what? What's Hecuba to me or I to Hecuba?

Now it is 4:30 A.M. and I have just written a poem based on the Seder song "Dayenu": "It would have been sufficient." The tradition calls it a song of degrees: Each blessing would have been sufficient and still the Holy One gave us more.

My theme, instead of plethora, becomes dissatisfaction! Where the insatiable confronts the Eternally Replenishing.

May 14, 1951

Too late to go downtown to the humiliating business of the rounds. I go out with Julian and Bapu (Julian's pet name for Garrick). I'm so busy that I forget how a sun-drenched river and early green tulip trees reveal art a pale artifice. But I am impatient, shrewish, a small soul, crowded and hurried.

I send Lou the poem to be sung, which I have entitled "Music" and dedicated to him on his birthday.

May 15, 1951

A note in Lou's exquisite script:

"Dear Julian, to thank you for the party, to apologize for my none too obscure idiocies and iniquities, and to say" [then to a line of music under which is written] "Happy Birthday to Garrick, Happy Birthday to you. Lou."

Through the whole day without demons or Eumenides: But I look down the street in anticipation of the dark forms' approach.

May 17, 1951

Why is a children's party so melancholic for adults? Julian says it's the memory of those parties at which we were hurt when we were children.

Garrick's second birthday is celebrated by a gala with all his little cousins: Bobby, Ricky, Teddy, Paul, their mothers and much giving of gifts. The children engage in a civilized form of enjoyment that Bernice calls "parallel play."

I'm curious about these people who have become my cousins, but my attempts at conversation are too self-conscious.

I imagine that's how Gauguin felt before fleeing Europe for his chosen Islands. Why did I start to write Van Gogh? Because I juxtapose the madness of the one with the flight of the other as though to signal to myself: This thought of flight is madness.

I baked a birthday cake with a horrible pink frosting that no one could eat.

May 18, 1951

Dicken shows me an article in *Vogue* by Peggy Glanville-Hicks about "Musical Explorers."

A closeup of Lou, only the features in the frame. He is a quarrel between what his mouth reveals him to be and what his eyes insist he is.

P. G.-H. writes of "his music floating and singing with an elegiac sweetness." And:

"His rather rosy-cheeked good looks and innocent blue eyes have sometimes caused him to be called the baby-faced intellectual. But the colorful impression, heightened by a truly hectic taste in socks and ties and a habit of writing his music in colored inks on handmade parchment is misleading. These attributes conceal an erudite and scholarly man, and one with an impressive creative talent."

But I must not spend my days in dolorous dreams of an unresponsive lover. "Must not"?

The clouds are soft and on the radio a song by Debussy and I am dreaming.

This afternoon Harold Norse comes with an issue of *Voices* in which we both appear.

Harold's "Poems for Plays" are luminous moments.

But I'm embarrassed at the sight of my words in print. A poem is as private as a letter, or a journal entry; it belongs only to me. But the printed poem looms up, a land discovered. Real and public, it belongs to everyone. Then the poem eats up the poet.

Spenser's phrase "In the Lion's House," which I use as title for these five lyrics, was chosen on impulse. Or perhaps the poems are little Daniels—fearing to be devoured.

May 19, 1951

Last night at Bill Drewes': parallel play for grownups. People reading, listening to music, classical and modern: Monteverdi, Varèse, Louis Armstrong.

Tony Leeds, an anthropologist, about to descend on the Brazilian natives, was a conscientious objector and talks about the decision to rebel.

May 21, 1951

The color of sky dark green, sky becoming earth and confusing the walker. His feet are in the clouds now.

This is the mind's landscape. The minutes reel backward; iniquities grow in the light of another's honesty as their shadows lengthen.

En route with Robin to a painting show on 9th Street, we meet Price Chatham, who tells the following tale.

He went to his draft board intending to declare himself a conscientious objector. Bullied through a physical and then interviewed by a psychiatrist while standing on line with other draftees, he was given a "psychotic" classification.

But then he thought it over and wrote a letter to the draft board saying that it was all a lie, that he had none of the aberrations to which he had admitted, and explained the moral basis of his action.

Now Price faces a sentence of two years for perjury.

"What they are doing is evil," he says, "but I am no longer part of that evil because I'm in control; I brought my prison sentence upon myself and I am responsible for it."

The art show is a great splash. Some wonderful painters have rented a large loft, painted it white, and hung hundreds of canvases in the bare rooms.

We seek relief from the intense night heat outside, under the sign painted by Franz Kline, lit from the window of a studio across the street. I talk for a long time with John Cage about painting and music and Lou.

After the exhibit there's a party at the Three Arts Club.

John, Merce Cunningham, and Morton Feldman stand in a little circle planning concerts.

Johnny Myers entertains with riotous sketches.

Clement Greenberg jitterbugs violently to Louis Armstrong's "I Ain't Rough." Sidney Janis jitterbugs conservatively and does a very suave tango.

I don't participate. I'm thinking of Price, this boy of nineteen who shames us with his example.

May 23, 1951

I make the rounds with a hopeless air. Yesterday, at Originals Only Playhouse, I saw an interesting arrangement for doing plays in a large room, used both for proscenium and arena theater. No admission is charged; contributions are made by the audience.

I walk along Washington Square Park where the outdoor art show is in bloom, sorry that among all these people not one of them is Lou.

A mounting wish for a ritual to cure the curse, complete with sacrifice and libation.

I stumble into a little café named Sages for an iced coffee and find that this tiny shop is owned by Harry Belafonte, a friend from the Dramatic Workshop, who after his success as a singer, now wants "to sing only for friends" and serve quick eggs to customers.

A discussion at Mount Morris House on the question "Does a group need to have a chairman or a leader?" Julian speaks for the autonomy of the group and the individual and is immediately accused of being utopian. I like the few minutes of meditation. I borrow *The Tale of Genji* by Lady Murasaki from their library.

May 24, 1951

Our fifty-dollar car, The Pardoner, has been destroyed utterly by neighborhood vandals.

Julian and I visit galleries: Twentieth-Century French Paintings at Rosenberg's, Bérard and Berman at Durand-Ruel. Why should I be so insufferably bored? It's not a bad life. I just . . .

On the bus home Julian points out Lou lighting a cigarette on the corner of Fifth Avenue and 57th Street. In Central Park I notice white blossoms dripping with rain. The poems in Lady Murasaki's novel relate all such events in nature to the emotions.

Dicken calls. Richard Miller is coming to use the piano to practice the pieces that Lou has written for Don McKayle's concert. I've gone to the room farthest removed from the music but I hear it still.

While Robin and Julian buy groceries, Richard and I speak of Jacob Boehme's visions, insanity and sanity.

A Thursday: Julian Sawyer tells gory stories of deaths en masse, and details a "prize-winning existentialist suicide." Gil Orlovitz and Sawyer feud. Tony Leeds and Alex Burdett are en route to Brazil and Paris. Dicken reports Lou as saying to Merce Cunningham, "We two will be the only people left in New York and it will be so exclusive!"

Julian Sawyer says that life is a meaningless farce, a magnificent "yak," and that true art exposes this meaninglessness. A devilish negation. I object.

Man is an embryonic state of godhood. We are in the process of becoming immortal. Evil is a vestige of archaic needs that we are outgrowing. Therefore we inhabit a paradox: Evil exists but nothing is evil.

Cannibalism was not thought wicked by right-minded cannibals at a certain stage of history, but then a struggle began (like ours to abolish war and capital punishment), precipitated by a few vanguard theorists, out of whose ranks emerge the revolutionaries, the catalysis, and then the change.

The way is often obscure. Eve's apple didn't do its work well enough. We know something of the difference between right and wrong but we are too confused to be reliable. We should have bitten deeper and swallowed the seeds.

May 25, 1951

After a great deal of difficulty about a baby-sitter, Julian's father consents to stay till 11:30 so that we can go to the "short" concert at the Ninth Street Arts Club to which John Cage invited us.

The movements of Cage's String Quartet are titled: "Slowly Flowing Along," "Softly Rocking," "Almost Stationary," and "*Quod Libitat.*" The piece is dedicated to Lou Harrison.

May 27, 1951

There was a thick crowd at the Remo. At closing time, Joe Martin asks me and Julian to come for a drink at his house.

He is toppling drunk but friendly as we steer him to the street. The air is clean after the rain and some drunken soldiers are climbing about the incomplete Law School Building of N.Y.U. On the way, we meet the people returning from the closing bars, among them the soulful, eccentric poet Ruthven Todd (Ruthven pronounced as in driven).

Our party of four arrives at Joe's house on West 10th Street, full of Picassos, a Miró, and the best Motherwell I've seen.

Ruthven is talkative. Joe resents Ruthven's way of life and flares up, condemning him for worrying about money.

"All I want is my rent paid up: That's the extent to which I want money."

"How much is your rent?"

"Nine dollars a week."

"Well, for Chrissakes, if you can't make nine dollars a week! Go out and earn it and pay your goddamn rent!"

Joe screams so loudly that the expensive things in the room begin to shake.

We proceed toward coffee and find the all-night Art Center Café full of nocturnal creatures coming and going (whence and whither?) as though it were mid-afternoon. Ruthven's baroque literary wit sees us through till dawn.

I enjoy such a night, but it would become sordid with frequent repetition; instead of watching the human show I'd become an actor drudging away at being wretched.

May 28, 1951

The approach of my twenty-fifth birthday terrifies me.

Stop. Stop. Stop. Stop. Stop.

The need to go out night after night frightens me.

I am a figure fleeing in the night, running from the image of Lou. I think of a knife with which I want to end this night demon forever.

My elaborate dressing is a symbolic representation of my preparations for Lou's arrival on Easter eve. My night-time adventure, a ritual enactment.

I'm uneasy if I return home before dawn. But if it's dawn, I'm not weary, and quite content.

May 29, 1951

Robin and I go to Fred Mitchell's studio on Bond Street, which runs at right angles to the Broadway Central Hotel. The sight of Great Jones Street and Jones Alley at night recall my childhood terror of the derelicts who lived there.

We are led up a creaking stairway past lofts smelling of leather, to a door with a combination lock behind which is a cozy garret.

Fred plays Bach on the guitar. He plays wisely. He calls Lou and Morton Brown the hopes of modern music.

We talk of the forms music is taking and of concerts which are not in "the concert world," of art not in "the 57th Street world." I begin to think and wonder. . . .

Robin talks about the theater, but the theater of which he talks is thoroughly corrupted by the inbreeding of a tradition that has begun to destroy its worthy roots.

There is a need for spontaneity. Everything else has been replaced by the film and other mechanical media.

Theater work is now so specialized that no one is permitted knowledge of another's activity. The stagehands paint the flats; the actors stand in front of them.

The only ones involved in all the aspects are the omnipotent and power-corrupted director and the nonartist producer.

There can be a *living* theater only in the work of small groups of people interested neither in effect nor success—except for the successful action.

Plays should be short enough to be easily rehearsed so that they do not deaden in the process. The plots simple. The style pure, direct; not too much scenery; music, but not too much; poetry, but not too many words; perfect tempo.

Attain the perfection of production through the perfection of immediacy.

The Noh is a perfect medium, but the Noh is too rigid.

Better than the Noh's strictness is the short enacted poem, the active, living poem. Gertrude Stein has clues. Work on this!

May 30, 1951

Garrick speaks several words in a row, shows deep understanding, and requests what he desires, but has his father's bad, sudden temper and my grueling, irrational impatience.

To the galleries with Julian. An exciting painting would be lost among the price tags and the code of gallery courtesy. But can one revolt against everything?

Dicken plays Lou's haunting score for Yeats' *The Only Jealousy of Emer*. The sight of Lou's florid calligraphy . . .

May 31, 1951

Today is Julian's twenty-sixth birthday. We don't make enough of the event.

To Hoboken to see Alex Burdett off to Europe. These recurrent leavetakings are so many little deaths—save that the departed pass into life, leaving the homebound in darkness.

Julian wants to travel but I want to accomplish something here first. I should find it dreary to go from place to place with a Kodak and an empty heart.

The idea of a room theater is the only thing that interests me now. It will further more than pursuing the commercial theater. We will do plays in our front room and call it the Theater in the Room.

There is an evil charm of which I have to rid myself. It has brought me untold sorrow from the day I made it. I will not describe it.

June 1, 1951

Looking for plays for the Theater in the Room; Stein and Yeats come readily to mind. And the Noh plays, new and old.

Finish *The White Goddess*, a work that can make changes in the reader, persuading, influencing. . . .

And I am vulnerable.

June 2, 1951

We hear that *Idiot's Delight* is playing its last performance and decide to go because it's a pacifist play.

Supper is rushed with a full kitchen: Remy weeping at onion cutting, Robin officiating over Spanish rice, Dicken washing dishes, Julian feeding the crying baby, and I'm only in the way among the aggregate of male culinary skills.

The seriousness of the comedy was misunderstood, but we applauded City Center for doing it at a time when pacifism is interpreted only as a lack of patriotism.

June 3, 1951

To alleviate the awareness of time passing, Julian and I give a party to celebrate our birthdays.

Am I really to be 25 years old? I feel such a child, such an apprentice. Others my age also seem to me children. Yet I wear my hair in a severe chignon to appear older. What strange old child am I, then?

Tonight I feel languorous, as if our home had changed into a sea kind of place. There are many guests and many gifts, and Julian Sawyer brings a cake with two candles.

Paul and Sally Goodman give us a pamphlet called "Childish Jokes: Crying Backstage," which Paul says is "not good, but very rare." I like this three-minute play, which in spite of the author's "not good" is a perfect piece for the room theater.

In a moment of abandon I show Paul some of my poetry. He is notoriously unkind in his judgments. He says to me, "I don't judge poetry, I discuss it. I don't care whether it's good or bad."

"But the author cares, and wants you to think it good."

"But he shouldn't."

I've been warned that he takes the poem as a psychological revelation and analyzes the poet's conflicts rather than the poet's expression.

Harold wrote us two acrostics, immaculate little lyrical poems. The one for Julian is about strength and goodness; the one for me about romance hidden under a mask of jest.

Dicken is writing us a piece of birthday music, as yet unfinished, and gives us a Japanese print.

There are Bill and Ethel Baziotes, Ethel fragile and Japanese, her sleek black hair drawn tightly away from her pale face; and there's Chester Kallman exchanging dirty limericks with Julian Sawyer.

Suddenly I realize that I'm enjoying myself and he who was not invited isn't causing me suffering.

With Dicken to Katie Litz's opera, *The Wise and the Foolish*. As we take our seats we pass Lou, and I answer his smile. He is with Remy and he is not only pleasant, but flirtatious.

Afterward, Lou walks arm in arm with me. I try to make the conversation simple. But soon, in the bus, his arm close around me, he speaks of *The White Goddess*.

"I know her third and fatal aspect, but it is the middle one that is difficult."

"But she's the important one. A man can't go about torn between his mother and his murderess."

The startled wide-mouthed laugh, "Why, Judith! A man can't be too careful." And he throws his head back in that terrorized, terrorizing laugh.

I'm tempted, but only a little, to tell him of the graven image I have made.

He kisses me fondly in farewell.

June 4, 1951

My hope had been to spend the day working and not let its being my birthday stand in the way.

Rounds in the heat. At Rockefeller Plaza, Bob Carricart, who is happily employed in *The Rose Tattoo*, one of the only two dramatic plays now on Broadway, spends his leisure reading the newspaper leaning on the marble parapet above the gilded Prometheus. He advises me not to be discouraged.

But I've just come from an interview in which I was promised a role if I would bed with a person of repugnant qualities and it's difficult not to be discouraged.

Ambition is a slow train and one gets so impatient with the scenery outside the window.

June 5, 1951

Laid low with a hemorrhage after the theater. It's painless and I'm told it isn't dangerous—only a symptom of anemia.

To the theater tonight—if it can be called that. Julian's parents bought benefit tickets to *Flahooley* for the entire family. There we were, thirteen in a row, exposed to a ghastly spectacle about the production of a laughing doll and the noxious twitterings of Yma Sumac, who is said to be descended from Inca kings. She is renowned for her range of three octaves and a tremendous publicity campaign. The show is riddled with capitalist jokes: "Your eyes are cuter than a thousand shares of American Tel and Tel. . . ."

I came home sick. While waiting for medicine from the drugstore, Dicken played "A Little Birthday Gamelon Processional to Accompany Judith and Julian on a Safe Journey through Next Year," graced with what Dicken calls "Satie-like comments": "a slow start . . . Judith was dressing"; and "the perilous part of the year," a rumble which he says represents danger because too much of it would destroy the music. It leads to love and joy when the danger has passed.

June 7, 1951

Bars are the only social places in this city. They are Court and Tavern, Ball and Marketplace.

Louis' Tavern: Dicken didn't want to go, but we seduced him. He drinks a great deal, but he doesn't get drunk.

From Louis' perforce to the Remo. Otherwise, one wonders what is happening at the other place.

Harold says there is an antipathy between "the dope fiends and the queers" and the "the dope fiends moved from the Remo to Louis' Tavern, but soon everyone followed."

Here is Karl Bissinger, all smiles and subtlety; it is disquieting how nice he is. We talk about the capacity for having fun. With grim faces we discuss it.

Still talking about fun, we go back to Louis' where David Sachs tells Dicken a gossip that upsets him.

All the way home, Dicken weeps, as we remember hundreds of rides in taxis up the West Side Highway above the black weeping river.

June 8, 1951

To what end is one alive?

The odor of summer's unendurable ripeness comes through this window after the rain on the blossoming trees. Birds, realizing the twilight, are chirping unseen.

Dumb as a pantomime, I move through the day.

Sadness of the death of love: no one dies; each goes on to another life.

The ripe hour is too much. The trees smell too green.

June 9, 1951

The Talmud says that a man is not responsible for sins committed in dreams. Freud shows us that we are responsible. Or then again, perhaps Freud has proven that we are not responsible.

Let sleeping dreams lie.

June 11, 1951

Synagogue this Shabbos morning. At the Society for the Advancement of Judaism they have instituted the custom of calling up women to the Torah, and the sight of a woman delivering that intensely masculine blessing shocks me. What's ingrained can't be changed without a struggle—even when the mind approves.

I am closer now to belief in God and prayer than I have been in years. I am certain that our collective presence is an extension of God and that this extension must be thought of as a collective presence.

This is a happy time.

June 13, 1951

Julian gives me two volumes of journals that he kept in the early forties. They are a portrait of confusion striving wholly toward good.

Do I take for granted his flight toward virtue and the beauty of his love?

I love him above all.

Read Harold's *Warnings and Promises*, extremely personal, strictly written poems. Is this a fault? Harold thinks not and speaks of a movement called "personalism."

Many of them are about Dicken, who reads them to me, sadly shaking his head, "Well, at least I'm in literature. . . ." "Three Songs for Plays" are dedicated to Julian and me, *après* the Lady and the Lioness song in *Damocles*.

A *Yahrzeit* visit with Mother to my grandmother's grave.

On the Staten Island Ferry the gray rain draws sky, air, and sea together. I dream of something I am seeking, the name of which I do not know, something I looked for in Lou, in Woody, in Walter McElroy; in Julian, in whom I seek it always. Which I look for in art, observed and practiced. Which I anticipate. In work. In creation. In acceptance. In society. In solitude.

June 15, 1951

Four A.M.: I can't sleep because I will not sleep.

Dicken and Rogers Albritton talk all night in the front room while I wander about the apartment like a specter and read an article in *Tiger's Eye* by John Cage. His dazzling eye, or ear, sees brightly through the dark that I can't penetrate. I watch the dawn come up.

Longing for the medieval stillness, Dicken and I go up to the Cloisters.

Among the tapestries Dicken speaks of his sad heart.

Thunder rumbles and I imagine Héloïse under such arches and the metrics in which her thoughts might sing. But only the thunder and the unicorns were real.

June 18, 1951

Yesterday we drove to the cemetery for a *Yahrzeit* visit to my father's grave. Spring full of melancholy.

We searched out wildflowers in the Ramapo Hills: cinquefoil and clematis and false Solomon's seal. We didn't pick them.

I go downtown to the library in the hope that Guillaume Apollinaire might have written a short play for the room theater or that Yeats has other plays to equal the *Four Plays for Dancers*.

At closing time the readers move through the halls into elevators, like sleepwalkers.

June 20, 1951

Rounds. I sit in an office at CBS and wonder what I am thinking about and realize, suddenly, frightened, that I am thinking about nothing whatever.

June 22, 1951   *Canterbury, Connecticut*

Waking in the country long before the others, I sit on a rock in a field of daisies and rose bushes. From this side the house looks ready to capitulate to the next storm.

How noisy it is! Birds and insects, and at night the whippoorwill, while the silent fireflies outshine the stars.

Now the sun breaks through the mist and sets the dew on the tall grasses adazzle. It is hard to write, I'd rather look and listen.

June 23, 1951   *Canterbury, Connecticut*

Old man Ames is a down-East classic; it's hard to coax him beyond the traditional "ayeh."

We buy dungarees in Willimantic, where a woman leading a leashed baby leopard through Woolworth's draws less comment than she would in a metropolis.

I've read half of the *Bhagavad Gita* in Christopher Isherwood's translation. Gandhi says "the battlefield is in the heart" and that the *Gita* is "the story of the conquest of evil by purity."

Arjuna's pacifist argument is clear: "How can I care for / Power or pleasure / My own life, even, / When all these others, / Teachers, Fathers, / Grandfathers, Uncles, / Stand here ready / To risk blood and wealth / In a war against us? / Though they should slay me / How could I harm them? / I cannot wish it. / . . . Evil they may be, / Yet if we kill them / Our sin is greater."

But the god Krishna answers the human argument by saying that killing is an insignificant act in a scheme in which life and death are equally part of a cycle without end.

For Gandhi, the *Gita* elucidates Karma Yoga, the way of action.

How can we reconcile the way of action with a philosophy in which the fruits of action are never to be desired?

Gandhi, interpreting the *Gita* as the central text of his religious philosophy, says that Arjuna's allusion to family ties shows that the battle exists interior to the warrior; that Karma Yoga is always a battle, but if we interiorize that battle, it is no longer in conflict with *Ahimsa*, the way of not hurting any living being.

June 24, 1951   *Canterbury, Connecticut*

Long flower walk this morning through the woods with Garrick on Julian's shoulders singing monotonous melodies in his father's ears. The smell of pine and cedar.

The well needed to be pumped and cleaned. The fire department did the pumping; however, no volunteer fireman was willing to do the cleaning and so Harold heroically undertook to remove the bloated muskrats drowned in the well. The woodsmen who have a shack up the road come down to watch the dangerous exploit.

The ladder is lowered. Harold descends rung by rung. The pail is lowered on a rope. A wet thud as the first rat strikes metal. Four times. Harold surfaces and I give him a warm beer from the kitchen.

Julian unties the knot and carries the dead critters to the garbage plot and buries them, without fuss or ceremony.

This is an example of Karma Yoga, duty done because it is duty.

Later, Harold speaks of the discipline necessary to accept the death of these creatures as part of their lives, but reading the *Gita* I am struck by my incapacity to do just that.

I read by the light of an oil lamp but the moths are attracted to it, especially the resplendent Io moth, whose beauty enchants us. I panic at their dangerous sport around the flame. Julian goes through all kinds of maneuvers to lure them outside.

June 27, 1951   *New York*

Back in New York, city of wonders and joys. O city containing the greatest number of creation's crowning form: people.

June 28, 1951

In this arrangement of modern furniture which I no longer care for, I am a swan on a lake feigning unawareness of the raw struggle under the surface.

Mother used to recite a poem of Schiller's in which the hero dives below the sacred precincts of the waters and returns with the warning that none should probe what the gods have tried to hide.

In the "know thyself" we dare it—and become gods. But like Jokanaan's mouth, the fruit of the tree of knowledge has a bitter taste.

Noon. They are testing the air raid signals. Death has new sounds and new heralds in our time.

The siren ceases. But the ears, by caprice of the aural memory, repeat it till silence is impossible.

I take some joy in Garrick and his repetitive chatter and his spillings and breakings. When he does wrong he grins up at me and says, "Funny?"

I feel guilt at leaving so much to Julian, who seems to have infinite patience.

Whatever I do, I feel that I should be doing something else.

Fabiola, a gory film by Blasetti about Christian pacifism. The hero kills the soldier who shot the fatal arrow that slew Saint Sebastian; the dying Sebastian reproaches the hero, who swears never to kill again. Later, in the gladiatorial arena he breaks the points off his weapons and defends himself with net and rod against the armed men. This so inspires the soldiers that they throw away their swords.

It's the kind of film that could move a child, as once I was moved by *Nurse Edith Cavell*:

> 1937(?):
> *Nurse Edith Cavell* at the Beacon movie house. Cavell shot by a German firing squad for tending the enemy wounded. At her apotheosis, Anna Neagle's pale and pure image floats over the choir of Westminster Abbey speaking the words she wrote on the eve of her death: "Standing as I do before God and eternity, I realize that patriotism is not enough. I must have no hatred or bitterness toward anyone."
>
> I come home and say to my father, engrossed in his work of enlightening the unlistening world to the plight of the German Jews, "Papa," I say, "you know, we must not hate the Nazis."

And I've been in trouble ever since.

July 1, 1951

In the midst of our planning for the Theater in the Room, the larger plans for the Living Theatre suddenly emerge after four years of struggle.

We can't wait. We can't put off the Living Theatre until we have a theater building of our own.

We decide: We will rent the Cherry Lane.

We make a deal with Leo Shull, with whom the simplest transaction becomes a game of smart moves.

For $1,800 we can have the Cherry Lane for two months.

Left alone with Leo in his office, I no longer have anything to say to this shrewd, ambitious man, whom I admired as the shrewd, ambitious boy who ran Genius, Inc., and from the basement of Walgreen's drugstore published *Actors' Cues.*

We plan three productions:

Faustina by Paul Goodman, which I will direct and for which I have asked Dicken to write the score.

Beyond the Mountains by Kenneth Rexroth, which Julian will direct and in which I'll play the triple role of Iphigenia, Phaedra, and Berenike (Electra).

Gertrude Stein's *Doctor Faustus Lights the Lights*, which I will direct and Julian will design.

And if I imagine the ideal scores they would be Lou's *Beyond the Mountains* and John Cage's *Doctor Faustus.*

July 3, 1951

The Theater in the Room still needs a major opening play.

Crying Backstage will be the curtain raiser followed by the three-minute *Ladies' Voices* for Helen and me. But the substantial play of the evening? We consider Brecht, Yeats, and Masefield.

We drive to Lou Harrison's to ask him for a copy of *The Only Jealousy of Emer* and about music for *Beyond the Mountains*, but he's not at home.

Julian, now that the theater is in motion, can't talk of anything else, never relaxes, nor allows me to relax.

July 6, 1951

Complete program for the Theater in the Room for the 15th of August:

Goodman's *Crying Backstage*, a comic invention; *He Who Says Yes and He Who Says No*, a didactic play by Brecht; Stein's *Ladies' Voices*; and two scenes from Claudel's *Satin Slipper.*

It is Harold's birthday and we celebrate modestly.

Lou's gone to Black Mountain until the fall when he will return here to teach.

July 12, 1951

David Sachs entertains in Bill Simmons' former apartment. He has removed the decorations and painted everything gray. He lives with Rogers Al-britton and Ruby Hill, an aunt who is no aunt.

Marguerite Young is an all-American type wearing a man's blue shirt, taut across great breasts. She has a homely face alight with a mischievous vitality.

She and Marie Menken gossip about Yaddo. Marie is a painter whom Lou admires—another big woman, direct, Catholic in a liberal way, quite attractive, though a shambles.

Willard Maas, her husband, flirts with the young men, especially Jo Jo LeSueur—"the perfect Attic youth"—white-blond hair cut short, a light-tanned complexion, and unblemished features.

Julian argues bitterly with Marguerite who is fervently pro-American and in favor of what she calls "the Iowa farmer." Vehemently anti-communist she calls us communists whenever we disagree with her.

She defends evil as a relief from the boring, sickly sweetness in life, and it is this that provokes Julian's wrath.

There is also much talk of grants and fellowships. I'm reminded of a story that I heard when I was working as a hatcheck girl at Valeska Gert's, about a man who listens to the poets and artists at a literary café talking about contracts, publishers, money, while at the door, he overhears the hatcheck girls discussing André Gide.

Letter and phone talks with Carl Van Vechten. He will permit us to do *Dr. Faustus* for a minimal royalty, providing we don't cut a word. We agree.

Remy will work with us on the Theater in the Room.

We read through the Brecht play. It's a good script, and a moral play. Remy's earnest gravity will lead the spectator to identify with the boy's ethical quandary. In the first telling the boy agrees to sacrifice his life; in the second he refuses. The audience makes its choice, shares his dilemma.

July 15, 1951

Today I made the directing book for *Crying Backstage*. Perhaps I have started on too simple a basis.

July 16, 1951

Driving downtown last night, Julian and I stop at the Broadway Central Hotel.

I return into a womb-world. We explore the dark ballrooms and the ornate halls on the second floor—my fairyland paradise—still embellished with mementos of turn of the century extravagance. I lived a floor above in room 330. The second floor was a layer of consciousness, to be visited only on certain occasions and reserved for special games.

"My mirror"—which resembles, as Julian points out, a dream of Jean Cocteau—still dazzles me in its enormous, sumptuous, though somewhat dusty, ormolu frame.

1938:
A small girl in a pink party dress, the ruffles stiffly reflected, the seed pearls on the round circlet brooch, the white flower, the girl who for the first time was me—a birth moment—and for the last time—a tran-

sition moment. My first inkling that I was, or rather was not but could be seen as, beautiful.

Thereupon some of my early misery vanished and new fears replaced them. A new fear of not being beautiful.

The moment is stamped on the mirror image in my mind. It seemed that I waited here a long time till Tommy Mabel, the doctor's son, came to meet me.

Now Julian's reflection joins me in the glass, a maturation of this rendez-vous.

Time lumps us together.

The tattered glories of the halls with their thick, odorous carpets, engulfs us. The banister of the great stairwell takes me dizzyingly downward as when I slid bodily. The painting on the landing that I recalled as a masterpiece of Adam and Eve fleeing the Garden is only Pierre Cot's sentimental painting *The Storm*.

The fireplace with ten gilt cherubs as large as life tumbling over and under the marble mantel.

I am on the outside, but the mirror, as Cocteau would have it, has drawn me back into itself. "Look into the mirror every day of your life and you will see death at work."

Then to a village bar.

Bang! Out of time into the timeless present.

July 17, 1951

Last night's Brecht rehearsal:

Dicken has the honesty without the stunts of an actor.

Victor Johnson as the Poet and the Great Chorus, has the sonorousness.

Remy, as I had suspected, works with great spontaneity, which enlivens every line that he speaks.

Dicken and Remy help Julian bring home some wood scavenged on the night streets for Julian's faw wood constructivist arrangement for the Brecht play.

July 20, 1951

The Brecht play is depressing and supports my theory that the rehearsal atmosphere is determined by the script, its glooms and gladnesses. Victor, on a ladder as the Great Chorus, kept dropping off to sleep.

But Paul's play is so much fun that it becomes corny if it isn't restrained.

I am petulant with stale, tenacious dreams.

Perhaps I have a fever. I go to the bars though I feel them to be blind alleys in the maze where dreams die.

"Let the world come to you," says Dicken to me. And so I shall. It must be learned. Restrain from plunging at the heart's behest.

Strength through renunciation? It's not honest, is it, to desire the fruits and pretend to disdain them?

Gandhi's admonition not to imagine the future seems stinting the imagination. Or do I confuse fancy with imagination?

But who can curb these horses of the heart without killing them? They'll bite through the bit and romp freely which way they want.

July 21, 1951

Richard Miller comes this morning as I'm brushing my teeth and we talk on the subject of God, about whom Richard has strong, though mixed, feelings.

He is shocked to hear Julian call himself an atheist. Of course Julian isn't, but he doesn't understand his own theology as theology: To say man is God is not to deny God but to welcome a divine existence.

The world. The Korean War continues. The peace talks go on. The U.S. press spills torrents of propaganda. The soldiers die.

July 23, 1951

We walk to 2nd Street to ask Bill Keck to play the Student in the Brecht play and the Angel in Paul's play. We bang on the rainpipe of the loft building and shout till Bill emerges. He played Galba the Gladiator in the anarchists' production of *Faustina* and Paul recommended him to us.

He is sitting on the floor in a Reichian posture, having dinner with a young woman in the sparsley furnished garret. Their barefoot style is soothing and precious.

He agrees to play the Angel and the Student.

July 25, 1951

Paul condescends but has so much to say that it's worth listening to his exaggerations and inversions to come to what's good in them.

We struggle over the moral position of *Faustina*. Paul says Faustina's morality is based on the fact that there is violence in the world, and in this case the violence becomes ritualized. The ritual sacrifice of the gladiator is intended to mitigate our revulsion toward violence. The procedure is not recommended; it is shown as existing.

Faustina transcends good and evil. Aurelius is trapped crying, "Help!" But Galba is dead.

Paul asks me, "What would you do if you killed somebody?"

Aha! Well, what? "Try to save my skin" is my only answer.

I have imagined it, and the imagining is an equivalent to the ritual. And the dreams.

Paul gives my poems back to me and dismisses them with "I can't talk about them because I don't dig them."

"Why?" I pin him down.

He says, "You see so much, that it's sad you can't see more. You are too excited when you write." He quotes: "Emotion recollected in tranquillity."

I dispute it. He calls it indisputable.

Paul points out that I suffer remorse and guilt. I call it a sense of responsibility.

Then Paul analyzed the psychological subtext of the poems.

I'm interested in his psychoanalytic process and he says, "I'll give you a couple of sessions when I come back from Canada."

Surprised and pleased, I accept his offer, though I'm afraid he won't be discreet.

"Why are you afraid to be discussed?" he asks.

I have no reply.

When I'm working on his play, will he think of me as patient or director?

And what happens when, with his condescension and his proud wisdom, he touches people's most private places, where the wound breaks easily? The idea fascinates and revolts me.

I am being extreme now. Oh, yes.

My hand trembles. Write faster.

Julian feels that Remy dominates the rehearsals and wants me to exercise more authority. I, on the other hand, am not eager for wrested authority.

When Julian and I struggle, I am usually wrong in logic, but I stand firmly on my wrongs.

Remy is not the problem. I am my own problem.

Bill Keck tells of his visit to the draft board and the questionnaire he filled out:

Occupation: *Observing nature.*

When did you begin this occupation? *Birth.*

When does this job conclude? *Death.*

Lou has written Remy that he is content at Black Mountain, where he can devote himself to work. He writes on onion skin paper in red ink. The letter like a raw, frail portrait of Lou: "I am so much in love with music. . . ."

Paul had suggested Lou for *Faustina's* music, but we already have given it to Dicken. Lou had said he wanted to do the score for *Beyond the Mountains.*

Van Vechten, who has complete power over Stein's work, rejects John Cage for the *Dr. Faustus* music. "He'd probably score it all for drums," he says disdainfully to Julian and suggests young Richard Banks.

July 27, 1951

The theater is paid for. The deed done. Eighteen hundred dollars spent.

Even Leo Shull, who handles the contract, breaks his businessman's reserve and says, "Gee. All that money."

"Let's hope we have an historic success," writes Kenneth Rexroth, giving us his permission for *Beyond the Mountains.*

Helen and I have grand fun with *Ladies' Voices*, a perfect duo portrait of *Vogue*-ish chatter in which the dressmaker's dummy is the scapegoat, the outsider. We know well how to treat her.

July 28, 1951

Farewell party for Julian Sawyer. Parker Tyler, Charles Boultenhouse, Robert Galster are entertained by Donald Mathieson's and Julian Sawyer's imitations of Bette Davis in various films, of which they know the dialogue by heart.

I look at my poems. I can't write the opera. There is no fiction. It is all true, even the plays and the films are real and open the vision to the other realities.

Death is not like something else. . . .

July 30, 1951

At this late hour we drop our plans for the Claudel piece for the Theater in the Room. It's too sentimental, too much heavy cream. Instead Julian and I will perform "The Young Man and the Mannikin," a scene from Lorca's *If Five Years Pass*, with music by Dicken.

Remy has gotten (I think from Jean Erdman) some fine Hawaiian lava stones for the percussion music in the Brecht play. They look like any other black stone, but make a more vibrant thud.

July 31, 1951

Dick Banks is modest, almost immoderately so. He brings us two "children's pieces": "Walking Pieces" and "Pieces for People." He will return in a month with "sketches" for *Dr. Faustus*.

Leo Shull gives us a lecture demonstration on how we could spend $250 on publicity for *Showbiz* and win instant fame. We refuse. He says this week in his gossip column that we have $5,000.

Reading excerpts from Gide's journals in *Kenyon Review*. How he conjures the quality of a person or place with an unadorned sentence!

August 1, 1951

At the Non-Objective Museum of Hilla Rebay, only the Baroness' and Bauer's work is really bad. While I try to enter the dimensions of Mondrian and Kandinsky, two bored-looking young people follow me, turning the light on as I approach a hall and turning it off behind me. [12]

Return to the Cherry Lane. We walk around the familiar premises planning renovations and repainting. We'll need to begin by cleaning up.

A good rehearsal of *He Who Says Yes and He Who Says No*. Bill Keck and Dicken use the stones skillfully and the whole play responds to the percussion.

Dicken is suffering from his prison experience, though he's never spoken much about it.

"I was young," he would say, "and when one is young one can stand a great deal that would be unbearable in later years." But now he talks about prison because he feels imprisoned in our house, feels his room intolerably cell-like, and sleeps instead in the studio.

He speaks of his analysis as a period of waiting which he confuses with his prison term, feeling he's doing "bad time."

His experiences in the prison strike in Chillicothe and in solitary fill me with premonition, fear that draws no line between anticipation and memory.

The worst moment for prisoners, he says, is the moment before the door shuts for the night.

August 2, 1951

Finish Apollinaire's *Poète assassiné*.
Tristouse Ballerinette pokes out the poet's right eye with her umbrella while

the crowd tortures him to death. The poet says "I confess my love for Tristouse Ballerinette" as he sees her with his last sight.

Surrealism has the appropriate metaphors for the world's madness and cruelty.

Read Charles Glen Wallis' brilliant article on *Blood of a Poet* in a *Kenyon Review* from 1944.

After a party at our house, Nelson Gurney borrows the book of Toller's plays.

"When I was in school we performed a play of his called *No More Peace* and Toller came to see it, and the next morning he was dead. We felt," he says, "somehow responsible for his suicide." Then he almost imperceptibly shrugs his shoulders.

Nelson writes copy for Lucky Strike. *Caveat Emptor.*

August 7, 1951

At a dance class given by Merce Cunningham, I watch Remy dance with boyish sturdiness. Merce keeps time on a set of drums with a very hard beat.

We work on renovations at the Cherry Lane. Then go to the Provincetown Playhouse whence we swipe—after some adventures—a dressmaker's dummy for *Ladies' Voices.*

Bill Keck dampens our spirits. "Life is different downtown," he explains. His friends are prejudiced against our West End Avenue address, against playing a thirties play by Brecht. We try not to show how much we are upset by this criticism. But the spirit, the group's self-confidence, suffers.

August 8, 1951

Never have I been so nervous at the approach of a play. In one's room one is so personally responsible.

I am atop the roof under a feeble, penny-sized sun, working on lines. The sky is chalky gray, I am a taut ball of twisted fiber.

I am afraid of the people we have invited to the plays.

August 9, 1951

Rehearsal of the Brecht play. Open hostility from the cast and condescension from Bill Keck. It is easy to love when you are loved, but otherwise. . . .

The Room plays demonstrate our intentions. We invite 20 people for each performance. A row of 10 on benches against one wall; in front of them, 10 cushions on the floor.

Remy creates fanciful invitation cards. Julian and he do a crayon and ink drawing on each one.

August 10, 1951

At Lou's apartment to fetch the clavichord for the Lorca play. It is fragile, as befits its maker. Now it is here on our foyer table. I wish I were able to play it.

August 11, 1951

The Lorca is not yet blocked for this evening's dress rehearsal. Madness, but I'm in good cheer.

August 14, 1951

Though most of the work is miraculously finished, dress rehearsal went as badly as possible.

Afterward, in the San Remo, we toast in champagne to commemorate Garrick's conception three years ago.
A ragged drunk approaches our table. In terrible shape. Ash blond hair askew. He lurches forward, his hands resting on the table. Directly to Julian: "What's your name?"
"My name is Julian Beck."
"My name is Maxwell Bodenheim. I'm an idiotic poet."
And he turns and moves off before we can speak.

August 15, 1951

"I hate the theater," I say to Dicken.
His expression like the look of a child discovering some disturbing actuality.
"Why?"
"Because she is cruel to me."
Cruel? Like a nightmare beast, with a lash and tongs, for striking and piercing. Like a man enamored of a vampire, I follow her fatally. Isn't there some way to break out of the fairy-tale's distorted landscapes?

August 16, 1951

Everything went better than I could have dreamed.
Remy arrived with Merce and John, while we were still at dinner. A thunderstorm broke. Rain is a good omen, as is a bad dress rehearsal.

I listen from the bedroom door to *Crying Backstage* and fret because I fear it is playing too quietly and without enough tempo.
Then I go on for the Brecht. Suddenly the sanctuary of one's home is full of judging eyes, observing too closely.
It will never again seem hard to act on a stage where the distance and the lights are so protective, where the audience can't see every flick of the eyelash, the motions of the tongue in speech, every trembling of the fingers.
Remy stands beside me at the opening. When I tremble he puts his hand on my shoulder, and when it doesn't calm me he presses tightly so that it hurts. As in some potent therapy, the tension vanishes in that moment of pain.

The staging as austere as the play. The striking of the lava stones and Remy's movements support the argument of the story, as does the bare wood construction of Julian's set. When we cross the narrow pass, the stone that hangs by the string wavers like a pendulum.

The Stein drew calls for encores.

During the Lorca, Julian and I scarcely see each other under the deep blue light. I wear a heavy veil, which protects me. But I regret my uneven steps in the presence of Merce and Sudie Bond and Shirley Broughton.

The music serves as a screen. Dicken plays the harp and Bill the bamboo flute. After our exit, the dying fall of the pavane ends the evening.

Then a whole happy hour of the pleasure of being appreciated.

John Cage and I continue the discussion we started at the Ninth Street Gallery when he said that the painters were getting away from the art world and the musicians were getting away from the concert world.

It was Robert Edmond Jones who first advised us to work in a room with no money at all—as we did—and it was Harold who read us Yeats on chamber theater.

And the night at Fred Mitchell's with Robin, when I insisted that a play could consist of an actor walking once across a floor, or making one perfect gesture, and that a play could be ten minutes long, an idea first implanted by Valeska Gert's satire on theater at the Beggar Bar.

This work tonight came out of these talks—the advice of Jones, and Yeats, and Norse and Cage.

But John says: "It grows out of a need more than anything else."

August 17, 1951

The second night of Theater in the Room. Though the audience's approval is wholehearted, it is as if this kind of theater outside of the commercial had always been one of the possibilities.

Mail: A letter from Claude, who is sending us his play *The Idiot King*, warns that he wants only the most sensitive production.

And a fancy note from Van Vechten to announce his arrival.

August 19, 1951

Julian starts to shout suddenly in the middle of the scene when he looks up and sees Carl Van Vechten straining to hear. V.V.'s a handsome, white-haired man, who speaks mildly and without affectation. His secretary, Saul Mauriber, and Milton Saul flank him like a guard of honor. He is pleased with *Ladies' Voices* and delivers compliments: I look like a dancer, like the great dancers.

And tonight another who "sells light," Karl Bissinger, with Johnny Nicholson and their gallantry. Only Peter Farb did not seem to like it.

Gene Derwood raves, "You are not and cannot play a real woman. You are a mask, a piece of poetry. Plays must be written for you. I'll write a scenario for you for one of Curtis Harrington's films. You are wasting your time as a wife and a mother. . . ." Oscar Williams thanks us with a silent nod.

After closing night, late into the night at the Remo. Then we wake early for Garrick.

A terrifying dream: I have told Dicken a secret and this knowledge has been discovered by a band of criminals. They have imprisoned us in our house; there are many other people, but they cannot help us. The criminals have a mysterious, immaterial murder device, a psychological method of killing with a look and a touch. The victim slowly loses his willpower; no matter what he does he will wither and die in a few hours.

Our four captors are jazz musicians. Their leader is a handsome man who wears a metal band on his head which holds a jackknife.

Julian searches wildly through some school notes which, he claims, contain a remedy, a simple antidote.

I can't bear to watch Dicken's slow death, and blurt out that I'm going to call the police. The handsome gangster comes toward me, touches my shoulder, looks into my eyes as with deep tenderness, smiles, and says, "Now you have it too."

I panic. We await death in Dicken's room. I see myself in a large mirror, half my hair dyed yellow. Remy, too, is there under the influence of this spell. Julian, who has some kind of immunity, suddenly finds the answer: light and cold water. As simple as that. A kind of awakening and ablution. We put on all the lights. I wash my face. I feel less numb. We go to rescue Dicken who is still in his room in the dark. He is slumped over. Asleep? I am terrified.

Julian awakens me. Even now, I'm shaken. For hours I panic when anyone turns the lights off.

August 21, 1951

The Theater in the Room is over. Immediately we schedule the Living Theatre's Cherry Lane opening for December, 104 days from now.

A note from Carl Van Vechten: He wishes to photograph *Ladies' Voices*. We're to go to his apartment tomorrow night with props and costumes. He will supply the dressmaker's dummy.

A letter from J. Laughlin this morning completes our royalty arrangements for all three plays.

August 23, 1951

Many wonderful paintings in Van Vechten's home and some bad ones, and a scintillating view of the twilight skyline across Central Park. Helen, who raves of Italy, is forced to exclaim, "No other city in the world has this!"

Inside are thousands of *objets d'art* fastidiously arranged. Many things of silver, which is fittingly the photographer's favored color.

A fine self-portrait of de Chirico from his best period reveals a determined profile and a phallic tower. An early full-length portrait of V.V. as a clear-eyed youth. Covarrubias, Stettheimer, Barthes.

We sit on couches covered with summer fabric. V.V. wears a white shirt falling loosely over his waist. He greets everything with deliberation. Saul Mauriber, aggressively polite to V.V., is cruel, condescending, and loving: making it uncomfortable for outsiders to watch them or be caught between them.

V.V. talks of Gertrude assuming that she is much less understood than she is.

No one addresses V.V. directly because of his deafness. One can only bring up a subject and leave it to Saul Mauriber to relay.

The lights are already set up in one of the innumerable rooms. A curtain is drawn and the dummy (Fania Marinoff's dress form) is readied. Quite by ourselves, Helen and I strike the attitudes of *Ladies' Voices* and V.V. says no more than "all right" and snaps. No poses are discussed. The lighting is flat, head-on. It seems the simplest thing in the world. Helen, who once was assistant to Erwin Blumenfeld, renowned for his endless fussing, is shocked.

Then he photographs Julian against a patterned cloth.

Van Vechten keeps a portfolio of postcard-size prints. His portraits of actors and artists are uniformly good. He says that his photographs document something, "As my writing documented something," but it isn't certain what.

He has not yet, he says, photographed everyone, but says he will do so sooner or later.

Van Vechten agrees to be on the Sponsor Committee for the theater.

Later at home, Julian makes a postcard collage with "Augustine the dummy" and all of her props for Van Vechten.

August 25, 1951

To a party at Larry Rivers' studio on St. Marks Place, decorated with streamers and balloons. Enormous windows open to the street a few feet below. The neighborhood people assemble outside looking up at the party. A guest to whom I was never introduced invites me to "escape the wrath of the peasants and flee with me in the troika."

The jester is not too wrong. The artists dance without shoes and play the jazziest records, but feel their separation from the neighborhood people.

Larry's two sons are tousled ruffians in constant motion.

Johnny Myers feels we should continue in the room and not go into the Cherry Lane.

"Obey the text," he says. "The theater today is interested in everything but the text. It is concerned with lights, with stars, with scenery. Forget lights, stars, sets. Give a perfect representation of the text. Be true to the play. Don't have actors rave and rant and fall on the ground. Don't worry about professionalism. Don't think about publicity or ticket sales. You have a beautiful thing. Don't waste it. Create a style of your own. Strip everything bare. Make it perfect."

To a version of *Potemkin*, which I recall as a great film but which has been edited into a modern paean to Stalin, courage, and World War II.

Two cards from Remy. One a wrapping-paper and ink collage of Black Mountain under the moon. The other a sad note: "Things are very black at Black Mountain. Lou is in a stew, drunk (now and mostly), and I don't want to be here when the pot blows off."

Ah, that I were the beneficent goddess who could bestow happiness on those I love.

August 27, 1951

Visit George Amberg in his home. He's the director of the Modern Museum's theater library. His neat manners, well-kept home, and correct wife stress his obsessive good taste.

We ask him what he would like to direct: Genet's *Les Bonnes*.

But Genet is in prison, he says. And Amberg doesn't know how to get the rights.

Two Cocteau films at the Thalia, *Orpheus* and *The Eternal Return*. Even when the magic becomes transparent it remains moving in the way that mathematics remains astonishing after the process is explained.

Cocteau's Death says, "What I am doing would not be understood in any world."

August 29, 1951

A telephone call from a man who says, "You don't know me, my name is Gershon Legman. I work on *Neurotica*."

But it is he who does not know me, nor that his magazine has published one of my poems.

His call concerns a translation of *Ubu Roi* which he and his wife have made.

We are, however, awaiting word from Walter McElroy on his translation, and in case he can't complete it in time, we've spoken to Paul Goodman about the possibility of his doing it.

I am full of prejudices about Legman, but he is unexpectedly sympathetic and ready to accept us as allies.

His work, he says, is an attempt to overcome the sadism in our lives by exposing the sexual motivation of our behavior. And the roles in which habit, propaganda, and the culture have cast us. He admits that his interest in sadism implies a sadistic trait.

Legman artfully makes fanciful paper creatures by folding squares of paper in intricate patterns. He says that he and the Spanish philosopher Unamuno are the only occidentals he knows of who practice this Japanese art. Its fragility seems at odds with the crude stories he tells as he folds the paper. Legman is all sensationalism.

A letter from Remy. He's sad. He describes Lou, sitting behind him in the kitchen, withdrawn. Remy doesn't want to do the *Beyond the Mountain* sets. He wants to concentrate on dance.

August 31, 1951

Clearing the Cherry Lane. In the scene dock, ancient things. Dust. Incredible amount of work.

Working on Stein's *Doctor Faustus Lights the Lights*. The over-simple words breaking the language to smithereens. The ideas, too, both dark and radiant.

How do you go to hell? "Kill something." What a brave declaration!

September 9, 1951

We work to capacity on the theater.

Death or glory.

Now we move ahead. On the Living Theatre letterhead, all the news is clearly printed in gray ink.

Dr. Faustus lights the lights in darkness and luminosity. The task, like the text: too clear and yet too obscure.

September 12, 1951

At Oscar Williams', Gene Derwood preaches most ardently the gospel as a solid humanism with which no one can argue.

September 15, 1951

Lou wants to do the *Beyond the Mountains* score. He did not know that we'd already promised it to Richard Stryker.

"It is so close to me," he said. "I mean the subject matter, especially after the Yeats."

We give him the *Faustina* script hoping he will find it as enticing as *Beyond the Mountains*. But who can predict him?

At Van Vechten's, we see our kodachromes projected on a large screen. The stranger on the screen seems gorgeous and ugly, the proportions juggling the eyeball.

September 16, 1951

Lou puts his desire aside and accepts Dick's doing the music for *Beyond the Mountains*.

He thinks that John Cage should do *Dr. Faustus*, even though Van Vechten has committed us to Richard Banks.

At a party at Larry Maxwell's bookshop, Charles Norman, the Marlowe biographer, is shocked when we tell him that Stein has treated the Faustus theme.

September 17, 1951

Work. Each day now a workday.

Bob de Niro lives in a garret on West Broadway. Legman was there and spoke incessantly of sex ("Subject B," as he calls it) with a fanaticism that cannot be gainsaid.

De Niro is a man of few words. His painting is tough, which is its virtue.

In the subway, Julian and I sit across from a thin, ascetic man dressed like a worker, clothes neat, but soiled, as from a day's hard work.

And monstrous, hideous feet. I fantasize the taking of a vow, perhaps twenty-five years ago, not to wash his feet or to remove the shoes that he was then wearing. The filth-coated feet are grown thick with sores, swollen, and hoof-like. The decaying shoes have merged with the skin which emits a gruesome, sickly odor. We did not leave the train. We felt bound not to.

September 18, 1951

Work on press releases, scripts.

Dick and Harold here with Howard Griffin, who restrains his talk as though testing the ground before treading on it.

September 21, 1951

Visited Lou; he has not read *Faustina* yet.

He plays us the music he has written during the summer: a chorale for Katherine Litz with heavy chords splashed with flutterings, like black moods threaded with joviality.

Tomorrow Lou will have gone back to Black Mountain.

September 25, 1951

A night at John Cage's.

His home is a bare white room, only the the black piano gleaming amid the ceiling-high plants that breathe a chlorophyll cleanliness into the air. On the floor, there is matting, a large marble slab as table, ashtrays, candles, and long strips of foam rubber against two walls for seating.

Both Merce and John have an unassuming way of living more in present time than we. Merce's renowned grace extends even to his speech.

Above all, an affectionate attachment to their creative powers, neither careless nor fanatic.

When art becomes pleasure it will find its function.

Outside John's windows, the East River and a fantasy of changing lights, glowing and flowing.

It's effortless—like Cage when he smiles and his eyes narrow to nothing and laughter crinkles his plain features to a look that the beholder wants to emulate.

He is explaining his newest work to a music writer named Slonimsky and the writer's fifteen-year-old daugher, Electra. The new piece is based on chance and on a Chinese "book of chance"[13] which explains the exactness and mystery of the random. Can mystery be explained or only discussed?

Each note is determined by the flip of a coin—pitch, duration and intensity are tossed for. The notation represents a spatial relationship to duration. That is, time and the millimeters of music paper have equivalent value.

Interesting and intricate. It would be boring if there were no faith in mystery. Slonimsky asks, "What if you have bad luck?"

"There is no such thing as bad luck," says John.

John plays a small piece, "Valentine of the Seasons." This is the first time I have heard the famed fixed piano: melody in rich unexpected tones, celestial in quality. I am tremendously impressed with Cage's work. And with his whole *esprit*.

There is a Goshen in this Egyptian darkness in which we live, and coming close to it we are filled with premonitions of promise.

Years back, walking in a daze of tears for some forgotten sorrow after a pointless revel in Val and Julian's room, I thought over and over in a tragic strain, "No, this is not it," as though detoured on some odyssey. Now I have a distant view, as of a place not yet visited with which I am already familiar by picture postcard.

Merce talks about their use of our theater for concerts and dance recitals.

John proposes a concert for a piano piece by Satie called "Vexations." The piece consists of 840 successive renditions of a minute-long composition. There are 840 minutes in 14 hours.

If John has the theater all day, from ten in the morning through ten-thirty at night, the hour critics must leave . . .

We enjoy talking about the ramifications of this idea.

A round ticket like a clock is printed. Audiences come and go all day long. The piece is played over and over. Admission is not charged but the entrance time is punched and the minutes counted at the exit. And the longer one stays the less one pays. That is: one pays according to how much one can tolerate, not for the space one takes up. For ten minutes, $14.40; for 20 minutes, $7.20; for half an hour, $3.60; down to five cents for 12 hours.

And a printed time-table of performing artists, for John can get all sorts of artists to play, from painters to renowned pianists. It might read:

A.M. 9:18–9:23 John Cage
9:23–9:28 William Masselos
9:28–9:33 Richard Lippold
9:33–9:38 Richard Stryker
9:38–9:43 David Tudor

and in this way use dozens of people.

The score is mimeographed on 840 sheets of paper each discarded after playing.

During the concert, talk, selling books, sandwiches, seat-hopping, etc. *Musique d'ameublement*, or furniture music.

We also talk of a David Tudor concert.

Merce is reading *Beyond the Mountains*, and would like to do the choreography, but his schedule is difficult.

John says he'd like to do a score for us.

John and Merce advise us not to use newspaper advertisements, but to concentrate on mailing lists. And to use sandwich men on stilts, or men with drums. . . .

They make us more alive.

On the river the lights move.

September 28, 1951

Julian and I return like pilgrims to the Chinese Theater under the Manhattan Bridge only to be told, "Disbanded forever. Nevermore in New York."

We solace ourselves with the ballet, but the dancers' gestures seem absurd; even Youskevitch and Alonso too forced.

Cocteau's *Le jeune homme et la mort*, about the goddess, the desirable woman who crushes and kills her lover—what Graves calls the "eternal" theme.

October 1, 1951

At Merce Cunningham's home we pick up his mailing list.

Sudie Bond, whom we met at Bonnie Bird's when Lou's *Eiffel Tower* was performed, wants to work with us. She has an extraordinary face.

Yesterday, Gershon Legman read his pneumatic translation of *Ubu Roi* to us.

October 3, 1951

In synagogue, I think during the silences which I no longer fill with prayer. It is necessary to be detached, stoic, distant. The problem is how to be detached, and still do what is necessary. To act with detachment when detachment contradicts "to act." Karma Yoga says: "Action without fruits."

October 5, 1951

The Cherry Lane is charged with unmanageable energies. I walk through webs of tensions and networks of danger.
Memory and desire catch me across the entrance to Commerce Street, permeated with the recollections of many loves.

October 8, 1951

Sometimes I'm frightened by the amount of work involved. No one can know how much we do in one hour, or how Julian and I plan our minutes.

Mother's illness has gone on too long for her to bear it uncomplainingly. She can't walk easily and grows sad at her disability. She'll come to live with us after Yom Kippur.

October 10, 1951

Many problems: We shall have to raise six months' rent for the theater. And pay for license fees, violations, water. . . .
Financial woes. Julian on edge.
Kenneth Rexroth sends several letters objecting to our doing all four plays of *Beyond the Mountains* in a single evening.

8/X/51

Dear people—

I think you are very mistaken in attempting the four plays at once. Such an idea never occurred to me. I think the audience would be worn out halfway through—as well as the actors. The more I think of it the less inclined I am to consent to such a program. There is no use in throwing away the effectiveness of the plays. . . . The dances, though not lengthy, do take up enough time to, for instance, fill up an evening with Hermaios and Berenike. The tempo should be leisurely—even slow—to get across the frozen, hypnotized effect of the people in *Beyond the Mountains*. The whole point is that, during the actual moments of the birth of Christ, they are living through the action of the *Oresteia* like sleepwalkers. . . .
[The music] *must* be kept extremely simple—diatonic—"white"—like Satie's *Gymnopedie*—and with a minimum of "effects." It is *very* difficult to get a composer to understand just how stark and hieratic it must be. . . .
I got an impressive letter from your musician. If he writes music as well as he writes about it, he should certainly do. . . .
Once again—put out of your minds the scheme of doing the plays all at once, straight through. I really know quite a bit about the theater and I assure you you will just be throwing them away. Ask anyone with practical experi-

ence—radio—burlesque—musical comedy, or vaudeville—or the movies—
NOT some highbrows—and you will get the same answer. . . .

Faithfully,
Kenneth Rexroth

He has no idea of how ambitious we are. Now we have to convince him of the plausibility of doing the full program.

Cage, Cunningham, and Johnny Myers are against our doing *Beyond the Mountains*. They abhor the intensity of its emotions.

Isn't it a sign of an overdeveloped culture, to search for a more and more bloodless stylization as in the cool Noh, or the unnatural attitudes of late Hellenistic sculpture?

John McGrew said that a symptom of a decadent period is always a futile attempt at pastoralism.

October 18, 1951

Casting. Every ten minutes a new face. Yet an extraordinary personality would not be lost among them.

Rexroth writes, in answer to Julian's letter saying that Goethe, too, wrote some long plays:

15 X 51

Dear Judith and Julian—

Goethe was wrong. Go ahead *BTM en gros* if you want—but I think you're ill advised. As to commercial vs highbrow theater, there is more theatrical sense in one old carnival or burlesque man—or in somebody like Jolson or W. C. Fields—than in all the O'Neills and Tollers laid end to end. You cut the plays as you see fit. This can only be done in rehearsal anyway. That is where you can tell if the lines will cross the footlights—beauty or dramatic profundity is worthless if the actor can't manage it or the audience can't follow it. I doubt if masks are actually desirable. Actors always mismanage them and actresses naturally hate them. They do permit dancers to stand in—also they are hard to hear through. As for the dancers—no Wigman, Graham or Pearl Primus, please! What I envisage is an extremely slow but dynamic movement—even more normal than a regular *pas de deux* and very hieratic—especially in the Phaedra and Iphigenia. There are books of Hindu and Buddhist *mudras* and of Tibetan Buddhas and Bodhisattvas in all the regular *mudras* which would give the dancer a hint of what I mean. And of course the two basic positions are those of the Buddhas and their Shaktis in Tibetan sculpture and painting—one of which represents sexual intercourse sitting, the other standing. You can see these things in any book on Tibetan Art. BUT—the end product should *not* look oriental. The Huns' dance at the end of the book is a typical Chinese military dance of the kind given in the plays based on the three kingdoms. If you ask at the local Chinese movie they can tell you when they are going to give such a movie. They're common enough.

Faithfully,
Kenneth Rexroth

Four designers.

Each of them has made a peculiar contribution. Each saw us on the basis of the letter we sent.

Donald Oenslager in his office in the tower of the Times Building is a portrait of security, framed behind his large desk by an enormous screen like a backdrop. He reminisces about the Provincetown, and Robert Edmond Jones and "the days when we were all dedicated."

The dedication has been lost in the old rarified air of our age of despair.

He scrutinizes Julian's designs and approves of them. He warns us about actors.

Do I delude myself that Oenslager seems envious of us? Not that he isn't proud and grandiose, but he seems to be struggling with a fond memory that threatens his complacency. For he has everything except what we have: a project to be committed to.

He says he will be on the advisory committee, that he would like to do real work for us.

"We were all dedicated then."

As if to say: "It is your turn now."

Horace Armistead, in his workmanlike studio on University Place conveys friendliness without smiling often. He's a craftsman interested in construction and the details of execution. We weren't aware when we went to him that he's production manager for the Metropolitan Opera.

On an easel, a soft-hued oil painting for Anthony Tudor's *Lilac Garden*.

How do these people have the time for it? And the time to see us? He manages all the Metropolitan's productions and designs independently, and yet shows none of the wear we show. The energy seems to flow effortlessly from those who have some measure of success.

Does the success bring about the calmness, or does the calm bring about the success?

Armistead too, will be a sponsor of the theater; He gives us the addresses of various theatrical suppliers.

Aline Bernstein. In a large, ill-furnished apartment on Park Avenue, the beautiful elderly lady lies in a small sunny bedroom. She is able to smile through her many troubles. In one hand a hearing aid stretched toward us, and the other went frequently to her face to shield the eye which is temporarily sightless from a hemorrhage.

Her backlog of remembrances: the Civic Repertory where she designed for Eva Le Gallienne; the Neighborhood Playhouse and the events there of which Thomas Wolfe wrote so innocently when he loved this lady.

She praises Julian's work.

She is sad, she says, to be "indisposed and out of things," but chats about the book she is writing and the sets she's designing and the rehearsals she's been attending. Next to her bed is a dictaphone (to which she said "excuse me" when we entered). This work she considers "not working."

Framed above her bed are her famous designs for *The Little Clay Cart* and, in a rack, designs for a book of costumes which she complains no one will publish.

What is most striking is the energy and the strength of this woman, ill and handicapped and yet so capable.

She agrees to be a sponsor. She gives us warnings and advice:

"Beware of light on the stage; it dims the actors, makes the text fade out into silhouette.

"I always underdesign. I make elaborate notes. I describe the whole room, all the details, but I always underdesign."

Aline Bernstein says that she knows no one who works as hard on a play as she does.

Frederick Kiesler is a small man whose expansive spirit towers like some fire-bearing Prometheus. His is a German rudeness-kindness. He ushers us in and growls, "Well, what is going on here? What is this all about?"

Immediately his eyes have discerned everything about us. All our secrets are revealed, filed, evaluated.

He calls in an assistant, a beautiful Chinese girl who obviously adores her teacher. And he deserves to be adored. There is something of Piscator in what he says, and in his self-esteem.

He speaks often of the beauty of women.

Listens with many interruptions to our story.

"This is very fine, but I have only this to tell you: You work very hard. You work forty-eight hours a day. Very good. Very fine. But if you are not geniuses, this does not mean a gott-damned thing. You have to be a *génie*. In this is everything. If you are geniuses, I guarantee you that you make a success. And if you are not, all this work is nothing for."

We were forced to choose the alternative of being geniuses—the tactic of a great teacher.

He leans heavily upon the *mise en scène*; considers the key to production what Johnny Myers calls obligation to the text.

Kiesler gives us ample space to boast, which is a great pleasure. He allows himself that prerogative also.

He recommends a play called *The Nineteenth Hole of Europe* by Cyril Connolly, a science-fiction fantasy set in a marsh fog that covers postwar Europe. With a eureka expression, he describes the scene: "The audience is given mimeographed pages of pictures of buildings—Westminster Abbey, the Cologne cathedral, all the landmark buildings of Europe—and the audience has, each of them, a candle and they can turn to whichever page they please, as this could be everywhere.

"On the stage, the actors sit on stools like my draftsmen, in very harsh light without costumes.

"How inspiring for the actors to look out and see all those candles in the audience."

It sounds like one of those ideas Piscator brought up in theater research classes, delivered with vigor and the pleasure of invention.

He places our success into the hands of chance, the chance that we have the *génie*. He understands us better than the other designers.

Kiesler knows how much depends on "the muse. She is a hard lady to please."

To the lady hard to please, then.

Kiesler is a sponsor of the Living Theatre.

On the wall, a painting in grays, browns, black, and dull lavender of a large chrysanthemum. Kiesler proposes a riddle:

"If you know who is the painter of that you will be a success."

Julian recognizes the Mondrian.

Let us hope it is prophetic.

October 21, 1951

Casting. Faustus proves a problematical man to cast.

Helen has fallen in love and consequently will not be able to play Marguerite Ida and Helena Annabel.

Still no music from Dick Stryker. Perhaps he is right in saying that we expect too much of people.

We do, we will, we must.

October 22, 1951

Dr. Faustus casting. Marguerite Ida and Helena Annabel: searching for someone who can convey Gertrude Stein's womanly view of this male legend: a Gretchen who does not redeem Faust, but dies in her own innocence.

Work on the directing book. Much freedom within the text. No stage directions in Stein.

Various printers: Trubow's little broken-down press for our tickets and stationery. And a fancy printer, who does work for Kenneth Patchen and other touchy jobs, for our announcements.

In search of a choreographer for *Beyond the Mountains* we call Tei Ko, the Japanese woman who danced the Noh dances at the Poet's Theater. Her little boy is named after Prince Genji, spelled variantly so as to mean Way of Peace; he was born at the signing of the peace between Japan and the United States.

Way of Peace was dressed as a most unpacific cowboy: toting two cap-guns, which he exploded incessantly, causing his mother much distress.

Tei Ko is surely the right person to choreograph *Beyond the Mountains*.

October 23, 1951

We have seen at least 350 actors. Not a moment's quiet. We eat in their presence.

Still no Doctor Faustus. No Marguerite Ida.

October 25, 1951

How a landscape can blacken, all light eclipse, all sun hopes vanish. How swiftly what was a garden is wilderness.

The pressures of the theater sustain me; my obligations steady me.

October 27, 1951

The play is cast: We find Donald Marye, who has just that look of soft Faustian wisdom that can allure Marguerite, and a cynical depth that is beyond his own comprehension.

Kathe Snyder, a poetic girl from the Workshop, is Marguerite.

Ace King for Mephisto—how fitting that the spirit of evil is played by a playing card, as if to say, "It's all a game."

Remy Charlip, back from Black Mountain, will play, will dance, will choreograph the Viper's role. No one else could bring it so much.

October 30, 1951

Luncheon with Eric Bentley. The hard critic intimidates me more than the accomplished artist.

Bentley seems not to be forming opinions, but we know that he is constantly judging.

One would think him less brilliant than he is, as he looks away in apparent disinterest, and then an astute observation reminds one that he is acutely present.

Later he warms and recommends several plays. Wishes to direct a play for the Living Theatre if he likes the early work.

Rehearsals: I feel this play under me. I can take its pulse act by act, scene by scene. I can move it, hasten it, slow it. I may do a good job on it.

The cast believes in the play and the work of the theater. Donald Marye's an extraordinary actor.

Equity makes things difficult for us. Three of our actors are union members. Equity will try to force these people to leave the cast.

We had a long disagreeable talk with Willard Swire, who is in charge of Off-Broadway at the Equity office. Equity shows total ignorance of the possibility of a theater not based on the financial standards of Broadway. Their demands—and even more so the demands of the "craft unions"—are impossible to meet.

Equity dictates that we must hire five actors who are union members, or no union members at all.

We don't know what to do; the actors want to appeal to Equity Council. The hardest days are now.

Hiatus valde deflendus:
Two lost journals: written during the period November 1 to December 21, 1951.

During this time, the Living Theatre opened at the Cherry Lane Theater with *Doctor Faustus Lights the Lights* on December 2 and began rehearsals for its second production, *Beyond the Mountains*. Despite the satisfaction which the work gave me, it was an unhappy and alienated period.

It is "lost time" since I think of the journal as time held captive.

All I have left to record the opening of our theater is a letter from William Carlos Williams:

December 15, 1951

My dears Julian Beck & Judith Malina:

I'm walking in a dream, the aftermath of what I saw and heard at your Cherry Lane Theater last evening—in all that snow. I'd be in there tonight if I didn't have a firm grip on myself—if I were younger nothing could hold me back. I belong there tonight but I dare not let myself go. And tonight is the last night of your play of Gertrude Stein's *Doctor Faustus Lights the Lights*. To me it was a wonderful, a truly wonderful experience to have witnessed it.

I want to tell you everything at once: about the excellently chosen cast, the evenness of their performance, the way they kept the interest up among them as well as the integrity of their individual performances (I was thrilled!) but there was something else that overshadowed all that. It concerned the stage itself, the overall conception of the play as something elevated, as pure entertainment, as something so well sustained, so far above the level of commercial theater that I tremble to think it might fade and disappear. I swear it lives in a different air from the ordinary Broadway show, it is as fresh as a day in the country, the first really serious, really cleanly written, produced and acted play that I have seen, well, in a long time.

I say I feel as if it was something, that someone were going to snatch it away from before my eyes—that is one reason I am so driven to go again tonight. I can't believe it possible that that cast, in those parts, just as they were acted, is going to be dispersed. I don't trust my contemporaries. Such a beautiful thing. Such a truly entrancing experience! it's going to be let die without anyone having adequately celebrated it. I want you to know that as long as I live I'll never forget it.

I realize that I'm speaking in hyperboles, I'm doing it of a set purpose. If I did not use that figure I could not show you how far above the usual conception of the stage you have set your mark and how I appreciate it. It's an almost impossible shot. But you've succeeded in communicating to me what you all together, as a company, have set yourselves and I want you to know and never to forget that you have succeeded. You HAVE succeeded and it is important, I do not want you to forget, any of you, that you did communicate to me the elevated achievement you had in mind when you first conceived such a theater as you placed before your audience last night.

I don't know whether you'll succeed in the fiercely competitive field which the theater in New York represents. There is a sordidness which corrupts playwright, producer, and actor alike which somehow, and sad to relate, brings in the coin while it strangles the entire range of what is offered. We all know this vulgarity, we all detest it. The only protest we make is to stay away from the performances—but there are plenty that go and so the appearance of success is achieved. I want to tell you that everywhere people are conscious of this state of affairs, that they long for something more satisfying to their sensibilities than these fifth-rate appeals to their emotions and intelligence represent.

You are young and, apparently, incorruptible. You know that there is a whole range of plays (not just Ibsen repertoire) waiting to be created for a public, actually to be created. And if you can maintain yourself by the skin of your teeth, writers will write more plays for you, poetic plays, excellent plays, the plays that an enlightened audience calls or will call for. I can't tell you how important it is for the theater that you want to CREATE new plays. It is the most thrilling thing that can be done on the stage today.

I wish I could give you a million to start at once on your plans to build a theater housed in the walls of a brownstone. I can't do it. But to begin with you've got the thing, the practical energy to have made a beginning at the Cherry Lane. May all success be yours.

Sincerely yours,

William Carlos Williams

Midwinter Night 1951

A wind from the moon. And a bitter taste. And a lost illusion.

As in my minotaur dance, I experience in myself all forms of violence.

Lou causes me great pain.

I fantasize taking Tei Ko's fabulous sword, the sword of a Japanese warrior, and performing the sacrifice of the Oak King, whose reign extends from Easter Morning to Midwinter Night.

This sword, Tei Ko tells me, is a national treasure of Japan, made by craftsmen with skills that no longer exist.

The action of Hermaios, the third play of the *Beyond the Mountains* trilogy, takes place Midwinter Night.

The mountains' cold invades me also.

Then suddenly my sullen spirits rise and I shake off those imaginings and I am newly created.

Yet at this moment, the "thin-lipped man with the narrow waist and long narrow face" saw me, smiled, and passed me by, like Lou. Reenactments.

The cold vegetables in front of me lose my needy mouth. I am revolted by intake. I spit everything from me.

His friends are at the next table and he is voluble with them, but he never voluntarily speaks to me. Though he answers pleasantly when I speak. Reenactments.

His embrace is warm. He maintains an impassive, passionless exterior.

Soon I shall learn to breathe.

Paul says that I'm a fraud. And then perhaps to compensate for my hurt he speaks of his own fraudulence.

He says, "Play the role."

I've learned why it's so tiring for me to write. I hold my breath during a sentence, and then inhale rapidly before the next.

I am like a room in great disorder. I want to straighten out everything at once.

Last night I wept and drank hot gin in great quantity.

Then I called Paul. Sally says I spoke to her. I must have passed out.

The lights went up on Mr. S, one of the San Remo waiters.

He lifted me from the floor of the ladies' room with its spinning tiles and told me it was four-thirty. I wasn't interested.

The three bartenders carried me out into the rain. I started a search for my journal, but couldn't find it. They drove me to 8th Street and put me in a taxi. They questioned me cheerfully.

"What were you drinking?"

"Gin."

"Another Bodenheim!"

"Not like that!"

"Hey, he's a very fine poet."

They were very defensive about their poet, whom they thought I underestimated. I was too tired to talk. I slept in the taxi.

This morning, sick and haggard, to Paul's quietness.

In an hour the rehearsal begins. I don't want to go back to the theater to face the cast.

There is something like music inside me, bursting like passion for a lover.

Now joy displaces both sorrow and calm.

I am in love with everything.

I've begun psychoanalytic sessions with Paul Goodman. I've been seeing him three times a week for a little over a month.

Paul tells me to remember two things: the acting offstage differs from the acting onstage; and to breathe deeply and exhale.

December 22, 1951

Let me praise Tei Ko who is goddess and child. I love to watch her in the mirror as she moves. She glides like a fish, her movements vanishing as though through liquid.

Dicken's fingers pointing up at the cues for the Chorus have a special authoritative air at tonight's rehearsal. I like him the more for this.

Day before Christmas, 1951

The pit of my stomach is raw. My guts want to fall out of me.
Where are my friends?
We start rehearsals of Paul's *Faustina* without a complete cast and without the proper spirit.

Christmas Eve, 1951

Everything breaks. Into pieces. Into place.
In the midst of hysteria this afternoon, we went to a Christmas party at Percival and Naomi Goodman's. I stayed apart and spoke to Paul's daughter, Susan. She is a wise child forced to use her young wits to contend with antagonistic adults.

Fritz Perls is an imposing German who conducts himself like a "Great Man." He approached me, however, like a seducer. Rumor has it that this is his custom. He admired my eyes and hands, but called my mouth "all wrong."

He claims that I despise people and should learn to spit at them.

There is not much to admire in this. His quick judgments irritate me. I dislike analysis as a parlor game. Especially in the hands of the qualified. Surely Fritz is more than what he is at a party.

December 26, 1951

Sardi's: 12:45.
We are invited to the "Luncheon at Sardi's" radio program to which I've listened for so many years. The dreams of glory become the most banal events.

A night with Dick Mayes. I feel a world of warmth from him and warn myself not to lean. He is ephemeral; time or circumstance will remove him from my orbit.

December 31, 1951

Now that the opening of *Beyond the Mountains* is past I can turn to my journal again.
Who has understood what burns in me? Not one person in the world

knows what I dream about. Paul Goodman dismisses all the important things as sham because he himself feels the menace of the abyss.

Rexroth, in *Beyond the Mountains,* quotes Walpole's epigram: "Life is a tragedy to those who feel, a comedy to those who think."

Why the limitations? We are heart-mind creatures, we bright ones.

1952

January 1, 1952

I am writing as I walk along the streets. The fog is unusually heavy, and the foghorns are making a pleasingly mournful sound. This bright morning is born out of my darkest night.

The Village is tranquil after New Year's Eve. The limits of misery stretched to the breaking point and then burst out into pleasure.

Like the Greek monster Antenor, who gained strength from his mother earth when he was thrown to the ground in battle; or as Rexroth says, "If the mountains gave us strength to carry them, we should carry a large mountain more easily than a small one."

It was the last of the year. I was playing Phaedra. Everything seemed to promise a good performance.

In the orchestra pit the girl who plays the oboe began to laugh uncontrollably at Phaedra's line: "Someday they may discover the moon's held in its orbit by the menstruation of women." I tried to finish the Minotaur dance, as I came downstage in the slow movement of the Etan Raknu to piano and cello alone. The laughter was audible. From under my veil I said to Richard in the orchestra pit in a hoarse whisper, "Get the oboist out of the pit." Then I lost control, retreated, discarded my veil, and ran off the stage.

In the wings I tried to pull it together. I said to Milton Macklin, the stage manager, "Bring down the lights, get the oboist out of the pit, and we can take up the scene."

Frantic faces from among the lights on the stage.

"Get back on that stage."

"I can't! Take the lights down!" The music almost at an end.

Mack: "Get back on stage or I'll slap you."

The music stops.

I see Phyllis Gildston move on stage, about to take my lines.

"Slap me."

He did. Phyllis is speaking my lines.

And then, as is my habit, I run.

I run out into the streets. The New Year's horns blow. The celebrants' inane glee seems the celebration of my sorrow.

I find myself at the doorway to Harald's house, where I spent one happy New Year's Eve. The door, always locked, gave way and I went up the stairs that I hadn't climbed in five years. As I wept at Harald's door, a neighbor appeared, a sculptor named Janio, and took me into his room. He spoke to me of Yoga and the Will, and of Buddhist principles.

Mahler's "Fourth Symphony" on the gramophone.

"Unhappiness is part of the process," he said.

On the wall he had penciled in broad letters: "If you know what is right, you will do your own duty."

I found this astonishing.

At eleven-thirty I left hurriedly for the San Remo.

There was an enormous crowd and no one was happy.

Who could be happy at San Remote on such a night? At midnight the room rocked with the blare of noisemakers. People kissed desperately and said: "A better year to you."

I sang "Auld Lang Syne" with them. I talked a long time with a young man called Phil Smith. He has a sad, sympathetic face.

Of hope, he spoke, and Pandora.

"There is no literature about hope because it is something man is never without."

"*Samson Agonistes* is a portrait of a man without hope."

I was trying to be drunk.

I ran on, down Thompson Street past Tei Ko's, where lights glowed in celebration. I thought of the Japanese sword. The vengeance ritual.

To Lou's home on Prince Street: Remy, Fred Mitchell, and Chip, but not Lou.

Remy is as mournful as I. . . . He tells me not to expect too much from friends. He is right.

Chip returns with me to the Remo where many people that I know are now assembled.

The black sky bleeds the new year and the celebrants' shouts are the cries of the wounded.

We go to Remy's, then return to Lou's, the circle closing closer and closer. The year has spiraled to a close.

I stay the night at Chip's. He leaves me alone when I ask him. A mother cat and her kitten frolic in angry play all night on the bed.

Nothing can be hidden now. The mask is shattered and we stand exposed before each other.

The clarity of the morning turns bitter in the afternoon. I call Julian and we confer. The cast has decided not to perform with me again. The play is to proceed without me.

Am I pained? I am, but I see what comes of expressing pain. It leads to hysteria.

I will have to face the actors. I will observe myself and the rising of shame. And anger.

David Tudor is giving a concert in the theater tonight and is preparing the piano for Cage's "Music of Changes." John has been tending the box office all day. The house is sold out, and they are selling seats on stage.

Later: The house just clearing after a brilliant concert.

The "Music of Changes" has changed music so that we can never hear the old music the same way again.

David Tudor's playing is miraculous.

I felt the audience like a monstrous heart.

This music has a divine precision which Tudor seems to feel physically as we feel warmth and cold.

Compared to it, the heartbeat's rattle is unsteady and spasmodic.

I think: This is the stage on which I will not again play Phaedra, Iphigenia, and Berenike. . . .

After the concert there's a party at Morton Feldman's.
Tudor in full dress. I am astounded at his ingenuousness.
The Harvard poets, John Ashbery and Frank O'Hara, are exceedingly chivalrous. They make a heroine out of me.
Lou gasps with a deadly fatigue. And my eyes follow him.
I think: The musicians are dancing in an exultant ring about the great mountain they have created tonight on my stage. But I am in exile and cannot draw strength.
"Take me back. You shouldn't have moved me."

January 2, 1952

I teach Phyllis Gildston my role. Not for a moment do I forget to fight my tears.

January 3, 1952

Everything is possible. Phyllis Gildston is playing my role. The theater runs without me, but it runs. I don't burn for it.
I begin *Faustina* rehearsals. Think like a director. Phyllis Castle's sensuality as Faustina contrasts excellently with Donald Marye's stoically composed Aurelius.

January 7, 1952

When the crisis was festering I wrote in small, ephemeral notebooks, perhaps hoping that I would lose them. Now I return to this sturdier journal, a bound book as anchor.
The theater is crumbling beneath us. No audience. No organization. No organism. How can I work? I see my role played nightly by someone else.
We rehearse *Faustina*. A sense of failure.
Julian suffers too, and his kindness is full of threats that make me feel my guilt. No one else even pretends to be sympathetic.
I look forward to seeing Paul Goodman again. It is Paul who had the most faith in me and I intend to prove him right.

January 9, 1952

The curtain rises on a three-people house.
Paul says I am wrong to cling to what hates me.
Terrible difficulties with *Faustina*. No money. No actors. No. No. No.

Paul says he has never known a woman who is an artist. He can't mean that. I think he meant to say more gently than directly that I am not an artist.

January 11, 1952

Postpone the *Faustina* production.
Whether we will now revive, close, change plans, I don't know.
Beyond the Mountains to close. False cheer backstage.
The theater is the great dead shell out which life can burst.
Norman Solomon from Black Mountain College says to me that to mourn is not to live for the moment.
I feel how I am tied to my own orbit.

Carnegie Hall: I came here alone. Maro and Anahid Ajemian play Mozart and Debussy; now it's time for Lou's piece.
Lou . . . Maybe I shouldn't write about these things.
I'm glad he's returning to Black Mountain. I need time to disremember the soft look of his conjuring hands when they conduct.
On the crowded backstage stairway, I meet the gifted Alan Hovhaness, introduced by his wife Serafina.
I want to go to a quiet center and proceed outward, but it's not up to me. Not up to me?

January 13, 1952

Suddenly falling through a period of feelinglessness, like Alice through darkness murmuring: "Do bats eat cats, do cats eat bats?" I jolt against something, I strike something there in the dark plunge. I fall in love with Philip.
When the Remo closes we take home the following motley: David Sachs, John Evans, Jo Jo LeSueur, Evan Rhodes, Dick Mayes, Vivian, Tom Cassidy, John Ashbery, Philip Smith.

January 14, 1952

The program is decided: Three plays to be called collectively *An Evening of Bohemian Theater*: Gertrude Stein's *Ladies' Voices*, Picasso's *Desire Trapped by the Tail*, Eliot's *Sweeney Agonistes*.
Julian says, "If this won't save the theater, nothing will." Stein, Picasso, Eliot.

Evening:
A terrible time with Paul. He is dreadfully angry at our postponement of *Faustina* and takes his vengeance by making me feel that I have betrayed him.
Paul says to me, "Don't talk to me about integrity." As if it were not our duty to question our teachers.
He is aggressively aware of his age and the number of years during which he's taken his stand. There is no reason why he shouldn't feel this pride, but he says it so often. He is paying the penalty for having attracted a group of admirers younger than he. Now, years later, as in a May-December marriage, the discrepancy shows, both to his advantage and disadvantage.
In my session with Paul, I cried and did not act it out. It's my habit to act when I weep, but I did not act it.
We never suffer enough.

We reach the bottom and say, "At last we can only rise, this is the blackest pit." But then we find new ways to feel pain.

Paul says to me outright now that I am not an artist, that if I admire *Faustina* as much as I say I do, I must hate it—out of penis envy, or envy of the excellent.

I know that he is speaking out of his anger at our being unable to do his play at this time. At our lack of faith that it will be successful enough to save the Living Theatre.

When we are in production and begin rehearsals, he will surely be different. Surely?

Three A.M. At these impossible hours I become ambitious. It must be some destructive impulse that makes me suddenly energetic.

I return from the Remo aware of the futility of this pleasure-seeking, this loss of time. Then I want to devote myself to work.

Dicken was in the Remo when I came in and hastily left with Remy. Frank O'Hara and Johnny Myers and Dick Mayes forced me into a conversation critical of *Beyond the Mountains*.

January 17, 1952

A letter comes from Anaïs Nin, who is withdrawing as a sponsor of the theater. She's gotten word of the "Evening of Bohemian Theater" and she objects to our writers, especially T. S. Eliot.

Dear Julian and Judith,

I feel as you do about the plays and I understand your position. But I cannot sincerely sponsor writing I do not believe in. I am a writer and I represent a kind of writing which is difficult to impose, and I can only do this by maintaining my position.

I know you will understand because you have integrity yourself: You believe in all these writers I do not believe in. I am sorry I cannot go along with your plans, because personally I like you both, and personally I believe you have the wit, the intelligence, and the polish, all the qualities for a modern theater. I know that you will succeed. I know also that my not being able to support what you do, as a writer who does not believe in Gertrude Stein, Rexroth, or Goodman, or Ubu Roi, or Eliot, does not in any way reflect on what I sincerely admire in you: your gift for design, synthesis, abstraction, stylization, in the theater, which I admired in your Stein production. I know you have an abundance of people who will back you up, in fact the majority is with your writers. It is I who am in the minority. I have to continue to say: Eliot is not a poet, and he is dead, until I myself die in the process. So I know my not lending my name does not in any way diminish your power in the literary world. You have everybody behind you. So do not hold it against me that I must maintain my difficult and solitary and precarious standing against such writers.

Anaïs

To Paul's session this morning, reluctant to face his anger. Sometimes I feel up to it but I can't always tolerate his lack of belief in me nor his self-deception as to the motives of his anger.

Michael Fraenkel at dinner last night. Behind his social altruism is the same personal canniness that I dislike in myself.

He brings with him an anarchist-adventurer named Harry Herskovitz, who was an editor of *Death* magazine. We talk, naturally, of the revolution.

Fraenkel says, "It is sheer cowardice on my part that I don't institute the revolution this very night."

Harry says, "The people are not ready. When they feel the need it will come."

Fraenkel, who calls himself "less rigid on nonviolence" than we, does not agree that a small compromise on arms could easily turn any revolution into a reign of terror.

January 18, 1952

The change must come now. It is the last possible moment.

Time is no longer an element to count on. It is now, the ever present now that I work in.

Therefore: I take upon myself all the minutiae of the moment, burden myself with everything at once.

. . . Even as I write I am interrupted. I can't finish anything.

We went to the Remo. Jake Spencer and Marge and Bodenheim. Harry Herskovitz knew them all.

I've never seen so grim a night at the Remo. Bodenheim was vindictive. Spencer shouted, and Death hung in the air.

Hours when I seem half mad, when nothing retains its logic, or appears a mathematics that my mind won't comprehend. I take care to appear calm, to justify, like a drunkard, any extraordinary word or action.

Now I am ready to cry out.

January 19, 1952

Jean Erdman, Erick Hawkins, and Merce Cunningham have rented the Hunter Playhouse for three concerts.

Last night, Jean's concert. Her women, heaving and contracting for all the sad women of our time, share each other's loneliness but never mitigate it.

None touched the male dancer in the company.

The dance called *Daughters of the Lonesome Isle* refers to this Manhattan where we live in terror of each other in this circle in which woman is an intruder.

Jean Erdman's body is sometimes too strong for the softness of her themes.

In *Io and Prometheus* the bound man and the hungry, tormented woman move toward each other, but they don't even try to touch. It's that hopeless. Music by Cage and Harrison.

January 20, 1952

Erick Hawkins' dances create a world which we recognize as having lived in long before we met this one.

Primeval symbols awaken responses whose origins are lost but whose evocations retain an inexplicable power. The goat, the single eye, the sword, the winged child, the gestures of the unremembered.

Lucia Dlugoszewski creates a startling, inventive percussion score for *Openings of the Eye*. Dorazio designs devices in which, and through which, Hawkins moves with an unhurried walklike tread.

January 21, 1952

Merce Cunningham's dance is the healthiest and the most pleasant modern dance. Instead of the sorrows, he dances the joyous discoveries.

A lady named Ann Lovett invites us to a small party: Jean Erdman and Joseph Campbell, Don McKayle and Erick Hawkins, Dlugoszewski and Dorazio.

I enjoy a long talk with the unsettlingly handsome Joseph Campbell. He speaks with uncanny exuberance when he describes the beauty of Sanskrit, in which each word is an actual expression of the concept.

"It is more than onomatopoetic language. The word is here"—and he makes a circle with his fingers—"And the idea here"—and does the same thing with the other hand. "And this equals this"—placing the circles together.

We touch on a variety of subjects: the arts, morality, Hindu sculptures, Lola Montez, witchcraft, insanity. . . .

He claims not to believe in progress and since he is an historian I'm at a disadvantage disputing.

Campbell believes in the power of magic and encourages me to experiment in the darker arts.

I say I would be morally obliged to practice only white magic.

"There can be no real power unless it is used for evil first."

He lies.

He tells me stories of magic and bewitchment.

I should not mind bewitching him in a much simpler sense. But no, the resplendent Jean Erdman is wearing a red dress. And I am quite powerless, even in my black satin. No, especially in black satin.

January 28, 1952

It was Remy's idea to raise money for the Living Theatre with a benefit performance by three artists: Judith Martin to dance; Paul Goodman to read poems; Alan Hovhaness to play his music.

Paul chooses a sequence from his *Anacreontic Poems*, which he says no one will publish because they are homosexual love poems. He was anxious about the audience's response, but they recognized the work as among his best.

Alan Hovhaness plays rapid and geographical music on an impossibly small piano.

Paul and Lou meet for the first time. I introduce them with jealousy already in my heart.

Lou allows me to clip a lock of his hair. Merce and John and Jack Heliker suggested that I put it in a "happener," a box containing sundry personal effects.

"And," says Lou, "you open it when you want something to happen."

John contradicts: "No. No. When you want something to happen you just shake it. You open it when you want all hell to break loose."

February 1, 1952

The Picasso play is cast, but the actors are afraid and approach it timorously. There's not much laughter during the rehearsal—yet. I am fortunate in finding a good actress for Tart, Sylvia Short, who reads in a stylized manner.

February 6, 1952

The actors are estranged by the surrealist style. Sylvia is brilliant but tries to play Restoration farce. Leonard Hicks as Big Foot excels in the long tirades but hasn't yet conquered the lyric readings.

Serafina Hovhaness, who is a novice actress, has touched me most extraordinarily. At twenty-two, she seems to be seventeen. Her looks are those of a child of whom it is said that she will be beautiful when she matures.

Onstage, I try to disguise her ingenuous acting. Offstage I disguise my own faults.

She sits in a darkened dressing room and reads the candle oracle for me.

She sees a cat in the flame. I am in Italy in a fishing village (San Remo?). She sees me visiting various monasteries.

"Were you a nun in another incarnation?"

"Probably every kind of priestess."

She sees me working on a large book. Living in a white house by the sea. There are cliffs.

Lou is there writing an opera with many, many bells.

The innocence with which she announces these things almost makes me believe her.

Alan works by her prognostications. Though he is wise and sophisticated, he seems a child like his child bride. They both seem to date back farther than most of us.

Serafina is his third wife. She tells me that as soon as he learned that Bartok had married a sixteen-year-old girl he began looking for a young bride.

"I was seventeen when we married."

We talk and talk, the four of us, at Mother Hubbard's after rehearsals. We talk of music, of the world's reception of the arts and of the jealousy of the artists.

Arrangements with Lucia Dlugoszewski for the Picasso music and with Jim Smith, sent to us by Charles Weidman for the dance. Lucia has an especially witty ear.

I think to myself that I must be much more provocative than other people since, within the past month, four people have been moved to strike me: Milton, Maurice, Richard, Julian. I look in horror at what I provoke.

There have been Remo parties that came home with us and included the unhappy Philip, all bleak, but easily stirred by sudden laughter. He is afraid of me but I am not afraid of his fear. And I tell him so.

February 7, 1952

At Paul's today. His psychotherapy is becoming more and more Hindu. He speaks of the wisdom of the East, of the fruit of action, of the need to set up no conflicts but to be in the conflict. He objects to my condemnation of wrongdoing and making distinctions between good and evil.

Paul and the awareness techniques. The problem of reality. Who is real? Julian is real when he speaks to me, more real when he screams, most real when he hits me.

At the post-Remo party, Dick Mayes laments that Vivian is leaving him on Paul's advice, while she sits by sullenly.

How clear Gide's journals are, and how stark Kafka's diaries.

Julian is preparing an exhibit of his paintings in the theater's foyer for the run of the Picasso play.

Lucia has a very personal way of speaking. She gets involved immediately and there is nothing I admire more. She is involved in art through people. Speaks intimately of Erick Hawkins and of his relation to Martha Graham.

The King of England dies. An Italian printer complains, "All over the papers it's all about the king dying. Soldiers, they die. Men dying in prison. Nobody writes that in the papers."

The night finds me alone in that infernal search, the object of which is to avoid what I am seeking.

It's a quiet night at the Remo. I meet John Myers, who is ill to the point of fainting, and accompany him to a taxi. He has, he tells me, "strained his testicles" posing for a statue by Larry Rivers.

Now I go back. My fantasies come easiest among the neons of the night when even my confused thoughts are in verse. And I like not knowing what I will be met with. En route I meet Philip going home. He has hatched a nest of hornets in my heart. The slow snow twists out of the sky.

February 10, 1952

Lucia's sounds make the play move as I had hoped: a farce ritual and the story of Pandora's bee of hope.

A David Tudor concert at our theater. These concerts arouse a special enthusiasm because among the musicians and dancers there is a more clearly defined community of artists.

The productive people have a marvelous elasticity. Merce and John laugh a great deal, whereas we work with angry haste. Merce chats and makes a game of cleaning the seats, leaping from row to row. The theater is crowded beyond the legal limit; Erick Hawkins gaily helps Stryker and Remy usher.

All with exuberance.

In the throng I find Stefan Wolpe searching for a seat and I offer him mine because I feel like a hostess. He suggests that I give him the seat of "whoever is sitting with you." I agree, if only because he is a composer whose work is being played. So I sit beside Wolpe who, with his contingent, including a sullen, hostile Dylan Thomas, constitutes "the opposition."

Cage and Tudor like the opposition to be assertive; it marks the work as being controversial. But it is another matter to sit beside them when listening to music.

Tudor plays the Webern "*Variationen*". John turns pages.

Henry Cowell's "Banshee" is a bit of play with the piano strings.

Cage's two "pastorales." Sound as we are not used to it, nailing us back to hearing as if we'd forgotten what sound is.

Wolpe and Dylan and their cohorts carry on, Wolpe making throaty sounds, passing notes, and entertaining his friends as loudly as possible.

How could I enjoy Wolpe's piece now?

Serafina threatens to boo it and asks to change seats with me so that she may kick Wolpe in the shins. Alan restrains her.

A small piece by Lou. An enchanting work by Christian Wolff (an astonishingly inventive young man) and the best Feldman work I've heard. Three intermissions.

Spoke to Richard S. a moment after the concert. He was holding the small lamp that he had used for the piano in *Beyond the Mountains*. I venture, "Ah, I see you're picking up the pieces."

"Yes, John will take the drums and other percussion things tomorrow."

"It's just as well they go. They have painful vibrations in them."

"They are silent unless struck."

"Richard!"

"That's a principle of percussion."

February 12, 1952

The seriousness behind the mask of farce in the Picasso play unifies the cast. The two Bow Wows, John Ashbery and Frank O'Hara, make a madly funny pair.

Jim Smith is somewhat graphic in his choreography. He says, "There is nothing funny in abstractions."

The Eliot is sheer somnambulism. Hazy like a sick remembrance. Perhaps it is even too humorless.

Morton Feldman conceives a sound setting for the Eliot play: the amplified sound of a ticking clock. We decide only the volume. The effect is the threat of time.

I hardly see Garrick. He relates too little to me and to Julian. Everything in the world outside the theater scarcely moves.

I want to be all things simultaneously, good and wicked, real and false, fine and vulgar, myself and my mark. I want to be indolent and busy, rich and poor, conservative and bohemian.

I won't give up any of it.

February 13, 1952

A newspaper scandal column written by Igor Cassini under the name Cholly

Knickerbocker, calls our production of the Picasso play "communistic" because the play is "naturally imbued with Picasso's warped political ideas."

He lists the sponsors because "the public should know their names."

Of Cocteau he says, "He has the political depth of a three-year-old."

Valentine's Day, 1952

A formal party at Maria Piscator's. It is beautiful, of course, to drink champagne in the company of all this elegance, but I keep thinking of the equally fraudulent but comfortable degradation of the *maudit* San Remo and the spirit of Valentine, patron of lovers. I leave in depression.

February 17, 1952

The mystery of the night: the rain with lumps of ice. The San Remo was warm.

Enchanted by the air, the odor. I try to draw around me the curtains of reality and am met by a series of improbabilities.

Seabrook describes an African image, a fan-shaped future. . . . Predestined possibilities radiating from the present. We freely choose the angle we travel. By foresight, therefore, Oedipus could have avoided his mother's bed. I'll make my maps carefully.

I promise Philip to find dance classes for him. And to talk to Paul about analysis. . . .

I dream of something distant and strangely spiced.

All day, Trudy Goth, the monarchical lady, oversees preparations for a Choreographers' Workshop program at the theater. Romantic in her harshness and queenliness.

February 18, 1952

Last night, Bodenheim's queer remembrance of poems past, and his terrible face. There was a mocking item about him in *Time* magazine, a story of his arrest some nights ago for sleeping in the subway. With it was a picture of him much as he looks now, though sober. He passed it around and confided to me that he will sue for libel. A recent benefit for him given by some Villagers put him in possession of some money, so he bought me beer, and gin for himself, and became quickly incomprehensible.

Then I went with a blond boy to a room I have been in before.

February 20, 1952

I go to Paul's with anxiety. And yet I look forward to this hour of what amounts to contemplation. He is very quiet; his manner is that of a Virgil guiding me through Purgatory. The session is more a mystical experience than an analytical one.

I try to be honest because Paul is. Why do I doubt my honesty? What have I done that is dishonest that I should suspect myself?

Paul agrees to talk to Philip, though he says he won't give him regular sessions without being paid. I try to persuade him to take me in a group session (since I do not pay him) and give my time to Philip.

I know I won't like group sessions. I'd be too competitive and too proud.

Paul is a balm on the wounds of the hysteria at the theater. *Theatre Arts* magazine wants to photograph a rehearsal of *Desire* tomorrow. This forces us all to try for performance level, at a formative stage when the whole thing is not yet pieced together.

February 21, 1952

I watch my work, disattached from it, seeing with the eyes of a spectator. I feel useless, like the placenta after birth, no longer the life source between the art work and the conception.

People from *Theatre Arts* are here. What was hilarious yesterday gets no laughs today. Julian improvises costumes on Sylvia and Shirley for the photographer.

Then I hurry to the Remo late. Only a few people. Among them Philip. A little party. There was Paul's first wife, Virginia. She has an impertinent, beautiful face. I had been curious. . . .

It snows lightly as we walk back to the theater. We are staying nights at the theater now; no time left for the luxury of home and sleep.

"It is yourself," says Julian.
"It is your reactions that matter," says Paul.
"It is a pattern," says Philip.
"It is the season," I say and never question the exquisitry of the path along the fan shape of destiny.

The theater is dark. I, too, gotta go home.

February 23, 1952

In the disheveled rooms of the Cherry Lane piled with straw and objects.

Still have not been home. Rare sleep. Naps in the tech room.

Jan Kindler puts it into my mind that I should have preserved the vulgarity of the pissing scene. I feel vaguely guilty, as if I had betrayed some cause. Frank O'Hara wishes it more tender.

I expect much of the Picasso. Eliot's *Sweeney Agonistes* has become intensely funereal.

I tried to make it funny at first. Soon we were trying to laugh inside the gloom. The laughter became weaker and weaker. The actors could not even laugh themselves, much less evoke laughter. Then we gave up and gave in to the gloom. Play it as a tragedy, we decided. It is a good example of terror. I wonder how it will follow the farce.

Saw Dylan Thomas last night at the Remo, boorishly banging at the locked door after closing time. Tomorrow night he reads at our theater.

February 24, 1952

Deafened, voiceless. And enchanted.

February 25, 1952

Racked with a fevered cough last night when Dylan Thomas read at the theater. I heard his priestly incantation through a veil of discomfort. Till I crossed into the depth of Thomas' thought beyond the cavernous grandeur of his language.

Dylan read only his own poems. Small panic backstage when Oscar Williams says that on this tour Dylan had been reading only other poets' works and has no text of his own to read from. I lend him my copy. He leaves in it ten little bookmarks, the names of the poems noted in his meticulous hand.

Afterward at the White Horse, Dylan's favored New York bar, the poet joins the circle at our table. Maya Deren is ebullient. She hardly stops to breathe between phrases. Her fantastic red hair shakes curls into the light; her features discharge sparks. She is boastful, but it's not offensive. She describes her witch's powers. She seems to weave spells then and there. I lose my voice entirely and sit mutely. Dylan is reserved, his inebriate manners held in check.

Maya tells us of the Haitian god of the dead and his magnificence.

"Is he an idol or a concept?" Julian asks.

"Neither. He is real. Because he is contemporary, he can assimilate both the modern images and the ancient customs. For instance, I asked him why he wore smoked glasses and he said, 'It is very dark where I come from and my eyes are not adjusted to the light.' Sometimes he wears only one lens so that he can look with one eye into this world and with the other into the next."

Maya cries out: "I am being battered, stoned, strangled, tied, pushed, mauled, burned thrice at the crossroads, and buried with a stake through my heart."

Suddenly I heard nothing. The noise of the pub snapped off. Maya's animated head wagged silently. Thus was I psychosomatically bewitched.

I couldn't talk to Dylan nor even hear him.

February 29, 1952

The last week of rehearsals we never went home. Previews now.

I didn't regain the use of my voice, so Jim Smith sat beside me, shouting my whispered notes to the actors. Before and after rehearsals I fell into spirals of fever.

I went through the last dress rehearsal hardly speaking, hardly hearing. Yet after midnight, for a few hours' respite (or spite, as the case may be), I answer the call of the Remo.

At four A.M. I find Julian and Frances working through the night at the Cherry Lane.

My direction of the plays is effortless. I am clear about what I want and outside the realm of articulation, I proceed without the least obstacle. I seem to be easygoing and amenable. Actually, I am stubbornly insisting on the hard and painful joy of creating the play.

March 1, 1952

Today, the day of the last preview. I went on a hurried errand down 8th Street and stopped at a jewelry store, where for a dollar I bought a silver ring which presented itself as a talisman, a plain ring with the initials S. E. P.: Stein, Eliot, Picasso.

March 2, 1952

I have it. I have what I wanted. The play is not only funny; it is sad. I have written a note for the program:
" . . . I will not have any audience: Only participants. Any play is a solemn circus of the triumph of love."

Only a few of us are aware of the significance of Picasso's *Desire Trapped by the Tail* and of this production.
The Bow Wows, Frank O'Hara and John Ashbery, do not know themselves how wise they are. They believe that they are in disguise. But it is part mask and part innocence. They will lose and gain when that form tarnishes. Frank is more sophisticated than John, though both are remarkably advanced.
The others work in dense incomprehension, unlike the characters whom they portray, the wretched lovers in occupied Paris who knew that they were destroying the enemy armies in the squalor of their deprivation.
Do the sad souls of the Remo wittingly defy a fiendish system, and when they love each other, do they overcome it triumphantly?
Those who know are always a little bit corrupted by the power that is knowledge.

March 4, 1952

Written by the red glow of the exit lights during the third performance of *Desire*.
I don't admit my feelings. Julian is right to feel for Frances all that he does. He admires her with every justification. I have loved far less worthy people far less well. I am jealous that his love is generous and that mine is hard and cold. We all get what we deserve, I suppose.
Julian is happy in her company. Adventurous and romantic. We go *à trois* to late films, undertake sudden excursions.
The sales indicate good futures. Julian is optimistic.

March 5, 1952

Philip's room is plain and bare. I'll describe it as I sit here on the bed and watch him in a maroon sweater standing by the window in a dancer's pose looking at the waterfront. . . .
There's only one bed and one chair. Mozart playing on a record player too ornate for the room.
Last night I lay beside him—Azrael asleep—and read Auden's ironical love poems, bracing the book on Philip's body. Poems of unfulfilled love.
We had gone from the Remo to the Waldorf singing in the streets. We had breakfasted in a dairy restaurant on Orchard and Essex, where my mother took me shopping among the pushcarts.
I had spent the day with Philip at the Cherry Lane, happy to be with him outside the absurd pale of the San Remo.

Pray always and only to the Inevitable. For the Inevitable will occur, thus all prayers will be answered.

On the fan-shaped path.

March 8, 1952

Philip is sleeping in our back room, the one Dicken used to live in. He sleeps like a mist on the city, heavy and damp.

Philip suggests that he assist me in directing *Faustina*.

Shirley Gleaner, who plays the Cousin in *Desire*, has come quite close to us. Now, at the theater, she turns her charms to diverting the license inspector who has been hounding us.

Philip is here at work with me painting the stage floor yellow.

In addition to a good review in the *Compass*, there's an interview by Elenore Lester in the *Newark Star Ledger*, which quotes me as saying that the Eliot play would "drive the audience crazy."

What would happen if I stayed awake, awake, awake, awake to the limit of my capacity? Would I fall down and sleep? Would my head burst with visions? If nothing had name or identity, but everything were only a part of an external flexing in an undifferentiated mass, would not that flexing be the world and a differentiated mass be God?

March 10, 1952

Manic phase.

The play rouses enthusiasm. Two nights of full houses and rising repute.

March 11, 1952

Garrick loves it at the theater, loves prancing about the stage, says he wants to be a dancer. I'm proud of his loving nature and adore showing him off.

March 12, 1952

Julian Sawyer seemed to have disappeared, but now we hear that he attempted suicide and was taken to Bellevue where he is being held for observation. And the authorities can't understand that it is a crime for them not to release him in time to see the Oliviers' *Antony and Cleopatra*, for which he bought tickets in August.

Paul Goodman calms my rages, soothes the storms. His messy house is peaceful and there are pauses to breathe in. Yet Paul is not happy. Is it necessary to be happy?

First I invent my world; then I step through the looking glass. No matter how fantastic the invention, there it is as world, and if it is unreality we invent, then it is unreality which greets us as world on the other side.

March 13, 1952

Day long I work in this dressing room that has acquired an air of myself.
At the foot of the daybed, Philip is reading *Faustina*.
In my ears, the sound of the performance of the Picasso play and music.
Above my head the queen of spades with the answerable prayer written on the wall.

March 15, 1952

Last night at San Remote, I talk with Kimon Friar, who didn't approve of my interpretation of *Sweeney Agonistes*. He introduces me to Christopher Isherwood.
I had met Isherwood briefly during *The Dog beneath the Skin*. Very much inside himself, he reaches outward tentatively. He says, "I am looking for complete directness and honesty."
There, in the heart's deaf and dumb house, there he dares to demand honesty.
We talk a long time. He warns me fervently against the practice of black magic, which Joseph Campbell has encouraged.
"It is because it does work that we must avoid it."

There are thefts at the theater and we know our thief is among the company.
Here we are, the few who have come together communally, and we know that our allegiances are variable and unstable. Who has never betrayed us? Who would never betray us?
And in the face of this knowledge and even while we are betraying ourselves, we have absolute faith in ourselves and others.
It is the impossible which we demand of ourselves.

March 16, 1952

I should like to train myself to the kind of concentration which enables Alan Hovhaness to write music in noisy public places.
Here at John's Pizzeria on Bleecker Street after the performance, Alan works while Julian, Frances, and Serafina talk and laugh. I open this book to write, but . . .
Alan pauses to complain that the Arabs want to harmonize their music, and that if they did they would become barbarians.

March 18, 1952

Mondays are empty without performances.
A rehearsal this afternoon in which I pull the play together, tugging at the reins and feeling a pull back.

The cast is restless. Only Julian is irrepressible, cheerful, optimistic.

March 19, 1952

When Paul talks to me of literature, I am pleased as a child is when a teacher discusses adult things with her. My respect takes undue proportions.

He says he would prefer that I made this an art work and not a diary. He believes that art is separated—not separate, but separated by a conscious act from the life of an artist. Cocteau, he says, suffers by not making the distinction, by making his life the art work. Why should this be detrimental?

Why not a life? I don't answer. He says that my poems suffer from this lack of separation.

On the way back to the theater, I write the following apology:

> All separation is a kind of pain.
> And yet he says: "The poem has to be a
>   separate thing."
> "It must be there." (He pointed with his hand.)
> "While you are over here." (His hand upon his breast.)
> "It must be sundered . . ."
> (Did he mean cut off?)
> The topmost leaf, by stem and tendril, touches root—
> But child, the higher being, sundered lives—
> Paul, by the navel cord,
> Judith, by swim of sperm,
> Are disattached that they may be alive.
>
> That separation is a kind of pain.
> And yet he says: "The poem has to be a
>   separate thing."
> "It must be there." (I'm pointing with my hand.)
> "While I am here." (My hand upon my breast.)
> It must be sundered.
>
> I draw my heart with bone-raw fingers
> Further from the page, until, quaking,
> I am alone. The poem is not mine.

The first day of spring 1952. Abruptly this morning men appeared in shirtsleeves. One would like a rite to celebrate.

March 22, 1952

BUONA PRIMAVERA!

We walked coatless in the new spring air to a gathering at Alan and Serafina's home.

The Hovhanesses have a room full of enigmas. Here Alan is strikingly gaunt and she an Egyptian princess. Hieroglyphic drawings on the walls by a Boston clairvoyant and two enormous black cats with Hindu names who are the guardians of their hearth.

Everyone present has his magical function: Serafina, the princess; Alan, the Oak King; Judith, the victim; Julian, the agnostic priest; Frances, Circe, the enchantress; Lucia, the muse; Philip, the prince of the waxing moon.

Among the objects in the room is an orgone accumulator. The marvels of metaphysics and the strictness of science meet in the zinc-lined interior of Reich's device. I sit stark naked on its little bench. Whether by science or suggestion I feel a flush of heat and excitement which pulsates through my body for a few moments and then abates.

Alan plays recordings of his "Rising of the Sun," the liturgy of an ancient festival of which only this musical memory remains—no, returns.

Here is a rite for the spring. The fire blazes consuming winter, the sacrifice.

Alan played "Janavar," with some reluctance because it is a death journey written for the Ajemians, whose parents vanished in an airplane.

The music immediately takes us off the ground.

At the beginning the hum of death's wings resembles the sound of the plane's motor.

Julian lays his head in the lap of the enchantress and, being unconcerned with death, goes to sleep.

Philip places his hands in the attitude he has been taught to pray in, palms together.

Alan says: "Death is one of the few things that interests me."

I leave suddenly and walk to the San Remo. An hour later Philip arrives.

There was a brawl in which John M. struck a man, and Philip, defending John, struck the man, and I defending Philip, struck the man, and the innocent man, whose only crime was not being "one of us," was thrown out.

A milkman drove me home.

March 23, 1952

John Santini, Remo manager, tells us he had a phone conversation with the lawyer of the man who was so unjustly thrown out of the bar yesterday. "Is he suing?" asks Johnny M. "Nooo!" Santini smiles, "He's asking for his client to be reinstated at the San Remo."

March 27, 1952

Ladies' Voices is so brief and tenuous that I forget that I am acting. The production of the Picasso play and the Sweeney are so "accompli" that little remains to be done on them. I am working on Faustina and putting my affairs in order.

March 30, 1952

Where are the lines I used once to divide one portion of my life from the other portions?

The I Ching says: "In time of increase work for the good of the commonwealth. The time of increase does not last, therefore take advantage of it."

I take this to mean that I must work hard while the theater is successful. No one understands why it is not financially successful, nor believes us that we cannot pay our debts.

March 31, 1952

I am surrounded by the labyrinth—and the way out is through myself.

I recognize that what I thought was my strength has been an illusion. I have imagined that my weaknesses were illusions which obscured the hard shell of good sense. I supposed that this was the foundation upon which I acted.

A LOVE POEM

x X xx XX x X
m m m M M M M M M M M M
N n n n
O
AAAAA aaaaaaaa
Z Z Z Z Z Z Z Z Z Z Z Z Z Z

Remy Charlip
Written in this notebook by Remy Charlip at the San
Remo   March 26, 1952

Unfortunately, from right thinking to right action is a better route than the one I take.

I learn much from the prescient *I Ching*.

This book of wisdom is perpetually encouraging. The gloomy oracles all contain encouragement. In decay is renewal. In the Abyss, there are adventure and conquest. Only the most satisfying signs carry stern warnings against optimism.

April 2, 1952

Our play is eminently successful in every way except financially. If the theater becomes a business, it will become totally uninteresting.

April 3, 1952

The amount of energy that is necessary is always available. We are able to fill every need. When more energy is made available than necessity demands, the creative act takes place. That's why we strain situations to summon energy. But we can't cheat. Or the surplus energy will be used in the strain and not in extending action.

Our child and our theater swing between Julian and me like skip ropes held by playmates. The tenuous swinging connection is always love.

April 4, 1952

There's a dark boy at the Remo, with almond eyes and thick black hair, whom we draw into our circle. His name is Johnny Parrish. There was Philip and a charming friend of Philip's, George Miller, who asks Johnny, "Do you swim alone?"

We wound and wove and sometimes sang our web, which twists to a knot.

I observe myself as I waste what I have in pursuit of what is unattainable.

"That night," I thought, dreaming of Duncan, "the students carried me home from the theater on their shoulders."

Johnny makes quickly clear what his desire is. Philip is the only one honest

· 219 ·

enough to display his anguish. There were three men with hungry eyes for Johnny and this Johnny with eyes only for me. But I wanted Philip.

I can't stand Philip's wan look, so I escape with George, whose first comment was on the envy he would evoke in Johnny.

In the end the unexpected happened to everyone. Julian is with Frances and with me. We are seven people in the bedroom drinking morning tomato juice like the coveted blood of one another.

April 8, 1952

I play *Ladies' Voices* with Frances.

Frances stays at our house. So does Johnny. And Philip.

I cry often. Paul Goodman is at the theater every afternoon. He has seduced Philip and is somewhat enamored of Johnny.

April 9, 1952

I sit across the street from the Cherry Lane. The sun lends everything the quality of permanence, of a hard terrain on which each animal seeks first the means to live, and second, another's incomplete companionship.

Johnny is a monument to the physical world.

Cast changes keep me busy. Oh, that I cared for what I do not care for, or that I did not care for the wrong things.

April 10, 1952

Tonight's *Ladies' Voices* went admirably. Yesterday's, horribly. The slightest loss of concentration and I can't repress the self-mocking laughter called "breaking." What means haven't I tried to overcome it? From Freud to dianetics, to Paul Goodman. I turn to Philip for solace. Julian attends to it with patient devotion.

At the Seder, my cousin Josie's vehement agnosticism throws us into short tempers. It is not a question of belief but of politeness.

After the Seder, we meet Johnny and Philip in the Senator Cafeteria, that 96th Street Waldorf.

We are a lovable quintet (quintangle, Julian says), tied together by the frustration we cause each other. These sorrows are not mutual, but interlocking; as in Sartre's hell, we are each other's torments, and yet we love one another.

Frances is playing the role of the Anguish in the Picasso play. She looks noble on stage, her thick black hair falling way down her back, acting in her eccentric exaggerated style.

Shirley Gleaner, now called "Nina Gitana della Primavera," has been badly shaken; she has seen what is not there. She is incoherent and wanders about in the red robe of Iphigenia.

April 11, 1952: Good Friday

I come to Paul, sleepless and still in last night's *Ladies' Voices* costume.

Paul walks to the theater with me. I like walking to the theater from his house, for then we talk very freely. The sessions take much pain out of me.

Eternal cleaning going on at the theater. The dressing rooms are constantly being redone. One person puts down carpets and another takes them up.

Paul compares my shame with Philip with my shame with the audience and my hostility to both. And the breaking, he says, comes from the same source.

He talks about his new book, *Parents' Day*, a novel about a school which is a community, as ours is a theater community. Which, he says, he may write about "if I become involved enough in it."

Easter Sunday 1952

Cycle of two Easters.

Philip hates magic, which he calls dramatization. But my memory traces the patterns of change.

Lou liked me for the mystery to which he believed I held the keys. Last Easter he gave me a painted egg, which is still atop my dressing table.

I was swept away and rode the crest of high spirits too recklessly. I said to Lou, "I know the answer. Ask me anything."

And Lou would wander in his mind and say, "T'other room."

Our Easter night was triumphant, but Lou was terrified. In the sunlight in the morning in Washington Square he said, "I will go to Black Mountain . . . to Paris . . . to California. . . ."

And so I lost Lou—because I was an idol who had been fool enough to turn into human female flesh.

Later that day at a concert Lou introduced me to Joseph Campbell. After that he refused to speak to me.

It was a week of concerts. Lou was at each one. To Bonnie Bird's setting of Cocteau's *Marriage on the Eiffel Tower*, Lou brought one of his students whom, he announced, he was going to marry. How terrible he looked then, with his sky eyes and his wicked mouth with a spiteful child's hysterical laugh that was distinctly "t'other room."

But soon we began to work on the Theater in the Room. Lou abandoned his hasty marriage plans and went to Black Mountain. Easter faded. Plans for the Living Theatre shaped my time; work quieted my passion. It was easy to find lovers and difficult to love.

Anxiously I awaited Midwinter Night, which ends the cycle that Easter begins. There was a *succéss d'estime* with *Doctor Faustus Lights the Lights*. Lou, in New York for Christmas vacation, came to the play Midwinter Night, and I sat beside him wondering in which direction the turning point would lead us.

The turn came where I least desired it, in the work. *Beyond the Mountains* rehearsals began to disintegrate. As I had determined to be governed by the seasons, so it had to be; for we create the mythology we live by.

During this time Paul Goodman became my analyst.

During this time Joe Campbell encouraged me in the pursuit and practice of magic, unaware of the object of my experiments.

On New Year's Eve, during the first act of *Beyond the Mountains*, I ran weeping from the stage, the glamorous garments of Phaedra dripping wet and golden. I ran towards Harald's house. A sculptor found me at the door streaming with tears. He made love to me by a red light. I escaped before midnight and arrived at the San Remo a few minutes before the hour. Philip kissed me at the magical moment.

"Life," he said, "is not literature." It occurred to me that this stranger might be someone I could love.

I told him how I had left the stage during the performance, of the mocking oboist and of Lou. It was an end and a beginning.

Remy took me in hand. He said, "You want everything from everyone and it's too much to ask."

In the morning I had to pull the havoc at the theater together. The theater was deeply in debt. We canceled *Faustina* and planned the *Evening of Bohemian Theater*.

During the rehearsals I went to the San Remo nightly. I let myself fall in love with Philip. Julian, to whom I had clung all my sorrows, drifted from me. Frances came to possess Julian's affection. Feeling helpless between my real love for Julian and my futile obsession with Lou, I drew Philip close almost by force. I brought Philip to our house, and thereby brought Frances and Johnny Parrish. As in the play, farce is the means by which we combat the poverty of our situation.

This year, Easter night, Bruce Duff Hooton, Marxist poet who is our house manager, gives a party. I weep; and Philip, who in his disdain for magic had derided by fear of this second Easter, cried out in anger, "I wish she were dead!" and then cradled me weeping. We all sleep through the coming of dawn. Easter is over at last. Let the magic pass, sorrow and all.

Everything breaks but the patterns.

April 21, 1952

I am breakfasting alone in a drugstore in excellent spirits.

We were up late last night playing cards. Johnny has taught me a good game of gin rummy. I rose early to do the laundry. This of all tasks gives me an archaically womanly feeling. In the cleaning of clothes, ablution of past sorrow. I think of Ulysses' Nausicaa and of Anna Livia Plurabelle by the Liffey and of Yerma—Paul says I'd be happier if I could identify myself more with the role of woman, rather than compete with men. I regret the distinction.

Receipts on the Picasso play have dropped. Julian says there's always a slump after Easter. We are going on with *Faustina* rehearsals. We plan to run the two plays in repertory.

I am pleased because it pleases Paul.

I work sans makeup. But I can't face going to Paul's without the security of cosmetics.

I go to the group session with great trepidation and considerable hostility.

The session provokes anxiety. Paul says that I make coalitions. Of course. I hedge, feel ground.

April 22, 1952

Paul asked, "Who am I in the quintet?" He thought a long time and then said, "The chronicler. That's right, I'm the chronicler."

At this enormous theater, the Brooklyn Academy, where Theater for the Dance is rehearsing, I feel the work-joy. Remember in times of discouragement the smile of John Cage, the cheer of Merce Cunningham, the inwit of Alan Hovhaness, the pleasantness of the dancers and musicians.

Julian, Bruce, Frances, and Philip are talking about a community of artists, which somehow we seek to be.

At the San Remo last night Philip said, "I have made my decision. I'm not going up there anymore." "Up there" means our house.

Here I am, whistling in the dark to bolster my spirits.

April 23, 1952

Paul and I have a good session. I trust him because I know that nothing I say goes unnoticed or forgotten or unobserved.

As I emerge from a taxi with Paul and Matthew Ready at the theater, Julian calls down, leaning from the office window, "We've been robbed."

The empty cash box had a quarter left in it. There had been twenty dollars. And Johnny Parrish was gone.

Let me ask the question Marcus Aurelius would ask, "What did I learn from Johnny Parrish?"

From Johnny Parrish I learned to play good gin rummy.

There is great relief at his going. I wish he had asked for the money. I wish I were certain that we would have given it to him. I wish he had left us a note. I wish that I could have been kinder to the good in him.

Faustina readings. Philip works hard and we smile much and laugh. The air is as clear as on Noah's fortieth day out. We send our doves forth and they return with olive leaves. We mail press releases and drink martinis.

Late, we all listen to Debussy's string quartet on the radio, our faces shedding light.

Philip comes home with us.

April 25, 1952

About five years ago, I spent a few hours at the Café de la Paix talking to a man with an overwrought passion for culture, a stranger in this country, en route to the West. His name is Cornelius Groot.

Later we corresponded awhile but then he vanished without an address.

A few days ago, I heard from him again. He is on Ellis Island, confined, awaiting deportation. For the past two years, he has been in McNeil Island penitentiary, for a political offense, the details of which are unknown to me. He is going to be shipped to Europe and hopes to go to the eastern zone of Germany.

I cross the bay in a ferry. Because Cornelius wrote that he has seen no woman for years, and asked me to dress up and wear high heels, I find myself absurdly conspicuous in white and jet among these troubled people.

Before the deportees arrive, we visitors wait in a big stone room in the center of which is an enormous cage made of glass bricks and wire screening. Through the barred windows, a view of the statue called Liberty.

The prisoners enter. It's the first time I've seen a man in a cage. The distance that the barrier creates is uncanny. I want to bring this man some comfort. He talks of the thwarted desires of his years of imprisonment. I can't resist talking to him about politics.

But it is impossible to argue with a Leninist locked in a cage when all he wants is affection. So we talk of affection and of meeting again in Europe.

We try to touch through the screen. It provokes frustration and outrage.

That which is truly revolting should cause revolt. I should have stood up and shouted. But I did not. That's why the cage exists.

By the time we are ready to shout, we are already utterly helpless.

May 3, 1952

The menace of *Faustina*'s opening three weeks hence hangs over me like Damocles' sword.

Julie Bovasso will be a strong Faustina. Her presence is a little too polished.

Leonard Hicks a lean, taut gladiator.

Philip's relationship with Paul has become heavily emotional. I'm inhibited in the *Faustina* rehearsals by Philip's presence as assistant director. Today when the cast disparaged the playwright, I couldn't defend him as I would have if Philip had not been present.

Faustina rehearsals coincide with replacement rehearsals for the Picasso-Eliot program.

May 4, 1952

I finish the blocking plan for *Faustina* this morning. But before I go back to work I want to hold onto this moment:

Across from me on Commerce Street is Harry Jackson's car loaded with canvases. Philip is with him and Harry's dazzling dancer, Joan. Everyone looks at the paintings in the sunlight. They stir the street. People stop and comment. His melancholy portrait of Philip upsets me. A magically exact resemblance.

Philip and Harry are doing rope tricks, lassoing one another; Joan rides along the street on Philip's back.

For all the striving toward a free community of artists and friends, the happy moments can be counted—that is, they are a rarity—and I am not enlivened anymore.

To work.

May 6, 1952

Alan Hovhaness' music addressed to Khaldis, an Eastern miracle piece with four trumpets and gong and piano. The little Cherry Lane shook with the ritual reverberations.

John Cage's sonatas encompass the minute detail of an aesthetically successful civilization. Alan's music is a primitive outburst of fear, passion, and arrogance. Lucia plays a loose piece—formless, yet nonetheless carefully drawn.

The audience is small but responsive. The Cherry Lane itself has a meaning. It is a place.

May 7, 1952

With his life's blood Paul Goodman hacked out a life of integrity (such as it is, or as he would say, the best he knows), and now, lines drawn, erased, redrawn in lifeblood, now he tries to tell me that it can be done without the agony.

> Is his moon rounder than the one the sky
> Pokes at us nightly?

Yesterday, we sat on Commerce Street and I worked on *Faustina*. Philip was splicing rope for Julian's nerve-and-vein setting, while Paul and Jo Le-Sueur stopped by to chat.

It is best to take the idyll and let it live a while. It dies soon enough.

En route to Paul's for a session. The subway.

May 10, 1952

The first act of *Faustina* flows cleanly from beginning to end.

Julie Bovasso responds to every suggestion; she is the ideal actress for the director. Sometimes I suspend my critical faculties altogether out of sheer admiration.

Donald Marye is cold and haughty. Perhaps in preparation for the stoicism of Marcus Aurelius. The warmth of his feelingful Dr. Faustus is gone.

Leonard gives the gladiator the strength to take on the whole corrupt Roman court.

The second act is untouched. I plan to work in my lunch break. But Paul comes and we spend the time talking.

In the second act the stage, like its Byzantine model, stands frozen, stiffly still. The theme is immobility.

Philip has gone upstairs with Paul and the awareness of their lovemaking stings me to jealousy. I burn. I try to rehearse, but I am aware only of the jealous rage of Aurelius whose words are Paul's words, while Paul takes Philip into his arms on my bed.

Why does the author do this during a rehearsal of his play at which this actor is needed? How much for destructiveness? How much for pleasure?

I try to have people stand in for Philip, but the stage falls apart. I call a break.

May 14, 1952

I bounce into a work rhythm full of practical energy. I am in contact with the actor's reality on the stage, his motions, his tone, placement, gesture, and the mystery of the ritual he performs. My mood echoes my work; my work, my mood.

If I feel pain, I desire satisfaction for it. This is the rehearsal atmosphere which dominates this play.

Paul calls *Faustina* a ritual tragedy because the ritual has in itself neither power, nor meaning, but from it power can be derived. This is true of the Mithraic bull sacrifice, of the eating of the host, as well as of the play.

To convey the idea of the ritual. As Isis, the soothsayer says, "Where else is the power to come from? I haven't got it."

Walter Mullen has replaced Edith as Isis. It was hard for me to deny Edith the role. The punishment of having authority is having to exert it.

I grow to love the play. This is the stage at which I love rehearsing and feel the play's promise.

Philip has constructed a model stage and I have made small figures of the players out of metal foil in the manner of Percival Goodman's sculptures.

Ten days till opening.

The last three nights we have slept at the theater. Julian and Frances on-stage in the prop bed. Philip and I in the tech room. Bruce on a mattress on a dressing room floor. Nina in the dressing room hallway.

May 16, 1952

In the swing of work. Even Paul saws away at the set downstairs in the camaraderie of Bruce, Philip and Julian. All night we address the opening announcements.

The pain about which I write is the energy that I use in the work.

Nina's pale figure, smiling through mazes, is a symbol of what I would not want to be. Her words are what mine would be if I spoke without the iron rod of my aspiration in my throat.

The play exhausts me. I believe its horror and beauty. Paul's presence and his sorrow underscore the legend.

I lie at night beside my lover who is not my lover. At rehearsal when the actors are guided by my feeling, the pain becomes fruitful and blooms in their mouths.

"I am the chronicler," said Paul.

May 18, 1952

I put a photograph of Modigliani on my dressing room wall because he has a beautiful face. No. Because his face shows his suffering. The sorrowful life of the bars and the unfulfilled art.

Do we idolize its victims and priests? Do we not idolize Maxwell Bodenheim although we are sometimes loath to talk to him and always ashamed of our condescension to him? The bartenders at the Remo have put a photograph of him over the bar.

What we admire is Bodenheim's refusal to resist. We fight all the time, resisting temptation. We admire those who don't. Even if it's suicidal.

Money harries us. Threatening creditors arrive with their own sad stories of deprivation. We quest even for food (a borrowed meal and peanut butter sandwiches).

A check bouncing at the San Remo upsets us. If we lost our credit at the Remo, what would become of us?

Last week at the group session I raved.

What is it that I demand of Philip, whom I do not love? Blessed are the numb for they are dead.

I express myself without consistency because I am inconsistent. I will not dissemble, but allow the lies I tell myself to betray me till the pain of lying forces me to the truth.

May 19, 1952

Six days till the opening.

I fall asleep on the library floor and feel guilty since Bruce, Julian, Nina, Philip, and Frances work through the night and are still working today without sleep.

Yesterday, Paul watched part of a run-through. I couldn't tell what he felt and he didn't say. I feel secure with this play and have joy in the making of it. I rise and fall with it in the most personal sense.

May 21, 1952

It is six A.M. of the night before.

A nightmare day and a night of no darkness.

Paul came in the morning, waking me out of the lonely bed that held Philip and me apart and together.

He was with George Dennison and when Philip and I went to rehearsal, they stayed behind in the tech room to make love.

Lunch with George and Paul. Paul says, "You dog, you ruined my pleasure. I would have enjoyed a threesome if Philip could have made love to me too, but your jealousy spoiled it for me. Don't imagine that he doesn't feel deprived because your jealousy spoiled his pleasure too."

"Paul," I ask, astounded, "is this calculated to make me miserable?"

"It is."

And it does.

But then we make amends with a friendly talk about schooling and what it is that learning is. Paul suggests that Julian and I go to Black Mountain to teach theater, that is, to run a workshop in play-making.

There is a sudden rush about the printing of the program and I hurriedly compose program notes.

I throw the coin oracle and the *I Ching* answers in the "Receptive" and I quote it in my notes without hesitation:

NOTES ON A RITUAL TRAGEDY

How shall I convey the emergence of power out of what has in itself no power? To underline the passion of the playwright and the priestess when they say (in holy concord): "It's a lot of shit but that's how we do it."

That is how we do it. Because in this play we speak out about the ritual with real brazenness, saying we haven't the strength and yet we can give the strength.

Here is the Taurobolium in which the initiate is bathed in the blood of the sacrificial bull and emerges from the pit reborn. The story places us in the pit and calls us to partake of the rites.

The arrogance of requiring the audience to partake! That is, to admit the *presence* of these hundreds of people.

We create in an art form in which every night hundreds of people are ignored: we pretend that they do not exist: and then we wonder that the actor has grown apart from society; and that art itself staggers lamely behind its hope of being part of life.

How shall I convey my belief in what the playwright says? The *I Ching* answers, "It is the Creative that begets things but they are brought to birth by the Receptive." And it says of me further, "The person in question is not in an independent position, but is acting as an assistant. This means that he must achieve something." I consulted this book of ancient Chinese oracle not only for myself but for my audience.

To allow ourselves to be assistants in the ritual, which hasn't any power, but from which the power is derived. The play does not take place in pagan Rome. Believe me, believe me that it takes place in this theater and *tonight*. How shall we (in concord) derive the power from the action? When the priestess says: "Where is the power to come from? I haven't got it"—say that it comes from the art of the play, and that it comes out TO us, and now we have got it.

That's how we do it.

Judith Malina

I wanted Philip to read it before I typed it out, but he didn't want to, and I cried in the wings while he embraced Paul and they skipped rope together on stage.

I could scarcely see the paper so Julian offered to type it. Julian, whose sturdiness is the foundation of my life in love and art, and the bosom of quiet.

Julie Bovasso feels that she cannot speak the last speech of *Faustina*, which is a direct address to the audience.

I tremble through the rehearsal.

May 24, 1952

We struggle with Julie to convince her to read the last speech, which is crucial to the play.

We talk for hours. She gives many and contradictory reasons, but her real reason is the fear of facing the audience in the light of real life. She says when she sees them sitting there in the naked light, she feels like a beast, like a wild animal let out of a cage. But she surely means that she is naked and that the audience is a wild animal let out of its cage.

May 26, 1952

The opening of *Faustina* is over. The play is ragged but beautiful. The reviews are wretched. Donald Marye, Leonard Hicks, and Walter Mullen hold the play together, but Julie is afraid and because she is afraid she is angry, and she doesn't read the last speech. Walter, always obliging, reads it in the character of Isis on the opening night, but the play loses. We have not succeeded this time.

After the opening, the depression. The preceding sleepless nights had turned Julian's face into a garish mask of exhaustion. Philip made a gruesome pact with me in which I was not permitted to speak with him unless he spoke first, impractical in a working situation. Paul, the playwright, the analyst, the sage among us, became my villain. When they are together (they are as I write this) I picture it and say to myself all that I do not say nor want to say when I see them.

May 28, 1952

After the second performance of *Faustina* Paul told me that his preparations for Black Mountain necessitate our not having our session at 11:30 this morning. I cheerfully thought no more about it.

This morning, Philip rises early and I ask him where he is going.

"To Paul's."

It was 11:00 A.M.

May 29, 1952

The actors, seeing empty houses, have no spirit for the performances. Walter plays the sorceress, Isis, with spectacular travesty. He stands unabashed before the audience during the final speech, but it is not the same as if the actress playing Faustina said it. The effect of the whole play is muted by Julie's talented coolness. She has given us notice and is playing her last performance.

The actors' lack of faith in the play kills it. I am watching it now from the last row and my pen falters . . . the gladiator and the emperor dance the fight in the arena. I leave before Julie's scene.

"Retreat inward to a quieter place."

I ask Philip to teach me Japanese, the quiet poetry that is their language. But I could not live it.

May 30, 1952

Rehearsals, I put Mary Montague through an ordeal in order for her to become Faustina in three days.

Then I'm tired. Nothing is left but weariness that grinds me like a millstone into a state of anger.

I break the mirrors in my dressing room with my fist and the crashing sound soothes me.

I go through *Ladies' Voices* without a flaw.

May 31, 1952

Mary, like Julie, refuses to read the final speech in *Faustina*. We are adamant about its importance to the play.

June 3, 1952

We make up our own horrors and then when sorrow comes, like Gertrude

Stein's tenderhearted people, we have a hardness of soul. The *I Ching*'s warning: the Abysmal, and I write the word "consent" on my wall. Consent to the abysmal.

I let myself fall slowly as through water into some depth. But I rise again; at the point of pain I lose the death desire, therefore the pain becomes pleasant because it stifles the death wish.

I fight with Julian. He leaves with a finality that terrifies me.

The theater is in my hands. I change my whole character suddenly. I know how to make the best of everything. I speak to the creditors. I plan productions, see actors, make decisions.

The cast agrees to work without pay.

I fear the night and being alone, so Philip takes me to Harry Jackson's place.

We walk the width of this island through the maze of the Lower East Side and the earthen odors of the markets of the Mediterranean in the Jewish and Italian ghettos.

Here in the slums, which are being torn down to make way for the projects, many artists are renting lofts.

Harry's studio is splendidly unhampered. I am able to rest and eat. (We steal rolls from a bakery and buy buns too.) Philip speaks to me for the first time in days. Coldly, but at least he speaks.

It is soon day.

Julian returns. He had not gone far. He was at my mother's.

We are going to be alone together. It's sad that what had happened was not the beginning of a community of artists, but a destructive situation in which our relationship—Julian's and mine—was in danger of being wrecked.

He tells a broken-hearted Frances this. He tells the five of us. It's painful, but he's right. There was more anguish than love in our house.

We both are close to weeping when we return alone at night to 789 West End Avenue.

"Enough of this," says Julian. "You must learn to do at twenty-six what we all learned to do at six."

He means that I must learn to master my emotions, but I remember when my mother said to me "Stop crying!" And I said, *"Der Wein kommt,"* in my childish German that didn't mean "the wine comes," but "the crying comes." I meant that it came in spite of myself. Even when I was six, Julian, I tried, and I couldn't. And I can't now. The crying comes.

June 4, 1952

The theater is in a desperate state. The creditors hound us and we are faced with no source of income. A half hour before curtain time, Julian cancels the performance.

I'm to rehearse Lee Alexander as Faustina: we must work from the basic principles upward.

June 5, 1952

The artist's problem is not only to be creative, but to be able to live.

"How will I live?"

"Artist's problem?" Nonsense. It is the outcry of the whole world.

I shout at a man on the telephone that I don't believe in laws and courts and money. I shriek at creditors, who look incredulous and say, "I should be the angry one." Philip refuses a subpoena for Julian.

The Con Edison company is prevented from turning off the lights in the theater by Bruce Hooton who interposes his body by sitting on top of the cellar door.

The marshal insists, and I say I'll get $25.00 in one hour. He says he'll wait right there. Bruce stays on the cellar door.

I race uptown and take from the shelf a parchment-bound edition—the first in English—of *The Niebelungenlied* that I bought for twenty-five cents at a West 3rd Street bookstand. . . .

I run on to a book dealer's on East 47th Street, where I show the dealer—who is very interested—the inscription: "To Jensen who's forfather [sic] was the Great King Jen—Richard Wagner."

I was sure it's genuine. Jensen was Wagner's American dentist, according to Newman—therefore it made sense that he gave him a copy of the first English translation. As to King Jen, I've no idea. . . .

Book dealer says, "Oh, yes, it's genuine. We have only to verify it."

"I need twenty-five dollars right now!"

"But it's worth ever so much more, only I can't possibly buy it without verification. I'm sure, personally, that it's genuine. . . ."

"Can you personally **give** me twenty-five dollars for it? I need cash."

I race back downtown **and give** the marshal, whom Bruce is still holding at bay, the twenty-five **dollars for** my twenty-five-cent book "worth ever so much more."

We founder in the boiling sea. We do not, in the midst of the struggle, have time to fear the next wave.

Philip must decide whether he will work full time on *Ubu* with me, or whether he will take a job. "How will I live?" He needs to dance and to have sessions with an analyst at ten dollars a week and I promise to call Merce and ask for free classes for him.

June 7, 1952

Julian and I are translating *Ubu Roi* ourselves. Time pressure. We imagine it is possible to work through the night, but it is really not.

Summer has come and I suggest that we work in Washington Square. The great moon and the lamps illumine the chess tables where we spread out the yellow pages of our typescript and the paperbound French version. Immediately, Ubu's crazy cheer overcomes Faustina's gloom. Can it happen so abruptly? Jackson Mac Low comes by adorned with maple leaves, looking like a boy without his dignified beard.

He has no sooner passed than the "delegation from Verve," heading out of the Remo toward a dancing place, sweeps us away from our table.

At the fountain there is a boy with a banjo. We sing together and everyone applauds.

Julian and I are carried away by dancing again.

June 14, 1952

I have been prompting the last few days because Lee Alexander, the new

Faustina, does not know her lines. I watch Philip play the soldier for the last time. We break off in a scene of violent anger.

June 17, 1952

Work on *Ubu* is our focal point. And John Ashbery's *The Heroes*, which we will do on the same program. John's play is a poetic dissection of the foibles of the figures of the Greek myths, like an 18th century play written by a young 20th century poet whose pen has been dipped in surrealism.

June 18, 1952

There's no one to do the lights for *Faustina*, so I volunteer and go to Jack Ferris' house, where he promises to teach me the light plot. But we got drunk and never got beyond the second act.

I thereby evaded a session at Paul's. Then, through the glassy dark, the road to the Remo and ruin. At the bar were Philip's friends. . . .

No, it is wiser to describe what Paul calls a "present memory—here and now."

Here and now: I am doing the lights for *Faustina*. I, who am afraid of electricity, am enjoying it, even though there is a thunderstorm.

Here and now, I am sitting up above the stage at the light board like an Olympian deity, while below the familiar Romans are frozen into immobility.

Julian is playing Philip's soldier.

A heavy, damp heat rises from the stage. I love this scorching weather as I loathe the cold.

I remember the fine snow through which I first walked toward the theater. . . .

Is it because it is the month of my nativity that it is the month of losses?

No . . . Get back to here and now: The heat rises up to the light board.

I am listening for my cue.

June 19, 1952

Begin rehearsals of *Ubu the King*. The script bears our pseudonyms. "Translated by Jane Warren and Arnold Devree." That's us.

Moe Moscowitz, the anarchists' Isis, is our Ubu. Frances, our Rosamund, is as sad as the sad queen herself. Sullen and silent, she is surrounded by the whole Polish army, played by Norman Solomon; they make a strange pair in their solemnity. Mama Ubu is Ruth Kaner. Walter Mullen plays Buggerlouse. Planning the directing book.

The closing night of *Faustina*. But after the first rehearsal of *Ubu the King*, I have no regrets at the end of *Faustina*'s run.

Moe Moscowitz is amazing at the first reading of *Ubu*. The production promises to be wholeheartedly pataphysical.

Faustina is ending now. I dim the lights.

I'm studying the Japanese alphabet. I love drawing the Chinese characters, and I take much pleasure, too, in the simpler figures of the Kana syllabary. I can write

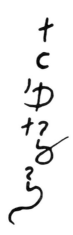

which means "if it must be so," or what we call good-bye.

Gandhi says that one should not make pictures of the future or the past, for in these fantasies we exhaust ourselves.

I think he meant that by dreaming of our desires we exhaust those very energies that could help us to realize them. I expend myself in fantasies.

June 20, 1952

Rehearsing *Ubu.*

Now the performance of *Ladies' Voices* and *Desire*. I'm running lights for all of these.

In *Ladies' Voices*, I climb up the ladder to the light board and dim the house, then clamber down to perform, then climb again to turn up the house at the end of the play.

How pathetic I thought Butler Davenport when I saw him do this at his Free Theater.

June 22, 1952

It was the closing night of the successful run of the *Evening of Bohemian Theater.*

My first taste of the effects of hash-hish.

A strangely dramatic fellow gave it to me, saying that it can take many different directions, and that I can choose the direction.

The intensity of this quietness.

June 25, 1952

After midnight, after rehearsals, to the San Remo. In spite of the ruthless violence of the current juke box favorites, one can sit still here.

With Weegee, the photographer of the Naked City, I go to his shabby, one-room home behind the Tombs and then to eat at Thau's. Joined by Norman and Nina and Julian, we prowl the dawn streets, and visit the catacombs below MacDougal Street and the Minetta Spring captured in the art nouveau fountain of a fashionable Washington Square hotel.

Last night in the Remo with John Cage and Lou Harrison. Lou, looking splendid in a white suit and a small Edwardian beard, boasts of his exploits like a child recounting his defiances.

Seven of the cast have left us. The recasting is arduous and boring.

And this is my good season.

"Why, this is hell nor am I out of it." The red glass bowls in the Remo's windows are little Cleopatra coals to comb through my hair.

Would we remember Faustus if he had heeded the good angel?

June 29, 1952

Obedience, not to circumstance but to the fluctuation of circumstances.

A great storm outside the San Remo. Water pours out of a raging sky and the glasses shake with the thunder.

But to be unshaken!

July 1, 1952

At rehearsals the contact with the actors gives me strength. To work alone on the directing book is much harder.

Japanese studies: Mr. Iwasake works with me on the alphabet in his oriental shop in the Village.

I practice calligraphy nightly in the San Remo.

July 4, 1952

A fire in the San Remo basement. I saw the smoke and called Johnny Mitchell, who opened the metal cellar doors, and the smoke billowed out into the street.

Philip orders everyone to step back, authoritatively (suddenly I remember he was a marine), lowers himself under the sidewalk with a deft movement and disappears into the smoke. My mind calls, "Philip"; and my mind answers, "He isn't there."

The fire is soon put out.

I dream about him, still and dead, and in the dream I call out, "Speak to me. Speak to me."

I always dream of those recently dead, that they return and laugh at my grief and say, "You see it isn't as you think. I am here." They don't say they aren't dead, just that they are here.

As in fact Philip is here. And still he refuses to speak to me.

The theater has many burdens. We play comedy, but cast ourselves in self-inflicted tragedy.

We are hungry a good deal of the time.

Still I live a life of pleasures. The theater is a bohemia and a lunatic fringe. It is infectious.

The barefoot rebels have taken hold here and move in wide slow circles around the theater. They work well, most of them, but they have a sound of star gazing in their voices that I associate with laziness.

Jackson Mac Low, who is rehearsing Ulysses in *The Heroes* and Captain Bordure in *Ubu*, has fallen desperately in love with Nina, who is playing Circe. But everyone is in love with her.

She sleeps through the days. Possessed, she looks frail and haggard. If she seems better, it is because we no longer expect conventional responses from her. She plays Circe with a melancholy grandeur.

Moe plays Ubu on a single violent note.

July 5, 1952

At the Halversons'.

Everything rises. A sudden small concussion enrages the senses. Leap over the last barriers. Rotation following soft velour wheels. Velours. Soft rotations. Dance. Music. Wine. Marijuana. A house filled with people. Björn and Hildur Halverson, Jackson Mac Low, Norman Solomon, Bill Keck, Bill Mullahly, Johnny Mitchell, Tchouki, Bruce, Frances. Sweet taste.

I like the delicacy with which one hands around the reefer while still holding the inhaled smoke. No thanks are said. It returns, shorter and bitterer, until it burns the lips and sears the fingers. Then someone makes a crutch out of a rolled matchcover and the last bit is finished.

This morning we eat in a stony courtyard with stunted trees like a Persian garden. The cooking done on kerosene burners. In the morning more hashish to soften the day. O food. O thirst. O summer heat.

July 7, 1952

Tolstoi's journal. He warns of the weakening of the self by "even such innocent means" as cigarettes and wine. I read this as I waken from my darkling hashish sleep. The hashish makes me ravenously hungry. The hunger is impractical as there is no money.

We all eat soup at Thau's Restaurant on Second Avenue, where Sam Thau, with the generous, arbitrary favoritism of a Jewish father toward a youngest child, often feeds us free—and superbly.

Tolstoi looks down on romantic love, rather favoring divine and social love as the more uplifting passions. But we function in terms of the particular because we ourselves are particular. We feel a kinship with the small because we ourselves are small.

At Paul's group session. Paul questions Norman Solomon. I feel he will say "next" and turn to me.

Attempt to participate. I am uncomfortable. Each talks in turn. Everyone has great burdens. I give up trying to participate. My head aches. They will not get to me today.

July 8, 1952

A time of splitting apart says the *I Ching*.

At a table at the Remo, the garish-shirted man who brought the marijuana to the party persuaded me to swallow a piece of cotton saturated in a liquid mixture of which I don't even know the name. The *I Ching* says "no blame," but if I say "whatever is done is well done" what shall impel me to do better?

I went sky high. Tchouki danced in the street, laughing at the approaching traffic.

We went to the circle in Washington Square and gradually revulsion overcame us. The horrors crashing over me in waves.

Maya Deren came by, walking an enormous black cat at five in the morning and shrieked like Hecate at the owner of a dog who attacked her pet.

The Swamp Rat passed.

At dawn we drank undrinkable coffee as the sickness slowly receded.

July 13, 1952

They sleep, the bohemians. Here in the tech room, Julian. In the dressing rooms, Frances and Bruce, and on the floor, Bill Kehoe. In the hallway on prop tables, Eric Weinberger and Bill Mullahly. In the lobby, Nina on the floor.

One night at the Remo Eric and Bill asked me if they could "flop" at the theater. They have been here ever since and they work hard. Eric, an exemplary person, is going to replace Larry Elfenbein in *Ubu*. He is admired by all. Bill Mullahly is stage manager.

Julian has gone overboard in his admiration for the haphazard way of life. He goes shoeless, which is all right, and dirty, which is not. He thinks he looks relaxed, but he looks a mess. I'm not troubled because it cannot last (this pose not being natural). Meanwhile, it's uncomfortable.

But the spirit—and that's the important part—the spirit is what matters. The work is done with communal enjoyment.

Still the communication is too superficial. Something more. Something more.

July 19, 1952

The dress rehearsal of *The Heroes*. No notes.

My handsome husband and the gossamer girl playing the love scene of Theseus and Circe. She fumbles her lines. He looks old-fashioned in a white suit. They look so distant, so unfamiliar on stage. How immediate this is.

July 21, 1952

Though nothing is ready for tomorrow's opening, the air is fraught with joyful work.

Jackson is hurriedly completing the score for *The Heroes*. The sound of recorder and harp come heavily into heavy air.

Absolutely no sleep.

In the center of the stage under a blazing worklight, Frances, in a bathing suit, coolly irons the 152 costumes for *Ubu*. Julian predominates.

Björn is like a railway worker in a film glorifying railway workers. Ellis, who directed the anarchists' *Faustina* with Jackson, helps day and night.

Tchouki sews fanatically on the old Singer machine.

Larry Elfenbein and Charles Lewis and Philip and Maury are all alumni of St. John's College and have in common a certain aloofness. Maury, of whom I cautiously say nothing . . .

There is much talk of drugs though they do not appear. There is jive talk of "hipsters and vipers."

The work is pleasurable at last.

Sleepless, dirty, hungry.

My wild look is proof of my triumph. I like myself in the role of the wild girl, though she is not humble. I could make these things compatible.

My head careens.

Go. Go. Go.

July 22, 1952

Last night's rehearsal was to have been the final dress rehearsal but I've decided to postpone the opening. No other way to salvage *Ubu*.

A grueling cast meeting. Group discussion is hampered by unnecessary notions of parliamentary procedure.

All the members of the theater expressed their feelings openly and some were with me and most were against me. Afterward I didn't want to talk about it.

At the San Remo, the talk was of the postponement, so I gave my beer to Bill and slipped out the back way. The park was lucid and hot. On one of the benches sits Sam with some people.

There are a great many dealings, waitings, returnings that lead to nothing.

We wait in Sean O'Neill's room. He is the playwright's son and I'm told he takes cocaine.

Sean lives in a large residential hotel in a tiny room containing bed and books. He is haunted by the same air of decay that I found so romantic in Pancho.

We wait for Jim and Mary. No one talks much. It's part of being "cool." I fall asleep, and when I wake everything is so still and mellow and distant that I no longer feel troubled about the postponement of the play. I go back to the San Remo with Sam. No tea.

Then I go to Maury and the night is tender to my wounds.

July 24, 1952

Paul says that I do not feel enough the self as a work of art. True. True. But he is contradicting what he has said about separating art and life.

I am torn: body, mind, and heart are splintered.

I don't cohere because death is a prolonged silence.

I cry out that communication is impossible. Therefore, silences are the form of torture that my friends inflict, having found my vulnerable spot.

Life as a continuous series of poems.

Julian and I grope in the dark. The prospects are bleak.

July 25, 1952

I can't settle down to the *Ubu* directing book, though I am more and more able to activate the actors. I've lost my rigidity with them.

The self as a work of art. I ponder this.

Constant entrances and exits. The intrigue of the barroom door through which anyone may walk at any moment.

A marvelous poem in Oscar Williams' anthology: Auden's "September 1939." I copy these lines from it:

> All I have is a voice
> To undo the folded lie,
> The romantic lie in the brain
> Of the sensual man-in-the-street
> And the lie of Authority
> Whose buildings grope the sky:
> There is no such thing as the State
> And no one exists alone;
> Hunger allows no choice
> To the citizen or the police;
> We must love one another or die.[14]

July 26, 1952

When the unbegrudging sun makes the mornings vivid as childhood hours, then I can draw from them some of childhood's energy. Washington Square has changed as have I, over the years of early Saturdays I spent at this fountain. But this morning the sun is the sun of my tenth year.

Yet it doesn't seem strange that I've come here from a lover's bed.

Till they wake up at the theater, I'll study Japanese in the park as once I did my homework. Lou appears.

I walk with him as he shops. At Womrath's he buys a book by Simone Weil. At Woolworth's, a shirt. In an 8th Street craft shop, sandals. And I see that the pain and the passion were disproportionate.

Where do they go, the passion and the prayer? In what realms of not-having-been do they lose themselves?

Ubu: The Desecrator. And the Affirmation. This follows.

July 27, 1952

In the Halversons' garret many people are sleeping. The gypsy way. The rootless way.

But if Julian, my love, should choose the gypsy way, even if it were wiser and purer than mine, I am not sure that I could follow.

I am in love with the world's bad dream.

If he can loosen his grip on tomorrow, I may envy him. But this tomorrow has her teeth sunk into me. I am driven.

July 29, 1952

I am finding, ever so gradually, an unwobbling pivot. I realize that the foundation stone is not oneself; it is a knowledge and sturdiness beneath oneself. So that even when the self is most vulnerable, this basis is not vulnerable.

It is necessary to keep oneself vulnerable. To make oneself the foundation is to turn oneself to stone.

July 30, 1952

The Chinese oracle says: "No blame."

I am bewildered as to whether or not I ought to chastise myself for smoking marijuana. That is to say . . . cease. Otherwise chastisement is nagging and useless reproach.

Yet I don't feel guilt about alcohol and its effects, because it is socially and legally acceptable. One can say, "I was drunk and . . ." The effects of the marijuana high are softer, less lasting, less upsetting to the system, but—and here's the rub—far more pleasant.

Do I feel guilt because I feel pleasure? Of course. Though surely:

> In a more perfect world we would not need
> the cozening solace of the weed.

Instead of anger at the lack of loyalty in the cast I feel a friendly spite. I wish to become, as it were, a legend to demonstrate my intrinsic merit.

In the end we are likely to be what we deserve to be.

August 1, 1952

A few days ago, the death of Eva Peron. The perfect tragic end to her Cinderella myth—adulated, enshrined, no decline to face, no descent from the pinnacle. I imagine that she would not be altogether disappointed, she who wore sensual black and jewels to see the Pope.

The play begins to cohere again after several stages of disintegration. I work like water in a stream—according to my own energies, avoiding, overriding, or dispersing obstacles. But without ever losing my rhythm.

"You accept only one kind of reality," says Paul, "and refuse to live through the other kind."

Yes.

"The cast" at the San Remo was so complete last night that one might have thought it a third act.

Even Paul was there, taken with Janet Jenkins from St. John's. I encouraged her for Paul's sake.

Marijuana. A light from beyond the smoke-filled dream. Less than sun, more than the glowing ash.

August 3, 1952

Preview performance of *Ubu*.

The dark, the stage, the sound: A net made of varying fabrics holding me close.

All I can hope for is a more comfortable mesh.

O dazzling multifarious world that I've brought forth in the dark auditorium. But here in the ardor of this fathomless room all things move out from a single circle, the pen, the ink, the candle, the clock, the tick of the clock.

Four A.M. silvery to sleep.

August 5, 1952

Tonight I will watch the play to learn what it means.

Julian has splattered the drab costumes with gaudy paint patterns born out of techniques discovered by Jackson Pollock. The process is exacting.

He is making the set out of wrapping paper. The wonders of our magical setting. The horrors of our farce.

August 6, 1952

The enthusiasm of the audience swept us away last night. Though the newspaper was insulting this morning, I am riding the crest of exultation.

I walk to Paul's. In the crook of my arm, my journal.

Writing as I walk.

August 9, 1952

The theater is closed! The new landlord, the rich Kenneth Carroad, has gotten the bureaucracy to close the theater!

No show last night. Today at the Municipal Building, we plead with many people in the various hornet nest bureaus.

For now, nothing can be done.

Is the theater really not going to reopen?

I want to come to myself again and take a soberer road. The deadening beauty of the netherworld is too sweet not to sicken.

Is the theater not going to reopen?

I didn't describe the opening night, putting it off to write in retrospect, but now I am at a loss about everything.

Lonely, lonely, lonely. Oh, Julian, I am so lonely.

August 10, 1952

The unpleasant sensation of having a powerful enemy. Even the authorities realize that this monied landlord is out to destroy us and they treat us with utmost consideration. But who can fight the green bait? We fight to remove accumulated violations. Clean. Repair. Plead. Fire Department. Electric Department.

The final incident:

We were all at work trying to repair the violations when the fire inspector came, in uniform, to give us final notice. We pleaded and, in the end, screamed, our fervor rising as his "no" grew more insistent. At last Julian grew vehement and with his bare hands tore the paper backdrop from the walls—ripping through his *Ubu* painting as though it were nothing.

Julian took up one of the bamboo spears that holds the canopy of *The*

Heroes and I seized it, menacing the unfortunate inspector; with shouts and cries I drove him from the theater like a furious Walkyrie, pursuing him down the length of Commerce Street to Sixth Avenue.

The neighbors laughed to see me with the ten-foot bamboo spear chasing the fireman—but I was crying when I returned. For a world ends . . .

August 13, 1952

A world ends.

The closing of the theater is irrevocable.

It was like a wake. We sat in the lounge and we talked of inequities.

Each actor came and took away his things. Packed clothes into valises. People took favorite props and costumes for their own.

Others came with condolences.

Paul came because "I come to such occasions."

"Sad occasions?"

"And to festivals."

He comes as priest to funeral and festival to bless, in his chosen role.

The clan reassembled. Only Philip was not there. Word came through Norman that Philip wanted his coat.

I left for the Remo with the coat on my arm, and the kimono I had given him.

August 14, 1952

Not often again. Not often will I sit at this window backstage at the Cherry Lane. Not often again.

Memory at work: the ice on the hedge at midwinter. And the carolers with candles in the courtyard at Christmas, and the light green budding at Easter, and the flowering of the honeysuckle in June, month of partings. . . .

Oh, all things concurred, in harmony with the seasons. But the seasons' harmony has proven out of keeping with the disproportionate universe.

"The reason for this disproportion is in the nature of the universe," quoth Paul.

I am sitting on the throne of Alexander the Great and lean my foot upon Faustina's couch.

We are taking home the relics of the theater—Phaedra's mirror, the costumes of *Ubu Roi*. Julian and Maury load them into a car and will drive them away.

Reading Coleridge. His preoccupation with ideas irritates me, while wicked Machiavelli delights me with his call to action. I have no more patience with theory.

Our future is unplanned. I want to make films. And I want to go to Paris where I would be more appreciated. And to forget Philip. And to gain weight and health. And to live with my child whom I have neglected.

August 15, 1952

Summer in New York. There's still the task of cleaning the theater. Nina stays uptown with us. Sometimes Maury sleeps at our house. Sometimes I stay downtown with him.

He is cautious of experience. His is an armoring that makes him seem like a small boy, which is not what I admire about him.

August 18, 1952

Images of wells. Dry wells and wells of rancid water. Stench of rotten well water.

We build with magic and destroy with stone.

As in Cocteau's image: In our hands the snowballs harden into lethal toys and really kill.

Julian is writing a scenario for a film.

August 20, 1952

Our circle is too wide and far too enclosed. It seems self-sufficient; actually it is incestuous and inbred.

Oh, for some self-sustenance.

August 21, 1952

One meal at Julian's parents. One meal at Mother's. So we live without money.

August 28, 1952

There was a party to close the theater that turned itself into 300 strangers and friends thronging, singing, dancing, drinking, smoking pot.

August 31, 1952

Julian is writing a film about love. Of Phaedra and Helen and Judith and Mary. History and personal life, the background and foreground of art.

Final cleaning out of the theater.

Garrick, playing, is told that we are leaving the theater. He shouts, "Good-bye, theater," and then adds with satisfaction, "It said good-bye to me."

Endings.

It is September 1952.

Lost. We are lost without the theater.

I move in a miasma of inconsequentialities.

Julian paints and draws.

After a quarrel last night, Julian and I walked down to the Village. At seven in the morning we reached Washington Square and slept an hour in the circle, on the stone steps of the fountain. Birds and buses for lullaby and a chill early fall wind.

Then, in the afternoon, to the Modern Museum to see Norma Shearer,

Leslie Howard, John Barrymore in *Romeo and Juliet*, which seemed, when I was ten years old, a golden legend enacted by the demigods. Now I see the lyric poetry lost in the garden scenery.

In the museum penthouse I find the decor as artificial as the Hollywood garden of the Capulets. But now even the cafeteria on Broadway's crassest corner copies the stonework of Frank Lloyd Wright's Taliesin.

I try reading Maury's copy of Hesiod. (Was Hesiod drunk on laurel leaves, this moral man, blessed by doves of peace and love . . . ?)

A group of well-heeled museum visitors walks by, praising Jackson Pollock: He is "proud," "admirable." He is "virile."

What end now does his fierceness serve?

September 4, 1952

I look with envy at the life of a nun, because to be dedicated formally is to simplify life, which offers so many possibilities that variety becomes an obstacle. Unable to control the shattering effects of a dispersed life, I want an outward form to bind me to a singleness of purpose.

What can't be achieved internally we wish to enforce externally. And that's the reason we consent to coercion and dependence.

I move toward a poverty of the soul.

I leaf through pages of unfinished poems. Send out to editors the poems of a year ago. Study a little French and Japanese. Dream about lovers. Read a little Hesiod. Theocritus. Sit in the San Remo Café. Scarcely sleep. Sparsely eat. Listen to Wagner or Purcell or Monteverdi. Procure the pungent marijuana. Dream.

I had a dream that was worth dreaming. I want it back. The feeling of being unquenchable.

Let me resolve again, and always again, and failing, still again, to be able and not to be consumed.

September 5, 1952

At night we experiment with our 8mm camera. I dance the minotaur dance from *Beyond the Mountains*.

We lit the front room brightly and hummed the Etan Raknu music. Maury counted the seconds. Julian ran the camera.

September 8, 1952

Julian's mother finds me a job in a pediatrician's office in the neighborhood. I squirm a little but cannot do other than accept.

I like the babies, the routine and the precision. The doctor is more concerned with his status on some state commission than with the children that crowd the office.

His brother shares the office. He is in "the medical insurance field" and tells stories of courtroom fraud and deception that disenchant me with the whole medical profession.

The doctor expects me to pose as a nurse. He could hardly hire a qualified nurse for twenty dollars a week. With my white uniform and a certain theatrical manner, I pass as a professional. But the ruse offends me.

To the river, where in the undercover comfort of trees and night Julian and I wander in the smoky mazes of the hemp dream.

September 9, 1952

Hesiod's concern with the poetical attributes of daily work.

Last night, filming. Julian constructs a set in the front room. Nina and I move through it as Julian shouts directions from behind the camera. Maury holds the lights.

September 15, 1952

Friday night we went to Julie Bovasso's; our first friendly meeting since she quit the cast of *Faustina*. Her husband, George Ortman, paints abstracts in the new, hard style. They live in a Second Street house.

We listen to bagpipe music. The pipes fill the room with a vast noise as the dirge cascades upward. The neighbors throw a glass at the window in protest.

Even here we find ourselves needing to defend the music of John Cage.

Things mean what we take them to mean. Superstition is the reality of the imagination. I see Carl Dreyer's *Book of Satan* at the Museum with Mother. Satan suffers over the evil he is working because it is his fate to work evil. An enormous idea. Thus Man and God are the villains and Satan the victim in a terrifying plot.

I dream dreams of guilt, dreams in which I am cruel, am found out, through which I flee into a dark maze.

September 16, 1952

I went back to the Cherry Lane to look for mail or memory. And now I'm in the Sans Remorse. A clean slate, the new leaf: Across from this page lies the clean page where all things are possible.

A la Gloire . . . !

Fallibility of the good resolve: As soon as I got up and walked across the room, someone said to me, "Tonight it can be done." And when have I ever resisted temptation?

September 17, 1952

En route to Paul Goodman's for an analytic session after the late summer interruption. I know that to go to him in high spirits means that he will break me down. But since I am in high spirits I am not troubled.

The interpretation of dreams. "But I knew this always. Why did I not know that I knew it?"

At night to San Remo. I write in subways; only in flux can I write. The pauses between are alive.

Twelve soldiers enter the train. All with guns. Hiiiii.

September 22, 1952

Rosh Hashanah prayer.

In the quiet hours when the doctor is not in the office, I work at my Japanese or read. Today, Gide's *Lafcadio*.

More and more I feel that right and wrong can be only defined as action. Buddha Gautama draws up the prudent borders of the middle path.

I know more than I admit to myself, less than I commit myself to, more than I am capable of.

I had best go back to Gide whose characters are possessed of a certainty so graceful that they are smug even as they waver. Or to George Miller's sardonic laugh and his sympathy, playing everything the British way, so much his own master, or as David Sachs says, "his own man."

In an Italian pastry place on Bleecker Street, Maury's friends talk passionately of the School of Korzybski and General Semantics. They manage to be idealistic and revolutionary without the despairing anger. I am happy to hear talk of a free (anarchist) society again. They call it a non-Aristotelian society. They mean not rigid. The jargon is elegant.

At Paul's today he said that I place blame, that I want to run both with the hares and the hounds.

September 25, 1952

I am not like Marcus Aurelius when he strives to be in all situations "still the same man." I want to give myself completely to the situation and not remain aloof from it. And though I have some of the stoic boredom, I have none of the stoic strength.

In childhood, when things touched me closely I could cry out and feel the hurt without pushing away the source of the pain. Now I can no longer say simply, "Here I am. It hurts." And so insidiously it comes about that I can no longer even say, "Here I am. It pleasures."

At the Metropolitan Museum of Art, there was an evening opening of a Rembrandt exhibit. In the gallery I come upon Van der Weyden's *Annunciation*, and am more moved by this stiffness than by Rembrandt's humanism. In the theater I seek the scope of the formalists in preference to the Ibsenic illusions of Rembrandt.

September 26, 1952

In the downtown morning subway, a crying boy and haggard mother with tear-stained faces. The scene suggests a recent death. His sister sits by apparently unmoved by the family tragedy.

Last night I read Garrick a Babar book in which an elephant turns green and dies from eating a poison mushroom. Garrick asked if he might tear out the page with the bad picture. He trembled, his eyes full of tears, not tantrum tears, but tears of grief.

Julian and I are amazed that our child knows the meaning of death, he who has just been born. We don't know where he learned the fatal sorrow before which all of us stand mute.

September 29, 1952

"The summer is over," says Dick Stryker.

At the San Remo Café the winter is already on us.

First there was a fight. Johnny Santini's face grew more and more brutal with satisfaction as he struck again and again his already unconscious opponent, crumbled on the tiles, inert. Johnny kept striking till they pulled him away.

That was the winter's start.

I gave some money for marijuana to someone who did not return but kept me waiting till four A.M.

Dick Stryker is friendly again and we flirt together and get involved with a bunch of thugs and sailors.

At closing time George walks me to Maury's.

September 30, 1952

Yom Kippur, 1952. Kol Nidre services with Mother. Enamored of inner progression I am full of resolves, vows, aspirations.

When I talk about religion with Maury, it irritates him that I can answer questions several ways. He argues by the firm principles of Aristotle while I insist on contradictions.

Maury grows furious. He blanches and his eyes turn a steelier blue. Afterward, he wreaks vengeance in a little torture scene and leaves me coldly, like a villain in a film.

This Yom Kippur I am fasting seriously.

October 1, 1952

To Paul's. I always write en route to Paul's. I am to pay him now out of my wages. To what more valuable purpose could the few dollars go? I feel with each session that, quite beyond psychology, what I am learning is tremendous.

October 2, 1952

Daytime: I write in the doctor's office, a world wholly dissociated from the boneless world of night.

Yet I've stayed away from the bar. It's been hard and easy. What I can do is easy. What I can't do is hard.

To deliberately avoid a net is to throw yourself into it. Oedipus running away from the predicted dangers. Avoiding the San Remo, I run into the barefoot party at Second Street.

Paul says that my difficulty is the integration of worlds. He says that in my mind there are several worlds and they are not compatible. But, in fact, I can't make up any world at all. No, Paul, there are no worlds to integrate, only glimpsed visions, a moment of rest between fears. A moment of ardent defense. A moment of happiness as painful as birth.

I began this passage in the daytime in the office, where what is true is bodily true. Now after midnight I'm writing in a 42nd Street movie house where I go through the nocturnal labyrinths of silences and abrupt farewells.

This morning I bought Pound's *Letters* for Julian, to say what I can't say.

Remo. I wanted to stay away a week. Failed.

What is art? What is life? What is speech? What is love? What is the human mind? What is discomfort? What is pleasure? What is sleep? What is marijuana? What is sexuality? What is literature? What is form? What is belief? What is experience? What is conscience? What is evil? What is daily bread? What is daily work?

October 3, 1952

The only question is, "How shall I live?"

We secure ourselves against the elements, we secure our children and build them storehouses of more than a lifetime's supplies. We organize states to protect the storehouses and systems to perpetuate their safety. And then the hunger of the heart roars in.

It is axiomatic that each one must find for herself the answer to the cry, "How shall I live?"

It is also axiomatic that we can only find it together, crying out, "How shall we live?"

October 4, 1952

Feeling lousy. Cold brought on by series of loveless events. To be ill is to say I have need of you, and be rejected. Cold. What a good word for an illness brought on by icy looks and unforgiving words.

Or by making love under an almost full moon on a tenement roof in October. Chill wind for a blanket.

And the next night in a fireless room under a single frail cover and an inhospitable atmosphere chill as yesternight's wind.

Well then, stay home.

No. With benzedrine and cosmetics and false wrappings I'll go to it. To what I have no idea. All day too sick to work.

October 6, 1952

At Alan and Serafina Hovhaness'. They live in an atmosphere of Before Completion. They do not need to be driven.

Serafina's mysticism is pure faith. Alan is, in his words, devoted to death.

Serafina regards death as neither desirable nor undesirable. Free of torment as an angel is, the seraph watches over the tortured musician. He says, "I am not afraid to die, but I am afraid to live, especially I am afraid of living long."

Why is there no gloom in their house when they speak like this?

October 7, 1952

I try to write poetry, but the words don't show me the way back to "the faith I seemed to lose with my lost saints." I'd like to do a libretto, an oratorical, religious libretto for Alan, lucid as his music.

Filming *Ladies' Voices* with Frances. Her languid and aristocratic bearing. I'm restless. And not for Aphrodite.

October 8, 1952

The inexpensive film we've been using is faulty. The third roll comes back spotted and faded, but Julian's inherent artistry shines through all flaws.

At Paul's the gigantic mess, the octopus is soothed. Things stretch evenly over compatible meanings. We talk about growth. He fills me full of hope though I don't know for what.

He lends me *Wilhelm Meister*, which I really ought to read in German.

October 10, 1952

Reading *Moby Dick*. Ishmael's sins don't horrify me, as we forgive those we love.

I read *Wilhelm Meister* in translation; Carlyle's antique style has its own charm. Julian is studying *Faust*. Goethephilia.

An Italian masterpiece, *The Path of Hope*, Pietro Germi's film about the migration of Sicilian sulphur miners into France.

October 11, 1952

Paul says there are no women artists because a woman is too much concerned with her own body. I get angry.

October 12, 1952

At Cooper Union. A concert called Music in the Making. Mostly to hear a piece by John Cage.

On the Bowery, in the Sagamore Cafeteria, after the concert the pioneers drink beer or coffee: Cage, Tudor, Cunningham, Heliker, Lippold, Stryker, Cowell, Norse, Beck. . . .

I speak to John in this noisy cafeteria. He drinks beer and we talk about Lou.

October 14, 1952

The gamelan and the dancers of Bali in a Broadway theater.

Magic and theater. What have we killed with our cautious fear of bad taste, our sophistry, and our criticism?

In its gold and red complexity, the theatricality entices the watchers to overflow with the dancers' motions and to rejoice with the insistent rhythm of the gamelan.

But I don't know how to go to the theater any longer. I am not able to decide between the simple act of watching, the complex duty of understanding, and the impulse to participate. When it is sublime, as are these dancers, I wish I could participate.

October 15, 1952

At Paul's. I described a nightmare in which monstrous forms of my own making menace me, but I cannot, or dare not, or will not waken . . .

Paul points out how I brace myself against pain instead of escaping from it. He puts pressure on my shoulders with his hands and I react by bringing up my shoulders to meet his hands with a return pressure till it stops hurting. Then he asks me rather to slip out from under him and squirm away.

I am literally unable to do this. My body will not move away. We repeat the attempt until, with effort, I can do it.

"This is the way you react. You brace yourself against pain and refuse to duck. So you grin and bear it, till eventually you will feel that because it must be borne you may as well enjoy it. Then it becomes masochism. That's also what your dream is about."

What Paul fails to account for is the real pain of the masochist, howling, "O God, how can you be so cruel?"

I want to be a woman, as Paul urges, and to have real life in me. That's modest enough.

October 16, 1952

In a small Madison Avenue shop, Julian and I buy white chocolates. A beautiful young woman enters and in a heavy European voice asks the shopkeeper if they have come yet.

The shopkeeper asks, "What?"

"The apricots."

Her voice emotes around the word. She says it simply. I knew it was Garbo.

"Oh, your glazed apricots? No, not yet."

"How is your cold?"

"Better."

"Ah, mine's still here."

She brought her hand up to her throat and moved out of the shop.

I learn this from Garbo's performance: to be fully present in the present, to desire the temporal (for what else is a glazed apricot?), and to smile as intensely at the shopkeeper as at Armand.

October 21, 1952

I have been all night with the weed, but I am not possessed.

I'll stay downtown because I enjoy the walk to Paul's in the morning through the Village.

Then I'll go to work without going home, very tired after twenty hours out.

At home at night, I arrange the back room as a work room where I can seclude myself and function in my own terms.

And I write a hundred little poems about silence.

October 22, 1952

Paul tries to make categories of my experiences and to correlate them. I prefer my system of counterbalances, which steady me within impossible situations of my own making.

Paul asks, "Where is your out? In your diary?"

We talk about this book. He suggests my reading back, making a typescript, preparing parts with altered names and editing for publication. Fear that it would make my writing self-conscious.

What do I want? It is what Paul calls "stepping out into the void." As he has it, there's a golden crown out there, but one must not—cannot—move toward the crown itself. It is necessary to step into the void with faith in the void and faith in the stepping self, but never with the hope of possessing the golden crown.

In the park that centered my childhood's play and my loves' flowering, I return like a Noh-play ghost.

October 30, 1952

A concert at the Museum of Modern Art began with Lou's suite for the Ajemian sisters.

After this very personal work, music for tape recorder. Stokowski came out on the stage and said, "This is a new kind of music, an experiment. Heretofore the musician has had to write first for the paper, and then depend upon the performers to make it into music. For the paper which we call music is not music. The sound is the music. Now the musician can make the sound directly with the new methods of electronics. Some people will say that this is not music, but they said that about Beethoven and Bach."

And he left the stage empty to the loudspeaker supplied by Maury's Electronic Workshop. Music of Luening and Ussachevsky.

Why do I feel so unnecessarily rootless?

I have a house, a bed, a husband, a child. But I have no work. I have no theater.

October 31, 1952

This is the anniversary of our marriage.

Children in their Halloween attire are on the streets.

I sing this song as I wait for the bus:

> The night is my friend
> And holds me in his black and loving hands. . . .

November 1952

As if happiness were a tangible thing.
The river is blacker than the night heavens. It is shinier. Dark park. Barges. Hudson. Very foggy Hudson. Peace. Night. Uneventfulness. Caught in a Japanese print, eternally immobile.
How dark it is. Barely see the pen.

November 4, 1952

A personal response to Paul's *Break-up of Our Camp*.
As I read the startling and familiar Talmudic question in Paul's book, I wanted to cry out: "*I shall. I shall.*"
"If I am not for myself, who shall be for me?" I have warm and tearful memories of these words in my father's mouth.
Then also I had wanted to cry out: "*I shall. I shall.*"
But the phrase continues: "If not now, when?"
And when I was a child I thought: "When I am grown up! Then."
But when I grew up I realized bitterly, bitterly, that then was the time, and if not then, never.
I have lived my life thinking this: I was false to myself and betrayed myself and betrayed my father by waiting, and when I was thirteen he died and left me to be forever unsatisfied and forever unable to answer: "*I shall. I shall.*"
Now I know with anguish that this is false reasoning. That now is the one thing we cannot be without.
Now I know that it is now again. I encounter this phrase exactly as my father spoke it. (With what rending pain do the tears come at this phrase, with what unsuppressed feeling am I at last able to give way to this!) And again I want to answer: not "*I shall. I shall,*" but "I am. I am."
It strikes me like a blow across the face. The knowledge that I cannot be for Paul, to whom I would give all my strength. To warm, loving Paul, who understands the tears of the universe and the plaints of my people and the wellspring of my streaming eyes. And I want to establish, as it were, a world for him to live in, in which he could fulfill his happier desires. (As I wanted to establish a magnificent temple for my father's congregation so that his greatness might not be wasted among the rented folding chairs.)
And I know like a blow that I cannot be for him.

I have not yet been able to eat my food without distaste and take what is given to me. Therefore how can I give?
I have not yet been able to speak my lines without laughing at myself. Therefore, how can I establish a city for him?

Beset with the pangs of the knowledge of what I could not do, a terrible ache came into my head. So I took headache powders, and the efficacious NOW became numb.
And still the pain persists. For where else but in my feeble head shall my heart cry out?
So I did not say: "I shall. I shall."
Nor better still: "I am. I am."
I reread what I wrote. And I add: "Lest he die, and it be again too late and I be left alone with bitter self-reproach."

Apply the words of his mouth to my mouth, my self-betraying mouth that has a distaste for the food that is given it and that laughs when I speak my lines, that laughs at me and is not for me.

Somewhere there is a turning. And if not now, when?

I want to cry out "I shall. I shall. I am. I am," until I am able in the ever-present NOW to build the magnificent temple and establish the happy city for him.

Somewhere there is a turning. And if not now, when?

The people elect the soldier, Eisenhower, to be their (the people's) president.

The majority has invited the invading force to rule.

They are all corrupt and I can't favor either side, even though I fear one side more. I fear the military. I fear the generals, who have dedicated their lives to war. Even worse, I fear "the people" who elect such a man in their majority.

No, it's not true. I don't fear the people. But I don't understand them either.

November 7, 1952

"Do what your father would have done," Paul says, "and keep him alive in that way."

Our talk had turned to what I had written after reading *The Break-up of Our Camp*.

Therefore, I think of gathering together my friends, as my father gathered together his congregation.

I talk at breakfast with Nina and Julian, and we arrange to meet next week with Charles Wellman, who has given much thought to the application of anarchist theory to revolutionary practice.

November 10, 1952

When I hear John Cage talk about music I feel I am part of the living world, but I can't sustain that strength.

John defends a piece by Morton Feldman at Cooper Union: "I love this music because there is a direct line between this music and myself. Nothing stands between me and this music. It is like a tightrope and to walk this tightrope is to ask oneself, 'Am I alive?' This is the question we must all ask ourselves: 'Are we alive?' "

The audience balked; they had no inclination to ask themselves this question.

John Cage is like a pale gray-white room, a shelter, a cloister, a haven.

November 14, 1952

Jean-Louis Barrault brings his troupe to New York. The pantomime "Baptiste" and Marivaux.

As a child I believed in art. Later I spoke only of "work," ashamed to use the word "art." This troupe has no particular virtue except their unashamed attachment to art, for its own perfect sake.

November 17, 1952

Participating in eternity I am only a part of things, therefore I am immortal.

In the theater, this urge toward participation leads to eliminating the line between the reality of the theater and the reality of the world outside the theater.

Barrault's production of *The Trial*, adapted by Gide, like Piscator's production, externalizes K's persecution.

Art itself is an externalization of the unspeakable cry.

If I did this play I would try to make it unbearable for the audience. Only when the audience realizes its impotence will it rebel. If I could drive them to such extremes of exasperation in the theater that their restrained outcries began to materialize in their throats, then I might drive them to enact their needs when they hit the air outside the theater.

The act of sitting in the theater is an agreement to tolerate the action as a demonstration and an enlightenment. The energy to change the unbearable situation mounts in the theater. Then we will go out and destroy the outer law and the inner chains: the state's yoke and the spirit's harness.

November 20, 1952

At midnight, at the Electronic Workshop in a well-lit cellar full of mechanical paraphernalia, Maury guides a T-square over a drawing board. His fool head is, alas, so handsome and his perception is, alas, so fine.

He is like a calculating machine measuring time, space, quantity, result or probability against a given standard.

I refuse to spend the night with him. I'll stop a while at the San Remo.

Jake Spencer and Marge, with two Spanish merchant seamen, Mario and Nilo. Nilo is beautiful, but it is Mario to whose sensuous flirtation I respond, and he imagines me won.

We all take a taxi to Jake and Marge's pad on Ludlow Street. We smoke. Vivian sings torrid songs of her own making, stroking her body, lifting her skirt, writhing in the murky glow of a single red bulb. Heat emanates from her.

These are, perhaps, sacred rites, but we can't be what we are not. I withdraw from Mario's attentions. I have no life in that life.

On various subway trains I lose my way, arriving home at six in the cold, wet morning.

Tonight in our gray front room some friends will gather. I will dress as hostess. I hear in my mind's ear a talk between Paul and Marius Bewly.

At work I dreamed, my head on the desk, little quick dreams of disorientation.

"I am addled," I said to Paul yesterday.

"You are better that way," he said.

November 26, 1952

Lucia Dlugoszewski plays the *Music of Everyday Sounds*—her music for

Ubu, in Ralph Dorazio's studio, behind a screen of newspapers. In this congregation there is neither the hush of undue reverence nor indifference. Lucia's orchestration of everyday sounds confounds the concert ear. We hear the clatter of teacups, the turning of the doorknob, breaking glass.

John Cage listens better than anyone because he exalts the very faculty of hearing.

The Barrault production of *Occupe-toi d'Amelie* is half art/half boulevard. Under the painted dome of the oversize Ziegfeld Theater the actors expend an excessive quantity of energy.

The National Theater of Greece's *Oedipus Rex*: The vitality comes out of restraint.

After seeing *Oedipus* for the third time, I realize that the meaning is not the inevitability of destiny, but that Oedipus and Jocasta could have pieced together the facts. The tragedy is that they did not.

November 28, 1952

The wedding of Bill Mullalhy and Janet Jenkins.

Janet's grandfather performed the ceremony with grandfatherly compassion and contempt. Bill's mother's wizened faith no longer cared. But Janet's mother was determined to make a traditional occasion of it. We posed with the wedding party in the portal of the church on Madison Avenue eating the nuptual cake.

Then to the engagement party of Peter Farb, at the Roerich Museum. He is marrying the daughter of the museum's owner, with whom Julian has been negotiating for the rental of the Master Theater.

Then to Peter Miller's Stuyvesant Town apartment. Andrew Chiappe, the Pousette-Darts, Helen Frankenthaler, Clement Greenberg. Greenberg heaps lavish praise on the Picasso play, and on me, in a manner to which I am not accustomed.

On to Janet's and Bill's. In their loft a blazing fire. Bob Kaufman beats time on the back of a guitar while he recites "The Love Song of J. Alfred Prufrock," translating Eliot's English into our dialect. Despite the ludicrous parody, we are drawn into the marijuana smoke while the evening was indeed "stretched out against the motherfuckin' sky like a patient etherized upon a motherfuckin' table."

"Eliot said that everyone should perform poetry in their own terms," Kaufman explained.

Am I beginning to integrate the world?

The new moon blows in December.

POLITICS IS A NATURAL WAR MACHINE. DON'T VOTE.	POLITICS IS A NATURAL WAR MACHINE. DON'T VOTE.

December 1, 1952

What is begun on the full moon, say astrologers, bears a good chance of prospering.

Julian met with Mme. Piscator about doing a series of plays at the Dramatic Workshop. It isn't now what it was, but only a remnant of Piscator's noble enterprise. Madame is dismayed by its decline and is hoping that Julian and I will produce work worthy of the old reputation.

Julian talks with Dr. Piscator (as she is now addressed) at the Capitol Theater Building on the Great White Way, where the Workshop occupies one floor.

She plans two productions, *R.U.R.* and *Murder in the Cathedral*, but wants to use outside actors rather than cast students as Piscator often did. *R.U.R.* is a faulty play with good inventions. Madame is anxious to be "conservative."

"We must allow the public to catch up with us."

Piscator is touring Europe while the school goes to seed.

I am eager for the connection to lead back to Piscator. My awe and affection have never wavered.

There's no other person in the theater with whom I should care to work save Cocteau . . . or Chaplin, who is currently being maligned by the press and the State Department and may choose not to work again in this ingrate land to which he has given his genius.

Livelihood: "How shall I live?"

Julian is working in Macy's toy department for Christmas demonstrating a toy fish, Swimbo, that does stunts in a tank. And I am forever at the doctor's.

I've come to dislike the doctors I work for more and more, especially since the day an epileptic had a seizure outside the office door. I called the doctor, who, seeing that the man was shabby and poor, refused to help. I went back to the man, who at last regained control with the help of kind, unprofessional neighbors.

If it were not for the pleasure of the babies which I weigh and clean, hold and medicate, I couldn't go on here, economic necessity notwithstanding.

At the theater tonight, Jean-Louis Barrault's *Hamlet* in Gide's translation. Oedipus and Hamlet: Hamlet's search culminates in murder and Oedipus' culminates in an atonement for murder. What can we make of this?

Looking at Auden's *Age of Anxiety, a Baroque Ecologue,* I know I want to stage this piece. It is a perfect Theater in the Room production.

No sooner do I suggest it to Nina and Julian than we are in production. Perhaps Walter and George for the two other men. Its simplicity makes it feasible.

The poetry is fluid in the mouth, for it is the natural voice of the heart (that is, the way we murmur to ourselves on dark streets, or what we hear inside while we consummate our banal conversations).

So it begins again. What if a bit "by time's fell hand defaced"?

December 2, 1952

Sleety snow. To the Remo at eleven.

George Miller is interested in *The Age of Anxiety.* "Auden has been haunting me for weeks."

Casting again in this bar. This time for a play about a bar.

George and I reminisce about our Saturnalian nights in Auden's St. Marks Place apartment. That disarray of the poet in which the anxieties are allayed.

A year ago *Doctor Faustus Lights the Lights* was running and life was a different life.

I'm on my way to Paul Goodman.

Soon we will be rehearsing again and it will be good.
Ad astra per aspera.

December 3, 1952

Read a little of Goncourt's journal in a French edition which I found on a Village street this cold four A.M. His littered pages, like Gide's tense little paragraphs, seem quite consistent with the illicit atmosphere of the predawn subway.

At Paul's. When he speaks of "us" and "our people," I feel like a disciple.

Paul says that I don't believe in the subconscious. It's not that I don't admit to its existence, but that I doubt its potential usefulness is helping us live with the lousy disproportion which is in the nature of the universe. We work so hard to establish an equilibrium.

In order to get through work I took more dexedrine:

Now night gives birth to death as if called sleep.

December 5, 1952

I want to escape the terrible thoughts that come to me, but I force myself into bitter acceptance of the bottle. What use is this need to grapple with horror?

To be strong? Why is that important?

To learn how? Why that?

To brace myself. Yes. To brace myself against the real pain to come.

Always this need to experiment with the soul.

No, I will not allow myself even a phenobarbital at this point.

The actor can't dissemble in real life because the spectators are too close, stage gestures fail, and worst of all the spectator is also a participant. And after the third act, the murdered don't go home.

December 8, 1952

Am I not addicted to the San Remo? To a mere atmosphere? I fight it, try to stay away, to taper off, to break away cold turkey. I fail. And are the passions that make us sick no more nor less than addictions to the desired one?

There's nothing to which one can't be addicted.

December 9, 1952

To the courthouse to testify for Mother, who was dragged along the street by a bus when the door closed on her ankle.

City Court is one of the dowager buildings, with a rotunda, whose columns and pilasters rise five stories high to culminate in a typically graceless glass and metal construction more like an enlarged skylight than a dome.

Heavy balustrades. Marble floors. Light fixtures converted from gaslight. Stolid people. The overcoated, hatted men amid cigar smoke.

"After all, you could say that it's the truth because it *almost did* happen that way."

Or: "In that case we'll show that it really has no bearing on the case."

We are briefed by several attorneys. At first they seem funny but I soon begin to adopt their false, mannered tone.

But Mother's inherent dignity is unscathed in the face of their flaunted corruption.

Working on *The Age of Anxiety.*

George Miller as Emble, the sailor; Walter as Malin, the Royal Canadian Air Force man; Julian as Quant; Nina as the Jewess, Rosetta; and I will play the Narrator.

In the first reading each actor shows a cerebral approach which is appropriate to the complex verse.

What is missing is the anxiety itself. The characters are so close to us that we treat them too informally. We shouldn't be more comfortable with them than they are themselves.

I take on problems of vocabulary, especially the botanical, geological, and geographical terms, and the structure and syntax: the characters lost in the words.

This is a merry company. Easy companions and full of cheer. But the play is a dark play.

Last night I wrote in my diary that I did not want to go to the Remo, finished the passage, and went.

December 10, 1952

Paul's wisdom in the morning. Much of the talk seemed at first not related to psychotherapy, but when we came at last to my dreams it was clear that not an irrelevant word had passed. It is impossible to digress with him—he tightens the reins so imperceptibly that one does not feel bound. Nor is it possible to feel any sense of hurry to get on with it.

December 13, 1952

December on the street. A cold night.

Philip spoke to me. I said. He said. I said. He said.

Before we parted, he kissed me somewhat on the forehead. I am satisfied with this business.

December 14, 1952

Party at Jo LeSueur's. We arrive after the rehearsal for *The Age of Anxiety* in time for coffee with Jo and Gianni and George and Paul Goodman and Don Wyndham and Jim De Vries and Ned Rorem.

When Dicken told me about Ned Rorem's adagio act, I didn't know he meant that I would find in it some of that demonic beauty that drew me to Lou; I liked his perverse attractiveness. He listens to music holding a yellow rose with his head thrown back in a pose as effective as he believes it to be. He is almost entirely turned inward; but if someone more his type had not been determined to possess him, I might have found a way.

December 16, 1952

Who says "if only" has bound himself, as it were, to a vow.

Reading: Apuleius translated by Graves. Sometimes I think it's the devil's work, this inconstant woman of three faces who would take up the remnants of the works of the fatigued god of love.

En route now seeking a substitute for the irreplaceable Remo.

It is the White Horse Tavern and scarcely a person is here. In the back room two men, one of whom is dispassionately criticizing the manuscript of the other.

I could sit here for hours hypnotized by the atrociously detailed mural of a woodland scene framed in bright gilt.

I think of my friends in the Remo with some longing. Like Alcibiades among the Spartans.

At Chumley's I play chess, a war game that I do not like, with a difficult young man.

December 19, 1952

Julian says that ugliness is a lie, but this implies that it doesn't exist. I prefer to believe everything exists and call the lie real, being as it is, a real lie.

To live through it. Not closing the eyes and clenching the teeth but instead opening the eyes wide (even if with horror), opening up the mouth, "Oh brother blockheads of mankind" (I'm reading Carlyle), breathing in the pollution, and living through it.

We've agreed to do *R.U.R.* at the Dramatic Workshop. I will direct, Julian will design. But now we learn that Madame Piscator has gone to Europe and that there is no money to pay us.

December 20, 1952

In the dentist's chair, I experiment with the relationship of sensation to thought. Precisely under nitrous oxide, the soul could be isolated, if I had the will not to be afraid of pain. Ah, but if I had the will I would not need the cool gas.

December 21, 1952

At Howard Johnson's at five in the morning, everyone discusses why there are so many people who go to Howard Johnson's at five in the morning, when nobody wants to be there.

"We won't relinquish the night," says Julian.

"We haven't found anyone to go home with and are unwilling to face it."

"It's a last attempt."

"It's nice here," says Remy, for whose sake we may all be redeemed.

And William Marchant, who was Gaugau Davis, when he introduced me to Julian.

1943, September:
I'm standing in a doorway on 45th Street in my red corduroy coat, watching the actors and actresses go by.

I'm eating a pocketful of penny Suchard chocolates I bought in the subway, when a good-looking boy approaches and says he's hungry. He finishes all the chocolates and is still hungry, so I take him next door to the Automat and watch him eat my next-to-last dollar, while he prattles in that exaggerated, sophisticated fashion. He calls me madonna and quotes poetry.

And tells me of the handsomest, most talented, wealthiest, most charming young man in the world to whom he will as a reward for my generosity, introduce me.

The following day he tells Julian to prepare to meet the most beautiful, the richest, the most talented, the most charming girl in the world and brings him downtown to me.

I wait in Genius, Inc., the actors' club which I frequent with devotion.

Gaugau (a diminutive for Guillaume) taps on the window. I dash out. He grabs my hand, pulls me across the street, and there, his head haloed with the neon "o" of the Holley Bar, a rugged raincoat tossed over one shoulder, stands Julian.

I'm introduced as Jody Malin(!). Julian takes my hand in both his hands.

Not a moment's hesitation. Instantly, I am in love. We spend a fantastic night. Gaugau and Julian filch my last dollar from my purse. We eat grapes and doughnuts, see *Beyond Suspicion*, with Joan Crawford, in a 42nd Street movie house, wander about Times Square without going anywhere.

We are determined to shock the world and succeed in shocking ourselves. But the constant shock keeps us constantly awake. And the energy!

Julian examines me through the night. He has heard that I say: "Calder should not be seen by the common people" (a typical Gaugau invention). In fact, I know nothing of Calder, nor was I familiar with any of the poets and painters of whom Julian speaks.

But in my mind, I note every name: Amy Lowell and Kandinsky, Gertrude Stein and James Joyce. The following day I go to work in the library. I research systematically and am astonished by what I find.

It seems there's this brave new world, different, brand new, stretching beyond the portals of our time, and certain privileged beings, members of a hermetic cult privy to its mysteries wander at will through the Enchanted Garden. I read fanatically. I cut my high school classes and sit in the library reading and skimming and studying and memorizing.

In a week I conquer the moderns. They change me completely, because what is learned out of love is learned most truly and most closely.

The years, strangely, seem not to affect Gaugau. Like Dorian, he is fairer with the passing time. He says he is taking an exotic youth drug that Stalin uses. He looks twenty and has an adolescent's flippant energy, enchanting in his porcelain soul.

Sitting with Julian between him and Remy, the world being round, everything finds, not its level, but its cycle.

December 22, 1952

Being the season, the concert of Maro and Anahid Ajemian: Anahid in blue tulle and green satin, Maro in white and orange. The bare concert stage made glamorous with their gowns and the dashing William Masselos turning the pages.

A suite for violin, piano, and percussion written for them by Alan. The percussion in mystic dialogue with the western instruments.

Lou, angelic, and distant as the angels, running past us constantly in inconstant motion. He spoke to Julian of his operas and the goddess.

Serafina invites us to a party at the Ajemians'.

En route we see a woman's form covered with a black coat lying on the subway platform covered with a black coat. Still and painless. The disquieted onlookers, the efficient police. Her painless state struck no horror.

Serafina and Alan had passed them on the earlier train, when her face was still uncovered. We talk of ill omen. Serafina feels the sight makes one prone to misfortunes.

Anahid plays with a kitten while Henry Cowell delights the company with witty stories of a child prodigy he is training, and of how he, Cowell, is most influenced muscially by early Cowell.

The apartment is furnished in the unassuming style of Washington Heights. Its prize, unrelated to the rest of the decor, a fine-lined Richard Lippold sculpture through which the kitten capers.

December 23, 1952

At Columbia, a concert of electronic music. Pierre Boulez, both reticent and dapper, and John Cage talk to the music lovers of the music.

No one mocked, for a change. Most of the audience were enamored of each other.

But all ears perked up when David Tudor and Boulez played together a piano duet by Boulez. Each sound, each note carved its space in the air.

We went to a Spanish restaurant with Remy and Norman and Nina and the notorious Nick Cernovitch from Black Mountain. He is indeed charming enough to be the subject of contention.

Returning home, as we emerge from the 96th Street station, there's a flash of light and Julian says, "Winter lightning."

The winter lightning was the flash bulb of a photographer taking pictures of a boy's dead body, bloody on the street. He lay in a plaid jacket in the gutter, his feet on the curb, his face exposed.

Not painless. Not this second corpse.

The crowds, the corpse, the efficient police.

A youngster of about nineteen stood with his hands raised above his head, his face against a lamp post. A plainclothesman held a gun at his back.

His face was blank and dull. His black eyes were turned down.

I didn't know the story until this morning, but it was clear from what was happening that the cop had shot the dead boy.

I wanted to speak to the boy standing there with his helpless hands raised, but I could not. I told myself that it was because a policeman pushed me away with his nightstick just at the moment that I would have spoken, and as he did I cried out to my astonishment, "I hate you."

He answered sadly, "Lady, I can't help that."

As we went away I looked back at the captured boy, and I imagined his blank look to mean, "Here I am. My friend is dead. I survived. I should feel something. Why do I feel nothing?"

Galba immobile. Guilty. "I hate myself. I hate myself."

This morning I read in the newspaper: three servicemen bombed a bar on Amsterdam Avenue. "Let's go to Spanishtown and raise a little hell."

A little hell.

All day I am haunted by the event. I see in Mark Sutter the living Galba of *Faustina* turning the sword in the bear.

"For everything, for everything . . ."

Our friends come here and we read from *The Duchess of Malfi*. Reading playfully this somber script. They, too, do not cheer me.

But what of the two corpses? Are they omens? Or are they lessons come at the moment when they must be learned?

December 24, 1952

I woke this morning with Mark Sutter in mind.

But I am late for Paul's.

The transference is intense. I feel more his disciple than his patient. My admiration for him strengthens my identity.

"What you admire and want to preserve is the stillness of the bodies and therefore you paralyze yourself," Paul says.

I'm not sure. In fact, I think not. He tries to make me cry out "No," but I can't. My voice becomes small.

"You hate the man, the *Mensch*," says Paul.

"Which man?"

"The dead man," says Paul.

For being dead.

What a terrible emphasis on doom this Christmas season.

December 25, 1952

Having weathered Midwinter night.

Having weathered two weeks away from the San Remo.

There were the old friends.

We talk about Reich and Whitehead till seven A.M.

December 29, 1952

Anton brings the *I Ching*. He reads, not by the coin oracle, but by the longer method, using ivory sticks as yarrow stalks. The reading was *"Chen Jen,"* the family.

"If the husband is really a husband and the wife is really a wife, the family will be in order, and when the family is in order, the state will be in order."

Through what Paul calls "the way that is hard because it is simple."

For the woman to remain enclosed within the family circle is a principle I have rejected.

Anton, Bill Keck and Nina seem to me like a frieze cast in the eternal light that such possessed people carry.

A wondrous night ensued. An easy meal, and long, long, easy talk.

We spend the whole night talking.

When Garrick woke, he came in and asked if we had been up all night. When we said yes, he said, "You could not have. You would have fallen asleep. What did you do?"

"We talked to each other."

"You must have fallen asleep while talking, didn't you?"

December 31, 1952

It is five minutes to midnight.

We all dress: Nina in white and gold skirt, black blouse, and Russian white fur hat; I am in gold and black with much jewelry; Julian in tabis, dungarees, and his bullfighter's bolero.

Julian opens the champagne.

1953

January 1, 1953

A blissful moment alone with Julian in the apartment, drinking to the year with wordless laughter.

Then four friends arrived: Jerry Newman and John Clellon Holmes, Allen Ginsberg and Jack Kerouac, and we drank port and got high on gage.

Holmes is the author of _Go_, a novel now popular among the vipers, and he it was who wrote that _New York Times Magazine_ oddity, "The Beat Generation," that has caused so much talk.

He seems uncomplicated and not like one who should be chosen to speak for his times. Unless the times are such that he is precisely the one who represents the spokesman.

Of all of them, he alone holds out against rashness of words or action. And smoking with us, he preserves a stable demeanor with uncanny hostility.

Jack Kerouac, whom he credits with inventing the phrase "the Beat Generation," is a novelist who was a contemporary of Julian's at Horace Mann. He was the football champ who surprised everyone by winning scholastic honors.

Kerouac is a hero, a free-flowing spirit. He can't do anything except display his talent. Sardonic and handsome to a fault, he became raucous, drunk and incoherent as the night wore on to morning. But a hero on the binge is still a hero.

Nina notes that he resembles the canoeist in Paul's _The Break-up of Our Camp_. His false, coarse talk hides nothing. Of the intoxicated intellectuals, he is the most interesting. Yet I am wary of him.

Jerry Newman plays Puck, but his instincts are accurate. He owns Esoteric Records, which put out Lou's _Only Jealousy of Emer_. At seven or eight in the morning, Jerry takes Allen, Jack, and me in a taxi to his studio to listen to music.

Allen shepherds the group, subtly leading, aiding them in small things like crossing streets, or remembering hats, or thanking their hosts.

Holmes splits without saying farewell.

New Year's morning, and the taxi takes the empty streets and snow-filled park by storm. Inside the cab, Allen sleeps and Jerry smiles while Kerouac and I dit-dat jazz.

The studio is cluttered with equipment. The three drunks and I seem external to it. We are not part of the music. Even to listen.

Flamenco, African, Algerian.

Allen goes to sleep under the piano with me.

Hell is many different things. Suffering is the least of these. Here are the elements of heaven: Every sweet thing.

When we waken, Kerouac, ever heroic, is waving a bottle of Sandeman port (he himself like the caped figure, but his cap hangs lopsided over one ear) and shouting obscenities.

We play some of Lou's _Only Jealousy_, but in competition with Kerouac's

· 263 ·

cries, it is better stopped. He gets so loud and vehement that he scares me. (The drag is that I'm sober.)

Elements of heaven and hell abrew in the cauldron.

Should they produce a cake of paradise?

Allen, walking me to the subway, is suddenly lovable. In this sub-super-human world, I long for the familiar talk of mother tongue.

January 2, 1953

Rehearsing *The Age of Anxiety*.

We are too loose and undisciplined.

Reading. Just finished *The Golden Ass*. Graves' translation interprets it as a White Goddess story.

Also Weigal's scholarly biography of Sappho. Whitehead. And an anonymous Victorian book on oriental drama.

January 3, 1953

Sure. Sure. Sure. Sure. This is self-silencing. Sure.

Chaplin films: *The Kid*. A film about the natural man. The police is the natural enemy of the natural man, and poverty his natural condition. With unashamed simplicity his dream is wealth and lavish living. And the happy ending is, alas, in terms of money. The natural man can break a window in order to be paid to repair it, and yet remain pure enough to dream about being an angel.

What can I learn from Chaplin? That art is simple.

January 5, 1953

I wake up early to work on *R.U.R.* but Björn Halvorsen and Bill Kehoe come to tell us of their vision of integrating man and the universe.

Kehoe, the poet-scientist, expounds in wild words the divinest logic.

That we have come to a crucial point in evolution. Man recognizes in physics and mathematics the compatibility of object and subject, or outside and inside, or micro- and macrocosm, and has created a fresh set of values.

Kehoe goes on to demonstrate that the purpose of organism is to create new organism. Relationship flowers into identification. We contain each other (no, literally: he quotes Whitehead, Oppenheimer, Huysmans, Newton).

It seems like the ultimate form of love.

He would like to make plays of it. I think he means to socialize his dreams. But I say to him that we must begin by creating the community in which such plays can come out of us. We need air to breathe in which such plays will grow because the players create them.

January 6, 1953

At the Dramatic Workshop there is no work fever without the beacon of Piscator's exacting seriousness.

Now there is only a view of Broadway, the glare of the Capitol Theater

sign flashing on and off outside the window. Passionless students com
out and read passionlessly.

January 7, 1953

Frances will play Helena in *R.U.R.* and Serafina will play either Sulla or
Nana.
In the cold, disinfectant-scented halls of the Capitol Theater Building, one
is inclined to walk secretly and sinfully.
Paul speaks more often now of "our people."

January 8, 1953

We search for actors and instead
Find a sea full of sad fish.
In the Remo a sailor comes and curses us:
He says that he hates life.
His body is tattooed with obscene designs.
He shows them off.
He insults everyone: He says: "You guys are faggots.
What you do for pleasure I do for something green."
"Envy?" asks Remy.

It's time to go to work: But Bill Keck comes: He tells a sorry story of his
girl: She "flipped": And they're giving her shock.
Artificial addling of the human mind.
And maybe of the soul.
Who knows what really happens when those dreadful waves pierce through
the fragile structure under the skull? Scientists don't know. It calms the angry
patients down. But what does it destroy?

January 9, 1953

I do not want to write in verse
But I can't stop.
I'll force myself. I'll just
Refuse to write in lines.
Still the form sticks:
My head jostles with beats.
It's sleep I need.
Sometimes this prose place
Makes the world outside
Seem like a cardboard dream;
Today, this office is the cardboard dream.
I no longer believe
that something is about to occur.
I believe something is
occurring.
I can't tell what it is.
O Paul, and O my father,

Rescue me.
          Someday I will go to Big Sur
among the houses that the
anarchists have built of
redwood, and live by
the sea.
          Someday I will go to the Aegean
And visit Lesbos and Crete
and across the Ionian sea.
I will see Syracuse and Sybaris,
the route of Sappho's exile.
And I will write about Akhnaton
sheltering from the sun
in a hot place where I can
see the Nile.
          Outside the rain falls.
Perhaps that's why
I think of sunny
places.

January 12, 1953

Lou conducts *Solstice*, a pagan dance. Jean Erdman is bride between the Sun Lion and the Moon Bull of Ronne Aul and Don McKayle, sexual warriors at solstice. A divine dance and a divine battle.

Lou also conducts a part of his new opera, *Demeter*. Goddess worship. Wicked.

At Jean Erdman's house, a party for dancers.

Joe Campbell is in the kitchen where I stay to serve, wash dishes, and talk with him. I tell him about the near disaster that his enticement to witchcraft brought about. Not until tonight did I tell him the name of the intended victim. And then, stunned, he agreed that the "experiment" would have been unjustifiably dangerous.

I talk with him all evening, nor mind not mixing with the dancers or even with Lou.

January 15, 1953   *Hoboken*

At George Dennison's huge, white studio in this crazy waterfront town, we see some films of Nick Cernovitch and Al Leslie.

A symphony of fog horns, sounding like the work of a contemporary composer.

But I keep hearing "Silent Night." When I am too keyed-up I hear the carol, high-pitched as if sung by a choir of a thousand children's voices, or perhaps even *castrati*. It is the carol of my inner ear urging sleep and rest for my overtired mind. It is the warning of overstrain.

Yet, strangely, I like the sensation of that hallucinated sound. Instead of scaring me, it comforts me.

In the Clam Broth House Paul entertains.

January 21, 1953

Julian has taken a typing job at the 42nd Street library and trudges mournfully off to work each morning.

Meanwhile, the electric company threatens extinction and the landlord presses for unpaid rent.

At the session, Paul said, "Because here you pay attention. That is why you are happy here."

He was exhilarated because he had just finished the chapter of *The Empire City* in which Horatio goes mad.

Superbly excited, with a wide smile, Paul speaks now of his despair and grief.

I pay attention.

When I leave I've caught the state of joy.

Paul suggests again that I edit a part of my journal. And again advises me to regard the whole journal as a work of art.

January 22, 1953

To Madame Piscator's to discuss *R.U.R.*

She is in her drawing room in a blue velvet robe behind the glitter of her discreetly cluttered desk. She speaks of her trip to Europe, of Dutch chocolate, of plans for a ten o'clock cartoon theater.

"I can see Malina as the dark lady in a decaying house."

She lauded *The New Yorker*, Piscator, women, and marriage. As to *R.U.R.*, "Ah, we shall see."

January 25, 1953

Erick Hawkins' concert. But once a year he performs his rituals and still there are only some 800 persons to see them!

Proud movements, precise as surgeon's cuts.

"If you like such posturing," says a corpse in the audience.

Laughing homage to God's economy of ends in a plethora of means. Out of a million motions, one motion is *le mouvement juste*.

"Isadora Duncan in a straitjacket," says the corpse.

Lucia's sounds challenge music. Surpassing its logic. Ralph's masterful setting.

John Cage and Merce Cunningham and Lou Harrison were not there. Who will love us if we do not love each other?

Backstage, Alan Hovhaness praises Lucia, "You are a great composer."

Erick's sandaled feet are the most perfectly proportioned feet I've seen.

He speaks with delight, but a sudden cramp in his hand belies his good humor.

"Where are John and Lou?" asks Lucia.

February 2, 1953

Frances Steloff presides at the Joyce Society meeting at Gotham Book Mart.

Padraic Colum runs the proceedings. Steloff introduces us to Colum and we sit beside him hoping to talk about *Finnegans Wake*, but he wants to talk only about his work on Arthur Griffith's biography.

Mrs. Joyce, the writer's daughter-in-law, describes his last birthday party.

"I tried to make the decorations sort of symbolical. You all know my father-in-law was fond of symbols. I had two mirrors on the cake representing the Seine and the Liffey. You know that he was very obsessed with rivers."

No doubt these earnest faces front earnest minds and they share a sense of romance, and all details about their beloved feed their devotion.

February 3, 1953

At night we visit the Remo and, omigod, there's Chester Kallman who has yet to be told that we are doing *The Age of Anxiety*.

The days runs thus:
8:00 A.M.: Get Julian off to work at the library and Garrick off to school.
9:15–12:00: Whatever morning chores or madness needs doing. Or a session with Paul.
12:15–1:00 P.M.: A fast lunch with Garrick.
1:00–5:00: To work at the doctor's office, the easy part of the day.
5:00–7:30: Dress, supper, Garrick to sleep, rush.
8:00–12:00: Business appointments, visits, events, or work.
12:00–3:00: Remo.
3:00–8:00: Five hours sleep.

Yesterday to Mme. Piscator's. A slight quiver of apprehension in Madame's voice takes the harsh edge off her pride. She begins many sentences, "One must . . . ."

In *Communitas* Paul writes in varied ways, but his soft Hebrew way is best.

He thinks of the Wisdom of the East as Talmudic calm with a puckered brow. When he makes the melody sweet for the very reason that it is sad, he is at his best. He thinks he writes well when sarcastic and that his philosophy is farther east than it is, but these are affectations.

The Brattle Theater is at the City Center with *Love's Labours Lost*. Amidst the satin capes Schildkraut says, "The naked truth is that I have no shirt," softly, in his *"Bühnen"* manner.

Talk to Bentley at intermission. Nina is taken with him, but Julian neglects to introduce her. We are immediately repaid when Chester Kallman steers Auden clear of us. Auden looks exhausted. I think of Paul's story, "Chester's Birthday."

February 6, 1953

I talk to Paul about my thoughts on the organization of pacifist-anarchist groups. Perhaps it's the way I say it that makes him respond without enthusiasm. Or perhaps it's the discouragement of failed attempts in the past. He doesn't understand how seriously we take the practical aspects of revolution. He says we are theorists and not men of action. As for me, I'm a woman. I lean too heavily on Paul.

February 12, 1953

Paul has assembled a new group. Noel Sokoloff is in therapy to clear up a "composer's block." Paul uses the psychodrama, that horrid concoction of artless acting, exposure, and a patina of Stanislavsky. I hate it. I do it badly. We "enact" pickups at bars. The whole thing offends me.

February 15, 1953

Paul says that when life becomes more secure the deeper problems surface. My mother would say, "One is too busy to worry."

At our party Madame Piscator conducts Mark and Nancy in a duo for recorders. She admires what she thinks I have become, as I admire what I think she is.

Bob Carricart tells us of Dan Matthews' death in a car smashup. The luminous boy who played the hero in Sartre's *Flies*. Orestes under the wreckage.

"I defy you to destroy me," Orestes Matthews said. I played a fly, the Fury.

Bob didn't want to tell Madame but asked me to break the news.

In the back room, kheef makes things sensual. Armand, one of Paul's young men, interests me.

Lucia comes with Erick Hawkins.

George Dennison stays the night with Nina.

Serafina tells me that Alan has adopted the title I suggested for his Egyptian piece, *Tel el-Amarna*.

John Cage sits on a ladder. Paul sits with Philip on the floor. He might have said hello.

Willard Maas asks us to participate in *Narcissus*, the film he's making.

Bill Young, in praise of Gestalt therapy: "If I had felt this way a year ago I wouldn't have felt it."

February 21, 1953

The pleasure of being loved, unlike the burning of loving, soothes, supplies, cozens, rests. Loving costs one's vigor. To be loved refreshes at little cost.

Pinned to my handbag, a damask rose. Armand brought it to me with a bunch of iris this afternoon. He looks at me with devotion.

He is married, stabler than most of our friends, about to be forty, very masculine, a war resister, jailed as a C.O., intelligent, even intellectual. He comes after our group session to take me out and away.

February 22, 1953

Paul laments that he does not live in the Golden Age.

I wear Armand's rose to the filming.

Willard Maas is making a film in a gay bar on the Brooklyn waterfront. Only men are in the sequence, which puts me on the sidelines. Julian plays the bartender, wearing the superior expression of that breed.

Maya Deren, drunk, shoots the film. Ben Moore, my handsome schoolmate, stars as Narcissus, fending off the embraces of a transvestite in gold lamé.

Standing on the sidelines, I'm suddenly popular. People approach me and seem compelled to say how much they like me.

Paul sidles up to me as I watch, and in a dime-novel voice asks, "Is that rose from . . . A.?"

We all go to the Remo.

It is Philip's thirtieth birthday. He's been crying. I run across the crowded room and embrace him. He reacts as if he'd been bitten by a snake.

All the men get amorous with me. It's almost funny.

Philip comes back and takes my hand, kisses me affectionately and tells me he regrets the pain he causes me. It doesn't matter.

February 24, 1953

It is reported to me by Julian through Frances, by way of Serafina, that Sunday, while we went to see *Misalliance,* there was a concert at the Modern Museum at which Lou's "Third Canticle" was played by Stokowski.

The ecstatic "Third Canticle" under Stokowski's hand and I not there to hear it!

Serafina explains, "I got a phone call: 'This is Leopold Stokowski. My wife and I would like you to have dinner with us.' We thought it a gag but at the last moment we decided to go and found ourselves welcomed by Stokowski and Gloria Vanderbilt." At dinner, Alan maintained that Sibelius was the greatest of the modern musicians and Stokowski countered: "I'll put my stakes on you."

We attend a preview of Johnny Myers' Artists' Theater.

Frank O'Hara's sexy "Try, Try" with a setting by Larry Rivers. An involved poem on the classical brutal triangle, climaxed when the lovers say, "This is where the wars begin. The suffering has to burst out somewhere."

Frank watches it with nervous excitement. He holds my hand as if he were in a dentist's chair, happy when I respond feelingfully.

A play by Jimmy Schuyler called *Presenting Jane.* Jane Freilicher asked that her full name be omitted from the title. The three characters, Frank, John, and Jane, speak the language of ephemera.

An allegory on sex by Kenneth Koch called *Little Red Riding Hood.*

March 3, 1953

With Alan and Serafina, I am able to talk about art without embarrassment. In the Golden Age, when artists were a community, it must have been like this.

I wish Serafina would act her role with the same directness with which she reads the candles.

We borrow Kafka's diaries from Alan.

Everyone comes to Dickie Mayes' party, where Philip uses Paul's phrase "a natural community of friends" or a "community of natural friends."

A wave of enthusiasm for the Living Theatre. In retrospect, we become respected. Now that the theater has been closed for six months everyone laments that they did not do enough to support it. Everyone has plans and suggestions for the theater's revival.

I tried to tell Chester Kallman that we are working on *The Age of Anxiety*, and ask him to get Auden's O.K. But he was in a bad mood, hobbling on a sprained foot.

Philip, blind drunk, fell onto him. Chester cursed and Philip responded with clenched fists. I had visions of losing *The Age of Anxiety*. But Philip only swore bloody murder, veered, cursed, and staggered out. I pushed Frank O'Hara out the door after him to guide him home.

Then a bloody fight in which Jeanette and her boyfriend beat up a boy she was making it with.

A community of natural friends? Yet it is so. Even so, it is so.

Today to court. A creditor is suing us for a debt incurred at the Cherry Lane. I run out of the courtroom because the arrogant tone of the policeman demanding silence makes me angrily defiant. Here is where, in Paul's sense, I cannot get along: this terrible fury at authority. Why can't I love these brutes too?

Clutching Kafka's diaries I note the judge's name is really Chimera.

March 4, 1953

All night we keep the radio on for news of Stalin, who has suffered a brain hemorrhage and appears to be dying. There are hourly bulletins.

March 5, 1953

Garrick at Purim looks around at the crowded synagogue and whispers to Mother and me during the reading of the *Megillah*, "There are a great many people in the world who don't know us."

March 6, 1953

Stalin dies.

Is history so uncertain that any one man, even a significant one, is no longer crucial?

We no longer think about war, as we don't think about death.

Group therapy. After the session, the group repairs to the Remo. Paul presides over our symposium at a long table over coffee and rum cake.

He picks up my journal and spots a line where I blurt out my despair at being unable to tolerate cops: "Why can't I love these brutes too?"

Paul says, "You divide the world into angels and devils. I divide the world into angels and deadheads. The trouble is philosophical. She"—he switches to the third person to rally the others against me—"believes in good and evil."

He had suggested that I keep still and I do. Unless I can be eloquent I'll be silent. He is eloquent.

"She does not mind my cruel tone," he boasts to Dickie Mayes.

This morning as I write this, the tears are coming down my face. But I don't need to defend myself against feeling.

Instance: Because Jeanette has started fights, Paul feels that she should be excluded from the group. "Every society has its standards and we must protect ourselves." So he proclaims that he will not attend a party to which Jeanette had been invited.

When we walked into the bar Jeanette was sitting at a table with Mike. None of them spoke to her: not the one who was once her lover, nor George, nor Paul, nor I. Because I didn't dare defy my friends. They don't understand why it makes me sad.

Then when we sit together, Paul reminds everybody that my affliction is my belief in good and evil, which is to say I didn't accept his solution.

In fact, I want a better solution than his and I haven't found it and am willing to suffer until I find it. I keep my mouth shut.

It's not necessary for them to understand what I feel; I know what I feel.

March 13, 1953

The condition which I call insight and which Alan considers a trance, Paul refers to as "perceiving the natural condition of things."

But this insight, when it becomes trance, does not allow for action because it destroys what Paul calls "the hierarchy of things," which I call differentiation.

Paul always finds the truer phrase. He says he learned it from Aristotle and Leibniz.

Rudely I seclude myself in the Remo's lavatory to write.

I look ugly to myself in the mirror tonight and intend to exploit it.

March 14, 1953

The "Theseus" of Gide: the man of action—guiltless because he knows nothing about guilt. What a vision of blamelessness!

An extraordinary stranger—dark-maned, ponderous—enters the Remo; I point him out and ask around "Who's that?" He has a snarling look, as though long ago abandoned by fate—to remorse-laden anger and anguished compassion.

Someone says, "James Agee." And the animal cry of "A Mother's Tale," and the transcendent poetry of *Let Us Now Praise Famous Men*—is what I remark in this handsome face.

I begged Julian to introduce me, for he had once met him, but that was years ago, and he was shy to approach him.

Agee had several drinks. Julian was still talking to Frank O'Hara/stray child of the Muses/when Agee left . . . .

Feeling thwarted and seething, I went off to Washington Square, to thoughts of the past, present, and future.

Of the past: how I dived for pennies tossed from the Fifth Avenue buses to the half-naked children in the fountain.

Of the present: I smoke a reefer and contemplate the motto on the monument, thrown into relief by the moonlight, "The event is in the hand of God."

Of the future: I want Jim Agee to be my lover.

March 15, 1953

Rehearsals: *Age of Anxiety* and *R.U.R.*
To love is to place the center of the universe outside oneself.

March 19, 1953

"Why do you say the world is terrible?" asks Paul.
And I ask him why he will not let me carry my burden.
"Carry it?" he asks astounded. "I'm trying to throw it to you."

After rehearsals, I go to the Remo. The center of my universe?
Paul has finished a crucial chapter in *The Empire City* and wants to talk about it. He repeats the climax from memory. It's enough like poetry to recite.
In this chapter the Paul-figure, Mynheer, "fucks his Only World." He has run away from her, fought with her; she has treated him cruelly. But she is his Only World, and when he breaks down and cries it is on her shoulder that he cries and then he "fucks his Only World."
Paul: "Like this bar. Here it is, your bar. Run away. Go to another bar and soon the horizon expands and there it is again, 'your bar.'"
"And then?"
"He goes underneath and becomes a sage."
Paul turns to me: "Good, no?"
And to Philip: "Sad, no?"
(At our session in the morning he had said to me, "I'm always aware of who's listening.")
And Paul's "Only World" and my "Center of the Universe" are siblings after all.
Then I quote a Talmudic story to allay Paul's fear that the sage cannot be a sage at fifty. But instead of calming Paul's fears, it roused in me thoughts of my father's death at forty-two.

March 24, 1953

R.U.R. rehearsal. Strain. Frances replaces Nina.
The better rehearsals get, the more the real weaknesses of the play show.

Easter, 1953

R.U.R. opens. After the final curtain Julian flees to the roof of the Capitol Theater. I follow. The atmosphere is macabre and lunar. Neon tubes stretch four stories above us; a beehive of construction all around; Broadway churns below. From horizon to horizon, electric messages explode in a mocking chorus. At last I find Julian. The long spell of work over suddenly; the end of the tension of many sleepless nights. The depression that follows a diet of dexedrine. He cries. I cry. We descend from the sparkling roof to the gloomy world.
Frances cries in the dressing room, dissatisfied with her performance in this impossible play.
At Alan Hovhaness' we meet Hyman Bloom, painter of ferocious visions.

Alan and the cats are frisky. He spills . . . no . . . pours milk on Bahai's
head and laughs loudly. Serafina says it makes the cat sad and she cries.

Everyone cries this season.

April 7, 1953

Fire in the theater building during rehearsal. We play a fine evacuation
scene. Firemen and dramatic smoke effects.

Julian rushes to evacuate us, but we all stop for our favorite possessions in
the dressing rooms. On the wet street Julian watches the firemen complete
their task, his arms piled high with costumes.

Paul says I must not make manifestos any longer.

I demand reparations from him. His criticism has inhibited my journal
writing and I demand a way to write.

April 9, 1953

Night. *R.U.R.* performance. Dexedrine breakdown. Groundless anxieties.
I tremble head to foot. The revolt of the robots begins with the beat of the
drum. Julian's beautiful set has vertical white lines made of clothesline. It is
surely a prison.

I'm reading Kafka's diaries. When I read Gide's journals, I describe the
weather and the scenery, not because I notice them, but because I notice that
Gide would notice them. But when I read Kafka . . .

Under nitrous oxide, I recall feeling: "Just for the experience, I'll scream
now. Not because the pain is unbearable without screaming, but just for the
hell of it."

Actually, the pain was unbearable.

April 10, 1953

I am too shaky to feel afraid. I did not sleep all night. Mother is sicker and
is to come to stay at our house.

This morning I sit here in a clean corridor of Mt. Sinai Hospital waiting
to talk to a social worker.

In the waiting room, a Puerto Rican woman and her little boy are pleading
for aid for his brother, who has broken both arms. It is sleety weather and they
say that they can't carry the seven-year-old to the hospital. No one listens to
her. The boy interprets hesitantly.

In disgust I get a toothache.

The social worker tells me, "Your mother has cancer. But she doesn't know
it, and it's best for her that you don't tell her."

I suspected it for a long time. All the symptoms. I try to say reasonable
things in the face of this confirmation.

I say, "But she will realize it. She is a very intelligent woman."

"She won't. They never do. We will give her radiotherapy. You know what
that is? X-ray treatments."

"Yes, I know. But then she will certainly know. It's a well-known treatment."

"If she knows, she won't admit it. I assure you . . . ."

When I walk out in this wet evening onto Riverside Drive, the dripping trees all have big birds on them.

April 13, 1953

Certainly.

There is certainly a world. There is certainly a life of people in this world and some of it is together.

Certainly R.U.R. goes well enough and this certainly does give me something to hold on to.

Certainly Walter Mullen is very charming and Frances certainly left her stole and jewelry in a taxi cab on opening night.

Certainly there is a life of art.

At a party at a dancer's studio, I doubt everyone's existence.

Certainly there is a concrete they.

Certainly I should respect them.

To Mrs. Loring who works here in this doctor's office I say, "Why not a ragpicker?"

But, deeply, I share her lack of comprehension.

Why not a dope peddler?

Why not a ragpicker?

Why not a hungry artist?

Certainly why not and certainly not.

This kick is certainly to bolster my enormous uncertainty.

In our front room, Paul reads to our circle of friends the last novel of *The Empire City* tetrology, possibly to be titled *The Holy Fright* or *The Holy Terror*. We are stricken with admiration, as well as with sorrow that we must kill in order to live, the final implication of the cannibalism of the Alger family.

It is intolerable. I cry. I am disgusted that this is my response. To cry like a baby. Helpless just like that.

"Great father, great artificer, stand me now and ever in good stead."

April 14, 1953

Mother coming to stay at our house means that Alex and Robin, who thought they had shelter, must leave.

Paul said, "Since it makes you unhappy, don't try to reason it out morally; just say it is your whim, because it is your need, that no more friends come to stay in your house for a while. That you require peace and quiet."

April 15, 1953

Breathe deep.

Walter and Frances on stage. The youngsters from the Workshop playing robots are the embryos of our new world.

Remy and Nick Cernovitch sit beside me. Across the aisle, my Julian. I count the persons of my only world.

Paul's Genet kick: "Sink to the lowest for then God is on your side."

It seems rather an unexpected way to get in His good graces.

April 16, 1953

What about outgrowing the infantile stage, Paulo, by changing it into something that satisfies us more?

You say we do not lose that which we outgrow. We lose our dependence on it.

I've been reading Eric Gutkind's *Choose Life*. It defies the infantile. Though even as an infant I had faith that I would grow to be a woman free of childish fury and childish spite.

What about childish faith? Must I lose my dependence on that?

I think of Dr. Gutkind and his wife, Lucy, and my mother and father in endless amiable discussion.

Kheef.

Agee was at the Remo and Julian had a friendly talk with him but I was not there.

April 17, 1953

The last performance of *R.U.R.*

Soon I can breathe a sigh and strike the set.

April 19, 1953

At Columbia University, two Kabuki dances and the Noh play *Hagaromo*, nobly attempted by college women.

Philip speaks to me in Japanese but I can't answer.

April 23, 1953

Here I am waiting.

The jukebox plays Tijuana music. I am not with friends and it is not the San Remo where something marvelous may happen at any moment.

Mother awaits me at home.

I am swinging with it in this small place on 17th Street. We are waiting.

April 24, 1953

On the way to Paul's in the evening, I pass through singing and dancing in the Puerto Rican streets. The doorways hold lovers or squabblers. The children, still awake, dart across the streets like crepe paper streamers at a fiesta. Many musics conflicting. Inside the curtainless windows, walls painted yellow and blue.

The life of these streets makes our somber manners seem long decayed. We have submitted and they have not.

The messenger (who is already one of them, though he has posed with us) enters shouting: "Attila is here. The Huns have come. The Goths are razing us."

And beyond the horror, the splendid cathedrals in the Gothic style rise, until that too decays.

April 27, 1953

Mme. Piscator agrees to our doing Genet's *Les Bonnes* at the Workshop's theater.

We work out a program which includes *The Age of Anxiety* as well as plays by Ashbery, O'Hara, Mac Low, Koch, Norse, Schuyler and Goodman.

Spring unleashes dangerous impulses. The tension of daily work at the Workshop, plus the job, the house, Mother's illness, is released in the night.

Armand brings a great branch of blooming cherry.

At the Workshop, Mr. Robbins gives us a business talk stressing "the cash." "I don't care what the standards of the school are, just so we make the money." I fix a smile on my face knowing I should protest.

April 30, 1953

San Remo bathroom. Closing time. The smash of tile against my face silenced me momentarily. I counted the hexagrams hopefully, expecting every moment that the nature of their secret would appear like the light Pythagoras must have seen through the sevens and nines.

May 1, 1953

She, Madame, laughed and said, "Piscator should be here. He would have a good laugh." She nodded her head tragically smiling at grief.

"It is nice that we are together here," she said.

But when I saw her carrying heavy bundles of costumes and draperies, or whatever the city marshal might remove for auction for a judgment debtor, then I thought (as she laughed): How all things equalize.

Under the portrait of Piscator, in which he is about to break into that sardonic smile, I always tremble.

But then I thought: How all things equalize.

But I was *kleine Judith* again and afraid.

May 8, 1953

At the group session I think, "If I leave my journal here it would imply that I want Paul to read it." I leafed through to see if there were a portion I particularly wanted him to read. There was not; nonetheless, I left the journal behind.

On the telephone he told me he had read it and that the writing was better. So that's what I had left the journal there for.

At the group we had talked for 10 minutes into the tape recorder about our lives. With a sigh Paul told his story. How hollow with grief his voice became!

His resignation was deep and troublesome. Like his writing it left me on the edge of tears.

May 11, 1953

Last night I started to Maury's and was waylaid by two men who dragged me into a hell of blows and insults. The blows gave me an excuse to cry about the insults, which I am too proud to repeat.

I screamed, "Hit me, beat me to death, I still won't!" To what purpose did I say that if not to rain down the blows? Why make such choices?

I end up bruised and shaken. Is that the answer? Pinch me and I'll wake up?

So I get myself pinched and the dream becomes a nightmare and I am *still* not awake.

I am fascinated by this side of the world where brute force is master: where rage rages freely and faking it is assumed to be the only way to live.

The difference in worlds (Paul says ain't such a thing) where the raised fist near the face succeeds better than seduction and persuasion.

But the raised fist didn't work. I was beaten but I was not raped. I was going to write "touched," but that wouldn't be true.

Julian works much too hard on *Aria da Capo*, sewing costumes at home on the machine, while my mother gives directions from her sickbed. Then he works at the theater all night. He is doing the sets and costumes for this production only to repay Madame's kindness in letting us have the theater for the summer. But I resent his wasting his strength on this.

May 13, 1953

I sit in the eternal tavern and wait for something wonderful to happen. Nina is here with Lester, Philip's love.

Lester has nowhere to go for the night and Nina has been asking various friends for a haven for him. Jackson Mac Low refuses rudely and then pulls a long face because she's angry at him.

I, too, refuse Lester our hospitality. I can't have strangers come in with my mother at home.

What has it to do with the fact that he is Philip's lover? He is aggressive—he is drunk—"You want me to tell you all about Philip, don't you? What are you so interested in *me* for?"

I am not sure I was really interested at all, for my eyes wandered around the bar expecting something.

"He kicked me out," Lester snarls.

I imagine Philip telling him about the theater—"She kicked me out."

Then Agee came in. At first he circled round our table, but I left no doubt that I wanted him to join us.

We talked about writing and about personal responsibility for the wars. I tried much too hard to communicate with him. My voice was high and pressing.

I wonder whether he is aware of me. One talks to many people, and I did not distinguish myself.

He is very talkative. He seems to distrust me; seems afraid we may turn out badly and that he will be disappointed; seems afraid of personal pain.

Agee says, "The only thing that makes me want to kill is the sight of outright vandalism, vicious purposeful destruction, those who smash things and tear up the pictures and destroy for the sheer hell of it."

I saw that he was sorry when four A.M. closed the bar. I am full of rash hopes that it is because of me.

In the subway a drunk runs into me and knocks me down. I have bruises on my knees and elbows. So I have become beating prone.

At home at five A.M. I find Lester in my bed. I'm furious!

Paul says we want to break down the ways of not feeling pain and get back to the Original Wound. Here are all the enemies of my nature. One of these demons was a black devil with a limping foot—the others include an ironing board, a toad, a 12-inch ruler (I especially fear him), a skeleton.

The enemies of my nature brought me relief as I let them carry the guilt, and let it make *them* hideous, as Dorian did with his portrait.

Now my monsters go with me like a caravan, accompanying me with my burdensome crime.

I see them, glorious and gruesome, in one of those imaginary landscapes by the Flemish painters depicting the temptation of St. Anthony.

Garrick says, "Time never stops." He means never stands still.

I would fly but it is against the laws of nature to fly (levitate). It is necessary to break the laws of nature in order to fly. Everything struggles toward this lawbreaking. What wins sets new boundaries, and is soon called the law of nature. So I don't fly because it isn't allowed.

May 14, 1953

Agee's smile in the hazy dawn on King Street on the stoop of his little red house.

This summery afternoon on the grass I recall it over and over, with the kisses. He is a balm to my cringings; he almost trusts me.

Sleepless, I go to help Julian on the *Aria da Capo* sets, and though I'm not much use, it is spring, and tired or not, dexedrine or no, I *am* in it.

The park is staid, cars whiz between me and the lordly Hudson. The sky is dull and damp and dreamlike, but it is a real dream where I am present, and feel my heart beat, and my aches, and how I desire him.

This time I'll make it without a whimper.

"*Verweile doch, du bist so schön.*"

Remo. Four. Agee.

He talks to Chester Kallman. I was with them but moved away probably in order to be followed.

Euphoria all night until a few moments ago. Tile. Chester, Agee, Remo. Soon it will close and the wide white curtain swing.

I won't tempt fate. Yes, I will.

The closing-time atmosphere.
And if I lost?

May 15, 1953

In Agee's white living room.
At seven A.M. the spring rains come down with a fury.
Agee talks to me about his marriage; tells me that he has hurt many women, and of the needless sacrifices that have been made . . . .
This then is his horror of vandalism. He dreads the destruction he imagines he wreaks. I am not honest enough with him. I feel that the jacket of my dress is too red and my eyes too made up.
The sliding doors are closed between us and the mother-in-law that we must not awaken. His black dog bit me and chewed my lavender glove to bits.
He sets up a barrier between us, a sexual taboo, that will become an obstacle. And what is more binding than an obstacle when it becomes a link?

May 16, 1953

Last night at Chester Kallman's farewell party. I saw Agee only for a few moments. He talked only to Harold Norse. They were both drunk and I was not.

May 19, 1953

King Street is one of those dark, quaint vestiges of old New York and the route to it from the cafe is dank with garbage pails and "the yellow smoke that curls."
The room on the first floor floods the street white.
It is fearsomely bright.
Inside, Agee sits at his typewriter acting out each sentence before he writes it. His face moving to the rhythm.
I watch for a long time before he sees me through the window and lets me in.

Jim reads me long portions of his scenario for a film on Gauguin. His simplicity seems incompatible with life in this world. I think it is.
He reads each line between Gauguin and Van Gogh with an exaggerated weight as though each one were an epigram.

May 21, 1953

At the Remo, with a stubby pencil, Allen writes a poem into my book.
Unpublished Rhymed and Iambic Set of
Stanzas by Allen Ginsberg
called
The Vision of the Shrouded Stranger of the Night

Bare skin is my wrinkled sack
When summer sun crawls on my back;

When winter racks me in these rags
I lock my lap with burlap bags.
My flesh is cinder; my face is snow;
I walk the railroad to and fro;
When city streets are black and dead
The railroad embankment is my bed.
I suck my soup from old tin cans
And take my sweets from little hands;
In alleys where the tigers wail
I steal away from the garbage pail;
In darkest night where none can see
Down in the bowels of the factory
I sneak barefoot upon stone:
Come and hear the old man groan.
  I hide and wait like a naked child,
Under the bridge my heart goes wild;
Hot in the body and soul ashiver
Flesh starts dancing by the river;
I dream that I have golden hair,
Arms raised up bloody in the air,
  The torso of an iron king,
And in my back a broken wing.
  Who'll go out whoring into the night
On the eyeless road where I stand in delight?
Maid or dowd or athlete proud
May wanton with me in the shroud
Who'll come lay down in the dark with me,
Belly to belly and knee to knee?
Who'll look into my hooded eye?
Who'll lay down under my darkened thigh?

1950–1952
Allen Ginsberg Fecit.

May 23, 1953

Agee's room.

He says to me, "I am a drunk."

We talk about sleeplessness. He says, "Alcohol is my substitute for both sleeping and fucking."

As soon as he said this, I stepped back.

There are not two worlds, but one world. I have to face the fact that this world has a night and a day.

Literally.

5:10 A.M.

At Herbert Berghof's studio a production with Sudie Bond and Julie Bovasso.

Geraldine Page greets me, "Don't you remember me? I played a Greek whore in one of your plays."

Sudie and Julie agree to play Les Bonnes. I am delighted. Both are highly skilled though too steeped in "the method."

I am surprised that the actors like the sinister script, whose appeal lies in the recognition it touches off.

May 24, 1953

Garrick has just seen his first play, Goldoni's *Servant of Two Masters*, at the Berghof Studio.

Genet's impact is felt among us. Allen's poem of a few mornings ago is surprisingly Genetesque, and Paul, too, declares himself influenced. Genet changes the atmosphere. Even I am touched to a difference by this criminal saint.

At work all day on the directing book for *Les Bonnes*.

May 26, 1953

First rehearsal of the Genet.

Sudie has an original and personal style and is impeccable.

Ironically, Julie does not read the final speech. The echo of the breakup of *Faustina* is ominous. But we don't mention it.

Ruth Kaner, once Mama Ubu, reads Madame.

May 27, 1953

In the small hours Bobs Blossom takes me to the Waldorf Cafeteria where we meet Arthur King. He is joyous and crazy.

It is Maxwell Bodenheim's 70th birthday. Max and his wife, Ruth, and a young fellow who is teaching her Hebrew celebrate. In honor of Max, Art steals a pie. A cop sees him, but is somehow content with my explanation that Maxwell Bodenheim is a great poet and that his birthday should be celebrated. The counterman is not so generous: "I ain't doin' this for love."

Bobs Blossom pays for the pie. We all eat. Ruth Bodenheim curses the cafeteria. Some junkies come and tell horrible tales of hospitals and arrests. One taps his eye with a knife to show us that it's glass.

Ruth Bodenheim smiles in an aristocratic manner: "I'd never have believed it wasn't real," as if she were consoling the owner of false jewels.

Paul tells me that Philip is coming to him as a patient.

"There is a boy," I said to Paul more than a year ago, "in whom I have an interest." So after a hard year on the rocky road we hit the flowery way.

June 3, 1953

Sudie Bond bows out of *Les Bonnes* because "the role is too taxing." Irma Hurley, whom Johnny Myers recommends, takes the role. She is suave and pretty, but evidently emotional.

Our plans for the summer at the Dramatic Workshop are in jeopardy. I plead with Madame Piscator for an hour. She silences me with anger, pity, fury, charm in rapid order. She functions superbly to my disadvantage. It looks like nothing will come of it.

I gave Julian the *I Ching* for his birthday, but I have been the one who has used it. It evades me by asking me (answering me) always to take a path easier than I would have wished.

Paul and Sally move into a big new loft on 23rd Street. Its expansiveness suits the author of *Communitas*.

Our session, which seemed disrupted and awry, was, upon reflection, useful.

Wrote a poem for Agee about time and age.

"Just As My Eyes See
A Glimmer, Everything Ends."

We are so fragile,
Why in twenty years . . .
  I was the thief who stole the jewels
That once were Nefertiti's eyes.
Being but mortal have I more
To lose than my antiquity?
You have your Catholic God!
You have your saints!
  But I?
  ". . . I only have a premonition of my past:
    (these are pearls that were his eyes)
Egypt and Sinai and a septal sea
That swallows chariots, opening for me . . ."
We are too fragile, why in twenty years
We will be old and all our glitter gone.
    (of his bones is coral made)
For you, who are a poet of the dawn,
(all gone, all old, wan dawns, and done)
Your early lights defend you
And your gods.
  But as for me,
Inside my hands the double gems dissolve
And I can see the thunder clapping shut your eye.

I write only when I am in love; not because this is my subject (it rarely is), but because only this state excites me to poetry.

June 4, 1953

We go to the Workshop this morning and Madame's blue jewels glitter in the blue light of her office. Our project falls apart. Oh, *Les Bonnes!*

It's my birthday, but it doesn't feel that way.

At Paul's, glumness. There was only Paul and David Andre and my gloom. David was tired and I lay intoxicated in his arms while Paul read to us, translating at sight, from Cocteau's *Opium*.

The kheef and the opium.

The young poet and the old poet.

June 5, 1953

On the first day of my twenty-seventh year.

Try to read Matthew Arnold, but nothing's as good as "Dover Beach."

Mullahly has a baby girl, Patricia Dierdre. If they go to Provincetown we may visit them this summer. A languid beach with friends would slow my pulse.

June 6, 1953

I put my feet into the lordly Hudson.

O Heraclitean motion, it is you who are the breath of beauty.

June 10, 1953

When I said to Paul in fun, regarding an ugly headline, "When *we* take over . . . ," he crowed, "My dear, we *have* taken over."

Read *Finnegan* seventeen pages at a time.

When Maury makes love and loses his morose look and his disapproving eye and tight mouth, he becomes wildly beautiful.

Mother's illness worsens.

June 17, 1953

Larry Maxwell takes us to a party at Norman Solomon's. Norman's paintings look rare and right in this environment without furniture, though very much clutter. There are the artists in their romantic tramp's clothing, and the black girls with their angry beauty. And there are David Walker, Philip, and his Lester.

The White Horse is full of friends tonight and in the course of the evening we speak to John Boyt, Joe Turner, Ruthven Todd, and Anaïs Nin (whose charm is touched with hesitancy since her note withdrawing as sponsor of the theater), Ian Hugo, Florence and Peter Grippe, Louis and Bebe Barron, and Yugi Ito, who sighs over his sorrows with Tei Ko.

June 20, 1953

At suppertime the news of the electrocution of the Rosenbergs.

Julian is horror-struck.

I say to him, "Why do we mourn especially for these? The same system kills so many people daily whom we do not mourn. We are hardened and insensitive to the senseless murders of children in Korea. Why are we moved more by the horrible murder of these two people?"

June 21, 1953

The Rosenbergs in their coffins. Their faces pale, like the divine masks of the Noh, which are embodiments of concepts.

The bridal white in which they are shrouded adds to the unexpected look of composure that seems to belie the turmoil and anger and agony which surrounds their deaths. I think my impression of them hallucinatory, because the newspaper photographs have been so pitifully crass, but I am told that all corpses have this peculiar glow.

Expecting to be horrified, I am instead so awed that my indignation vanishes. In the presence of the dead even the many police in the street do not upset me.

Many people mill about at three o'clock on a Saturday morning on an obscure corner of Brooklyn, reluctant to abandon the dead.

Inside the funeral parlor a rabbi's prayers sanctify the night while a guard (one does not know whether it was of honor or dishonor) stands among the American flags that mock the murdered.

After all the macabre fuss about not executing them on *Shabbos*, the exposure of the bodies is a contradiction. It is alien to Jewish custom to uncover the dead; that's why I've never seen a corpse in a coffin before. But this is well done in the spirit of Mark Antony's, "If I were to show you Caesar's body. . . ."

Their very looks proclaim them innocent; their innocence rouses rebellion.

June 24, 1953

At three A.M. I stop by Agee's to see if he is home. For all the *I Ching*'s warnings ("Retreat"), I watch him typing for a while in the white square of his window. When he sees my face, he leaps up. He looks tired, is unshaven, but invariably beautiful. We go to the Remo for a closing-hour drink. No one is there but we two. We talk prettily and wittily. He is writing a film about love in its many variations. Babies and marriages and adulteries.

We walk in the open air; I am hungry and suggest food. Instead he asks me if I want to go to bed. Clearly and out of the clear black sky. I say yes.

He doesn't take me to his house on King Street, but to a small room in a backyard house on Cornelia Street. There's no electricity. Candlelight flatters.

He makes love with the skill with which Marlowe turns a line. He makes me very happy.

If anything stands between me and complete happiness, it is the awareness of the ephemeral moment.

In this candlelight there is that *"Verweile doch"* pounding out the silence of Agee's sleep and my contentment. As dawn comes and we talk, I talk too much of his harsh furies and his passions. I can't be wise with him because I'm still afraid.

No danger in this fear, but a barrier; more love would be dangerous. Knowing he is vulnerable, he has developed a hardness that seems more real to him than the vulnerability. And while he always acts gallantly, he often refers to himself as "hard-boiled," aware that he will be disbelieved. But I believe him.

June 28, 1953

I've just left Jim. He talks only of the Gauguin film. He works with ferocious absorption.

Earlier, at Frank O'Hara's birthday party at Grace Hartigan's, I was overcome with melancholy that only Paul's presence mitigated.

Everyone left early and Paul and I went to the Remo, where Weegee took posey photos of us. I dressed elaborately in low-cut black with a red sash, orange shoes, a bright scarf and long green earrings. And there was Agee admiring an ocelot that Davido had in a box. And these are the years of my nights.

June 30, 1953

Alan Hovhaness calls and asks me to have lunch at the Russian Tea Room. He feels a need to talk to me of those oppressive things that tear, each one in its own way.

He asks of me the kind of dialogue and the bitter cheer that Paul gives me. He does not omit a prolonged discussion of the white goddess.

His suffering is genuine, and he feeds his heart and body to his suffering but leaves his spirit free to work.

We are the only people in the Tea Room, talking amid the waiters restless in their Russian blouses of Serafina, of the work of the artist, of the beauty of accepted grief, of Alan's new piece about to be performed, of being torn apart, of the goddess and the lover.

Later, I listen to Alan's *Tel el-Amarna* played on NBC. The announcer identifies the title as "the ancient name of Cairo."

July 19, 1953

I stopped writing when I was having trouble with James Agee.

Paul says about him, "He's big, he's talented, and he's a pain in the neck."

Agee puts me in a position where I can only retreat or be torn apart and I'll not be torn apart.

I won't give him up because he's going to continue to hurt me. Let that be his problem.

We find a kitten crying in the street. I bring it in. He treats me with the same coy affection.

He simply can't reject me—though he both wants to and doesn't want to.

Agee wants me to share his being torn apart.

Again he reads his scenario to me.

I read him a poem I've done on his piece about guilt in the "Religion and the Intellectual" issue of *Partisan Review.* I am brazen on the most touchy subjects. It's this that frightens people of me. Through his stumbling and clumsiness, which is his "act," he does everything with an effortless perfection. And an expression of pointless agony.

Alan Hovhaness comes in from Cummington to get his passport for his trip to Greece. We walk around the Village, then drive around in Alan's old broken-down car. He drives like a cautious madman. Halfway to Nyack we stop to talk on the edge of the Palisades.

And still he has not talked. I try to move him, but he hesitates. We chat about metaphysics. Long after the sky turns light, he turns to the subject—haltingly, untruthfully, but with good intent.

July 20, 1953

Having despaired of getting a theater, we hope to find a loft to do the plays we want to do, free of the bondage of high rentals, royalties, budgets. In the

smallest way, we may do the best work. We'll begin with *The Age of Anxiety.*
The small money needed is being asked of friends. Ten each from Julian and
me, ten from George Miller, ten from Larry Maxwell, ten from Frank O'Hara.

I waited in the Remo till three last night.

I knew that he would come.

July 22, 1953

This is the second morning that I've spent here in Agee's white room with
David Bradley, who is to direct *Noa Noa,* the Gauguin film.

I am an intruder between these people and their work. Bradley tolerates
me with the barest politeness, but Jim seems glad I'm there as though I were
an old, secure friend.

July 25, 1953

Searching for a loft for the plays, we visit Beauford Delaney in his loft,
which resembles a gypsy or Arab tent with swirls of cloth, and objects suspended from walls and ceiling. Julian hesitates and I am disappointed.

The doctor's office is closed for the summer so I've gotten a job tinting
photographs. Staring at the sepia faces lulls me into a dreamy state while I
work, like the state of the melancholy maidens at their looms.

I enjoy watching the *Noa Noa* script take shape under David Bradley and
Jim's hard-pressing work. But if I ever so cautiously contradict Jim, he is furious with me.

He is describing a scene when I suddenly exclaim, my attention caught by
a fly about to be devoured by a spider. He spitefully will not return to the
subject.

"I don't mess with divided attention."

"Please go on. Don't be offended."

"No. I'm not in the least offended, no."

"What happened to Gauguin after the fight with the sailors?"

"Well, he was laid up in the hospital for a while and . . ."

So it goes.

It is Saturday. Julian works at Hearn's. Garrick is with Julian's mother and
I'm to pick him up.

> Sleep.
> Nature needs five hours,
> Custom takes seven,
> Sloth takes nine,
> And wickedness eleven.
>
> New England adage
> quoted by Agee.

July 26, 1953

We are on our way back from a drive to Philadelphia with Mother and
Garrick when we hear the news of the Korean armistice. There is usually joy

at a war's end, but the end of this wasteful war brings only a hard-drawn sigh of relief.

Among the relics of Independence Hall I was saddened by the failure of those noble libertarian aims; "and more than this is tyranny."

The tourists passed in respectful ignorance before the Liberty Bell. Which is wisely mute.

July 27, 1953

A party at Marius Bewley's. Marius, affectionately drunk, is fearfully witty. His words flow generously. He talks of Peggy Guggenheim's gallery and those salad days when he was Peggy's secretary and Julian one of the promising young artists in her Autumn Salon. He asks, and I answer that I did not care for Peggy and he is shocked.

Perhaps now I would like her better.

Today, a copy of *Poetry Manchester* arrives in the mail with my "Song of Degrees." I thought it too simple, but it looks splendid in print.

July 29, 1953

Jim scarcely knows how dear he is to me. The night is very long. David and Jim talk only of films. I sit in the white room watching his animation, his pedantic mood, his mimicry. When David goes to bed it's raining hard and we can't leave. Jim recites some of his poems—much softer than the movie writing, which is firmly polished but edgy and unyielding.

I try to give him a little of my optimism, try to let him feel more freely. He is afraid to sacrifice a little reality, though he can toss away the Big Reality without a sigh.

I had waited for him in the Remo. John Cage was there and it was the propitious moment to introduce Saville Clarke to John. I'm relieved that Saville didn't meet Lou Harrison first. Lou would have tormented him, whereas John will teach with a clear head.

August 5, 1953

The need for achievement is itself pernicious and is its own obstacle.

Thus John Cage at the Remo explains the notes he wrote for the *Ladies' Voices/Desire/Sweeney Agonistes* program.

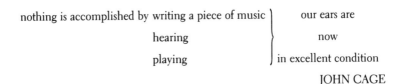

Written in response to a request for a manifesto on music 1952 } instantaneous   and unpredictable

nothing is accomplished by writing a piece of music } our ears are

hearing   now

playing } in excellent condition

JOHN CAGE

The point is not nihilism. But only when accomplishment is no longer the aim are we ready to begin work.

Not stoic, but a kind of brave and happy action without fruits.

At 4:30 A.M. Jim called and I went to meet him.

He talked incessantly and I never said a word. Julian says he woos me like Othello with tales of his adventures.

"You would not care for him if he were not James Agee."

But of course. Who else should he be?

And he is beautiful and loves me as a man should do, all certainty and ease.

With a single stick of marijuana, he rattles a blue streak of intelligent nonsense.

When I leave him he lies sprawled like a great dead Greek hero.

All day I am happy.

August 6, 1953

Every time I leave Jim I am certain we will not meet again. It seems inevitable.

Now he is going to the country and "may or may not" return to the city for the rest of the summer. Then in the autumn perhaps to the Philippines to make a big film, for half a year, and/or to Tokyo. Conjectures. His image breaks over me this evening in waves of warmth. Then why do I say I do not love Jim Agee?

He said to me, "Of course, it is only natural that such lovemaking leads to love. In this large sense, I love you. But what we do not feel is the sharp cutting-edge of love."

I, too, am resigned to not calling it love until it hurts.

Of my poems, he liked those that I had hoped he would like. He refused to disparage the others, insisting that he could not understand "the idiom of contemporary poetry."

A kind of idyll this morning in his greenery-bound breakfast room. His kitchen opens onto a backyard garden enshrining a glass-encased Virgin, slightly disintegrated, left by the former tenants, a devout Italian family.

And Jim plays Beethoven's Fourth Concerto on the piano with passionate distraction. Never has the music been so clear to me.

I ask him to play Holofernes in Julian's film project and he agrees.

We have a futile disagreement on a subject that touches us both, not in our actions but in our hearts. He rages vengefully against the killers and the "moral idiots," says he'd be willing to kill them. He thinks I am merely sentimental. I think he does not know his own heart: In reality he wants to kill that aspect of himself that wants to kill himself (his suicidal self). We argue until noon. All along I feel too buoyant in his presence to be deeply hurt by our quarrel.

August 9, 1953

Paul and I, spurred on by my happy mood, continue to probe in deep water.

Julian found a loft for the theater on 22nd Street, exploring Paul's neighborhood during my session.

We will rent the loft as a "rehearsal hall" and hope that we will not have troubles.

One year ago *Ubu* closed. And one year later we begin again.

August 12, 1953

At the Maases' for dinner, in a penthouse-garden set with plants and plaster goddesses, overlooking New York harbor, Willard and Marie rake legendary ladies like Hilla Rebay and Peggy Guggenheim over their witty coals. A dinner of delicacies, but I find myself sinking out of contact. I take a book by Mary McCarthy from the bookshelf and scan a few pages about Jim which increase my malaise but wake me, and I appreciate the return to the present world.

We did not get the loft. Damnation.

Reading Emerson. Good.

August 14, 1953

After Paul's session, we go to the Rienzi Café. Paul shepherds a tableful of young southerners, friends of Saville Clarke and Murray Hargrove. Then I love him and am happy to be his special friend among friends.

At the San Remo, Richard Stryker tells me he saw Agee at the Remo till four the night before when I was at Willard's.

I run to King Street. Sure enough, the white windows shine and I "stick my snout over the geraniums." He seems pleased but embarrassed. I realize that he has a new lover, which makes me—what?

We work on a letter concerning the rights to *Noa Noa* and then walk over to the San Remo.

Racing another couple for a table, they turn out to be John Cage and a friend. We drink until four.

John is admiring of Jim's work, but even more of Jim. The affinity between these two flatters me. In the complex conversations of Cage and Agee, Cage takes the Zen view, which rarifies and quintessentializes, and scares the bejesus out of me.

We return to the white room in King Street.

All morning Jim reads in a painfully pure voice his beatific, "The Morning Watch."

I am transported, not only by the story, but by the grace of the writer who senses the proximity of God to little boys and the funny inability of little boys to know they are so proximate. Then he, the little boy, and I, who magically become the little boy, come nearer to our honor and falseness and precious striving, and our holy self-deceptions.

Then I love deeply this deep-feeling lover.

August 16, 1953

At eight-thirty, Jim calls to say he is going to be away until the middle of next week. I feel for the first time (bad portent) that he'll be back. His image fills the dull day.

I am afraid of the finite tasks of a day like this because right beyond the end of accomplishment lies the awful void. And in this vacuum I must present an account, so I avoid conclusions and seek infinite tasks:

I keep a journal, I collect things, build dream empires spiraling endlessly toward the need for need.

I read Emerson and feel his ardor for all things. I close the book and plunge down from his height.

In my ecstasies I know how to feel. But then I am mute and can't say what I feel. Afterward I can't remember.

When I read the words of Beethoven in Agee's *Let Us Now Praise Famous Men*—"who has understood what I am doing can never be completely unhappy again"—then I rise for a moment to a breathless place.

With Julian, to a film on the Warsaw ghetto, a horrifying document that cannot be judged on cinematic merits. I cry because I understand that there is no blame. And even if we all die in this way—murdered by our fellow men—there is still no blame. The battlefield is in the heart.

August 18, 1953

It is noon and I take the subway to my prosaic job, tinting photographs.

The night before last was a bad one at the café. Going there when Agee is not in the city destroys the alibi that I go there to see him. Saville Clark and I sat talking about George Miller, who was out with Iris Love and his other society friends. Then George comes in, bringing the friends whom he has carried safely in a separate compartment, leading them across boundaries, uncomfortably, painfully mixing his worlds. He was visibly in the middle of a nightmare. Iris Love is a charmer; she picked her place and played along with the other players and outdid most of us.

Then, unexpectedly, I saw Jim Agee with one of the California golden people. I sat with them. We put up with the drunken antics of Dick Mayes and Dicken Stryker and an aggressive sailor named Al, who took an unwelcome fancy to me.

Through the window I see George lachrymose on Saville's shoulder.

Last night the sailor returned in civilian clothes, looking like the tough he is. He took out his knife, threatening those who used foul language in my (a lady's) presence. He was genuinely hurt when I told him that his threats and knife offended me more than foul language. Then he gave me the knife.

Jim had a scene with an angry anarchist. He spoke with the most genteel invective, but his face got vicious.

Jim loves another very much, which saddens me because it deprives me. I am not honest with myself at all. I push myself over dishonest cliffs and am amazed that the fall and thud are real.

August 19, 1953

I sit in this fear-inspiring hospital waiting for Mother.

The stone floors and the hideous architecture of a clumsy era evoke deep unease. Occasional nurses walk by humming. My anxiety mounts. I will never lose it all.

I think of Paul. Of such wistful, pristine, and blessed love as his, which extends to "his sunsets" and "his Hudson River" and "his Milky Way" and touches us all.

Of the session in his friendly loft where Paul constructs a better world, and of that white room where Jim embraces me, and of Julian who makes everything possible.

These thoughts enable me to endure my anxiety in the hospital. Sometimes when everything loses its context like this I get scared. I want to get back to a road, even if I have to imagine one. Now contexts don't exist, only disconnected states of being in an eternal vacuum unbroken by the recognition that there are others in this void, which is all we have of one another.

August 25 or 26 or so, 1953

Agee asleep and the image that he evokes of Agamemnon Dead. His posture and his heroic body and the breath heavy as a dying gasp. Nothing is limp in his sleep, but stopped as if in action. His elbow rests against mine as I write; his hand to his forehead. To the vivid and virile odor of him I am most deeply drawn, but wisdom girds me not to love too well.

It's nine-thirty. Julian is bringing Garrick downtown to stay with me while he goes to work. I think I'll spend this day in Washington Square.

Last night Dicken and Larry Elfenbein came home with Jim and me. We all had much to drink. The talk was thick and literary. Agee, always opinionated, covers anger and arrogance with charm.

Garrick cavorts in the charmed fountain of my childhood. I am full of superstitions about the place. So much has route and source here.

Group session: problems. The problem is always its own problem. The circumstances are only dramatic incidents.

One August noon, 1953

At the session, Paul talked of Kafka till I fell asleep. It is hot. The night was spent at Jim's: Julian, Dicken, David Harris, Jim, and me.

An idyll in which all are content with their modicum of happiness. Jim likes my friends and evokes their spontaneous love.

September 2, 1953

With Jim, our friends talk lightly about God.

Jim says he wants his children to have a Catholic education to give them a basis from which to deviate rather than to leave them floundering. His own search for faith is evident in all he says and writes. He believes in God but fears the rigors of his forsaken church.

Julian argues atheism. David Harris says he is an atheist in fear of God. David asks for a "good and just God," refusing any definition of "good" save what pleases him.

Dick Stryker, who has been listening to Gutkind and reading Buber, sides with me—and God. I talk nonsense like the others.

David notes the sunlight on the leaves of the heaven tree, ailanthus, in Agee's backyard. We ponder the crumbling Virgin in her glass case, and the significance of our inhibited worship.

Now that *Noa Noa* is finished, and *Moby Dick* postponed, Jim may go to the Philippines. I wish he wouldn't. "Let him write his poems," I repeat to myself like a prayer.

John Cage says: "One should think effortlessly. . . ."

September 3, 1953

A night with Jim. He pours out his troubles with his love. My concern annihilates my jealousy.

Not till six in the morning does a more portentous note creep in.

Jim tells a peculiar version of the Chambers-Hiss case. Chambers is his friend. I didn't think that Chambers was anyone's friend. Jim gets aggressive as though I had attacked him.

His politics are flawed.

At the group, Paul is formidable when he confronts the two young Puerto Ricans who live with David Andre. Speaking beyond their vocabulary, though not beyond their comprehension.

September 7, 1953   Boston

Faneuil Hall, Cradle of Liberty. Marked: veal 49 cents. It's a meat market. Sunday morning the people of this pious city are in church.

Walden. They make much of it as a site:

"No one shall utter abusive, threatening, profane, or indecent language," say the regulations. And no person "shall annoy another person, do any obscene act . . . preach or pray aloud . . . disturb any bird's nest . . . throw any stone."

The pond emerges pellucid out of the pines.

The site of Thoreau's cabin is marked by stone posts, and his ruined hearth by an inscription. Even the woodshed is commemorated. There's a cairn made of the stones that pilgrims had piled to mark the location of the hut before the heavy posts were erected.

The trees rustle, but I dare not write about it. Who would dare to say one more sentence about this place?

I sit on a hillock overlooking the site. Julian and Garrick have gone to fetch Mother and I wait here and write.

It was Thoreau's intense commitment to the actual that made him a visionary. All the trees here are young, and none remembers Thoreau.

I think of my circumscribed life.

And I look up from the notebook toward the small space defined by the stone posts.

Afterward we film Garrick playing house in Thoreau's hut. It is his first impulse on seeing it and reduces it to its real proportion.

In Concord, the lady who conducts visitors through the Wayside Inn is the daughter of Margaret Sidney, who lived in the Inn when she wrote *Five Little Peppers*.

She speaks with equal loyalty about Hawthorne, her mother, and Bronson Alcott. She rattles off tales about Whittier, E. E. Hale, and Julia Ward Howe. And the sweet things that they said to her. Garrick sits restlessly on Hawthorne's "fully authenticated" footstool.

As we leave, our guide points out three pictures of Hawthorne: one young and romantic; two old and grumpy.

"Forget the last two. That wasn't he. He had humor, spirit, charm. His family loved that first portrait. Copies on postcards can be purchased as you leave. Reread him with *that* portrait in mind! That was the man!" Her voice rises. She really cares.

The Alcott house is full of diminutive examples of the girls' work. Their father, Bronson Alcott, is shamefully ignored. Our guide lingers among Louisa May's delicate paintings, so we have to trudge through the mud unguided to find the School of Philosophy that Alcott built behind his house. Here he developed Transcendentalism, whose basis in Indian thought reopened the *Bhagavad Gita* for Gandhi, enabling him to establish through Emerson and Thoreau the link between his tradition and social action.

By the time we reach Emerson's house, I wish the old woman would stop telling us to whom all the furniture belonged, and let me walk through the sage's rooms and savor the shape of things in silence.

Driving on, we took the Salem route.

Salem is eerie, highly cultivated, pretty, rigid. I don't wonder that they feared the supernatural.

We are staying in a fine small house where an old lady lets rooms to tourists. The sound of rain, then crickets.

I think of Agee because here there is hardness, virtue, ability, honor, vigor, righteousness, work, progress, tradition, America, literature, architecture, whiteness, endurance, sea, road, pilgrim, pioneer, church, mind, meaning.

September 8, 1953   *Salem*

In Salem, "the witch house" still stands where the trials were held and the supposed witches condemned, perhaps in vengeance on the sea.

"It's because you were born in a seacoast town," says Julian, explaining why I'm so moved by the harbor and by my terrible and loved gulls.

Perhaps I remember the circling gulls in Kiel.

On the road back I realize how the trees shelter us from the too big sky.

September 9, 1953

Small birthday party for Paul. He reads "The Emperor of China," a complex piece cut from Paul's moral structure.

September 10, 1953

The Bride Comes to Yellow Sky may be a charming film, but there seems no reason why a splendid poet like Jim should squander himself on it. Especially as he says he can't work on more than one project at a time and feels time's pressing limitations.

But how exciting it is for me to see him up there on the screen among the golden people. The camera reproduces him with an exactness that is more than verisimilitude, as though he looked more like himself than he does.

Will I ever see him again? With no one else do I experience this awful sensation that every meeting is the last.

September 20, 1953

Paul says I'm not willing to put myself in the care of God. This pride is the root of my torment. Of what am I afraid?

Of annihilation.

I must learn to say, "You're wrong, but I won't argue." I can say it, but I can't stop the tears.

Last week at the group Paul complained that Philip is imperturbable. I suggested that Paul ask him to a group.

"But I can't if you're here. It will perturb him."

"We'll see."

Tonight.

September 22, 1953

I cannot withstand attack.

I left quickly at the end of last night's group and didn't even stop to taste the cake Sally had baked for us during the session.

Then, after crying it out in the doorway, I trudged back upstairs, apologized cheerfully, and had my coffee and cake.

Went to the Remo. That waxworks.

Gianni Bates introduced me to a group of people of whom I have forgotten all but one.

John Goodwin looks like one of those frontispiece portraits in collections of the romantic poets.

"They tell me you have written a book about magic. . . ."

"No, I wrote a novel about Haiti."

"What's the opposite of black magic?"

"I . . . I don't know." And then, "Christianity, I suppose."

Later, surrounded by coy Remo talk, he turned suddenly toward me and confided, "I wish we could make tenderness and honesty smart."

September 23, 1953

Last night at the Remo, Martin Corbin, our anarchist friend who had wanted me to meet Jim, criticized him for his article in praise of Roosevelt. Jim raged a minute in guilty fury but soon simmered down to treat his admirer more gently.

Do I not love him?

The madcap nymph Mary John, known also as Bridgit, an Irish fable of a creature, drunk and poetical as Anna Livia, took Jim and Martin and Julian and me home for coffee, where we listened for some hours to her soft obscenities on sex and Hemingway and women and the Catholic church.

Over more coffee in a neon-bright place, we made up a mock musical version of Abe Lincoln's life. Insatiable, we went on in search of an after-hours place on Downing Street.

Jim treats me so tenderly. And does he not love me?

This evening I went to see Harry Jackson's paintings in his studio on Broome Street. He seems impossibly hearty. He produces unflaggingly robust work.

September 25, 1953

Blood of a Poet again at the Thalia.

This morning I woke thinking of Cocteau after a disturbing, yet pleasant dream in which I was the lover of André Gide. In this dream Gide had prepared a dinner at which Julian and I and Tracy Woodward were the guests. A mirror image of the long night with Julian and Jim and Martin.

Jim had said, "I would rather dance with Cocteau than with Sartre."

September 27, 1953

Very dark. King Street. Inside I see Jim asleep. In houserobe. A book on his belly. Hands folded. A cigarette smolders to ash in the ashtray while I watch. I've taken some beans from the streets—remnants of this morning's kids' bean-shooters—and tried throwing them vainly at the geranium-guarded panes. He is as far as Eden. Now as I write he extinguishes the light.

The moon is so full and the air so fresh that I feel quite exhilarated.

September 28, 1953

We may—I hope so much, I dare not hope so deeply—rent a loft tomorrow. It is ideal: close to home, perfect in feeling and atmosphere. I must dismiss it as too good to be true.

October 2, 1953

The loft is rented. In a three-story wooden building on 100th Street and Broadway, it occupies the top story. The street floor is an open-air fruit and vegetable market, the owner of which rents us the loft. A beauty parlor has just vacated the second floor. A social club formerly occupied our story and we spend this evening trying to discover inexpensive ways of undoing their floral wallpaper and silver woodwork.

Julian plans a brown wrapping-paper wallpaper like the *Ubu Roi* set, using salvaged paper, and a curtain of patchwork *Ubu* costumes.

There is some phoenixlike meaning in this.

We will probably begin with *The Age of Anxiety*.

October 6, 1953

Fifteen people are staying in our apartment. My headaches grow more frequent. George Miller and Tom Williams and Saville Clark, who is trying to finish a harp piece, Renée Gerson, her baby Lydia, Dick Gerson, and Nina Gitana. A few days ago Johnny Parrish, looking even more sensational than usual, stayed two nights and made off with Julian's best corduroy jacket and pants; Richard Miller wanders in and out playing his angelic pieces on the piano, insisting that they are not worth writing down (it makes one mourn). Then there are Nina's lovers: Bill Alex and some others. Mother.

October 7, 1953

At Larry Maxwell's party I scarcely knew a soul and went up to the roof to smoke.

Then, at the Remo, Agee is all smiles and embraces. At closing time we go to Dicken's room where we three sprawl to watch the leisurely dawn waft into Charles Street in a haze of weed smoke.

October 11, 1953

Julian loses his job at Hearn's. I'm glad. It was a lousy deal. But how will we pay the rent on the loft?

I dread being all alone with myself and facing the quiet, so I fill my time up with duties. Now I flee it by writing it here. When I put down the pen I will flee it in housework.

At least I have not fled it in the Remo lately.

I fled it at the movies.

I took Garrick to *Houdini*, which he watches more intently than any previous film and censors my attempts at explanation with "Watch the picture." All day he does "magic" and makes things disappear by tossing them away after a count of three.

And all his life he will look for it—the sense of magic, or "gullibility unrecapturable."

So I flee my quiet moment and like the Hound of Heaven it follows.

October 14, 1953

It's impossible to dissemble in the group without being discovered. Paul asks us each to write a description of another member of the group. Paul assigns Philip to me, himself to Philip, and me to David Andre. I've been reading the letters of Keats, Byron and Browning and draw upon their restraint in my analysis of Philip. Still my voice stuck, reading what I wrote.

"It would have surprised me," said Philip, "if she did not keep a journal which I have read."

"Is it like you?" asked Paul.

"It is more like me than I want to admit."

And then suddenly and in a louder voice, accusingly: "But it was *she* who set it up!"

Of me, David Andre says, "Judith is a swell girl. She seems to act from a solemn desperation."

October 18, 1953

The Boat: The Boat has become the subject of all our talk, and the center of everyone's fantasies.

Nina brought the strange Mr. Nason to our house. He tells us the story of his yacht, the *Romalorie*, which is to hunt the South Seas for a treasure for which he has the map. He is recruiting for the trip, and all our friends are making plans to join the crew.

Julian and I neither plan to go nor do we believe there is such a boat. It is for Rosemarie Louise, his lost love, that Mr. Nason has named her, and he says that she is between Florida and New York, to dock soon at 23rd Street. Everything about the *Romalorie* is connected with the number 23, which Nina claims is the "perfect" number "because it contains the duality and the trinity."

Among those whom Nason has recruited: Paul and Lester and Philip. Our whole community is in the throes of this false hope.

Julian says outright: She's a fantasy. But everyone says I disbelieve because I don't want Paul and Philip to go.

Everyone—especially Paul—is offended that Julian says it's a hoax.

Our house is headquarters for mustering the crew. Nina dances blissfully through this dream of a miraculous voyage.

October 21, 1953

The ship fantasy continues to keep everyone spellbound.

Nina flips into a state of manic joy. She is convinced that she is Aphrodite.

October 22, 1953

Watching Nina, I see how what is called madness is a breaking down of hierarchies. The vast differences and minute similarities merge.

Doubtless the hierarchy on which we base sequence and communication, survival and action, is not the only one possible. The mad construct a different hierarchy, while we secure ourselves inside the limits of the world we've made.

Nina draws a coin of which she suggests that she is both sides. She draws radii out from the center and far beyond its circumference.

"But I cannot stop there. I am out here [her pencil careening off the paper into space], that's why I am a god."

Later I meet Alan, who talks familiarly of gods and the land outside our ken. He has seen visions of the northern gods amidst the aurora borealis from the windows of a plane. His, however, are household gods in human scale, and not the tigers in Nina's mind.

Her excesses make me unsympathetic even to Alan's kindly gods—and aghast at my own mystical proclivities.

She rants of Manfred and the heroes.

"Who is this Man Fred?" she asks, and answers: "Freed-rich Nietzsche. He probed the poet's lie too much. But I am the s. sense of Nietzsche. I AM Nietzsche."

October 23, 1953

How can I work on the loft while Nina dances in a frenzy?

Last night Philip and Lester found Nina dancing in the Village in an impossible situation and brought her home. Bill Alex returned from Philadelphia with a fifth of Schenley's, which he has almost finished by the time I return from work.

He plays the piano with abandon and then recites Shakespeare's angrier soliloquies. Between Richard III and Othello, enter Philip, harried; Lester, drunk; Nina, mad. Lester!

October 24, 1953

Nina goes into a stage of quiet, exotic pantomime.

Her Earth Mother, Anna, a big blond beautician whom Nina met on the street, arrives this evening with her dog, Tinya. Earth Mother wags her great blond head, spoon feeds Nina while cradling her in great embracing arms.

"Now is my little girl going to eat the way her mama tells her?"

In a black gown, with her black silver-streaked hair falling round her like a veil, she dances the "pale white lilies" of the romantics she so much admires.

Yesterday we went to Noel Sokoloff's. He played a record of his string quartet and we were proposing he do music for our theater when Dick Stryker called: Nina, at Rienzi's, had been asked by the management to leave . . . could we come? He kept her in the kitchen where he has taken a job washing dishes. Since then she has steadily darkened her demeanor. She sings, dances, gestures slowly.

How can I do the work?

Her spinning makes me spin.

I flee to the White Horse Tavern. Dylan Thomas quaffing and holding court.

Martin Corbin is at a table with his political friends. Since they are arguing about Trotsky and the Makhnovites I don't say much.

At that moment I regret it because one of the arguers is a good-looking boy with a tone firm for his age and a bright eye. He catches the meanings sharply. I like this. I learn he is a socialist pacifist. Despite my silence he notices my interest. We feel immediately acquainted and leave too quickly. He lives in the house where Harald lived, on the floor below our very room.

This Mike Harrington is brilliant and turns out to be a friend of Paul's and others of our gang; he describes a recent change of character. We are very casual but I talk too much of Jim. Soon, excited by my own chatter, I leave Harrington to get to the Remo before closing time. Sure that Jim will be there. He is.

The family at the bar: Paul, Julian, Maury, Philip, Dicken, Jim.

But the question was: How can I work?

How can I work when I chase phantoms, and the house is charged with anger and madness.

October 28, 1953

Julian, at home, is trying to convince Nina to visit Alison Montague, a psychiatrist friend whom Paul recommends.

Last night we began painting the loft.

How can I work without calm?

Jim clings to me, tells me his troubles and the troubles of the women who circle him like moons. He has no commitment to me; therefore he trusts me. He thinks I am not very clever but very kind. In fact I am more clever than kind. I listen to his troubles and feel the sorrow he deals out.

All the while I am patiently waiting for my moment. In the dirty Cornelia Street hideout I feel strong with him. In his King Street home I feel timid, cowed by his castle.

How can I work?

Nina sees Dr. Montague. She goes willingly and does not disguise her behavior.

We cannot follow his suggestions nor heed his warnings. Jackson Mac Low and Norman Solomon stay with us, watching over her.

October 29, 1953

Willard Maas conducts a film symposium, at which Maya Deren, Dylan Thomas, Parker Tyler and Arthur Miller talk on "Poetry and Film." The ennui is indescribable. Dylan is contrary but doesn't push it to the point of being interesting. Four vibrant personalities bored to death.

Then at Dorazio's studio with Paul, Lucia, Ben, Willard, Julian, and Marie, we heatedly debate the same subject. I insist on going to the White Horse afterward if only to hear Dylan carry on.

At Paul's I am angry at the world. Love bears me up. Looks on tempests and is never shaken.

Jim's film, *The African Queen*. How he must see himself in the prehistoric manliness of the Bogart role! The symbols that he complains Huston obscured are clear enough.

October 31, 1953

On the night of our fifth anniversary, we traipse among the rubble of the houses being demolished on Amsterdam Avenue to find wood to build our stage. I become discouraged by the splintery edges of this romantic notion. It would be more romantic if I were seventeen again. But I am years too late. Feeling old. And yet we build the loft and begin again with nothing.

Halloween. The nightmare season. I try to order the bedlam at home. The kitchen has become Nina's domain. She and her friends decorate it fantastically. It is colorful, but creepy and not beautiful. I long for it to be clean.

November 2, 1953

To Paul's in my very narrow orange shoes with the extremely pointed toes and thin heels.

Now on the subway I open my notebook to write and wonder that my only thoughts are about my clothes: black lace, silver belt, Chinese brocade jacket, rhinestone necklace and earrings, white beaded handbag. Gaudy, because I want to be out of place in the subway. Every item was bought at the Salvation Army.

Nina says to me, "What is a fact?"

I try: "A fact is an arbitrary condition that we set up among a hierarchy of conditions in order to survive."

She stares, asks: "Is the ship at Twenty-third Street a fact?"

November 3, 1953

The phantom ship has vanished. Everyone had worked themselves into a frenzy of preparations—and then Mr. Nason was no longer in room No. 23

at the Terminal Hotel on Twenty-third Street—and the treasure hunt was over.

Julian and I are blamed, especially by Paul, for our disbelief—as if it were our fault that there never was a ship, because we didn't have faith in the dreamer's dream.

". . . There could be no excuse for blaming anything other than oneself any more than one could blame the sea for man's inability to live within it." John Goodwin in *The Idols and the Prey.*

November 4, 1953

At work I read Stendhal and make up a production schedule for the loft.

Last night in my black velvet cape to the Artists' Theater at the Amato. A good production of Lionel Abel's *Death of Odysseus.*

At intermission Duke Ellington in his white greatcoat towered above the mortals.

My private sessions with Paul become more and more serious and dangerous. I mean that what I have been protecting is endangered because I no longer want to protect it.

November 6, 1953

Finish *The Red and the Black.* It makes clear how the emotional mechanisms we devise turn on us like the robots in a science fiction story.

Alan has been trying to teach me to play piano. He uses the Béla Bártok *Mikrokosmos.*

I am not quick at this, but Alan expresses delight at my slightest progress and ignores my obvious faults.

Jim does not call. In a week he will tell me with the fiercest sincerity how he has missed me.

The snow is splendid.

Nina has had two sessions with Fritz Perls. He has frightened her. She is fleeing to Provincetown. In this storm—and by bus.

Philip says he envies her. Paul points out that my dreams indicate that I envy her too.

November 10, 1953

The sudden death of Dylan Thomas in New York City.

> We are robbed of the unwritten poems.
> Because we have mocked his drunken laughter,
> We will, ourselves, intoxicated by his lost songs,
> Cry how amiss the bars can be without him.
> I am here, as if in the cold, as if
> After the first sniff of heroin,
> When the body in horror, and dread pleasure,

Freezes in memory of all remembered deaths.
The first great death to come.

And this, the poet's death.
We are now forced to admit that he was the flower among us, the drunken, sweet singer, screaming like a child and penning like a prophet. We are left to regret our hard thoughts and the futility of our contrition. "And death shall have no dominion."
Here, in the White Horse Tavern, where he drank, it's a crowded night.

November 11, 1953

Put my right hand through a pane of glass in a fit of fury and emerge bloody but only scratched. I take satisfaction in such violence and no little pride in the ability to be so reckless and unthinking, though I think of myself as a cautious person.
Yesterday I could think of nothing but Dylan.
Dark, flamboyant letter to Oscar and Gene.
Today Dylan Thomas is already one of the dead poets.
Scored for an ounce of the weed at great trouble and expense. And mostly to entertain Jim.
My self-wounded hand hurts when I write.

November 13, 1953

Dylan Thomas' funeral.
In St. Luke's Chapel, a block from the Cherry Lane, where I went to sit quietly on days when the theater's worries pressed too hard.
Though the full roster of writers and artists is here, there is neither ostentation nor the unease evoked by coffin and flowers. It might be a mass in any church where all the parishioners know one another, nod, and afterward stop in the winter sunlight to exchange a few benign words.
No eulogies.
Gene and Oscar are teary-eyed, but everyone else—save for Caitlin—is cheerful enough. We know well enough what it is we have lost.

November 20, 1953

Several nights with Jim. One ice-cold night at Cornelia Street with only the fireplace red with old *New York Posts* for both light and heat; once in King Street where we made love fearful of every sound.
Jim is much troubled by Dylan's death. He makes efforts to cut down on his drinking, boasts about it less, attends a meeting of Alcoholics Anonymous, rations himself to five drinks a day.
It is as it should be that he talks ceaselessly, for he is a wellspring of ideas and the source is abundant, so that the poet takes the poet's part and gives us a fabric for the world.
I am hardly able to absorb it all. I watch his maned head and how the loving and vicious expressions alternate as his voice softens and hardens.
Of me he always talks softly. But when he tries to touch me softly his hand

is tentative, like a giant trying to play with a mouse without mangling it. His hard movements come more naturally. He can suddenly, in a tender moment, lash into a swift painful move at which his face contorts. He does it quickly as if not to notice it himself. Noticing, he stops.

As Philip paints the loft ceiling, I look up to his ladder from where I'm working. And looking up, I understand that the myths don't hold up in the face of the paradoxes.

November 22, 1953

A memorable party at our house begins quietly with Willard, Ben Moore, Philip, Lester, Perry Roth, Dick Hillman, and a few others in conversation with Fritz and Laura Perls.

Fritz opposes Willard's niceties and I defend them. Then the room fills and the conversants break into groups. But when Jim comes I take him aside into the library, to reserve him for myself.

Fritz soon joins us. They take to each other immediately. Fritz proposes a film of *Fidelio*; Agee embroiders on the idea as they warm up to one another with mounting enthusiasm: two heavy-talkers engrossed in each other's style. Laura Perls joins us. Then they proceed to concoct a film on the life of Heine.

Jim and Fritz advance on *Hamlet*; I work myself up to quite a pitch refuting Fritz' contention that the divided, indecisive personality is never deep. I point to the depth of the abyss that looms between the decider and the decision, arguing that the indecisive personage in the drama dares not cross the chasm, but that we, the audience, cross it for him, with full knowledge of his fears. And as I speak Jim greets someone behind him and I see Mia Agee.

Mia is a tall, sternly beautiful woman.

I try a few times to speak to her, but timidity overcomes me.

Fritz asks me, "Who is that woman? What a marvelous face. I must meet her."

In the front room, a party atmosphere of ease and liquor. Joan Hunt is the attraction of all eyes. Harry Jackson talks art with me, the lovely Joan, and Chester Kallman. In the library Agee and Perls, Mia and Laura form the center of a brilliant discussion. Jim and Fritz make up ever more scenarios, enjoying each other's irreverance.

Later the liquor veers the party to excess. Philip is put to bed in the studio. Stryker goes out and gets mugged by two angel-faced toughs in the street. Chester is angry after a fight with a sailor, who left cursing him. Willard falls drunk on the floor having tried unsuccessfully to seduce all the young men. Rose Anderson flirts vainly with Julian.

And the party is over.

Lester stays and we talk about Philip (as once Remy and I talked about Lou). Each longing for the absent one that both love, each seeing in the other's love for the beloved a reflected light of love, as a sun worshipper might love the moon. In the end honor is the threat of guilt tattooed across our lovemaking.

Discretion alone troubles me, but this pretense at the need for discretion is itself a form of indiscretion.

November 26, 1953

A summons from the U.N. comes about a "film group," which we, as "film makers," are to attend. Paul points out it is like K's "Castle": That we go there uncertain of whether we really are land surveyors or that we will ever really find out. With Maya Deren and Willard and Ian Hugo and many others, we meet in a smooth-walled room. The parliamentary procedure is childish and inefficient among these people. Maya says the necessary things in a manner that sets everyone on edge. Her little flaming frame all red and gaudy in the smooth-walled room that she revolts against.

Jim Agee looks ill at ease, shifting in the smooth plastic seat. He smiles at me often, secret, flirtatious smiles. The devouring and the devoured talk about film careers . . .

Jim whispers to me, "You never gave a damn about anybody's career, not even your own."

November 27, 1953

Alan James and Ross Vaughn open Shaw's *Simpleton of the Unexpected Isle* at the Davenport Theater. The old man, Butler Davenport, sagacious and splendidly aged, looks on from an aisle seat while these children play in the little gold theater to which he has devoted his life.

I remember his gray-sheeted figure at intermissions cajoling us to support his effort, promising a rebirth of the arts in return for our patronage. Now with narrowed eyes and set jaw, he observes another generation's inadequacy.

At Alan and Serafina's I make some drawings of them. Serafina's face seems to move through space, Alan's face is fixed and unmistakable.

Ramascura and Bahai, the cats, fare better because, Julian says, a black cat can't look bad against a gold background. And the ghost cat on Alan's shoulder paints herself.

November 28, 1953

Jane Freilicher's birthday party. All the painters are very affectionate toward us. In retrospect, they forget their bitter disapproval, as the good old days gleam in the mellowed light.

December 4, 1953

We work on *The Age of Anxiety*, but there is insufficient progress on the loft.

There is a vague sustenance in kheef and the loveless loves which seem like satisfactions, while they only make us forget the dissatisfactions.

At home a little world begins to cohere which I nurture like a wee fire in a windy place.

December 11, 1953

Julian works in a studio called the Medium that makes decorative stuff for window displays.

Ruth, the director/boss, who claws at the hostile world with all her youth and femaleness, hires me and Joan and Harry Jackson and Philip to help with the Christmas rush.

We work among plaster cupids, puffy angels, gilded ballerinas—a window display version of a Cocteau dream.

We make reindeer for a candy store chain.

The Jean Erdman concert signals my annual encounter with Joe Campbell. He makes no errors. I am infatuated with the idea of his weaknesses, which I have never seen, as a man might be infatuated with the body of a woman whom he has only encountered in clothing.

Remy is Jean's leading dancer. Dancing the Lover with lithe, strong limbs.

At the party after the dance, I am mostly in the kitchen, where Joe does a host's duties. This season we don't even engage in philosophical discussion.

From his study lined with the printed knowledge of a hundred languages a window looks down on the Waldorf Cafeteria, the seamy life of Sixth Avenue and 8th Street and the women's prison.

December 15, 1953

We are discussing the possibility of starting our own theatrical props studio with Harry and Joan when Philip brings in an order from Ballet Theater for the new Hemingway ballet, *Capital of the World*. We find ourselves thrust suddenly into activity.

We make four bull's horns, molded on an original, banderillas in velvet and flowers, and knives of rubber and celastic.

We name the venture Malina-Hunt. Harry's loft is hastily rearranged to look efficient for the conferences with the designer, Esteban Francés.

December 31, 1953

I have had to relearn, by a laborious, painful process, how to think.

Paul so shook my faith in my capacities—as an artist, as a poet, and as a thinking person, that in order to recreate a balance I have to return to former ways of thinking which supported me long ago.

Till I have my hand again firmly on the guide-ropes along the road of reason.

I have by no means overcome fear of the dark.

I stayed away entirely from the San Remo except when Agee has called me to come. For all that he gives me, he is too torn for me to lean on.

The Ballet Theater project ended dreadfully. Harry and Joan are angry with us. The ballet was lousy, pantomiming the brash Hemingway sentiments. Our props looked fine. The decadent benefit audience loved everything. I liked only Alonso; not even Youskevitch. We watched from a box in the Metropolitan's crescent. In Mrs. Vanderbilt's box, next to ours, four young balletomanes sat eating cheese sandwiches.

A pudgy man sporting a fake diamond tiara caused talk. When yet another crazy crank loped by in red satin, the dignified matron who shared our box whispered to her companion, "Why, it's a drag!"

Paul said: "We have taken over." But what we want to change must be changed by revolution and not by camp.

Two plays: *In the Summerhouse* by Jane Bowles, in the Williams-Mc-Cullers style, shows a trend toward a formula as rigid as Clyde Fitch's.

In thirty years we will be unable to read them, much less to play them.

Richard III done in the dark Margaret Webster style. Heavily thumping along.

"Stand by and let the coffin pass." It contains the drama, dead.

And our loft is so slow getting started.

When theater is good theater I feel crushed and left out; when it is bad I feel angry and impotent. I can work with the anger. When it's great, I'm inspired.

1954

The containment of all in any part is our greatest solace.

The clues that the criminal leaves show that even when a person tries to disassociate himself from his action everything leads to him. And the way in which the master detective can trace an object, a word, a gesture, an omission, a slip of the tongue, a look of surprise, shows that if we follow any road persistently enough we get what we deserve. Or, as it may be, any road leads to God.

Tennyson:

> Flower in the crannied wall,
> I pluck you out of the cranny,
> I hold you here, root and all, in my hand,
> Little flower—but *if* I could understand
> What you are, root and all, and all in all,
> I should know what God and man is.

Our limited perceptions never let us participate in the whole universe; what my five senses show me is too partial to make a coherent structure.

But the actual world is not a myth; it is simultaneously ours and its own.

> Little flower—but *if* I could understand
> What you are, root and all, and all in all,
> I would not pluck you out of the cranny.

Paul reads to our little group of friends "The Galley to Mytilene." He says that it is the pacifist piece I urged him to write. And I suspect he thinks it will irk me that his pacifism speaks so differently than mine.

It's a wonderful story and yet I am distracted by the loveliness of our friends listening attentively to our acknowledged teacher: Murray Hargrove and Marjorie, Saville Clark and Richard Miller, Dicken, David Andre, Rose and Bob Anderson, Sally, Julian, Lester, Philip, and Glenn Lewis.

I care for them all very much. Last night we let the year come in unnoticed and toasted it later. It wasn't a party; it was a community. Glenn Lewis, whom I have long admired from a distance, made love to me as if in promise of good omen for the year.

At Merce's concert the air is clean in contrast to the posturing at the Met a few nights ago. Merce has rented the little Theater de Lys on Christopher Street where he can barely break even. There he dances with a freedom that frees us.

Remy dances with him.

I understand these movements.

The music for *The Age of Anxiety* should be like Schaeffer's tape piece: *Symphonie pour un homme seul.*

Jackson says he can't write like that.

January 2, 1954

Julian tells me they've invented an all-annihilating bomb. I imagine a lifeless earth, with a sense of helplessness of which I cannot rid myself. How useful then a certainty of God.

January 3, 1954

With the help of Henry Proach and some friends, the skeletal form of the stage begins to rise in our loft. The lumber fitted and pieced together,

> that was dragged as packing cases from the streets
> or carried from the lots on 98th Street
> where the houses are being razed, or
> made of "lifts" from Germany
> with the wood of German forests
> the big crates that contained all the worldly goods
> of the refugees from Hitler
> and of the floors of brownstones now decayed
> that were, a hundred years ago, the residences
> of the rich uptowners:
> our stage.

And as I see the form become like a stage I shout like a child and jump with joy at seeing the theater begin.

Dick Edelman, of whom I have heard much, is here. And he has heard of me. Strange feeling (almost *déjà vu*) at our first meeting. As though old friends.

January 4, 1954

Alan Hovhaness with his satchel of music. He is embarrassed and fidgets. I don't fidget.

At our therapy group I am tired and can't really listen with attention as I listened to Alan. Their ponderous statements about human nature mean less than Alan's fidgeting.

Julian, angry at my going out when the work presses hard, tells me that Jim called.

Alan's discomfort solaces me. Paul's comfort disturbs me. Julian's anger flatters me. Agee's call troubles me.

January 6, 1954

Rehearsal ran late last night. Afterward to Paul's to pick up some lumber for the stage. We stop awhile to hear Paul tell how the writer's plight is economic.

When we return home longing for sleep, Jim calls.

At Cornelia Street we keep the cold in check by burning newspapers, and

I see they are the notices and reviews of Jim's work. He complains of his age, of his wife, of his work, of his sexuality. And when he makes love to me, he seems indeed an old man and his age tires me.

In this disenchantment I love him no less. What happens when Cocteau's tightrope walker finds herself on the ground going firmly?

I return home at eight A.M. taxiing through a morning-fresh city with the night's taste still in my mouth.

But I go to work, and then to Paul's for a session about childhood and parents and those sickening details of childish eating habits.

Chairs for the loft, scavenged from trash piles with icy, numb fingers.

January 8, 1954

An interview at the Bethsabee de Rothschild Foundation, arranged by Vivian Fine, a composer friend of Paul's. The baroness is straightforward, very spirited, and apparently has faith in us. Craig Barton, another official of the foundation, is with her.

They are planning a chamber theater in a large dance studio now used by Martha Graham. Noguchi had begun the plans for a transformation to be made in such a way that the space remains flexible to suit both dance and theater. A big wooden model of it sits in the room.

But Noguchi, they explain, won't return to this country as the State Department will not grant a visa to his wife, Shirley Yamaguchi.

I suggest Kiesler, but Craig Barton says he's too formidable. "He sits at a perfectly clean table, perfectly lit by fluorescent light, surrounded by many men, all of whom hold T-squares."

Our informal meeting at his house had been quite different, and at the opening of *In the Summerhouse*, his small bustling figure admonished us with encouragement.

In the foundation office a Noguchi sculpture in thin gold wire, designed as a costume for Graham, shook its tentacles.

Barton says nothing about the possibility of a grant, but suggests we might "use the room."

On our way out we glimpse "the room" through a glass door. Martha Graham is rehearsing her intense, stiff-necked work. Everyone inside keyed to a terrible pitch. A boat by Noguchi in the center.

January 9, 1954

A marvelous rehearsal last night. The depths of the Seven Stages of *The Age of Anxiety* emerge radiant from the poetic fog.

Each actor brings to our play the conclusions of his and her peculiar contemplations. Ellie Munro, Dick Astor, George Miller, Henry Proach, Julian and I. We are all spirited and read with excitement. Bobs Blossom understudies all the men.

January 11, 1954

A light snow falls as we go into the ruins of the Ninety-eighth Street tenements to pick up stage lumber, pulling floorboards out from under the bricks.

I wish I could retreat from these tracks which hurt my pride and make my fingers blue with cold.

Henry Proach is hammering the top planks onto the supports and Saville Clark stripping someone's ancient woodwork down to usable wood, while Garrick sleeps on a cot in front of a portable heater.

The Perls give a party. Most of the guests are from the Gestalt group. Laura earnestly plays hostess, much the way I do, while Fritz divides his attentions among the younger ladies. He singles me out, however, in a more serious endeavor and corners me upstairs in the bedroom. He does not for a moment drop his role nor I mine. This is singularly European. Our culture requires that at the first love-pass, one drops one's role, or at the least, takes on a different role, that of simulated sincerity. Though this is customary, it does seem more honest not to attempt it. He catches hold of me and murmurs, "Tell me, Judith, do you have orgasms?"

Drunk on champagne and whiskey, I talk jauntily with Isad Fromm and Paul Weisz. Laura comes, rustling black taffeta against pink velvet (a rose with dewdrops of rhinestones suggestively at her bosom), to whisper loudly, "Agee just phoned. He is coming." Whereupon everyone plunges into a discussion of Jim.

Two hours later it's two o'clock. We've had Chopin on the piano and have run out of fresh talk and people are leaving. Fritz even had his back-talk tape machine out to affright us with our own voices.

Then Jim arrives and several people put their coats back into the closet, and sit down to listen to him talk about his New York film. He's rather bitter and hostile, though maintaining a certain courtesy. The theme of adultery is thrashed about till Fritz asks Jim, "How much of this is confessional?"

And that launches Jim on a tirade. Paul Weisz restores equilibrium, his incisive advice marred by a sardonic streak.

An inept discussion of the nature of tragedy ensues; so many fine minds incapable of a single insight. I wish Paul Goodman had stayed, but he would not put his coat back in a closet for anybody. Paul knows something about the nature of tragedy, and even when he is maddening he is enlightening.

We rant, each defending some set of personal propositions. Fritz brings back his voice machine into which Jim and Julian now talk; Julian closing his eyes in confusion, Jim furiously beating the monster at its own game by roaring slowly and deliberately back at it.

We leave them at five in the morning. Fritz glares at me. Laura kisses me good-night. Fritz kisses me good-night. Julian and Laura kiss good-night. We taxi west with Jim. I kiss Jim good-night.

January 14, 1954

Last night a party at Herbert Machiz' for Dwight Ripley. A crusty crowd. The De Nagy painters: Jane Freilicher, Al Leslie, Grace Hartigan, Larry Rivers, Harry Jackson and Joan, the de Koonings. And Dick Astor, Harold Rosenberg, and Willard Maas, who turns all discussions to sex.

I talk at length with Marie Menken about Ezra Pound, in the kitchen, while a shy maid is abashed at our forthright vocabulary. I wear black lace; Marie towers over me in lamé. She promises to write to Pound about permission for us to do *The Women of Trachis*, which he has translated into a heady vulgate.

January 22, 1954

These are the best rehearsals. In our living room where the furniture is disarranged to approximate a stage, the actors move easily and securely, and the static poem becomes a moving play, the meanings clear. I am in love with what I am doing; therefore the actors work well.

Every night after rehearsals we plunder the ruins for floorboards, dodging the ubiquitous policemen.

Alan comes to talk with me about the two realities. He divides his world into the spiritual and the actual and dares not let them mingle. The only bridge is the music, which actualizes the spiritual, dissolves conflict, and unifies. But when he does this in any other area he is seized with terrible cramps in the stomach. (I suspect it's a shrinking terror of the entrails.)

He writes to me passionately, includes me in that special sphere of music and mysticism where the worlds meet.

January 11, 1954

To Judith

> Out of the ocean of waves of strange bell sounds.
> Bells of unknown varieties in unnumbered unknown
> mikrokeys with mysterious rustling sounds below
> and weeping of mikrotone voices above. This is
> my world and my love chant.

Alan

He might be better off with someone who could reject his spiritual world instead of containing it in a philosophic scheme. But he would suffer stomach pains.

I no longer fear Jim's irrational temper. We talk about poetry and vision, Joyce and Dante. He reads me an indelible chapter from his typescript, describing the visit of his family to a surviving ancestor.[15] I ask him how, given his brazen disgust with people, he can portray them so lovingly?

"No, it is not really people I care about"—we had discarded ideas, concepts, and atmospheres—"I'm interested in them, but I don't really care about them deeply. It's more the sense of smell and touch and, and"—here his hands reached out, each feeling for, blindly and sensitively, the other—"that's what I care about."

I left him at four, not enamored but happy.

Reading Whitehead's *Process and Reality*, and the splendid *Enchafèd Flood* by Auden.

January 24, 1954

To hear Lou's Mass. Done, not only badly, but erroneously by the Collegium Musicum and the Cantata Singers.

Through the vague rendition I remember only Lou standing at his rose-wood piano singing in a tenuous, ecstatic voice.

February 1, 1954

Fear at the prospect of beginning. Where do I feel it? As a constriction in the chest (high, right below the shoulders), as a weakness of the wrists, as a sexual urge of an unpleasant (unyielding) nature, as a slight palpitation of the heart, as a sense of suffocation.
Paul says, "Breathe."
That can make me frantic.

February 3, 1954

Jim loosens my flow of ideas and allows me to expand until I speak with certainty. We go to the San Remo where I seldom go now.
We soon leave and talk till six of a horror story Jim means to write. The time goes quickly. I borrow Melville's *Journal*.

February 4, 1954

The Immoralist, with Geraldine Page, adapted from Gide's story. The play portrays a corrupt refinement which makes the audience consider, "I am not half so genteel as these people, but I could never be so depraved," or "These people are so much more genteel than I, but they are just as depraved." *The Age of Anxiety* cast occupies a whole row at this preview performance.
Backstage we find Billy Rose talking to Geraldine at the dressing room with the gold star Scotch-taped to the door.
We collide belly to belly with Billy, as Geraldine greets us with shrieks. She talks high and fast. "Gerri," I crow, "you've become such a genius!"
And she: "Yes!" (Six octaves up.) "Isn't it wonderful!"

February 10, 1954

The hideous death of Bodenheim blankets the Village in a funereal spirit. Who dares confess to the wrenching excitement of seeing a companion's mauled corpse on the front page of every newspaper, and all of us knowing that the worst has again triumphed?
Max and Ruth both murdered by a boy to whom they offered a bed. The ranks of the dead poets swell.
Even self-contempt when fierce enough is magnificent. The virtue of the extreme is its extremity. Nature loves extremes as much as she loathes a vacuum.
So it was for his very last birthday that Art stole the pumpkin pie from the Waldorf Cafeteria counter.
Alan plays the *Two Orbits* for me. The second is remarkable for what Alan calls his new style. Ecstatic and Byzantine, with less of the European folk rhythms.
Jim reads me hot off the typewriter the latest chapter of his autobiographi-

cal book. It revives the torment of children's teasing games. A boy like himself, mocked by his playmates for having a "nigger-name."

The more I come to enjoy these all-night talks the less tired I am by day after them.

February 16, 1954

Jim is cynical now even about his sufferings. We talk till dawn of Don Juan's sorrow. I can't be useful.

The Bártok is wonderful. I work slowly. Lose myself in the idea of the music. Even understanding the notation is fantastic.

Everyone works hard on *The Age of Anxiety*, though rehearsals err on the side of too much sociability.

To concentrate is to put oneself in the center of it.

February 22, 1954

The stage is built, and covered with carpeting found in the ruins, using the reverse side (the strong side) as a ground cloth and patching the tears with celastic. The proscenium is made of black cloth stretched on wooden frames. The ramp is built, the wings begun. We are ready to begin onstage rehearsals. The curtain of patched *Ubu* costumes is ready. After a music conference with Jackson Mac Low and a light conference with Bob Anderson, we feel relatively equipped.

But as Paul says, when things are a little better the deeper problems come up.

I don't want to continue work in the doctor's office. The doctor's prejudices, his discourtesy to the nonpaying patients that the law requires him to accept, appall me. After the 15th of March I will work only mornings.

I smoke a good deal. Dick Astor and Ellie and George press me to turn them on and I do, though I wonder if this is prudent in the presence of Joe Kraft, Ellie's friend from the *New York Times*. They make much of it.

I make discoveries. With discipline, the inner eye ceases glancing at the passing landscape and acquires depth perception.

This week another passionate letter from Alan that I can neither answer nor ignore.

Boston
Dear Judith,

On the train, to lose myself—going north forever north in pain I drink the thought of you whom I love with my life's fire burning at the center with burning mouth along gray oceans or amid mountain pines. This is a love song but night closes in around my hand and your eyes ever pierce my darkness.

Alan

Yet when I see him, his restraint makes such extravagant words seem impossible. I am of no use to him.

Alan is trying to win by magic.

Tonight we hear his piano concerto at Carnegie Hall. Barzin leaps about when he performs. We sit in the second row beneath the cellos where only their sound and the heavy brass could be really heard.

We go afterward to Alan and Serafina's with some of their Boston friends, and I forget my Freudian handbag which Alan will be bringing home.

Paul spends entire sessions insulting me. Why does he do this? Occasionally I get angry, but I've gotten so used to it that I often merely observe it.

"You are not qualified to discuss this," he says of precisely those things I know best.

Paul won't see this as his problem and insists on playing the Zen teacher.

Garrick says, "I don't have to learn. I know everything."

February 24, 1954

Time goes too fast.

The Auden play engages me fully. There is no impatience during the work.

The actors imagine that they are moving very spontaneously and doing very worldly things in their scenes. Actually they are performing as stylistically as the Noh players. They are so absorbed in the play that they do not see how we are only transmitting the content and not representing it.

Alan returns my handbag. We talk, not in the passionate idiom of his letters but about his meeting with the dead Prokofiev in Switzerland.

The composer emerged out of the stage candles at *Romeo and Juliet* and conversed awhile with Alan about his music and about his demise. Alan tells me the dead composer assured him his was a calm death not hastened by political persecution.

I am tempted to tell him about the doll.

I give him the Victorian map of Egypt that I intended to give him at Christmas.

Jackson Mac Low's music for *The Age of Anxiety* seems to come out of Webern. But Jackson says I'm wrong—it's Schoenberg.

February 26, 1954

Julian in *The Age of Anxiety*: He does it the way he does everything. With awkward strokes, unconventional methods, he creates seemingly haphazard, impossible moments, and then suddenly he places the last stroke and we marvel at the whole composition.

First rehearsal on stage in the loft.

Jackson huddled in cap and overcoat in the cold.

Pulse rises.

An approaching storm turns the air to a color it hasn't been since I was young.

Yesterday Dicken mentions in passing, "Lou will be in New York around the fifteenth, en route to Rome to live out his year on the Prix de Rome."

Alan in the drenching rain talks of magic. I show him the doll, an ugly graven image. It's plain to see why we are commanded not to make them.

March 2, 1954

In the group. Philip lying on the floor, talks of his insane fear of chickens, explosives, and a woman's hair in his eyes.

Paul, lying on the floor, central and vulnerable, doesn't play the antagonist that he has been of late. He accepts everyone's remarks.

Then I go to work on the loft.

When I reach home Jackson plays the record Alan has left for me, *Hanna*. I hear in it a whole elucidation of music. The line launched, adrift, bolstered, wrecked, reborn, subsumed.

Having written this in the Café Dome, she cleared her throat, sat up in her seat, brought her napkin to her lips (a token gesture, she was wiping nothing away) and prepared to close her book and her pen. Now, back to the world.

March 5, 1954

En route to Paul.

I am pleased with the first run-through last night, which took four hours. Friends drop in to watch. Feeling of an audience. No strain. Ellie does her long monologue with penetrating simplicity. I would rave and rant like Sarah Bernhardt.

It's as well that they don't worry the abstract quality of the play. Pat Woodul to stage-manage. Blossom, who had left us to fight Senator Joe McCarthy, returns from Washington exhausted.

Now all our energies are bent to *The Age of Anxiety.* Everything goes smoothly—except that the music is not yet ready. Jackson works a blue streak. The dissonances all day make me want to scream. Dick Stryker comes to organize a recording session. He hopes to have Grete Sultan play the piano part; Tui St. George Tucker, the recorder; Larry Rivers, the saxophone. Larry calls from Southampton having received the score and plays it over the telephone for Jackson to O.K.

Jim Agee, in his best southern speech, will play the radio announcer. He likes the idea of reading Auden's lines. I have still to tape his voice.

I bring the leftover cover-paper for the old *Doctor Faustus Lights the Lights* programs to Milton Saul. On it he and Claude Fredericks will print programs for *The Age of Anxiety.*

Bob Anderson wires the lights.

Eric Weinberger fixing chairs, and recalling the warm *Ubu* nights when we all went barefoot in the streets. Now Eric is a messenger for a banking firm. Wears sturdy shoes, good clothes.

"I feel as though I'm in costume," he says. But it will pass and we will all take off our masks.

The world goes to pieces. We are its only adhesive:
Frank O'Hara is shot in the thigh by a robber's bullet.

The Goodman children discuss the differences between "legal marriage" and—what? Paul shrugs.

On our block they find 40 cases of ammunition on the premises of a shop supposedly manufacturing boxes.

When the enraged Lolita Lebron shoots down five congressmen shouting, "*Viva Puerto Rico libre,*" not one newspaper dares use the adjective "beautiful" describing her.

March 11, 1954

Jackson works all night and all day. The music I scarcely understood on the piano sounds marvelous orchestrated.

Recording in the Amato Opera at three or four A.M.: Jackson and Tui St. George Tucker, dressed like an urchin, with a tired, pugnacious look.

March 13, 1954

Recording Jim Agee.
Jim wakes up with a whale of a hangover. Eggs and coffee.
We rehearse the lines of the Radio Announcer and record at the Amato. The sound man, George Jacobs, is impatient. Jim staggers, retches, moans. Anthony Amato stands by asking, "This won't take long, will it?"

March 22, 1954

The Age of Anxiety opening was both miracle and ordeal. The theater is itself a wonder. Its black-lacquered chairs, its brown-papered walls, its minute size, its proportions. Its Ubu patchwork curtains. And this we have built. We have built this sea with our hands.
The ordeal is my old monster, pouncing upon me after so many years. I am frightened onstage and I laugh at my fear. It strikes at the least loss of concentration. I am determined to take measures against it.
The play tells the story of everyone at the opening night including the actors, but it speaks neither to nor of the Mexican peasant. Yet it does, when Auden says, "The sullen South has been set on fire."
The set Julian devised is a world in itself, of symbol, sign, and actuality. It is a collage of somber objets trouvés: left over bits of life, like history washed up on stage. Jackson's tambourine placed on an orange crate at the door is full of coins and dollar bills.

Paul Goodman says I suppress the terror. I do, as he says, fear a loss of ideology. We are caught in a net of superstitions, dogmas, obsolete creeds, bungled scientific "conclusions."
Squeaking like drowning kittens we sink without knowing what water is, or death, or our own fear. I think of the stiff-bodied fish who can never see any portion of his own anatomy; has he the sense to feel himself as a force of moving matter, or even as an area of energy? We are, like him, invisible.
Such gloom, Malina.

March 25, 1954

Writing to a friend in prison. Repelled at writing the number after his name.
Read Dylan Thomas' Under Milk Wood.
Letter from Alan Hovhaness:

Dear Judith,
May I compose music for Spook Sonata? When I was in Sweden the feeling of Strindberg's hell was with me. And most deep my love for Strindberg.

Will you come to Town Hall Sunday Eve April 10? I conduct Concerto No. 9. Will send you tickets.

Alan

In answer to a plea from Cornelius Groot, we made up a package of winter clothes, then found we had no money to send it. Now it's on my conscience. I'll change it to spring clothes.

Reading, on and off: *The Poetics; The Unwobbling Pivot;* Jung; *Ars Poetica;* Horace; Hobbes' *Digest of the Rhetoric.*

Jackson has written Pound that we want to do *Women of Trachis.* Pound himself has written music for it but writes Jackson that he has not the patience to notate it. Jackson is thinking of going to St. Elizabeth's Hospital in Washington and doing the notation for Pound from his notes.

The Circle in the Square Theater is closed by the fire department. An ill omen. We tremble in our unlicensed loft.

March 29, 1954

I visit the hypnotist, Dr. Mor Lewinsky, in whom I have no faith though his diagnosis is not uninteresting. He does not regard it, as I always have, as a psychological problem, but as a neurological phenomenon. As I lie on his couch, he lectures me at length on the vagus nerve, catechizing, "Now tell me again, Miss Malina, what are you?"

And I must suppress a smile to answer solemnly, "I am a vagus neurotic."

He says, "You are now in a deep sleep"—and I wonder whether I should protest that I'm not—when it seems terribly rude, as if I were calling him a charlatan. When he says, "Raise your right arm, it is very heavy," I do so, even though it's not particularly heavy, and I wonder whether I should argue with the man or do as he says.

I do as he says.

Then he tells me marvelous things. That I will be strong and able—that my concentration on stage will never waver—that I will never again laugh at myself on stage—that I will be cheerful, confident—

He prescribes belladonna "for all vagus neurotickers" and implies that it will work miracles. He says, "You will be full of confidence, energy, and pep," and while the words awaken me to a sense of absurdity, either the belladonna or his suggestions seem to affect me favorably.

The problem during the performances disappears.

Thursday we play to an audience of three; it was hard to keep the actors from fretting.

Friday night we have a good audience and invite them to some punch at our house after the play. I like to talk to the audience after the play—to break down the separation into a friendly scene. And we learn much about how our work affects people—they talk freely—both praising and criticizing. We decide to make these invitations a regular event. It makes many friends.

Among the audience who come home with us after Saturday's performance are Fritz Perls and Frank Hale. Hale is a practicing analyst who collects art, sees all the theater, was connected with *View* magazine, and speaks of his Sullivanian therapy in precise words, pausing between every word with an irritating emphasis. He seems to admire whatever is extravagant. He liked *The Age of Anxiety.* He argued patiently and cautiously with Fritz. Fritz, however, expresses himself more poetically so that whether or not he was right I tended to side with him.

I enjoyed watching their careful exchange, uncertain as to what they were trying to achieve in stressing the divergent tendencies of their respective schools.

Fritz says, "Nowadays nobody tries to be god," and reminisces about the Romanische Café where Grosz, the Bauhaus artists, Marc, and the *Blaue Reiter* group, gathered to become gods. Hale didn't contradict Fritz when he fell into the romantic exaggerations to which he is vulnerable. I suspect he was more interested in studying Fritz than arguing with him. Perhaps he was even serious when he took my arm to lead me to Fritz and suggested, "Come, we shall sit at the feet of the master."

Joe Kraft is one of those people who functions with a strong objective awareness. But they make me uncomfortable.

April 5, 1954

On Friday Joe Campbell and Jean Erdman in the audience. They recognize the play's relation to *Finnegan*.

Leaving the theater we see a dying cat and I wish for a Schweitzerian patience. Calling the ASPCA, I fear that they will kill it; they will either kill it or help it.

Holy indifference is not mine.

"Nor," points out Joe Campbell, "is faith."

He relates the story of Buddha's horse ascending to the thirty-third heaven and being established there as a saint.

Joe is studying Hindi. He will be going to India for a year. We talk of the character of languages, but mostly of Japanese.

On Saturday we had a packed house with ten standees. Paul, Philip, Fritz and Laura were there. Fritz gives me a copy of his book *Ego, Hunger and Aggression*.

Paul interprets Reich's "He cannot be a great man, I had breakfast with him"; or Hegel's example: "No man is a hero to his valet"—not because the man is not a hero, but because the valet is a valet. Because we project our self-disdain on those around us.

Warning: Get on your high horse if you would inspire affection. My whole being, my ethics, and what Paul derogatorily calls my "ideology" rebels at this. Yet in *Spook Sonata* I'll play the role of the Director. People will call me Malina. I'll keep my weaknesses to myself, put my best foot forward, and if lonely, play solitaire.

Am I beginning to feel myself in the ambience of *Spook Sonata*? In the annotated script made for my production at the Dramatic Workshop I find a quote from Piscator: "The spook house destroys itself like society."

Sunday at the Caravan Gallery my drawing, *The Leaves of One Tree and the Fruit of One Branch*, is awarded an honorable mention. Mother and Julian attend and Garrick, who, hearing my name, calls out, "That's you, Mother, that's you."

Then we attend Larry Maxwell's "Spring Festival and Defloration of Virgins."

As there are no virgins present, the bridal crown is passed from me to Jean Erdman, to Anaïs Nin, to Maya Deren.

Our faces have a masklike look, and when we talk we grimace too much. Julian talks to Anaïs.

Maya asks Joe Campbell to take her to a hypnotist to discern the difference between hypnosis and possession.

I had left my hypnotist only a few hours earlier but keep my secret.

> Ach, wie gut, dass niemand weiss,
> Dass ich Rumpelstiltskin heiss.

April 7, 1954

Alan comes to discuss the music for *The Spook Sonata*. We talk with Jackson of the power of evil. Alan believes that Maya Deren is trying to harm him and is the source of a present illness. He played at a party given by Joe Campbell and felt Maya's presence hostile. Jackson suggests exorcism but the idea of bringing the weight of the church on that hell-bent young woman's head is appalling. Jackson: "This is the disadvantage of a liberal church."

April 12, 1954

Alan conducts his concerto as if in trance.

The rest of the program is Bach, Brahms, and Liszt.

Later, Alan admits that he fled to Hector's Cafeteria during the Liszt, a composer whom he accuses of ruining the piano as an instrument.

Last night in Claire Goll's little room in the Master Institute. "High in her tower to the west" with a sweeping view of the Hudson, surrounded by rare books, by Chagalls, Picassos, Légers, Dalis, she conveys an impression of protracted loneliness. She thrusts book after book by Yvan Goll into our hands, scarcely letting us see one before another is presented. They are all fine illustrated editions, in three languages. It is the struggle of a woman still beautiful, though no longer young, trying to make contact with a world grown cold and strange.

She is superb as she speaks tenderly and much of Yvan Goll, and proudly of her liaison with Rilke. But she takes pains to specify the unadulterous sequence of her relations. She mentions no one who is not an international figure; yet there is no sense of boasting, only an attempt on her part to reconstruct a world which she has known and lost. She thinks "Goodman is a genius who ruins himself with his perversity" and adds, "I think maybe he does not like me very much because I said I do not believe in all this psychoanalysis. He said, 'I don't invite you to tell my patients this.'"

Claire Goll cannot imagine why people don't seek her out more when she is always so *disponible* and makes herself interesting, or why someone like Laura Perls is so outspoken in her dislike of her. The truth is, she would gain greater acceptance if she became an old woman and took the liberties of the aged.

"How terrible to lose so close a partner, how empty," Julian says, and we cling closer to each other.

A few minutes later at the crowded Remo bar, Ben Moore tells us of the death of Gene Derwood. Oh, Oscar!

April 14, 1954

There are only a few people at Gene Derwood's funeral, and besides Oscar, only Paul Goodman and Sally of our acquaintance.

The chapel is bright with Easter lilies. I can imagine Gene a ghost, but can't imagine her immobile and cold inside the draped coffin.

Perhaps because she always insisted that she was entirely a creature of the spirit.

When the young priest read her poems they were strangely ecclesiastic. "I am not a poet," she said to me the first time we met, "I am a preacher."

Chatting with Paul and Sally and Julian over luncheon—we lose too quickly the sense of Oscar's sorrow.

The group session this week was somewhat diminished because David Andre has gone back to his hometown where his father has just died and Philip home to Ohio where his sister died.

Work on *Spook Sonata*.

April 16, 1954

The Medium goes out of business and Julian is unemployed. They haven't paid him for weeks and the bad checks accumulate in a useless pile.

April 17, 1954

Read history. Ault's *Middle Ages*, Boulanger's *France in the 17th Century*, *Finn McCool*, a pamphlet of the Catholic Truth Society of Ireland.

At the White Horse I meet Mike Harrington again. He has a sharp mind, and knows more than I do, yet I treat him like a child. He had an article on the waterfront strike in the *Catholic Worker* incisive in its analysis and just sentimental enough to be effective. I find him attractive and promising, but he may be too hard-headed.

April 19, 1954

Dick Edelman will probably play the Student though he reads Old Hummel better. I admire him but am afraid of him. We would work better together if he were afraid of me. I can see that he takes every advantage.

Paul is angry with me.

April 20, 1954

At the White Horse, Mike Harrington and his friends talk; most of it is chatter, but it's never the solemn defeatism of the Remo. At the White Horse people seem to have some life outside the bar.

Mike is heroic enough. That is, he takes in the environment and its people and includes them in a generalization of which he is the center. Thus the hero is in control without needing to be in command.

Mike is handsome and doesn't rave in extravagant adjectives about what he likes, but smiles acceptingly, and his approbation is highly valued. What he scorns he scorns outright. Sometimes he says flippant things: "The only trouble with Dylan Thomas was that he was ruining a perfectly good bar." But then, he comes to himself. "But now I already eulogize him."

When I say to Mike that I am reasonable, I realize what pride I take in this. Not to create problems. To be simple with him. But when it's really important I am not simple and make many problems.

Why did I go on to the Remo when the night was already finished?

Perhaps I hoped to meet Jim. Or my eternal salvation. Four A.M. Closing time.

April 21, 1954

On the rounds in my bandbox clothes, my sparkling disguise, I have no identity at all. I could be a mechanical doll. In the offices the receptionists say: "Try next month"; and on Broadway simple-hearted, ugly men make idiotic pleas for affection and companionship that sink to a beastly lechery if one so much as answers in a monosyllable.

For Saville Clark's concert at the loft, a grand piano is placed at the back of the house, all the seats reversed, and chairs put on the stage because Julian is afraid that the stage might not hold the weight of the piano.

Saville's cool, honest music, played by the prim, young Lalan Parrot suits the Stein *Meditation* and the Pound song.

How slowly the day begins. I sit here answering the doctor's phone, writing of the events of yesterday, feeling hunger, and anxiety about casting *Spook*. Tension in my body. I'm waiting for what Auden calls "the absolute instant." I anticipate something. I hear the siren and wait for the bomb which might fall and crush me out of hearing.

April 22, 1954

A second concert at the loft last night. Dicken has woven the *Beyond the Mountains* and *Thirteenth God* themes into a suite.

Dicken also played Lou Harrison's *Pastorale*.

In the *Tribune* I read a tribute to Lou on the editorial page about the Prix de Rome, praising him almost as if he had died.

In the candle readings, Serafina has seen him in Italy under very blue skies and heard the sound of bells. That she included me in the Italian idyll does not ring false. I'm somewhat there.

April 26, 1954

This weekend unflawed performances: no self-mocking laughter, no loss of concentration. I credit the hypnotist.

The cast for *Spook* begins to shape. Serafina Hovhaness will play the Mummy, and Louis Criss, the Student; Edelman will play Hummel, and Irma Hurley, the Young Lady.

Energy directed at an object has an energizing effect which eventually moves the object toward the original source of energy.

If one has mastered this technique, there is nothing one cannot do.

April 27, 1954

First rehearsal of *Spook Sonata*.
Read-through. I read all absent roles.
I work with Irma on the Young Lady's desperation and with Edelman to structure Hummel's Stages of Evil.
I work with Serafina on the Parrot's voice. (She cannot trill an "r.")
I must work with Louis on the rising bitterness which the student needs in order to make possible the "bitterness redeemed" at the end.
Trying to help Moe find a slower, threatening nature. He expresses disappointment in the small size of the role, which has only two speeches, but the person of the Cook sets the sinister tone.

May 3, 1954

The Age of Anxiety finishes its run.
After the final performance, at a party at John Ashbery's, I was angry at all the artists who were at the party and never attended the play.

Louis Criss has dropped out of *Spook Sonata*. Edelman will play the student.
Irma finds an actor, Joseph Leberman, an older man who has spent seventeen years at the Hedgerow Theater. He's not really quick, but with a well-rounded technique for Hummel.
Closing night, Garrick comes to the theater accompanied by my mother. Afterward he says he doesn't wish to attend any more children's plays because grownup plays are so much better. As to the acting: "Mommy was terrific. Ellie, the same. Dick Astor, medium. Daddy was the best of all. No, George Miller was the best of all because when he fell down I really thought he was dead."

Tea at the Lees': Francis Lee and his wife, Michel, invite us to tea with Claire Goll. Lee asks me to bring Garrick to play with their five-year-old, Michael.
Their European-style apartment is covered with Michel's big, splashy, nervous canvases, all like shouts of anguish.
The children take one look at each other and each feels that this is the person he has really wanted to hate all his life.
They proceed to try to kill each other. Conversation is impossible. To calm the children a cowboy picture is put on the television.
Michel moves toward the phonograph, saying, "I'm sure we can hear Mozart over the television."
Between Mozart, the cowboy film, and the children's cries of anger, we try to say a few words.
Francis shows us an album of his Paris photos taken in 1944. He took the first pictures of Picasso and Stein after the liberation, in which he participated as an American private.
Claire leaves close to tears. The children are in tears. The parents smile bravely, each holding their bloody boy out of reach of the other's fury, and we say: "They don't seem to get on well, do they?"

May 10, 1954

Resume *Spook* rehearsals. Joe Leberman has a somewhat preconceived notion of Hummel, but it is not a bad notion.

Edelman: "You'd be surprised what a *heimische* boy I really am," he says. And I am surprised. I thought him not very human.

Irma is almost ideal for the Young Lady; she achieves the poetic effect.

Angelo is Johannson. Frank McGuire is Bengsston.

Joe Leberman says to the method actors: "When I appeared in the crowd scene in *Julius Caesar*, I stood downstage right in extreme profile; I cried only with my right eye. No sense wasting tears that the audience couldn't see."

May 11, 1954

Alan asks me to write an opera libretto for him! Searching for a theme, we talk about Akhnaton, Cagliostro, Nostradamus, Sappho. . . .

After the opera Alan will be setting St. John Perse, and that should occupy him for almost a year.

May 13, 1954

My schedule is hard. I proceed as though driven. I try to treat each hour as though it were my last. Would that I could live the moment as more than a step to the future.

Now that I work mornings the day begins at eight. Julian goes off to Brooklyn where he is working in the display department at Namm's department store. This depresses him and he is impossible to talk to.

At 20th Century-Fox, in a gigantic office with Tutankhamen architecture of brass and Nile green tiles, the casting director ignores me while watching the McCarthy hearings on television. I try to talk through the government debacle, but the state of the union interests us more than whether or not I get into the movies.

At MGM, Mr. Wilkinson suggests that my severe hairdo limits me and wants pretty photographs.

"But," I murmur coyly, "I can't compete with the glamour girls."

"Look as pretty as you can and let them compete with you," he says. "Come back with pictures and a softer hairdo."

When I come home this afternoon, Dick Edelman is asleep on the front room couch and he takes me sweepingly in his arms. I don't regret my resistance.

May 14, 1954

At Murray Korman's for photographs. Lots of show-girls, phones constantly ringing. Murray bustles like the queen bee, dropping a word or a name, selling, building up, getting out a bit of information. He serves each client like a press agent. I get into evening gown and then wait two hours while being introduced to people. My virtues and theirs extolled, exaggerated. A small, tough man, Murray uses his vulgarity as another man might use his refinement. He appears to single out each woman as his pet, muttering a "hiya, baby, ya inspiah me" or stroking her hair as he walks by. When he takes pictures he works fast, gesturing and exclaiming like a madman. Though he strains and twists me, and almost breaks my back, he certainly makes me feel gorgeous.

Frances Clarke's wedding takes place in a scented little church of the Greek Orthodox faith.

She wears her grandmother's wedding dress. Bride and groom wear wreaths of white lilacs on their brows.

The church is covered with ikons. Above the altar a great painted eye with spikes of golden light.

The service is elaborate, but then, where Rome elaborates the spirit, Byzantium elaborates the ritual. Two old women in black go from ikon to ikon, kissing the feet and garments of the saints and martyrs.

We all go to the Café Rienzi. Early Sunday morning MacDougal Street is faded like an older woman in too strong a light. Where is my night-sick street? I left an unturned corner. I'll run after it.

May 20, 1954

At the group on Monday, I can't remember Philip's name. And Paul presses me to feel my qualms.

The night is cool and spring is in it and I walk with Philip. Our talk is intimate. We stop like lovers in front of a row of old houses with wrought-iron balconies on 12th Street, admiring the architecture, but talking of hostility. I explain that he misunderstood what happened at the Cherry Lane.

I rally my best resources to move beyond the proscenium into my own needy world.

Paul sees that my romantic passions, as well as this passion to immerse my life in the art work, are facets of the same need. But only when work and love mingle is it possible to make life creative.

Philip asks me the name of "this boy" of whom I speak, but I put him off. My affection for Richard will be known soon enough. They are both St. Johnnies, whose world of logic is always in precarious balance. Each of these men thinks he has solved his world in terms of Aristotle when he has succeeded only in buttressing his illusions. Edelman, however, is safeguarded by his intense Jewishness.

At rehearsals I work at refining the structure of the play. The important thing seems to be to build the house and then rot it. All the characters must serve this purpose. The structure like Piscator's spidery traps.

In the coffee shop after rehearsal, Leberman tells of his life in the C.O. camps with the Brethren and the Mennonites, Edelman of his experiences in Mexico with a group of workers on a public service project.

When we all say good night I go off with Edelman. Our talk turns to hilarity. We are so overcome by laughter we can scarcely kiss. It's important for me not to press him. Yet I do.

We return to the empty theater. We have some secret shyness. I feel a little incestuous with him. He is too much "my people." He would not admit that our laughter was anything but amusement. We were not amused.

I close the curtains to lie on the stage floor with him.

I muddle, shy and ashamed, but he disarms me.

It remains a stage—the most exposed place in the world—and I'd never been naked on stage before.

The Japanese lantern houselight shone through the curtain. He is nobly proportioned, not too passionate, but gallant and romantic. Above all, I care that he is affectionate.

The stage floor is harsh on my skin. But I could bed so every night.

I had been warned—he himself said that he is not to be trusted. He said, "Trust my loyalty, trust my admiration, but never trust my love . . . ."

Who spoke of love?

Earlier the same day, Paul said that I must be brave. I try to be discreet.

In the all-night Bickford's Richard and I talk. His Jewish name is Tobi Rivka. He is an adventurer but denies it.

I'm still afraid. I don't want to make life hard.

May 21, 1954

Alan writes:

Boston
May 19, 1954
Dear Judith:

The feeling is with me that soon knowledge will come so that I may take away the image for you and you will be released from it. Without harm to anyone. During this trip I will ask about it and then if you wish me to I will take it away to the high mountains.

The opera *Cassandra of Ilium* you wrote would be beautiful for the kind of music I want to write. I need your friendship deeply. No matter what I become, what madness I perpetrate have mercy on my soul.
I love you

Alan

Finished a duet in three movements today in one day for a European tour. A very mysterious piece of scattered clusters.

The Strindberg will be finished next week.

Called New School about our future opera. Told them I wanted a small chorus to sit with the instruments and augment the orchestra while the solo singers sing and act on stage. It will be O.K.

May 23–24, 1954

At rehearsal I stage the love scene between Irma and Edelman with some bother. He tries to control the character by logic, but I want him to give it his passionate feelings.

We argue about logic and metaphysic.

I ask him to play more passionately. He wants to impose form on feeling. A kind of artistic rape.

Julian is making a black cavern of the stage, deep, dense, charred.

Saturday afternoon we rehearse and Edelman helps Julian build the chicken-wire framework.

We bought some fancy costumes for near nothing in the Salvation Army and the Opportunity Shop.

Edelman tells us a little about his life, hiding behind hints and half-said things. There is a woman in England and her husband, the brother of his lover . . . .

I make too much of it. I am not in love.

Today at Paul's I say that I wish I were strong. Once I wished to be good, but now I want to be strong. If I'm strong I can afford to be good.

I am not in love.

The session at Paul's confuses me completely.

May 25, 1954

Last night we three worked on the set, papier-mâchéing the chicken-wire construction for the stage. There was a happy kind of sleepiness under our glue-covered aspect.

At five A.M. we return home in an oncoming dawn that excites us. Edelman stays over on the front room couch. I stay chastely away.

This kind of closeness is not altogether healthy. I think of the maelstrom Philip was drawn into. I am counting on Edelman's superior strength.

Money presents a major problem. There is not enough food.

Tobi Edelman sleeps most of the day. Though sleepless, I go to work happy. Julian works too hard, careless of the amount of energy he expends.

We go downtown with our Chinese tapestry hoping to sell it for enough money to redeem our invitations from the printer. But we do not succeed. I hate this scrounging business.

We rehearsed two acts last night amid the growing set. Fourteen people on that small stage seem like hordes.

To accommodate the stage, we place the lanky Leberman in a child's wheelchair, and in this his macabre Hummel looms up enormous.

Henry Proach's Ghost is formidable. Irma is unearthly. Alan returning from Boston today.

It all coheres.

Eight days to production.

Edelman says, "We are both directors because we want to impose a form onto life that we cannot find in the life around us."

But he does it all the time. He imposes the form. He feels the spontaneous harmony in the world as formlessness.

May 27, 1954

I enjoy the emergence of the clear form of the play, sitting beside Alan, who comes to hear the scenes with music.

Julian's gaudy crater is stained with luminous points of violet, orange, green, gold.

Afterward I go to Tui's for the long-awaited treat. Edelman goes with me. First he waits outside and studies lines under a lamp post, but the hospitable Vera Lachman invites him in for coffee.

Spencer Holst and I smoke. Tui is not there. There are six Siamese cats and exotic birds caged in geometric forms made by Spencer. We stop in Vera

Lachman's room to admire her treasures: some Chinese pottery, an old Persian rug, a Greek motto.

I have estimated Tobi Edelman incorrectly. And I'd be a fool not to alter my attitude. I am sad and angry. I feel as if I've been taken in, swindled.

It's seven days to opening.

Dollie Chareau sends a vital ten-dollar check.

May 28, 1954

Rehearsals proceed uncannily well. The muse is with me.

Alan's melody is so deeply connected with the words that it seems like a miracle. Alan recorded it himself, playing all the parts.

I feel very gay; the set is such a masterpiece—and the sight of Tobi dispels my anger. Jed Duane frets with Method terminology at rehearsals. Joe Leberman frets. Still, they're good.

I go to the river with David Harris for a smoke.

The sky is pink and gray with soft round clouds.

I ask him about Tobi.

"He may be greedy," he says.

May 30, 1954

Rehearsal. The play is beautiful. Tobi is beautiful. The set, the music is beautiful. Irma is beautiful.

I am not in love.

Except when Tobi sings Alan's song.

May 31, 1954

All the churchbells are ringing in their various timbres. Here on the roof of the theater I hear them change and mingle. The sun is going down. And below me the actors are trying their new costumes and makeups as the transformation begins.

Tobi has not yet come and I am up here to lengthen the day.

A dead pigeon reposes in the dying sun.

And the grace of contentment surrounds me.

Julian feels the strain of production. It is his birthday and he has spent the day in hectic, last-minute work. He says that's how he likes to spend his birthdays.

June 2, 1954

Tobi singing Alan's song.

This is for me so perfect a light I do not care to describe it.

And then it is I who am left, the dark center in its penumbra.

I credit Tobi with all the noble qualities of Arkenholtz, the student.

And if his faults are many, it only makes me want to redeem my own, for I identify with him.

The play excites me. I have never had such joy in work.

I don't question its success. I have succeeded and now it remains only for others to experience it.

June 4, 1954

Twenty-eight.

The play opened: It is a dream, this *Spook Sonata;* when the Ghost, the Milkmaid, and the Cook enter, it is a nightmare.

It had the mystery I aimed for when I directed it years ago at Piscator's.

Even John Cage and Merce Cunningham, usually so restrained, praise it extravagantly.

Paul Goodman tells a Zen story in clarification of Strindberg's third act: A student comes to a Zen sage and asks: "What is the meaning of life?"

The sage asks: "Have you had your breakfast?"

The student says: "Yes."

The sage says: "Go wash the dishes."

June 7, 1954

To hear Tobi sing the song is a constant joy.

We bring Garrick to the play, which he sits through enraptured.

I am given a role on "The Goldbergs" again. Mrs. Berg greets me affectionately. She casts me as her pregnant niece, on the verge of giving birth throughout the script. Dreading the end of our four-week run, when *Spook Sonata* will be over and we have no new plan.

Julian suggests our doing *Phèdre* and that Tobi direct it. Tobi agrees; they discuss the settings and the production.

Alas, Tobi is getting the better of me.

June 9, 1954

Alan writes twice from Boston, ill as he is. He has consulted with his oracle regarding the image of Lou.

June 6, 1954
Boston

The knife should cut 3 times. Once on the left edge. Once on the right edge. Once on the point. For the treacherous use the left. For the misguided use the right. For the loving use the point.

Some shall wear scars like the marks of claws and a few wear scars like the dents of rain. He who wields the weapon decides the mark. Against whom are you sharpening the right edge? If there is no countermeasure there will be another sword to reach the mark.

The image is dead but the force is living in its dark regions. You must give it a ceremony of resurrection like that of Osiris. The tomb must be stone. The garments white. The flowers blue. And it must be arranged by the hands of women. The time must be right after the new moon before the summer solstice. The one instrument for the music should be a wooden flute. And any music you find in you for the ceremony will be given without rhythm.

After the ceremony the image must be given to the person of its origin, of whom it was made. Evil spreads to him who only wades and washes as well as to him who swims.

Tell these instructions to the cause of evil and the decision must be on that head.

Dear Judith:

During May when I was here in Boston, I consulted the god. The answer is terrifying and I withheld it, but now in this weak condition I must send it. It is not my answer, not my wish, I could not help it. If you wish to do anything I will play the music if you wish it. If you wish to go through the ceremony and keep the image it might render the image less dangerous although it still must be kept carefully. Or you might keep the image and ask the gods to bring about a meeting in which it could be returned.

The other night (Friday) while bleeding violently I was transported to your theater and the play. It was wonderful.

With love,
Alan

June 10, 1954

At the Empire Hotel rehearsing "The Goldbergs" in a banquet room under crystal chandeliers.

Gertrude Berg sits in the center of this long table as at the Last Supper. All attention is on her. The scripts, our very selves, are her instruments.

She rewrites lines, sweats, smiles. She has changed from an ecru shantung suit to an apron, but her fabulous diamonds sparkle on her house dress and on her fingers.

She admonishes overambitious acting with: "Sarah Bernhardt! Sarah Bernhardt!"

June 11, 1954

Each day consists of work at the doctor's office, "Goldbergs" rehearsal, *Spook* performance, and Tobi.

Last night Lilli Bennett missed the performance and I played the Milkmaid. Once I met the sincere look of Tobi as Arkenholtz I was calmed. After the play a rehearsal with Julian, who is replacing Jed as the Colonel.

We walk home along the Hudson, Julian walking with Irma and I with Tobi. Under a crazy orange moon we lose ourselves.

Tobi reads in French from *Phèdre*, as well as some poems of Campion and some of WS's sonnets.

When I ask him if he is my lover, he speaks of another. That will teach me to be cautious.

June 12, 1954

I went to the group elated, which usually bodes badly at Goodman's. Tobi had made me happy and I felt secure. Paul turned the talk to *The Spook Sonata*.

After some quick praise Paul says, "But the boy plays the final scene as if it were a scene from *Awake and Sing*. Like Odets' *Awake and Sing*. You know that play?"

And I am furious at a world where—in Strindberg's words—"any praise you get always is accompanied by blame—the art of tearing people down has been developed to such a point."

So that when Paul says, "After all, here was Strindberg pouring out a life-time's suffering, giving his guts, his bowels—this is a great speech—"

I reply (burning quietly), "At least you got that much."

Paul throws his lit pipe at me. Rises out of his chair. Raises his arm and strikes me hard in the face.

Tears come to my eyes.

Then we talk about it. Paul asks me, "Why did I hit you?" I say, "Because I'm a woman," and the answer offends Paul so much that he refuses to speak to me for the rest of the session.

It causes much discussion, gossip, and analysis, but I doubt that Paul's misogyny will ever be uncovered.

Alan returns from Boston looking and feeling better. He is seeing Hyman Bloom's analyst. He brings us a copy of the score for *Spook Sonata*.

June 15, 1954

Here I sit, fat in a pregnancy harness and a costume from Lane Bryant.

The old Central Opera House, only recently converted into a modern television plant, is cold and drab.

The first time on "The Goldbergs" set, I was nervous, but today I fell asleep sprawled on three chairs, harness and all.

Unfortunately there is no one here to talk to. Actors only repeat incidents out of their careers.

Dora Weissman talks about her theatrical past. Arlene McQuade talks about movie actors.

They all work with a sense of driven monotony.

I walked this morning, from Eaves Costumes on 46th Street to the studio at 67th Street, elated by the summer.

June 16, 1954

Once begun, "The Goldbergs" seemed to be over in a few minutes.

Following a hectic dress rehearsal, the floor man says "three minutes" over the mike and a hush descends. Everyone freezes. After an interminable si-lence he says: "Two minutes." Then after a few hours of frost and deaf and dumbness: "One and a half minutes." We can hear distant watches tick in the silence, and our own pulses. "One minute." In the last hush Arlene McQuade lets loose a shattering whisper: "It's like an execution."

"Thirty seconds. Fifteen seconds. Stand by."

After my first entrance I am at ease.

The flattering attentions of the stagehands, as well as that of my stage husband and of the older ladies of the cast, give me confidence.

It's a tradition that popularity with the crew implies the best reception by the audience.

Afterward Gertrude Berg came back to kiss me and congratulate me. Everyone thought it an exceptionally funny episode. How dark the night was after all the lights and sounds. How quiet the world really is, I thought.

June 20, 1954

Day at South Beach with Julian, Garrick, Tobi.

Julian, Tobi, and I talk all the time of *Phèdre*. I recognize the scope of such ambition. From our bedroom wall an engraving of Rachel in the role looks calmly down to reassure me.

Tobi fusses about an adequate translation. But this is a problem with every play in a foreign language.

Boultenhouse said it of Strindberg last night. As did Mr. Paulson of the Strindberg Society. Anyone close to any language says it of plays that they care for. I say it of *Faust*. And it's always true.

Irma and Julian flirt cautiously with love.

We approach midsummer, taking up our positions for our midwinter madness. And the spooks on the stage of our loft include my husband, his mistress, and my lover. *Schon wiedermal.*

Disturbed to hear that Cocteau is ill.

June 23, 1954

Willard Maas says that he feels life is more bearable after seeing our play. This is a cause I am pleading. But it is not enough.

If I'm to play Phèdre in the fall I will need to be very brave.

I look at the various translations of *Phèdre* in the library at 42nd Street. Beyond the three translations we have at home (all inadequate), I find only two "libretto" translations: bilingual paperbound pamphlets sold in the theaters when Rachel and Bernhardt played *Phèdre* on tour here. They are crude and obsolete. I find, not only a certain historical interest in them, but also a warning against my *chutzpah* for daring to play the role that those two played.

In a bookshop I read a passage from Simone de Beauvoir's diary in which she describes our Dramatic Workshop production of *The Flies*. She distinguishes between Piscator's theater and Broadway and says that in New York a production in a small theater cannot expect recognition even when it's better than a Broadway production; in America one works "either in total obscurity or amid the acclaim of crowds." That was 1946 when we sat on the stage of the President Theater listening to her expound Sartre's philosophy in her faltering English. And I am still far from the crowds' acclaim in the obscure theater; it has grown even more obscure. Sometimes I think that in Europe people might care.

Our production of *Spook Sonata*, so worthy of recognition and support, can get none. And next week it will do its last four performances to an unmoved world.

June 24, 1954

Downtown to two useless theatrical offices. Stop on the street to hear a fine drum solo by Cozy Cole on the sidewalk in front of the Metropole, meet Philip Schrager:

"I'm off to Las Vegas with a show, then to Hollywood to direct a film. Saw you in Sardi's one night but couldn't wave because you were sitting next to Franchot."

Visit from Alan. He presses me to choose a theme for our libretto. I feel closest to Sappho, but Julian advises against a Greek theme. I too would prefer an oriental story.

A few days ago in the dressing room, Serafina said, "Alan says he identifies with Strindberg and feels he is like him."

"But Strindberg was cruel to his women."

And Serafina reported this to Alan who sent back word that he is not cruel to his women.

Alan and I sit on the banks of the Hudson and smoke marijuana. There had been thundershowers all day and the air was clear and the river bright. As the benches were wet, Alan insists I sit on a handwritten manuscript of *Yenouk*.

We listen to the sounds of the boats and talk of the colors around us.

June 26, 1954

Joe Campbell, who has used *The Spook Sonata* as a text for his classes, came to the theater last night and pronounced the production's iconography accurate.

He congratulated Julian on an explication of Strindberg's choice of the hyacinth: the banks of the River Styx were clotted with them.

At the second intermission Joe and I stood together on the fire escape. The night was very warm. I confessed that it was I who had sent him the Japanese love poem.

He is going to India and Japan next month for a year. He promises me a pine come from Kyoto.

June 28, 1954

The closing of *Spook Sonata*.

Saville Clarke comforts me during the last performance. I weep when Tobi sings Alan's song:

> Seeing the sun, it seemed to my fancy
> That I beheld the spirit that's hidden.
> Man must forever reap what he planted:
> Happy is he who has done no evil.
> Wrong that was wrought in moments of anger,
> Never by added wrong can be righted.
> Kindness shown to the man whose sorrow
> Sprang from your deed will serve you better.
> Fear and guilt have their home together.
> Happy indeed is the guiltless man.

July 1, 1954 — Maryland. En route

We're crossing the Susquehanna River Bridge. Julian and Mother and Tobi.

The day is hot. I am dirty and sticky from the long ride, but at last I'm on my way to Washington.

My father promised long ago to take me on a trip to Washington. Some sort of fulfillment of that promise is implied in taking mother there now.

We make o'erreaching plans with Tobi for a worldwide theater tour, though there is as yet no evidence that any of these schemes can be carried out.

A letter from Alan in Boston suggests that an outline of our opera may bring a commission. Sappho?

July 2, 1954   *Washington, D.C.*

Here is a pompous city, proud, wide of avenue, overbearing, fearsomely grand.

I sit on one of the side streets on the stoop of a dingy hospital where Mother, who developed sudden pains, is being given some tests. She has symptoms of appendicitis and is in no condition for us to take her back to New York. We await the diagnosis.

Yesterday, Tobi showed us Baltimore, its scrubbed white stoops that say, "In here we do not sin," its gaslights, and its painted window screens.

We picnicked on the road, then drove on to Annapolis to visit St. John's College, which I've heard described with devotion by a dozen loyal alumni.[16] Tobi lectured us on the architectural details of the Georgian buildings set among sylvan groves.

Each low-ceilinged classroom has a seminar table around which the students gather in philosophical discourse. Wooden geometric forms lie about as if demanding that the young men emulate their solidity.

Tobi asks again and again, "You will send Garrick to St. John's, won't you?" Garrick will decide that for himself.

We left Tobi behind in Annapolis where he will stay six weeks.

On the road I read aloud from Pound's *Women of Trachis* and Genet's *Les Bonnes*. And talked of repertory and touring. And of Tobi as a codirector of the Living Theatre.

We reached Washington at night surprised by its cosmopolitan air.

Mother was impressed by the well-lit Capitol, but I thought it like an oversize wedding cake, all white frosting, with "Armed Liberty" as both bride and bridegroom spotlit against the night.

We spent last night in a modest tourist house on U.S. 1, the busiest trucking thoroughfare in the nation. No one slept.

We rose early to see the city: The decorative Capitol with its overabundance of patriotic murals. In the House Chamber where the recent shooting by Puerto Rican revolutionaries occurred, we were questioned on entering and observed as we went about.

At the Library of Congress, among a mass of documents; the monumental aesthetic of the Gutenberg Bible and the modest Thoreau diaries.

At the Corcoran Gallery, Blakelock and Innes and some Italians. After lunch, the National Gallery masterpieces: *Les Saltimbanques*; Manet's bullfighter lying dead in his black costume; and an uncanny carved head of John the Baptist, by Donatello, painted in soft colors, the skin ashen, the lips a pale lavender tinted pink, the whole giving an effect of the supernatural and the possible merging.

Sated with the accumulated splendors of the ages, we came upon the wall with five tiny Vermeers, unostentatiously hung. They eclipse all the rest. In the center, *The Woman Weighing Pearls,* flanked by *The Woman in the Red Hat* and *The Woman in the Striped Hat.* Mother says, "The genius of these works is that they are so far in harmony with nature that nothing disturbs."

At the Folger Shakespeare Library, we lament that the Elizabethan stage is not put to use, because the directors are unwilling to mar the building's exterior by cutting through the marble for the exits required by the fire department.

Between the Lincoln Memorial and the Washington obelisk Mother took ill and we came here to the hospital.

She has been given medication and the pain alleviated. They make no diagnosis.

We spend the long night and dawn driving back to New York.

July 7, 1954   *New York City*

I have decided on the subject for Alan's opera: Buddha Gautama.

The theme: We never really have that which we are afraid to lose.

The plot: Act I: Gautama goes out of his house to work out his salvation, abandoning his wife and newborn child. Act II: Gautama at the Bo tree, years later. Act III: Yashodhara, the wife who is left behind, makes peace within her domestic confines on the night of his departure.

In *The Spook Sonata* the Buddha dominates the action of the third act: "Thou wise and gentle Buddha sitting there waiting for a heaven to sprout from the earth, grant us patience in this our ordeal."

Alan says, "This play has brought me close to the Buddhist spirit."

The love I felt for Tobi when he sang the song in that golden light, the occult music and the sacred words; a love I can scarcely understand; an epiphany which recalls only one other moment in my life.

> 1930:
> In the setting sun at the shore of the Atlantic
> a dark figure that I long for comes
> toward me in the golden light to bring me home.
> My father.

I try to call Alan in Boston, but can't reach him.

I call Joe Campbell, who is after all an authority on Buddha. He not only offers advice but offers to lend me some of his texts.

I dress with special care in my plain green dress. Julian drives me downtown and we eat at the Jabberwock. I arrive at Waverly Place so anxious that I have to stop to catch my breath at the entrance of the house.

Joe is editing Heinrich Zimmer's book on Indian sculpture and, with the enthusiasm with which Garrick shows me a favorite picture, shows me his work.

The dozens of photographs of erotic sculptures inundate us, in wave after wave of onrushing excitement. Joe is in transports. A big smile like that on some of the Hindu goddesses appears and remains on his face.

I cry: "Enough, enough!" We sit down to great balloon snifters of brandy.

He tells wondrous tales of the life of the Buddha, and he lends me three books, thick with his intricate annotations: Coomaraswamy's *Life of Buddha,* a volume of the *Harvard Oriental Studies,* and one of the *Sacred Books of the East.* His notes are not comments, but scholary summations of each paragraph. The loan (till he needs them to check his proofs) is a gesture of reckless generosity.

Tobi is disdainful of my interest in the Orient, as if it were some form of affectation. Saville explains that St. Johnnies are bound to regard Eastern religion as a kind of fortune telling.

I get high at Jake Spencer's with some weird people, still clutching the precious books.

Richard Miller comes the next morning to play his music: "I know why I don't write music. It's because I'm schizophrenic."

And then tells a mystical tale about the need to "slay desire" while he plays wonderful sounds and writes nothing down. But his talent makes me patient.

July 11, 1954   *Gaspé City, Québec, Canada*

In Boston at the Fine Arts Museum, I come agape upon the small Cretan statue of a snake goddess in ivory and gold, almost hidden among a hundred vases. Her tight-waisted body is erect and her outstretched arms hold the golden sacramental snakes.

Gauguin's epic *D'où venons-nous? Que sommes-nous? Où allons-nous?*

Manet's *Execution of Maximilian.*

We visit Alan Hovhaness, with an image of the Buddha in his little room at Hyman Bloom's. He says he put it there just before my call came from New York. He values such omens.

Mother and Julian go to look for lodgings while we talk about the libretto. He wants an orchestrated vocal line. I'm afraid to rob the theme of its simplicity.

He tells me also his torment at the prospect of hurting Serafina. He seems so determined to leave her that I ask him outright whether there is another woman whom he wants to marry, and he tells me of his passionate attachment to Phyllis. There is nothing for me to do but to lighten his burden.

Ultimately it will be something entirely different and not a passionate attachment that can give Alan peace. Fortunately he is productive regardless of the circumstances.

Alan suggests we stay at the Brunswick, inhabited mostly by mediums and mice. The latter scamper noisily, and one gets crushed under our door.

On the way north we pass through Salem and Gloucester. Eating on beaches, or in groves as the scenery becomes harder and pines replace the softer trees.

In Portland, at a book sale in a big church, I find an old set of Racine, for one dollar, sold to us by Miss Maine, the minister's daughter, who, returning from the pageant in Atlantic City, is helping her father in his church work.

I think too much of Tobi, though I know from the start that I will not love him for long.

But just now this love is young and happy; when it grows a little older it will, like all that ages, grow a little more desperate. So I implant the idea of its transience to spare me sorrow later. Perhaps this is the very way we grow old. Losing our fervor, with foreknowledge of the pattern that we make for ourselves.

When we enter Canada at Van Buren, the architecture changes to a poverty-stricken grayness. The land is unyielding. The people are poor. The pebble road is almost impassable.

We stay the night in Campbellton, which consists of a street facing a stretch of railroad tracks, beyond which industrial plants spew vile odors over the city.

On the Gaspé Peninsula, hills give way to mountains and gorges, and the sea breaks against great cliffs. The slanting roofs of the houses glide toward the earth. The Gaspésian men look of the weather, with tanned skins and heavy brows. The fishing villages are small and poor. Prices are high but it becomes clear that these people pay highly for what they sell us.

And our landlady says wages are low and nods bitterly, "Life is hard here."

July 15, 1954   *En route home*

At Percé: Coming to a bend in the road, we are met with a view of the sea from which a vast rock juts upward in the shape of a ship. Into this rock an opening has been worn away by the sea like a miraculous tunnel.

We climb one of the cliffs facing the rock. Julian wants to go on when the road breaks away and I am shamed into continuing in spite of my fears. I cling to a shaky little barbed-wire fence. The sea beats the rocks far below.

Feeling remote from home, I feel remote from myself.

Leaving Rimouski, we pick up a priest who is hitchhiking to the next village to conduct a funeral. The dead man's family is poor and the priest still a poor student at the seminary, therefore he hitchhikes to his priestly duties.

On a stretch of road between two villages the children hail the passing cars to sell wooden boats that they carve out of birch. We stop to buy one for Garrick and talk with the youngster who sells it to us. The Gaspésian dialect limits us, but it is clear the boy is saying he is not happy.

His name is Aurélien and he has never been away from the Gaspé.

Julian says that the country here is beautiful and Aurélien says *"pour vous."* The smallest children sell dried *étoiles de mer.*

July 18, 1954   *New York*

At the Metropolitan I examine the books on Barabadur that Campbell had recommended. These remarkable volumes contain no hint of the story of Yashodhara's conversion. In the museum's oriental collection, many Chinese Buddhas but scarcely any Indian sculpture.

We visit Garrick in Camp Waquasset. He looks magnificent with his sunburn. A tear escapes him when he first sees us and just before we leave, but he will not admit these tears are there.

We watch him, the shyest in the pool, shivering in the water, yet brazenly persevering. He is pleased that we play with him all morning, staying apart from the other children and enjoying him for ourselves.

July 19, 1954

Rounds. Last night I fell asleep at the library table to avoid starting the outline for *Gautama.* However it has taken a clear form in my mind. The orchestral voices are the Devas, whose chant Gautama heard in the wind.

Julian says it's too simple. But I like this.

July 20, 1954

An affectionate letter from Tobi Rivka, though he makes no mention of *Phèdre*. He writes instead of a production of *Much Ado about Nothing* in which he is involved. He plans to return in late August, in conflict with our rehearsal schedule.

Julian is my lover. This is a great comfort and makes life easy and domestic.

July 28, 1954

Boston
Dear Judith,

This room is called the whirlpool.
Enclosed is what I am sending to Louisville.
May Buddha help us both!

Love,
Alan

August 3, 1954

My head is full of Tobi.

If he plays Orphée . . . And Julian has decided that Cocteau's *Orphée* will be our next play. . . . The role of Death is small enough not to obstruct my view of the production as director.

Saville is jubilant that we've asked him to compose the *Phèdre* score.

August 5, 1954

In the mail today, Claude's *The Idiot King*. The play is religious and pacifist.

Claude's church, like his kingdom, is mythical, though the language of *The Idiot King* is Christian. But I'd prefer to play the Nun as a Buddhist. No Christian could say, as this nun does, that she is good and certainly in grace. In fact, the Prioress calls her heretical. But I am perhaps swayed by my current concern with Buddha.

August 8, 1954

To Joe Campbell's to return his books on Buddha, as he's about to leave for India.

He is pleased at our doing *Orphée* but *Phèdre* gives him pause. He calls it a "nutty play" because the villain is the nurse, but I argue for Phèdre's villainy. Everyone his own worst fiend.

Joe, Jean, and I drink gin and Schweppes, and talk of Buddha and of politics, and of the hatred and the fear that other peoples feel toward the United States.

Joe claims not to have noticed it.

He says, "Of course everyone envies our strength. But what does one do when one finds oneself in a field of conflicting powers?"

I answer, "One chooses a religious position." Joe accepts my meaning but finds the word "religious" objectionable. However, he admits to a respect for Buddhism: "Yes, it's the only one, the only possible one, the best one."

Alan has asked Serafina for a divorce. He no longer has that wan and lost look. He has rented a room on East 10th Street "in order to work." Creative people justify every move they make with this phrase.

We go to the river in a cloud of hemp.

It becomes increasingly difficult for me to cope with his feelings, which I can neither requite nor reject completely. I am constantly making small retreats.

He must return to Boston to work on the Stokowski and St. John Perse pieces before he can begin on the opera.

August 9, 1954

Orphée seems to be available in New York only in the Columbia University Library, where I copy it out in longhand.

Late last night, we struck the Spook Sonata set. I asked for a moratorium on sentimental remarks so that it should seem less painful, as we coldly crushed underfoot the black chicken-wire structure.

Now it is gone, mashed into neat piles of wire and paper.

August 24, 1954

How we came to translate Phèdre:

When Tobi got too involved in Much Ado About absolutely Nothing to work with us on the Phèdre script, we decided to ask Paul Goodman.

Paul says that Phèdre is a great play but Corneille's Horace is the greatest play in French literature and asks us not to proceed until we have read Horace.

The end of the play, as Paul forewarns, is a blatant apology for the court and glorifies the king, who has caused the tragedy. But Paul wants to change that. When we call Paul back he is full of talk of Horace.

We agree to do it if Paul will translate. He says he will start immediately and that it will be ready for next season.

Nothing further is said of Phèdre. But our interest in Horace does not diminish our desire to do Phèdre.

So Julian and I go to work on our own translation.

August 25, 1954

Last night to The Cretan Woman of Jeffers.

Richard Miller is preparing to do the Orpheus score.

Nina is home from Provincetown, strong and eager to act, but Orpheus is already cast. Till Irma returns from summer stock she will stand in for Eurydice.

Very late, Jim Agee calls, at his sweetest, at his warmest. He has been reading Zen and the Art of Archery and talks of little else.

July 19, 1952: "Dress rehearsal of John Ashbery's *The Heroes*....
My handsome husband looks old-fashioned in a white suit."

With Paul Goodman at the San Remo Cafe: June 28, 1953: "After Frank O'Hara's birthday party Paul and I went to the Remo where Weegee took posey photos of us. I dressed far too self-consciously in low-cut black with a red sash, orange shoes, and a bright scarf, with long green earrings."

November 1, 1954: "At the *Idiot King* rehearsals I begin to realize the character of the Nun. . . . Claude (Fredericks) asks us to consider each personage as a segment of humanity. . . . Julian is heartbreaking as the king."

Tonight We Improvise. February 11, 1955: "True to Pirandello I no longer know who I am, Mommina or Malina. . . . When I weep do I weep for Tobi Rivka (Richard Edelman) or for Rico Verri?" (Behind JM and Tobi Rivka: left to right: Dorothy Olim, Nina Gitana, Judith Graves, Judith Lennet)

July 25, 1955: "Alan Hovahness and I drove up Mount Equinox. . . . I do not like the height that divorces me from the warm good earth. . ."

August, 1957: "In the street: The street, I thought, as the brighter light of freedom flooded my eyes, is the place that surrounds the prison... I am not free because I am in the street that encircles the prison."

Christmas Eve: Caroling in front of the Women's House of Detention. JM, JB, Garrick center, Dorothy Day at extreme right.

August 27, 1954

The Racine translates slowly, but is a great pleasure. I work in the park while Garrick plays.

We are using the twelve-syllable line, and often, but not always, a real Alexandrine, with frequent assonant rhymes.

August 29, 1954

We translate *Phèdre* all weekend.

I plan to leave the doctor's at last. Not to return.

If only people knew what empty-headedness the charming office manners of the doctor hide. What lack of compassion. What lack of learning. I'm glad to be out of it.

Tonight I hear an atonal piece on the radio and hate it till I learn that it's Lou's string quartet. Then I excuse myself; it was a bad performance, badly reproduced.

The set for *Orpheus* begins to rise.

September 1, 1954

George will play Heurtebise. It is practically his true self.

And Philip consents to play one of the angels. He prefers Raphael to Azrael. "I dreamt that I saw Azrael lying in the snow." Dead poems. All things are mortal.

September 2, 1954

I've left my job at the doctor's. Never to return.

Work on the Racine. Constantly, the three of us, Julian, Nina and I on the subways, in the park with Garrick. We make a rough of the whole play before polishing.

September 6, 1954

It is six o'clock and I admit to having counted the hours of this day on which at nine the first rehearsal of *Orpheus* is to take place.

O God, give me patience. Let me work when no one watches. Let me be able to plant and wait.

How will I maintain my good intentions to be marble and ice when I am so easily transformed into tinder and fire and consume myself so readily?

September 7, 1954

The first reading was good, but not more than that. It's a play that requires action. Auden and Strindberg come alive with the words alone, so that I was a little disappointed in *Orpheus*.

Tobi hasn't gotten the Shakespeare out of his Orpheus and it clashes with this cool, white play.

Nina reads poetically but not yet with spontaneity.

George is still oversimple, but endearing.

Frank McGuire as the Detective is ready to open.

Henry Proach is the ideal actor.

Philip is Raphael.

I read poorly. Tobi Rivka made me edgy despite he brought me roses.

I woke this morning from a nightmare of murder, of a horse, a woman, and a child. Chosen by lots in which I cast a vote.

September 8, 1954

Attend to the play. Very well. Engage in combat if necessary.

There is no temptation to disclose the real secrets.

Tobi be damned.

But one can never wash one's hands of anything.

Attend to *Orpheus*, but I am distracted because I really want to do *Phèdre*.

Yet yesterday in a sunlit world, Tobi, Garrick, and I walked along the East River and lunched in the Museum, stopped to see some armor, and held hands.

Then it grew dark.

September 9, 1954

Orpheus shapes slowly and surely. Each reading is a little firmer. Tobi doesn't work with me. He says, "I let you intimidate me as Arkenholtz and did not experiment enough."

He wants to make more mistakes in rehearsals.

September 10, 1954

Instead of rehearsing, we go to Paul Goodman's forty-third-birthday party. Paul reads his newest poetry; in the birthday poem, which is an annual affair, he complains how he is ill-treated by his city—her loyal son. The listeners concur, Matty and Susie among the familiar faces of their father's circle.

Jo Jo LeSueur tells me about the Huxley-popularized mescaline with which he experimented this summer.

Playing chess this afternoon with Norman Solomon, I realize the discomforts of excitement. I respond well enough to the challenge of real danger, but gambling or competing turns my bowels inside out. A similar excitement in the sickening feeling when I expect Tobi.

September 13, 1954

Tobi hovers protectingly around us, full of grand, absurd, unrestrained ideas.

"We must buy a house. . . ."

"We must do much Shakespeare. . . ."

"We must settle in a small town. . . ."
"We must seek renown thus and so. . . ."
"We must play the festivals. . . ."
His Orpheus becomes better and better defined. Irma is nervous and impenetrable. She isn't sure if she will do Eurydice. Nina works very hard. Tobi undermines everything and then rebuilds it in shining colors.

Parker Tyler reads us his play on a transvestite subject about Tiresias, hermaphrodite, and a mythical androgyne named Hippolytus/Hippolyta.

September 14, 1954

Garrick's first day in P.S. 75, the Emily Dickinson School.
We start blocking *Orpheus* with George and Nina. Irma is gone. Nina is a promising Eurydice.
The set will be harsh white, like a Greek village.
Ten dollars from Willard Maas for the Living Theatre.
Death rehearsal last night.

September 16, 1954

When Tobi frowns I have little fits of melancholia. When he is kind or makes love to me, all's well. When I am sleepy he tends Garrick so that I can rest. He cares for me in a peculiar, loving way, alternating with bitingly cruel humor.

Tonight, Ruth Kaner, who is working in theater in Mexico, came to see us and her childhood friend, Richard Edelman. In an empty cabaret, the Old Europe, assisted by a pianist and violinist, we danced and capered till it was too late to see Agee. I had wanted to bring Tobi to meet him.

September 18, 1954

Three-thirty A.M. after an excellent rehearsal.
Richard Miller had not yet brought the music. We wired him last night and today he calls confessing that he has only two minutes of "unformed material" ready.
Saville promises to take any vestige of music that Richard has and make a score out of it. And if there is not enough he will compose or "improvise" it.

September 20, 1954

Yesterday afternoon, rehearsal for my Death Scene. The scene is intricately timed, each step and each action done to a count, so that Death and the Angels of Death move with metaphysical precision.

When we reach home, images of violence overwhelm me and I fear again another Philip Smith, another Lou Harrison, another Woody Parker, and I am not willing to experience, this humiliation, this self-destruction, this masochism again.

September 23, 1954

Tobi's Orpheus is a pompous, impossible, lovable pain in the neck, adored for his good intentions, or his bad ones.

As I identified Tobi with Arkenholtz, I now identify him with Orpheus; not the pure singer of the legend, but the ill-tempered, well-meaning brute of Cocteau's play.

Tobi and I take Garrick to the thrift shops to look for costumes, the while we talk of our problems.

Alan calls about an ambiguous letter from Louisville about *Gautama*.

Six days to the opening. I'm worried, but Julian is not.

September 28, 1954   *Rosh Hashonah*

Julian plays Azrael, Julian and Philip—uncanny poetry of my Angels of Death.

Dress rehearsal last night. The holy days and the opening coming together.

October 1, 1954

The first night of *Orpheus.*

The play proceeds without flaw.

Nina's Eurydice is formal and unearthly. Tobi's Orpheus is erratic, idiotic, magnificent. George plays without effort the unblemished sweetness of the angel Heurtebise. Frank and Henry circle like comic moons.

Working frantically during the last days and nights, Julian embellished Orpheus' villa by sculpting nine muses, the whole height of the stage; they resemble those thin figures Giacometti creates and their impassive gaze inspires us.

Saville's music sparkles like little waves and moves under the play like the tide.

For my scene, I prevail. When I enter, thrusting my hand through the mirror, a vacuum cleaner is plugged in backstage and roars through the scene like the persistent sea. Julian and Philip give me assurance and we move in concord, timed exactly to Saville's exacting score.

I love this company.

October 3, 1954

In the Death Scene, Julian gave me only one glove. The scene hangs on Death's second glove. I conjure an invisible glove and convince the audience that they see it.

I go to Tobi's where he lets me lie fretting beside him.

October 7, 1954

Three days.

Tuesday night group session.

In the dawn I visit Jim Agee. Jim is sick with depression over his film work and roars at me when I suggest that he work on the novel. Yet the dawn-begun day is exuberant.

Wednesday. Kol Nidre. Distracted during the service, I am incapable of prayer.

Difficulties with the opening aria in *Gautama*. I find no words for the alien compassion. I fall asleep Kol Nidre night still dressed and thinking of the aria.

Thursday, an easy fast.

The audiences are small but elite. George Freedley is at the theater to-night. The de Rothschilds are to come. Wallace Fowlie writes for reservations.

October 8, 1954

In the *Geographical History of America, or the Relation of Human Nature to the Human Mind*, Gertrude Stein shows us what human nature cannot know and what the human mind can know.

With my human nature I perceive Tobi's weaknesses. But my mind is dazzled by his deceptions and he knows he can swerve me from my resolutions.

Basho says, "Granted that all is God's and that all is equally God's, yet . . ."

October 13, 1954

The glitter of our first encounter wears off and underneath is a hard, me-tallic stratum that hurts even to think about.

There is no world. Sometimes I am caught by the attraction of a cat with varicolored eyes. Sometimes hope flashes for a moment, a mirage in the dark.

There is no poetry. Sometimes I imagine I am in pain, but soon I see that even that is an exaggeration.

There is no feeling. At times I mistake my fleeting obsession with someone who attracts me for a feeling, but these are watery images, meaningless in their impermanence.

Everything is impermanent. Yet everything is concrete. Hard and uninter-esting.

October 14, 1954

The play is all it should be, but to play for seven people, or even eleven, is discouraging.

I have no real hold.

Standing in the park under the cascading black clouds of Hurricane Hazel, I seem to take hold. If only of the wind, as Shelley took hold of the West Wind and found his spirit in it.

The sky seems very domed as the black clouds move in a sharp arc.

Saville is going to be musical director for the theater. Tobi donates $100 for a sound system.

October 16, 1954

Yesterday, we canceled the performance because of the hurricane. I spend the night at Maury's, where I sigh that the least likely of men is the best of lovers.

At last the opening song for the opera comes. I eke out twenty good lines.

Tobi is directing *The Idiot King* and he works in a trying manner which pleases him, because he believes that all the great directors treated their actors horribly. It is certainly ugly. But it works.

October 21, 1954

The Baroness Bethsabee de Rothschild is a reserved, suspicious, complex soul who speaks in a crisp Franco-English Oxonian, with its characteristic emphasis of too many words per sentence. She is with Craig Barton, and her plainness is all the plainer for his show of style.

The baroness liked the production but did not extend herself to praise. Treating her with exaggerated deference, I launch into our hopes and complaints, trying to temper one with the other so as to put our case most earnestly. She says she is interested in rural theater and talks of doing the classics in the Bronx.

She is proud.

C.B.: "Gielgud has asked Isamu Noguchi to design his Stratford *Lear* and largely through Mme. de R.'s efforts. . . ."

B.B.deR. (opening her eyes very wide): "Largely? Entirely!"

The Idiot King. We meet Claude at Jimmy Merrill's house on West 10th Street. Claude is doing some bold revising.

We have a production conference which looses such a barrage of ideas of an epic nature that Claude leaves breathless.

Lester woos me with a heartwarming pursuit. Unable to find "a place to meet in the dark," we finally go to the romantically sordid Christopher Street Hotel, a waterfront place.

Lester is too vigorous for me. I am not accustomed to such ardor. I like him, but he unsettles me.

October 22, 1954

Garrick ill. A high temperature. I worry.

The play goes well. Arduously.

Wallace Fowlie at the play. Julian talks with him before the performance, but we are disappointed that he does not come backstage afterward.

October 25, 1954

Claude's proximity lends an air of grace to *The Idiot King* rehearsals. Tobi is dissatisfied with my Nun, but I feel sure of her. Kathe Snyder, the Marguerite of *Doctor Faustus Lights the Lights*, is the Queen. Julian reads the King splendidly.

October 26, 1954

An encouraging review by George Freedley. He gives us the air of an institution, speaks of our previous work in our "various homes." Tobi, he writes, looks like the young Jean Cocteau.

Julian gets a window display order from Franklin Simon's department store to keep us busy. And fed.

An unexpected laudatory letter from Wallace Fowlie.

Paul reads us, and Nick Cernovitch, Murray Hargrove, and Merce, his new play, *The Young Disciple*. Its style is daring, expressionist and allegorical, based on the Gospel of St. Mark.

October 28, 1954

I visit Dudley Wilkinson and get my Screen Actors' Guild card, making me a member of a union in a profession in which I have never worked.

In a taxi to an interview at Music Corporation of America for a television job. On either side of the rain-spotted windows, the frantic autumn leaves. So turbulent, sexual. Those hectic, dying colors.

Last night Willard showed his films: *Geography of the Body* and Nina in *Mechanics of Love*. Marie Menken and I try to define pornography: that which excites to desires which it cannot gratify.

Marie's *Noguchi* film, a very swift, fluid film, rushing by with Lucia Dlugoszewski's windswept music, which uses words from *Doctor Faustus Lights the Lights*.

Nell Tangeman is going to sing the opening aria of *Guatama* in concert.

Nina is sullen. She can't stand Tobi. She's just right for Eurydice. She sleeps all day.

Rehearsal. My Nun is closer now to what Tobi expects.

October 30, 1954

Our sixth wedding anniversary.

We waken to a phone call from Kathe saying that she won't play the Queen.

Lester amuses Garrick with a chess game while we select actresses from the files.

Lester stayed overnight and complained in the morning that I did not come to him.

In the afternoon we rehearse with the children.

Sharon Stock, daughter of anarchists Robert and Harriet, is a sophisticated eleven-year-old actress.

Peter Ernster, who was recommended to us by Jackson Mac Low, comes with his father, Deszo Ernster, the magnificent Wagnerian basso, the Metropolitan's Wotan.

Ernster puts his hands on the child's shoulders, lectures him with solemn resonance on his responsibilities toward us. I think, however, that his fatherly purpose is to make us aware of our responsibilities to the child. Ernster will not see the production as he is leaving to tour Europe in December.

Immediately following the rehearsal, we have a Halloween party for Garrick. Skeletons and candles in the form of black cats inside pumpkins. Julian's mother, Garrick, Julian, Sharon, Tobi, and I, all masked. Even I, who am cold to these displays, was drawn in.

October 31, 1954

Lester and I go to the theater, to Orpheus' villa. The tradition that Orpheus/Arkenholtz established flourishes again on the great hard bed of the stage.

Lester loves me with an appalling warmth. If only I could accept such simplicity.

Why do I hold the thorns dearer than the rose?

November 1, 1954

Alan calls to say that the New School wants to do *In Gautama's House* in May, if it can be ready. He is busy with the Odets play *The Flowering Peach*.

Judith Graves, the Tarakaia of *Beyond the Mountains*, comes to read for the Queen. Tobi fears her tigerish looks, but as soon as she is out of the room, George pantomimes ecstasy and Tobi says, "Call her back. The role is hers."

At rehearsal I begin to realize the character of the Nun. Tobi helps enormously and I can't resist the temptation of passing him notes of praise.

Julian is heartbreaking as the King. Nina is heartbreaking as the Prioress. Judith Graves is heartbreaking as the Queen.

Lester at night. Much too young for his thirty years. He should be a boy.

November 3, 1954

Paul is right. I use my busyness as a screen against the fearful something that could happen in the empty moment.

When life makes no demands on me, I feel my blood circulate, my wrists throb. Often I get the headaches. It is as though inaction were death.

Claude, at rehearsal, asked us to consider each personage not only as an individual, but as a whole segment of humanity, as one defined way of living in the world. Claude's soft-spoken explanations are very positive both in intention and effect.

The whole of my madness is that when Tobi says he loves me, I feel that I ought to despair.

November 8, 1954

We play *Orpheus* to full houses this week and have extended its run through next weekend.

November 10, 1954

The more I know, the more burdensome the knowledge. The circle half completed is further from completion than at the start. The return, the inward arc, is a homecoming. Meanwhile the regions grow colder and colder.

"I will stay here a little while longer and rest."

"I am gathering strength."

November 11, 1954

Polar regions.

Not dark. A blazing cold light on the snow. Relentless light without warmth or cheer.

We go to the Metropolitan Museum, Julian and I, to see the Dutch show. Dozens of blinding masterpieces. Three Vermeers.

The Little Street. The patch of white above a broken arched doorway. The breath catches.

Hans Hokanson coming upon us exclaims, "You look infatuated."

Today Julian accompanies me to Paul's for a session. Paul says it's tragic that Julian has no men friends. As for me, again he says I am not an artist. More and more I see the futility of arguing about anything.

November 14, 1954

Tonight is the last night of *Orpheus*. I am sad but not as sad as at the closing of *Spook Sonata*.

At *The Idiot King* rehearsal, Tobi directs in the grand manner as we huddle around a heater. Julian, as the King, finds protean satisfactions in acting. Claude follows on book. He has been a saint about changes.

Nina gives the Prioress an unexpected power. She is responsive to Tobi's direction despite herself.

Jerry Wellish as the Prince allows Tobi a wide range for his temper, his domineering shouts, the gamut of power acts.

Judith Graves is calm and self-possessed, but her presence recalls the nightmare of *Beyond the Mountains*. As *Phaedra/Phèdre* nears there is too much talk of *Beyond the Mountains*.

November 15, 1954

How marvelous what we are doing in our small, icy loft is. Is. We are so alive. Our hard work is so perfect.

November 26, 1954

Ich muss es ganz allein tun, und darf nicht vor der Kälte Angst haben. So lange es mir schwer fällt, kann ich es nicht tun, und, so lange es mir schwer fällt, habe ich es nicht getan. Wenn es möglich ist, werde ich es ganz einfach und ohne Anstrengung tun. Dieses "Es"? Im Moment bedeutet "Es" die Selbstständigkeit. Das heisst: Selbst zu stehen, mich nicht mehr an Andere anzulehnen.

November 28, 1954

Alles geht langsam und fällt schwer.

December 2, 1954

The Idiot King is to open tonight.

Seven-thirty: dinner alone. Julian still involved with the technical difficulties. Tobi's gone to dress. Nina's making up.

Julian whips himself into his desired pattern. He drives himself without pity.

I pray. I want so much to do this well. I think of Rachel's classic grace, which they say was simplicity. I don't know how to do a simple thing.

December 3, 1954

Trauma. I throw myself at the role in desperation.

December 6, 1954

The Constant Crisis.

I put aside the preceding notebook, I am disturbed that I've let the opening and the events that followed go unrecorded, as though it were my duty to keep a log.

I have never wrestled so hard. I have never wrestled for my soul. I am doing that.

I have loved only once in my life.

Ashamed, not guilty but ashamed, of my inability to control, even to transcend feeling . . .

It is impossible for me to speak to Julian till the crisis abates.

Perhaps now I can keep my mouth shut. Without clenching my teeth.

I see now that I must deliver myself over totally to the playing. Only dedication will enable me to perform.

I have stayed away from Paul. I have wanted to work alone, as though any aid weakened my own power.

Julian, Paul, Tobi, Lester, Rachel . . . Rachel . . .

I think obsessively about her. From two gold and black oval frames she looks down on me from my bedroom wall, in the engravings torn out of my father's *Brockhaus Encyclopedia*. I read about her. I would emulate her devotion, her classic art, her daring composure, her nerve, her Jewishness, her Greek poses, her Frenchness. I am obsessed with her.

Her Phèdre.

I am afraid and ashamed. But I am not guilty. I wrestle. And I must not lose.

It is 4:15 A.M. To sleep.

December 7, 1954

The Constant Crisis.

I tell Paul that I want no sessions with him for a while.

December 8, 1954

Paul on *The Idiot King*: "No one has this problem. At the most crucial moment this King talks about his soul. No real mystic talks about his soul; the mystic never even uses the word 'I.' If one secedes from the social order it should only be because one has found a better expedient."

He cites Gandhi's expedients.

"If one is concerned with one's soul," he claims, "it is because one is hiding from the real problem."

At Nell Tangeman's concert, our aria "May the lids of your eyes" occupied the main place on the program.

Alan has given the words a broad scope. The music is almost too hard for a lullaby and for Yashodhara's nature. But Alan has used delicate instruments: gongs, a harp, reverberating drums, soft bells.

The aria rises out of a cushion of sounds, concise at first, the song only gradually dominating the music, then sinking back through repeated words.

Tangeman sang with pungent clarity.

Alan is upset over the omission of my name from the program. I don't mind the anonymity. But Alan telephones the *Times* and *Tribune* immediately after the concert, making his concern for me too transparent.

Frank O'Hara in Johnny Myers' new magazine, *Semi-Colon*: "I am out on a limb and it is the arm of God."

December 10, 1954

The Constant Crisis: a few hours of self-pity.

Last night we didn't perform, the audience being too small: four people. Instead we had a rehearsal and a production meeting.

Our first Christmas card is a poem and a photo of Gene Derwood, sent by Oscar.

In the freezing winds off the Hudson, Tobi and I read the second act of *The Infernal Machine*, which ends with the line: "He has not understood a single thing."

December 11, 1954

The Constant Crisis.

If I lose a lover, it is still I who remain. "Medea superest." But if I lose myself . . .

Sitting in a coffee shop with Julian, I see outside the window a hobbling, old woman gesticulating and declaiming to herself. And I think how it is that we cannot see ourselves; for how could we live if we saw ourselves?

But Julian is here, and how shall I not have hope? We rehearsed our second act for heart and feeling and the real stuff. We will try to play it tonight.

December 13, 1954

Julian and I work on *Phèdre* which is not too awkward in its first draft.

Tobi is at St. Luke's Hospital for minor surgery.

December 15, 1954

We divided for two concerts. Julian went to the John Cage/David Tudor piano recital at Carl Fischer Hall. I went with Alan across the street to Carnegie Hall to hear the Collegiate Chorale do his "Glory to God."

I didn't like all those voices singing together.

I wanted to be at the other concert across the street.

I wanted to be with Tobi at St. Luke's.

Halfway through the concert Martha Graham arrived, sending divine sparks through the hall. When Alan's piece was cheered Martha turned to him and raised her eyes to heaven, "You have reason to feel uplifted."

At intermission she talked a great deal; she often raised her eyes to heaven this way. She is the Priestess, expressing noble sentiments about even the simplest things. She said she envied Alan's prodigious energy and he said he envied hers. For a while they admired each other's productivity. When Alan introduced me she said, "You are doing all those wonderful plays. How wonderful to meet you."

I enjoyed her wonderfuls and suggested that she see some of the plays soon. And then she ran away across the street to put up a poster in Carnegie Hall.

December 19, 1954

Peter Ernster was giving a beautiful performance in *The Idiot King* and his father was well pleased with him. But yesterday Deszo Ernster flew to Stockholm to sing the *Ring* cycle and will not return to the Metropolitan till January.

This morning Peter's mother calls to say that Peter can't continue in the role, it's too much of a strain and interferes with his schoolwork. We sit at dinner fretting at the problem of replacing an eleven-year-old actor at such short notice.

Garrick says, "I know all the words if you tell me where to stand and to move."

At first we can't believe him, but he recites the text and quite well.

And then we adjust our notion of the role from an eleven-year-old to a five-year-old. And we rehearse with him and he seems able to do it.

It changes the play. His tininess makes the killing much more pathetic.

The adults will have to play their roles less emotionally lest the second act become like the death of Little Nell.

I am anxious for Garrick. He doesn't know the terror that awaits him when the pleasant rehearsal atmosphere changes into the uncanny arena of the performance. He doesn't know this fear and I'm not going to tell him for he may be spared altogether.

I hope he will draw closer to us and feel the theater as a part of us instead of as a rival for his affections.

Visit Tobi at St. Luke's. He has many visitors, is surrounded by friends.

I find Bob Bart there, working on the directing book for *Phèdre*.

December 21, 1954

Garrick plays well. Strong and clear and without fears.

In the frieze in the first act where he must stand stock-still for a long time, his attention of course wanders. And he plays squinty-eyed games with the glare of the stage lights.

But when in action he is somber and conscientious.

December 27, 1954

I've developed a racking cough, which gives me an excuse to remain in bed.

Yesterday with Julian to *The Flowering Peach*, the new Odets play, for which Alan has written the music.

Julian and I gasped to hear the Isle of the Dead theme from *The Spook Sonata* as a flute solo; it transforms for us Gorelick's mountaintop into that shimmer of silver on black silk evoking Böcklin's *Toten Insel*.

Serafina was seated between Franchot Tone and Gloria Vanderbilt. Alan conducted with Saroyan sitting directly behind him and Julian spoke for a moment with Tennessee Williams. After the play, we went with Alan, Serafina, and Midi Garth to Schrafft's . . . instead of Sardi's.

Today I finish the "Chorus of the Winds" for *Gautama* and give it to Alan, who comes for dinner.

The reviews of the Odets play were good, but Alan is singularly unexcited by success. I have to excuse myself from the table early because of my cough, then stay in bed reading *Père Goriot*.

December 31, 1954

Julian reproaches me with creating the constant crisis, not realizing that I cherish the crisis as a refuge from the polar frost. To ride the whirlwind bespeaks a kind of strength.

If I had a thousand years I might hope to become what in childhood I thought I would become in a week. To complain of the slow grinding of these mills is to be in disharmony. Love the process.

Impatience is my greatest vice, not indolence.

Impatience is an infirmity of faith.

On the stage I am enveloped by mysteries. Every night that I perform I am both nearer and farther from actuality. Farther because I plunge deeper into the murk of the subconscious, and nearer because the world we create on the stage is actually the one we live in.

1955

January 3, 1955

Refrained from writing while I had only gloom to record.

New Year's Eve, I drank toasts while friends crowded around mingling cruelty with levity. After the turning hour, Sharon Stock in her sweet child's voice read psalms to us, chosen at random. Songs of praise and despair.

The last three performances of *The Idiot King* were canceled on account of insufficient audiences.

No word from Tobi as to whether he will do *Phèdre*. If not, we will do Pirandello's *Tonight We Improvise*.

Today, he arrives with a decidedly unattractive new beard. He brings penitent daffodils, spring flowers, as a New Year's gift. He is divine, and impossible. He swoops up my gloom with the dramatic gesture of Cagliostro dispelling a cloud.

Julian mentions our lack of money and Tobi invites us to lunch. We talk for hours over coffee. They want to do *Tonight We Improvise*. I hold out for *Phèdre* as our next production. I argue feebly.

But when we three are together I feel protected.

January 5, 1955

It is decided to do *Tonight We Improvise* before *Phèdre*. I think the real reason is that Julian wants me to play a particularly challenging role to prepare me for *Phèdre*.

Julian will direct *Improvise*. I will do Mommina; Tobi will play Rico Verri.

Tobi is asked by an Annapolis group to direct Molière's *Miser* this spring. He claims that he has not made his decision, but it is clear to Julian and me that he has.

He claims it will not interfere with our schedules, but I know it will.

January 9, 1955

Yesterday afternoon we went to 57th Street. We saw Dali, extraordinarily like a caricature of Dali. His paintings, however, dispel frivolity. Even the ridiculous moustache curled up to his eyes is furiously sincere.

His subject is Man and Madonna. Through Gala, a glorification of Woman like that essayed by the poets but rarely by the painters, at least not with their wives. Dali's religious passion and real madness is some sort of nondebilitating schizophrenia. Among our friends he is decidedly unpopular. We look a while at the paintings, awed by the profundity of his contribution.

Dali walks from picture to picture with Emily Genauer explaining each one to her critic's eye.

Afterward, an exhibit of Bob Rauschenberg's. What Julian sees as full of vitality I see as full of death. It is a bright doom that hangs over these paintings. He's at odds with form, as I am, but I could not exist embracing the philosophy that makes this painting possible. Rauschenberg is not at the gallery and I leave him an unsigned love note.

Preparation for *Tonight We Improvise*.

January 10, 1955

The Idiot King closes. Tonight we begin rehearsals for *Improvise*.

A self-conscious little East Side party full of painters and people who talk about "who has the money."

Claire Goll talks about her garnets. ("Rilke gave them to me.") Willard of young men. I talk of myself. Everyone was absolutely detestable, especially the hostess, full of brainless twaddle while her beautiful blond daughter bore with her parents with a resigned smile.

January 15, 1955

The production of *Tonight We Improvise* is underway. Julian works with lightning strokes, skillfully using Pirandello as a cue for invention. The cast of twenty-two is assembled and rehearsals have been smooth. Julian is playing Dr. Hinkfuss, the director, not as a satire on Reinhardt, but as a satire on himself, as avant-garde director; Dorothy Olim plays an overweening mother; Judy Lennett, Judith Graves, Nina, and I are the four daughters. Leonard Hicks is the father; Henry Proach is the Ruffian; Garry Goodrow, Jackson Mac Low, Bob and Harriet Stock and Sharon are hecklers. And Tobi's Rico Verri.

Alan writes that he is very ill: "My doctor wishes me to live since that is his art."

When I play the final monologue in the Pirandello, the desperation is real. The scene with Tobi is still artificial.

January 16, 1955

Our only real problem is money. Unpaid rent. And today the last cash goes to the Edison Company.

We send Faith Rose, an art collector, who is Michel Lee's sister, a direct appeal for $175.

Try, but fail, to work on *Gautama*, instead I write a Sicilian blues song for the Chanteuse in *Improvise*.

January 31, 1955

Only pain assures us of life. Pleasure is illusory. Then why is not pain illusory?

February 1, 1955

In rehearsals, when Rico Verri speaks of passion, dare I, in Pirandello's manner, remember that it is Tobi's hand, not Rico's, which is, with hatred and passion, crushing my mouth? This is Pirandello's subject matter. The illusion that is no illusion. Like waking to find in my hand a token given me by a figure in a dream.

All my life I have lived as if my life were a prologue, as if it were all yet to come.

Today to the doctor. I am frightened by mortality. Dr. Jane talks in her woman's way and I trust her and death seems so possible. And I am forced to think of what my whole life was and is and can be, and how lightly I have treated it.

The Pirandello is a comedy and I die in the last act, wishing for and dreaming of a theater. At some moment it must all become real. There will be Phaedra. I stake everything on *Phèdre*.

February 2, 1955

Because it snows, I can't resist walking. First to an appointment for an X-ray, then to the Fourth Avenue book shops.

As I pass the enormous clock suspended over Klein's on 14th Street, the minute hand suddenly began to move noticeably. I watched with horror thinking it a flaw in my perception as the activities on Union Square proceeded normally. They proscribed a full half hour before the clock again resumed its normal pace.

That's how these days have been with their threat of death.

February 10, 1955

The doctor proclaims me a healthy specimen of 84-pound womanhood.

I am happiest during the rehearsals.

To love Tobi is to make myself his target. He has taken on the violent character of Rico Verri, losing even his reserve of charm.

Acting. The impossible art.

February 11, 1955

Rehearse my last monologue intensively with Julian. True to Pirandello, I no longer have any idea who I am, Mommina or Malina. For half an hour I am immovable. Then I begin to be able. I resist. I want to be swept away. I want to be possessed. And is this not a form of laziness? I want it to happen to me whereas I must go out and be it.

February 15, 1955

There is a bitter kind of satisfaction in the growth of the role of Mommina. I still don't understand this art of acting.

When I weep, do I weep for Tobi Rivka, or for Rico Verri? And if Tobi Rivka were kind (which he is not), would I nonetheless weep for Rico Verri?

Mark Klein, Garry Goodrow, Nina, and Jackson Mac Low come home after the rehearsal, and while I lie in bed they smoke and laugh till I fall imperceptibly into unconsciousness. Imperceptibly because I am already on the fine line between awareness and illusion of which sleep is a vague modifier.

I do not love this state. My energy was meant for something better. I have lost my road.

Corneille. I will read Corneille. For a little more spine and less clenching of the teeth. I am growing too solemn. Everyone seems childish to me.

February 19, 1955

Before the play opened, I plunged into rapidly alternating moods—the hope for glory, the weight of my sins, the faith in my desire for virtue.

I worked very hard.

Tonight We Improvise opened. Plaudits on all sides.

I am praised for Mommina, but I am only beginning to act. It is as though I were eighteen years old. I lost ten years somehow. I squandered them.

In the theater scene, during which we enter the audience and displace some spectators, Tobi and I throw Remy Charlip and Nick Cernovitch out of their seats. They play the scene expertly.

Garrick is wonderful, a real actor on stage.

We are not going to have receptions after each performance but did have an opening night party.

I left to lie down when the world began to spin. Tobi came unexpectedly to talk to me. We spoke of the details of the performance, actor talk, while in the dark studio he brushed my hair. How should I not take this for an act of love?

He is dissatisfied with his performance and says he wants to stop acting, but he always says this while he is in a play, and when he directs he wants to act. When I'm acting, I only want to act.

Thank heavens I played Mommina before Phèdre.

Why do I try to please everyone in the world? Gene Van Grona and Philip Smith in the audience are mementos of the way I waste my tears. And I haven't learned a single thing.

Lionel Abel full of praise.

At home, the frantic vipers.

February 22, 1955

Acting is really a combination of possession and cold awareness. Who is standing there? Who am I standing there?

Saturday night Harriet and Robert Stock gave a costume party. Lots of children. Garrick and Christopher and the incredible Sharon.

Jackson Mac Low performs with her a play she has written. She takes her opening line from Dante: "Halfway along the path of life I found myself in a dark forest lost."

She plays a ballet dancer; he, the statue of a philosopher—the living and ephemeral artist encountering the rigid statue of the tradition.

February 27, 1955

I woke this morning and didn't know my name.

Nothing cohered. For a long time I existed in this manner. Then I realized it was the first day of the *Phèdre* readings.

4:45 rehearsal: awe of the occasion.

We begin.

An ominously good first reading.

We used the Henderson translation provisionally. Tobi Rivka followed in the French. I read plain.

March 1, 1955

Read *Phèdre* last night with some passion. I see her clearly.

It is not Hippolytus but Phaedra who possesses Phaedra. She knows her hope of possessing him is delusory; the more fantastic the delusion, the more cherished. She is in love with the crime. No, she is in love with her abhorrence of the crime and uses Hippolytus to feed the flame of her perversity. She describes herself as a victim of Venus, but she herself is the altar to which she "brings victims" and in this role she sacrifices Hippolytus as an offering to her passion.

I want not to lose the lusting woman in the immorality of the Queen and the possessiveness of the Priestess.

March 2, 1955

Escudero. Stripped of extraneous theatrical trappings, Spanish dance is a chaste art. Pepe La Matrona sings with an oriental heartrending wail like the best of the Jewish songs, except for the strict beat native to Spain.

From our first row seats, Escudero appears older than his 62 years. His sparse hair is parted down the center in the old-fashioned manner. And his cheeks, sunken into his face, heighten the look of scorn. He is very tall and exceedingly thin. The stage darkens so that we barely see him though he is all in white. The white boots alone are spotlighted. There is no other music as he makes a rhythm with his feet. Masterfully he develops and changes the rhythms. The boots creating the sound and the echo from the back of the theater are hypnotic. He sits and taps out a rhythm on a chair with his hands and fingertips, stands and moves to the sound of his own fingers snapping, and finally clicks only his fingernails, still moving ever so slightly. Then with an arrogant look at the audience to assure them that he has them in thrall, he stops, makes us hear our anticipation, looks at his hands and clicks his nails once more, turning to bow for his applause.

To Merce's advanced class with Remy. Merce teaches coordination rather than precision.

John Cage is a sight at an old player-piano chopping out bits of Chopin and simple 1 2 3 4 rhythms for two solid hours! He did it with great humor and suggested I come again because "sometimes the music is even worse."

Rehearsing *Phèdre*. I must not be overawed by the play or by its structure.

Why doesn't Tobi cast George as Hippolytus? He would look so handsome. I feel warmly toward him, even if he is harsh, and he reads so heroically.

March 5, 1955

Readings on the seventeenth century.

Yesterday with the whole cast to see Jimmy Merrill's *The Immortal Husband* at the Theater de Lys.

The mythological tale becomes psychological science fiction. We see the ancient Tithonus bear the burden of immortality as he grows infinitely older, while the goddess Aurora, whose love won him the precious and hideous gift, mocks him with her eternal youth. The gifts of the gods are two-faced, says the comely, gifted, wealthy Jimmy Merrill.

Fritz Perls is so enthusiastic about *Tonight We Improvise* that he offers to subsidize our taking it to a larger theater.

March 8, 1955

Phèdre rehearsals. I have to remember that whatever Phaedra and I may have in common I am not Phaedra. Nor is . . . better not.

Tobi directs slowly. He points out the crucial moment at which Phaedra's "*vous*" to Hippolytus becomes "*tu*." Since we cannot translate this fatal transition into English, I wanted at this point to touch Hippolytus, letting the gesture replace the words.

Tobi says, "No, let her try to touch him, let her try to stop him from leaving, let her interpose her body between him and his exit, and let him step back in horror at her touch. Thus he humiliates her by saving her honor."

March 10, 1955

Yesterday spring burst out. Off with the polar winds.

Spring is like a new love, innocent of its doomed future.

Phaedra. Phaedra. Phaedra. And Racine. Baffled by the grandeur.

March 17, 1955

The air is dark with promises of success. The signs are constant. Full houses on weekend nights; change in the kind of praise we receive.

We have not a penny for food. We work at breakneck speed. For the first time since the year began I stop into the Remo to be with Glenn for a few moments. But I ignore the friends who are still here: Stryker, Elfenbein, Ashbery. Only Lester upsets me because I don't have a reasonable excuse for him.

In the group I am asked what I think of my body.

This week my father-in-law tells my husband: "Judith could be a great actress, but face it, she hasn't got the looks."

Plans for another theater.

With Julian, life is an adventure.

Tobi, thank goodness, is in Annapolis.

Tobi, thank goodness, returns tomorrow.

Phèdre. Phèdre. Phèdre.

This is the spelling they have adopted. "We decided."

March 20, 1955

Phèdre rehearsal. Tobi strives for effects. The Henderson translation weighs us down. Tobi works without regard to feelings. I am less close to Phaedra because of his Phèdre.

March 23, 1955

All day I work alone on my Phaedra and in the evening with Julian when he comes home from work.

Paul Goodman is angry that our plans don't include an immediate production of *The Young Disciple*. Julian should not have spoken to him of a production date. Paul's bitterness makes it necessary for him to condemn us more violently than he intends.

"Your theater has no idea."

This is the way that Paul has antagonized the whole world. Why has he become so bitter?

"Seminar" discussion with Robert Bart on *Phèdre*. He is academic but instructive.

"Is Phèdre to blame?" he asks, suggesting that she is.

I am listening to Alan's *Khaldis* played on Fleetwood's radio program, "Music through the Night." A fierce four-trumpet, gong, and piano piece, unsettling, brutal, savage.

March 24, 1955

My performance as Mommina renews my mother's faith in my work. She says, "This is the first time Judith has really acted since she was a little girl."

March 25, 1955

For what is Phaedra to blame?

Julian says she has no alternative. Corneille would have given her an alternative.

Her only choice is to keep silent. That is to say, *"la gloire."* Nothing is so hard to do as nothing, to resist what seems to be nature, to abide by this decision against all forces that propel us to do otherwise. Isn't this *"la gloire"*?

Paul and I talk about the human struggle with passion. He says that he wishes to be a dog, an animal.

We blame Phaedra because she does not control her passion. Who is this "we"?

March 26, 1955

Tobi and I go to Queens to talk to Ruth Kaner about playing Oenone. Traveling along roads through woodlands now massacred by an encroaching city, ugly with pilings of earth and cranes and tractors and man-made gullies. Nor will it ever be as beautiful as the woods were. But will it at least be a human habitation?

Ruth, is svelte with crew-cut hair as a result of her recent operation, tells us sanguinary stories of her fall from a horse and her ensuing weakness.

Tobi steps out of the room for a moment and before the door closes Ruth asks, "So you love him?"

I deny it.

We read Oenone and Phèdre. Ruth's Oenone, Tobi says, is a *"yiddishe mamme."* I find her easy to respond to, feelingful and alive, evil in her solicitude.

March 30, 1955

At luncheon with Alan. After a nightmare under nitrous oxide in the dentist's office, I oppose Alan's mystical world. The illusory strength of "another view" weakens the mind and body.

Tobi Rivka on his twenty-ninth birthday joins us in the Russian Tea Room. Alan changes the subject to Handel.

In despair today at the nothingness of all things, till later at the Automat I encounter an old man, extremely affable and quite deaf, who for two hours expounds a reasonable view of life. The significant thing, he says, is that we are "here" and have a certain number of tasks to perform; nor does he neglect to say that not performing these tasks is one mode of performing them. It is true and the tediousness of it comforts me. As sheer horror could comfort me for the feelingless void.

Thus, Alfred Harding tuning his hearing mechanism in the noisy Horn & Hardart is a comfort to me.

April 1, 1955

For Tobi's birthday, I, who never cook, prepare a Japanese meal: dashu-soup, tempura, rice and chestnuts, served very formally for Tobi, Julian, George, Saville, and Bob Bart with Murasakian attention to detail. Pretty, but artificial.

A good *Improvise* tonight. Tobi feels that his most abandoned performances are his best. I like playing opposite him in this state, but it is a sin of lust on my part.

April 2, 1955

Yesterday we went to look at the Japanese Gardens, that fabulous theater hidden above the Riviera movie house on 97th Street and Broadway. Its pseudo-oriental splendor in dusty decay. On that enormous stage what visions could unfold, and in the vast spaces of the auditorium that seats 1700, among the plaster flamingos and crumbling lanterns, what masses could be moved. But the money required . . .

Work on *Phèdre*.

Working from our translation. It is less "poetical" than the Henderson, but this is its virtue. It's very close to Racine. Robert Bart is on hand with scholarly advice.

Alan writes that he "can hear celestial musicians singing our new opera."

His music is too much for me. I think of death incessantly. It's not this that saddens me, but the vanity of my efforts.

April 7, 1955

Tobi goes to Annapolis to direct Molière's *L'Avare*. He says he will divide his time. And his heart?

Easter, 1955

The same sudden morning warmth, an uncanny sun breaking too quickly on a dark, cold season. Light and reason, falling upon the darkness, should illumine and lift it, and yet contrast with their sweetness its immutable terror.

The years between don't lighten the dark Easter Eve that I spent with Lou Harrison, nor the condemnatory brightness of the people in Washington Square, nor the hardly perceptible glow of guilt, an accusation of adultery, nor fear in the sunlight, like a black poodle.

We rehearse *Phèdre*. Can she be redeemed?

April 11, 1955

I feel my strength in the rehearsals. Tobi has one idea, then another. The ideas are good and dominate the whole rehearsal. With great enthusiasm he suddenly discovers in a scene some truth for which I have been working for months. He then propounds it in a new way and then asks me to try for it.

Dicken Stryker appears at the theater and says: "Lou has a farm, a vegetable farm in New Mexico. He's writing a piece for Louisville. I'll get you his address." And he's gone.

Jackson Mac Low and I eat some matzohs alone in the kitchen and he talks of an ugly bruise that Tobi suffered in the first act of *Improvise* and how he bore it without complaining.

"It was the first time I admired him."

"He is like that." I say, "His heroism is not really seen."

"Then it's his character."

I think, "But he always has a wound."

Until five this morning, Tobi, Julian, and I confer. In a burst of clarity I describe the conflict of our efforts and Tobi's. I even suggest that he not do *Phèdre* if he wants to devote himself to Annapolis.

We compromise. But I changed the balance.

Julian is horribly overworked. He takes no pleasure in anything, and I don't know how to relieve him.

We work on *Phèdre* till it's time to take Garrick to his play group. Then Julian goes to work. I'm in the park to write this and study Phaedra.

Rain clouds approach our sunny Paschal skies. The Hudson darkens.

Phèdre not Phaedra now.

April 15, 1955

Do I write what is true?

Only fools and fantastics can. The mystics write what is true because their genius supplies them with inspired language in which to couch their astonishing souls.

Tobi points out how my panic at crossing busy intersections reflects my whole character. I try to achieve some equilibrium, but confronted with the traffic, I see the abyss and lose control. This is exactly what Phèdre does when confronted with Hippolytus.

April 17, 1955

I identify pitilessly with the role of Phèdre. I play my own reflection. If Racine intended that we be instructed by the representation of vice, he succeeds.

April 19, 1955

Attendance at *Tonight We Improvise* has dropped. We play to small houses which means that we don't have enough money for *Phèdre*.

April 20, 1955

Dinner with Claude. He lives in a little room atop one of those smart Village houses.

We speak of the reality of the present moment. Julian and I live for the future. Claude has the fortune (he calls it a kind of grace) to live in the moment and savor it.

When Claude describes his journal, and the pains he takes with it, he makes me want to take more pains with mine.

I find it difficult to write because a recent interest in calligraphy has made my handwriting self-conscious. Copying an early uncial that I found in a manuscript at the Morgan Library.

Alan showed me today a series of postcards from Lou Harrison in California. He has become a mythical being.

Was it I who misused him? I forget how brittle people are. I imagine they are as brazen as I.

April 23, 1955

Phèdre inundates me as she struggles for control over rebellious passion.

Yesterday Tobi patiently let me weep. He is neither kind nor cruel. But what he is is not my problem. It is what I am. And what I am not.

I gather my determination for this afternoon's rehearsal, but Ruth faints after my first line and the rehearsal is over.

Only two more performances of *Improvise*.

Hideous dreams of passion and carnage.

This morning a useful talk on Phèdre/Phaedra and her passion—and of passion in general. We talk, as if theoretically, of need and rejection.

Tobi washes his shirts while we talk, infuriating me.

George's Hippolytus will be icily desirable. The play directed coldly, but with great integrity. Leonard Hick's Theseus is too formal. Judith Graves' Aricia is constant.

April 25, 1955

Tonight We Improvise has closed. Having worked on *Phèdre* all day under the handicap of a fierce headache, I am too tired for sentiment.

It did occur to me during the third act that I would not play it again and that these kisses, which, whether he willed it or not, were Tobi's as much as they were Rico Verri's, would never be repeated.

May 1, 1955

I enjoy this day with its flowering trees by a sunlit river canopied with gulls because of a postponement of *Phèdre*. I'm glad for extra time on this enormous role. Tobi warns me, I'm too awed by it.

Our translation is finished. Tonight we will polish the verse and send the whole to Bob Bart for academic review.

Completely submerged in *Phèdre*. I no longer identify with her but devote my own life to hers.

Tobi is playful. His jests burden me.

Wasn't our lovemaking always accompanied by laughter?

May 4, 1955

The entire night polishing the translation with Julian. For hours the phrases seem good and poetic. And then there are hours when the whole thing seems heavy and lifeless. In the morning we have only two acts ready to send to Annapolis.

In Macy's. They have stuffed the ground floor full of flowers and ranged caged birds and statuary among the merchandise. On a platform above the blouse counter they employ a Japanese man named Shinichi Uize to play the koto and "perform" the tea ceremony. I am impressed by his courage but could scarcely hear his music above the clanging of the cash registers. The tea ceremony takes apart a simple process and emphasizes the perfection of each separate act. During the deliberate pause in which "nothing" happens, the actor is renewed for the next action.

Tonight Philip brings two wonderful swords for *Phèdre* from the prop house where he works. He tempts me to go to Paul's group session, but the truth is that I don't want to. I won't worry about the rumors that I am mad at Paul.

May 5, 1955

When I came to the theater tonight, a pale pink moon hung full in a pink sky. The glorious green of the church steeple clear as the bells of St. Michael's, which tolled in the thick warm air. I was glad to be going to a rehearsal. I was glad of all things.

All day we make extensive changes in the *Phèdre* text.

May 6, 1955

Rehearsal this morning during which I could do nothing but fight against putting personal meanings into the lines.

At lunch, Tobi quotes Baudelaire: "It is the pleasure of pederasts to love intelligent women."

May 10, 1955

Philip calls two, sometimes three times a day, "just to chat."

Alan has been having numerous successes, which keep him too busy to work on *Gautama*. Sunday at the museum concert, he used the Isle of the Dead theme as an introduction for an English horn solo, around a chorus of lines by Thoreau about the stars. Alan promises to dedicate the piece, which is called *The Stars*, to Julian and me.

After Alan's piece they performed Lou's Mass. Though it was a good performance, it was not the sound of Lou in his house on Prince Street.

May 17, 1955

Garrick's sixth birthday. He celebrates with Stephen Stuchin, Sharon Stock, and his cousins. Davy Crockett seized the minds of all American children. The coonskin cap appears on the cake, in the decorations, games, favors.

We rehearse.

May 19, 1955

Yesterday, returning from rehearsal, George tells me the news. I do not believe him, cannot believe him. But I write it down. Jim is dead. Jim Agee. My Jim.

He will not write the poems he has put off too long. He will not read them to me at dawn. I will not see him again.

Bitter self-reproaches that I did not hold closer to so dear a friend.

Jim who said: "The only reason we are not in love is that we cause each other no pain, and the world is so crazy that we don't call it love unless it hurts."

I had planned to call him soon, to visit again the white room on King Street and hear the end of the novel of Rufus. And return perhaps to the dark room on Cornelia Street. I had fancied that when I saw him next I would greet him with "Hello, Rufus."

We should hold the present dearer, should hold closer to each other.

The transience makes all encounters holy.

Just
As
My
Eyes
See
A
Glimmer
Everything
Ends

A profusion of images:

The night he read *The Morning Watch* to me till the morning indeed did come as though we had lived through the book.

The night we talked of God with Julian and the day came into his little garden, lighting the blue dress of the madonna.

The night when it was so cold on Cornelia Street that we burned his old reviews and articles in the fireplace to keep warm, and I could barely prevent him from burning manuscripts.

The morning that I encountered his family as I woke him from a terrible drunken sleep to record the *The Age of Anxiety* newscasts.

The nights. The nights.

May 20, 1955

I am already accustomed to it. I think of Jim as having died.

I give him up. Did I love him? Very much or not at all.

Cecil Willis has left the cast suddenly and Julian is playing Theramène, which he should have played from the outset.

Julian has made the stage a box of light. A white velour floor. Luminous rayonese walls and wings, lit from behind. Mark Klein has constructed an ingenious lighting system with three dimmers.

Today the first costumes appeared on the stage. Julian's grand flair is apparent in the men's superb capes.

He has put me in red velvet and gold lamé, Oenone in black brocade and dark purple velvet, Hippolytus in pure white and silver, arrayed like a bride. Aricia in metallic silver and blue. All glorious in Louis XIV style.

I struggle, go through agonies, exhaust myself at every rehearsal. It is unimaginable what I am doing to myself on that stage.

I am possessed, utterly frenzied, yet controlled. It could be vile; it could be splendid. I dread Tobi's criticism.

Yesterday, crushed by Jim's death . . .

(I shake when I write it. I don't believe it again. Oh, my dear drunken darling. Oh, my big black-haired beauty who was such a panther in bed . . .)

Yesterday, Willard and Ben came to rehearsal. And later we sat in the park and smoked kheef.

Willard said, "Are you not glad that you knew him before he died?"

Strange how we don't think of that.

May 24, 1955

Phèdre is postponed two more days.

I try not to think at all. The reality is all right, but the values are shaky.

There is vast satisfaction in playing this role. Never have I done anything so enervating, and so fulfilling at once.

May 29, 1955

Tonight we open *Phèdre*.

I approach it as if to perform some reverential ritual, as if I have the power to convey to people the secret mysteries, to demonstrate their passion by my art.

Ô cieux, aidez-moi!

May 31, 1955

I am not what I was.
Thunder rolls. Ominous.
Three days ago *Phèdre* opened.
Even the thunder is helpless.
I expected a door to open, but the latch I reached for was an illusion.

The costumes were still being sewn or pinned on as we stood in the wings awaiting our cues.

George in icy white and silver, his scorn for me become real, as if Hippolytus has to hate Phèdre in all incarnations, clinging to Judith Graves, the two conspiring against me. Leonard, the rash Theseus, tall in beige, an ally in my troubles.

Ruth's mystical force in diabolic black. At the end of the labyrinth scene when Oenone lures Phèdre with Hippolytus' sword, Ruth faints in my arms.

The day after the opening we rehearse again. But I can't take Edelman's pressure and cruel banter. I leave the rehearsal distressed and I wander in the streets of the Puerto Rican district, where the old houses are being torn down and where the world bears the stamp of ruin.

I wander into a dark and empty church. Here I recite the jealousy scene from the fourth act with great emotion. The pews tremble under my intense whisper.

When I leave the church, a vendor, seeing my tears, asks me into a tiny store. We do not speak the same language. Yet he manages to sell me, for fifteen cents each, two bottles, two potent fragrances: one is called "Azucena" and the other "Cleopatra Oil." I refuse a bottle marked "Money-getting oil," which he assures me I need regardless of my other troubles.

He wishes me good luck and cheers me considerably. Who can weep with a bottle of "Cleopatra Oil" clutched in her hand?

I return to the rehearsal.

Luther L. turns out to be an alchemist. He has the famous mescaline, which he has manufactured from peyote. It hasn't been available and is the subject of much curiosity. Luther has refined it into a powder and put it into capsules. The dosage differs by body weight. I swallowed a capsule and waited in that eerie room where three years ago I shared Luther's first stick of kheef. There is a tangle of tubing and the glassy apparatus of the chemist amid the haphazard arrangements of a bachelor room straightened for a lady's visit. Sauterne and two green glasses on a small table. We listen to Beethoven quartets.

First nausea, then hilarity, then hunger. We grab cakes and avocados with bare hands and stuff them into full mouths. We are still flying when we return uptown. It is four in the morning, but I find Julian, Judith Graves, Ruth Kaner, Nina, and George Miller drinking champagne. They lie about drunken and delighted. But we boast of something better and Luther and Nina go downtown to fetch the mescaline. They return and the capsules are distributed. Meantime I am struck with the full force of it.

It is schizophrenia, the real and unreal incongruities glare at one. Yet I am not afraid.

There is pleasure, but the horror is beyond telling. I try to flee, but in private or in company it is equally horrible.

I deny, even to myself, the frenzy that possesses me. The fierce colors that surround me and that I become. The vibrancy of everything.

I give myself over to it. I am the green and the blue green. I am thick and damp. I am hard and hard skinned. I become the green, hard, thick-limbed plant. The peyote cactus.

But where do the colors come from? I burst through the hard green skin into the blazing desert sun, violent with hues invisible to the unaided human eye. Peyote worship is sun worship. We are back at Ra. Back in Egypt. We are back to the "glorious author of an unhappy race" . . . Phaedra's too-bright sun . . . Akhnaton's monotheist sun whose mystery traveled from Egypt to Crete and from Crete came with Phaedra to Greece. And our autochthonous Indians are linked in common worship with them.

Nina gloats, "You thought I was mad."

"Yes. I thought so. Now I know it."

She wants to be vindicated. But instead we are all condemned. What does it profit her if we are mad too?

Julian and Luther lie on the floor howling with laughter and sudden shrieks of terror. Ruth dresses to join her family at the beach. Judith Graves strews flowers, Nina utters pronouncements. Having lost all, I cling to the marrow, as even the bones are dissolved. I call on Sweet Reason in this bedlam and become more rational. I bathe and dress, clean the kitchen, tend Garrick, shop, scrub the floors. While they glide past still vibrant with hallucinations. I speak to them of Sweet Reason, whom they spurn. The whole day passes thus.

I saw the other side and I like it better here.

They say I'm afraid but I'm not ashamed.

If there is pure ecstasy and pure sensation let me come to it with sanity, and if it's not compatible with life, then I'll choose life.

June 8, 1955

Phèdre persistent.

A few pages ago I lost my journal; a letter arrived from a pathetic old woman who found it on the Broadway bus. I went to her sordid room with Lester. He gave me a dollar for her. It seemed too little, but I had no other money and she took it eagerly. In her crone's voice she said, "Such things should be kept under lock and key."

June 9, 1955

Late night. Till six A.M. with kheef and Alan Hohvaness. We listen to Fleetwood on the radio.

The play went badly; Julian says I should work harder. What he says is true. I fail to give myself. I can't admit that I'm afraid.

Julian says: "Spite."

I am lost because—*tout ou rien.*

Alan believes that I am strong.

But Edelman says to Julian, "If you break with her we will work together. We could achieve much, you and I."

Am I to admire his devotion to the Living Theatre or consider him a traitor?

Group: I am more interested, less interesting.

It is Phèdre who matters.

I am twenty-nine years old.

Julian's honesty and beauty.

Not troubled. Yet not at peace.

June 11, 1955

Ruth manages to get through her lines, but totters about the stage and faints at the end of each scene. This constant state of emergency intensifies our acting.

Leonard must leave the cast. Julian will replace him as Theseus. We propose Jackson Mac Low for Theramène.

June 13, 1955

"I think I should resign my directorship," Tobi says to Julian and me.

A long silence follows. So long, so ludicrously long, that it is broken only by our mutual and strained laughter.

We do not protest.

This morning, a letter from Alan.

Dear Judith:

It is so difficult to put into words what has happened. I feel it has changed everything, my entire life. . . . Your beauty could call me from the dead to the living. . . . Your eyes and lips speaking from great opera houses . . . Boxes, many boxes, and gold behind your face. And time was not, and then was again. And I heard the sound of the dust on fingerboards and bridges of Haydn's string instruments, especially the cellos and basses.

The lines you spoke in the play are the lines I would speak in silence. For my voice is too ugly for the beautiful and the passionate. Your eyes and lips will haunt me forever.

With deepest love
Alan

He comes uptown this afternoon. He has set Gautama's entrance magnificently. Tonight during the play he sits in the front row. My voice is better, but I get carried away and throw myself into a frenzy.

After the play I talk to Alan at Rosenbloom's Restaurant. He wants to take a trip to Pakistan with me. He has these impossible desires.

June 20, 1955   *Pawlet, Vermont*

What saints and monsters I have seen since my last entry!

I have been part of hell.

I wasn't allowed to have my notebook with me, and though I had paper and pencil, I was told I could not keep anything I wrote.

There are things that can't be remembered. I've forgotten the anguish; I recall the facts:

Jackson Mac Low, whom we have asked to play Theramène in *Phèdre*, called Wednesday morning about the role. Then he added that he was on his way to picket City Hall with some of the pacifists to protest the air-raid drills.

How blithely I went!

It was new to me.

I am not a demonstrator. At lunchtime in City Hall Park I searched for Jackson, and not finding him, I stopped to hear a sidewalk evangelist under a statue of Benjamin Franklin denounce the Jews for the death of Jesus.

Then I saw folks distributing copies of the *Catholic Worker*; I introduced myself and offered to help. Ammon Hennacy gave me some to hand out and despite my religious difference I did so gladly. Ammon had seen *The Idiot King* and treats me like a friend. I like his ornery plainness, and Dorothy Day, to whom he introduced me, won all my heart instantly. She is a tall woman, strong boned and sharply molded; her white hair wound in braids around her head and a face and a glance that are fire and poetry. She wore a Hopi cross and a locket that contains a relic of St. Anthony.

We talked for a few moments. A CBS cameraman asked us to step further into the sun. Everyone accepted the newspaper. When we had given them all out, we proceeded to the office of the War Resisters' League to plan our protest action.

Warned of impending arrest if we refuse to take shelter when the sirens go off, Richard Kern advised that we all go limp. Bayard Rustin, who is organizing us, objected that the emphasis must not be taken away from the issue and become a question of resisting arrest.

We go down into the park. I see Jackson picketing separately with a sign asking for the end of H-bomb testing.[17] I greet Jackson and then join the others, who are sitting on two facing rows of park benches.

The siren begins its wail as I talk to Quaker Kent Larabee. The park clears in a few seconds, except for the newspapermen, photographers, policewomen, and policemen who surround us. Placards are held up for the photographers.

One of our young men is chosen (it seems to me arbitrarily) by the police and taken to a wagon which appears on the park pathway.

Bayard is approached by a policeman and asks him if we are under arrest.

Then Bayard announced quite loudly, "We are under arrest."

We all rose and the twenty-nine of us piled into the wagon. I found myself sitting on Kern who was seated on the floor, so as to let the older members of the group take seats. Jackson was in the front with the police. The sirens still wailed as the van started. I could see the deserted streets out the windshield. I was in the highest spirits. Knowing what I know now I would not be so gay at the outset nor so weak later in the face of fear.

At the Fifth Precinct stationhouse our communal feeling was strong. I noted less jollity among those who had been arrested before. I talked mostly with Jackson and exchanged a few words with Dorothy Day. I called Julian at work to make sure he would be at home when Garrick returned from play group. I felt confident that Julian would be able to get me out in time for the *Phèdre* performance!

Among us was a bootblack named Parilli. At two o'clock, it seems, he had picked up a cigar butt, and finding it bitter, walked toward a water fountain in

City Hall Park, just as the sirens started. Parilli, not having read the newspapers, did not know why the park was emptying. He was asked by a policeman to take shelter, but saw us sitting quietly, ignoring the police, and felt discriminated against. Why should he leave the park when others were sitting there in the sun? So he was arrested with us. As he was the first one called for questioning, our case came to be called "The People vs. Rocco Parilli and twenty-eight others."[18] One by one we were called in. First the men were arraigned and taken away and we didn't know where to.

A brisk policewoman asked me to open my blouse and my brassiere while she spilled the contents of my purse and looked closely at all my possessions. An unaccustomed modesty overcame me, and I complained when a policeman's face peered down from a window across the courtyard. The policewoman grumbled about her colleague's indiscretion, about the lack of window shades, and the lack of facilities in general. Then we were arraigned but not "booked" (we were not fingerprinted); the only pictures that were taken were for CBS, which, I later learned, were shown on the evening news.

I was glad I'd worn the pretty white lace dress that Ruth Kaner gave me for my birthday. At that point there was still a certain element of the performer left.

After the arraignment we were returned to the wagon. We sang en route. Dorothy distributed leaflets to passersby through the grating. Helen Russell held up a copy of the *Catholic Worker* to indicate to starers who we were.

I am awed by Dorothy, her fervent face, her silence, and her speech.

At the Fourteenth Precinct we were put into small green cells, each with a wet wooden board, an exposed toilet, and a sink.

Again that extraordinary sensation—the change between inside and outside. The sensation of imprisonment that is comparable to no other sensation.

Thoreau asked if they think him only a body to be shut up and put behind a wall. The mind is not free of the body, nor the body of the mind. What hurts the body, hurts the mind.

Dorothy was reading psalms and I would have asked her to read aloud, but it seemed presumptuous.

I tried to read, but Saint-Simon's account of the corruptions of King Louis' court, useful for the study of Phèdre, failed to obliterate the unnatural green of a prison wall.

Julian had warned me not to take my journal lest it be confiscated. I made a few notes in the endpapers of the Saint-Simon.

Dorothy suggested sleep, but I soon began to talk to my fellow inmates. And didn't return again to my book or my writing but stayed attentive to these ten women, who out of eight million came forward and remembered their womanliness. In all of New York there were only eleven women to protest when the siren sounded, and I counted myself fortunate to be one of them.

As we emerge from the cells, I see Julian with a bailbondsman. Julian insisting that I must be at the theater in a few hours. The police captain almost agrees, but says it's too late as they are moving us. He lets Julian ride downtown in the wagon with us. Julian brought the newspapers which he reads aloud to us; the story is being treated as a major item.

We parted again at the Tombs, still in the hope that I could play that night.

At the Tombs, we were all put in one tiny cell. At eight I grew restless about getting out in time for the performance. At ten past eight I was fatigued with suspense. Once it was too late my anxiety diminished; I had, after all, only to sit still.

What did we say those hours in that cell? Dorothy spoke very little. Edith told how she brought to court an albino who attacks women's legs with a compass point in the subways. I argued that neither jail nor the insane asylum is a real solution. Dorothy spoke for my view. "We have had psychopaths at the *Catholic Worker*," she said, "and we lived with them."

We sang some, for by then our spirits had weakened somewhat.

At Dorothy's urging, I told the story of *Phèdre* and recited the speech that seemed appropriate: "O heavens, what have I done today?"

Various poor women were brought in, taken out to court and brought back, invariably in tears. The judge was hard on all of them. All of them protested their innocence. They were accused of shoplifting, brawling, gambling, streetwalking.

Finally we're led to the courtroom—panelled, dim, and civilized after the impersonal tiles of the jail. I am weak with hunger. I see Julian, wave to him, and am reprimanded by a policeman. I apologize. I see many friends out there. Julian and Nina and Ruth and Mark and Robin and also Mike Harrington—his pale face reminds me irrelevantly of Jim—because we talked so much of Jim the night we met.

It is this that I am thinking while the court reads the names of the defendants. Of Jim Agee who is pure and beautiful and dead. Of Mike Harrington and his pale handsomeness, for which he seems sometimes to hate himself. I don't even notice the sleek judge, clothed in authority, up on his altar. Now as I try to remember, he seems all black and white. His black robe, black eyes and brows, and black hair against a stark white face, lipless and featureless.

I hardly listened to the names being called nor did I notice that Ammon Hennacy was called "Ay-mun Hanackee." But some of our friends laughed at the mispronunciation.

I became aware of the judge's sudden angry voice, "What's so funny?"

I came to the defense of the others: "We're hungry and it tends to make us giddy."

"You," he barked, "come up here!" I stepped up.

"What's your name?"

"Judith Malina," and then, "Beck."

"Where do you live?"

"789 West End Avenue."

"How long have you lived there?"

I thought, "Several years." I tried to calculate—four? three? five?

I turned back to Julian.

He said, "Six," and I turned back to the judge.

"Six."

"I asked you, not him!" he screamed.

I asked him please not to shout at me.

Then he said menacingly: "Have you ever been committed to a mental institution?"

I answered quietly, "No . . . have you?"

"That's enough!" he shouted. "You are hereby committed to Bellevue for psychiatric observation."

For a moment I didn't breathe. Then fear and rage and panic all at once.

"No!"

I heard a tempest break around me. The spectators rose.

Julian's voice above the others . . .

My book slammed out of my hands onto the table. I moved toward the judge and in my panic blurted (of all things), "You are a rude young man!" and seized the edge of the tribune.

Behind me Julian's voice roaring . . .

Two police came to take me, and I climbed on a bench to elude them. As they reached for me, I leaped from bench to table; I saw my copy of Saint-Simon spill onto the floor, the pages fluttering. Funny, the images that stick.

As they carried me out, holding my trembling, struggling body up above their heads, I called out to Julian, and saw that he too was being held aloft by four policemen, as he shouted in his heroic voice (and when moved, his power is immense), "No! you have no right, no legal, no moral right to do this!" And then he disappeared, still raving in praise of my accomplishments, my beauty, my worth. . . .

They brought me back to the cell; it was quiet after the shutting of the door, all the turmoil behind me.

It is a kind of ecstasy to fulfill one's fears, as it is to fulfill one's desires.

I needed an excuse to shout. An open window inspired me, for I heard street noises outside, and if I could hear them they could hear me. I took my shoe off, struck it against a metal partition and shouted my protest with all my voice, over and over, till the rage left me. And then I had to reckon with the dread.

Later I learned that Julian was not alone in protesting and in the confusion escaped arrest. The riot squad was called, but by the time they arrived all was quiet. The courtroom had been cleared because the judge said he feared for his life. Only the press and the prisoners were allowed to remain to hear the judge pronounce us all "murderers" and responsible for the hypothetical deaths caused by the H-bomb.

His name is Louis Kaplan, and among prisoners he has a terrible reputation. Of us he said in a prepared statement: "These people, by their conduct and behavior, contributed to the utter destruction of the three million theoretically killed in our city."

Some of this I learned when our friends returned to the cell. I was afraid they would reproach me but Dorothy reassured me. Desperately, I wished I could go to prison with them.

Bail was set for them at $1500 a person. As for me, I knew not what hope I had. I felt I was going to hell.

Someone miraculously got an apple to Dorothy which she gave me. It assuaged my hunger and my heart.

Dorothy said she would pray for me; if her prayers were meant to calm my fears they were already partly answered by my knowing of them.

When Dorothy and the other women were taken out of my cell to the women's jail and I found myself alone, it seemed indeed like a tomb.

I tried to breathe slowly.

I tried to imagine what all the wise ones would advise me. Suddenly calm, I understood what I must do.

A policeman and a husky attendant in a blue uniform from Bellevue came for me. At first they took me by the elbows, but they accepted my assurance that I would walk peacefully.

In the ambulance I entertained my captors with an account of my arrest and the courtroom story and confessed my fear of what was in store.

The policeman seemed sympathetic. "They'll let you go in ten days."

Ten days!

At Bellevue there was an hour of red tape before I was escorted by two policemen to the Criminal Psychiatric Observation Ward. Again the clanging of bars.

It was two A.M. as I went through a routine that I had often administered in Hartford: name, age, address.

Everything kaleidoscoped: doctor, stethoscope, pulse, a wet jam sandwich, a tin cup full of milk, an open beltless smock, a páir of ill-fitting cotton mules.

A tough policewoman named Sweeney lectured me: I am a traitor to my country.

I'm too tired to argue. Please don't talk about politics. Everything swims before my eyes. The heavy door with the small glass window like the gate of hell. And Sweeney moralizing. She examines the contents of my purse and takes offense at the diaphragm she finds there. I try not to argue.

A nurse comes to take my temperature while she tells Sweeney that two days ago her eighteen-year-old son was drowned at Orchard Beach. In a flat voice she tells how she prayed and hoped in vain, her face showing no emotion. I express sympathy but restrain, of course, an impulse to embrace her. Her unhappiness seemed to complete a picture of a world of unending miseries that stand as milestones between the first catastrophe and the last.

Sweeney led me to a second gate, opened it, and her flashlight led my slippered feet along the slippery floor to an empty bed. I closed my eyes as I heard the last gate shut.

Closed my eyes, but did not sleep.

Waves of dread came over me. I let myself cry.

Nothing I had known before followed me here. Stripped of what I owned and sequestered from all I knew; having only myself with me, I found myself wanting.

I watched dawn break just as I fell asleep. Most of all, I longed for Julian.

We were awakened by an attendant in a blue smock who went from bed to bed crying, "Up, up!" The room, which I saw for the first time, was not a dormitory, but a corridor filled with beds for lack of space.

My companions rose: Here a seventeen-year-old and there a seventy-year-old; all shared a certain numbness. And I, who had always prided myself on never being afraid of people, was afraid of them.

Everyone bustled as though to some purpose. I wanted to dress but I was told to make my bed first and did as I was told. Then I realized that I had no dressing to do. Everyone wore the same kind of cotton smock. A tin mirror recalled the last scene of *The Cenci*, when Beatrice and her mother tie up one another's hair en route to their destiny.

I took down my hair.

A slight, young girl with cropped hair and a cruel, pretty face approached me. "I'm Francine. Ask me about anything you want. And tie up your hair. They'll give you a piece of ribbon."

I nodded. Francine shook her body in a lewd, itching movement, and raised one hand to her head. "Bugs—you know what I mean. Bugs."

I tied up my hair.

When a food wagon came, everyone settled onto the benches. Francine motioned me to her table. The girls at the table asked what crime had brought me here. When I told them, they didn't seem interested. They were more interested in Lucille, who was just then being dressed and wheeled out. She had thrown her two children out of a window, killing them both. After some speculation they have concluded that she is crazy.

After breakfast we washed our tin cups. Then a frantic cleanup. An attendant brought mops and brooms, but it was Francine who directed the hectic activities. Her open smock revealed full breasts on an otherwise boyish body.

She was clearly the supreme boss of the ward. I started to scrub, but Francine set me to cleaning tables, an easier task. I obeyed her.

Throughout the cleaning and scrubbing everyone moved at an unnaturally high speed, and then the mops and pails were removed and the day began.

Everyone settled in silence on the benches and the floor. I looked around the square day-room with windows onto 31st Street and onto First Avenue. There are three long tables, six benches—and nothing else. There were two incomplete decks of cards, three books, and a few mystery paperbacks. Nothing else. We sat. Someone started playing solitaire. Later a gin rummy game with the ten of hearts and the queen of spades drawn on wrapping paper. Nothing else. The activity of the morning was over. We waited for lunch. Then for supper. Nothing else.

I began talking to the others. First we tell each other what brought us here. Each one, like me, told stories of her innocence. There were fourteen women, of whom half spoke English and half spoke Spanish.

Olga, a very pregnant Spanish beauty, danced till everyone shouted for her to stop. "Hey, Olga, you'll drop your baby!" She enjoyed the bantering, laughing at their fears.

A stout girl sat on the floor pounding out mambo rhythms for Olga. When she stopped there was that deadly, boring silence.

Carrie, an old woman suffering from advanced cancer, asked me to read to her from the Bible. She was obviously in much pain.

She told me she'd been taking care of a six-year-old girl, and one day in the playground, the child climbed the sliding pond and threatening to jump down, called out, "Come and get me." Laboriously (for she can scarcely move her right arm as the result of a recent mastectomy), Carrie climbed the steps of the sliding pond, and as she approached, the child, to spite her, jumped down. She was not severely hurt, but when treated for bruises she claimed that Carrie pushed her.

I read from the psalms, but Annie, a hardened woman who has spent thirty years in jails, snarled, "Shut up, you're in jail. If you'd been reading the Bible when you were arrested, you wouldn't be where you are now." Francine intervened to avoid a fight.

I asked for and was given a pencil. I wrote:

> Why doesn't it help me
> To remember Gandhi in prison
> Or to think of Thoreau?

I read through two chapters of *Pride and Prejudice* but couldn't concentrate on such refinements.

My lunch companion told me her misfortunes. She had pierced out her husband's eye with a kitchen knife one night when they were drinking. A mild, elderly Irish woman, she is not too distressed by her fate, since her husband now forgives her and is trying to free her.

It was visiting day and I could see Julian but dimly behind the heavy screens that stretch across the bars.

He spoke lovingly, passionately. He was doing everything possible. Paul Goodman had told him to call Dr. Alison Montague, who knew the Dr. Cassidy who is in charge of the psychiatric wards. He promised Julian swift aid.

Meanwhile he says there's a great to-do in the newspapers about our protest and the arrests and Judge Kaplan's courtroom scene.

We were only allowed to speak for a few minutes.

A psychiatrist named Nachtigall came to interview me. It took some effort to dispel her condescending manner, though she had seen the Picasso play. "How does that speak for my sanity?" I joked. She asked me to explain Julian's paintings, which she said puzzled her. We swung round slowly from examination to conversation.

And though she assured me of the certainty of my release—she was sure I would have to remain ten days.

I asked about Dr. Cassidy and she said he had left, that he was never in the building in the evening, and as this was the weekend . . .

At supper I offered the girls the meat on my plate in exchange for their vegetables. Francine divided the portions. Table talk: the profits of prostitution.

Suddenly a nurse called me to go to see Dr. Cassidy. A nervous, thin, young man, he was businesslike and abrupt. He had returned to the hospital after going home and seemed annoyed. He sat atop the desk to look down at me. He questioned, took no notes, but watched me so closely that it was funny. He asked me why I was there. Halfway in my narrative he asked if I had been drinking. I said "Certainly not" in such a hurt tone that he got angry and shouted at me. There was a method to this man's observations.

When I related the courtroom events, he laughed a good deal, loudly and abandonedly. Then he suddenly resumed his abrupt manner, "Can't do anything tonight. I'll see you're released in the morning. I'll make out your papers now."

He didn't stop to hear my thanks.

With relief I returned to the outer room, where Francine told me that she had arranged for me to sleep, not in the hall, but in the dormitory, and in the bed next to hers. As soon as the lights went out, Francine ordered two accomplices, Esther and Olga, to the door with an imperious gesture. The girls stood at either side of the dormitory entrance watching for the approach of the attendant.

Then Francine came into my bed and despite my reluctance started to fondle and kiss me. I was alarmed by her lovemaking. I saw no hope but submission, but just then the girls at the door whispered a warning and rushed to their beds and Francine to hers.

A nurse and an attendant with a flashlight, brought me a special-delivery letter from Julian, full of tender reassurances. I can't imagine why they delivered it after lights out, instead of waiting till morning.

I read the letter by flashlight over and over, standing in the corridor between the guard and the nurse. When I returned to bed Francine and the others were asleep.

I looked out the window for some hours watching the lovers pass arm in arm on the street below.

Mrs. Kelly woke up shouting. She is a large old woman who had had a minor operation for a festering sore on her leg. During the night her bandages had pulled up around her thigh and hurt her. As no nurse appeared, I tried to untie the bandage. The guard came to the gate and ordered me back to bed. I insisted on staying with the old woman till a nurse came.

Kelly howled the night long in anguish until she was taken out of the ward.

In the morning I learned that Kelly is one of several here who are serving long prison sentences but have reason to prefer the mental hospital to jail. And so this night, taking advantage of her hurt thigh, Kelly put on her mad act and was committed to psychiatric, whence she will be shipped to one of the state mental institutions. Of such is the kingdom of hell.

In the morning as I waited for release, I had my hair examined for lice and gave the money I had with me to Francine for the girls.

Returning my belongings to me, Sweeney saw that I was reading *The Memoirs of the Court of Louis XIV.* She was, she said, descended from the kings of France. And this heritage, she went on, accounted for her proud carriage; people thought her "snooty" when she was really "patrician." And she demonstrated her "patrician walk," her nose high in the air, swinging her jailer's keys as though they were a lace fan. I was glad to leave this vestige of the royal line of France for the policewagon which this time meant release.

They brought me to the Second Street precinct, where Julian awaited me. The cop who asked me my name told me I had a prominent lawyer, a former judge, Morris Ploscowe, who was "running around like Groucho Marx" getting me bailed out. The cops talked (God help us!) about torture devices. I joined in this talk, perhaps too lightheartedly.

While the court recessed for lunch, I was locked in a cell with a young girl who said she had taken a girdle from Macy's but was going to plead innocent.

She asked me what I had done. I said "civil disobedience." Her eyes widened. "Man," she exclaimed, "that sounds like a crime!"

Alan Hohvaness brought $500 in cash, and the bail was made out in my name.

Dorothy came with some of the *Catholic Worker* people and we all had ice cream sodas.

That night I gave an excellent performance. I was told it was my best Phèdre to date.

I am sitting in the soft summer of Vermont in that same white dress as I write this, and the dark horror of that prison ward is unthinkable, yet it was so. And it still is so. Those women still are there.

July 5, 1955   *New York City*

The night before Tobi's departure I went walking with him in the ruins of the demolished houses.

We stopped in the shell of the Carlton Theater . . . .

An empty theater in the bleakness of destruction. The last film I saw here was Jim's *African Queen.* Tobi said, "And to think that I had once hoped we might make this place into our theater." The plaintive tone was for our abandoned collaboration.

We parted with vague references to the future. I saw him again at a replacement rehearsal the next evening. He came with his baggage packed. There was no farewell.

July 6, 1955

A meeting at the *Catholic Worker,* a place rich in poverty where the poor are fed and the needy clothed.

Dorothy and Ammon and the Workers have decided to plead guilty.

The War Resisters have decided to plead not guilty and make a test case on a constitutional issue.

I am inclined to plead guilty rather than to fight the law. But I am not certain.

The case is postponed until September.

July 25, 1955   *New York City*

We've been traveling.

To Newport, where a historical pageant unleashes a fireworks display.

To Plymouth, where we stay in the Oldest House, still inhabited by the descendants of the Pilgrims who built it.

To Provincetown, where the dunes fill me with vitality.

To Boston, where the Isabella Gardner's "plaisir" is a superb Vermeer.

To Salem, where we live right on the shore, inviting me to finish the Salem poem, begun two years ago.

Then one night in New York, and the next day I go to Tanglewood with Alan.

We sit near three gigantic perfect birches waiting for the afternoon rehearsal. Alan talks as though silence would reveal a deadly secret.

But at night the overwhelming applause for the *Easter Cantata* and the hundreds who crowded for autographs and congratulations elated him and he beamed with delight.

Alan is excited by the mountains, and next morning took me to the scenes most significant for him. We drove up Mt. Equinox, which is 3816 feet high. And at the foot of October Mountain I wrote a madrigal for him, in six lines following the form of Orlando's "Gibbon's Swan."

The last night we got lost in the woods. The forest grew ancient as we ventured deeper. Alan made notes for a piece to be called *October Mountain.*

I rejoin Julian in Canaan, where we parted from Alan. Glad to be free of his difficult heart.

Julian and I slept in the woods and washed in the morning in a brook and ate berries.

Claude's house on the hill. Peace sits on it. Claude and Jim Spicer seem suffused with the immortal beauty of the country. The smallest cares take their place in the divine pattern.

The eternal landscape forms the background, thereby permitting one to live in the present.

Here the terror that cries *"memento mori"* is modulated by the natural world into a mere whisper in the dying flowers, the picking of vegetables, the singing insects.

I began to be happy there. We swam in a stream like the one in Hopkins' "Epithalamion," full of happy youths.

We walked in the woods, past lazy cows in open fields, past brooks and hills. I grew quiet.

A sudden storm over the house at night shook the great pines—Zeus, Agamemnon, and Orestes.

But I was quiet again.

Back in New York, we try to arrange our lives. How hard.

How unnatural everything is here.

August 2, 1955

I need quiet. But I can't find a place in myself which is not filled with noises.

I want contact with the immediate world.

I want to work like a happy nun.

I dedicate this book to her.

Last night at Stratford, on the banks of the Housatonic, at the big teak theater where they play Shakespeare, I said to Alan, "I will not give way to envy." But the pink envious moon finds the weakness in my hypnotic state and shines on my envy till my head aches.

The Tempest is a gaudy pageant which is also a mystery. It promises us the fearful light that, wiser than Semele, we dare not invoke lest it consume us in our frailty.

I envy the actors: the pompous Massey, Roddy McDowell almost succeeds as Ariel (but who could satisfy that role?), Jack Palance as Caliban (it means Cannibal, says Alan). But have they really understood?

Costumes by Bob Fletcher. Scenery by Horace Armistead. These whom I have met and who are part of my history but have not become my friends.

And Juno appearing suddenly in peacock feathers is Virginia Baker, who filled me with awe when she read Strindberg's *A Bridal Crown* at Piscator's. And I have never been the same.

All the way home I fell into an envious half-sleep while Alan piled up proofs that Shakespeare was the Mason Francis Bacon, secret son of Queen Elizabeth.

I, too, in disguise, in Sycorax' bond, hoping for Prospero's magic before I learn I am not Ariel but Cannibal.

August 9, 1955

Friday was the tenth anniversary of the bombing of Hiroshima.

We gave out leaflets in front of the Empire State Building where the Japanese Consulate is located. This is an annual observance of the Catholic Workers and War Resisters. Ammon and Dorothy deliver a letter of penitence to the Japanese Consul. Julian, too, gives out leaflets and we both find a peculiar satisfaction in this new kind of activity.

I thank Dorothy for both the praise and the chiding in her article in the *Catholic Worker* on the arrest and hearing.

She is enlivening to me the way someone I love is.

She tells of Saint Theresa of Lisieux, who bestows roses when answering prayers. Dorothy had prayed that morning that her daughter and grandchildren be provided for in her absence, and lo, someone had just brought her a bunch of roses and she was certain all was well at home.

Saturday I joined for one day in a fast for the sin of the A-bomb. Ammon will fast ten days, picketing, as is his annual custom, in front of the Internal Revenue Building because it is the tax money, after all, that pays for the bomb. Carol Perry joins him in both the fast and the picketing. Jackson Mac Low has already fasted four days since Hiroshima Day and has taken some fruit juice today. He has a large, informative sign concerning the H-bomb tests, surplus food, and the tax dollar.

I distribute *Catholic Workers* and Jackson's leaflet down at Bowling Green. I like the contact with strangers.

August 13, 1955

Long philosophical talks with Julian. Too many activities.
Wednesday I join the pickets with a sign I have made:

LOVE & LIFE

NOT

DEATH & TAXES

Judge Ploscowe passes me twice.
"I thought I'd scared you away from this sort of thing. You're incorrigible. However, if there's any trouble I'm right down the street."

To the Remo and the White Horse and Mike Harrington.
His single-mindedness is enigmatic. He's like an early Huxley hero. His whole life, his whole energy devoted to his politics.
Thursday night Julian and I had dinner at the *Catholic Worker* with Dorothy and then went to see a 1938 Russian film called *Volga, Volga*, on a double bill with a socially significant tragedy called *The Lady in the Deathhouse*.
To walk on the streets with Dorothy is a pleasure, for she notices everything, finds interest in everything.
A rain began to fall and we enjoyed the wetness. Its name is hurricane Connie. Much ado in anticipation of her.

August 18, 1955

A busy week of planning for the coming season. Every third Monday we will do a reading of new and old plays:

October 11: Montherlant's *Queen after Death*.
October 31: *Venice Preserved*.
November 21: William Carlos Williams' *Many Loves*.
December 11: Strindberg's *Easter* or *Bridal Crown*.
January 2: Goodman's *The Theory of Tragedy* and *The Theory of Comedy* and Frank O'Hara's *The Houses at Falling Hanging*.
January 23: Tieck's *Puss-in-Boots*.
February 20: Shelley's *Prometheus Unbound*.
March 12: Beckett's *Waiting for Godot*.
April 2: Synge's *Dierdre* and Yeats' *Dierdre*.
April 23: Toller's *Masse Mensch*.
May 14: *Troilus and Cressida*.
June 4: New American Play.

We draw up this list with great excitement.
Meanwhile, we make our plans for *The Young Disciple*, spurred by Merce's choreography.

August 23, 1955

Typing stencils for *The Young Disciple*.

To "The Goldbergs" to be *looked at* for a role. I feel helpless. If only I could audition, but to be merely "looked at"!

August 24, 1955

I did have to read and I did get the role. I'm all disguised to look forty. I get a role I'm much too young to play as a reward for a good reading.

August 26, 1955

Alan has set the madrigal. He calls and writes daily. His intensity overpowers him.

August 20, 1955
Dear Judith:

Just one mad utterance—
I am one of the few composers who don't write "industrial" music. And now I am forced to join the million of composers on wheels and pistons—piss—the unhappiness crushed the brain—and knowing I have been sold a slave to the enemies of humanity and music, to those who make slaves. I hate myself that I am false. You are my ideal of courage and beauty and intelligence.

All my love,
Alan

They also make mistakes in timing and I have to do this shit over again because of their mistakes.

August 24, 1955
Dear Judith:

How do you write "courageous" music? Even "fifteen seconds of courageous music"? Or rather "fearless music" as has been ordered? I can write heavenly music by the barrelful, but my "fearless" music only moved along fast and brightly but not fearlessly.
Now as night journeys into the holiness of dawn a melodic heaven opens and gushes forth to meet my inquiry. My search, which had seemed so hopeless. Will this be the idea? It has wings of whiteness.
I love you most dearly and deeply, you who are my heaven upon earth.

Alan

August 30, 1955

The television work is exciting and humiliating. A complex of pressure, glamour, and vulgarity. The human situation and the art are pathetic.
I play a caricature of a woman Mrs. Berg's age, whose son, played by the comedian Arnold Stang, woos Mrs. Goldberg's daughter, Rosalie. The joke is this woman's hypermaternal concern with her son's health and well-being.
I ask myself if this exercise is more instructive or more destructive.

Mrs. Berg, like all the celebrated people I've met, is fiercely energetic, egocentric, and obsessed with whatever she's doing.

She demands total attention and concentration on the scene being played from everyone in the room. She is centripetal and in her presence the banality of the text dissolves.

August 31, 1955

Reading Marston's *The Insatiate Countess*, a bawdy work. Isabelle is painted extreme. The comedy is lewd, but Isabelle doesn't participate in the lewdness. Reading also: *The Critique of Pure Reason, Letters of Mme. Récamier,* and the crude biography of Rachel that Alan gave me flatteringly inscribed.

Nina is back from Provincetown, verging on complete breakdown or breakthrough. She is aggressively talkative. She wants to shut out all sadness from her consciousness. Speaks of her revelation of two years ago as incomplete, and now is certain that all will be fully revealed. Her euphoria is full of reproaches. She can breathe and we cannot. She is searching and we are not. Yet she is graceful and joyous.

Casting *The Young Disciple*. A Disciple is hard to find. An innocent young man. Is there one? We hear several people: singular among them, a lithe dancer recommended by Merce, Paul Taylor, whose fluidity is interrupted by the words.

Lester has been here for some weeks. He is devoted, loving, kind. I meet Philip, friendly and sullen, in Bryant Park. We will take classes with Erick Hawkins together. So I fulfill the last of my three promises to Philip.

A new season. A new life.

September 3, 1955

One hundred years ago this date Rachel played her first performance in New York. The play was *Horace* and the role Camille.

Hearing many actors read for *The Young Disciple*.

Walter is typing the scripts for *The Insatiate Countess*.

Lester is here all the time. His affection. I cannot return it and do not reject it.

Garrick is home from camp.

A nightmare just before awakening this morning. A man who is really a cat. A prison which is also a palace. I am trapped there. A fantastic escape through corridors and gates.

September 9, 1955

Nina. Over, out, and back in three days. Two days of barbaric madness which she considers revelation. Doesn't she go into that dark night and look into a dawn too bright to be compatible with life itself?

When I go there, I hide my strange sails from the hostile world. Those who do not are barred and locked from the sun. She is angry with me because I criticize her.

Erick Hawkins' dance class is a Zen archery lesson. The movements come out of what is learned rather than being what is learned.

Devoutly a dancer, he wants to instill in us the knowledge of how "to move with passion." Not the borrowed passion of Spain or India, but our own. I don't know if in this environment I can convey my own passion, though I'd like to. "The dancer resists gravity while yielding to it."

He is very grave, with sudden bursts of merriment.

I am buoyant, but I am clumsy.

A marvelous lad named Hooper Dunbar comes to read for *The Young Disciple*. He is astonishingly simple, and above all an extraordinary actor. Undespoiled ability such as I have not seen before. The cast is amazed at the reading. The play which I had feared is wondrous.

September 10, 1955

Yesterday was Paul's birthday. He seems gloomy and pained. His party simmers with longing. We go with Søren and Lester.

Søren is a pale, poetic young man who has fallen in love with the Living Theatre. He came first to the evenings after the performances of *Improvise*, and attracted much attention at the opening party for *Phèdre*, where I misunderstood his sociability. He has become close friends with Hooper Dunbar, and they and Paul engage in long, emotional conversations.

Everyone at the party is bent on tinkering with each other's affections. Alison Montague, who got me out of Bellevue, has a forlorn look. I feel fondly toward him, and not only because he has done me a service.

Marie Menken and Lester talk with much wit together in a public way.

Everyone friendly enough to pretend very little that is not felt. This friendliness becomes a way for us to use each other. We become subtly involved and interwoven. In the end, too many are sad and we are hurt by each other's sadness.

I am saddened by Monty's sadness. He says, "Lend me Lester tonight. Tell him I'm safe." And I cannot. Lester and I talk all night of this.

September 12, 1955

Communal picnic. Paul's people on Wards Island under an everchanging sky, our city's skyline close at hand. We crossed the footbridge over the East River to this island which everyone ignores. No one was there save our group on this perfect Sunday. Part park for pleasure, another part is fenced off for various municipal prisons and/or hospitals. The surrounding bridges in all directions frame us. We play baseball. No troubling under the blue sky. How different from Paul's nervous birthday party, the sad shaking of the aspen leaves.

September 13, 1955

Number One Wall Street is a skyscraper in the financial district. Here our shabby band of protesters gathers on the top floor to talk with some prominent lawyers.

It seems that the Fund for the Republic is paying for an expensive legal defense of our position.

Harrop Freeman and Kenneth Greenewalt speak, as important men, of making this into a "great case" to be taken, if need be, to the Supreme Court.

They plan to call in atomic scientists to testify that there is no defense against the atom bomb.

But—here's the hitch—in order to do this, to conduct this great case, the defendants must plead "not guilty" so that they can be tried.

Dorothy is very firm in her statement of the position of the Catholic Workers. In the spiritual sense of the word they are not guilty, but in terms of the law, they broke the law deliberately because it is a bad law. There are eight of us who want to plead guilty.[19]

The lawyers harangue us. They say that our plea of guilty "weakens the case," that we have "the opportunity to be pioneers and clear the way for others to speak freely."

I am tempted to an interest in "the case."

But I feel with the Workers. I will plead guilty.

Judge Ploscowe says, "Question that on advice of counsel."

September 14, 1955

In the evening I go to Erick Hawkins' class. As soon as I see myself in the mirror I cannot concentrate even on the simplest counts and movements. It's then that my feeling of nonreality and nonparticipation begins.

I make a collage with stones called *Political Prisoner*.

Reading Kitto: *The Greeks*.

September 16, 1955

At an NBC recording session of Alan's music for the India film. Alan plays the celeste. The score is gorgeous, but gets sentimental because of the overemphasis on the strings.

A good many new actors last night: Jean Barr, Shirley Stoler, Ace King, Katherine Lurker and Mark Williams. Ruth K leaves us, offended by the play, as many will be. We have as yet no Master. Hooper reaps new wonders at each rehearsal.

Fall comes. We prepare the theater. Søren and I take up the old carpet that Tobi put down and lay down a new season's ground.

We take up also the last of *Phèdre*'s silver background while listening to the *Phèdre* and *Spook Sonata* music.

September 19, 1955

September 18, 1955
Dearest Judith:

My music is my offering to you. And then to the world. And it is my deepest concern that I protect the excellence and honor of this music which is for you.

The sound of lushness was far removed from my wishes and my music.
. . . The conductor, being a Broadway theater conductor demanded more and more lushness in the strings. What happened was similar to a modern lush

orchestra arrangement of Purcell's *Dido*. It was not at all what I had written at first. Bowings were changed from my Purcell bowings, upper octaves were added. . . . When they suppress the music under spoken words the strings will tend to disappear completely, especially during trumpet or horn solos, leaving only the wind sound bare. . . .

The music was *not sentimental*. . . . The only possible exception being the five fearlessnesses which I rewrote many times and all of which were rejected. Considering all this torture, I did not stoop to anything cheap and still satisfied their insane demands. . . .

But it does not touch either me or my music. It is very important that you understand me rightly. The others do not matter. I care nothing for their chatter. As it adds nothing and detracts nothing to or from my music and its destiny.

You I love and you alone I want to understand.

My deepest love always,
Alan

September 21, 1955

Autumnal equinox.

In dance class I learn that I am not in my body.

Nina's state is closely akin to religious ecstasy.

Yesterday I read in Englebert's *Lives of the Saints* a life of Quirinus whose feast day is on my birthday and who was martyred for civil disobedience.

Sts. Judith and Salome were both recluses, supposed to be princesses. They lived in seclusion in one of those dimly remembered medieval forests.

We have not found Our Master for Paul's play. Philip has read for the role and is here tonight rehearsing.

Alan lends us $180 for the rent.

Julian directs *The Young Disciple* with certainty of meaning.

September 25, 1955

Ploscowe surprises me by agreeing to a plea of guilty, after a long and reasonable talk. I had even been willing to concede to a lawyer's argument, but apparently our cause does not look "good" to him. That is, the possibility of acquittal looks dim.

Money is terrible. Dwight is going to help us, thank heaven, and Willard and Marie. Also Stryker, of all unimagined sources, who has come into an unexpected inheritance.

Søren's friend Albert Urban comes to look at Julian's paintings and offers him a one-man show at his gallery in November. So soon, and so sudden after waiting so long.

Yom Kippur. Fasted well. Broke my fast badly.

Class with Erick. His devotion is also a form of fanaticism. But what art is there without some madness?

Philip is strong tonight. We decide he will play Our Master.

Merce is at rehearsal to plan his choreography. He paces our little stage to see "how much room." "How little room," I correct him. "No, no," he says generously, "lots of room."

Late to Alan's to listen to Schaeffer's *Symphonie pour un homme seul*. It seems less unsettling now, despite its radical form. Then Alan plays a new composition of his own and the completed portions of *Gautama*.

September 27, 1955

Garrick lights a memorial light to Albert Einstein. Seeing the lamps for sale in a store, he asked Julian what they are for, and being told that they were in memory of someone who has died, he immediately asked for one for Einstein. It is this sort of respectful tenderness that is his most singular trait. He has a very somber, rigorous, but extremely rational *Weltanschauung*.

September 28, 1955

Judge Bushel, having decided that our case is within his jurisdiction, does not want any of the defendants to plead guilty. But he does not take into consideration that we are eager to plead guilty as an expression of our commitment, rather than as a judicial maneuver. Five of the *Catholic Worker* group and Richard Kern and I are the only ones to so plead. The lawyers, in the end, all opposed this plea and even at the last moment tried to convince us to change our minds.

I said nothing. Ploscowe spoke for us. Again and again as the others made their pleas, Ploscowe turned to me and whispered, "Do you still want to plead guilty?" The judge and the lawyers thought us merely stubborn, and a throbbing tension mounted.

Dorothy is a mountain when she is determined. Her marble pallor exaggerated, her square jaw set sharp beyond human reach.

The trial is set for next month.

Tonight Paul is at the theater to see the rehearsal.

A check for $150.00 from Dwight Ripley, with a kind note, solves our finances.

A postcard from Pound about *The Women of Trachis*:

"O.K. Ez. P. as to yr 'hope' " [that he was well and happy] "I ain't, but yu can do nowt about that. Taint yr. fault."

September 29, 1955

The play shapes. Hooper resists Julian and himself. Paul's presence disturbs even while it disciplines the rehearsals.

The papers carry the story of our plea of guilty and they falsify everything. This, however, is to be expected.

October 8, 1955

Merce is here teaching Philip the dance of Our Master, a simple choreography which Philip executes eloquently.

October 10, 1955

Alan has spoken to Stokowski of *Gautama's House* and Stokowski has offered to conduct it!

Julian, as always, has used himself up in preparing the production. He is tired and haggard. His set is an extraordinary series of movable panels made of corrugated cardboard, painted and collaged.

The police have spoken to cast members about trouble on opening night because we are doing an "obscene" play. Where they got that notion I don't know. That they might consider a play of such devout purity obscene I do not doubt, but I don't know how to prove to anyone's satisfaction that direct language is less obscene than veiled remarks.

Here we are in a crisis. The real gains are intangible and can neither be confiscated nor diminished. They are also constant.

Hooper works from his feelings and by feeling I mean sensation and not passion. He is undisciplined (how does the word relate to "disciple"?), but when he weeps or suffers the spasms of his anguish, he is apart and unreachable.

He and Søren are rival friends. They sport like naughty children and are jealous. Both think me their mother, but Hooper says so outright and asks to call me Mother, while Søren, who feels his survival depends on his contempt for mankind, dreams I am his mother and is astonished by the dream.

October 14, 1955

The police harassment has increased. They stop actors on the street and ask, "You doing a dirty play up there?"

We decide to go directly to the local precinct, and we ask them if they have any objections to our work. We bring the script and ask if there's anything there that they won't allow.

The cynical sergeant behind the desk says, "If we raid you we'll raid you. We ain't gonna tell you about it ahead of time."

I'm sure there's something illegal about this remark, but there's no reasoning with the man. He's a lemon.

We talk half the night with the cast. What to do? What if we're not just stopped but arrested? It seems possible. We try substituting the word "censored" for the word "fuck" with hilarious results.

"Our Master is censoring his Only World."

After the laughter we all soberly talk about the risks and everyone is cheerfully willing to brave the only honest course. We begin to feel like the harassed disciples in the play. It increases our ardor.

October 16, 1955

The Young Disciple has opened. Audiences are small and astonished, sometimes surly, sometimes cautious, sometimes enthusiastic, and sometimes repulsed.

There was no interference from the law.

A great release follows the opening and everyone is wildy elated.

October 17, 1955

I begin to give acting classes. I insist that the student go quickly into the heart of the matter. I teach well because I become avidly interested in the immediate problem.

At this moment we are rehearsing *Queen after Death*. Leonard and Julian and Irma and I and Bill Fletcher and Hooper. But Garrick, sitting at the foot of the stage with his coloring book, is my center of attention.

October 30, 1955

Today an anniversary of our marriage.

But I scarcely see Julian. He is painting for his show.

Tobi came to the theater with a psychoanalyst named Rachele Thomas. He was eclipsed by her brightness and played rather the fool than the hero.

November 6, 1955

I sit here in this theater which my persistent distress has built out of nothing at all. *Venice Preserved* is being read on the stage. In the glow of Julian's genius, the loft has become a little sacred grove.

November 10, 1955

Alan surrounds me with the magic of the sounds he knows how to create out of numbers. When I am with him I am confounded, knowing he takes my clumsiness for grace and my embarrassment for profundity. Meanwhile he can only utter inarticulate speeches of love, which I answer with silence and respect.

And mirroring this love *sans reproche* is Lester's. Concrete and sexual. I disdained him at first, and slowly, by power and persistence, he has won me. Won me despite myself, despite all prejudice and preconception. As the hero conquers.

We cast the next program. Pound-Sophokles' *Women of Trachis* and Fielding's *Tom Thumb*—tragedy and comedy. Everything's difficult.

At a Village party last night with Walter, Lester and Julian. Walter is drunk and affectionate and makes Lester jealous. Lester, drunker still, steals a silver bookmark that I had been admiring. The bookmark is engraved with a portrait of Othello and the date 1864. I have it here now in my hand, aghast at Lester's recklessness, though his desire to please me makes me happy.

Lester and I wrangle all night over how to return it. The jealous Moor. My love for him enlivens me, makes my days lightsome and the nights too short.

We work hard. All sorts of problems.

November 15, 1955

God, let me see how this moment is precious in Your History. In my classes I bring the students my best self, all that I know and feel. Only to them and to the lover can I give myself so unstintingly.

I teach a simple girl named Beverly how there is nothing without feeling.

Lester and I talk with ease of "forever" as if it were in our power to carve ourselves a slice of eternity.

We are alone in the theater, making love on the stage floor, the way we used to long ago before love came to be between us.

There's a knock on the door. We break apart. I'm flustered and try hard to appear casual as I open the door.

The man says, "I am a licensing inspector." He has come to close the loft. I decide against anger and draw him over to the theater, for it's a freezing wet day, and the loft is cold. Lester stays in the dressing room, as the inspector sits down by the electric glow and writes out a "Notice to Appear and Show Cause." It may be the end of the loft.

I look at the fatal paper and I say that we can't appear in court on Thursday as we must appear that day in another court for a civil-defense protest.

He is staggered.

"Are you one of The Twenty-eight?"

"Yes." He reaches me his hand, smiling warmly.

"My name is Charlie Solin, I'm a member of the War Resisters' League. . . . Do you know Bayard and Ralph and Ammon Hennacy?"

So this enemy of the people turns out to be, after all, one of us.

Charlie expresses chagrin at having to be the agent of our troubles and tells me his story. The story of the civil servant. He was working in another city department—I don't remember which—and:

"One day they pass a new law—we have to carry guns. As a pacifist I protest and refuse to carry a gun. So they change my job and I become a building inspector—and the first thing I have to do is close the theater of some fellow pacifists—now how do you like that?"

I thought it appropriate, for it is the way of the world.

November 18, 1955

It looks as if they will succeed in closing the loft. The premises, they say, may not hold more than 18 people at a time—including actors and audience.

Nina calls Lester "Lustra": true, he glows, especially in the dark.

Alan's intensity sheds shadows, somber and stiff.

Julian is the underlying reality. By day or night equally to be counted on.

First day in court for the civil defense case, where the judge behaved like a Daumier vignette. He is drunk, and we recess for the judgment to be soberer, but he returns even more tipsy and makes jests and vulgar insinuations.

The Reverend Muste, as if in a pulpit, declares that "Man's personality is to be revered and respected and this respect is impossible in the conditions of war."

The judge replies, "Do you know this girl? She's good-looking, isn't she? You're under oath now—where have you seen her before?"

And to the charitable girls who work for the poor in Harlem and live in voluntary poverty, "Who pays your rent? Come on now, I want to know—who pays your rent?"

November 23, 1955

Julian's show:

He looks at the paintings hung on the gallery walls and plunges into an abyss of despair.

Because the theater closed, because he doesn't feel his paintings accomplish what he had hoped. He says, "They don't really signify anything."

I don't think he's disappointed with his painting, but with all painting.

It is the disappointment of the moment at which the dream is fulfilled, and all we can say, if we can speak at all, is, "I never dreamed it would be this way."

I learned it at 14, when I graduated from school; and at a moment which I had anticipated all my life, my white gown only betrayed my father's death.

Always.

The loft is done with. With a spiritless enthusiasm we try to raise money, to do a play elsewhere, and sooner or later we will succeed. It is not a bad time. It is a time of germination.

November 28, 1955

Julian talks about himself. He is desperate. And I am unable to alleviate his despair.

The fact is, we can say with faith that there is more in life than we can comprehend, and we can live for the mystery. Or we can devote ourselves to love, social change, art, pleasure, the search, the ego and pretend that *it* is a meaning. But seeing the difficulty of the former and the narrowness of the latter . . .

There is no sadness. It is simply so. And as such it does not interest me.

Ambition eats me up, and lusts possess me. But I am not interested.

There is a pattern and a harmony, but I lost sight of them. I have forgotten how to suffer.

I lost my details. It were better to have lost my generalities.

Tonight's reading will be the last performance in the loft. It doesn't make me sad. I'm sad already. Irma got sick and I'm replacing her in the four roles in *Many Loves*, the William Carlos Williams play.

December 4, 1955

Jimmy Merrill sends us $500 to start the theater again. Meanwhile we live with no source of income, excepting $6 or $8 a week from classes.

December 16, 1955

I am bounded by ecstasy and by ennui. There is Lester and there is the world of abstractions.

Lester and death. Lester and art. Lester and time. Lester and home. Lester and daily life. Lester and the world of men. Lester and God.

I made my love a tower from which I survey the world. It holds me up, raises me to a vantage point above the distances between myself and the scenes of the spirit and the senses.

He yields to my touch as a sight yields to the eye that sees it. And therefore he is compared to the light.

We are both in this ecstasy. And the world is a distraction.

But the clear light of reason shines through the illusion. Love is ephemeral, the teachers say, and I listen, unwilling to believe.

My household is a shambles.

Garrick has the chicken pox.

Mother is doing poorly.

There is no money.

We continue to try, without too much encouragement, to further the Living Theatre.

December 29, 1955

The judge simply gave us suspended sentences. He read a lengthy opinion pointing out that since this group consisted of religious and nonreligious persons the issue was not one of freedom of religion. Beliefs, he went on to say, however well-motivated, may lead to actions which are unlawful.

He read in a stumbling manner, but what he read was a reasonable opinion supporting the general view: the view which we hold to be erroneous and by its nature unreasonable.

The judge praised Dorothy at great length, spoke of her kindness, her repute, her devotion, and how he was loathe to impose any sentence upon her. Like Gandhi's judge who wept while he sentenced him. And then I felt that I was on the side of the angels.

December 31, 1955

At year's end.

Julian says, "You played Phèdre. We had a successful season. Did the Goodman play. I had a painting show. . . ."

I listen with respect.

But death is so soon.

And joy consuming.

Sometimes ambition—and even glory—is a shadow receding in the light of a passionate embrace.

Then I cry in a pained voice, "I love you. I love you." And wonder, "Why in a pained voice?"

Mother is horribly ill and in pain. We tend her.

Last night when Julian was out she was in such a state that Nina and Lester and I were frightened.

Here is a conversation that is exactly preserved:

He: "I wish we were old. . . ." Long pause. "Maybe by that time you will have no objection to being happy. . . . Do you really live for one thing only?"

I: "Yes."

He: "That gives you a narrow field."

I: "No, it is catholic and contains all things."

He: "No one thing is that great."

And I wish he would ask me what it is. But I cannot say, "*la gloire*." Even if asked I would not.

He: "Evangeline. . . ."

He called me Evangeline. "I too have lived in Acadia." His head is in my lap and we have so little time.

He: "What are your plans for tomorrow?"

I think to myself, *"La gloire."*

And now it is to be a New Year and I who always wish for new beginnings am to have my wish again.

Nothing holds me back. Nothing prevents me. I make resolves again.

This year I will be thirty.

The house is newly painted and the fresh smell of paint covers old sins with bright colors.

There is sound and laughter. I will soon join it.

1956

January 1, 1956

Caught in the hub of my mother's nightmare. I am nevertheless not unhappy, though I am increasingly sad.

I want *la gloire*. And my mistake is expecting to reach it through others.

January 4, 1956

Mother, in her pain, makes great scenes. Julian is stern with her and now
there is a truce in her favor. No one can oppose her, for her weakness is her
strength and she needs us.

Lester circles me like a constant moon. In him I forget my constant crisis.

Lester tells me that Philip says of this house: "They will destroy you there.
She breaks down everything and everyone."

And Lester said: "Was it because she was looking for me?"

And Philip: "You don't see it."

And Lester: "And I was looking for her."

January 8, 1956

Last night *King Lear*. Orson Welles in a wheelchair, incapacitated by a
broken foot. Majesty but never madness. Viveca Lindfors enraptures me.

Sylvia Short, the Tart of our Picasso play, played Regan, and Bob Fletcher
is playing Edgar. We visit backstage.

January 14, 1956   *Wappinger Falls, N. Y.*

In an old house and at leisure, I still deny myself breathing space.

Dwight Ripley's voluble affection doesn't scare me here.

Every room is full of paintings. My bedroom has Mirós; Julian's bedroom,
a Motherwell, a Pollock, and a Jimmy Ernst. Downstairs are a Tanguy, a Max
Ernst, Picassos, an ivory Hercules without fig leaf, two Gothic cabinets lined
with striped silk from a shirt of George Sand (how do such myths arise?), and
of course Dwight's famous collection of grotesque bird cages. They are dirty
and empty, or worse, tenanted by dusty stuffed birds.

Dwight, whose brilliance only sometimes glimmers through his relentless
chatter—"Darling, it's so tedious, it drives me absolutely frantic"—is kind and
hard and terrible and lovable.

But Rupert Barnaby's gentle intelligence makes a revealing contrast to
Dwight's grossness.

Rupert is a prominent botanist and he looks like one of his dried flowers, a pale and tenuous memorial of a blossoming. In another world, I could have loved such a man.

The conversation last night was a series of battered comparisons: "Such and such is divine, but such and such is so tedious. So and so is absolute heaven, but so and so is such a bore."

The liveliest talk was of Lester. Dwight and Rupert swooned as Julian and I praised his virility.

We visit the greenhouse filled with specimens of rare plants, and Dwight tells us their origins. He calls his plants "she" with the same disdain with which he talks of effeminate men: "Oh, she's an old Portuguese rare old thing."

On my night table a pile of "physique" magazines. In my closet hangs a policeman's billy club.

Dwight says, "It is put to *use*, honey!"

O tempora. O mores. He writes poetry in twelve languages. This afternoon he read some amusing satires to us. I laughed a good deal.

Two nights ago we saw the Kabuki dancers and the red mane and the white mane of the two tiger costumes startled me amid my dark dreams here.

The art of Picasso decorates this country house where winds out of hell blow away the fumes of alcohol.

Yesterday afternoon I read "Manfred" and was disgusted by its lurid mystic nonsense.

There is a room on West End Avenue, 100 miles away, where my mother cries in pain.

Now I must go downstairs to force conversation with good people who can't give or take anymore.

January 17, 1956

Glancing for a moment into Kafka's *Diaries*, I notice with what care K noted the small attributes of his fellow men. Of course, an exaggerated concern with detail is an earmark of paranoia and his affliction no doubt sharpened his perception.

I looked into Thoreau's *Journal* yesterday in a fancy edition at Brentano's. At the drama library, I looked into several actors' diaries, notably Macready's—detailed, boring, interesting.

Today at the American Jewish Congress Chapter meeting at my mother-in-law's house, I will read a few selections from Shakespeare and Auden and Wilder.

I have yet to rehearse, then to teach a class, then the reading, then another class.

Yesterday we saw Howard Schott about drawing up new incorporation papers for the theater. After the Cherry Lane bankruptcy we will need a new corporate name. Howard suggests a membership corporation.

We go to Stamos' opening at Betty Parsons'. Many people going through the same dance in front of the same picture using the same words.

At Dollie Chareau's, the Continental atmosphere.

She greets us in French. Julian responds in French.

Dinner in her tiny dinette, divided from the kitchen by a chintz curtain. The hostess sat in the doorway in order to make space and spoke of her husband's contribution to architecture.

She takes seriously what I think of as play. She believes in culture as a separate phenomenon. She believes simple faith is mysticism, talks a great deal and, to her credit, mostly in praise of people and their art, sympathizing with everything.

January 21, 1956

My ladies' club program: "Shylock: Was he a villain?" "Juliet: Potion scene: A fiery Italian girl"; "Rosetta from *The Age of Anxiety*: Hiding her simple Jewish background from her elegant friends"; "Sabina of *Skin of our Teeth*: There are two kinds of women."

The assurance of being well-received allows one the freedom to act. In these recitals I am freer than on the stage because I know I can please these women, whose aim is to enjoy what I do, not to pass judgment on it. In this way the critic destroys the artist because he makes the work an ordeal.

We visit Nina at Søren's. Pale and sad, she huddles near the stove with Søren's books of mystic lore. She doesn't want to go home but wants to go to live at the Buddhist Temple on Staten Island.

Welles' *Othello* on film. The jealous Moor lost in a maze of arches. Julian says Othello is a domestic tragedy like those we read of in the *Daily News*: "Jealous Husband Strangles Wife in Bed."

January 25, 1956

Tamburlaine the Great. Tyrone Guthrie's company with Anthony Quayle. A big, fierce production—Reinhardt and English surrealism. They rant, they sing, chant, dance, leap. All beside the point of the story of the madness that urges to power and the madness that power urges.

At the *Village Voice*, Ed Fancher has grown himself an editor's beard. He suggests that I write reviews and introduces me to Jerry Tallmer.

I refuse to review Equity Library's *My Three Angels*.

"I could only write why that sort of play should not be done."

J.T.: "That might be a good thing."

Nice people.

Home later. Lack of Lester. L. gave J. five dollars for me. Is it to save or for sweets?

In the evening. Howard Schott's. One feels the tumblers turn in Howard's mind. He likes the connection with Jimmy Merrill. But my heart likes schemers.

As for the theater. We think of names and variations for hours.

"The Living Theatre Associates . . ."

"Living Theatre Productions . . ."

"Living Theatre Company . . ."

Howard favors "Living Theatre Foundation" with a board of trustees. Meanwhile the check from Jimmy Merrill is in the hands of a lawyer named Ulysses S. Grant.

Last night Lester said that he would like to burn the old journals. "Not for the style, but for the content."

By this he means my life.

Lester, like all men who choose actresses, artists, or uncommon women to love, now wishes to turn me into a drab. They pick the most exotic women they can find and try to make them into obedient wives. Lester chooses the word "Oradel" as the symbol of his bourgeois dream home. Oradel is the burial place of my family; thus what represents home to him represents burial to me. He will not succeed with me, but it will be a point of contention.

January 26, 1956

Rooftop Theater. Memories of Piscator's *The Flies* and *Spook Sonata* and *The Aristocrats* as we look over this old auditorium for new possibilities. They have done it over to conform to the endless regulations that are imposed upon Off-Broadway houses. Frances Adler dressing in the basement underneath the stage lingers in my mind like a theater ghost.

February 7, 1956

Bus. Notes on Cleopatra and Lady M.
Study of their images.
Telephone Alan. Russian Tea Room. Tomorrow 2:30.
Chas. Kibbe at Ted Bates Agency:
"An actor's success depends on his salesmanship."
"Above talent."
"Yes, above talent."
NBC Casting. Saw Anderson. Asked nervily to meet Begley. Thursday between ten and ten-thirty.
Ask more often. And ask more easily.
Call Chandler Cowles.
Redgrave: *The Actor's Ways and Means*.
Seligmann's *Mirror of Magic*.
The Encheiridion: Epictetus.
Jung's *Archetypes in Drama*.
Bus. Sleep. Home. Sleep.
M.G.J.L.
Class. Mae Crane is my only student today. We start work on *Anna Christie*. With a parallel of Mae's own story: Mae studied voice, went to Columbia for a master's in musicology, and fell in love with a homosexual composer. . . . Then left it all for "security." And Anna's motives . . . ?

February 8, 1956

I read that Rachel in the sleepwalking scene of *Macbeth* tried to lick the blood from her hands.
Lady Macbeth is more carnal than Cleopatra because for Cleopatra sex is conquest. For Lady Macbeth conquest is sex. She wants Macbeth to be the man she would have been were she a man, and forces her husband to be ruthless. Cleopatra makes of her lover a coward.
As I'm thinking of Cleopatra, I meet Cornell in a fur coolie hat in the elevator at 1270 Sixth Avenue. She says coolly, "It's very beautiful now in the country."
At Dollie Chareau's. European intellectualism. Conversation is a commodity.

At Consuelo Sides'. Rich widows. The Eskimo custom of letting grandma perish in the snow. Talk and talk.

Erick Hawkins: "No regrets. Here there are no might-have-beens. Forget 'should' and 'must.' What you are is here and now this instant."

He doesn't let us talk during class.

February 13, 1956

Gordon Craig on theater art: The makeup mirror deserves a chapter.

Tauroboleum. The theater and the bullfight.

I hate the bullfight because I love the theater. They are incompatible. The actor does not kill the bull, nor take the bull by the horns, he becomes the bull.

February 16, 1956

Bankhead on her first entrance: "I was told to take a streetcar named Desire" gets a derisive, challenging laugh from a disrespectful audience. She fought valiantly, a performance of tiredness and age, with her breath, her body, and her grating and often incomprehensible speech. In the second act she began to win. In the big scenes she always won. The battle was more interesting than the play. Her final scene was triumphant and she was awarded her tremendous ovation at the curtain.

I mention to Julian that it was like the bullfight the way the spectators spurred on the actors. Tennessee Williams at the Puccini Restaurant comes over from an adjoining table to greet Julian.

Julian: "Judith says it was like a bullfight."

T.W.'s face lights. He likes this image and soaks it up visibly like a sponge.

"Yes, yes. Like a bullfight. Like a great last fight, like watching Manolete."

I love the theater because I hate the bullfight.

February 20, 1956

Love, you are as beautiful as though I had created you with my own hands. Do I dispraise God this way?

Praised be God who made me that I may praise you. For the sake of my love, God, redeem the judges who condemn those who are your especial concern.

February 23, 1956

I have a sense of anniversary
and celebrate the solstice
like a heathen
For though they say I lack
a sense of time
I have a sense of season.

On Tuesday, the twenty-first, the signing of the corporate papers for The Living Theatre Productions, Inc. For signatories: Søren and Alan Hovhaness and Howard Schott and Dollie Chareau. While waiting for Dollie we admire for a long time the view from Howard's window, which overlooks half our dear city. The theaters, the cathedral, the river and in the distance, the wastes of New Jersey, the twilight and then the nightfall. At last, Madame Chareau arrives and affixes her name.

So we are a corporation. Again. And anew.

February 29, 1956

The actor and the bullfight.

The ideal prototype for the actress is Pasiphaë, costumed by Daedalus, inside her wooden cow.

A Trojan Cow!

Voltaire:
There are three things that are difficult:
To keep a secret
To suffer an injury
To use leisure.

March 1, 1956

Rupert Barnaby, at Dwight's exhibit, stands in front of a portrait of himself. In the picture an exotic Himalayan plant blossoms from his headgear, accompanied by a botanical description of which every other line is written upside down. The whole a mysterious mandala. At the party afterward at John Latouche's, Rupert and Dwight invite Lester to come with us to Wappinger Falls in April.

We work slowly and persistently on the Living Theatre. Now that we are incorporated, we are about to launch a membership drive.

Lester makes a bold advance to Julian. That will change the atmosphere.

March 6, 1956

Goat—Dionysus—tragedy—goatsong.
The Ram. Daedalus. Mask.
Thespis—solo.
The ritual meaning of the harlequin story.
The social reassurance of folk theater.
Punch and Judy.
18th century purity: (fem.) and bravery (masc.).
Broadway: permissiveness within the mores.
Pageant. Masquerade.

March 7, 1956

Bought a Tiepolo drawing, at an absurdly small price. I spend the evening reframing it.

Dinner at Chambord with Dwight is expensive. Lunch with Dwight at the

Gladstone is dull and social. Lunch with Tobi's Rachele yesterday is lively and pleasurable. We had not time enough to talk.

Saturday at home with Jean Adra, Joachim Streseman, and Alan Hovhaness. Then, a public reading of *Thirty-Love* with music by John Latouche at the B. de Rothschild Foundation; it is done here as well as it can be done and not uninteresting. *Tout le monde* was there and one feels if Denmark's a prison then the whole world's a prison.

And so we make a smaller orbit in which our real life is contained. I said Lester circled me like a moon. But no, Julian and I both circle Lester, whose gravity (though it is lightness) draws us toward his loving nature.

March 9, 1956

Dinner at Herbert Machiz' and John Myers': Irma Hurley, Lionel Abel, and John and Alice Griffin of *Theatre Arts*, Julian, and I. Lionel is brilliant. His intellect asserts itself with audacious oversimplifications which imply that he has already coped with and conquered the subject at hand.

"Intelligence," he says, "is the ability to see what's right in front of your nose."

Tallulah Bankhead calls Herbert while Lionel, Irma, Julian, and I alternately listen on the extension. She is unhappy over a letter from Tennessee Williams to the *New York Times* suggesting that he had shown her how to act. She is planning a retaliatory note and incidentally seeking a ghost-writer for her memoirs. Herbert suggests Waldemar Hansen.

March 16, 1956

I found a curious volume of Sacher-Masoch's *Die Liebe des Platon*, a love story between two men, one of them disguised as a woman. It has peculiar pseudo-Beardsley illustrations, and the story is told in the hero's shameless letters to his mother. I'd like to translate this odd mixture of prurience and prudery.

March 19, 1956

The vernal blizzard.

Mother tyrannizes by her helplessness and anger. We are happy despite. Lester is a solace. Julian leans on him and subtly imitates him.

Julian's desire centers around our trio and anything, work or pleasure, that interferes with that, seems like lost time to him. They are both annoyed by my ambition. But love holds us in a strong bond and I am stronger, too, than I have ever been.

Night. The city is under deep snow drifts.

When Dwight first met Lester he said to him, "You are the image of Jim Agee." It is reasonable that I should not notice it. Lester hates memory, tries to deny history, and is jealous.

He gave me a little heart-shaped candle on the day of the trial. It lights our nights of love; I pray that it lasts a while.

I've started work on the translation of *Die Liebe des Platon*—to be called *Platonic Love*.

I've done a rough version of Act II for *Gautama* and changed much of Act I. Alan is in Boston.

March 29, 1956

There is pain in the house, agony and distemper, but love soothes me.

Mother's hysteria has calmed, but Julian is irritated by her constant demands and Lester balks and grows sulky when I play cards with her. Then I must be as patient with them as I am with her. I cannot reconcile them to her. Nor can I desert her. The complexities of the Passover ritual add to the anxiety.

Easter 1956

I pursued my life's geography this morning, to be rewarded with a kind of peace. Julian and Lester have gone off to work, leaving me alone after a night of love in an idyllic little apartment on Mott Street that we borrowed from Dick Mayes on his wedding night.

Only once was the peace broken, by a painful headache that attacked, then faded. The shadow of my mother's agony.

Lester hates my migraines and reproaches me for them.

Lester hates my journals. They imply that the events in them are still incomplete. He wants me to burn them (i.e., my bridges behind me) so as to complete them.

I set my course by the landmarks of my history, for I love monument, memorial, anniversary, and poem, cherish inscription, symbol, and ritual drama.

In the doorway of St. Patrick's Old Cathedral on Mott Street is a fresco of naked sinners burning in pink hell-fire; white-robed angels around the throne of Jesus, pour thick red drops, which I presume to be Christ's blood, from golden beakers down upon the burning souls.

Then I turned into Prince Street where Lou's house faces the north side of the cathedral. Here I counted the years since Easter Eve. I think they are five, between me and all that ancient stuff: the pagan egg and the drunken musician who, thinking he was Orpheus, led me into, not out of, hell.

For Lester I will be simple. He hates the mysteries. "Don't give me that shit about Easter."

Neither does he care that we came out of Egypt. He hates the bread of affliction.

For Lester is a Mason and that is the only ritual he does not despise.

The Masons' mythology is of the building of the temple, by secret numbers and geometry, cutting stone when cane and thatched hut were still all there were of dwelling places.

Pythagoras, too, worked in secret, and what he taught openly was the shell of what he kept hidden.

When the mysteries were dispersed and only the remnants remained, the Masons held on to their solemn rites. Officially organized in the Renaissance, they trace their origins to Egypt and the East, to Ishmael and Pharaoh, from whom we were delivered.

The Orphic rites included men and women. Orpheus was not torn apart by the Bacchantes because he was the soul of music, but because he was the tutelary genius of homosexuality. It is noteworthy that he could charm the beasts of the field but could not dissuade the women from tearing him apart.

Julian remarks that Lester, with his black curls, resembles our image of Dionysus. (Ariadne's black lover, whom Rexroth caused Phaedra to see reflected in a cup of wine: "People who see them go crazy," she says).

But Lester, thinking of Bacchus in his fat, satyr aspect, rejects the resemblance.

Lou, on the other hand, was offended that Julian did not choose to paint him as Orpheus.

The musician Lou Harrison is not Orpheus and the Mason Lester is not Dionysus. But it is not by coincidence that these archetypal stories are reenacted, for they were acted first out of our primal needs and express our lives and so we reenact them because they are the fabric of life itself—no, the pattern.

This is the five-year path around the corner.

Like the wandering of my people in the desert. In the Haggadah, we are admonished to say, "It is I myself whom the Lord brought out of Egypt."

On Bleecker Street I walked past Rachel Falk's restaurant. Once a strictly kosher local haven for the pious, it was owned by my best friend's parents. Here Ray and I played every day. And twenty years later, though the exterior bears a ghastly sign reading Hero Sandwiches, there is not the slightest change inside.

I drank coffee out of the same thick cup. I didn't dare ask to see the backyard full of the debris of the surrounding factories, where I once persuaded Rachel to try to plant a garden. We cleared a square of space of layers of refuse and found a patch of ashes and soil into which we poked beans and potatoes and other growing things. But every day the factories, whose high windows entirely surrounded the yard, would dump their wastes down on our agriculture. Many times we cleared it away, but after a while we gave up and forgot our garden and went back to the Broadway Central for our game.

This game which we called "The Game" was the enactment of fantasies. It might have been cops and robbers, or playing house, except that our plots were sophisticated, sometimes sordid and cruel, sometimes sensual, historical, or mythical. It depended on what movies we had seen. I tended to play the Man or the Queen despite (or because of?) Ray's advantage in size and age.

Now, when it is arduous to improvise, I think of the freedom of The Game and its abandoned preadolescent sexuality. I did not yet know how intercourse was consummated and yet we were setting scenes in brothels, unperturbed by our ignorance. About to be slain, I might look up and shout through the empty ballrooms, "Aha, here come the horsemen of my brother's army to rescue me!"

I looked into the hotel lobby today and saw it spoiled, the murals gone, the giant staircase covered over. I didn't go in to mourn my childhood paradise.

In those days when I was unhappy I thought of the future glory which alone would compensate me. Now, in the season in which I will reach my thirtieth year, I have no glory, no fame, no victory, only a moment on Mott Street where it is so sweet that Lester says he expects to find apple branches growing out of the walls: only this to compensate me for my consuming unhappiness.

Alone I still play The Game. No it is solitaire and I am ashamed of it.

Voltaire was right. At seventeen a man makes plans to build a temple; at seventy he begins to gather materials for a shack. And it is enough. *Dayenu.*

I thought to have lunch with Rachele and went to her office at N.Y.U. Between Rachel Falk and Rachele Thomas there was interposed the other Rachel, La Félix, whose picture fascinated me in my father's Brockhaus Lexicon. After his death, the day we abandoned his office to the creditors, I was told to take anything I wanted. I was fourteen and chose to tear out my favorite pictures from the Brockhaus volumes, among them two portraits of Rachel, one of them in the character and costume of Phèdre.

The rare and valuable books of philosophy and theology were left on the shelves. What did a fourteen-year-old know of rarity and value and philosophy and theology?

Yet I took the significant thing.

Here in the fountain these events took place:

First I cried out for pennies to the passengers of the double-decker buses when I was still young enough to appear unashamedly in only a pair of panties among my contemporaries.

Later I watched Garrick play in this pool on hot summer days.

Here were also countless dawns and twilights.

The Cherry Lane days when this was our vacation from the theater. Debauched nights on the benches waiting to score weed. Industrious nights at the chess tables, translating *Ubu*. The night I met Jim Agee and made my vow alone in the circle. And how it is all too late now. "All gone, all done, dead dawns, and wan."

The childhood play. The adolescent adventure. The artistic endeavor.

There, during the annual art show, on the steps under the church's square tower, I sold my pastel drawings—a landscape; a self-portrait called *Judith, the principal's daughter*; a charcoal scottie named Fala, after Roosevelt's dog, whose custom it was to be walked in this park. And my sign reading Judith Malina, Artist, Age 10 (and the next year, Age 11).

And all those I have loved, I have walked here with them. And Easter morning with Lou.

And today again, the brightness that makes clear outlines blazons this time into memory.

Not "revisited," for I was never away.

April 10, 1956

The lessons of Easter Week on Mott Street.
Lester says: "Heaven."
I prefer the word "Eden."
We three, naked, playing, eating, laughing, loving. Or Lester playing the radio and cursing the static, Julian asleep, or frying an egg, or telling hilarious stories, while I sit in a wicker chair, finishing my translation of Sacher-Masoch's *Platonic Love*, smoking a Chinese pipe that I bought at the other end of Mott Street for only twenty-five cents. It has a yellow metal bowl and mouthpiece set on a foot-long bamboo reed tinted red brown and painted with concentric circles.

Lately I can feel the drive like the application of a whip.

Whatever I touch becomes a straw to clutch at.

April 15, 1956

Yesterday at a film forum, Joe Campbell and Parker Tyler speak of myth and film, and Maya Deren of the god of the dead in Haiti and the ritual in drama.

Joe Campbell says of Freud: "He describes what might be called the 'family romance,' that ghastly little story about poppa, momma, and this little midget. This is a reflection of the larger religious myth of God the poppa and God the momma. And the Judeo-Christian religion has barred God the momma. And that's why we're in trouble. Where is she?"

I try to hide my enthusiasm from the jealous Lester.

Joe apologizes that he did not bring me the pine cone he had promised me from Japan.

April 30, 1956

I enter the last month of my "twenties" full of rash resolutions, maxims, goals.

Play out the shadow, I say to myself. But I imagine that this shadow is not a shadow but a prince like the Beast in *Beauty and the Beast*.

As Paul says: "When one is happy, then the *real* problems emerge." So it is now. I wrestle with an angel for my soul, like Jacob; both contenders desire to lose, but both are too noble to throw a fight and fight all the more avidly.

> Wisdom begins
> Where the loser wins.

Last night I said to Julian, "I'm not interested in anything but virtue."
And he said in a melancholy tone, "I'm not interested in anything either."

May 7, 1956

Wrestling like Jacob for my soul, O virtue and desire, shall I leave off praising the one, or enjoying the other? Now I am fatally entwined.

I lie abed with my books. Graves' *Mythology*, Wooley's *Ur of the Chaldees*, *Finnegan*. Lord Raglan's *The Hero*, and a dual biography, *The Marquis and the Chevalier* by Cleugh, a sensationalist, but the only book on Sacher-Masoch in the public libraries or, so far as I can find, in the bookstores.

In the afternoon I'll work on *Platonic Love*.

Every night we have gone to plays and afterward to coffee or parties. Every night the same people. Of whom I care only for John Cage, the warm and mad and unquenchable, with his hearty, heartless grin and the look of his eyes that should be but are not full of tears. A blond model with short hair sits on his lap and asks him, "And what do you do?" He replies, "I compose music but mostly I'm a mushroom identifier." She bursts into laughter.

Yesterday, when I asked him whether he had ever made an error with dangerous toadstools, he said with the same grin, "You only make an error once."

Knowing his love of chance, I wonder whether he is making an outrageous demand that fate prove that it side with him. Is this the heroic demand?

Cleugh says of Masoch: "He was a lover of humanity and therefore one of its predestined victims."

Also at these evenings, the rebellious Bob Rauschenberg, who is so talented and who flirts with me. But he is not serious. And David Tudor, and virtuous Remy, and Bentley at the plays, unyielding behind his peevish beard.

May 11, 1956

Such quiet. Life is at a hush. If I burn at all, it is like a smoldering coal, no flame.

Paul warned me that my busyness is an evasion of the confrontation with myself. I shed garment after garment. The dreaded exposure threatens me but I will survive it. Without desiring the fruit of the action. But what then impels us? I am almost immobile. Sometimes it feels like annihilation, but again and again I survive.

It is either an end or a beginning. And for the chance that it is the beginning, I risk the danger of its being the end.

May 15, 1956

"This room," says Julian, "is like a room described by Cocteau."

I begin a new notebook with a description of this room:

Very small: an immediate consciousness of the class problem, that because it was designed for a servant it deserves no architectural aesthetic. A door. A window. Another door to the tiny lavatory. A washbasin and a radiator pipe.

A Chinese embroidery hangs above my head. I don't know its history, value, or period.

On a red silk panel the empress appears, sitting in the center of a Turquoise pavilion in a pink and gold robe. Forty-eight figures of which no two resemble one another surround her. Their faces express a mildness of temperament that Western art always fails at imitating. On either side of the pavilion stand seven musicians playing flutes and cymbals. No one is doing mundane things; they are engaged in courtly activities. In the upper right-hand corner I see what I take to be a monk, followed by a servant holding a banner. He sits in his yellow robe cross-legged upon a small ox. *I Ching* trigrams are embroidered in gold on his robe. He displays a gold plate emblazoned with the yin-yang. This is possibly his beggar's bowl. In the opposite corner another yellow-robed figure sits on the back of a great white bird. He holds a flower in his lap. His head is larger than the other heads. He might be the Lord Buddha hovering above the scene.

The figures are embroidered on the red silk except for the heads, which have been sewn on separately. Four of them are missing and in their stead are Chinese characters.

All around are designs, a whole universe that I look at in the mornings when I lie here and wrestle with my soul on the untidy bed still ardent with a night and sometimes a morning of love.

Sometimes I catch glimpses of the tapestry when I am embraced and embracing, and then, quite without thought, divorced from idea, its light joins the brilliance of feeling and form.

Next to the tapestry hangs my guitar with its sober, raw wood, white pegs and metal strings, waiting for me to work on *Gautama's House*. I strum and sing the words to an irrelevant tune which gives me an idea of their singability.

One string, broken by a student in my acting class, dangles down into the love light, the candle Lester made using the remains of the red heart-shaped candle. Now the wick is gone and either he will replace it or it will gather dust indefinitely here by the bedside.

Next to it is a pile of five books and my Chinese pipe and the Kodak film can for smokes.

Behind me is the black desk, which forms a headrest for the bed. On it Jung's *Psychological Reflections* to help me wrestle, my last completed journal, the *World Almanac*, a rare edition of Sacher-Masoch's *Aufstand in Gent*, *The Devil and God Almighty* by Sartre, a *Yale French Review*, *Finnegan*, and a clock that says I cannot describe more because it is time to do what has to be done. To do it before I have finished what I began. To break off in the middle. To meet Coleridge's person from Porlock. To have miscalculated again. To have been able neither to describe the window, the Tiepolo, nor the essential poetry, the realms toward which these are only the means of transport, or the bed.

Yesterday, *Hedda Gabler* played by Jane White as a recognizable portrait of the plight of the married woman. Beyond the problems of physical need and economic necessity, how shall we live? Debauch like Brack? Immerse ourselves in studies of the Middle Ages like Tesman? Destroy ourselves like Lovberg and Hedda, or shall we breed and live in the hope that after several generations something as yet unforeseeable will occur?

Evening. The B. de Rothschild Foundation. Three scenes from *Il Ritorno d'Ulisse in Patria*, a Monteverdi opera performed in America for the first time. Half-sleeping; Ulysses and Penelope and Minerva float through my mind.

Then Geselher Klebe's *Roman Elegies* with Goethe's rhetoric. I clutch Julian's hand and want to go—out into the warm air of Rome or the ruined streets of Pompeii and fall on a heap of historical stones to be ravished by a surviving god who haunts the ruins.

But I am on a hard chair hearing a trio for violin, cello, and piano which is very good and does not interest me in the least.

After the concert, the first thing Paul says is how he hates the Goethe elegy: "Goethe is so great when he is great, but he shouldn't write things like this." And then he adds: "These Germans!" And then, in a quieter tone: "He swallows all of antiquity and then he complains it rejects him."

"Yes, yes," I said, thinking it an inappropriate reflection on the Elegies.

"But who asked him to swallow it? Who asked him?" And he stamped his foot in childish petulance. We were walking to the car to go for coffee. Paul and Sally and Kurt Stone, a musicologist who is an authority on Monteverdi. Stone is very mild and says that Paul is a very mild person.

I am overjoyed that Paul is friendly to me again. Perhaps the storm is weathered.

I've dreamed about him, dreams of affection, sensual but not sexual, in which he forgives me and this forgiveness remedies all.

We go to Geiger's Café, where Kurt discusses Monteverdi under the violin of the *Kappelmeister*, who grates out the old sentimental numbers atrociously.

The conversation is between two scholars. It is not music that they discuss when they discuss music, but certain universal attributes.

I think back to Adolph Giehoff, my first lover, whom I met here.

And further back to when I was six years old and crawled under the tables every Sunday afternoon when my parents met their friends for *Kaffee und Kuchen*.

Today is Mother's birthday and we celebrate.

Lester is drunk and lies sprawled on the front room floor. "But," said Alcibiades, "inside this satyr is an image of the god."

May 16, 1956

Hedda Gabler is only a latter-day Medea, and Tesman is, like Jason, a betrayer, but so insensitive have these men become through the years between Jason and Tesman, that Jason seems a hero in the light of Tesman's bungling. It is clearer in *The Doll's House*, where Helmar's guilt is specific.

Tonight is the first anniversary of Jim's death. I will not sentimentalize the occasion.

He never wore that cold mask, never once; learn *that* from him.

But he was so much an Eilert Lovberg, with his manuscripts destroyed in the fire; his best work never, never, never born. How then am I to remember not to hurry?

May 17, 1956

Garrick's seventh birthday. A family party. Garrick is adult and restrained. All the mothers try to be informal and charming and no one succeeds.

A day of anniversaries. Memorial service. Temple Ansche Chesed.

The prayers, recited in the tone of the rabbinical seminary, seemed distant. Until the Torah was taken down among the congregation and people kissed their fingers and stretched out their hands to touch it, or touch the fringe of the *talis* to the white-robed, crowned scroll, and a mother stretches out her little one's reluctant hand to the Torah and then brings it to his lips. The custom is more folkloric than ritual and verges on superstition, but I felt I was participating in their reality.

How hard a task is demanded by a religion which allows no concrete symbols, no saints or images! To what shall the mind cling when abstraction seems so much like emptiness? It's easier to recognize an idol than a precept.

The prayers for the dead are so tactfully worded that I suspect a modern adaptation.

I had two thoughts during the memorial service:

The first, that I had forgotten on June fifteenth how proud my father would have been, and how well he would have understood our action.

The second, that when I saw Jim for the last time—it was at the last performance of *Orpheus*—he assured me, "No matter how long we don't see each other, I'll never grow cold and distant toward you."

I wonder whether it's true.

But nothing is for nothing. Nothing is wasted. And therefore nothing is forgotten.

May 19, 1956

To visit Fritz Perls and Laura. He wishes to build an Off-Broadway theater, as a real estate investment. We suggest several possibilities, including the Japanese Gardens. The talk is of large sums of money. Of course his domineering personality and his personal views are frightening in terms of a collaboration. There is something distinctly unbelievable in all this.

Laura in a spring green dress serves coffee with rum. She shows me the jewelry her daughter is making while the men discuss the cost of the installation of plumbing facilities in a Second Avenue location.

Some of Fritz's theater ideas derive from Germanic taste and some are in the same spirit in which we work.

We suggest Frederick Kiesler as architect for the project.

May 20, 1956

We photograph the loft theater as record and memento of days past.

It is a leave-taking; as yet I see no ghosts, not even Phèdre's. It is only a lit proscenium platform before me with the set for *The Young Disciple* still intact and the curtains still bearing the spatter marks of *Ubu Roi*.

Time is a flat plain on which we are small winds rippling the tops of the grasses, thinking ourselves whirlwinds containing the voice of God.

Today we went to Inwood Park with Garrick, and Julian showed us the glacial potholes and explained how over the aeons the melting ice caused these geological phenomena. There were Indian caves—small and uncomfortable homes they must have been, and unlikely shelters against the Manhattan winter.

Garrick could not quite believe that Julian and I remembered the last Indians who were allowed to live in Inwood Park. They were regarded more as curiosities than as inhabitants of their rightful land. They had a small hut in a wooded section.

I recall an old woman who sold souvenirs: moccasins, fake wampum, postcards. But what ages her wrinkled face conjured up!

"Were they wild?" asked Garrick. "Did they paint their faces?"

Julian is reading to me. Spinoza's *Ethics*.

I am reading Darwin's *Descent of Man* and *Sexual Selection*.

Kiesler agrees to work on the theater project. The money Fritz proposed is not enough to build a total theater and Kiesler suggests renovating a garage, a movie house, or a loft. He discourages the Japanese Gardens.

May 22, 1956

The marvelous warmth of the first real spring day is appreciated the more because it comes so late.

Tobi asks me to work with him on Shakespeare scenes for an audition. We do some *Hamlet* and *Richard III*.

Tobi says, and it is so startlingly true: "You did not play Phèdre, you played Rachel."

May 26, 1956

The breakup of our theater. The time has finally come for us to move everything out. And as I tear up the boards and extricate the nails that I and my friends only a short time ago drove in, my sense of anniversary does not let me forget that it was a year ago that *Phèdre* opened.

And where tonight I stand in workclothes tearing apart the stage, I stood in gold and red velvet, and crowned.

But I'm happier now.

June 1, 1956

We look at theater locations. Julian points out that I like every one and it's true that I see every place as a potential theater and the image is as strong as my desire to realize it immediately.

At John Cage's concert. The big piece for four pianos, played by John, Grete Sultan, Maro Ajemian, and David Tudor, is a mustering of heretofore unheard overtones and undertones.
Everyone in the audience has seen our plays and we have seen their pictures, dances, concerts, lectures, books, soirées, openings, mailings, posters, crafts, songs, parties.

June 4, 1956

It is my thirtieth year to heaven.
When I complain of how hard I work, Lester says, "Don't complain. You're dedicated."
It's like childbirth, the fortress of despair that is creative pain.
I don't allow myself to revel in it because I think it's sacrilegious, but as an artist, I must give myself beyond myself, and reach out into something external to myself, and be it.

June 6, 1956

At our birthday party the subject matter is the superhuman while everyone struggles to approximate humanity.
Glenn Lewis talks of mathematics, cybernetics, and the incredible feats of his superb superhuman and subhuman "machine."
We drive Garrick to visit his little friend, Steven Stuchin, in the country. He is still enamored, though it is more than a year since Steven moved out of our neighborhood. His loyalty is such that no one else has ever been considered as a replacement for his best friend.
Then we drive to Cedar Park and converse in the clichés of the cemetery.
Under the palisades, at the ferry slip, we meet Paul Goodman, George Dennison, and Jerry Raphel and drink coffee and weave tales about our friends till the world becomes an intimate family affair.
Yesterday I met Tobi, accidentally, on the street. We romped like children. What have I really learned for all my wrestling?
As soon as I've learned something, I forget that I ever didn't know it, therefore I seem never to learn.
We meet Kiesler at his studio. While he instructs a young architect in his informal maestro manner, we wander among the paraphernalia of his studio penthouse, a mixture of Bauhaus purity and contemporary clutter.
We go with him to 3rd Street to look at the old Cleon Throckmorton Studio, with the hope that his genius will discern a way to remodel it, but it's discouraging. He says a theater on the second story is certainly illegal. Is it? The tenant below says many groups have tried and failed to get it licensed.

To Fritz Perls'.

June 7, 1956

Fritz seems interested in buying the property for $60,000! And he speaks of an additional $5,000 to $10,000 for renovation. This gives us hope that we will be able to license the premises because we'll have the finances to repair violations. Kiesler is not too well-informed on this. We'll have an estimate made.

June 10, 1956

At the 4th Street Theater we see *Uncle Vanya*, a play stricken with the emptiness of life. I am sad without being moved. Not because the play is bad, but because it is good.

Yesterday we drove to New Jersey to bring my mother to Mrs. Adel's country place for a few days. There, as in Uncle Vanya's, there is the delusion of peace. And when this delusion is destroyed, what remains?

Mother talked about accepting the delusion as "the true harmony of all things."

The wave of rebellion called juvenile delinquency is the cry of the kids that nothing in our world seems worth their aspirations.

Another gloomy production, Julie Bovasso in *The Maids*.

She is a good actress and the play is stunning, but this production is less poetical than psychological, and the meaning disappears.

June 17, 1956   *Wappinger Falls, New York*

Across the pond Lester and Julian are lying on a lawn listening to music, and behind them the hill on which the rock garden is laid rises like a painted backdrop of subtle colors.

We play as we did this morning when we climbed the apple tree, happier, far happier than children.

But Dwight and Rupert are not playful, for they conceded the game and are now forlorn losers, tediously playing out their hands.

Rupert, the gentle one, submits to fate, seems to be part of an eternal process, like the bud, blossom and withering of one of his plants, whereas the caustic one yields neither to this world nor to the next.

There are photo albums full of castles on the Riviera, and there we see the dashing boys, the millionaire from America and his English pal, as chic as they come. But they were naughty, and danced past the boundaries laid by their closeted set, until one by one the doors closed. And they fled to America.

An air of frivolity pervades the house. A frivolity that never for a moment hides the disgust and despair.

Dwight pretends to rule here as in a palace. Rupert cooks and keeps house and "takes care of him." Occasional friends come up and Dwight paces the floor and talks a rapid barrage of deviltry, telling over and over a few stories in which he refers to a half-dozen people as "all New York."

Yet he expects to be seen through. He expects us to admire his real intellect and to understand his suffering.

He punctuates his speech with schizophrenic patterns, spelling out words, abbreviating three-syllable words to one, using puns, obscenities, foreign phrases, all at a fast clip.

This weekend, his blissful *agonia* is inflicted by Lester's rampant masculinity.

What compassion can be felt for the *flagellante*, whose shrieks of pain instruct his paid Master to strike harder and pronounce his pleasure.

One can pity him, but not for the pain of the whip, for the whip is the least of his pains, the pain chosen to obliterate the unchosen, deeper pain.

As once, when I was suffering from my migraines, I pressed a handful of tacks in my hand so as to experience the pain in my head less sharply.

He is a good host and we are in fact happy here.

Last week I bought a drawing "attributed" to Michelangelo at an auction. It is a set of three fragments that depict the arms, shoulders, and legs of a muscular male nude, toughly penned on brown-tone paper.

The night before, Lester went to Harlem and negotiated for $160. We celebrated his homecoming with a triumphal ceremony and have been celebrating ever since.

One night, a year ago, I looked out the barred window of Bellevue, and one sight only moved me—the lovers who were free.

June 20, 1956

To the Limelight Café for the *Village Voice* presentation of the Obies, the Off-Broadway awards. I applaud especially for Julie Bovasso and for Lionel Abel.

I have a strong partisan feeling that *The Young Disciple* is really the best play of this season, but *Absalom* is a good, serious, poetic work and Julie is a good, serious, poetic actress.

Bobs Blossom sat next to me and we talked about directing. And I talk of the ritual roots of the theater in my private metaphor.

Bobs says: "I'm talking about theatricality and you are telling me about a mystique." Yes.

June 22, 1956

John Cage calls to suggest that Paul Williams might finance a theater for us that would have a stage large enough for John and Merce's concerts.

The Rooftop is mentioned as an autumn possibility and there is talk of building. Williams is an architect.

June 26, 1956

Sunday. In a yellow-brick apartment house in the Bronx whose second-story windows look out on a cemetery, we meet with Lester's parents. They are the epitome of their world. And their conventionality radiates ancient wisdom and ancient warmth.

They are the Chinese plowmen who say: "So long as the rainfall is good what care I who rules the nation?"

The mother is pleased with us. Lester has nice friends now. He works steady and not on those dangerous jobs in the shipyards, coming home with steel splinters in his eyes—what she calls "rusty eyes"—and when Lester and I are out of the room the father says to Julian: "He used to drink terrifically."

We drink grape juice and go on to the beach.

June 27, 1956

In Stony Point with John Cage and the Williamses. They have built there an idyll out of the theories of Paul Goodman, and the Shakers and the anarchists. They have built themselves houses on the hill made of stone and plywood, corrugated metal and glass.

John lives in a room attached to a wooded hill in his simplicity. No furniture. On the floor, spread out to dry, the myriad mushrooms which he has collected. The "oyster mushrooms," cooked in wine, are served for dinner. All the food is highly spiced.

John has poison ivy.

We talk only of business. No gossip. No aesthetics. But his immediacy is in itself aesthetic.

July 1, 1956   *Pound Ridge, New York*

Mourning in advance my own demise, I gather strawberries in the woods. Then angry, and Lester and I quarrel. Then calm and quiet.

A clearing in a birch grove with a stone lean-to and a fireplace that looks like an altar.

Lester tends the fire and cooks. White birches lean the way the wind has bent them. And I want to lean with the wind. Again and again I try and again and again I ask myself, why do I refuse to lean with the wind?

July 11, 1956   *Rodanthe, Cape Hatteras, North Carolina*

The cape is an endless beach. Wrecked derelict ships stand as monuments to the sea's sovereignty. The terrible ocean whose roaring breakers are vast jaws biting down on the land.

Beyond the beach are dunes with their sensuous slopes. I am sitting on one now, near the cabin where we live, while the sun takes his pleasure in me.

July 12, 1956   *Rodanthe, Cape Hatteras, North Carolina*

Lester frightens me by swimming out too far. Everything here frightens me.

I feel too strongly my kinship with the sea. My fear of drowning, which I take to be a desire to submerge into that bottomless primeval matter, only to rise like the Cyprian, Apollo's sister, out of the sea, like the sun.

And the night is moonless and starry, with winds near to hurricane strength blowing the sharp sand like gusts of stinging needles into our faces.

I am terrified of the enormity of this which cannot be mastered. We hide in houses to forget it; no, to postpone remembering it.

We climb the 265 steps to the top of the Cape Hatteras lighthouse, the tallest in the land. It is painted in a dramatic black and white spiral. A strong wind frightens me. I seem unable to spend a day here without terror.

Along the beach, every few miles, lies a wrecked ship, its deck and mast rusting among the elements.

Chicamacomico was the Indian name of this village. The family that rents out the cabins has adopted it for their inn to keep the name alive but no one around here remembers what it means.

We play cards.

Make love.

Walk.

Smoke.

Make love.

Sleep.

I read *Damocles* to Lester and Julian. It stands up, but I wouldn't write that way now.

Before we left I wrote, after all these years, the poem about the San Remo.

At an amusement park I want to take photographs in one of the coin machines, but Lester says, "No, someday I'd look at that photograph and feel bad. I don't want to make memories."

How afraid he is to grow old.

Perhaps that's why he isn't afraid of the sea.

July 17, 1956   *New York*

At the Warwick Hotel in a room full of crones for a movie. A collection of age and failure. I, among them, prematurely uglied, am cast as an extra in a film I don't even know the name of.

Before we got into this Greyhound bus that takes us to location on the Lower East Side, I learned what Lester meant when he describes the "shape up" at the docks where some are chosen to work and some are sent away. We were lined up in our costumes while three men with clipboards came in and pointed: "This one. That one. Her. Her."

At Orchard and Rivington, we are surrounded by those whom we are trying to imitate. We stood under a huge banner that said Jimmy Walker for Mayor. The director stood on a ladder and shouted; we cheered as directed.[20]

July 18, 1956

We look over the Nut Club[21] on Sheridan Square. Julian budgets weekly and monthly costs. Merce and John beam at the prospect. But Fritz balks at anything short of ownership of the building. So we are at an indecisive point again.

July 20, 1956

The siren, like the world in pain, screams unendingly and still endures.

From the window here I still see many people on the streets not yet taking shelter.

But Dorothy and Ammon and the others expect a year's sentence. "What's a year?" says Dorothy on the phone. They are in Washington Square Park now and I would that I were with them.

But I can't risk arrest with Mother so sick and so dependent on us.

The streets now in silence after the screams. No traffic noises of any kind. Suddenly I hear the birds in Riverside Park.

Now a policeman comes and orders lingerers off the street. The people go into houses as he directs them with his club.

May Dorothy and the others who are resisting accomplish their cause without being punished.

This is a deadly silence.

It is made to frighten us.

The all-clear.

Evening. Centre Street. Here they are, prisoners in this cold modernity. We saw them tonight on television going into the patrol wagon like early Christians in the hands of Centurions.

July 25, 1956

Merce says the sight lines at the Nut Club are inadequate for a dancer. In view of the high price it seemed there had to be an end to this project anyway.

Now we stand nowhere.

My atmosphere is changing somewhat—rarer, of a light blue-violet hue, but very bright and piercing.

We went to court and after a long line of vagrants and assault and theft cases, our friends were released on bail of $100 a head (why not like cattle?). Ammon and Dorothy were cheerful, thanks to a polite, straightforward judge. Greenewalt was on hand, and Bayard Rustin, in charge of his imaginary army, while Arthur Brown clutched a valise containing $8,000 in cash for the bail.

Dorothy and I kissed when we met in the complaint room.

July 26, 1956

All night we listen to the news of the collision of the *Andrea Doria* and the *Stockholm* sixty miles off Nantucket. The terrible sea.

July 31, 1956

"Whatever a man does in reality he himself becomes": Jung.

Is the theatrical reality defined by the performer's action, or does the reality of the performance define her action? In the theater, as in the dream, as the surrealists discovered, the contradictory realities are woven by the actor in the single fabric of her art, a never-ending process of becoming.

In this hospital room, surrounded by suffering, I notice that the sufferers are more passive than the onlookers, for being victims they have no choice. The terrible comfort of having no choice.

I want to say, "It is unbearable," but I find that I am bearing it and that they are bearing it and I remember that it has always been borne and that it always will be borne.

Last night we saw Garbo's *Camille* again and I cried at the romantic death. With it was *The Quiet One*, with Jim's eloquent poem of narration (how he would hate to hear me call it a poem), and I cried at his words about longing.

But here in the face of the hardest facts there is nothing but the coldness of the knowledge that it must be bearable and that anything, including tears, that would make it less easy to bear is superfluous.

August 7, 1956

The sameness and difference of days.

Yesterday was Lester's birthday. I gave him a ring with an ivory and ebony yin-yang; Julian gave him a recording of *The Magic Flute*. We ate marrons glacés, smoked, and made love. Same and different.

August 12, 1956

I am clinging to something with a grip that destroys me, but I cannot let go. I don't know what will befall if I let go, except that it's disastrous. Nor do I know why it is so important that I do so.

Pain and disease groan and shout their complaints in accompaniment to our laughter. Yet what can we do but take the joy, knowing what waits whether we take joy or sobriety.

My mother's agony and the deaths of friends. John Latouche's funeral in the Little Church Around the Corner—a crowd of theater people, an almanac of his orbit.

Then yesterday in the Museum of Modern Art, John Button tells us of the deaths of Jackson Pollock and Bunny Lang. Pollock the night before in a car crash, Bunny in the hospital of cancer.

The actor's priestly function is to make an identification with every one in every case, and to communicate this psychic sympathy.

The actor's craft is to create an image of the perfect action. In performing an action for which her gift has equipped her, she communicates the reality of the action to the spectator so as to enlarge the action from the specific to the universal.

The actor's art is to transform herself and the spectator from being the object of this action into being a participant in all action.

Enlarging here also means condensing into the center. Because the more personal, direct, and internal the movement, the greater the reality. As though a globe were to expand (out from the center) the more deeply one pierced toward the center.

In the actor's terms: The deeper I can pierce the personal reality of the moment, the closer I get to the broadest and most all-embracing action.

The way in is the way out.

August 16, 1956

Rachele tells me on the telephone that she and Tobi were married in March.

She has converted to Judaism and is pregnant. They were married in a garden in California.

August 21, 1956

Yesterday I lunched with Alan who told me of his pleasure in his new wife, Phyllis. Also talked much of Mozart.

How he, Mozart, struck the balance between the formal and the feelingful; I called it the classical and the romantic. But he said these mean different things in the musical jargon.

And speculations on Man, Masonry, Music, and Mathematics. Alan says Masonry's "a good allegory."

To Rachele's and found the door locked.

Going down the stairs I thought of Rachele's conversion to our hard faith and envied for a moment the pleasure of the Catholic for the burden-easing rituals of confession and absolution. As I came to the bottom of the stairs, I was met by an old Italian priest who lives in the front parlor of this brownstone. I gave him a note for Rachele.

Father Capitani insisted that I come in to see his studio. He has a parlor full of landscapes: Lake Como by moonlight ("I am very much interested in the moonlight"), Verdi's house, Venice, Rome ("From Roma comes all the great art, all the great *musica*"). Many photographs of opera stars who have bought his paintings. (Who could resist the sentimental moonlit scenes of Italy painted by an aged painter-priest?) Sometimes as he talked he forgot what language he spoke; lapsing into Italian, he spoke at great length of Europe and the Vatican and *"personaggi preminenti."*

Finally a large, unpleasant man in a gray overcoat burst into the room and the little priest all but pushed me out of the room whispering, "Come back, I like to talk to intelligent artists. Come back. Visit Father Capitani."

I went to Max Richards' office and was cast as a "long-haired Village intellectual type" for a film called *Bachelor Party.*

August 23, 1956

Movie job.

An enormous crowd gathered on Greenwich and 10th. Lights strung up on the houses as for a festa, but unearthly bright. We worked from eight P.M. to five A.M. just walking up and down in front of the women's prison. The night was unseasonably cold; we froze in the early hours.

The police kept the onlookers back, but since they were Villagers, we were again in the midst of what we were imitating; we were unreal and inauthentic. Many friends passed by and stopped to talk: Lucia Dlugoszewski and Erick Hawkins, Bennes Marden and Pancho.

A Greyhound bus that served as a place to stay between shots. Pancho went into one of his long, attention-getting tirades, reciting my history in hyperbolic verse to the crowd.

The actors were friendly, clever, cheerful, and young.

Tonight. At work. In the bus. This time there are 150 of us and the crowds on 8th Street are dense.

September 5, 1956

Terrible days and nights.
Mother worsening.
I do cope.
Julian is infinitely patient with her, but not with me. I am kept at bay. Nothing now. Just try to get through day by day.

September 14, 1956

Mother worsening. It is terrible to watch. How terrible it must be to suffer it. A nurse comes three times a week and gives her a testosterone injection. If she is angry, she has some cause to be.

September 21, 1956

Mother is in Harlem Hospital. After a harrowing series of events, begin-ning with the brutality of the policemen who threw her into the ambulance and then dissolved into the monotony of this dark and alien place. A sudden turn for the better and she makes plans and brightens a bit.

Autumnal Equinox, 1956

And already I yearn for snow.
Now it is necessary to respond to each moment with an entirely new set of postulates—as if history didn't exist. The scientist and the pragmatist pretend to examine a real world. In what space and time?
Today, at a French lesson with Dollie Chareau, I exposed myself as a neo-phyte patient exposes dreams to a psychoanalyst. I saw myself. But I could not do otherwise. She was patient, pointed out my impatience again and again.

September 24, 1956

The emergency is easy.
Then I say, *"Ja, es muss sein."*
Pain is a great prompter, and fear a discipline.
Yesterday at our group's annual picnic on Wards Island, Garrick got a solid hit out of every good ball pitched to him, even with a lightweight bat that added no power to his arms.
Matty Goodman cried because he felt reprimanded, even though he wasn't, for not hitting well.
The handsomest man there was Bertolt Brecht's son, Stefan, who wore a fanciful avocado-colored shirt and socks, and is not a good ball-player.
Paul and Sally and Julian and I left the picnic for our respective hospitals: they to see Susie who has been stricken with polio, we to my mother.
We speak of the difficulty of finding a hospital for my mother.
"No one wants a terminal cancer case," I said.
Paul shrugged and in a Jewish voice said, "We, God be thanked, we have a good disease. For polio they roll out the carpet."

September 26, 1956

I notice at Dollie Chareau's that when I feel stupid I pretend to be even stupider so that I shall be held to account only for my pretended stupidity and not for my real stupidity. What cowardice!

Last night there was an artists' party at Grace Hartigan's studio. Everybody. Nobody. Fatiguing.

At the hospital.

Only now am I beginning to believe in the immortal soul. But immortality, which seemed to me the most personal eventuality of all, is the most impersonal. It is the dissolution of what I am into all that is.

Still, it is hard to believe, hard to pray.

At the Theater Guild: In this monumental mansion I am resentful, like an ambitious servant girl.

The bronze bust of Shaw enshrined like a Roman household god between the two grand stairways tempts me to idolatry and perhaps brought about the solemn thoughts that I attributed to the hospital.

September 28, 1956   Pawlet, Vermont

Dear God, let me take some of this silence back with me to my city world. For here rest is not indolence nor talk a waste of time, nor thought a shirking of duty. Amen.

Last night with Claude and Jim we talked of the death of Jesus, and whether it was the Jews or the Romans who killed him.

I recalled how once when I was nine or ten a crazy old woman in Washington Square whispered to me: "Don't you believe it when they tell you it was the Jews who killed our Lord. It was the wicked Romans." I hadn't the least idea what she was talking about, but her voice scared me, like Goodman's crones: "Lórdy, Lórdy, seóolie Kóoris / ínkoménie dópssi óoris."

Now I am in the woods.

I came here following a cowpath up the hill past cornfields into a wood of recent growth. Now and then I hear a cowbell.

My fear is ebbing now, slowly.

What do I fear?

Distant gunshots. Is it that?

A cow lows far away. Is it that?

The comforting trees mediate between the sky and me. A fallen birch leans into the distance.

The wind accelerates. I'm back at my old trick, fleeing into description.

If only I could meet my fear face to face and pass the ordeals. Meet it and not call out.

This is why I want to act. And why I want to excel.

And even, perhaps, if I examine my motives, why I want to love and be loved.

The sinking sun makes shadows. Soon it will turn everything to gold and then to gray and then to black, but I will be back in the safety of my friends.

Am I thinking of comfort to forget the wish of meeting my fear?

Shall I go on a short way and then go back?

On the other side of the woods I saw a big red barn and turned round and tried a footpath through other woods. On a garbage heap a dead baby deer lay curled up as if in sleep.

The woods were darkening but I was not afraid then. Yet I walked fast, singing my favorite song.

Came back at nightfall, my stockings, borrowed from Claude, full of burrs.

October 1, 1956   New York City

Yesterday, *Sehnsucht* for the calm of Vermont. Home seemed cluttered and I seemed to myself a mess of contradictions.

The last night in Vermont, Claude read to us from his meticulous journals. The exactitude shows his reverence for the moment and also his reverence for the sovereign importance of the detail. And I read aloud the contents of this notebook.

Jim Spicer declined to read his journals because they are "too sexual." Was he apologizing or boasting?

Julian read from his journal, of deaths and of my mother's disease, until the gloom was thick. And I watched a hornet crawl across the floor and tangle in a spider's web at the base of a brass lamp. The spider rushed out and began to weave around the struggling hornet. Julian read on describing the agony of cancer death.

I wanted to interrupt him and rescue the hornet and I don't know which of three motives impelled me to sit still: 1) because I feared being derided for my hypersensitive empathies; 2) because I feared the hornet, who was likely to sting me for my trouble; 3) because I know that the spider must eat and the hornet is its food and I cannot expect the spider to be vegetarian even if St. Francis did convert the wolf.

So I sat still while it struggled to death.

October 5, 1956

I meant just now to complain of the route to the hospital, but then I thought that if I call the route to the hospital long, slow, and torturous, what shall I say of the route from the hospital?

"Death is too much for anyone to live through." "The dying has to be borne."

I'm eating my heart out with these stupid puns en route to visit Mother. It is intolerable to see her suffering. And I am horrified that I am able to do it.

At Julie Bovasso's Tempo Playhouse, *The Lesson* and *Escorial*, in which Bobs Blossom plays the mad King. I never believed the King's madness, but the actor's . . .

I thought: "He is really mad. He thinks he is acting out his own soul. Didn't I try that as Phaedra and didn't I learn that the soul will not be acted out?"

In the lobby, two bright paintings of Julian's stood out among the gray and drab people. And Brooks Atkinson among us like a mortal. Like the Voodun god of death, who is one of the villagers in every respect except that he happens to be the god of death.

I worked one day in a film at LaGuardia Airfield for Kazan's *A Face in the Crowd*. Kazan directs a hundred screaming teenage girls from local parochial schools with earnest pleas through an electric megaphone, "Come on, girls, now, with feeling!"

October 10, 1956

Daedalus' vow: "Silence. Exile. Cunning."

Under nitrous oxide I felt the world, the universe, as a continuous series of choices, and every choice had a value predicated on the preceding choice, so that each one was of the utmost importance to all the eternal values. Every error was fatal, every choice mine alone. The existence of the world was endangered or assured by these choices.

Only one possibility had to be avoided: the ridiculous. She was a tall girl named Helga, clumsy, lanky and the unwitting object of ridicule.

Helga is my ego fear, what I must at all costs not be.

At every choice, Helga interposed herself in her homemade dress, pathetically unaware.

But under nitrous oxide all the superfluities had been eliminated, and I was face to face with Helga alone, and had to choose Helga or Helga, I or Helga, I or I.

And then there was nothing anymore.

October 11, 1956   Hot Indian Summer

The evocative odors that the heavy air carries are too warm, too sentimental. And I turn myself to steel so as to be able to bear the sight of the haggard face and the mangled features and the hideous stench of what was an object of love. If I felt my love now I would pity her, and if I really pitied her I would break under this slow torture.

November 1, 1956

What is past is past absolutely. How enslaved we are when we realize that we belong to the inevitable. Hating the inevitability, we are nonetheless part of it, bound to it, wracked by it, until the time comes when we no longer rebel against it. Then we are one with it. And only then can the real grief end.

At death what is present becomes instantly ancient, becomes one with all history and all memory.

I knew she was to die, but I couldn't mourn beforehand. Nor could I look at her fast-withering face and believe it could be so still. And I dared not think of the day which was to come. She had long ago forbidden me to love her openly. And so I was cold. That is, skin-deep I was cold.

On Friday I had been watching a Chekhov play on television and came late to the hospital. Each day the difficulty of the visit increased. There were no words for a week. Only an eye that blinked from under the bandages and sparkled yet at the sound of Garrick's name.

Every day we approached the door with greater anxiety, but today Julian was scolding me for my lateness and we entered unprepared for the image that met us.

I will not describe how she looked; if only it would leave the foreground of my memory where it hangs like a painted scrim clouding my vision.

It is something that I want to remember and something that I don't want to remember and something that will never be erased from my mind.

We could not be sure. We stood for a moment and then went to call the nurse. The time stretched out very thin. Julian went back into her room. I never went back. That was not what I wanted to remember.

The nurse called an aide and went in.

In the endless wait that followed I observed a small gray spider scaling the gray corridor wall. Sometimes Julian spoke.

The nurse came out and told us to wait until they called the doctor. I followed the course of the spider. He was hard to see, being so small and gray on gray. I marveled that he was visible at all.

Dr. Tolati and his assistant came and went in and I watched the spider so intently that I hardly heard Julian speak. The doctor was in there a long time.

He came out.

"Oh, my dear. Oh, my dear. Oh, my dear," he said to me. And he touched me and I don't remember exactly what else he said, but I thought it a strange thing for a doctor to say: "Oh, my dear. Oh, my dear. Oh, my dear." It was so very unpracticed, as though he had never announced a death before and as though he were terribly moved.

Julian and I gave very specific instructions that no one touch or move her so that the last religious practices might be scrupulously carried out.

We left Harlem Hospital for the last time. Only now that I can cry about it can I remember the scene, but I cannot evoke the cold coldness that covered me. I said to Julian, "I feel nothing." He said he felt only a slight trembling.

At home there were arrangements to be made. Julian diligently made calls and did what needed to be done. I don't know what I did.

I had meant to tell Garrick, but at the last moment I couldn't and Julian told him and he hid his head in a pillow. And then he was cheerful again.

The next day was *Shabbos*.

The next day was Sunday, the funeral. It had its forms to be followed and I had only to keep to the path, and since there was no choice and no turning, everything was easy and blank and empty.

Now I have no roots. I am supported by nothing but my own being. Love is ephemeral. I am deserted and alone.

Julian contacted the *kehilla*, who perform the *tarah* as my mother had requested. She had given Julian specific directions for everything. We carried out everything. Five women prepare the body so that no man should touch it. They cleanse and dress it according to the religious prescriptions.

A taciturn chauffeur drove us to the funeral parlor in the Bronx. Julian and I stood in the lobby of what should have been a funerary temple but was only a commercial establishment. One of the undertakers stood by clinking the change in his pocket. Relatives whom I scarcely recognized spoke to me and we moved into an anteroom, too tastefully decorated, and everyone was very nice and simple and talked kindly. I liked these relatives for the first time now that they are all that is left of my family.

The ladies of the *kehilla* came out in single file, severe and determined of look. They all wore the *sheitel*, small hats, and hideous suits and looked like the poor dressing up. The chief priestess came to us with a grim cold smile: "Everything is in order." I thanked her. They gave me the creeps. It amazed me how these ordinary Jewish housewives were able to rise to their difficult task, which they perform not for pay but only for the *mitzvah* of it.

Rabbi Carlebach came late, his white beard shaking under a sad smile of real compassion. I was so embarrassed by the surge of feeling that I only looked at him hoping to say silently what I could not say. He addressed me with formal warmth.

We went into the chapel. Only now at the sight of the coffin covered with its plain black cloth could I feel why I was here. But I could not (I cannot now) understand why *she* was not here. Or how it was that I saw her visible in the hospital and yet she was not there. I cried then for the first time, protesting against the cruelty of her lost, brave, proud life. Her unrewarded constancy, her unmerited sufferings. Cried like a child protesting the injustice of her father.

She had instructed Julian, "Simple, no praise, no eulogy."

But Aunt Jenny said, "Let Rabbi Carlebach say a few words, he loves to talk."

Nonetheless, Julian instructed the rabbi, "No praise. No eulogy." He read the service.

And it was in my father's voice. Even the accent, the dramatic emphasis, redoubled my tears, as though it were my father reading my mother's funeral rite.

Julian had called him because Rabbi Jung told him that Rabbi Carlebach had been my father's teacher in Berlin. And when he read the Twenty-fourth Psalm, it was my father's reading of the Psalm. With a pang I realized that this she could not know. Except in the way in which all things are known to all of us and whatever is immortal in her knows.

But in the face of death I cannot believe in immortality.

The closest I can come to that comforting hope is the feeling—now she is part of everything. And I know this to be true despite the fact that I cannot understand it.

One morning after she had had a dreadful, painful night, she told us how she had awakened from her drugged sleep, woke so drugged from a sleep so deep she thought she was dead.

She questioned herself, "Am I dead?" and then answered, "No, I am not dead, for I don't believe in reincarnation, and if I were dead I wouldn't know it."

The last time at the hospital, I recalled that dream while waiting for the doctor. And did she ask herself that question? And was there an answer? And did she know it?

Rabbi Carlebach said that she requested simplicity and no eulogy, but that this was the highest praise for it bespoke a great modesty.

(Yet she was not modest; she was very proud. Too proud to have herself praised for what she had not fulfilled. She waited always for her hour of happiness, her day of fulfillment, and it never came. She never accomplished that which would have made her seem to herself praiseworthy, and that is not modesty.)

And Rabbi Carlebach went on praising her by speaking of not praising her, and then I saw that he looked like my father with his beard and hair turned white.

We drove to Oradel, to Cedar Park Cemetery. Rabbi Carlebach rode with us. He spoke to us of charity, of lies, of the Jew's plight. He held Julian's hand and my hand. I cannot remember any more / so numb and distant.

I cried very much at the burial. Ismar and Julian covered the grave. My mind understood and I cried. But my human nature cannot understand. If it is not she, what is it in the coffin? What do we bury? Over what do we say the blessing?

It is not she, because I called to her in the hospital and I knew—it was then that I knew! —that I was speaking to no one, that she was not there.

Where then?

This is the feeling that defies description.

There were less than ten men and we had to seek a *minyan*. While we waited (here in the greenery and sunshine around our sorrow it did not seem so long), Rabbi Carlebach spoke to Aunt Jenny and then came to me and put his hands on me and said emphatically, "*Ich war dein Vater's Lehrer.*"

We were standing at the foot of my father's grave—now 16 years covered.

And I could not say more than yes, and if I had not just then stopped crying with grief, I would have cried for joy. Because I didn't speak he didn't know whether I had understood him, and so he told me again that he was my father's teacher and that this was the reason that he had said "*du*" to me, and I said I knew; and then the ten men were found and the prayers said. In the ritual he instructed me what to do and where to walk and called me Judith publicly.

When we rode back he spoke more intimately. About olden times, and the surroundings became clearer and realer, and the griefed ebbed. Only once did Rabbi Carlebach refer to funerary subjects, to explain that tradition forbade comforting a mourner until the deceased was interred, for until that time the mourner, like the mourned, is between earth and heaven and not at rest. Only afterward can we say: "Be comforted."

Does this mean that to be put into the earth is to be consigned to heaven? Is this the significance of returning to the elements and "becoming part of everything"?

"Drink wine," he advises, "for wine must be drunk at sad and happy occasions. Therefore we say '*L'chaim*'—'To Life'—or 'May you drink only to life and not in mourning.' " And he was very close and said he would come to preside over a *minyan* during the *shivah*.

Then began the *shivah*. Despite the context of my life I found myself absorbed in traditional ritual. In the front room the memorial light flickered and I sat on a stool and received visitors. The family I hardly knew came with cakes and jams and talk. Some talked about my mother, but mostly it was friendly, pointless talk. I recall myself as I see myself in dreams—large and distant, distinct but unavailable, like a far-off mountain. Only the mountain is in another world and cannot be climbed, no, not ever. I was neither happy nor unhappy then.

Midweek we held a service to say *kaddish* in the house. Rabbi Carlebach came and men I did not know who were the husbands of Mother's friends and, unexpectedly, my father's brother, Uncle George. He was visiting from Detroit and Aunt Jenny told him. How cold he was, and how formal. I tried to talk to him, but long ago he gave me up and I couldn't draw out the old delight in his eyes. Despair of being misunderstood. Alien. *Allein.*

"But," I wanted to cry out, "*Ich bin Judith, Judith!*" (Not Jewdith but Yoo-dit.)

All I could do was recall the old times, hoping to move him. He was cool and unswervingly polite. I recounted more and more intimate stories. And he only smiled a restrained smile of recognition. Uncle George never knew how much I cared for him and now he will never know. I will probably never see him again.

The rabbi spoke of the edict: "The Lord has given and the Lord has taken away."

"There are two words," he said, for the Lord, "and the one means the Stern

Judge and the other means the God of Love. And in this phrase not the two forms but the same form is used. It is not the God of Love who has given and the Stern Judge who has taken away, but the God of Love has given and the God of Love has taken away."

And he said it is the ones who are God's special children whom he makes to suffer, for they can bear his trials and love him for all their agonies.

I understood with my mind, but my nature hardly knows what to do with these things.

Not wisdom, but a "*heart* of wisdom."

We held the service after we determined which way was due East, everyone turning in circles and pointing in various directions. *Kaddish* was said for my mother.

Then the rabbi came and took my face in his hands and said, "*Ich liebe die Judith wirklich. Ja, Ich liebe sie wie mein eigenes Kind.*"

He pronounced the German so familiarly that for a moment I was not lost. How quiet it was in that moment. Like waking in a peaceful room before returning to the nightmare.

He has called me twice since then. I say so little, but it is because I am understood and therefore he says, "*Du hast eine ruhig und eine beruhigende Stimme.*"

Oh, that I were what I am in the rabbi's eyes! Oh, that I were what I am in his presence!

Shabbos I go to his synagogue. He expects me and I want to be there. I mean, I am wanted where I want to be, where there are no ulterior motives.

As though in the death of my mother I found an image of my father to comfort me.

Yet after the *shivah* ended I felt no comfort; it was like bursting into an implacable reality. I was alone. Earth was hard, unremitting.

In everything I saw the imprint of its end. I heard decay at work in everything. Saw the futility of temporal hopes, of love and labor. As clearly as the outline of an object sets its limitations to the eye, my heart discerned the limitations of life.

Every man's death was writ on him visibly, and the death of his children's children and the death of his memory.

Everything was an encompassing zero in which the world of spirit, hope, faith, meaning, life, and immortality were little weeds sprouting inside mortal minds too weak to admit the reality of death, minds in need of the comforting abstractions.

No hope. No God. (Yes, that is what it was; it was true doubt.) No self.

Why not then that desireless nirvana? Because there was pain.

Meaningless pain without object, without subject. Pain without end and without beginning.

Then after seven tearless days, three days of tears. Three days and three nights, for I could not sleep. I cried for her, for her unfulfilled hopes, for her sorrows, for my lack of love, and I cried for myself, and for everything and everyone and then, finally, I cried for nothing.

December 3, 1956

The month began auspiciously on *Shabbos*. I went to Rabbi Carlebach's synagogue. After I had seated myself in the women's section, Julian and Lester passed by to find their seats, and when I saw them in the *talis* with *machsorim* in hand, my eyes filled with tears.

Carlebach's son, Shlomo, embellished the service with joyous Chassidic melodies, heightening the participation even beyond what is usual in an orthodox *shul*.

This Shlomo is a modern intellectual under his bushy, dark brown beard, a sophisticated Chassid who has struck out a singular path for himself. Though when he heard Julian's paintings described as "unstudied," Shlomo nodded approvingly: "Sophistication spoils the genius."

I like his fervor.

Only age can fulfill his desire, and waiting is hard. But a good doctrine has been given to him and he has not forsaken it.

The father preached, with apologies to us, in a Yiddish liberally garnished with German and English. Of the ingratitude of Pharaoh's butler, who allowed Joseph to linger in prison, of the ingratitude of the nations who do not fight to defend Israel, of Chanukah as a feast of gratitude.

After the service, a *kiddush*. Carlebach showed us the silverwork on the Torah's garments and Shlomo talked to us of his experiences as "religious adviser" for *The Dybbuk* at David Ross' theater. Mrs. Carlebach brought cakes.

December 10, 1956

In the evening we prepared dinner for Joe Campbell and Jean Erdman.

Joe told us of his fire-walk in a Buddhist temple in Kyoto. He walked across a pyre of burning logs with a sprained ankle—and not only was the fire cool, but the ankle healed.

He said he prefers no explanation. Finally, at my urging, he said hesitantly that maybe there was something which protected his feet in the sand he had to step on before he entered the fire. But he prefers no explanation. He prefers illogic. He can't trust it, but it *must* be so.

He is impressed with Morey Bernstein's sensational book, *The Search for Bridey Murphey*, the story of a girl's memory of an earlier existence, unearthed through hypnosis.

Yet he is capable of profundity. In *The Hero with a Thousand Faces* he writes, "Woman is life. The Hero, its knower and master." A subtle choice of words progressing from knowledge to mastery. But is the mastery of life the knowledge of Woman, or is the knowledge of life the mastery of Woman? When he explains the symbolism of dreams he falters, like any professor, but when he plunges into his own myths, he emerges triumphant like his own hero.

He is under the delusion that he is a kind of a scientist, but he is a kind of poet, and if he were brave he would be a kind of sage.

We talked about matriarchy and patriarchy, and about Eve and the Serpent—the "proper mate," he said, whom Eve chooses over Adam. The happy fault. And I said I agree that Woman represents the priestess, but I have searched in the Old Testament and can't find it there.

"You won't find it there," said Joe.

"But it must be there if—" I began.

And Joe interrupted, "From the standpoint of comparative mythology . . ."

"But I am a good Jew," I exaggerated.

"And I am a good comparative mythologist," said Joe.

My boast was less true than his.

"As a Jew," I went on, despite his interjection, "I believe what is written there, even if it makes absolutely no sense to me."

"That," said Joe quite solemnly, "is faith and it is the road to heaven."

Then it dawned on me that I have not lied either to others or to myself when I said that I both believe and do not believe. Therefore let me thank God, who has kept me from sin when I could not hold myself upright.

When we say "there is no good and evil" do we mean that God's bounty is so great that we cannot do evil because his mercy makes it good?

And what of the apple? And the cruel edicts of Deuteronomy?

There is a Moslem sect, says Joe, which worships the devil, honoring Lucifer as the angel whose sin of pride consisted of his refusal to obey God's command that he, with all the other angels, bow down before man. For Lucifer so honored God that he would bow to no other.

December 18, 1956

The removal of the mask, or the assuming of the mask.

I alter an aspect of my face. My nose.

Who am I? Am I what I look like? I am not what I was.

I wonder whether it is not the proverbial "spiting of the face." Paul says spite is my gravest flaw.

December 31, 1956

For 1957:
Tolerance. Even of myself.
Gentleness as a feminine virtue.
When feeling secure: Keep silent.
When feeling insecure: Keep silent.
    Neither boast nor apology.

New Year's, 1957

Dream: On an espionage mission into enemy territory with Julian and Lester. I am sent on ahead to our destination, a vacant department store, but am diverted by a fortune teller who stops to read the Tarot for me. I see the cards showing the four seasons in splendid procession, laden with promise of fulfillment, but she says, "I don't understand this. I won't charge you for the reading."

I steal the Tarot pack.

I think: Is the stealing of the cards really the equivalent of carrying out our mission?

Last night. The New Year's gathering. The strangeness fades, but it requires faith. Faith that even if I let go (of my individuality, my pride, my self), the world will not disappear. But it's too much like daring to die.

Everyone says it was a wonderful party. Champagne, and I wore a new white gown from Bonwit's.

Just when I stopped caring comes the long-desired dress as I dreamed it, with a wide white sweep in which my childish presumption is fulfilled. And as with the oracle, it is true but so different from what we expected.

If Oedipus was so skeptical as to distrust the oracle, why didn't it occur to him to suspect Jocasta?

Because he never thought it would be this way.

Oscar Williams commented on my lunar gown and I said I was espousing the new year. And after I said so, I meant it.

They say the owl was the baker's daughter.

There were:

Jean Adra with two young friends.

Søren Agenoux declaring his love for me in a clumsy and frantic embrace.

David Sachs: philosophy/Princeton.

Rogers Albritton: philosophy/Harvard.

Both searching for some passionate affection.

Remy Charlip, giving out handbills for Merce's concert.

Maya Deren, dancing to Haitian drums in a purple and gold gown; talking to Lester of voodoo and Masonry.

Teiji Ito in his black silk shirt, always near Maya.

Richard Edelman and Rachele, very pregnant.

Paul Goodman and Sally.

Nina Gitana, sad of face, and cheerful of manner.

Oscar Williams, growing constantly wittier, looking through everyone rather charitably.

Frank McGuire, with his small book of lyric poems.

Francis and Michel Lee, she like a brightly enameled steel spring—sharp, coiled, painted.

Sala Staw dressed and tense and greedy for love, taken and given, enamored of everyone, her hopes for the Living Theatre looming like a promised land.

Larry Kornfeld also in love with the future.

Lee Hoiby, gay, with friends.

Steve Feldman, taking tranquilizers for hallucinations.

Gene Thornton, ponderous and omniscient.

Shirley Stoler, splendid in brown velvet.

Glenn Lewis, always wise.

Walter Mullen, always unwise.

Saville Clark, George Miller, Prising, Burdett. (A string of darkening pearls.)

A new year.

January 11, 1957

With Julie Bovasso and George Ortman. George is quiet, as if he were taking mental notes. She has become very proud and talks of "Malina and Bovasso," as if we were great stars. She is full of plans and schemes, practical and fantastic. She sees herself, somehow, historically.

She is renting Tempo Playhouse. She owes a great deal in taxes and meanwhile is seeking work. "I've thrown myself on the open market."

What a bold way to say it! I can't help but admire her.

She talks of us both in *Dark Eyes*, a commercial play.

We are so different. Yet surely her vigor, like mine, must be balanced by despair, unfulfillable needs.

But she can be hard. Harder than I can be.

January 14, 1957

At Merce's concert. The Brooklyn Academy subscription audience is outraged at John's daring music. Lester, of course, is against all music written since Mozart, but even Claude and Jim and Paul are critical.

My eye paces the movements with pleasure. Rauschenberg's sets, Remy's new dancing, Cage's slow *Winter Music*.

Nocturnes which look like aubades. Merce's movements grow purer and more precise. He does a pantomime of the inner man. He leans forward slowly from the hips and his arms and legs follow, then by their agility seem to outstrip the trunk and lead him, head back, into new territory.

John and Merce, after the performance, laugh all night like mischievous kids who have succeeded in some tremendous boyish escapade.

January 16, 1957

Garrick's pet parakeet Pokey dies. But Spring is well despite the bitter cold that even steam heat can't thaw.

This morning the five "guilty" defendants in the civil-defense trial were sentenced.

Providentially, as Dorothy says, Judge Kaplan, who was so harsh on us 2 years ago was not, after all, the presiding magistrate.

After hearing the case, the judge gave them a choice of twenty-five dollars or five days. They all chose jail and made their statements.

Ammon: "I gladly accept this sentence as a penance for our bombing of Hiroshima."

Dorothy: "God gave us free will and therefore we are responsible for our acts."

Deane Mowrer: "I'm happy that in the middle of a wasted life I can do one good thing."

I'm glad that they did not get the year that I supposed Kaplan would have given these inspired people.

Then I think: They are like everyone.

A few days ago at a meeting that Dick Kern organized, Ammon talked of his experiences as a Catholic anarchist, in and out of prison. And Julian and I acted out the prison scene from *Masse-Mensch*. And tonight, Ammon is again in prison.

He is in prison for me, because I wasn't there when he made his protest in the park.

And Dorothy is in prison for me.

And tonight I am going to the theater. I will dress up and laugh at a musical comedy, wishing I were in the cell next to Dorothy's and she reading psalms.

January 27, 1957

Paul Goodman says: "It seems to me that the world is a provincial enterprise: Our culture, my friend Moses, my friend Sophocles, my friend Dante; it's all a provincial enterprise. But then I get into trouble because there is a Big World somewhere, but where?"

I understand him, but it does not lessen my aches of mortality. He implies that if there is a real culture then there is no futility. "But if the culture itself is futile?" I ask.

He says: "I know that people die."

January 29, 1957

Kama Mara—the tempter of Buddha under the Bodhi tree:

> Kama—desire.
> Mara—hostility.
> Kama Mara = love and death.

January 30, 1957

Tennessee Williams with a day-old black kitten in his hand. At Maya Deren's. And then Maya weeping in Tennessee's arms that she doesn't get pregnant.

Joe Campbell on judo and geishas. I make him blush by asking how he came to be invited to a geisha house. He, at least, does not pretend that his relation to these ladies was chaste. "But you judge them by Western morality." I don't.

Earlier in the evening, introducing Tennessee to present the awards to the filmmakers, Joe made an effusive speech in praise of Williams' work, singling out *Camino Real*, as the best.

They all shook hands and were photographed against an American flag.

The awards, rolled up like diplomas, seemed appropriate to the high school auditorium with its forceful W.P.A. murals.

Willard's *Narcissus* was shown.

We talked to hundreds of people and I thought: This is my world, want it or not, love it or not.

Only in Paul's presence / who doesn't much attend these functions anymore / do I seem to find some core.

February 4, 1957

"But," I said, "didn't the Buddha say that he would not say what he learned under the Bodhi tree?"

"Yes, he did," said Joe Campbell.

"And do you know what the Buddha learned under the Bodhi tree?"

"Yes."

Then he made two circles with his thumbs and forefingers and brought the two hands closer slowly. Then he opened one circle.

"Taking the bait of love, we are caught by the—"

And he opened the other circle and then closed them into each other and then moved his hands away so fast that they seemed by this gesture to vanish.

"—hook of death."

Thus he explained the Kama Mara.

Thinking of the opera, I asked if they were one person or two. He insists that they are one person, for "life is death."

He again made two circles with his fingers.

"Standing in *Samsara*, we see the goal *Nirvana* and move toward it, but when we arrive—"

The circles becomes concentric and vanish.

"—it all disappears: *Samsara*, *Nirvana*, and all; it is all equally illusion, it is all one, and he, the Buddha, saw those who stand in *Samsara*, and he knew they were already in *Nirvana*, and because they could not know it he felt the great compassion.

Soon Joe called me a daughter of Kama, but thinking I might take offense he changed it to the consort of the Gautrava, whose name I have already forgotten.

Noh music on the phonograph with long, slow, piercing sounds that take me from the surroundings into an immutable place where everything is always the same. Where I feel myself moving as though I were not moving; as though motion were itself the illusion of motion, and speech a trick of the unhearing ear; and the music swallows itself, dissolved in the twilight from his high window as it covered the Village in vermilion, and then in darkness, the kisses and touches are all lost: happening indeed to some Gautrava and his consort, as distant from us as those Hindu deities.

Joe Campbell never stopped speaking of the myths. He claims that he does not believe in God. I asked him like Gretchen and he answered like Faust. But I don't believe him.

Except when he cries out with tears: "I'm so ashamed of myself. So ashamed."

February 19, 1957

The theater. With Fritz Perls and Paul Williams we'd been trying to negotiate for Jimmy Walker's old speakeasy. The terms grew harder and harder. They tried on every side to cheat us. Finally it came to a matter of $9000. And it stopped there. Julian called everyone. Dwight refused. Rich men whom we don't know refused rudely by letter and phone.

We gave it up—after months of being on the verge of something. Loss is the final relief.

February 22, 1957

Having just lost one potential theater—the nightclub on Sullivan Street— we start on another, a garage on Minetta Lane. Howard is closely advising us on everything. The anxiety and suspense are terrible.

On Washington's Birthday, Julian and I take Garrick to Fraunces' Tavern. The mementos of this "provincial enterprise"—the shoe (one, yellow silk) worn by George Washington's mother; a piece of wood from his pew in St. Paul's Church. The revolution, a minor bloody skirmish, ugly, provincial indeed, is melodramatically glorified into the Great Cause.

Garrick enjoys history, but I see the lies in every line, the sunsets painted too orange in all the pictures of Valley Forge. Yet I also disdain the worn shoe on display. What I want is the heart of the matter, neither magnified nor made homey.

No echoes here.

The most authentic thing here is this old washroom where I write to rest.

The more I tell Paul the truth, the less I am honest. He speaks of "mental reservation."

I say, "It was Jim Agee who first spoke to me of 'mental reservation' as a Jesuit doctrine. He hated it but seemed to believe in it."

Paul says, "That was what killed him, wasn't it?"

February 24, 1957

Idyllic weekends. Garlands of pleasure painted by Fragonard or Boucher, dazzling, lively, bound up with allegory and metaphor. For this is a self-conscious joy. Lester and Julian and I play with more freedom, more ease than Garrick and his friends, with their competitive, angry games and their solemn and bitter cabals.

Tonight to hear Tebaldi. Glorious in green chiffon draped from broad white shoulders, with diamonds blazing at ears and bosom. Long white gloves. A white flower in her hair.

Tireless when she sings; she gives herself with pleasure.

February 28, 1957

To see the MacDougal Street property with Fritz. He plays some sort of role. I don't know what it is.

We really don't have the finances for this venture. Paul Williams will help toward the remodeling, but will not "finance real estate."

March 3, 1957

Extra on Camera Three's "The Organization Man," about the loss of ego in the corporate world. Hired by CBS to sit at desks and pantomime office work, we sixty-three extras are acting out what is in fact the case.

On Friday night at Fritz and Laura's party, there was the constant battle with the right and wrong remark, the tactful and rude response, the interested look and the yawn, the boast, the lie, the exaggeration, the evasion, the conciliation, the endearment, the parry, the false laugh, the forced frown.

Ah, sweet submission. O fatal submission.

The theater situation looks hopeless. The city has not yet approved the rezoning of the MacDougal Street building. Fritz is going to Europe and will leave the final decision in his lawyer's hands; his lawyer is cautious and does not know what the theater is about. "Other people" are bargaining for the property. I'm tired of waiting and apologizing and explaining. I want to get on with my work.

March 8, 1957

Fritz has put his money elsewhere. It was a fond hope, but farewell to it.

March 11, 1957

We arrange with Julie Bovasso to rent the Tempo Playhouse. We want to do *Improvise*, but the rights are held by Marta Abba, who is in Italy, and we cannot, even through her lawyers, get in touch with her.

We decide for the William Carlos Williams' play *Many Loves*.

Purim, 1957

When the lease arrived in the mail and we saw that Julie had set terms that we could not meet, I was in tears. To go through the same disappointment again. Everything breaking into fragments, nothing cohering.

March 25, 1957

Nothing on the theater.

At a reception after Jean Erdman's concert, Meyer Kupferman proposes our directing and designing two operas he has composed: *The Curious Fern* and *Voices for a Mirror*.

Afterward, Joe Campbell keeps to the kitchen where I and a bright Bard student keep to him.

It seems I'm always speaking to Joe of the myths in the kitchen. It must be the witches' kitchen.

People wander in and out with questions on symbology, bits of information about the Shakers, the Kabbalah, the Book of the Dead.

It is astounding how much belief a man who doesn't believe in God is capable of investing in myth.

"I'll keep your bracelet for a while."

March 26, 1957

Nothing on the theater.

Lester brings flowers because it is payday.

Garrick has turned from geology to astronomy. Star charts. Trips to the roof on clear nights with Julian.

March 27, 1957

Read over *Voices for a Mirror* and *The Curious Fern*. We're on our way to Kupferman's now.

Last night to Cinema 16. *Nicht Mehr Fliehen*, Robert Frank's scary film on the zero point which we have reached. Of two women and Herbert Vesely in the barrenness of his soul, and the cold goddess who escapes even from nowhere and whose luggage he carries because she is hard and shallow and dresses in rayon acetate at the zero point.

Also Kenneth Anger's ritualistic, passionate *Pleasure Garden*.

March 28, 1957

Nothing on the theater.

Yesterday Meyer Kupferman sang us all of *Voices for a Mirror*.

Wisdom is the residue of passion. After a great feeling has altered the course of our soul and spirit and body, its ecstasy disappears and what remains is the knowledge born of passion, but outliving passion, the immortal consequence of mortal circumstance.

April 1, 1957

Wake in the middle of the night unresigned to death. Specters of mortality fall on everything and everyone. The well-polished lamp is already thrown in a tangle of metal and plaster into discard, the cities already ruins, the smiling face skeletal, half-decayed but not yet clean bone, the art is ashes and the language lifeless as antiquity.

Was I thinking of the secrets I have with the dead, which once we shared and now exist in me alone?

> I feel too mortal
> "and I do not approve,
> and I am not resigned."

I say to Paul, "If you know what it means that people die, how can you be so calm?"

And he says—"I have said often—and written it—that I am in purgatory—I feel I am saved but I am suffering now. This is because I know that my work is as good as it is. But you are in hell."

I had, indeed, a headache.

April 2, 1957

Today we heard auditions for *Voices* and *Fern*, quite formally at the Nola Studios. Kupferman is searching for "great" voices. We heard accomplished voices and fine voices.

We attend a lecture by Joe Campbell on *Finnegan* at the Y. He talks with no pretensions at all, carried away by the intoxicant of his scholar's enthusiasm. He piles meaning upon meaning and forgets us all, racing through the channels of his mind, making rapid associations, lapsing into foreign tongues.

He said that *Finnegan* brings one to the point where there is nothing that a man can do that you cannot love.

Of the sex crime in Phoenix Park and its elusive nature, he says: "Schopenhauer says, 'Life is like nothing so much as a punishment for something we have done.'" And Joe stretched out his arms, "But what have we done?"

April 4, 1957

Dinner with Alan at the *Kleine Konditorei*. He describes his feeling of possession when he played earlier this afternoon while we smoked. I had asked him to improvise. He was reluctant at first, but began a curious passage in an unusual rhythm.

He wants to find "the man" who was playing, but I can't even get him to admit that this "man" or "demon" lives inside him. He contends that it is because of his capacities he was especially chosen.

I don't, however, insist on rationality because Alan is such a "mad genius" as could produce unusual work under unusual circumstances. Like "Kubla Khan."

He assures me that his demons are somber (depressive) demons, and can be coped with, not frenzied (hysterical) demons, which are more dangerous.

April 11, 1957

Work on the Kupferman operas compensates us for no news on the theater.

April 18, 1957

I remember you, memory, with your dim face and your veiled eyes and your game of obscuring, and your pretended fickleness, and your heart-rending constancy. I remember you in the small hours, memory, and first thing on waking.

I saw you again in Gaugau's face, tired but brave to be so false. Now he has achieved a measure of recognition, and though endearing still, he exemplifies the successful playwright.

Gaugau approaches us with a spelling game at Jim Downey's.

"Randolph Churchill got 11 out of 12 wrong."

Pencils and papers and words frequently misspelled. Herbert Machiz does best. Gaugau buys brandy.

It is the first night of *Pesach*.

We had been to the Seder at Julian's parents' which my father-in-law conducted with an iron hand. The family read from the *Haggadah* in turn, in English, though I was asked to read in Hebrew when my turn came.

Garrick did me proud with the *Mah nishtanah*.

Fireworks. Everyone left the Seder and took to the roof. A wonderful display, though they say many called the police to ask if we were being bombed. But the Japanese, without reference to Hiroshima, were only lighting the sky with color to advertise a world trade fair.

Then to a lecture by the stage director Robert Lewis. Small, bald, bold, comical, he talks on the Method to an audience made up entirely of actors. Many illustrious. The trend in the theater is to be a serious student throughout one's life.

Lewis acts a great deal, imitates Moissi and Ben Ami in *The Living Corpse*, favoring Ben Ami's psychological formulation over Moissi's theatrical expression, though his imitation of Moissi was far better.

At the lecture we meet Herbert Machiz who tells us we must "meet the right people, go to the right parties." And, on a note of desperation, wins our agreement.

Herbert led us to Downey's, full of actors, crowded and comfortable. And there Gaugau came stealing back out of our history, out of memory to face what has come of his matchmaking.

I was wearing a red coat like the red corduroy with its pockets full of penny chocolates that I had worn the day I met Gaugau, the day before he brought Julian to me as a reward for a Horn and Hardart's meal.

There was a long night, frivolous talk. And memory, the unwobbling pivot.

April 22, 1957

The long concert of new European music. Breaking up the silence too deliberately. David Tudor expertly striking the doom out of this convulsive music. He makes little vocal noises as he plays.

But borne away by no image, I am stuck here wondering how they paint this intricate ceiling.

What determines this need?

This afternoon, when I went to Fanny Bradshaw's Shakespeare class, I had the same thought.

Fanny stays close to the line, puts Shakespeare first. Perhaps I will learn something. But what determines this need?

We read *Richard II* and talk more somberly than real scholars would need to. We discussed accents and rhythms. Gerri Page was there. She has acquired a preoccupied look, which could equally well be intensity or ennui. She read Lady Anne's first speech flatly (I would have raged) but with great regard for the verse. Boris Tumarin read well and heavily. There were twelve of us, so we all read much.

As I look around this concert hall at this small audience of 90 people, all the faces are as sad as they are old. The youngsters aglow with a mortal hope;

the adults declining in grace; the middle-aged engraved with bitterness, as though they had been eating bitter fruit (they have), and the old ones regaining a peculiar freshness like that of the young.

What I really want to know is why we are here and what this music is.

David Tudor is playing, for the second time, Karlheinz Stockhausen's *Nr. 4 Klavierstück XI.* It is the best (most alive) of the work tonight. He is transfigured, mumbles the climaxes vocally, is sharp with his hands. In the audience, no one is transfigured except for the few who look from their own depths at subway trains and concert halls, passive, unreceptive, as the dead are to the rain.

Yet they like it. I do not very much like it. It has not John Cage's yielding softness (he peers down intensely from the balcony, Juliet enraptured), nor Lou's ecstasy, undimmed as Easters pass. Remy leans down over the balcony rail. Merce dreams into his hands. Jean Erdman examines, like me, the ceiling.

At the Playhouse Theater. Robert Lewis under five pink lights. Here the audience is young, but successful; the cast of virtually every play on Broadway is in attendance. They are too similar, but nonetheless expressive.

He prepares the listeners for a formal exposition of the Method: "This will sound forbidding, but next week we will be back to the fun of loose opinion."

April 24, 1957

At Fanny Bradshaw's. *Richard III.* Fanny has set up a kind of altar to the bard in honor of his birthday. Bowered in greenery, a bust high on a pedestal, toasted with sherry. Poor key cold figure of a holy king.

Fanny: "Now let's all stand and drink a toast to Shakespeare who—who—who brought us all together."

Last night to Jimmy Waring's dance concert at the Master Institute. It was one of those young dadaist programs, which Garrick called "not at all grownuppish because I enjoyed it very much."

In one of the pieces the audience supplied the accompaniment. The Armour sisters, Toby and Rachel, danced random, humorous sentences. Garrick on a trumpet, which Earl Browne and John Cage taught him to use during the intermission.

Nick Cernovitch projected his film onto the audience's faces. This dada device, which Garrick called a mean, dirty trick, delighted and angered everyone. Nick says it was merely the simplest solution to the lack of a satisfactory screen surface.

April 25, 1957

No news on the theater.

The operas are almost ready for rehearsal. We met today at Milton Feist's for a discussion of the production. Feist is a delightful, benevolent tyrant in a wheelchair. One more role to cast, then I must face those ogresses, the opera singers, with a strong hand. (Feist says, "With an iron fist.")

Cocteau replies to our request for permission to use one of his drawings as our theater signet: "I am your friend and agree to anything that will give you pleasure or render you service." And a sublime drawing of Orpheus with oak-leaf laurels on the same page.

April 26, 1957

We've seen hundreds of lofts, stores, spaces, but either zoning, exits, columns, or costs prevent us. Constant discouragement.

At the St. James Hotel (I remember you, memory, with your neon lights and your pianos) to look at Genius, Incorporated, as a theater space. Wouldn't it be poetic justice if it worked out? Not even a "for rent" sign, but we asked and were shown in. In the clutter, ghosts lay littering the battleground.

April 29, 1957

At Robert Lewis' lecture:
"But it would take a lifetime to perfect this method."
Lewis: "Yes, but so does any work the artist chooses to do. We always die too young."

April 30, 1957

Another concert: Pieces by Browne and Cage and Feldman. Illustrious pianists: Masselos, Cage, Grete Sultan, and Tudor.

But there is no air here.

Today I thought: Why can I not give myself over? But then I want too absolute a change. It may be that with each such mood I am already more given over than before.

Across the glossy expanse of the piano, Edgar Varèse stares glumly. His mouth is drawn down. He perks his head up at all the important sounds. At the third piano, John's face is devoutly solemn. They attend to the profundities with raptly blank faces.

I write because the writing makes it real. Till I am given over.

May 2, 1957

Walk from Paul's to Alan's, past the forbidding windows of Bellevue. There's new construction on every side, and in an empty lot, the interns playing lacrosse. Past the shining U.N. which we visited two Sundays ago with Garrick. Its glowing architecture meant to inspire us to an ideal less pure than its alabaster, but as hard.

Alan has returned, ill, to Serafina, who feeds and nurses him with ostentatious solicitude, bringing him horrid mixtures of malt and herbs and baby foods.

I bring him the complete version of *Gautama*, Act I and of the little Sappho poem that I wrote at Dwight's which he wants to set. He has visited Mytilene and seen the very cliff.

Eric Gutkind: "The Bible mentions immortality, but once: It is said, 'Ye certainly shall not die,' and these words were in the mouth of the negative principle: They were spoken by the serpent."

" . . . What Freud showed us is that the subconscious life is not a granite foundation but an abyss."

" . . . A meaningless life is the acme of suffering."

Lucy Gutkind sits beside me and with wifely indifference pays little attention to the talk but a great deal of attention to the listeners and their reactions, as if, having accepted the philosophy, it now matters only that it be understood.

Gutkind's is a positive view. He calls it existential, though his context seems more altruistic than other existentialist expressions.

There are, Gutkind says, the private answers of psychoanalysis (which Campbell calls "that boring little family romance"), but these cannot replace a philosophical view. The meaning of life is to partake.

There are two alternatives that the existentialists offer to the destructive impulse of our times.

The religious existential view: "Accepting God, we stand at every moment before the very countenance of God," and this, as Kierkegaard saw, "makes life almost unbearable."

And the atheist existential view: Since God is dead (Nietzsche) or nonexistent, there remains only one absolute—death. And freedom consists of not fearing death.

Both views are struggles to overcome fear.

"We must see this clash of ideas not as the great fear but as the great opportunity. This takes courage and optimism."

Gutkind says that Freud showed us how, when we suppress the animal savagery, we become neurotic.

But when asked what the alternative to savagery or neurosis was, Freud always answered: "I have no advice."

But Gutkind says if the subconscious is not a granite foundation, but an abyss, then we must rise out of this abyss by a vertical movement.

Gutkind speaks with the perspective of a mind of genius. Not a word out of place. He seems to digress into long descriptions of diseases—of cancer and schizophrenia—but then he demonstrates that these two diseases physiologically mirror the disease of our times.

Before the beginning of the lecture Lucy Gutkind asked about my mother and when I told her of Mother's death, her immediate troubled response was, "Don't tell Eric." And then, clutching my hand, "Later, after the talk, tell him later."

May 18, 1957

Yesterday was Garrick's eighth birthday.

The opera is in rehearsal. We have a gifted cast. Helen George analyzes everything from the psychoanalytic view; she won't sing facing upstage at all; she admires Callas' temperament as well as her voice. Ellen Faull has an uncanny voice and loves the work.

We rehearsed at Ellen's apartment in the Eldorado. Its lavish lobby recalls the days of our plush poverty after my father died.

1942:

We have no place to go, and no money, mother and I. An eccentric lady, Doctor Oshlag, invites us to live for some months in her terrace apartment in the Eldorado, amid a musty luxury.

Paul says I live in hell because I make constant judgments. How can I think without judging? I want the whole truth, and trying to see the whole truth I am torn apart by the possibilities, as though there were many truths and they could not survive together. If they cannot survive together, they are not truths.

Thus I complain to Paul: I am not endowed with the sage's powers and yet, on the other hand, I am not stupid. It would be better to be stupid than to be stuck in this position. If I were stupid I would act. If I were wise I would know. I cannot become what is not mine to become, but if I accept what I am, as I accept what I am not, I can cling to the dramatic truth.

The dramatic truth is one kind of feeling that translates into action.

The Tao of movement from sensation to motion.

May 20, 1957

Helen George is too emotional, plays her own intensity instead of the role. Ruth Kobart and Monachino are troupers. Ellen's voice is glorious. Larry Kornfeld is assisting me at bridging music and staging. During the blocking I apologize too often. Perhaps I am trying to call attention to the fact that I am being considerate.

I am too aware of death. This consciousness disturbs my every action.

May 21, 1957

At Fanny's. James Daly quotes Stark Young: "In the old days the actors didn't understand the plays but they knew how to act them; nowadays they understand the plays but they don't know how to act them."

Could I empty myself to be as unthinking as the oracle, and like the oracle utter words that are not mine from a source I do not know?

And at night after the Robert Lewis lecture I talk to the actors at Downey's about acting, very wisely, knowing that all my knowledge is worthless. Worthless till I let go.

May 26, 1957

Rehearsals proceed miraculously. Both operas are almost completely blocked. Good *esprit*.

June 1, 1957

When I work now I am so much in the center of the problem that I am not conscious. I work like a medium, instinctively, without questioning myself, as though I were alone. The performers exist only as extensions of my own possibilities. I can either make them yield or not.

The good *esprit* has broken down. Mounting tensions have taken quite a toll.

Helen George's soul is in turmoil and wracked with frustration and anger. She screams.

It was a rehearsal at the Fraternal Clubhouse, and my eyes went round and round the tiled floor divining Masonic patterns, and in this way I kept quiet while she raged. Later she telephoned and was apologetic, and since then she has been almost too fond of me.

June 5, 1957

The last few moments—ironing costumes, adding a bow to Ruth's shoes, etcetera. For the last time it is my stage, and then I will give it over to what is outside myself, and those strangers will inhabit the empty seats and devour my work.

June 13, 1957

The events of my life move me too little since the ones for whom I wanted to prove myself are gone. Through my mother there was still a vicarious means of pleasing my father. They were my audience; they were my purpose. There was something that I had to show them. Now I look at everyone, asking, "Who are these people?" And have no answer.

The operas: The designer's work, like the performer's, blossoms out suddenly on opening night. The director fades away at that moment into the oblivion of the harmonious whole.

June 16, 1957

Again hopes aroused by another theater that we can't possibly finance. A large, old theater, once Miner's Burlesque House, decrepit but perfect in every way.

With $60,000 we could have it. But it could as well be 60 million.

Climb to the top balcony with Merce; look down over the little horeshoe of the first balcony to the stage in the distance with its three-story proscenium.

"Like a miniature opera house," says Merce.

A hot day, and we perspire there in the dusty heights.

A gang of five kids comes in as the house opens, to see the Saturday movie show. The screen lights up with cowboys as we come down. Merce gives me his strong dancer's hand for balance. I think of Remy saying, "He is now at his peak. He must dance now," as the Western rolls on.

Business has dropped at the movie house and the friendly keeper of the door tells us that they scarcely break even. He has a black cat. I do not hope.

Yet Merce is enthused. He will report it all to John and Paul Williams.

A few days ago we visited John Cage at Stony Point. He was making strawberry jam, of which he gave us a jar. And showed us Lamb's Quarters, an edible weed like a tasty spinach, which we picked and had for supper the next night, and we picked mint and watercress by the stream.

"It's not that I don't care about the arts; it's that I'm so interested in botany," he says.

Still the theater rouses him.

Julian wants to do an opera with him. John prefers to call it theater. But then he thought a while, a habit he has of stopping to consider, and said: "Yes, opera—that means 'the works'!"

Vera Williams, on a terrace, was nursing her new baby, which they have named Merce, while the other children danced around in carefree circles.

Still I wouldn't want it, that realer life of the green world. It is too close to the earth, which swallows us only too soon.

June 18, 1957

Yesterday Alan made a remarkable tape recording of improvised piano music under the influence of several goddesses.

First we smoked a long time and then I read to him from Graves' *Greek Myths* the story of Zagreus, even the story of the frenzy. And when the tiny room where there was scarcely space for us became stifling in the heat, Alan sat down to play what he called at first A *Preamble*. He claims again to be possessed. He believes it is an oriental master who is performing through him. He works fiercely and with a look of just having been struck unconscious by a blow on the head. I have seen prize-fighters on the television wear exactly this expression at the moment of staggering just before they fall senseless to the canvas.

Alan maintained this expression throughout the meditation.

Simplicity of sound alternated with moments of extravagance that used the piano as though it were an organ.

Indeed some somber-voiced angel could have sung spontaneously among these voluminous crescendos.

At lunch we talked over the attributes of the spirits and the implication of believing in such heathenish creatures.

I read again, this time of Poseidon. The heat was tropical, and we sweated like the sea.

He played again. A long piece. The overtones combating one another with such violence that it has the effect of orchestral armies clashing in some musical Armageddon.

Alan hurt his fingers on the keyboard trying to fulfill the requirements of the mystical master and left a trace of blood on the ivory.

When we heard it played back, we could only laugh with enthusiasm.

Later, I read again, this time of Dionysus whose story is coincident with that of Zagreus, but even more possessed of frenzy, and dedicated to an intoxicant—like ours.

June 21, 1957   *Midsummer Day*

With John and Merce and Paul Williams to look at theaters. Merce needs enough space to leap. John is full of impossible schemes and his beneficent smile is so guileless that it seems no thinking person could smile so purely. He drives the Volkswagen bus in which we go from columned loft to aerie garage; the strain of New York traffic never seems to disturb him.

We see a building about which Paul Williams is positive, an abandoned department store on 14th Street.

June 23, 1957

Sitting with Larry Kornfeld over beer in the Remo, Julian and I see Jim Agee's ghost at every table, big and beautiful and drunk and full of wit and deathly despair. A few old friends wander over to our table.

June 24, 1957

At the cemetery to say *kaddish* for my mother. The new grave is bare beside the tended one. We feared the visit, but the fear gave way to the vague stoic feelings that cemeteries bring on.

Because it is not acceptable to human feelings that the one who was warm and real is there, cold, in the earth. The living memory is real: of my mother at picnics or in the car driving out to Cedar Park, or at home, or away from home, but not there. No, not there under earth, where one cannot imagine her physical presence without the specter of decay.

"Human nature cannot know this," said Gertrude Stein, "but the human mind can." Therefore feeling stops, and suddenly there is a void. And in this state we say our prayers at the grave.

Then we leave hastily. We picnic with Garrick at our old spot on Hillside Avenue. We'd gotten lost, and winding toward the Hudson, we found the wooded nook where we had often picnicked with her, and where she was more readily memorialized than at the grave.

Then, for the third time, we climbed High Tor. The climb more strenuous at thirty-one. When we reached the top I did not like the wind and the long vista, was afraid of falling.

We looked down upon the top of a plane circling below us. This, too, disturbed me.

Michael Fraenkel, editor of *Death*, they tell us, is dead.

Last night we had Ellen Faull and Dr. Gordon and his daughter, Marsha Joseph, to dinner.

We talk about magic. He does not believe in it. Yet, he says, if we grant we have come from the anthropoid apes, why should we not in 10 million years be men with brains as large as this room, deriving strength to fulfill our every need from the solar energy?

The earthworm, he says, has four brains and not one of them can think. But none of them the size of this room.

June 26, 1957

The Gutkinds have just left. We talked of the great and the small things with equal liveliness.

His abstract look makes me imagine that he is not listening and I turn my eager eyes toward Lucy. She answers more to the point; when he speaks, it is out of the obscurest depth.

Garrick came in and Gutkind said that he sees in him a great Jewish scholar. A reflection, perhaps, of my father in the old seer's eyes?

But we do not speak of the past or the dead but of the times we live in and the division of our lives.

A letter from Alan:

June 22, 1957
Rochester
Dear Judith:

Many thanks for being my white goddess and bringing forth such an astonishment.

As to the tape, I made another copy and a record. But may I keep all of them long enough to study and make a score on *Meditation on Poseidon?* Something strange is going on. And I have been warned that if this is played at present (except to you and that is all) that I will lose the power which is in this new yet infinitely ancient music. The "guide" who used my hands and mind is not a human, but a "blue flame," a kind of Aztec being who carries a symbol of human sacrifice.

Tonight in this dreadful hotel the room filled up with spirits of black dancers who were singing and dancing for me, yet were chasing me. And they wished to get the "stuff." This means I must insulate this power for about a month, and study and work on it until I can master these new principles. I am holding your record for you, however, and as soon as I can make a score of it, I will give it to you. Only even then, please keep it very secret until I get a go-ahead signal from "blue flame."

My deepest love to you always,
Alan

July 9, 1957   **New York City**

A letter from Alan:

July 2, 1957
Dear Judith:

Your beautiful letter received and cherished. In Boston . . . my piece *Kohar* went marvelously. . . .

Then late, around 1:30 A.M., I was walking Serafina to a friend's house in the South End when it happened—my initiation. It started with our day at 40 Union Sq. with *Meditation on Poseidon.* Human sacrifice. My bloody hand was the symbol when I played. Now it came to its climax. A man stepped up to us as I was leaving Serafina at the door. The man put his hand in his pocket and said, "This is a .38. This is a stickup. Hand over your wallet or I'll blast you."

I did nothing. He said, "Are you going to play games? Do you want to die in the street?"

Suddenly I said quietly, "This is as good a time as any. Go ahead."

At this he was surprised. He tried to shake hands. I said, "No thank you."

I feel that I passed the initiation.

The *Meditation of Poseidon* is now written out in pencil and I have started to put the *Preamble* into notation. Every day I have played the tape until my machine is worn out. It can be done and soon I will copy it.

You are the white goddess who made all this possible.

All my love,
Alan

The street, I thought, as the brighter light of freedom flooded my eyes, is the place that surrounds the prison.

The people walking "in the street" lost the enchantment that they had had when seen from behind the mesh screens and gratings of the Women's House of Detention, because while from inside they seemed to be free, as soon as I stepped out they were as I was, and I was not ever again to be free while prisons exist, and I am not free now.

I am not free because I am in the street that surrounds and encircles the prison. The street that squeezes its misery into the prisons as if to rid itself of pain by compressing it into its innards.

"In the street" on a farm, or at sea, or on the road, or in the metropolis. "In the street" is on that narrow strip around the walls that enclose the secret sins of the world and the elemental human. Here we hide away our untamed part, instead of letting our minds know how our hearts feel, free and un-ashamed and compassionate.

I looked from the outside and waved up at the barred windows (Joan, Deane, and Dorothy were still inside) and felt myself divided between free and not free. Then I chose the better part and I am not free. Within that contradiction, choosing freely to be not free, is the only possible freedom.

Julian and I had come out of the north, which the Masons call the land of darkness, but which the aurora borealis crowned with sparkling lights for us.

Garrick was safe at camp. We drove north with Lester. In Maine there was the spectacle of the still-raw sea, as wide as before the advent of the machines; washed up on its shores, not refuse, but clean, tangled sea things, a school of baby sharks come to grief, lying with their sharp tiny teeth exposed to the sky, starfish vibrating in their breathing skins, sea urchins, weeds and shells and shapes not catalogued on land.

The shore grew rockier. We crossed into Canada; at Pocologan we stayed in a log cabin poised over the Bay of Fundy.

I went out into the cold night (we were far north enough to need a fire this summer night) and I sat on the rocks bared by the prodigious tide, wishing I were not afraid of the sea. I was troubled, and I could not turn again.

When the moon set, the aurora borealis lit up the sky in waves wider than the sea's waves, and whiter than the sea's foam.

That was the first light.

We drove up through Nova Scotia to Pugwash, where we came across a Gathering of the Clans. Girls in feathered tartans and brilliant plaids played on bagpipes, while kilted men danced for the assembly.

A week later the Pugwash Conference on War in the Nuclear Age was in session, and the name Pugwash was spoken all over the world. Scientists gath-ered to talk about A- and H-bomb fallout, nuclear testing, and the hope of peace between the larger clans.

As we neared the Gaspé peninsula we watched night fall among the pines on a cliff overlooking the *Baie de Chaleur.*

And that night, too, the aurora borealis. This time in rays from the zenith, like a celestial tent of light. Four nights with lights. That was the second light.

On the Gaspé we lived like vacationers in a foreign film, in a little hotel run by three pretty *Québecoises.*

Returning to the United States, we picked up two soldiers hitchhiking back to their air force base in Maine. They told us about the Nike rockets in readiness at their base. Rockets that seek out, follow, and destroy their targets. They said they hated the base out in the middle of nowhere. They hated the rockets and their potential destructiveness. They expressed their despair in a vain attempt to cheer each other up with the usual soldier's gripes.

"The woods here," they said as we approached the border, "are all thick with radar plane-spotters. The whole coastline is like that but especially up here. This whole area is restricted territory."

To our right and left, the road wound through thick pine forests. Not even telegraph poles or wires ran along the road. But they showed us where some of the rocket stations were. And among the treetops of those seemingly primeval woods, we could see the launching equipment.

Nike, the winged victory, the ruthless, strode flying through the sky. Athena was meant to temper her warlike aspects with wisdom. But Nike is the spirit of power and conquest. And it was terrible to see her return, out of an oblivion which only the artists' necrophilia had penetrated in ornament and masterpiece. After the servicemen got out at their destination, we drove on in silence, in discomfort at Nike overhead.

Soon a lightning storm burst around us. Brilliant streaks flew toward us as we drove into and out of the storm. The landscape changed from forest to farm and I saw the bright light hit the fields. That was the third light.

And the lightning seemed Nike's. But it was not, for as we drove out of the storm in the dawn, a rainbow stretched across the farms, its unbroken arch dissolving at either end in the trees that border the fields. We stopped by the side of the road to watch it fade.

And I gave thanks for God's covenant with Noah, promising that the earth will not be destroyed. That was the last light, the comforting one.

The day we returned, Dick Kern called to ask what we were going to do tomorrow during the air raid drill. Julian spoke to him, and then told me that we were going to participate in the protest.

We wrote cards to be mailed to Garrick in camp every day for ten days. I took Shakespeare, some extra money, and a notebook. It grew late and we took a taxi to Chrystie Street to the *Catholic Worker*'s House of Hospitality.

The exact time of the drill was not specified, but was to be between twelve and two.

The atmosphere before the event was a vacuum of small actions and expectations. Get used to waiting, I thought, it is what life is.

Dorothy pinned a red rose on me. She and Deane Mowrer wore red roses too. Bearded Dan O'Horgan showed me how to operate a Gandhian spinning wheel.

Wrapping sandwiches, Ammon told us about his picketing in Las Vegas against the bomb tests.

Outside the windows we saw the police gather. Reporters appeared.

Dorothy speculated that since there were so many police, they might try to prevent us from going outside when the sirens sounded. And if they forcibly kept us inside we would be foiled in making our protest. So we walked out toward the park before the sirens. As at the protest two years earlier, it was a bright, clear, perfect day.

The park is called Sara Delano Roosevelt Park after the mother of the man who approved developing the bomb but was spared the decision to use it.

Reporters ran toward us, cameras cocked. They pleaded with us to return so that they could photograph us coming out of the building. Dorothy refused to pose for them. They railed: "You promised us you were coming out when the sirens sounded!" Dorothy smiled.

A Japanese reporter, attracted by the Catholic Worker's statement that this demonstration was in penance for the destruction of Hiroshima and Nagasaki, followed us with a tape recorder into which he spoke, in his poetical, staccato language, a description of the proceedings.

Julian handled the newsmen valiantly. We sat.

As the CBS cameramen assembled their equipment, I thought of the coming silence in the cells, against which this moment's celebrity shattered like the sunlight under the park's trees. But I was wrong. The cells are noisy. In prison there is no quiet.

Sirens. The Japanese reporter shouted into his machine above the din. Faster and louder.

Our gray-haired friend, Colonel Hearn, in his dazzling uniform, approached each of us individually: "Will you take shelter?" And each of us answered no. The Japanese reporter thrust his microphone between Colonel Hearn and each answerer.

Under arrest, Dorothy and Julian walked side by side to the van.

There were ten of us in the wagon: Julian, Dorothy, Ammon, Deane, Kerran Duggan, Dan O'Horgan, Sandy Darlington, Michael Graine, and a youngster named Karl Meyer, who had decided that morning to join us.

With us also was a friendly cop who often stops for coffee at the *Catholic Worker*. A cheerful tone prevailed.

We are embarrassed by real action. We are ashamed lest we appear heroic. So we gab and joke and mock ourselves lest others mock us.

Then the monotony began, the routine procedures that filled our next days.

The all-clear sounded as we were booked at Elizabeth Street Station, asked name, age, address, and whether we used drugs.

Then, in the van again, we rode to 151st Street where Judge Bayer immediately heard our case.

We all pleaded guilty.

The courtroom was empty except for 2 court-appointed lawyers, a reporter from the *Post*, one from the *Times*, and one from the *Daily Worker*. And the assistant district attorney was there to prosecute us in case we did not plead guilty.

Ammon spoke of penance. Dorothy spoke of psychological warfare and penance.

The judge shuffled his papers.

I saw the judge's face harden, his eyes flash in contemptuous anger. He worked himself up to say foolish things; he turned to Dorothy and said:

"Go home and read the Bible and find out what our Lord Jesus Christ would have done for penance. . . . You are a bunch of heartless individuals who breathe contempt of the law. . . . I have no sympathy for you or for your cause. Thirty days in the workhouse."

Because, as I set down these last words, the thirty-day sentence again seems long, as it did at first, I stopped writing and paused to remember those who are serving not thirty days but thirty years. And if I reread these words, or if anyone else reads them, and thinks that thirty days is long, it would be fitting to stop and to remember what we are doing to one another.

I was concerned for Julian. It's easier to go to jail than to imagine someone you love as a prisoner. I kissed him quickly as we were led out of the courtroom.

We were sentenced and taken to jail a few hours after the sirens. I think they were prepared for us.

Joan Moses, tall, pale, blond, was brought into our cell while we were waiting to be taken to prison. She told us later that at first she thought Dorothy a shoplifter, Deane a slum landlord, and me a prostitute.

Joan is 22. She and her husband expressed their protest in the tradition of rugged American individualism. He, a conscientious objector, had been a medic in the war. Stationed in Germany, they had become pacifists while living among the conquered people. They made signs which read We are Preparing For War—Why Not Prepare For Peace? and drove to Times Square when the sirens sounded to parade with their signs. They had not expected to be arrested. She was astonished to discover there were others.

We were put into another van, completely closed save for heavily meshed slits.

The men were in the front, handcuffed to one another, we four in a small cubicle in the rear. The metal bench jogged unmercifully and we were thrown with every roughness of the road.

At Bronx County Prison the men were separated from us. Through the small slit I called to Julian, "What about our visit to Garrick?"

"It's too late to worry about that. Write to him!" And again, "Write to Garrick!"

Now the feeling of captivity began, and till the moment I stepped out into the street again I was not myself but under a spell. One cannot act but can only be acted upon; not move, but be moved. It is the spell of Sleeping Beauty, of Brünhilde, of all princes transformed into beasts and toads. It is also the nonfictional story of all slaves, all the oppressed, and of all prisoners.

We rode on in our metal compartment to our new home in Greenwich Village.

First they took away our possessions. Then our clothing. We tied our clothes into the dresses we had been wearing. We were showered and given cotton robes to wear. The guard who guided us through these things asked me why we were arrested.

When I told her, she sneered incredulously, "You mean for ideals?"

"Yes, for ideals."

"You don't know what you're doing," she replied. "Why, if you knew the filth, the scum, the dirt you're going to mix with up there, the kind of filth that's up there"—she kept pointing to the ceiling—"you wouldn't want to mix with that dirt for all the ideals in the world."

I was sitting, naked, on the stone floor of the shower room, tying my bundled dress with the string she had provided. It was my first encounter with the guards; none of the others that I later met shared her outspoken contempt for the prisoners.

Different forms were filled out. We answered the same questions over and over. We signed a paper saying that the prison authorities had the right to read our mail. If we didn't sign it we didn't get mail. Then we were given numbers.

58601

58602 (Deane)

58603 (Dorothy)

Finally we were searched for drugs. The rectal and vaginal examinations were so brutal that I screamed in pain and Dorothy bled and had to be treated for the bleeding. After this torment we were taken by elevator to the seventh floor where we were to be confined.

The door opened on a hectic scene. A hallway filled with shouting girls, who gathered around to see the new arrivals. Almost all of them were colored. They wore plain print cottons, were curious about us, friendly. And I was amazed to find them so free and wild.

The block-long hall has concrete floors and yellow, glazed-tile walls, at either end a mesh-covered window, one to Greenwich Avenue, the other to Sixth Avenue. In the center two entranceways: to the dining hall and the recreation room. And from this hall four gates led into "the corridors" A, B, C, and D, where were entombed the cells.

A very young girl with short hair and a leather wristband (a sign of masculinity in the prison) pointed to me and cried out to the guard who was assigning us cells: "Put her in my cell." Her look was unmistakably desirous. Dorothy, who until now had borne everything with only quiet complaints, suddenly assumed her grave look. She spoke with authority: "She is to be put in my cell."

I was given cell number 23, together with Dorothy. Deane was in another corridor.

Yet Dorothy was to recall the small tough girl with the wristband and to regret what she called "interference."

We went to our cells and tried to find what comfort we could for the night. A low bed slips out from under the cell bed, for the cells were built for one, and the prison is horribly overcrowded. There's a sink and a toilet and a tin table and a shelf, a clothes hanger and a window. Of the twenty-four small panes of the window, six open partially. But this opening is covered with a heavy screening that has been painted over so many times that it is almost solid with paint and dirt. One pane, below this opening, is clear glass. Out of cell 23 I could see an inch of the Nedicks' facing the Village square, and I looked at length at the people "in the street."

The first night was a noisy night. Some nights it's calm, but on some nights a touch of madness overcomes everyone; some nights there's an air of melancholy, and on some nights a desperate gaiety. It was a gay night the first night. Before lights-out, one is locked in one's corridor with the cells inside still open, so that there is a social hour of visiting, dancing, gambling, putting up pin curls.

Because of Dorothy I was embarrassed by the obscenities, though they sometimes became wildly poetical, like Jackie's crooning complaints, or her dissertations on God and fate. The Oedipal adjective precedes every other noun. Deane suffers, but Dorothy says, "I have a deaf ear and at such times I turn my deaf ear."

The first night I cried and enviously watched the people walk in and out of Nedicks'.

Was I ashamed? Yes, somehow, without having committed what I counted as a crime, I was ashamed. I shared in all their guilts: the prisoners', the judges', and the guards'.

And these thoughts turned my tears into little lights containing images of courts and Julian's and Dorothy's minutest actions.

We found a New Yorker magazine with Auden's poem "First Things First," which ends with the startling line: "Thousands have lived without love, not one without water."

Except for the sick and the drug addicts, the prisoners are provided with most of their external needs. We were kept moderately clean, fed, bedded, dressed, and given ordinary consideration. But internally and psychologically, it is the hellish image of the modern world where we die gasping for the air of love. We drown in the baptismal waters. . . . We drown in little drops of blood.

The image is religious because, as in a true initiation, I was provided with a psychopomp, a Virgil of the highest rank who made the ordeal itself beautiful.

Dorothy Day guided me without preaching. Except for her daily readings from her breviary, most of our conversations were either practical or long, narrative chapters out of our life stories. It was by her actions and her restraint that she showed me what to do.

She doesn't step forward to do a thing, but knows the need will make itself known. When the sirens blared, the need was so great that it called out to her and she didn't refuse it; stepped out into the sunlit park.

The first day is called isolation day and one is not let out of the cell. Since we had only our cotton robes, the girls gave us clothes. They looked upon us as their responsibility and gave us everything we needed, including advice on what attitudes we should adopt and how we should behave. They were curious about us and respected our cause. They understood easily why a bad law must be broken.

But when we spoke of the abolition of prisons, they immediately told us horror stories, as if we did not know what terrible crimes there are and how badly people treat each other.

Dorothy is patient. She does not try to teach and thereby we all learn from her.

I see now that I cannot write down the essence of Dorothy's influence on me. Only that I felt myself to be in the presence of someone in whom I could have complete faith, someone who does the right thing, even the holy thing, at every moment.

Deane adores her and studies her. Deane seems much older than she is, for her small, crouched frame is the image of resignation. She was a teacher of English literature at the University of New Mexico, but her eyes failed her and she could not read well enough to do the work.

But her love of God grew and she determined to become a nun, till at the *Catholic Worker* she found a secular religious focus, and in Dorothy a model and a saint. She has "given up" this world, but she suffers from it, which means that she has given up its pleasures but not its sorrows. The fear of blindness haunts her.

Deane, in her gentleness, is trying to make her faith a fortress against the world, while Dorothy uses her faith to sensitize her to all the feelings of heaven and earth.

Our day of isolation was broken up by fingerprinting, a visit to the clinic for a Wasserman and other crass medical procedures.

In the infirmary, a young, wide-eyed girl who tried to talk like Humphrey Bogart flirted with me. . . . "I'd like to . . . you know . . . take you out when we're in the street. But I expect to do about three or four, so we can't make a date."

Her name is Annette and she is in detention awaiting trial for larceny. (She broke into a car, had been arrested for the same offense several times in a few weeks, she said.) She talked a lot about her mother.

Detention girls, like Annette, who have not yet been sentenced, wear their own clothes, do not work, and are kept isolated from "sentenced girls." One of the only ways in which a "detained" prisoner is shown the courtesy of being treated as if she were innocent until proven guilty, is in being protected from the corrupting influence of sentenced girls.

This girl is in prison because she wants to defy, to cry out, to disobey, to be chased, caught, caged, in order to show that she can't be subjugated and that she doesn't fear their threats. Yet she becomes sentimental, and regrets that she is causing her mother sorrow. She inquired after my mother and reacted to the fact of her death as though she had known her. Then she toughened and talked like Humphrey Bogart again. I saw her later while I was working. She was waiting to be punished for cutting a girl with a broken bottle during a "general fight" on her floor. A guard whisked me away before I could hear the details.

"Don't talk to the detention girls."

Many girls said they never looked out of the windows because it depressed them. But I loved to watch the people below as they started out gaily each night to the Village life, then bedraggle as the night wore on, till only the after-hours stragglers were left.

Is that someone I know? Everyone might be someone familiar—from the seventh story.

Our cell was changed to number 13. Now below me was the alleyway of Patchin Place, white flowers planted at the entrance of the house where we visited e. e. cummings. And in the distance the Empire State Building.

And along Sixth Avenue on 14th Street I could see the windows of the abandoned Hecht's department store that we visited with Merce and John and Paul Williams, and where we hope to build our theater.

Cell 13 faces the shower room—deprived even of that feeble stir of air that cross-ventilates the cells. I spent a day poking the dirt and paint out of the screen that was the only access to air, but the window opens in such a devilish way that it's nearly impossible for air to penetrate.

The temperature went up to 98 and still no breeze. Dorothy was gasping. I fanned her when I was not too hot and weary myself.

Dorothy was put to work in the laundry. It was hard, hot work and her distress increased every day.

One day in exasperation she wished that the window were broken so that some air could enter. In keeping with our half-joking mood, I took off my shoe and threatened the pane (the six-by-four-inch clear one for looking out to the free world).

"Break it," said Dorothy, "break it."

Certain that the glass was heavy, even invulnerable, I struck it rather lightly with the heel of my shoe and it shattered into a spiderweb. We looked at each other in horror. Surely breaking a prison window is a serious offense. If we were found out, I knew that, should I say I did it, Dorothy would say that it was she who instigated it. We even discussed the possibility of saying it was broken by a mop handle while we were swabbing the cell.

We were spared the need to lie. It was never noticed. We were entitled to five days off for good behavior and we worried the whole time that that broken window would cost us our five days' good time.

This is the viciousness of authoritarian liberality, of a progressive state, of beneficent tyrannies.

The more beneficent, the more we have to lose. Every "good" law chains us more firmly to the idea of law itself, which is, in the long run, repressive, because it holds us back.

For the prisoner, five days off for good behavior only means five days more for bad behavior.

The broken window became a secret little crime between me and Dorothy that bound us even closer together.

Joan Moses shared the cell next to ours with Deane and worked in the laundry with Dorothy. Deane was assigned to sweeping the roof and I to mopping the offices and the downstairs lobby.

We were given work clothes, print dresses, socks, shoes, and our daily routines began.

We rose early, at six. Breakfasted at seven in the mess hall. The food was substandard: coffee (mostly chicory), cereal with powdered milk, jam, and a pasty white bread. The mess hall, like the cells, crawled with cockroaches. The din made conversation impossible. The meals were rushed because of the overcrowding.

I went to work early while the others were locked in for a count. The endless counting. Every change of guards means two countings, one by the guard who is leaving, and one by the guard coming on, and the count is always wrong and is done over and over again while we are kept sitting in the cells with our gates partially shut.

My work hours were short. I mopped and dusted and swept and polished the brass in the lobby and the offices. A good-natured colored woman, hearty, pleasant, and serious, was my "boss." She was patient with my clumsiness and taught me to use and wring the mop properly. She stood close beside me while I cleaned the rotunda, which lies outside the bars and is the foyer to the street, "guarding" me as I worked.

I liked the work on the main floor. There were many people—police, visitors—comings and goings to and from the street. I liked the connection with the outside. I saw and learned much, which I reported to the prisoners upstairs.

I saw the detention girls on their way to court in the morning, dressed in the evening finery in which they had been picked up, escorted by their arresting officers. These vile men appear in the mornings in their uniforms, but when the girls saw them last they were in plainclothes, seducing, cajoling, lying to entrap them into a prostitute's jail sentence.

Most of the girls are arrested for prostitution. Most of the girls are drug addicts. Most of the girls are arrested by the dishonorable men of the vice squad.

I watched these sad processions. I watched the cops and heard them talk about wages, pensions, and vacation. I overheard their conversations about the girls, whom they regard with horror.

Dorothy says we must win them over with love, and that it is not enough to do civil disobedience; we have to show them (and ourselves and all others) that we do it for love of them.

My conversations with my boss, Miss Ogilvie, grew longer and more subtle. She was not impatient even with our radical views but tried to point out our error. Her views are sophisticated, conventional, and implacable. She is not a stupid woman by any means.

On Sunday I went with Dorothy and Deane to hear mass in the chapel, which is the best room in the house of D., high ceilinged and well designed. The chapel and the rotunda are the only rooms built with an aesthetic idea. The rotunda fails with its brass bars weakly disguised as stalks of wheat. But the chapel has dark wooden walls and an arched ceiling. A tripartite altarpiece turns a different face for the Catholic, Protestant, and Jewish services. For the Catholics there is a crucifix. The priest wore a green chasuble with a golden cross; a youngster assisted him. The mass was spoken quickly, and almost inaudibly. The priest read a portion of the Gospels in which Jesus instructs the Pharisees: "If you have rancor in your heart against your brother, first make peace with your brother and then bring your sacrifices to the altar."

He narrowly interpreted this to mean that his congregation should prepare for confession by proper observances. He spoke without feeling.

It was not until the next weekend that I could attend the Jewish service. The crucifix had been turned to the wall and the Ten Commandments were in view. Though it was one o'clock on Friday afternoon, the *Shabbos* candles were lit. There were only two others in the congregation, both elderly ladies who lived on our floor. Their names were Ruth and Rachel. Both were diabetic. Both were gray-haired. Ruth had lost 60 or 80 pounds during a year in jail. Rachel was white and plump.

Rachel owned a general goods store on Second Avenue and was convicted of marketing stolen goods. "How could I know those sweaters weren't legitimate?" she complains to everyone. Ruth never told me what she was in for.

Both ladies considered all the other prisoners despicable, vulgar creatures. One claimed to be innocent. The other admitted she had erred but did not think that this rightfully placed her among prostitutes and drug addicts. Their special charge was the cat, Jimmy, whom they fed and looked after.

These two formed the whole congregation for many weeks. The rabbi read from the Union Prayerbook, with *Sh'ma Yisroel* the only Hebrew words. Then he talked gently to the three of us of repentance.

The first ten days I had no word from Julian and no news of where he was. It was said that prisoners could not write one another, but Mrs. Glantzberg, the social service worker, arranged for us to write each other.

One day Miss Ogilvie assigned me to washing the walls of the rotunda with a long-handled brush. As I was working, Charlie McCormick, who was managing the *Catholic Worker* while its editors were in jail, came in for a business conference with Dorothy. As he came up to greet me, Miss Ogilvie restrained us, "You mustn't talk to a visitor." So I stood there grinning at him while he looked at me helplessly. He was made to wait there, and so I scrubbed in silence while the guard stood between us.

"It's very frustrating," I ventured, "to keep quiet in front of someone you want to talk to."

"I realize that," she said, "but you can't talk to him. . . . But I can." And she turned to him, "How is everyone?"

"Fine," he said.

"He says everyone is fine," she said.

"I want to know how my husband is—and where he is."

She: "How is her husband?"

He: "He's at the Tombs. His number is 483326."

She: "He says he's at the Tombs and his number is . . ." and she couldn't remember.

He: "483326."

She: "You mustn't speak to her."

And so on.

After twelve days Julian's first letter reached me. He wrote exuberantly of contact with his fellow prisoners. At first he was on Hart Island, and then he was transferred to the Tombs, where he worked in the kitchen for thirteen to fourteen hours a day, seven days a week. He did not complain.

He has written Garrick the whole story of our civil disobedience and arrest. Dorothy said it was right that this should be explained not by the mother, for whom sentimental sympathies were reserved, but man-to-man by the father.

In the afternoon those who are not working may go up to the roof. Again after supper there is a roof session. A wall nearly six feet high surrounds the roof. One can almost look over it, but not quite. There are, however, brightly painted benches, and standing on these we could see all of the Village and much of Manhattan. A metal mesh overhead enclosed the roof so that even the sky is covered lest one take flight, or lest manna fall on the imprisoned.

In the distance I could see the Tombs, a stark slab of a silhouette among the fanciful obelisks of lower Manhattan. Julian wrote that he saw no sky at the Tombs.

I saw them building a bank on the site of the notorious Waldorf Cafeteria where we stole a pie for Bodenheim's 70th birthday.

Too many dead already.

And the ships moved on the Hudson. And I saw all those roofs that cover those yet to die, as though they had already crumbled under the bombs from which I sought no shelter.

There was Joe Campbell's house, from which I watched the same river when I learned what it was that the Buddha learned under the Bo tree, and there the arch of Washington Square. I repeated the legend though I could not see the letters from my roof: "Let us raise a standard to which the faithful and honest may repair. The event is in the hand of God."

And I saw the New School, where from Piscator I learned the ritual art that drove me to think deep on the motives of men and of my own heart. And Morton Street where Valeska Gert danced and I checked hats and sang.

My history spread out before me like a map. The dead and the living were one in this tapestry as I gazed for hours at the past and the future.

Sometimes on the roof we played basketball, Dorothy's tallness proving a greater advantage than my youthful agility.

The evenings were spent in the recreation hall where an ill-tuned television set screamed over the cries of the card games. The popular programs were crime and prison dramas.

Where are the prototypes of these fictional criminals? They are in the prisons watching the TV portray caricatures of themselves.

During the heat wave there was no air and we talked about air as we waited for sleep and we walked about half-nude and took frequent showers. We called the roof and the showers our havens. Air and water.

We prayed for air in the stifling cell. And Dorothy told me the story of St. Vincent Ferrer who performed so many foolish miracles, like making a homely woman beautiful so that she might find a husband, that his superiors forbade him to work any further wonders. But one day Ferrer was walking past a church when a scaffolding on which a workman was repairing the upper structure broke. St. Vincent cried out, "Stop, stay where you are!" And the workman remained suspended in mid air while the Saint ran to his superior, begging permission to perform one more miracle, especially in view of the workman's occupation in repairing the house of God, and permission was granted. Ferrer hurried back, waved to the workman with the words, "Float down gently," which the happy workman did.

Dorothy then chanted: "St. Vincent Ferrer, send us some air."

And though the heat continued, there was, at least, a thunderstorm.

Every evening Dorothy would read to me the daily portion from her missal. Many priests visited and gave her various religious books, which, like her rosary, she was allowed to keep.

The saints passed nightly before us in humble penitent's sackcloth or in jeweled splendor, as she read to me in her unecclesiastical voice. How many of them were in the prisons! Starting with Peter, who broke his chains when he walked with the angel out of the prison where he, like Dorothy, was put for preaching.

After the lights were put out, Dorothy would recite a bedtime prayer and I would say, as she taught me, within the sanctions of our religious difference, "Thanks be to God."

Such piety as is hers does not swerve one away from one's own faith; rather in her faith I strengthened my own and through her saw how far a trust in God can take one.

There is a well-stocked library from which we borrowed far more than we could read.

Dorothy read first Stalin on Lenin. She reads quickly, a book a day.

I read Tolstoy's stories and *Anna Karenina* and Thomas Mann's *Doctor Faustus*.

Dorothy read part of *Doctor Faustus* on my recommendation, but she didn't want to finish it. She told me that when she tried to read *The Magic Mountain* she put down the book in distress and rose and sprinkled the whole room with talcum powder to dispel the odor of evil that she sensed all around her as she ascended the *Zauberberg*.

Deane feared even the mention of witches and witchcraft and refused to listen when I told Joan of Maya Deren's pranks.

Instead of dark books, Dorothy read of the sea. She read *Kon Tiki* and fled to the ocean. "This cell," she said, "is like a raft where we have so few of the usual comforts and yet we make an adventure of our voyage, and make a little world for ourselves."

Every prisoner decorates her cell with the few things that she is permitted, tacks a greeting card on the wall, puts up drawings, clippings, makes things of wool in the sewing room. "And decorate the place and call it home."

We four, always together, came to be known as "the air raid ladies." Dorothy leading us, looking like a monument to womanhood, erect like a country woman. And Deane beside her, bowed and tiny, cautiously measuring her next step, peering through heavy-tinted glasses. Then Joan, her innocent blond head announcing the respectability of her polite Methodist manners, and I with a pink and blue ribbon bought at the commissary, trying to look pretty.

"Judith Beck. Visitor."

I went with happy heart only to see Lester drunk and desperate.

The distance between those "on the street" and those "inside" widened.

He told me how his vows were broken; I saw how weak he really is. I realized how all our determinations are at the mercy of our weak wills, how insecure we all are, always, in each other. Not he, but I. Not he, but everyone.

Then, to calm myself, I thought of Julian keeping faith in the kitchens of the Tombs, and of all the C.O.'s in all the jails. And of Dorothy sitting a few feet away at that barricaded visitors' table where the inside and the outside meet.

Yet Lester asked me to keep faith with him and said that he would come to Patchin Place where I could see him—I would light a match so that he could see from where I was watching. "Come one night a week," I said. "I'll come every night," he said.

Put not your trust in princes.

After the visit I fell into a miasmic night of despair. I lay in my cell and wept till even the saint was out of patience with me. But it was grief "for everything, for everything."

Dorothy went to the next cell where Deane lived and together they recited a litany of the saints for me.

One by one the girls opened to us. They would come to our cell and drink Kool-Aid and eat Ritz crackers and tell their life stories.

These histories formed a dark background to our lives there.

The stories of the drug addicts. Each time they are arrested, usually for prostitution, they are put on the fourth floor in cells that are designated as "the tank." Here in solitude and darkness they undergo the "cold turkey cure": the skin crawls as though covered with vermin, the extremes of hunger and nausea, the freezing cold, the fevers, the fear of death, and at the height of the agony, the hope for death.

They become, in their sickness, incontinent, and they vomit and lie in their filth till the cell is hosed out.

Every girl knows girls who have died there and each fears that sooner or later it will be her turn to die in that dark, bare tank.

Telsa tells of being in the tank, and in the midst of her suffering another girl, sicker than she, was put in the same cell. The other girl was dying. Telsa tried to help her, tried to call a guard. But the tank cells are soundproof so that the victim can scream "to her heart's content." And no one came. The girl died. All night Telsa cowered in her sickness in the cell with the dead girl. In the morning the guard came and gave the cold body a shot of morphine.

Which might have saved her a few hours earlier.

There are stories of brutality, both credible and incredible. But whatever we choose to believe, the deaths are not necessary. There are treatments to relieve the withdrawal syndrome. They don't use them, with the excuse that "this is not a hospital."

There is the legend of a doctor so sadistic that two girls tried to drown her by forcing her head down into the cell toilet. She suffered ever after with an affliction, a constant twitch. Her abuses were part of the folklore of the House of Detention.

These stories are garbled and incoherent. They come in outbursts like the girls' life stories.

Sherry, 20, is a tall beauty; only her scarred arms attest to her sorrows. And her scarred hands too, for she takes heroin in any vein she can. At nine she had started a dope habit. At twelve she ran away from home and became a prostitute. Sometimes she worked in nightclubs as a show girl, but usually she lived with a man who found men for her, to support the habit of both. Some years ago she had a child, but the father deserted her in her seventh month, and the infant was placed with foster parents who are willing to give the child to her if she ever "cleans up."

Many of the girls have such lost children somewhere and have a poignant attachment to these remembered sons and daughters. But Sherry does not hope. She has been arrested sixteen times in the last two years. This time the judge wanted to send her to Westfield for a year, but Westfield is for "rehabilitation" and Sherry's record is marked "incorrigible."

"Sometimes I think of cleaning up, but then I see another girl and decide that what I want is to make it with her on the street and live the junkie's life because men are so disgusting. A square John is no man to me."

She has been brutally beaten by the cops. The despised vice squad is not as feared as are the sadists of the narcotics squad.

The addict, known through previous arrests, is never free again. Her door is broken down suddenly, and she is beaten until she tells where "the stuff is stashed." When there is nothing there, she is likely to be killed, so they say.

When we are asked about these abuses by the press, whom shall we believe? These disreputable junkies or the police officers who deny that such things happen?

They show us the strangulation marks on their necks, tell us of being hit with the butt of a gun, of a girl who had a hidden syringe and needle removed so brutally from her vagina that the officer dared not arrest her because of her wounds. And the tale of the infamous woman called "the Kitten" who lived with a junkie in Harlem, hustling so that the two of them could support their heroin habits. She lived for six months with this man as his woman and then, when she was known and trusted by the junkies, she arrested them all, for she was a policewoman and the wife of a notorious narcotics squad agent.

Many, many such stories. We don't know if all of the stories are true. What is true is that they live in terror—and that their image of terror is the brutal bust and the death in the tank.

Sherry was only one of these who told and lived out her anguish before our eyes. She drank dozens of cups of black coffee in our cell. One moment penitent and talking of her child, the next moment tough and calculating. She cried like a baby when they moved her from the cell which she shared with her friend Telsa.

Our closest friend was Thelma Gadsden. Her rich humor loud in uttering her desperation. Every night after lights-out Thelma gave her little lecture:

"Ladies and otherwise, this is the day when I got only 98 more precious little days till that there precious day in O-C-T when I get to see the street again." (Thelma never looks out of the window.) "Only 13 more precious weekends, 13 more precious Saturdays, 13 more precious Sundays . . ."

Every night after her *spiel*, the noise and giggles started. But Thelma's little sermon for the night was respected and everyone listened attentively, substituting their own count for Thelma's, and S-E-P, or A-P-R for her October.

I didn't know all the girls' names, but I knew the months of their release by heart. Except for those who would say sadly, "Nineteen sixty."

Many, many stories.

They are the outcries of all the women betrayed since the world began. They are Eve blamed, Hagar cast out, Hannah accused of drunkenness for the tears of her barrenness, Tamar deceived, Bathsheba widowed, Ruth exiled, Esther vengeful, Vashti cast away for her pride, Lot's wife in salty tears for her lost home. They are Deane and Dorothy and Joan and I, and the jailers, aghast at their reflection in their charges' eyes.

The girls came to our cell for sweets and cigarettes. But in Dorothy's presence they began to apologize for the curse words that escaped them in our cell, and gradually to curse less. They were not ashamed for their sins when they spoke to her of them, and therefore their burden was lightened and they could dream of putting it down.

Yet she reproached me when I cried for them. I must bear what I cannot change. She pointed out how prideful it is of me to want to change everything.

Why should I feel that I can help them all? "Do what you can." She did not cozen or press, as I did. What she did remains the mystery of sanctity. She was there and heard them and talked to them of the work in prison, of the problems of earning a living, of her world, of their homes and their children, and through it all, without too many words, of the great goodness of God.

Dorothy and Deane and I talked to each other of our lives too. And how intricately wrought they were, like iron grillwork. We all spent a portion of our lives in the barrooms of Greenwich Village. Yet the chronicle of our lives is so arranged that though each of us frequented those barrooms for almost ten years, we could never have met there. It was in the twenties that Dorothy knew the Village in what legend calls its Golden Age, and in the thirties that Deane drank in the Minetta on MacDougal Street, and in the fifties that I went my nightly rounds to San Remote, disdainfully passing the then passé Minetta Tavern.

We formed, as it were, a historical pageant of Bohemia. Now we lived together on the Village square and surveyed together from the roof the landmarks of our lost years, pointing out to one another where our ancient loves were spent.

Dorothy told us of the days when O'Neill was said to be her lover. But though she loved his plays, she could not love him. For he lived, she said, only for his muse, and a selfish man was not a man for her.

Her life unfolded before me. In those days she haunted with "Gene" the waterfront cafés, where they made friends with the longshoremen and she and Gene and Michael Gold and Rayna Prohme, whom Vincent Sheean immortalized, had all those nighttime adventures that only night people really understand. She related many incidents, and how in the morning hours Gene would fall asleep on her breast reciting "The Hound of Heaven" as he dozed in her virginal embrace.

Later she became a full-time reporter for the *New York Call.*

And then she met Forster, the radical with whom she fell irrevocably in love.

When their child was born she found her religious persuasion. The fact of birth convinced her of divine purpose and she turned to the church. Her husband, or as she says, "the man I call my husband," hated the Catholic church and refused to marry in it.

And so she left the man whom she never ceased loving. In thirty years she saw him only once, when she was sick in the hospital. She called him each time that Tamar, their daughter, gave birth to a child, his grandchild. But the woman Forster lives with doesn't want him to visit Tamar. Tamar was pregnant while we were in jail and Dorothy was full of self-reproach, feeling that she should be with her daughter at this time. It is Tamar's eighth child.

When she talks of Forster her voice grows warm with admiration. "And if he were to come to me and say, even now, after all these years, let us recommence our life together, I do not know what I would say."

She has been faithful to him and chaste, though many men have loved her.

After struggling as a movie writer and as a cook for a group of priests, she met Peter Maurin and together they founded the *Catholic Worker*, which became her happy vocation.

Yet wistfully she says, "A woman's true vocation is marriage."

The work she has chosen is not in her nature, and it is greatness because it is not her natural bent; she admits that she has to grit her teeth to eat with some of the derelicts that the *Worker* shelters. In this gritting of the teeth is the battle of compassion and repulsion and the victory of love over indifference.

Some years later, Ammon came and fell in love with Dorothy.

"Men are so vain," she sighs, "it was almost impossible to convince Ammon that I could not love him. The day I met him he was publicly advocating birth control and wondered why I did not like him."

She and Ammon met again and again in their travels and one day Ammon went to a priest with her and spoke of baptism. The priest told him the story of Philip and the Ethiopian whom the apostle met on the road. The Ethiopian asked him: "What hinders me to be baptized now? See here is water." And Philip said: "If thou believest thou mayest." And then and there Ammon was baptized Ammon St. John the Baptist Hennacy, Dorothy being his godmother.

She is distressed by the implication that Ammon became a Catholic only for love of her.

What sweeter raisin?

I told my story too and what Dorothy could not approve she nevertheless heard with compassion. And when I cried she stood over me and said, "Stay me with flagons, comfort me with apples, for I am sick with love."

Then every night I built a seat of books on the little metal table under the windows and perched there after lights-out.

I couldn't see any clock and I couldn't tell minutes from hours. Patchin Place was quiet and dark. I counted the lovers walking entwined along the street, stopping to kiss, innocent of the cells looming above them.

Lester did not come. He never came once, though I watched every night. Dorothy told me right away he wouldn't come and shook her head at the selfishness of "men." She pronounces the word man or men most gently when she speaks of the brotherhood of men, or man's love for God, but often contemptuously when she speaks of men in their relationship with women.

"They have always leaned on me. They always see me as a mother. A man to me, to any woman, should be the person *she* can lean on, depend on. Only once in my life, one night when the police were dispersing our picket line with gunfire, that night Forster . . ."

Sometimes I was still sitting at the window when the dawn came.

Dorothy's snoring lightened my loneliness. Sometimes she woke because of the heat and said, "Don't lean against the broken pane." In the morning I cleaned the little glass slivers away.

Life seeks an even keel. Even prison is life.

Our friends made a picket line in front of the prison. They paraded every afternoon at the main entrance from noon till two.

We heard about it immediately over the prison grapevine. We were elated. We were not forgotten and their presence on the street constituted a kind of freedom for us.

The signs read: Twelve Pacifists Jailed; In Jail for Peaceful Protest; Free the 12 Pacifists; While They Are in Prison We Walk; Dorothy Day, Apostle of the Poor, Jailed.

Dorothy said immediately, "That last one must go!"

The startling news reached us that Forster, after all the years, had come to picket in front of the jail for her.

Dorothy laughed when she heard it, first in disbelief and then more and more with embarrassed delight. She has titled her autobiography *The Long*

Loneliness and for 30 years has loved at a distance, and now the one she loves was there outside the wall for her sake. Her laughing calm a measure of her true chastity.

The pickets endowed us with a kind of notoriety in the jail. The guards spoke more seriously with us.

The warden came to see us. The "rec room" was cleared and we were ushered in for the interview. The girls stood around the screened room watching.

"I do not consider you in the same class with the other prisoners," the other prisoners heard him say.

Like a fool, I argued. One should not argue, I thought, even as the words were leaving my mouth.

Dorothy kept her eyes lowered to her crocheting and said hardly anything. I brazened:

"Do you, as the warden of a 'correctional institution,' believe that drug addicts, whose only crime is their addiction, belong in a 'correctional institution'?"

"No."

A pause. Then he said what they always say, "We obey the courts. We only carry out the judge's sentence."

Still I did not keep still. I urged him to tell us why he became a prison warden. He began by pleading his economic position, "It was during the depression . . ." and ended by defending his work as an honest job.

But finally he said, "How can I believe in peace? I'm a Hungarian."

Afterward I told Dorothy I regretted my contentiousness. And in answer she read me Lawrence Scott's directive to the pacifists who were going to Nevada to walk into the bomb test area.

"We must meet everyone with love. We must not harass officials but convince them of our good intention."

She explained all this to me with great patience, saying "we" as though she too had harassed the warden, so that I should not bear the blame. She explained it to me as though it were new to her and she had not been saying the same thing time and time again.

Learning is slow. Long after we think we know, we still don't know. Even now I don't know. Dorothy reminds me that we must forgive our brothers seventy times seven.

The routine of prison is constantly broken by dramatic events. The newspapers are a source of excitement for the *dramatis personae* of the bloodthirsty tabloids, who are our neighbors. To be written up means little, but to have one's picture in the paper—that is celebrity. The girls read the papers carefully, paying close attention to their own concerns.

An article is passed from cell to cell in which a judge discusses the futility of "punishing" prostitution with prison terms. The problems of the Puerto Ricans and the desegregation struggle are followed fervently.

One item stirred the whole floor. Everyone began talking at once, irate, opinionated. A wave of indignation spread through the corridors. Maria, the girl with the leather wristband who had asked that I be put in her cell, had been released at the end of her sentence and a few days later shot herself in the stomach. According to the *Daily News* she'd gone back on drugs and decided to take her life because she couldn't find the money to support her habit.

She was arrested for possession of a gun!

She was in Bellevue criminal ward and not expected to live.

Dorothy felt that if she had not "interfered" by speaking out, I would have been put in this girl's cell and might have helped her, have influenced her in some way—and saved her life.

Tolstoy's story "The Godson," which I read the day before Maria's suicide attempt, tells of a young man who, by trying to be helpful, interfered where he should not have, bringing about grievous harm to those whom he wanted to help.

Dorothy had only tried to protect me. There was no reason to believe that I would have helped Maria. My initial response to her had been more like fear than compassion.

Dorothy prayed for her. The papers on the following day reported her condition to be favorable.

She was soon recovering from her wound. We learned that she was downstairs in detention, awaiting trial.

Maria, it was said, was first given narcotics in the Women's House of Detention. Rumors of "hard shit" persist in the jail. All "contraband" is symbolic of the forbidden narcotics. The cells are raided regularly to find and confiscate anything that is not issued by the authorities. Yet contraband keeps appearing: a pair of lace panties, a bright lipstick, a razor blade (cherished for beautification), a cuticle scissors. Nutmeg was the only intoxicant commonly available in the prison during my stay.

Another newspaper item got everyone excited. A girl arrested for prostitution grabbed at the wheel of the police car and veered the car into a truck, risking death rather than face the cold-turkey tank. She was injured. The policeman died. He was described as the young father of three. The girl faces a manslaughter charge. She was in detention on the floor below. Dorothy added her name to Maria's in her prayers.

All the girls expressed their sympathy and admired her courage, the way that they admired Lolita Lebron, the Puerto Rican woman who fired into a room of United States congressmen to protest the United States' exploitation of Puerto Rico.

A copy of the special edition of the *Catholic Worker* describing Dorothy's good works and the reasons for her imprisonment appeared and was passed around.

Though they thought us idealistic fools, the girls did believe that we were on the same side as they against the world of laws, against the world of prisons. But as Sherry said to me, "No matter how much I like you, let's face it, you're a square."

And so we were. Squares.

But it was somehow not insulting.

My other visitor was Rabbi Naphtali Carlebach. I'd asked the jail rabbi to send for him. He came in great distress, for he couldn't imagine what crime I had committed. He visited in a small booth reserved for lawyers and the clergy, a guard sitting outside. His bearded, noble face seemed unreal in the setting of glazed brick, down where I washed the floors and carried my buckets of water.

"*Mein Kind, was ist denn geschehen?*" he cried out. When I told him my offense, he raised his hands half in belief, half in blessing, and said in his theatrical way, "I came to see a criminal and I find one who would redeem mankind." He brought me a *siddur*.

As the rabbi left we passed one of the supervisors. Carlebach paused and asked, "Are you 'the boss'?" He said it in a slow, rabbinical tone, emphasizing "the boss" as if it were an awesome title. It was not Miss Ogilvie but one of the redheaded Irish guards with whom I was on good terms. She giggled and said, "I guess I'm the boss," and then tried to look at him soberly.

Carlebach's dramatic eyes closed and he very slowly shook his head in a tragical movement. His beard bobbed up and down before her startled face.

No sermon could have told her more clearly where she stood and why she stood there. We walked on.

Thereafter I read my prayers out loud to Dorothy as she in turn read me her novenas.

In the course of our conversations I described *The Idiot King* to her. She asked if we would do it as a reading at the *Catholic Worker*. I wrote Julian about it and he wrote back.

Thus we began planning the future.

We received the new issue of the *Catholic Worker*, which contained Dorothy's first prison letter (how embarrassed I was to see that she described me as crying all night). Also a poem of Deane's called "The Women's House of Detention Welcomes You."

Because of the mice there is a cat on every floor. A large, black and white cat called Jimmy lived with us on the seventh floor. The girls hate the cat because at night, perhaps on the scent of a mouse, Jimmy runs across the horizontal bars of the cells and leaps into the sleeping girls' beds. This results in screams of terror followed by strings of curses and the din of objects tossed at the fleeing animal.

Ruth and Rachel decided that Jimmy's bad behavior was a sexual problem and offered to pay to have him castrated. At first the authorities refused permission. The girls were angry. The captain was consulted. The warden was informed of the situation of the seventh-floor cat.

Only Dorothy and I defended the cat. But we were not heard. People feel no compassion for an animal that they castrate. The trial of the cat seemed like a reenactment of the prisoner's trial. The defendant was so mute, so incapable of expressing his needs, so ignorant of the judge's motives, so maltreated for something that neither the prosecutor nor the prosecuted understands or admits.

Fear everywhere in the sheep's clothing of justice.

The cat was taken upstairs to the hospital and altered.

When Jimmy came back to the seventh floor, Dorothy said, "Call him Abelard."

He responded to the name and came like a docile domestic cat, the old wily jail-cat no longer.

More and more I clung to Dorothy. We ran the gamut of moods. Some days were hard, others were easy.

A television program called "Nighbeat" asked Dorothy for an interview. Her modesty prompted her to refuse. We talked about the influence that the program has, and the need to tell people not merely of our action in civil disobedience but about the girls here and about the tank, how it feels inside and what it means. The girls came to Dorothy and pleaded with her to speak.

Tessie stood in the doorway of our cell, waving her arms like a soapbox speaker: "Tell them about us. You got power behind you! We got nothing! No one will ever know, for we don't see nobody with power behind them, and they don't see us either. But *you* see us, how crowded we are, how airless this place is, what they do to junkies. . . ."

So Dorothy agreed to appear on "Nightbeat" the day after our release.

I warned her of the nasty treatment that the guest receives on "Nightbeat." We rehearsed all the harsh questions that I thought John Wingate might throw her.

As we sat in the cell talking about this, Sherry came from the recreation room, whose televison set blared down our corridor. "Come to the rec room. There's a friend of yours on television." It was Bob Gilmore of the American Friends Service Committee, who was arrested with us in 1955, describing the CNVA protest against the bomb tests in Nevada. They were entering the testing grounds and expected to be arrested.

The day before their protest, a telegram in the old revolutionary tradition came for Dorothy. It read: "On the eve of our protest we send greetings and fellowship to you who are in jail for your protest. Committee for Non Violent Action Against Nuclear Tests."

There were two entertainments during our sentence:

One was a lecture by Eleanor Roosevelt.

Toward seven in the evening, I was called down to the main floor, given a broom, and told to sweep the same lobby floor that I had swept that morning.

The supervisor said, "We're having a visitor. And we want to look *nice* for our visitor. Don't you clean up your house at home when you have a visitor?"

After I swept, I returned to my floor till we were finally called by the guard. We were already late.

As the four "air raid ladies" entered the chapel, the warden approached us with outstretched hands like a European host.

"What happened? I'm so sorry, there was some misunderstanding. I was looking for you. I knew you'd want to come. Especially I was looking," he pointed over the heads of the girls, "among their heads for your white hair."

Dorothy remained stony under his flattery. We were seated during a long silence while men with earphones and microphones and wires moved among the audience.

Mrs. Roosevelt stood in the pulpit, tall and motionless, even surprisingly beautiful, she who was not considered beautiful in her youth. Her gray hair faintly tinted with gold, her manner regal.

The lecture was over. It was the question period. We soon gathered that her talk had been about her travels in the Middle East.

The men with microphones approached a girl who formally stated some improbable question about the problems of the Near East. Mrs. Roosevelt answered elegantly, patiently, indisputably. She answers as she does in her magazine column, with an icy warmth, hewing the liberal bourgeois rut with undeniable precision and an unfading smile.

"There is good in everything. Necessity forces us to difficult decisions, but virtue, which is always victorious, will guide us to do the right thing. . . .

"For those who put trust in God, we add the words 'with God's help.' Those in doubt can leave out this clause. . . .

"You cannot imagine," she said in answer to one question, "how difficult it is to get visas both to Arab countries and to Israel. The Arab nations refuse to issue visas for passports already stamped with a visa for Israel, and one has to go to Malta to get a new passport if one travels from Israel to Arab territory. I was made an exception. I had a passport good for both."

I'm sure the girls in the House of Detention couldn't imagine how hard it was to go to Malta for a visa nor could Eleanor Roosevelt imagine the feeling of not even being able to go to the corner drugstore.

She spoke also of integration in the South. She exhorted the colored girls:

"Stand up for your rights. Freedom has to be fought for and you must stand up for what you believe in."

Not too many girls attended the lecture. It seems she comes often and is not popular. In order to fill the chapel all those who go to hear Mrs. Roosevelt are given a portion of ice cream and may stay up an extra half hour after lights-out.

The other entertainment was *The Summer Show*, an original musical created by the girls.

The theme was "Travel in New York." It was an undisguised outcry for freedom. The backdrop, a crude drawing of "The Street." The numbers: a steamy dance to a record of "Slaughter on Tenth Avenue"; a calypso number with bongo drums; a primitive dance—"In the jungles there is a goddess so beautiful and powerful that she holds the lives of her subjects in her hands"; and a few sophisticated songs: "Black Magic," "You Don't Know Me," and the favorite, "Autumn Leaves."

Most of the numbers were very sexy. The girls in disguise as boys played up the implications of their roles and the spectators shrieked their approval. If a girl wriggled, everyone applauded. A deep lust was released and everyone grew edgy.

The show stirred everything up. The sensuality of the dances, the girls in drag, the music, the sentiment, all conspired to raise rebellious longings. After the play there was a fight on the sixth floor in which several girls were severely cut by broken glass.

On our floor, too, there was a brewing storm. The violence of the censored sexuality was loosed. Tears and fights between lovers. Quarrels over nothing. Railings at infidelities. Hot flashes of jealousy. All in the uninhibited language and violence of jail.

I believe them that they hate men, for even in their lesbian relationships the girls who play the woman's role are always full of resentments, sulks, and pouts, while their girlfriends enacting the man's role are cold, demanding, and cruel.

And *The Summer Show* set them all acting.

"Autumn Leaves" described their imprisonment. "You Don't Know Me," their loneliness, "Slaughter on Tenth Avenue," a sacrificial rite in which their prototype was slain for their redemption. It is their history in which their salvation is foreseen as death in the barroom, killed by man's hatred. This is my body and this is my blood.

And the savage queen, whose power made them fall prostrate in a hypnotic death at the wave of her hand?

They have the courage to act out the drama of the old goddess raging in the libido. But they do not make her a villain. Our cellmates dressed up as natives of the Congo, for it is to the homeland that the goddess returns, the death-dealer, and dances again. And such is her power that she can resurrect the dead and they rise again to worship her; thus she, who slays, becomes redemption.

A miracle play!

I returned to the cell elated. When Deane and Dorothy and Joan came, I conceded that the show was immodest.

All the gates clash around us. All the time. It is time to be counted. Every moment is the time to be counted.

O heavenly Father, may I be found in my cell.

Mrs. Glantzberg, the social worker, said she liked me and sent for me often to tell me long stories about her life in Maine.

She called the social service workers in the Tombs, Hart Island, and Bronx County Prison and arranged for Julian's release to coordinate with my own. She also arranged for my going to meet him—I was to wave at a man in a red Mercury as he drove into an entrance with an iron gate on 161st Street.

The whole thing seemed absurd. I did not trust her and thought I should go straight home when released. Dorothy scolded me for even contemplating intrigues with men in red cars. "Are you going to listen to her or to me?"

But Mrs. Glantzberg gleefully told me that Julian had already been informed that I would be there.

The day of our release we followed a complex routine like the routine at our arrival played backward. Our prison clothes were taken away while we waited in those gray and green robes.

As we sat in our emptied and newly scrubbed cells—for one must mop and clean one's cell on leaving it—a call came for me. I was told that I was to go first.

A count was about to be taken. The girls were in their cells.

I called good-bye as I went down the corridor. For the last time in the hideous prison garb I saw the three air raid ladies stand together in the sunlight that crept through the screened window and the translucent, mottled glass.

Dorothy called back: "We love you."

I was rushed downstairs and told I must be processed hurriedly because I had a date with my husband. My clothes came quickly, forms were rushed through, my papers were not examined, so that I had my poem and all the little notes I had made in jail. Everyone was possessed with a sentimental passion to reunite me quickly with Julian.

The warden came and warmly pressed my hand and wished me happiness. I might have been graduating from school.

My own dress was bitter to me. My cosmetics seemed silly. My purse, my books, seemed superfluous. The gate closed behind me. I waited for my money to be returned in the rotunda where I worked long ago—long, long, long ago when I was a prisoner.

Because time is immeasurable between freedom and captivity. Once we were slaves in the land of Egypt.

As I waited I thought: "I could step out into the street but I am waiting for money."

Everything was like a parable.

Behind the gates the guard said he had no bills and asked if I would take two silver dollars. I took the silver and went out.

I stepped into the street and said a prayer that I might remember the inside. As I went across Seventh Avenue I thought, "Now I am one of them." And then I wondered if I meant them outside or if I meant them inside.

I waved toward the seventh floor and wondered who was behind the screens.

So at birth we begin to doubt heaven, and near death we begin to dread hell.

For the last moment I was between two worlds.

I took a cab to Bronx County Prison. A long ride all through Manhattan, through Times Square, through the gorgeous summer park.

I waited outside the iron gate for more than an hour. I waved to the man in the red Mercury. Then vans of prisoners, unloading our friends even as I saw them last, and Julian, different—beautiful and different. His voice was not the same, but an echo of his voice fourteen years ago when we first met.

The day after our release was Hiroshima Day and we picketed in mourning for the dead of that city and Nagasaki.

Dorothy ate lunch with us at Thau's Restaurant (where they often fed us free in Cherry Lane days) after the picketing.

In the evening there was a Town Hall meeting against the atom bomb at which Norman Thomas said of Dorothy, "If I don't approve of all her ideas it may be because I am not as saintly as she." She did not attend the Town Hall meeting because she was on the "Nightbeat" program.

We saw the program replayed later. Dorothy spoke slowly and acquitted herself on the side of God. How deliberate and how graceful she was, speaking of the sufferings of the junkies.

Asked about Cardinal Spellman, she praised him for permitting so radical an element as the *Catholic Worker* to exist.

Asked about her child, she said it was the child of a common-law marriage.

Asked about communism, she said that St. Gertrude said of property that "the more common it becomes the more holy it becomes."

This notebook was written on Claude's Pawlet farm where I sit overlooking the valley, remembering that I had written a journal of the Bellevue experience here too, and both times found it difficult under the wide, free sky to imagine that at that moment those among whom I had moved in confinement but a few days before still walked that narrow space.

We did do the reading of Claude's *Idiot King* at the *Catholic Worker*. Several priests applauded our effort, though one said that he feared that evil won because all the virtuous ones were killed.

There in the backyard of the St. Joseph's House of Hospitality we read to the poor and the wise. Ranged around the yard were the destitute in their attitudes of age and despair, the intellectuals pressing in close to hear that "love is eternity," while the retarded boy who lives in the shelter of the *Catholic Worker* grunted and shouted and then quieted and listened in a doorway. Dorothy was there, our bond still strong in the air of freedom.

And Claude's brave words and our cries echoed over the roofs to the imprisoned spaces in the world. And to those who walk in them and stand in them and sit in them and lie in them and die in them:

Where there is love
There is only love.

1. The Dramatic Workshop, which I attended from 1945 to 1947, was founded by the German director Erwin Piscator in 1940 as part of the New School for Social Research. By 1947 it had moved to the President Theater in the heart of New York's theater district.

2. The On Stage Company was founded by Al Hurwitz and Bob Ramsey. Bob had been working on the Living Theatre as technical director but grew impatient at TLT's long gestation and formed On Stage.

3. Valeska Gert: dancer and actress. As the inventor of a visceral vocal and dance style whose "unevenness" (*Unausgeglichenheit*) immediately entered the mainstream of Expressionism, she had an acknowledged effect on the work of Eisenstein and Piscator, among others. Her pre-Artaudian "outcry" (*Schrei*) had a profound influence on Julian and me and, consequently, on the Living Theatre.

4. A film by Carl Dreyer made in 1927 with Mlle. Falconetti as Joan of Arc, and among the inquisitors, Antonin Artaud.

5. Produced at the Dramatic Workshop, May 31, 1946.

6. This name, and the names of the other patients at the Institute, have been changed in deference to the Florence Nightingale Pledge.

7. In 1981 Rober Jastrow became Director of the Goddard Institute of Space Studies, and The National Space Agency's Lunar Exploration Commission.

8. I suspected that I was pregnant. I was afraid to write this in the diary lest my mother see it.

9. Rabbi Jerome Malino, my first cousin, is also a chaplain at Danbury Penitentiary, where Julian was to encounter him again in 1965 when he served sixty days there for protesting against the closing of the Living Theatre on 14th Street.

10. On September 16, 1968, the Living Theatre opened its American tour with *Mysteries and Smaller Pieces* at the Yale theater.

11. Cocteau completed the cycle, returning in fact through the mirror in *The Testament of Orpheus* in 1960.

12. Baroness Hilla Rebay was the militant director of a small art museum called the Solomon R. Guggenheim Museum of Non-Objective Art in a re-modeled private house on 54th Street, where I spent many hours. Its banner was non-representational painting. Its cornerstones, Kandinsky, Mondrian, and Rudolf Bauer; its patron, Solomon Guggenheim.

Frank Lloyd Wright was later commissioned to build the museum on Fifth Avenue which now houses the collection.

13. I meant, of course, the *Book of Changes*, the *I Ching*, which I encountered here for the first time.

14. I was shocked to find, years later, in Auden's *Collected Poems*, that he had deleted this stanza.

15. *A Death in the Family*, Chapter 13.

16. St. Johnnies: Rogers Albritton, Robert Bart, Richard Edelman, Larry Elfenbein, Janet Jenkins, Charles Lewis, Glenn Lewis, Maury Logue, George Miller, David Sachs, Philip Smith, Gene Thornton.

17. From *What Happened on June 15?* (pamphlet issued by the War Resisters' League during the course of the ensuing trial); "One member of the group . . . wanted to raise the issue of the deadly effects of preparation for nuclear war. [He testified in court that he] thought the occasion of a hypothetical danger the right time to warn against the real danger."

18. The defendants: Henry Babcock, Judith Malina Beck, Robert Berk, Sterling Borowski, Dale Brothington, Hugh Corbin, Dorothy Day, Ralph Di Gia, Eileen Fantino, Robert Fisher, Joan Hamilton, Ammon Hennacy, Edith Horowitz, Richard Kern, Michael Kovalak, Kent Larabee, Jackson Mac Low, Mary Ann McCoy, Henry Maiden, A. J. Muste, Andrew Osgood, James Peck, Orlie Pell, Segrid Perry, Mary Roberts, Patricia Rusk, Helen Russell, and Bayard Rustin.

19. "The *Catholic Worker* Group had pleaded guilty on religious grounds. . . . They felt that they had made their witness of conscience when they were arrested and wanted to express that witness further by accepting suffering under a bad law rather than becoming involved in a complicated legal process. However they made it clear that they stood firmly behind the other defendants who wanted to test the law in the courts." From *What Happened on June 15th?*

20. It was "The Jimmy Walker Story."

21. Later "The Circle in the Square."

INDEX

· 482 ·

· 484 ·

OTHER GROVE PRESS DRAMA AND THEATER PAPERBACKS

17061-X   ARDEN, JOHN / Plays: One (Serjeant Musgrave's Dance, The Workhouse Donkey, Armstrong's Last Goodnight) / $4.95

17083-0   AYCKBOURN, ALAN / Absurd Person Singular, Absent Friends, Bedroom Farce: Three Plays / $3.95

17208-6   BECKETT, SAMUEL / Endgame / $2.95

17233-7   BECKETT, SAMUEL / Happy Days / $2.95

62061-5   BECKETT, SAMUEL / Ohio Impromptu, Catastrophe, What, Where: Three Plays / $4.95

17204-3   BECKETT, SAMUEL / Waiting for Godot / $3.50

17112-8   BRECHT, BERTOLT / Galileo / $2.95

17472-0   BRECHT, BERTOLT / The Threepenny Opera / $2.45

17411-9   CLURMAN, HAROLD / Nine Plays of the Modern Theater (Waiting for Godot by Samuel Beckett, The Visit by Friedrich Durrenmatt, Tango by Slawomir Mrozek, The Caucasian Chalk Circle by Bertolt Brecht, The Balcony by Jean Genet, Rhinoceros by Eugene Ionesco, American Buffalo by David Mamet, The Birthday Party by Harold Pinter, and Rosencrantz and Guildenstern Are Dead by Tom Stoppard) / $11.95

17535-2   COWARD, NOEL / Three Plays (Private Lives, Hay Fever, Blithe Spirit) / $4.50

17239-6   DURRENMATT, FRIEDRICH / The Visit / $4.95

17214-0   GENET, JEAN / The Balcony / $5.95

17390-2   GENET, JEAN / The Maids and Deathwatch: Two Plays/ $5.95

17075-X   INGE, WILLIAM / Four Plays (Come Back, Little Sheba; Picnic; Bus Stop; The Dark at the Top of the Stairs) / $7.95

17267-1   IONESCO, EUGENE / Exit the King / $2.95

17209-4   IONESCO, EUGENE / Four Plays (The Bald Soprano, The Lesson, The Chairs, Jack or The Submission) / $4.95

17226-4   IONESCO, EUGENE / Rhinoceros and Other Plays (The Leader, The Future Is in Eggs, or It Takes All Sorts to Make a World) / $4.95

17485-2   JARRY, ALFRED / The Ubu Plays (Ubu Rex, Ubu Cuckolded, Ubu Enchained) / $9.95

17744-4   KAUFMAN, GEORGE and HART, MOSS / Three Plays (Once in A Lifetime; You Can't Take It With You; The Man Who Came to Dinner) / $6.95

17016-4 MAMET, DAVID / American Buffalo / $3.95
17047-4 MAMET, DAVID / A Life in the Theatre / $6.95
17043-1 MAMET, DAVID / Sexual Perversity in Chicago and The Duck
         Variations / $3.95
17264-7 MROZEK, SLAWOMIR / Tango / $3.95
17092-X ODETS, CLIFFORD / Six Plays (Waiting for Lefty; Awake and
         Sing; Golden Boy; Rocket to the Moon; Till the Day I Die;
         Paradise Lost) / $7.95
17001-6 ORTON, JOE / The Complete Plays (The Ruffian on the Stair, The
         Good and Faithful Servant, The Erpingham Camp, Funeral
         Games, Loot, What the Butler Saw, Entertaining Mr. Sloane) /
         $6.95
17019-9 PINTER, HAROLD / Complete Works: One (The Birthday Party,
         The Room, The Dumb Waiter, A Slight Ache, A Night Out, The
         Black and White, The Examination) / $6.95
17020-2 PINTER, HAROLD / Complete Works: Two (The Caretaker, Night
         School, The Dwarfs, The Collection, The Lover, Five Revue
         Sketches) / $6.95
17051-2 PINTER, HAROLD / Complete Works: Three (The Homecoming,
         Landscape, Silence, The Basement, Six Revue Sketches, Tea
         Party [play], Tea Party [short story], Mac) / $6.95
17251-5 PINTER, HAROLD / The Homecoming / $4.95
17885-8 PINTER, HAROLD / No Man's Land / $3.95
17539-5 POMERANCE, BERNARD / The Elephant Man / $4.25
17743-6 RATTIGAN, TERENCE / Plays: One / $5.95
17948-X SHAWN, WALLACE and GREGORY, ANDRE / My Dinner with
         Andr9 / $5.95
17884-X STOPPARD, TOM / Travesties / $3.95
17260-4 STOPPARD, TOM / Rosencrantz and Guildenstern Are Dead /
         $3.95
17206-X WALEY, ARTHUR, tr. and ed. / The No Plays of Japan / $7.95

GROVE PRESS, INC., 196 West Houston St., New York, N.Y. 10014

Selected Grove Press Paperbacks

B442	CRAFTS, KATHY, & HAUTHER, BRENDA / How To Beat the System: The Student's Guide to Good Grades / $3.95
E869	CROCKETT, JIM, ed. / The Guitar Player Book (Revised and Updated Edition) / $11.95
E190	CUMMINGS, E.E. / 100 Selected Poems / $2.95
E808	DURAS, MARGUERITE / Four Novels: The Square; 10:30 on a Summer Night; The Afternoon of Mr. Andesmas; Moderato Cantabile / $9.95
E380	DURRENMATT, FRIEDRICH / The Physicists / $4.95
B342	FANON, FRANTZ / The Wretched of the Earth / $4.95
E47	FROMM, ERICH / The Forgotten Language / $4.95
B389	GENET, JEAN / Our Lady of the Flowers / $3.95
E760	GERVASI, TOM / Arsenal of Democracy II / $12.95
E792	GETTLEMAN, MARVIN, et. al., eds. / El Salvador: Central America in the New Cold War / $8.95
E830	GIBBS, LOIS MARIE / Love Canal: My Story / $6.95
E704	GINSBERG, ALLEN / Journals: Early Fifties Early Sixties / $6.95
B437	GIRODIAS, MAURICE, ed. / The Olympia Reader / $4.50
E720	GOMBROWICZ, WITOLD / Three Novels: Ferdydurke, Pornografia and Cosmos / $9.95
B448	GOVER, ROBERT / One Hundred Dollar Misunderstanding / $2.95
B376	GREENE, GERALD and CAROLINE / SM: The Last Taboo / $2.95
B152	HARRIS, FRANK / My Life and Loves / $12.50
E769	HARWOOD, RONALD / The Dresser / $5.95
E446	HAVEL, VACLAV / The Memorandum / $5.95
B306	HERNTON, CALVIN / Sex and Racism in America / $2.95
B436	HODEIR, ANDRE / Jazz: Its Evolution and Essence / $3.95
B417	INGE, WILLIAM / Four Plays (Come Back, Little Sheba; Picnic; Bus Stop; The Dark at the Top of the Stairs) / $7.95
E259	IONESCO, EUGENE / Rhinoceros & Other Plays / $4.95
E496	JARRY, ALFRED / The Ubu Plays (Ubu Rex, Ubu Cuckolded, Ubu Enchained) / $7.95
E216	KEENE, DONALD, ed. / Anthology of Japanese Literature: Earliest Era to Mid-19th Century / $7.95
E552	KEROUAC, JACK / Mexico City Blues / $4.95
B394	KEROUAC, JACK / Dr. Sax / $3.95
B454	KEROUAC, JACK / The Subterraneans / $3.50
B479	LAWRENCE, D.H. / Lady Chatterley's Lover / $3.50
B262	LESTER, JULIUS / Black Folktales / $4.95
B351	MALCOLM X (Breitman, ed.) / Malcolm X Speaks / $3.95
E741	MALRAUX, ANDRE / Man's Hope / $12.50

E697	MAMET, DAVID / American Buffalo / $3.95
E709	MAMET, DAVID / A Life in the Theatre / $6.95
E712	MAMET, DAVID / Sexual Perversity in Chicago & The Duck Variations / $3.95
E801	MARIANI, PAUL / Crossing Cocytus / $5.95
B325	MILLER, HENRY / Sexus / $5.95
B10	MILLER, HENRY / Tropic of Cancer / $3.95
B59	MILLER, HENRY / Tropic of Capricorn / $3.95
E789	MROZEK, SLAWOMIR / Striptease, Tango, Vatzlav: Three Plays / $12.50
E636	NERUDA, PABLO / Five Decades Poems 1925-1970. Bilingual ed. / $8.95
E364	NERUDA, PABLO / Selected Poems. Bilingual ed. / $6.95
B429	ODETS, CLIFFORD / Six Plays (Waiting for Lefty; Awake and Sing; Golden Boy; Rocket to the Moon; Till the Day I Die; Paradise Lost) / $7.95
E807	OE, KENZABURO / A Personal Matter / $6.95
E687	OE, KENZABURO / Teach Us To Outgrow Our Madness / $4.95
E359	PAZ, OCTAVIO / The Labyrinth of Solitude: Life and Thought in Mexico / $7.95
E724	PINTER, HAROLD / Betrayal / $3.95
E315	PINTER, HAROLD / The Birthday Party & The Room / $6.95
E299	PINTER, HAROLD / The Caretaker The Dumb Waiter / $4.95
E411	PINTER, HAROLD / The Homecoming / $4.95
E606	PINTER, HAROLD / Old Times / $4.95
E641	RAHULA, WALPOLA / What The Buddha Taught / $6.95
B438	REAGE, PAULINE / Story of O, Part II: Return to the Chateau / $3.95
B213	RECHY, JOHN / City of Night / $3.95
B171	RECHY, JOHN / Numbers / $3.95
E806	ROBBE-GRILLET, ALAIN / Djinn / $4.95
B133	ROBBE-GRILLET, ALAIN / The Voyeur / $2.95
B207	RULFO, JUAN / Pedro Paramo / $2.45
B138	SADE, MARQUIS DE / The 120 Days of Sodom and Other Writings / $12.50
B313	SELBY, HUBERT / Last Exit to Brooklyn / $2.95
E763	SHAWN, WALLACE, and GREGORY, ANDRE / My Dinner with Andre / $5.95
	SILKO, LESLIE / Storyteller / $9.95
B456	SINGH, KHUSHWANT / Train to Pakistan / $3.25
B618	SNOW, EDGAR / Red Star Over China / $8.95
E785	SRI NISARGADATTA MAHARAJ / Seeds of Consciousness / $9.95

GROVE PRESS, INC., 196 West Houston St., New York, N.Y. 10014